Zanzibar
Pemba • Mafia

the Bradt Travel Guide

Chris & Susan McIntyre

edition
8

www.bradtguides.c

Bradt Travel Guides Ltd, UK
The Globe Pequot Press Inc, USA

D1330699

70001612961 3

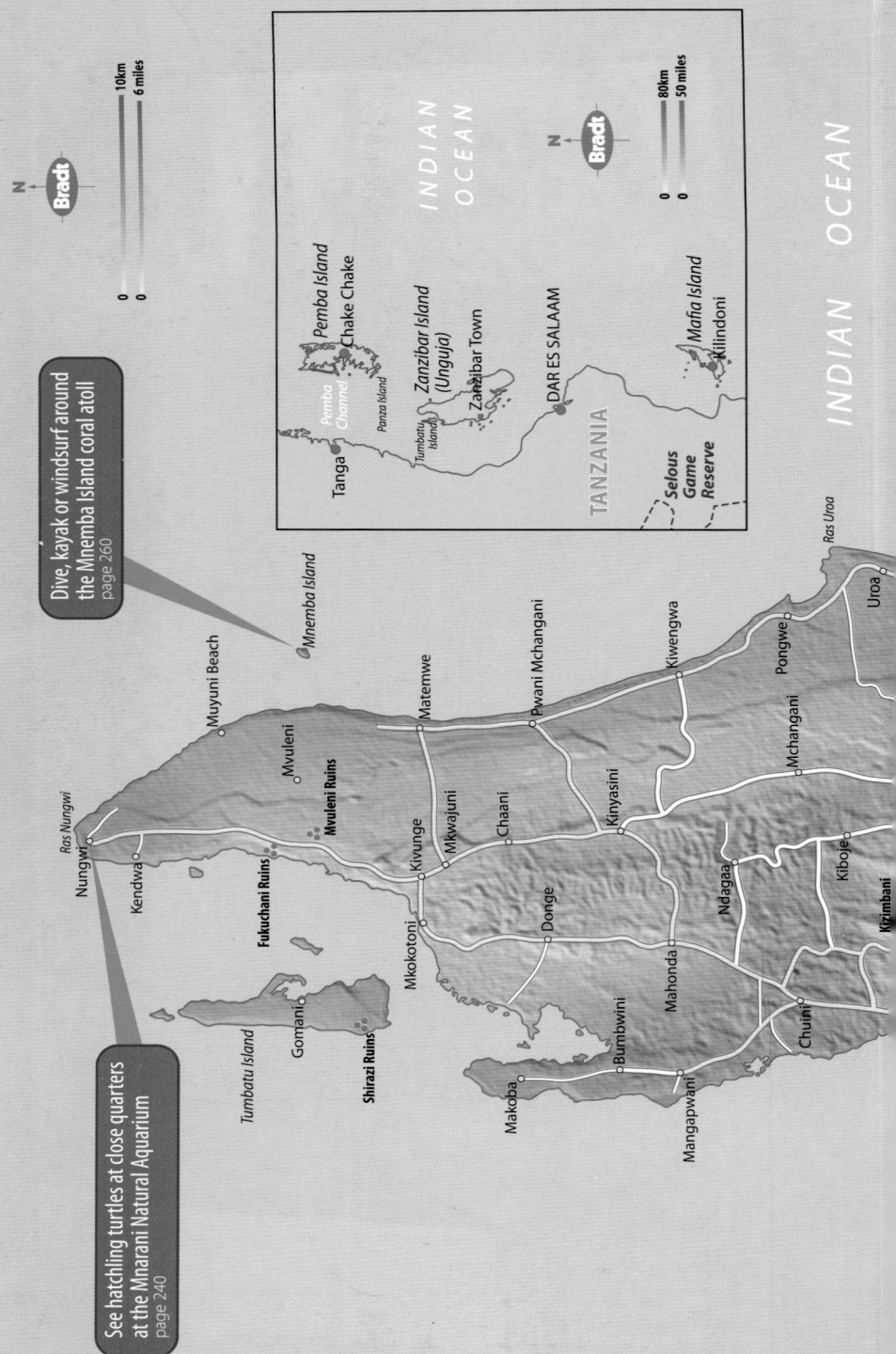

Dive, kayak or windsurf around the Mnemba Island coral atoll
page 260

See hatchling turtles at close quarters at the Mnarani Natural Aquarium
page 240

10km
6 miles
0
0

Bradt

N

80km
50 miles
0
0

Bradt

N

INDIAN OCEAN

Pemba Island
Chake Chake

Pemba Channel

Panza Island

Tumbatu Island

Tanga

TANZANIA

Zanzibar Island (Unguja)
Zanzibar Town

DAR ES SALAAM

Selous Game Reserve

Mafia Island
Kilindoni

INDIAN OCEAN

Ras Uroa

Uroa

Mnemba Island

Muyuni Beach

Mvuleni

Mvuleni Ruins

Matemwe

Pwani Mchangani

Kiwengwa

Pongwe

Ras Nungwi

Nungwi

Kendwa

Fukuchani Ruins

Kivunge

Mkwajuni

Chaani

Kinyasini

Mchangani

Kiboje

Kizimbani

Tumbatu Island

Gomani

Shirazi Ruins

Mkokotoni

Donge

Mahonda

Ndagaa

Chuini

Bumbwini

Makoba

Mangapwani

INDIAN OCEAN

Discover native wildlife and underground caves at the Ufufuma Forest conservation project *page 277*

Encounter the colobus monkey colony in Jozani-Chwaka Bay National Park *page 329*

Make coconut paste and learn about village life on the Jambiani Cultural Tour *page 318*

Gain an insight into rural life in Zanzibar on a spice tour *page 136*

Walk in the footsteps of Princess Sayyida Salme at Mtoni Palace *page 206*

Wander the labyrinthine alleyways and atmospheric market of Stone Town *page 139*

Embark on a snorkelling tour to the protected reef around Chumbe Island *page 339*

Explore uninhabited islands and sandbanks in the Menai Bay Conservation Area *page 335*

KEY

■ Capital city
● Main town
○ Village
✈ Airport
∴ Ancient site
▬ Main road (tarred)
▬ Main road
▬ Other road

Makunduchi Village
Makunduchi New Town
Jambiani
Kizimkazi Mkunguni
Dimbani Mosque
Kufile
Muyuni
Kitogani
Zala Park
Pete
Zanzibar Butterfly Centre
Jozani Forest
Paje
Bwejuu
Dongwe
Michamvi Pingwe
Michamvi Kae
Ras Michamvi
Chwaka Bay
Chwaka
Ufufuma
Jendele
Bi Khole Ruins
Ungúja Ukuu
Unguja Ukuu Ruins
Uzi Island
Menai Bay
Kiwani Bay
Fumba
Kisakasaka
Tunguu
Fuoni
Heritage Conservation Park
Dunga Ruins
Dunga
Bambi
Welezo
Mtoni
ZANZIBAR TOWN
Mbweni
Chukwani
Chumbe Island
Zanzibar Channel

Zanzibar
Don't
miss...

Wildlife
Kirk's red colobus
(*Procolbus kirkii*) is
native to Zanzibar
and can be seen in the
Joanzi Forest Reserve
(AZ) page 54

Diving and snorkelling
The seas around the Zanzibar
archipelago offer coral reefs,
sandbanks and plentiful
marine wildlife (SS) page 110

Beaches
Fine-sand beaches such as this one on the east coast are a major draw for visitors
(CM) page 281

Zanzibar Stone Town
The islands' largest settlement features whitewashed houses, bazaars, mosques and the House of Wonders, now a museum containing fascinating exhibits
(AZ) page 139

Culture
Locally produced paintings can be found for sale throughout Zanzibar
(AZ) page 44

Zanzibar
in colour

left & below   The large, billowing sail of the traditional dhow is a typical sight off Zanzibar, and dhow builders can be seen at work up and down the coast
(AZ) page 48

bottom   Women fishing on the northeastern coast
(SM) page 251

above   Maruhubi Palace was once one of the most ornate on the island; following a fire in 1899 and poor maintenance, it has fallen into a state of picturesque ruin (AZ) page 205

right   The Kidichi Baths were built in 1850 for Sultan Said; they owe their Persian style to the sultan's wife, a granddaughter of the Shah of Persia (AZ) page 211

below   Mtoni Palace was home to Sultan Said's wives, their children and hundreds of slaves, and is now a conservation area (AZ) page 205

| *top* | **Leaf fish** (FJ) | *above right* | **Juvenile angelfish and big eye** (FJ) |
| *above left* | **Flat worm** (FJ) | *below* | **Black snapper** (FJ) |

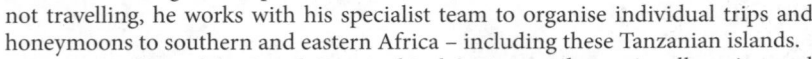

Chris McIntyre went to Africa in 1987, after reading physics at The Queen's College, Oxford. He taught with VSO in Zimbabwe for almost three years and travelled extensively, before co-authoring the UK's first guide to Namibia and Botswana for Bradt Travel Guides. He now has three Bradt guides to his name: *Namibia*, *Botswana* and *Zambia*, and co-authors three others: *Tanzania*, *Northern Tanzania* and this guide, *Zanzibar*.

Chris is also the managing director of Expert Africa, a leading tour operator to Africa. When not travelling, he works with his specialist team to organise individual trips and honeymoons to southern and eastern Africa – including these Tanzanian islands.

He is a Fellow of the Royal Geographical Society, and occasionally writes and photographs for UK magazines and newspapers. Based in west London, he lives with his wife, Susan McIntyre, and can be contacted by email on chris.mcintyre@expertafrica.com.

Susan McIntyre spent her formative years living in Zambia and Saudi Arabia, which gave her a tremendous enthusiasm for travel. After returning to the UK to attend university, Susan spent a further year globetrotting before joining the travel industry in a professional capacity in 1999. Having created communications strategies for tourist boards, hotels and tour operators, Susan sought a career focusing on African travel, the area about which she is most passionate. She has acted as a consultant for Expert Africa and has co-ordinated media campaigns for a number of southern Africa's finest independent safari camps and boutique hotels.

Susan spends several months each year in Africa with Chris McIntyre, and many more instilling a sense of adventure in their two children. She can be contacted by email on susie.e.mcintyre@gmail.com.

MAJOR CONTRIBUTORS

Philip Briggs provided the original base information for the *Southern Tanzania Safaris* chapter and additional facts and figures. He is the co-author of the Bradt guides to Northern Tanzania and Tanzania Safaris. He also wrote their guides to Uganda, Ethiopia, Malawi, Mozambique, Rwanda, Somaliland and Ghana, as well as their *East African Wildlife*, and Highlights Guides to Kenya, South Africa and Ethiopia. He also contributes regular travel and wildlife features to *Travel Africa*, *Africa Geographic* and *Wild Travel* magazines.

Sarah Chanter wrote the original *History* section and many of the historical items for early editions of this book. She has a keen interest in the history and culture of Zanzibar, has worked as a teacher in Kenya and has travelled extensively throughout east and southern Africa.

Said el-Gheithy lives and works in both Zanzibar and London. As director of the Centre for African Language Learning (London) and the Princess Salme Institute (Zanzibar/London), he kindly provided information for the *Language* and *History* sections in early editions of this book.

David Else is a professional travel writer. He first reached Zanzibar in 1985, sailing by dhow from Dar es Salaam. Over the next two decades (and using more comfortable transport) he visited Zanzibar regularly and wrote the first five editions of this guidebook. David now lives in the north of England – a long way indeed from a tropical coastline.

Jeff Fleisher is an archaeological researcher in the Department of Anthropology at the University of Virginia, and provided valuable information for the historical and cultural sections of this book.

Angela Griffin has a love of travel kick-started by a trip to South America before her degree. A post-university journey from Nairobi to Cape Town led to her joining Expert Africa in 2009 as a Namibia specialist and she has recently added Tanzania and Zanzibar to her expertise after spending several months researching there. Angela is also a major contributor to Bradt's *Namibia* guide.

Tricia and Bob Hayne researched and provided the base for the current section on Pemba. Formerly editorial director of Bradt Travel Guides, Tricia is now a freelance travel writer, and a member of the British Guild of Travel Writers. She and Bob have also helped to update Chris's guides to Namibia, Botswana and Zambia.

Dudley Iles is a keen ornithologist and conservationist, and provided information on the wildlife of Zanzibar. From 1993 to 1995 he worked for the Commission for Lands and Environment in Zanzibar, helping to set up environmental clubs and train conservation officers.

Christine Osborne wrote the original text on which this book's *Mafia Archipelago* chapter was based. Born in Australia, she has travelled widely through Africa and the Indian Ocean islands as a writer and photographer. Christine now runs the multi-faith and travel image libraries www.worldreligions.co.uk and www.copix. co.uk. She is a member of the British Guild of Travel Writers.

Gemma Pitcher is a travel writer who has lived and worked on Zanzibar, and travelled widely throughout eastern and southern Africa. She provided content for the early editions of this book; some of the text originally appeared in *Zanzibar Style* which was written by Gemma, and is reproduced with permission.

Dr Matthew Richmond is a marine science and fisheries expert who has lived and worked on Zanzibar and around the western Indian Ocean since 1989. Matt is involved in numerous marine education and biodiversity projects in the region, is the author of *A Guide to the Seashores of Eastern Africa and the Western Indian Ocean Islands*, and provided the text on marine wildlife for this book.

AUTHORS' STORY

Holidays in Africa have long concentrated on game-rich safaris on the mainland. Visitors since Livingstone have travelled from across the globe for great wildlife spectacles set in vast tracts of wilderness, sometimes accompanied by strange and fascinating traditional cultures. Many find themselves bitten by the Africa bug, returning as frequently as possible, but it is only recently that Africa's islands have been viewed as final destinations their own right.

For us, the transition from bush to beach followed a similar pattern. We have both lived in southern Africa, Chris teaching in rural Zimbabwe and pioneering Bradt's travel guides to Namibia, Botswana and Zambia; Susie spending a happy childhood in Zambia. Our early experiences were concentrated in the heart of Africa; any travel focused heavily on the national parks and wildlife wonders of neighbouring countries.

Years later and still hooked on the continent, Chris used his experience to establish Expert Africa, a UK-based tour operator. Slowly, an opportunity became clear to offer exotic beach hideaways: relaxing ends to more traditional safaris. Keen to understand the options, we explored all the archipelagos from southern Mozambique to Tanzania's Pemba. Our first trip took us to Zanzibar and its idyllic neighbour, Mafia – we were enchanted! So when the opportunity arose to take on the Bradt guide to these islands, we leapt at the chance to research in more depth, and get a deeper understanding of these islands.

Now, as we sign off our third edition of this guide, we're pleased to have been able to completely overhaul some sections of this guidebook and extensively update many others. We remain humbled by the helpful individuals we've encountered, amazed at the marine life in the turquoise seas, and also concerned by some of the less responsible developments that we've seen. We hope that this guide may help ethical travellers to contribute towards a better future for these striking islands.

PUBLISHER'S FOREWORD   *Hilary Bradt*

My association with Zanzibar goes back to 1976 when the newly 'Africanised' and socialist government of the island was hostile to foreign visitors. I have since returned many times as lecturer on board expedition ships and have relished the changes I have seen. The beaches are still superb, and while Stone Town still has the intimacy and total otherness that I loved, the buildings have been renovated and tourists now receive a warm welcome. On my last visit I escaped my group and wandered the narrow streets away from the tourist centre, stopping to watch a small child play with a toy car made from wire and bottle tops. His father, seeing my interest, came forward with a broad grin and asked me to photograph the two of them. That brief encounter epitomised all that I love about Zanzibar.

Chris McIntyre's talent at knowing what Bradt readers are looking for has made him one of our most praised writers on Africa. Once again, he and Susan McIntyre have extensively revised one of our flagship titles, bringing their inside knowledge to an ever-widening audience of travellers to Zanzibar.

Eighth edition published April 2013   First published 1993

Bradt Travel Guides Ltd
IDC House, The Vale, Chalfont St Peter, Bucks SL9 9RZ, England
www.bradtguides.com
Print edition published in the USA by The Globe Pequot Press Inc,
PO Box 480, Guilford, Connecticut 06437-0480

Text copyright © 2013 Chris and Susan McIntyre
Maps copyright © 2013 Bradt Travel Guides Ltd
Illustrations © Carole Vincer and Annabel Milne
Photographs copyright © 2013 Individual photographers (see below)
Project Managers: Maisie Fitzpatrick and Kelly Randell
Cover image research: Pepi Bluck

ISBN: 978 1 84162 458 7 (print)
e-ISBN: 978 1 84162 749 6 (e-pub)
e-ISBN: 978 1 84162 650 5 (mobi)

British Library Cataloguing in Publication Data
A catalogue record for this book is available from the British Library

Photographs Farhat Jah (FJ); Chris McIntyre (CM); Susie McIntyre (SM); SuperStock (SS); Ariadne Van Zandbergen (AZ)
Front cover Sailing dhow approaching Ras Nungwi (SM)
Back cover Diver in a shoal of glassfish, off Zanzibar (SS); House of Wonders, Stone Town (AZ)
Title page Colourful textiles for sale in Stone Town (SS); The Old Dispensary, Stone Town (AZ); Citrus swallowtail (*Papilio Demodocus*), Zanzibar Butterfly Centre (AZ)

Maps David McCutcheon FBCart.S

Typeset from the authors' disc by Wakewing
Production managed by Jellyfish Print Solutions; printed in India
Digital conversion by the Firsty Group

Acknowledgements

Susan and Chris McIntyre have extensively updated and rewritten the guide for this eighth edition. However, thanks are due to the many people who have helped with advice, information and contributions throughout the book's many years of life.

Some are already listed as major contributors (pages ii–iii) and others are named in the text. Of the rest, special thanks go to Peter Bennett, who helped research and gather information for four early editions of this book. Further help has come from many others, including Javed Jafferji, John da Silva, Balkishna Gorolay, who greatly benefited our *History* section, and Fiona Clark and Jim Boggs, for input on wildlife and culture. For wildlife contributions, particular thanks to Rob Wild, Dr Nadia Corp, Lorna Slade and Dr Per Berggren. Thanks also to Toufiq Juma Toufiq, Ali Addurahim and Ali Khamis Mohammed for local insights; and to Adria LaViolette for historical, archaeological and anthropological input. Hildegard Kiel and Yusuf Mahmoud helped with the *Music and dance* section, whilst Haji Hafidh and Robert Pasiani of Eco+Culture gave great insight into community tourism initiatives and practical help with local transport details.

For this eighth edition we're very grateful also to all those who have so willingly offered information, insight and a place to rest our heads: Salim Abdullah, Nassor Ali, Christian Chilcott, Nicola Colangelo, Joel Crossland, Elies Hagedoorn, Bas Hochstenbach, Tammy Holter, Niccy Kiefer, Nicolas Konig, Kassim Mande, Elly M'langa, Dr Aviti J Mmochi, Hashir Mohammed, Mohammed Naushad Mohammed, Flo Montgomery, Mustafa Mukame, Ali Mwinyi, Thomas Norberg, Illa Peters, Stefanie Schoetz, Paola Sibilia, Abdul Simai, Emerson Skeens, Emilie Viand, Tom and Gloria Zimmermann and Edwin van Zwam.

On a personal note, thanks to our children, James and Charlotte, for their patience during days of writing, and to their grandparents, Mike and Margaret Shand, for outstanding and inspirational childcare.

Contents

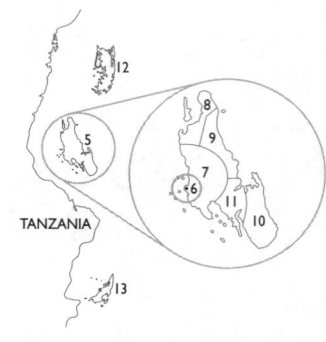

TANZANIA

LIST OF MAPS

THE NEXT EDITION

We're aware that guidebooks start to go out of date on the day they're published – and that you, the readers, are out there in the field doing research of your own. You'll find out before us when a fine new family-run hotel opens or a favourite restaurant changes hands and goes downhill. So why not write to us and tell us about your experiences? Email the authors on e susie.e.mcintyre@gmail.com and e chris.mcintyre@expertafrica.com, copying to Bradt on e info@bradtguides.com. You can also contact Bradt on ☏ 01753 893444. We may post 'one-off updates' on the Bradt website at www.bradtguides.com/guidebook-updates. Alternatively you can add a review of the book to www.bradtguides.com or Amazon.

Introduction

Zanzibar is one of those magical, evocative African names, like Timbuktu, Casablanca or Kilimanjaro. For many travellers, the name alone is reason enough to come. Yet although expectations run high, awareness of the reality on Zanzibar and its neighbouring islands is often rather hazy.

Like many visitors, we discovered the islands relatively recently. We both had friends who had sailed from mainland Tanzania to Zanzibar decades ago, and returned eulogising about the intoxicating aroma of spices, the amazing beaches, and just how cheap it was – but somehow neither of us made it there.

When we eventually visited at the start of the new millennium, stylish lodges were flourishing alongside backpackers' beach hideaways, and flights around the islands were becoming easier. On that first trip we also discovered Mafia – a smaller and quieter archipelago to the south, with fewer visitors and spectacular diving.

It's now close to nine years and many trips since our first encounters, and a tremendous amount of change has taken place, both good and bad. It remains impossible not to be enchanted as you approach from the air, looking down on sparkling turquoise waters, darkened only by patch reefs, and punctuated by the billowing triangular white sails of passing dhows. We still always smile as we step off the plane, to be enveloped by Zanzibar's exotic blend of warmth, humidity and aromatic spices.

For many, the islands offer a quintessential Indian Ocean experience: palm-lined stretches of powder-white coral sand line the coast for miles, while below the waves, reef fish flit amongst colourful coral gardens, overshadowed only by the occasional pelagic looming out of the blue. From the turtles that nest here, to the whalesharks seen annually off Mafia, there is always something unexpected awaiting the diver and snorkeller. On land, too, these islands can enthral. Kirk's red colobus monkeys can be seen in the forest, Arabian architecture provides an exotic urban backdrop, and village life remains steeped in tradition. Yet, despite the stunning raw material and depth of culture, aspects of Zanzibar have the potential to disappoint.

Development along huge swathes of Zanzibar's coastline, by both foreign and local investors, has been astonishingly fast, and much of it is lamentable. In general, there appears to be scant regard for environmental impact and a disturbing lack of real community development. The islands are also handicapped by a largely autonomous government which, at best, has combined inefficiency at regulating development with ineffectiveness at providing even the most basic of public services. At worst, and in stark contrast to the more positive situation in Tanzania, it seems to conform to the most negative stereotypes of African governance.

Despite these issues, we have found much to hearten us on recent research trips, mostly due to a sprinkling of dedicated, forward-thinking individuals who are determined not to give up on the islands and their people. A handful of interesting, ethically run hotels and lodges do exist, even if they need to be carefully sought out in advance of visiting. (Planning well will invariably improve your overall island experience.) For those who want to escape to simple, small lodges with great diving and snorkelling, the lodges on Mafia are firm personal favourites and less visited simply because the island is less well known. On Zanzibar, Fumba Beach Lodge in the southwest is trail-blazing a new part of the island in some style; the top-end Matemwe Bungalows continues to impress; and Casa del Mar in Jambiani has also adopted some excellent community initiatives. Meanwhile, trailblazing models of responsible tourism, like Chumbe Island and Mafia's Chole Mjini, continue to force the pace.

Away from hotels and lodges, opportunities for visitors to enrich their holidays whilst also making a positive impact on the people, range from original and high-quality souvenir shopping, which also happens to be fair trade, to local village restaurants with impressively high standards of cuisine, and the eclectic island tours run by Eco+Culture, who are dedicated to funding community development. We love these primarily because they're all very good indeed – but also because these initiatives are responsible in their approach. If you take time to look beyond the gaze of most visitors, and vote with your feet to support them, you might find your trip taken to a whole new level.

While researching, we arranged to meet with Mr Kassim Mande, founder and leader of the Jambiani Village Cultural Tour. A kind and knowledgeable Zanzibari, he is totally dedicated to his community and their surroundings. With Kassim to guide us, we met and talked to ordinary, hard-working Jambiani residents: nursery children and teachers, young boys climbing for coconuts, women preparing seaweed for sale, the revered traditional healer and local restaurateurs. As we were welcomed into humble homes and learnt about daily life, it became patently clear why Kassim is so passionate and dedicated to educating tourists about Zanzibari village life and generating funds to improve the lives of his community.

Jambiani has a proud history and a deep culture. Kassim is determined that both must be protected, but he is equally resolute that it should have a happy, prosperous future. He believes that, by encouraging visitors and community members to engage with each other and understand local sensitivities, he can start to break down some of the negative barriers which have arisen from a lack of knowledge and respect, and in doing so bring in some much-needed cash to their economy.

Kassim's enthusiasm and warmth is infectious, his mission commendable, and the generosity we encountered humbling. This was one of our favourite days on Zanzibar, quite simply because it offered one of the archipelago's most genuine and accessible opportunities to interact with local Zanzibaris.

The message is clear: don't discount the less well-known areas of Zanzibar, Pemba Island or the Mafia Archipelago. And for some of the best experiences, get off the beaten track, ideally with knowledgeable residents. Your choices will make a difference not only to your stay, but also to the communities that you encounter.

These islands already receive more than 140,000 visitors each year; fewer than one in every 50 will have a copy of this guide. We hope it helps you to get there, to choose the right places to stay, and to make the most of your time on the islands. But more than that, we hope that it will open your eyes to some of the more offbeat and responsible travel opportunities on the islands, and give you the confidence to venture off on your own, away from the lodges that we've so carefully described, to explore and to meet people like Mr Kassim Mande – for their sake, as well as for the good of your holiday.

Part One

GENERAL INFORMATION

Islands Zanzibar Island (Unguja), Pemba Island, and surrounding islands
Location About 40km off the coast of east Africa, in the Indian Ocean, about 6°S of Equator
Size Zanzibar 1,660km², Pemba 985km²
Climate Wet season mid March to end May; short rains November; rest of year generally dry. Average temperature 26–28°C
Status Separate state within United Republic of Tanzania, governed by Revolutionary Council and House of Representatives
Population 1,193,383 (2008 estimate)
Life expectancy 57
Main town Zanzibar Town, population 205,870 (2002)
Economy Fishing, agriculture, tourism
Languages Swahili (official), also Arabic
Religion Islam
Currency Tanzanian shilling (TSh)
Exchange rate £1 = TSh2,547, US$1 = TSh1,611, €1 = TSh2,156 (February 2013)
International telephone code +255
Time GMT +3
Electrical voltage 230v 50Hz; round or square three-pin 'British-style' plugs
Weights and measures Metric
Flag The new flag, inaugurated in 2005, consists of three horizontal stripes in green, black and blue, and features an inset of the United Republic of Tanzania flag.
National anthem 'Mungu ibariki Afrika' (God Bless Africa)
Public holidays 1 January, 12 January, 7 April, 26 April, 1 May, 7 July, 8 August, 14 October, 9 December, 25 December, 26 December (see also page 109)

1

History, Politics and Economy

HISTORY

Sarah Chanter, with additional contributions by Jeff Fleisher

The monsoons that blow across the Indian Ocean have allowed contact between Persia, Arabia, India and the coast of east Africa (including the islands of Zanzibar) for over 2,000 years. The first European arrivals were Portuguese 'navigators' looking for a trade route to India. They reached Zanzibar at the end of the 15th century and established a trading station here and at other points on the east African coast.

At the end of the 17th century the Portuguese were ousted by the Omani Arabs. During this period, Zanzibar became a major slaving centre. In 1840, the Omani sultan Said moved his court from Muscat to Zanzibar, and the island became an Arab state and an important centre of trade and politics in the region. Many European explorers, including Livingstone and Stanley, began their expeditions into the interior of Africa from Zanzibar during the second half of the 19th century.

Zanzibar was a British protectorate from 1890 until 1963, when the state gained independence. In 1964, the sultan and the government were overthrown in a revolution. In the same year, Zanzibar and the newly independent country of Tanganyika combined to form the United Republic of Tanzania.

FIRST INHABITANTS AND EARLY VISITORS The first human beings, *Homo erectus*, evolved in the East African Rift Valley, within 1,000 miles of Zanzibar, about 1.5 million years ago. They migrated throughout Africa and later Asia and beyond, becoming hunter-gatherers. Near rivers and coasts these people developed fishing techniques, and it is possible that Zanzibar's first human inhabitants were fishermen who crossed from the African mainland in dugout canoes sometime during the 1st millennium BC.

At around the same time, or even earlier, the east African coast (including the islands of Zanzibar) may have received visitors from many parts of the ancient world, such as Mesopotamia (present-day Iraq) and Egypt. The Egyptian pharaohs sent expeditions to the land they called Punt (present-day Somalia) in around 3000BC and again in 1492BC; these possibly continued southwards down the east African coast. This theory is supported by carvings on temple walls at Luxor showing sailing boats with slaves unloading gold, ivory tusks, leopard skins and trees of frankincense.

Other visitors may have included Phoenicians, a seafaring people from the eastern shores of the Mediterranean. Around 600BC, a Phoenician fleet sailed south along the coast, past Zanzibar, and is believed to have circumnavigated Africa before returning to the Mediterranean three years later.

By the 1st century AD, Greek and Roman ships were sailing from the Red Sea down the east African coast, searching for valuable trade goods such as tortoiseshell, ebony and ivory. Around AD60, a Greek merchant from Alexandria wrote a guide for ships in the Indian Ocean called *The Periplus of the Erythaean Sea*. This is the first recorded eyewitness account of the east African coast, and describes 'the Island of Menouthesias' (most likely the present-day island of Unguja, also called Zanzibar Island) as 'flat and wooded' with 'many rivers' and 'small sewn boats used for fishing'. Another Alexandrine Greek, Claudius Ptolemaeus (usually called Ptolemy), also mentioned Menouthesias in his book *Geographike*, written about AD150.

At about the same time, it is thought that Arab and Persian trading ships from the Persian Gulf were also sailing down the coast of east Africa. They sailed south on the northeast monsoon between November and February, carrying beads and cloth, and even Chinese porcelain that had come via India. Then, between March and September, after the winds changed direction, they returned north on the southwest monsoon, carrying the same tortoiseshell, ebony and ivory that had attracted the Greeks and Romans, plus mangrove poles for timber and other goods. The Arabs and Persians traded with the local inhabitants but they remained visitors and, at this stage, did not settle.

During the 3rd and 4th centuries AD, other groups of migrating peoples started to arrive on the east coast of Africa. These people were Bantu (the name comes from the term used to define their group of languages); they originated from the area around present-day Cameroon in the centre of the continent, then spread throughout eastern and southern Africa. On the east African coast, they established settlements, which slowly grew into towns, and eventually became the major trading cities such as Kilwa, Lamu and Mombasa on the mainland, and Unguja Ukuu on the island of Unguja (Zanzibar Island). These coastal settlers traded with the Arabs, exporting ivory, rhino horn, tortoiseshell and palm oil, and importing metal tools and weapons, wine and wheat.

The Arab traders called the east African coast Zinj el Barr, meaning 'land of the black people', from where the modern name Zanzibar is derived. 'Zinj' comes from *zang*, the Persian word for 'black', and *barr* is the Arabic word for 'land'. The Arabs may also have derived the word from *Zayn za'l barr*, meaning 'fair is this land'. Zanzibar remained the name of the whole coast, including the islands of Unguja and Pemba (which together make up the present-day state of Zanzibar), until the late 15th century.

EARLY ARAB SETTLERS The 7th century AD saw the rise of Islam in Arabia. At the same time, wars in this area, and subsequent unrest in Persia, caused a small number of people from these regions to escape to the east African coast, where they settled permanently, bringing the new Islamic religion with them.

There are several accounts of emigrations from Arabia to east Africa – the history of this period is largely based on stories handed down by word of mouth through generations, which are difficult to separate from myth and legend. One story tells of two Arab chiefs from Oman who arrived in east Africa with their families around the end of the 7th century, and settled on the island of Pate, near Lamu. Another story tells of an emigration from Shiraz, in Persia, some time between the 8th and 10th centuries. The Sultan of Shiraz and his six sons migrated with their followers in seven boats. One of the sons stopped at Pemba, while others settled in Mombasa and Kilwa. The 9th-century Arab tale of Sinbad the Sailor, one of the stories in *The Arabian Nights*, was most probably inspired by accounts of journeys by Arab sailors to east Africa and southeast Asia.

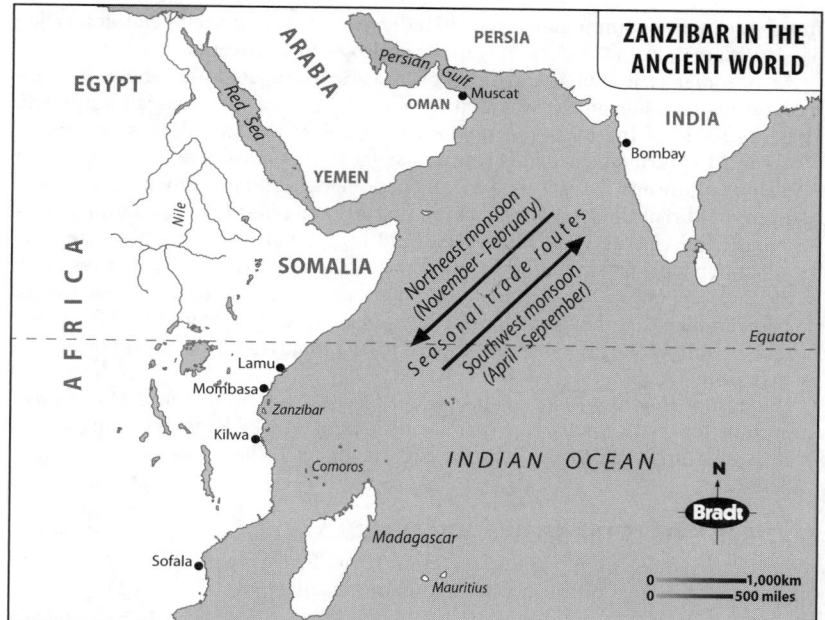

THE RISE OF THE SWAHILI During the second half of the first millennium, the coastal Bantu people developed a language and culture (in fact, a whole civilisation) which became known as Swahili. This name came from the Arabic word *sahil*, meaning 'coast'. Their language, Kiswahili, although Bantu in origin, contained many Arabic words. It also included some Persian words, mainly nautical terms. There was some intermarriage, and the Swahili adopted many Arab customs and traditions, including the Islamic religion. On Unguja (Zanzibar Island), Shirazi settlers are believed to have married into the family of the island's Swahili king. Several centuries later, the Mwinyi Mkuu (the great lord), the traditional ruler of Unguja, continued to claim descent from a Shirazi prince.

By the 7th century, the Swahili people were trading regularly with Arab and Persian merchants. In the same way, Swahili dhows (traditional ships based on an Arab design) also became involved in the trade and sailed regularly to and from the Persian Gulf, carrying gold, ivory, rhino horn, leopard skins, tortoiseshell, and ambergris from whales. African slaves were also carried to the Persian Gulf, probably to work in the marshlands of Mesopotamia.

Over the following centuries the trade between Africa and Arabia increased, as did trading links between east Africa and Asia. Ivory was exported to India, and later China, while Indian cloth and Chinese porcelain and silk were imported to Arabia and Zanzibar. At around this time, Indonesian sailors from Java and Sumatra are thought to have reached east Africa and Madagascar, possibly introducing coconuts and bananas.

From this period (7th to 10th centuries) archaeologists have discovered a very distinctive kind of local pottery, known as Tana Tradition, which looks the same at sites along the whole east African coast, from northern Kenya to southern Tanzania, and out to the Comoros Islands. The similarity of this pottery over such a large area shows how closely linked the people of the coast were, and also shows – for the first time – a sense of commonality and shared experience. Imported ceramics, called Sassian Islamic, from the Persian Gulf, have also been discovered.

Archaeological, linguistic and historical research conducted since the early 1980s has also led to a shift in the way that the early history of the coast is interpreted, rejecting some of the ideas put forward by scholars working during the 1950s, 1960s and 1970s. In essence, this research suggests that at its core – its foundation – Swahili culture and history are African phenomena. Until recently, archaeologists had proposed that the large towns of the east African coast (such as Kilwa, Lamu, Mombasa and Unguja Ukuu) had been built by Persian or Arab settlers, and the local Bantu people had then intermarried and 'Africanised' the Arabs, thus resulting in the Swahili people. But, through extensive excavations at many of these towns, it is now known that they were founded by people from the interior of Africa and, instead of simply starting as grand towns, were actually built up slowly over time by these same people.

Unquestionably, the links to the Indian Ocean trade were some of the most important for these towns, but there is little evidence of large-scale migrations from Arabia or Persia to the coast of east Africa until the middle of the second millennium.

ZANZIBAR ENTERS THE SECOND MILLENNIUM On Unguja, one of the earliest remaining examples of permanent settlement from Persia is a mosque at Kizimkazi, on the southern part of the island. It contains an inscription dated AH500 (Anno Hegirae), which corresponds to the Christian year AD1107, making this the oldest-known Islamic building on the east African coast. From the end of the 12th century, Omani immigrants also settled in Pemba. At around the same time, the settlement that was to become Zanzibar Town also began to grow.

As the trade between Africa, Arabia and the rest of the Indian Ocean continued to expand, Zanzibar became an increasingly powerful and important commercial centre. Major imports included cotton cloth, porcelain and copper from Dabhol, a port on the west coast of India, and exports included iron from Sofala (in present-day Mozambique). By the 13th century, Zanzibar was minting its own coins, and stone buildings were starting to replace more basic mud dwellings. In 1295, the Venetian traveller Marco Polo wrote of Zanzibar: 'The people have a king ... elephants in plenty ... and whales in large numbers', although he never visited the island. Other writers of the time noted that the kings and queens of Zanzibar and Pemba dressed in fine silks and cottons, wore gold jewellery, and lived in stone houses decorated with Persian carpets and Chinese porcelain.

Many Chinese imports had come to Zanzibar via India, but in the early 15th century the ports on the coast of east Africa were trading directly with China. Gold, ivory and rhino horn were transported to the East, as well as a small number of slaves. In 1414, a dhow from the city of Malindi (in present-day Kenya) carried a giraffe to China as a present for the emperor. The trade came to an abrupt end in 1443 when the new Ming emperor banned Chinese merchants from going abroad, but the demand for ivory remained, supplied by Arab dhows via markets in India.

By the mid 15th century, the islands of Zanzibar, along with Mombasa, Malindi, Lamu and Kilwa, formed a chain of thriving Swahili Islamic city states, each with its own sultan, spread along the east African coast. These cities had close trading links with Arabia, Persia, India and southeast Asia. Commerce between Africa and the Indian Ocean had become very profitable, and it seems that the sultans of Zanzibar and the other city states were more than happy for their territories to remain as gateways or conduits for it. At the end of the 15th century, though, the situation was severely disrupted by the arrival of the Portuguese on the coast of east Africa.

PORTUGUESE RULE By the mid 15th century, Prince Henry 'the Navigator' of Portugal was encouraging voyages of exploration around the African coast. He hoped to find a sea route to the East, as well as the Christian kingdom of the legendary Prester John (or 'Priest-king') of Abyssinia. With the rise of the Ottoman Empire in 1453, all goods from the East, including the increasingly valuable spices, now reached Portugal via potentially hostile Muslim countries.

In 1487, Prince Henry's successor, King John II, dispatched two expeditions to the East led by Bartholomew Dias and Pedro da Covilhan: one by sea around the southern tip of Africa, the other overland through Egypt. In 1497, another Portuguese navigator, Vasco da Gama, encouraged by the reports of Dias and da Covilhan, rounded the Cape of Good Hope and sailed northwards up the coast of east Africa, on the way to India. He passed Zanzibar and landed at Mombasa, where he received a hostile reception from the sultan. But he got a warm welcome in Malindi, an old enemy of Mombasa. Da Gama built a pillar of friendship on the shore at Malindi and employed an Omani navigator called Ahmed bin Majid to guide him across the Indian Ocean. On his return from India in 1499 he moored for a day off Unguja.

More Portuguese ships followed in the wake of da Covilhan and da Gama. They needed safe provisioning and repair bases for their voyages to and from the Far East, and so garrisons were established in the harbours of Unguja, Pemba and Mombasa.

Any early friendship was soon forgotten when the Portuguese took control of Unguja in 1503. A ship commanded by Rui Lorenco Ravasco moored off the southern end of the island while Portuguese sailors captured over 20 Swahili dhows and shot about 35 islanders. The Mwinyi Mkuu (ruler of Zanzibar) was forced to become a subject of Portugal, and agreed to allow Portuguese ships free access to Zanzibar. Additionally, he was required to pay an annual tribute to the Portuguese crown.

Portuguese domination of the region continued. In 1505, they took control of Mombasa, and in 1506, Pemba. Between 1507 and 1511, the Portuguese also occupied territories in the Arabian Gulf, including Muscat and the island of Hormuz.

By 1510, Unguja's tribute had fallen short and the people of Pemba had also become hostile to the Portuguese. Under Duarte de Lemos, the Portuguese looted and set fire to settlements on Unguja, then plundered the town of Pujini in Pemba. They soon regained both islands, and by 1525, the whole east African coast, from Lamu to Sofala, was under Portuguese control. Gold, ivory, ebony and slaves from the interior were carried to Portuguese colonies in India or back to Portugal. Iron ore and garnets from Sofala, and coconut fibre and gum-copal (a tree resin) from the islands were also exported. Cloth, beads, porcelain and metal tools were imported to the east African coast from Oman and Portugal.

Around 1560 the Portuguese built a church and small trading settlement on a western peninsula of Unguja. This was to become Zanzibar Town. But although the Portuguese occupied Unguja, and forced the local people to trade under their supervision, the islanders continued to pay allegiance to the Mwinyi Mkuu, their own king.

Portugal was not the only European power with interests in the Indian Ocean. In November 1591, the *Edward Bonaventura*, captained by Sir James Lancaster, became the first English ship to call at Zanzibar. It was supplied with fresh food and water by the Mwinyi Mkuu. Soon, more European ships were calling at Zanzibar on their way to and from the Indian subcontinent and islands of the East Indies.

John Henderson, a Scottish sailor from one English ship, was reportedly held captive on Zanzibar in 1625. He later escaped, but not until he had fallen in love with a Zanzibari princess who escaped with him back to Scotland. Today, their portraits are in the collection of the Scottish National Portrait Gallery in Edinburgh.

With the advent of English ships in the Indian Ocean, the Portuguese needed to strengthen their position on the coast. In 1594, they built a fort at Chake Chake in Pemba, and from 1593 to 1595, Fort Jesus in Mombasa was constructed. Settlers arrived from Portugal, and a Portuguese garrison was established in Fort Jesus, brutally suppressing the local population. Mombasa became known as *Mvita*, 'the place of war', and the Portuguese governor as *Afriti*, 'the devil'.

Despite these fortifications, however, the Portuguese position in east Africa began to weaken. In Arabia, Hormuz was regained by the Persians in 1622, and in January 1650, Muscat was regained by the Omani Arabs. Following this victory, the Sultan of Oman's navy sailed to Zanzibar to help the Mwinyi Mkuu, Queen Mwana Mwema. The Omanis raided the Portuguese settlement on Unguja, killing many people and imprisoning about 400 in the church. They also attacked and burnt the Portuguese settlement on Pemba. By 1668, virtually the entire coastal area was in Omani hands. The only garrisons still held by the Portuguese were at Fort Jesus in Mombasa, and on the western peninsula of Unguja.

In 1682, the Portuguese persuaded the Queen of Pemba, who was living in Goa, to return, but this attempt to install a friendly ruler in Pemba was frustrated when her own subjects drove her out. The last Portuguese inhabitants were expelled in 1695.

By this time, Queen Mwana Mwema of Unguja had been succeeded by her son, Yusuf. After his death, towards the end of the 17th century, the island was divided between his two children, Bakari and Fatuma. King Bakari ruled the southern part of the island, with Kizimkazi as his capital, while his sister, Queen Fatuma, ruled the northern part. Fatuma supported the Portuguese, so her capital was built near the garrison on the western peninsula which later became the site of Zanzibar Town.

When the Omani fleet arrived at Mombasa and laid siege to Fort Jesus in March 1696, Queen Fatuma sent three dhows full of food to help the Portuguese defenders. The dhows were captured and burnt by the Omanis, who then attacked Zanzibar itself, forcing Queen Fatuma and her followers to flee into the interior of the island.

THE PORTUGUESE LEGACY

Zanzibar was occupied by the Portuguese in the 16th and 17th centuries. They introduced many new foods, brought from their colonies in other parts of the world, and the Swahili words used for these today are borrowed directly from the Portuguese language: cassava or manioc is *muhogo* in Swahili (from the Portuguese *mandioca*) and the cashew nut is *mbibo*, from *bibo*, both plants originally grown in Brazil. Avocado is *mpea* and guava is *mpera*, both from the Portuguese word *pera*. The Portuguese also introduced the use of dung (Swahili: *mboleo*, Portuguese: *boleo*) for cultivation, and the iron nail (Swahili: *parafujo*, Portuguese: *parafuso*) for boatbuilding.

Source: A History of East Africa *by Oliver Roland and Matthew Gervase, Oxford University Press, 1963*

The siege of Mombasa lasted until December 1698, when the Omani forces took Fort Jesus and installed an Omani governor. Once again, the Omanis attacked Zanzibar. They drove out the last of the Portuguese settlers, captured Queen Fatuma and took her to Oman, where she spent the next 12 years in exile before returning to resume her rule. While she was away, her son Hassan took the title Mwinyi Mkuu, but paid allegiance to Oman.

Thus the Portuguese were finally ousted from the whole east African coast, and the Omanis were firmly in control of the entire region as far south as present-day Mozambique (which remained in Portuguese hands until 1972).

OMANI RULE
Early sultans and the rise of the slave trade
From 1698, the Sultan of Oman ruled the islands of Zanzibar from Muscat, his capital, through appointed governors and occasional armed raids to put down minor rebellions. To consolidate his grip on the islands, a fort was built in Zanzibar Town, on the site of the Portuguese church, and by 1710 about 50 Omani soldiers were garrisoned there.

By this time, Oman had become a major trading nation. One of its major exports was dates, and the expansion of date plantations created a demand for cheap slave labour. The rules of Islam forbade the enslavement of Muslims, so Africans were imported in large numbers, many of them transported through Zanzibar. It is estimated that there were about 5,000 African slaves in Oman at the beginning of the 18th century, with about 500 new slaves arriving each year. Although most slaves were used on the plantations, others were employed as domestic workers or concubines, and some were re-exported to Persia or India.

In 1744, in Oman, the ruling Yaa'rubi dynasty (which had been in power since 1624) came to an end after a long civil war. It was succeeded by the new Busaidi dynasty led by Ahmed bin Said al Busaidi, an Omani merchant and ship owner. Ahmed was made Sultan of Oman and the east African coast; one of his first moves was to install a new governor in Zanzibar.

At this time, the governors of the east African city states paid allegiance to Oman, but in practice they enjoyed a great deal of autonomy. Zanzibar, Pemba, Lamu and Kilwa were all ruled by members of the Busaidi family, but Mombasa was controlled by a rival Omani family, the Mazrui. In 1746, the Mazruis declared Mombasa independent of Oman, and overthrew the Busaidi force on Pemba. In 1753, they tried to capture Zanzibar, but the governor here remained loyal to Oman and repelled the attack.

During this period, the Mwinyi Mkuu, King Hassan, had died and been succeeded by his son, named Sultan, who in turn was succeeded by his son Ahmed, and then by his grandson Hassan II.

Zanzibar was now a major commercial centre and had also become very important strategically. From the middle of the 18th century, there was a flourishing trade in slaves from Zanzibar and Kilwa to the Mascarenes (present-day Mauritius and Réunion). By the 1770s, these numbered about 3,000 slaves a year. In the same period Dutch ships came to Zanzibar in search of slaves to work on plantations in the East Indies.

Until this time African slave traders had brought captured slaves to the coast, but by the end of the 18th century, the demand for slaves had increased to such an extent that Arab and Swahili traders from the coast and islands were penetrating the African interior. By the 1770s, caravan traders had already travelled inland as far as Lake Nyasa, present-day Lake Malawi (for more details, see box, *The east African slave trade*, page 190).

Sultan bin Ahmed and British involvement In Oman a new sultan, Sultan bin Ahmed, came to power in 1792. He needed a strong ally to help him combat the Mazrui of Mombasa and also to keep the Persians out of Oman. He found this ally in Britain, by this time a powerful maritime nation with an empire expanding all over the world. In the late 18th century, Britain was at war with France and knew that the French emperor, Napoleon Bonaparte, was planning to march through Persia and capture Muscat on his way to invade India. In 1798, Britain and Oman agreed to a Treaty of Commerce and Navigation. Sultan bin Ahmed pledged himself to British interests in India, and his territories became out of bounds to the French. He allowed the British East India Company to establish a trading station in the Persian Gulf, and a British consul was posted to Muscat.

As well as defeating Bonaparte, the British had another motive for the treaty with Oman: they wanted to put pressure on the sultan to end slavery, which had been declared illegal in England in 1772. At this time, the trade from Africa to Oman was still buoyant.

At the same time, Zanzibar's position as an important trade centre was bolstered further when the supply of ivory from Mozambique to India collapsed because of excessive Portuguese export duties. The traders simply shipped their ivory through Zanzibar instead.

Sultan Said and the birth of the spice trade In 1804, Sultan bin Ahmed of Oman was killed in battle, and his sons Salim and Said (aged 15 and 13) jointly inherited his kingdom with their cousin Bedr acting as regent. Two years later the young Said killed Bedr, who he believed was plotting to kill him; in 1806, he was proclaimed Sultan of Oman and the east African coast.

Said ruled his kingdom from Muscat and did not visit his African territories for several years. He maintained good relations with Britain because, like his father, he hoped for British help against the Persians and the Mazruis. During this period, wars and drought had drained Oman's economy, and many Omani merchants migrated to Zanzibar to participate in coastal trading and the caravans to the interior.

Meanwhile, in Europe, a campaign led by William Wilberforce resulted in the abolition of the slave trade within the British Empire in 1807. The USA passed a law against slave trading in 1808; the French and Germans did the same a few years later.

In east Africa, however, about 8,000 slaves were brought from the mainland to Zanzibar every year, many of them carrying ivory. The resultant surplus of slaves was addressed in 1812, when a Muscat-born Arab called Saleh bin Haramil al Abray introduced clove trees into Zanzibar from the island of Bourbon (now Réunion). The slaves were diverted to work on clove plantations and demand increased once again.

As the demand for slaves and ivory continued to expand, Arab traders from the coast pushed further inland. In 1820, they established a trading centre at Kazeh (near present-day Tabora, in Tanzania), over 800km (500 miles) from the coast. From Kazeh, trade routes branched north to the shores of present-day Lake Victoria, northwest to Buganda (now Uganda), and southwest to the southern end of Lake Tanganyika (see map, *Zanzibar and the slave trade*, opposite).

Early British anti-slaving attempts To combat this expansion in slavery, the British consul in Muscat continued to put pressure on Sultan Said to end the slave trade. In September 1822, Said signed an anti-slavery treaty with the British captain Fairfax Moresby which prohibited slave transport south and east of the 'Moresby line', drawn from Cape Delgado, the southern limit of the sultan's domain in Africa, to Diu Head on the coast of India (see map, *Zanzibar and the slave trade*, opposite).

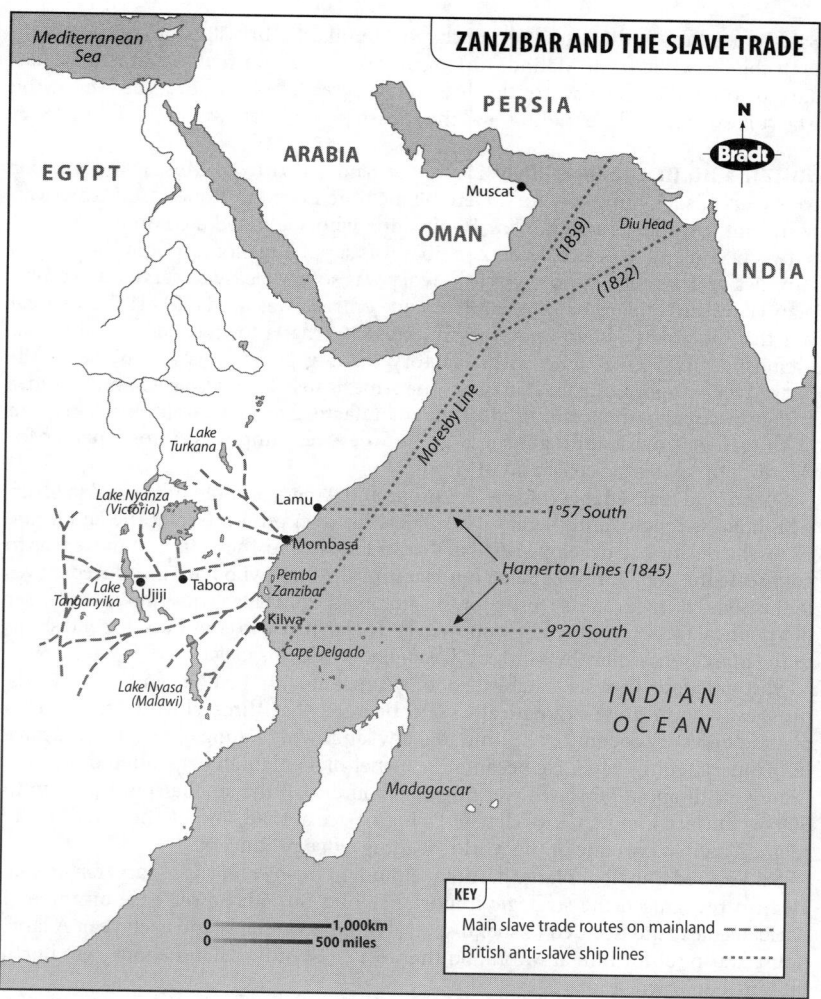

ZANZIBAR AND THE SLAVE TRADE

KEY

Main slave trade routes on mainland ------

British anti-slave ship lines ....

This treaty meant that the transport of slaves from Zanzibar to the Mascarenes and India was banned, but still permitted between Zanzibar and Oman. The sultan was also banned from selling slaves to Christians, which included the French for their Indian Ocean islands. British warships gained the right to confiscate any dhows found carrying slaves in forbidden waters. Ironically, British prohibition of the slave trade to the Mascarenes only led to an increased development of the slave trade in Zanzibar itself. Sultan Said lost the revenue he would have received as duty on all slaves sold, so to make up the shortfall, he encouraged the development of more clove plantations.

Meanwhile, Sultan Said continued his attempt to oust the Mazrui Sultan of Mombasa. In 1823, the sultan asked for British protection against Oman. Captain William Owen of HMS *Leven* saw that he could use this local dispute to Britain's advantage: he sailed to Muscat and informed Sultan Said that he intended to grant the Mazrui request for British protection unless Said agreed to end the slave trade.

Said refused to do this, so Owen declared Mombasa a British protectorate, along with the coastline from Malindi to Pangani, on condition that the Mazrui sultan agreed to abolish the slave trade. The sultan agreed, but within a few years, the Mazrui reverted to slave trading, and the British protectorate was lifted in July 1826.

Sultan Said in Zanzibar

In 1827, Sultan Said sailed from Muscat to Zanzibar to inspect his far-flung territory. Here he met one Edmund Roberts, an American merchant from Portsmouth, New Hampshire, who suggested a commercial treaty between Said and America. Soon Zanzibar was supplying large amounts of ivory to America and western Europe. African ivory was soft and easy to carve into combs, piano keys and billiard balls. Asian ivory, in contrast, was hard and brittle. So great was the American demand for ivory in the 1830s that a town called Ivoryton was established in Connecticut, with a factory making piano keys and billiard balls out of ivory imported from Zanzibar. The Americans also purchased animal hides and gum-copal, a tree resin used in the manufacture of varnish. In return, cotton cloth (called 'Amerikani'), guns and gunpowder were imported into Zanzibar for distribution along the coast and to Arabia.

Sultan Said realised that trade with Europe and America would increase Zanzibar's wealth and strength, and thereby consolidate his own position, so at the end of the 1820s, he decided to develop Zanzibar's clove industry further. His first move was to confiscate the plantations of Saleh bin Haramil al Abray, who had introduced cloves to the island in 1812. Said's reason for this stemmed from Saleh's position as the leader of a political faction competing for power, and Saleh had also continued to send slaves to the Mascarenes after the Moresby Treaty had made this illegal.

Vast plantations were established on Zanzibar and Pemba, and the islands' prosperity soon grew dramatically. Said decreed that three clove trees must be planted for every coconut palm, and that any landowner failing to do so would have his property confiscated. He became the owner of 45 plantations scattered over the islands, with about 50 slaves working as labourers on the smaller plots and up to 500 on the larger ones. Cloves fetched a high price abroad, and by the end of Said's reign, Zanzibar was one of the world's leading clove producers.

Said valued Zanzibar's large harbour, abundant freshwater supply and fertile soil. He also recognised the strategic importance of a Busaidi power base on the east African coast, and decided to spend several months on the island each year. A large house was built for him at Mtoni, on the west coast of the island about 5km north of Zanzibar Town.

Over the next few years, Said came under increased pressure from the British to abolish slavery. This call was strengthened in 1833, when the Emancipation Act abolished slavery throughout the British Empire and all slaves in British territories were freed. Recognising the need for strong allies, in the same year Said formalised the trade agreement suggested earlier by Edmund Roberts and signed a Treaty of Amity and Commerce with the United States of America. This gave the Americans freedom to set up trading posts at Zanzibar and on the mainland. In return, Said hoped for armed assistance against the Mazrui and for British anti-slavery pressure to ease. In 1837, Said finally managed to oust the Mazrui from Mombasa and install his own garrison of soldiers in Fort Jesus. His presence along the coast of east Africa was finally complete.

Links between Zanzibar and America became increasingly cordial, and a consul, Richard Waters, was appointed in March 1837. Said presented him with a horse and a boat, and Waters was often the sultan's guest at Mtoni Palace. In November 1839, Said sent his trading ship *El-Sultani* to America. The ship arrived in New York in May 1840, the first Arab boat ever to visit an American port, and returned to Zanzibar with a cargo of arms and ammunition, china, beads and 'Amerikani' cloth.

Zanzibar becomes the capital of Oman
In December 1840, Sultan Said established his capital in Zanzibar, transferring it 3,000 miles from Muscat. He made this move at a time when Zanzibar's prosperity was increasing rapidly, and Oman's was in decline. Said also believed that the dual power base of Zanzibar and Oman would help safeguard his territories on the African mainland and maintain his dominance over Indian Ocean trade. Many of Oman's most influential merchants were already based in Zanzibar, and more followed him in the move from Muscat.

Said's title was now Sultan of Zanzibar and Oman. He ruled Zanzibar directly while his eldest surviving son, Thuwaini, remained in Muscat as Governor of Oman. Zanzibar's own king, the Mwinyi Mkuu, presided over local matters but Said's government took control of trade and international affairs. Zanzibar Town began to expand: when Said had first arrived in the 1820s, the buildings were mostly huts of mud thatched with coconut fronds, but by the 1850s many impressive stone buildings had been constructed by the new immigrants from Oman.

Said was also followed to Zanzibar by Captain Atkins Hamerton, who had originally been installed in Muscat to act as British consul. In December 1841, he became the first British consul in Zanzibar. France also established diplomatic relations with Zanzibar: a French consulate was opened in 1844.

Meanwhile, despite the restrictions imposed by the Moresby Treaty, the slave trade continued to expand. In 1841, Arab traders had established a trading colony at Ujiji on Lake Tanganyika, almost 1,600km (1,000 miles) from the coast, and in 1843, the first Arab caravans had reached Buganda (now Uganda) on the shores of present-day Lake Victoria. By the end of the 1840s, Arab traders had gone even further, reaching the Upper Congo (now eastern Democratic Republic of Congo), the Central Highland area around Mount Kenya, the Rift Valley lakes of Baringo and Turkana, and southern Ethiopia. About 13,000 slaves a year were arriving in Zanzibar from the mainland (see map, *Zanzibar and the slave trade*, page 11).

Britain's opposition to the slave trade
Sultan Said became increasingly concerned that British attempts to abolish the slave trade would weaken his power in the region. In 1842, he sent his envoy Ali bin Nasur to London on the ship *El-Sultani* to plead his case. Said's gifts for Queen Victoria included emeralds, cashmere shawls, pearl necklaces and ten Arab horses.

In reply, the British government told the Zanzibari ruler that it wished to abolish the slave trade to Arabia, Oman, Persia and the Red Sea. To soften the blow Queen Victoria gave Said a state coach and a silver-gilt tea service. The state coach arrived in pieces and had to be assembled. It was still unused a year later, as Zanzibar had no roads, and the tea service was considered too ornate to use and was taken to the British consulate for safe keeping.

Britain continued putting restrictions on the slave trade. In October 1845, Said was virtually forced by Captain Hamerton to sign another anti-slavery treaty, which allowed slave transport only between lines of latitude 1° 57' S and 9° 20' S (between Lamu and Kilwa, the northern and southern limits of Said's dominions on the coast). This meant slaves could still be imported into Zanzibar but could no longer be exported to Oman.

Ships from the British navy were employed to help enforce the treaty by capturing any dhows carrying slaves. When a dhow was captured, it was set on fire and the slaves were taken to Aden, India, or a free slave community on the mainland coast, such as English Point in Mombasa. However, with only four ships to patrol a huge area of sea, the British navy found it hard to enforce the treaty, so the slave dhows continued to sail. Ships from France, Germany, Spain, Portugal and America also continued to carry slaves, as there were still huge profits to be made. On the mainland, slave traders continued to push further into the interior.

Early European explorers In the 1840s, European missionaries and explorers began to venture into the east African interior. In Britain, an Association for Promoting the Discovery of the Interior Parts of Africa had been formed as early as 1788, and had since merged with the Royal Geographical Society (RGS). In the following years it would play a leading role in the search for the source of the River Nile.

Zanzibar became the usual starting point for journeys into the interior. Here, the European missionaries and explorers paid their respects to Sultan Said, who 'owned' most of the land they would pass through. They equipped their expeditions with supplies and porters before sailing to Bagamoyo on the mainland. Many explorers followed the established slaving routes into the interior, often employing slave traders to act as guides.

In 1844, the English Church Missionary Society, unable to find any British recruits, sent the German Johann Krapf to east Africa in an early attempt to convert the local people to Christianity. He was joined by his missionary colleague, Johann Rebmann, who arrived in Zanzibar two years later. They travelled widely across the areas now known as southern Kenya and northern Tanzania. In May 1848, Rebmann became the first European to see Kilimanjaro, and in December 1849, Krapf was the first European to see Mount Kenya (see map, *Exploration in east Africa*, opposite).

Meanwhile on Zanzibar the slave trade continued. By the 1850s, about 14,000 to 15,000 slaves a year were being imported into Zanzibar from the mainland, providing Sultan Said with a large income from duties. Zanzibar traders pushed even deeper into the interior, reaching what is now northern Zambia. In 1852, a caravan reached Benguela (in present-day Angola) having completely traversed the continent from east to west, while the following year another group reached Linyanti, in the present-day Caprivi Strip of Namibia.

Through the slave caravans Said had become the nominal ruler of a vast commercial empire stretching along the coast from Mozambique to the Somali ports, and inland to the Great Lakes of Nyasa (Malawi), Tanganyika, Nyanza (Victoria) and Turkana. By the end of his reign, Zanzibar's empire covered about 2.5 million km² (1 million square miles), or 10% of the African continent, including the whole of present-day Tanzania, plus sizeable parts of Malawi, Zambia, the DRC, Uganda and Kenya. The Arabs had a saying: 'When the flute plays in Zanzibar, they dance on the lakes.' But it was an empire in name only, and Said never attempted to conquer or develop the area.

The end of Said's reign Sultan Said made periodic visits to Muscat, leaving his son Khaled as Governor of Zanzibar in his absence. Khaled had a predilection for French goods and called his principal country estate Marseilles, after the French Mediterranean port. When Khaled died of tuberculosis in November 1854, an order came from Said in Muscat appointing another son, the 20-year-old Majid, as governor.

In September 1856, Said sailed for Zanzibar again in his boat *Kitorie*. He travelled with his family, including his son Barghash, now 19 years old. Said ordered some loose planks of wood to be loaded onto the ship, saying that if anyone should die on board, the body must not be buried at sea according to Muslim custom, but embalmed and taken to Zanzibar in a coffin. Said seemed to know it was he who

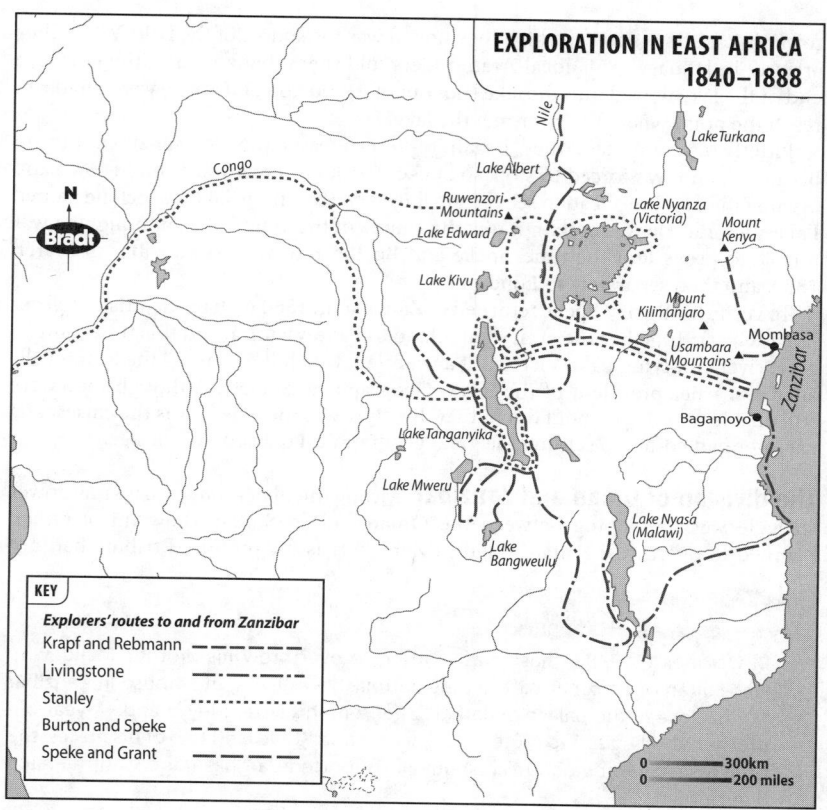

EXPLORATION IN EAST AFRICA 1840–1888

KEY

Explorers' routes to and from Zanzibar

Krapf and Rebmann — — — — —

Livingstone — · — · — · —

Stanley · · · · · · · · · · · ·

Burton and Speke — — — — —

Speke and Grant — — — — —

0 ——— 300km
0 ——— 200 miles

was about to die: he began to suffer severe pains from an old wound in his thigh followed by an attack of dysentery. On 19 October 1856, he died on board the ship. He was 65 years old.

Barghash put his father's body in the coffin and took command of the fleet. He knew his elder brother Majid would succeed his father as the new Sultan of Zanzibar, but he also realised that Majid would be unaware of their father's death. On the night of his arrival at Zanzibar, Barghash came ashore secretly and tried to take control of the palace at Mtoni and the Fort in Zanzibar Town, but he was unable to muster enough supporters and his attempt was thwarted.

On 28 October 1856, Majid bin Said was proclaimed Sultan of Zanzibar. A ship was sent to Oman with the news, but Said's eldest son Thuwaini refused to acknowledge Majid as sultan, believing that he was the legitimate successor. Majid agreed to pay Thuwaini 40,000 Maria Theresa dollars annually as compensation, but after a year the payment ceased.

Later European explorers By this time, the reports of early explorers like Rebmann and Krapf encouraged the Royal Geographical Society to send an expedition to east Africa to search for the source of the White Nile. The leaders were Lieutenant (later Sir) Richard Francis Burton and Lieutenant John Hanning Speke.

In December 1856, on the last day of mourning for Sultan Said, Burton and Speke arrived in Zanzibar. They sailed for Bagamoyo and followed the slave route towards Lake Tanganyika, which they hoped was the source of the Nile. When they arrived, in January 1858, local Arab traders told them that a river at the northern end of the lake flowed into the lake (not out of it). Burton and Speke were unable to reach the point where the river met the lake.

Bitterly disappointed, they began to return eastwards to Zanzibar. Burton became ill and was forced to stop, so Speke struck out northwards on his own and became the first European to see the great *nyanza* (meaning 'lake') which he named Lake Victoria. He was certain it was the source of the White Nile, although he was unable to prove it at the time. Speke and Burton returned to Zanzibar in March 1859, and then separately to London.

To verify his theory, Speke returned to Zanzibar in 1860 with the Scottish explorer James Grant. Together they travelled inland to Lake Victoria, and this time found a great river emptying Lake Victoria at a waterfall, which they named the Ripon Falls after an earlier president of the Royal Geographical Society. Although they were still unable to prove without doubt that this river was the Nile, it was the closest any explorer had gotten to settling the great geographical question of the age.

The division of Oman and Zanzibar Meanwhile, back on Zanzibar, a power struggle was developing between the Omani rulers. Sultan Thuwaini of Oman planned to overthrow Sultan Majid of Zanzibar, as his promised tribute had not

THE ESCAPE TO MARSEILLES

In October 1859, Barghash was plotting to overthrow his brother, Majid, who was Sultan of Zanzibar. At the time Barghash was living in a house in Zanzibar Town, close to the palace of Beit el Sahel, with his sister Meyye and 11-year-old brother Abdil Aziz. Two more sisters, Salme and Khole, and two of his nieces, the princesses Shembua and Farashuu, all supported Barghash and wanted Majid overthrown.

Majid, aware that his brother was plotting against him, arranged to have their houses watched and ordered Barghash's house to be blockaded. Several hundred soldiers were posted outside the front of the house with strict orders to shoot any suspicious person and cut off all communications. But Barghash had plenty of provisions, and his fellow conspirators smuggled water to him through the back of the house.

Meanwhile, at the fortified plantation of Marseilles (so named by another brother, Khaled, who had a predilection for all things French), in the centre of the island, the conspirators stored arms, ammunition and food supplies in preparation for a siege. Princess Salme played an important part in the preparations because she could write, and prepared secret messages to be carried between the other conspirators. She later referred to herself as 'secretary to the alliance of rebels'.

At midnight on 8 October 1859, Salme and Khole went to Barghash's house with a large escort including Shembua and Farashuu. Bluffing their way past the soldiers on duty (Arab women did not normally speak to strange men), they were allowed to pay the prisoner a short visit. They brought women's robes and veils and Barghash wrapped himself in a voluminous black robe, which left only his eyes free. The tallest women walked alongside him to make his height less conspicuous, and the guards on the door made way respectfully for the royal party when they left the building.

been paid. In February 1859, Thuwaini sailed southwards but was intercepted by a British cruiser at the eastern tip of Arabia. The British government wanted to keep control of the sea route to India, and did not want a civil war to develop in this area. Captain Hamerton, the British consul, had died, but Thuwaini was persuaded to submit his claims to the arbitration of Lord Canning, the Governor General of India. Thuwaini agreed and returned to Muscat.

But Majid was in danger from another member of the family. His brother Barghash was still plotting to overthrow him and proclaim himself Sultan of Zanzibar. Majid learnt of the plot but Barghash escaped to the Marseilles plantation. He was finally captured and exiled to India for two years (see box, *The escape to Marseilles*, below).

In April 1861, Lord Canning declared that Oman and Zanzibar should be completely separate. The annual tribute from Zanzibar to Oman was reinstated, and in March 1862, Britain and France signed an Anglo–French declaration which recognised Majid as Sultan of Zanzibar and his territories as an independent sovereignty.

Although the Mwinyi Mkuu still lived in the palace at Dunga, his power was now negligible. Hassan II was succeeded by Mohammed, who died in 1865, aged 80. He was succeeded by his son, Ahmed, who died of smallpox in March 1873, leaving no male heir. The line of the Mwinyi Mkuu of Zanzibar had come to an end, and its passing was hardly noticed.

Once outside the town, Barghash threw off his disguise and headed for Marseilles with his supporters, while his sisters returned to Zanzibar Town. Majid soon heard news of Barghash's escape, and mustered 5,000 soldiers, while the British consul, Sir Christopher Rigby, provided nine soldiers and a gun from the British warship HMS *Assaye*.

Majid marched to Marseilles and started to bombard the house, but Barghash's supporters emerged from their fortifications, and fought off Majid's troops until sunset. Several hundred lives were lost. Majid retreated for the night but, as he and his army slept, Barghash and his supporters slipped back into town. On the morning of 16 October, Majid re-advanced on Marseilles and smashed open the gates, only to find it abandoned.

By this time, Barghash had returned to his house. Realising that his plans were thwarted, he remained concealed, refusing even to go to the window. Rigby arranged for HMS *Assaye* to be anchored just offshore, and a detachment of marines landed and marched to the front of Barghash's house, calling on Barghash to surrender. When there was no answer, the marines started to fire their guns at the front of the house. Khole, calling from her house across the street, persuaded her brother to surrender. Contemporary reports describe how cries of *Aman!* (Peace!) were heard from inside the house and how, after the firing had stopped, Rigby rapped on the door with his walking stick and demanded immediate surrender. When Barghash emerged, Rigby arrested him and put him on board the *Assaye*. He was taken to India, where he lived in exile for two years. Abdil Aziz insisted on accompanying his elder brother and stayed in India after Barghash's return in 1861.

Princess Salme was rejected by her family, and in 1866, met a German trader called Heinrich Ruete. They became lovers and moved to Germany, where Salme changed her name to Emily and later wrote a book about her life at the court of Zanzibar (see box, *Princess Salme*, page 208).

In 1866, in Oman, Thuwaini was murdered in his sleep by his son Salim, who succeeded him. Majid discontinued the payment of the tribute on the grounds that Salim was a usurper, and Oman withdrew into isolation. This isolation lasted for over 100 years until the accession of Sultan Qaboos bin Said in 1970.

DAVID LIVINGSTONE AND 'STINKIBAR' In 1866, the Scottish missionary and explorer David Livingstone arrived in Zanzibar. He had already travelled across much of central and southern Africa, and written at great length about the horrors of the slave trade. He wanted to introduce what he regarded as essential elements of civilisation – commerce and Christianity – to Africa as a way of defeating the slave trade. He had also been asked by the Royal Geographical Society to clarify the pattern of the watersheds in the area of Lake Nyasa and Lake Tanganyika and their relation to the source of the White Nile (still an unsolved problem for the geographers of the day).

By this period, Zanzibar's increasing trade and growing population had created its own problems and Livingstone did not enjoy his stay:

> No-one can truly enjoy good health here. The stench from … two square miles of exposed sea-beach, which is the general depository of the filth of the town, is quite horrible. At night, it is so gross and crass, one might cut a slice and manure the garden with it. It might be called 'Stinkibar' rather than Zanzibar.

During the same period, other European visitors arriving by ship claimed they could smell Zanzibar before they could see it. In the town itself, the freshwater springs were not particularly fresh. Dr James Christie, an English physician who arrived in Zanzibar in 1869, reported that the springs consisted of the 'diluted drainage of dunghills and graveyards'. Not surprisingly, this led to frequent bouts of dysentery and epidemics of smallpox and cholera. Malaria and bilharzia were also problems. Cholera epidemics had occurred in 1821 and 1836, and smallpox in 1858. Later cholera epidemics in 1858 and from 1869 to 1870 killed one-sixth of the population of Zanzibar Town, and 35,000 people throughout the island.

At this time, slavery had still not been abolished on Zanzibar. In the early 1860s, an average 15,000 slaves a year were being imported into Zanzibar from mainland Africa, and by 1866 this had grown to 20,000 a year. The slave population had reached its peak and clove production entered a phase of overproduction and stagnation, so prices dropped.

As a result of the declining profitability of clove production, there was a greater interest in the production of coconut and sesame seed oils, mainly for export to France. There was also a revival of sugar production, and rubber plantations were established along the coast.

LIVINGSTONE, STANLEY AND THE RELIEF EXPEDITIONS David Livingstone had left Zanzibar in March 1866. Lack of news in the outside world led to speculation on his whereabouts, and in January 1871, the American journalist Henry Morton Stanley arrived in Zanzibar, having been commissioned by the *New York Herald* to search for the 'lost explorer'. In November the same year, Stanley arrived at Ujiji, where he found Livingstone and greeted him with the now immortal phrase, 'Doctor Livingstone, I presume?' (for details on the explorations of Livingstone, see boxes *David Livingstone*, page 192, and *Henry Morton Stanley*, page 20).

After Stanley had found Livingstone and returned alone to Zanzibar, Livingstone stayed at Kazeh until August 1872, then set off southwards on another expedition to find the source of the Nile, which he thought would take no more than a few months (he had already been in the interior for six years at this stage).

Meanwhile the RGS in London was unaware of Stanley's 'find', so in February 1872, the Livingstone Search and Relief Expedition, led by Lieutenant Llewellyn Dawson, was dispatched to Zanzibar in the steamship *Abydos*. Two months later, the expedition arrived in Zanzibar, where their ship was caught in the freak hurricane of 14 April. Every ship and dhow in the harbour was driven ashore except the *Abydos*. The town was wrecked, many people were killed, and over two-thirds of the coconut and clove trees on the island were uprooted.

A few weeks after the hurricane, in May 1872, Stanley arrived at Bagamoyo, where he met Dawson and told him that Livingstone was safe and would be arriving after a few more months. Dawson cancelled the Search and Relief Expedition and returned to London. But by the end of 1872 Livingstone had still not arrived back at Zanzibar as expected, so in February 1873 a second Relief Expedition, led by Lieutenant Verney Lovett Cameron, set out from Zanzibar to find him.

Unknown to Cameron and the rest of the world, Livingstone had grown ill, with a recurrence of dysentery. On 2 May 1873, he died in the village of Chitambo, near Lake Bangweulu (in present-day Zambia), 800km (500 miles) south of Ujiji, and even further from the actual source of the Nile. Two of his companions carried his body back towards Zanzibar. In August 1873, they reached Kazeh, where they met Cameron.

Cameron decided to march on to Ujiji, which he reached in February 1874, and where he found Livingstone's papers. From Ujiji, Cameron continued westwards, eventually reaching the Atlantic coast in November 1875, thereby becoming the first European to travel across this part of Africa from east to west.

SULTAN BARGHASH AND JOHN KIRK By this time, on Zanzibar, Sultan Majid had died, aged 36. His only child was a daughter so his brother Barghash (who had twice already tried to seize the throne and had returned to Zanzibar from exile in India in 1861) finally succeeded to the throne, and was proclaimed sultan on 7 October 1870. In the same year, Dr John Kirk (who had originally come to Zanzibar as a medical officer on Livingstone's expedition) was made acting British consul.

After the hurricane of April 1872, Sultan Barghash had announced plans to grow new plantations, and the slave trade picked up once again. By late 1872, around 16,000 slaves had been imported into Zanzibar. The hurricane hit only the southern tip of Pemba, leaving most of the clove trees on that island untouched. By the 1880s, the island was producing about 80% of the total clove harvest from Zanzibar and Pemba.

At the same time, the anti-slavery movement continued to grow, fuelled in America by the publication of *Uncle Tom's Cabin*. In January 1873, Sir Bartle Frere, a special envoy from Queen Victoria, arrived in Zanzibar to negotiate a treaty which he hoped would finally put an end to the Arab slave trade. Sultan Barghash was naturally reluctant to end slavery and Frere sailed for England at the beginning of March 1873 without a treaty. Almost immediately the British navy began a blockade of every slave port on the mainland. The number of slaves passing through the Customs House in Zanzibar Town between January and March dropped to 21, compared with 4,000 in the same period the previous year.

In June 1873, Sir John Kirk informed Sultan Barghash that a total blockade of Zanzibar Island was imminent. Reluctantly Barghash signed the Anglo–Zanzibari treaty which provided for the complete abolition of the slave trade in Barghash's territories, the closing of all slave markets and the protection of all liberated slaves.

Transport of slaves was forbidden, and slaves could no longer be exported from mainland Africa to Zanzibar and Pemba, except for domestic purposes.

The large slave market in Zanzibar Town was closed immediately. The site was bought by missionaries of the Universities' Mission to Central Africa (UMCA), and

HENRY MORTON STANLEY

The man known to the world as Henry Morton Stanley was born John Rowland on 29 January 1841 in Denbigh in Wales. He spent nine years in a workhouse and two years as a farmhand before joining a ship from Liverpool to New Orleans, which he reached in 1858. In New Orleans he was adopted by his employer, a cotton merchant, from whom he took his new name, Henry Stanley. 'Morton' was added later.

By 1869, Stanley was a correspondent for the *New York Herald*. The manager of the newspaper, James Gordon Bennett, dispatched him to Africa with orders to cover the inauguration of the Suez Canal, and then find Livingstone if he was alive, or bring back his bones if he was dead.

Stanley arrived in Zanzibar on 6 January 1871. He borrowed a top hat from the American consul, John Francis Webb, and went to visit Sultan Barghash, who gave him letters of recommendation to show his agents in the interior. Stanley set off from Zanzibar in March that year, just two days before the start of the rainy season. His provisions included American cloth, beads of glass, coral and china for trading, plus two silver goblets and a bottle of champagne for the day he met Livingstone.

Stanley finally met Livingstone at Ujiji, on the eastern shore of Lake Tanganyika, on 10 November 1871. According to Stanley's own description of the meeting, Stanley took off his hat, held out his hand, and said, 'Doctor Livingstone, I presume?' When Livingstone answered, 'Yes,' Stanley continued with, 'I thank God that I have been permitted to see you,' to which Livingstone gravely replied, 'I feel thankful that I am here to welcome you.'

After these traditional English niceties, and the seemingly mundane phrase that was to dog Stanley for the rest of his life, Stanley and Livingstone travelled in the area together for some time, but Livingstone was still determined to discover the source of the Nile and pressed on southwards alone. Stanley returned to Zanzibar on 7 May 1872, before travelling to London.

Two years later, Stanley gave up journalism to return to Africa as an explorer. He reached Zanzibar again in September 1874, and left for the mainland in November the same year. On this expedition he rounded the southern shore of Lake Victoria, went through Buganda (now Uganda), and followed the Congo River (through present-day DRC) to the Atlantic Ocean, which he reached on 12 August 1877, thus crossing Africa in 999 days.

From 1879 to 1884, Stanley returned to the Congo for King Léopold II of Belgium. He established and governed the Congo Free State (which was to become Zaire, now renamed the Democratic Republic of Congo), and the town of Stanleyville (now Kisangani) was named after him.

After another expedition from 1887 to 1889, Stanley returned to Britain a celebrity. He was married in Westminster Abbey in 1890, elected to Parliament as a Liberal Unionist for North Lambeth in 1895, and knighted in 1899. He died in London on 10 May 1904.

work started on the cathedral which can still be seen in Zanzibar Town today (see *Chapter 6*, page 189).

One of the main effects of the treaty, now that slavery was illegal, was to push up the price of slaves and the trade continued in a clandestine manner. Through the 1870s smugglers were estimated to be exporting between 10,000 and 12,000 slaves a year.

In 1875, Kirk brought Sultan Barghash an official invitation to visit Britain to ratify the Anglo–Zanzibari treaty. In June the same year, Barghash and Kirk arrived in London where Barghash received the Freedom of the City at the Guildhall and attended a state banquet at Mansion House. While Barghash was in London, his sister Salme had come from Germany (see box, *Princess Salme*, page 208) hoping to be reconciled with her brother, but Barghash refused to meet her. After four weeks of intensive sightseeing and entertainment, Barghash and his party returned to Zanzibar via Paris and Marseilles, arriving home in September.

For the British, Zanzibar was no longer a distant, obscure island, and links between the two countries became even more firmly established. In 1869, the Suez Canal had opened, making the sea voyage between Britain and the coast of east Africa much shorter and simpler. In 1872, the British India Steamship Navigation Company started a monthly mail service between Zanzibar and Aden. It brought the first scheduled passenger and cargo service to Zanzibar, which allowed merchandise to be exported quickly. Communication was again improved in 1879, when the Eastern Telegraph Company completed their cable from Zanzibar to Europe via Aden, and a telegraphic link with Europe was established.

Inspired by his visit to Europe, Barghash decided to make many changes on Zanzibar. Advised by John Kirk (now firmly installed as the power behind the throne), he appointed Lieutenant William Lloyd Mathews (see box, *William Lloyd Mathews*, page 214) to reorganise his army and enforce his sovereignty over the interior.

During his exile in India, Barghash had seen the opulent wealth of the Indian palaces and he tried to emulate them on Zanzibar. Many luxurious palaces were built, including Chukwani, to the south of Zanzibar Town, and Maruhubi Palace, to the north, for his harem. Another palace in the town became known as the Beit al Ajaib, or House of Wonders, as it was the first building on Zanzibar to have electric lighting. In all of his palaces, Barghash upgraded the dinner services from silver to gold. Divan coverings of goat and camel hair were replaced by silks and taffetas, and French carpets covered the floors.

Barghash introduced Zanzibar's first clean water system to replace supplies from local wells and rainwater: aqueducts and conduits brought pure water from a spring at Bububu into Zanzibar Town, a distance of some 6km. Other developments introduced by Barghash included a police force, an ice-making factory, electric street lighting, and telephones to connect his city and country palaces. Barghash also built and improved the roads on the island, and every year he provided one of his private steamships for Muslims wishing to make the pilgrimage to Mecca.

THE SCRAMBLE FOR AFRICA In 1884, Dr Karl Peters, founder of the Society for German Colonisation, arrived in Zanzibar, then sailed for the mainland where he made 'treaties of eternal friendship' with the local African chiefs in return for large areas of land. By the time he reached Kilimanjaro he had annexed more than 6,000km² (2,500 square miles) of land, which were still nominally under the control of Sultan Barghash.

Britain was concerned at the presence of a rival European power on its patch, but was distracted by events elsewhere. In January 1885, Khartoum, the capital of

Anglo–Egyptian Sudan, fell to the forces of the Mahdi. The British general Gordon was killed and the British governor of Equatoria Province, south of Khartoum, was cut off (ironically, the governor was actually a German called Eduard Schnitzer, although he had adopted the name Emin Pasha and was working for the British).

Otto von Bismarck, the German chancellor, saw the Mahdi's victory as a sign of Britain's weakness and believed that Germany could consolidate its claims in east Africa without British opposition. In February the same year the General Act of Berlin, signed by Kaiser Wilhelm of Germany, officially proclaimed a German protectorate over the territories annexed by Karl Peters. Sultan Barghash was only formally told about his loss of land in April of the same year. He hoped for support from the British, but Britain did not want to make an enemy of Germany, and so declined.

In June 1885, the Germans claimed another protectorate over Witu and the mouth of the Tana River, near Lamu, and in August the same year, five ships of the German navy, commanded by Carl Paschen, arrived in Zanzibar harbour. Paschen demanded that Sultan Barghash recognise the German protectorates. Kirk, on the recommendations of the British government, persuaded Barghash to submit.

A few days after the arrival of the German fleet, another German ship entered the harbour, carrying Barghash's sister Salme (who had eloped to Germany in 1866). She was with her son Said-Rudolph, now 16 years old, and two other children. On Kirk's advice, Barghash tolerated Salme's presence. Barghash sent his formal recognition of the German protectorate to Carl Paschen and two months later, the British government arranged for a joint commission between Britain, Germany and France to establish their own boundaries in the mainland territories that were still officially under the control of the Sultan of Zanzibar.

After lengthy discussions the first Anglo–German agreement was signed in late 1886. Barghash's lands were reduced to Zanzibar, Pemba, Mafia, Lamu and a ten-mile (16km) wide coastal strip stretching around 1,200km (about 750 miles) from the Tana River, near Lamu, to the Rovuma River, near Cape Delgado. The rest of the mainland, east of Lake Victoria and Lake Tanganyika, was divided between Britain and Germany. Britain took the northern portion, between the Tana and Umba rivers, which became British East Africa, later Kenya. Germany took the southern portion, between the Umba and Rovuma rivers. This became German East Africa, later Tanganyika (see map, *Zanzibar and east Africa*, opposite).

Given no option, Barghash agreed to this treaty in December 1886 and the French government signed it a few days later. In June 1887, Barghash leased the northern section of his coastal strip (between the Tana and Umba rivers) to the British East African Association (BEAA), which had been formed by William Mackinnon in May the same year. Meanwhile the Germans and Portuguese met in Barghash's absence to discuss their own border, and Portugal gained more of Barghash's land in the south.

In February 1888, Barghash sailed to Muscat, to recuperate from tuberculosis and elephantiasis at the healing Bushire Springs on the Persian coast. He returned to Zanzibar on 26 March, but died five hours after his arrival, aged 51.

On 29 March 1888, Barghash's brother Khalifa bin Said was proclaimed sultan. In April the same year, the British East African Association became the Imperial British East Africa Company (IBEA), with its capital at Mombasa, which was beginning to take Zanzibar's place as the commercial centre for Africa.

A BRITISH PROTECTORATE In September 1889, Khalifa signed an agreement with the British government agreeing to abolish slavery in his territories. Anybody who entered the sultan's realms, and any children born, would be free. Britain and Germany were awarded a permanent right to search for slaves in Zanzibar's waters.

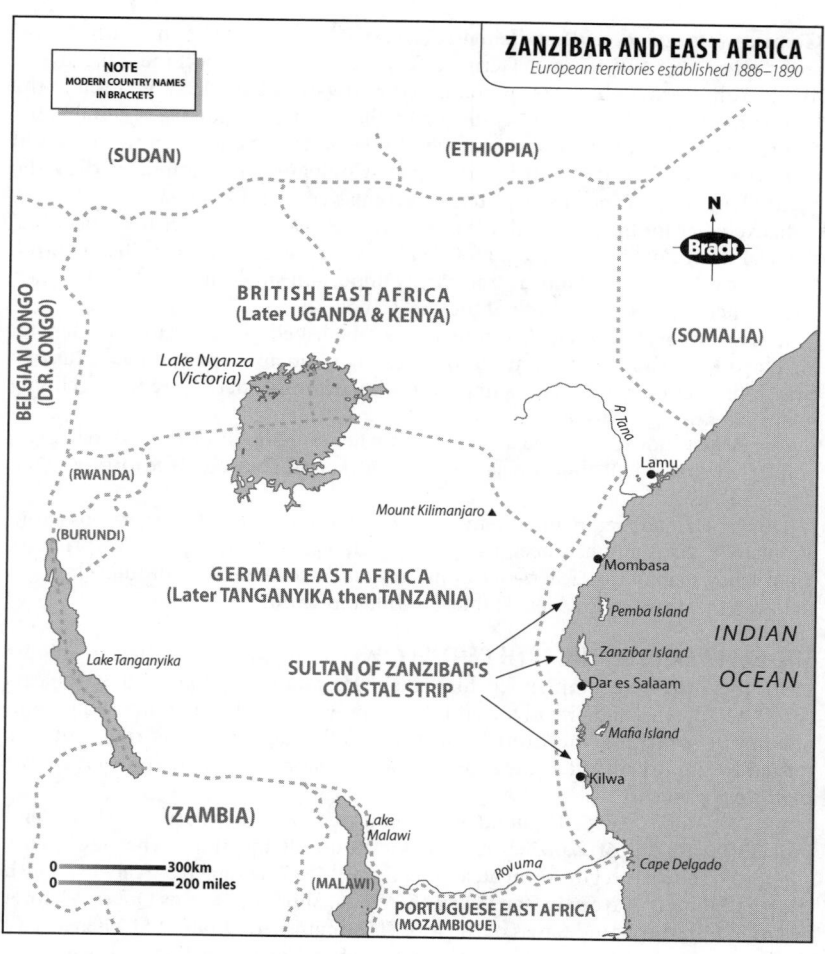

ZANZIBAR AND EAST AFRICA
European territories established 1886–1890

NOTE
MODERN COUNTRY NAMES
IN BRACKETS

(SUDAN)

(ETHIOPIA)

N

BRITISH EAST AFRICA
(Later UGANDA & KENYA)

(SOMALIA)

BELGIAN CONGO
(D.R. CONGO)

Lake Nyanza
(Victoria)

R Tana

Lamu

(RWANDA)

Mount Kilimanjaro ▲

Mombasa

(BURUNDI)

GERMAN EAST AFRICA
(Later TANGANYIKA then TANZANIA)

Pemba Island

INDIAN

Lake Tanganyika

**SULTAN OF ZANZIBAR'S
COASTAL STRIP**

Zanzibar Island

OCEAN

Dar es Salaam

Mafia Island

Kilwa

(ZAMBIA)

Lake
Malawi

0 ——— 300km
0 ——— 200 miles

(MALAWI)

Rovuma

Cape Delgado

PORTUGUESE EAST AFRICA
(MOZAMBIQUE)

As a sign of Britain's appreciation, Khalifa was knighted, but less than a month later he died, aged 36.

Khalifa's brother, Ali bin Said, was the fourth and last of Said's sons to become Sultan of Zanzibar. On 1 August 1890, Ali signed an anti-slavery treaty forbidding the purchase and sale of slaves. With the end of the slave trade, the only viable export from the interior was ivory, by now a rapidly waning asset.

Meanwhile in the interior, Karl Peters entered Uganda in February 1890 and claimed the territory for Germany, just ahead of Sir Frederick Jackson from England. The British politician Lord Robert Salisbury realised that control of the Upper Nile could lead indirectly to the control of the Suez Canal and thus the trade route to India. Germany was persuaded to renounce any claims over Uganda in return for British support of the Kaiser against the major European powers of the day, France and Russia.

By the second Anglo–German agreement (the Treaty of Zanzibar) of 1 July 1890, Germany agreed to recognise a British protectorate over the Sultanate of Zanzibar, and to abandon any claim to Witu and the country inland as far as the Upper Nile.

Germany also abandoned any claim to the west of Lake Nyasa but, in return, gained sovereignty over the coast of German East Africa, later to become Tanganyika. The British–German border was continued westwards across Lake Victoria to the boundary of the Belgian territory of Congo, thus securing Uganda for Britain. The British coastal strip (which still belonged to the Sultan of Zanzibar) was removed from the control of the British East Africa Company and administered by the British East Africa Protectorate, later to become Kenya and Uganda.

In exchange for the thousands of square miles of east African territory, including the islands of Zanzibar (Unguja and Pemba) which it gave up to British control, Germany gained Heligoland, a strategically important small island off the German coast which lay near the mouth of the Kiel Canal.

In 1891, a constitutional government was established in Zanzibar, with General Sir Lloyd Mathews as first minister. But although Zanzibar enjoyed the status of a British protectorate, the island's importance as a commercial centre was declining further in favour of Mombasa.

The British now controlled Zanzibar, so when Sultan Ali died in March 1893, without making a will, they proclaimed Hamad, son of Thuwaini (the former sultan of Oman), as sultan.

During Hamad's reign, in November 1895, Zanzibar issued its first stamps (from about 1875 the island had been using Indian stamps with 'Zanzibar' overprinted). Then a newspaper, the *Gazette for Zanzibar and East Africa*, was produced. It was followed by others in English, Arabic, Swahili and Urdu.

THE LAST YEARS OF THE 19TH CENTURY When Sultan Hamad died in August 1896, the British recommended his cousin Hamoud as sultan. But Barghash's son, Khaled, who had already tried to seize power from Hamad, made a second attempt at snatching the throne. He was briefly successful this time but was ousted by the British, after 'the shortest war in history' (see box, *The shortest war in history*, page 26).

On 27 August 1896, Hamoud was conducted into the Customs House and proclaimed Sultan of Zanzibar amidst the salute of the ships. The new sultan supported the British government, and on 5 April 1897 he signed a treaty to abolish the legal status of slavery in Zanzibar and Pemba. Shortly after this Queen Victoria awarded him the Grand Cross of the Most Distinguished Order of St Michael and St George. Hamoud sent his son Ali to school at Harrow in England, where he represented his father at the coronation of King Edward VII.

Sultan Hamoud died on 18 July 1902 and the British proclaimed the 18-year-old Ali as the new sultan. From his school days he spoke English fluently, and continued to travel in Europe during his reign. In May 1911, Ali attended the coronation of King George V in England. While in Europe, his health deteriorated and he abdicated in December 1911. He spent the last seven years of his life in Europe, and died in Paris in December 1918. Khalifa bin Harub, a cousin of Ali, became Sultan Khalifa II on 16 December 1911.

ZANZIBAR ENTERS THE 20TH CENTURY Sultan Khalifa bin Harub proved to be a moderate but influential ruler, and proceeded to guide Zanzibar through the first half of the turbulent 20th century with skill and diplomacy.

Soon after Khalifa gained power, changes were made to the British way of overseeing their interests in Zanzibar. In July 1913, responsibility for Zanzibar was transferred from the Foreign Office to the Colonial Office. The post of British consul became British Resident, subject to the control of the Governor of the

British East Africa Protectorate. At the same time a Protectorate Council was established. This was an advisory body with the sultan as president and the British Resident as vice president.

During World War I, the German and British armies, with conscripted African soldiers, were involved in several campaigns on the mainland. The war did not affect Zanzibar directly except for one incident when the British ship *Pegasus* was bombarded and sunk by the German ship *Königsberg* in Zanzibar Town harbour (graves marking the bodies of sailors killed in this incident can still be seen on Grave Island).

Towards the end of the war, in 1917, the British army drove the Germans out of their territory and marched into Dar es Salaam. Khaled, who had tried to seize the throne of Zanzibar during 'the shortest war' in 1896, was still there and was captured. He was exiled to the Seychelles, then allowed to return to Mombasa in 1925, where he lived quietly until 1927.

After the war, the German East African territory was administered by Britain under a League of Nations mandate and called Tanganyika. Later, in 1920, the British East Africa Protectorate became known as the Kenya Colony.

In 1925, the British Resident on Zanzibar was made directly responsible to the Colonial Office in London, and a new Legislative Council was established. The ten-mile (16km) wide strip of land along the coast of Kenya, including Mombasa, which had been leased to Kenya in 1895, was still technically 'owned' by the Sultan of Zanzibar and the new Kenyan government continued to pay the lease of £11,000 per year.

During World War II, Zanzibar was not involved in any military action. The war's main effect was to interrupt the supply of rice, a staple food for the Asian and African people, that had until then been imported from Burma.

REVOLUTION AND THE ROAD TO INDEPENDENCE After World War II, Britain gradually allowed the local people of Zanzibar to become involved in the islands' government. Several local political parties were formed and Zanzibar's first elections were held in July 1957. The Afro-Shirazi Union (which later became the Afro-Shirazi Party, or ASP) defeated the Zanzibar Nationalist Party (ZNP). Broadly speaking, the ASP was dominated by Africans, the ZNP by Arabs.

In October 1960, Sultan Khalifa died, after ruling for 49 years, and was succeeded by his only son, Abdullah. In November the same year, Zanzibar was granted a new constitution which allowed for the elections of the members of the Legislative Council. Elections took place in January 1961, producing no clear result, and again in June 1961, but these were marred by serious interracial rioting. Nevertheless, the ZNP, along with the aligned Zanzibar and Pemba People's Party, won 13 of the seats on the council, while the ASP won ten.

Britain realised that internal self-government for Zanzibar was inevitable, and this was finally granted in June 1963. In July that year, Sultan Abdullah died following a reign filled with personal pain and involving the amputation of both legs. Abdullah was succeeded by his eldest son, Jamshid.

On 10 December 1963, Zanzibar became an independent sultanate, and the coastal strip was finally ceded to Kenya, which became independent two days later. Zanzibar was made a full member of the British Commonwealth and on 16 December became a member of the United Nations. But the new sultanate was short-lived: on 12 January 1964, the Zanzibari government was overthrown in a violent revolution.

The leader of Zanzibar's revolution was a Ugandan called John Okello who had been living in Pemba. The local African population supported Okello with great enthusiasm, and went on a rampage through the islands, during which more than 17,000 Arabs and Indians were killed in one night. As a result, the leader of the Afro-Shirazi Party, Sheik Abied Amani Karume, was installed as president of the newly proclaimed People's Republic of Zanzibar, which included the islands of Unguja and Pemba.

Karume and other prominent ASP members formed the Revolutionary Government of Zanzibar (Serikali ya Mapinduzi ya Zanzibar, or SMZ). Most of Zanzibar's Asian and Indian people left the islands; their property was confiscated and their land nationalised. On the mainland, Sultan Jamshid was given temporary asylum in Dar es Salaam, then went to Britain where he lived in exile.

Meanwhile, Tanganyika had also become independent in December 1961, with Julius Nyerere elected as president the following year. Nyerere had known

THE SHORTEST WAR IN HISTORY

Sultan Hamad died on 25 August 1896 while the British consul, Arthur Hardinge, was on leave in England. The acting British consul, Basil Cave, recommended that Hamoud (Hamad's cousin) be appointed sultan, but when Cave and Sir Lloyd Mathews reached the palace of Beit el Sahel in Zanzibar Town, they found the doors barred. Khaled, the son of Barghash (and another cousin of Hamoud), had arrived before them with about 60 armed men, entered the palace by climbing through a broken window, and been quickly joined by more than 2,000 supporters.

Khaled proclaimed himself sultan, and raised the red flag of Zanzibar on the palace roof. But Basil Cave refused to recognise his claim: British ships in the harbour landed guards of marines, which were posted at the British consulate (where many British women sought refuge), the Customs House, and elsewhere around the town. Many foreigners gathered on the roof of the English Club, where they had a clear view of the harbour and the palace.

On the morning of 26 August, the three British ships were reinforced by the timely arrival of two others, and the following day, at dawn, the British fleet under Rear Admiral Harry Holdsworth Rawson delivered an ultimatum: Khaled was to surrender, disarm, evacuate the palace and be at the Customs House by 09.00, or the British ships would open fire. At 08.00 Khaled sent an envoy to Cave, asking for a chance to discuss peace, but his request was refused.

The palace clock struck three (09.00 British time) and at 09.02 the bombardment started. In half an hour, Beit el Sahel and the adjoining palace of Beit el Hukm were badly damaged. The lighthouse outside the palace was in flames and the nearby House of Wonders was also hit a few times. Many of Khaled's supporters had fled, leaving 500 dead and wounded lying about the palace grounds.

At 09.40 Khaled surrendered. He lowered the flag, the firing ceased and the war was over. This dispute over the succession is listed in the *Guinness Book of Records* as the shortest war in history.

Khaled escaped through the narrow streets and fled to the German consulate, where he was given asylum. As the steps of the consulate led onto the beach, Khaled was able to board the German warship *Seeadler* without risking arrest and was taken to Dar es Salaam, where he lived in exile. He died in Mombasa in 1927, aged 53.

and supported Karume since the mid 1950s, but the Zanzibar Revolution created problems in Tanganyika, inspiring an attempted coup in Dar es Salaam only a few days later. (To suppress this coup Nyerere received help from Britain in the form of a battalion of commandos.)

Once Nyerere had regained control, he approached Karume to discuss a political union, and on 24 April 1964 the two countries joined to form the United Republic of Tanganyika and Zanzibar. In October the same year the country was renamed Tanzania (from 'Tan' in Tanganyika and 'Zan' in Zanzibar). Nyerere became the president of the new state while Karume became vice president. The SMZ was to control all local affairs on the islands of Unguja and Pemba, while foreign affairs would be handled by the Tanzanian government.

During the negotiations, John Okello had gone to the mainland to meet Nyerere. On his return to Zanzibar in March 1964 he was sent back to Dar es Salaam. He made no further public appearances.

Despite the so-called union, Karume kept Zanzibar separate from the rest of Tanzania in many respects. The clove plantations on Unguja and Pemba were developed and the earnings from exports continued to increase, but this revenue was not shared with mainland Tanzania.

After the revolution almost all of the European and Asian residents had left Zanzibar. To fill the vacuum caused by the departure of these skilled people, Karume attracted technical and military assistance from Cuba, China and the then Eastern bloc countries of East Germany, Bulgaria and the Soviet Union. Engineers from East Germany designed and built new blocks of flats in Zanzibar Town, and in 'new towns' elsewhere on the islands of Unguja and Pemba. In 1970, Karume's government was accused of human rights violations against political opponents.

On 7 April 1972, Karume was assassinated while playing cards in the ASP headquarters in Zanzibar Town. Aboud Jumbe Mwinyi, who had been a member of the ASP since before independence, became the new leader of the Revolutionary Government. Mwinyi was less hardline than Karume and introduced several reforms. He was also more sympathetic towards Nyerere and mainland Tanzania. In February 1977, the ASP united with Nyerere's party, the Tanzania African National Union (TANU), to form the Chama Cha Mapinduzi (Party of the Revolution).

After this unification, both leaders began to relax some of their policies on nationalised industries and state financial control. Relations with some Western nations, including Britain, slowly improved. In July 1979, as a sign that Tanzania was regaining some international respect, Queen Elizabeth II visited Zanzibar. Then, in 1980, the first presidential elections took place, and Aboud Jumbe Mwinyi was officially elected as President of Zanzibar.

POLITICS AND RECENT HISTORY

Zanzibar is a semi-autonomous state within the United Republic of Tanzania. It is governed by its own Revolutionary Council and 50-strong House of Representatives, whose members are elected or appointed for five-year terms. The President of Zanzibar is also the Vice President of Tanzania.

Zanzibar has seen many changes on the political front since the early 1990s. Along with the rest of Tanzania, Zanzibar ceased to be a one-party state in 1992. For the first time in almost 20 years, Chama Cha Mapinduzi (CCM) was faced with several new opposition groups, which quickly coalesced into parties. The Civic United Front (CUF), led by Seif Sherif Hamad from Pemba, became the major opposition party for Zanzibar. Elections were planned for October 1995, as all parties agreed that a gradual transition to a multi-party political system would be beneficial. Salmin Amour remained as Zanzibar's president and CCM leader, while on the mainland the CCM chose a new president, Benjamin Mkapa, in July 1995. This followed the resignation of Julius Nyerere, the 'father of the nation', who had ruled since independence, although he remained an important figure behind the scenes.

Elections were duly held in Zanzibar on 22 October 1995, a week before the mainland vote. It was a simple two-horse race between Salmin Amour and Seif Sherif Hamad for President of Zanzibar, and between CCM and CUF candidates in the islands' parliament. There was a very high turnout (over 95% of registered voters) and voting passed peacefully, but the counting took three days for just over 300,000 votes.

Although the ruling party's control of the government structure gave it an in-built advantage, it soon transpired that the CUF was polling strongly. Complaints by the CCM that the election process was flawed were withdrawn when it transpired that Amour had won with 50.2% of the vote, but then the CUF picked up the claim of unfair procedures. International observers agreed that there was evidence of serious irregularities, but the nominally independent Zanzibar Electoral Commission refused to hold a recount or to compare their figures with some of those recorded by the UN. On the mainland, a divided opposition and an even more shambolic election, not to mention the possibility of vote-rigging, meant that the CCM and President Mkapa stayed in power. The CUF brought a high-profile legal case against the CCM on the grounds that the results and the whole election process were not representative of the wishes of the people, but this was bogged down in the courts and finally dismissed in 1998.

In the lead-up to elections in late 2000, Amour rocked the boat by announcing he would stand for a third (and unconstitutional) term as president. The instant response among the people of Zanzibar was a sharp swing in support for the CUF. An equally quick response from CCM high command meant Amour was relieved of his post, and Amani Karume, son of President Karume who had been assassinated in the 1960s, was ushered in as Zanzibar's new CCM leader and presidential candidate.

At a grass-roots level, there was still considerable support for the CUF, but the strong Pemba following this party enjoyed meant that ostensibly political differences stood in danger of degenerating into inter-island (or 'tribal') conflicts. This sense of grievance also translated into separatist aspirations; since the end of the 1990s, the desire of many Zanzibaris to be independent of mainland Tanzania has been stronger than it had been for many years. The urge for separation is also partly due to the death in 1999 of Julius Nyerere.

When elections were held in October 2000, President Mkapa and the CCM romped home with huge and increased majorities. The people of mainland Tanzania seemed happy (in fact, many seemed indifferent) about the result, and international observers agreed that voting had been free and fair. On Zanzibar, however, it was a different story. In the period leading up to the election, fist-fights erupted on several occasions between CUF and CCM supporters, local party offices were attacked or burned, and CUF demonstrations were broken up by the police and army. On election day, things were so bad in 16 constituencies that the whole process was cancelled, and a re-run vote arranged for 5 November. CUF demonstrations turned into violent protests, especially in Zanzibar Town, to be met with police tear gas, rubber bullets and even live ammunition. In disgust, the CUF pulled out of the election process, leaving the November re-runs to be easily won by CCM candidates. In response, the CUF announced its continued boycott of procedures in the House of Representatives.

In one of his first moves as newly elected president of Zanzibar, Amani Karume called for peace and reconciliation between the two sides, which he backed up by releasing from prison the group of CUF leaders who'd been held on charges of treason since 1998. Hopes for peace were dashed shortly afterwards when a series of bombs exploded in Zanzibar. The trouble simmered on, with more CUF street protests in January 2001. This time the police used even stronger tactics to break things up: in a single day, between 20 and 70 demonstrators were shot, one policeman was killed, and many more were injured. The events were reported in media around the world, the USA and the donor nations of Europe expressed concern, and aid money which had been frozen following the discrepancies of the 1995 election remained firmly out of reach.

In March 2001, at the direct behest of President Mkapa, leaders from the CCM and the CUF tentatively started to discuss their differences, and in October that year, after a long series of negotiations, the two sides signed an accord to end their dispute over the election results. By 2002, the islands had returned to their traditional calm and peaceful atmosphere, and Zanzibar was fully open for business once again.

In the elections of October 2005, the CCM and the CUF were once again vying for power, with rallies held across the island throughout the summer of 2005. Although there seemed to be little in the way of party manifestos, and despite claims by the CUF of vote-rigging and other irregularities, this time the election passed off comparatively peacefully. With a 90% turnout of the electorate, the CCM retained control, with the CUF polling 46% of the total votes, and Amani Karume retaining the presidency. Tensions remained between the parties and their supporters, with the CUF claiming in both 2000 and 2005 that election victory had been stolen from them and the Zanzibar Electoral Commission citing many irregularities in the voting. Sporadic negotiations to agree on power-sharing terms and secure a peaceful resolution took an immediate back seat. However, in April 2008 a major setback stalled the process completely: the CCM called for a referendum to approve a contentious power-sharing agreement resulting in the CUF abandoning the negotiations altogether. The political future seemed murky with the poor rural population suffering from the lack of real commitment to bettering their future.

But then change did come, and on 1 November 2010, Zanzibar formally formed a government of national unity, known as the Revolutionary Government of Zanzibar. Overwhelmingly approving a constitutional change in July 2010, Zanzibari leaders paved the way for a possible power-sharing government. Subsequent general elections were broadly peaceful, in contrast to many previous violence-charged years. Good, orderly voter turnout was recorded and the Zanzibar Electoral Commission was praised by international observers for its improvements in election management.

Now headed by President Ali Mohamed Shein, of the ruling Chama cha Mapinduzi, and Seif Sharif Hamad, of the Civic United Front as vice president, the two main parties involved in the coalition government have pledged to work together and have divided up ministerial posts accordingly. Whilst the majority of old-school politicians effectively remain in power, there is a tangible sense of hope and positivity about this move amongst the population. With luck, the infighting and diminished political violence will lead to some practical good governance and improvements for the average Zanzibari.

ECONOMY

For the people of Zanzibar, fishing and farming are the main economic activities. From the beginning of the 19th century to the mid 1970s Zanzibar exported a large proportion of the world's supply of cloves, and the islands' economy was based largely on this commodity. Some diversification has occurred since then as the world market price for cloves fell dramatically in the 1980s, but cloves are still a major export, along with coconut products and other spices. In recent years, seaweed has also become an important export commodity. The potential for tourism to be a major earner of foreign currency has been recognised and has been developing apace for the last decade.

In 2006, Tanzania, and by association Zanzibar, was one of the 32 countries worldwide designated for HIPC (Heavily Indebted Poor Countries) debt relief.

HISTORY OF ZANZIBARI AGRICULTURE

The earliest peoples on Zanzibar are thought to have been hunter-gatherers who made little impact on the natural vegetation. However, the first Bantu settlers, who probably arrived sometime in the 3rd or 4th century AD, started to clear patches of natural forest to plant crops such as millet and sorghum.

At some stage, plants such as bananas, coconut palms and yams were introduced, possibly by peoples from Madagascar who in turn had originally migrated from the islands of Indonesia. As these crops became more popular, more indigenous forest was cleared.

In the 16th century, Portuguese traders established bases along the east African coast, including those on Zanzibar and Pemba, and introduced plants such as cassava and maize from their colonies in South America. More forest was felled as local people cleared the land required to grow these crops.

After the Omani Arabs gained control of the islands in the early 18th century, and the trade in ivory and slaves expanded, Zanzibar became an important import and export centre. Cassava was used for feeding the vast numbers of slaves who passed through the island's infamous market. Another major export at this time was copra (produced from coconuts) which meant more land was cleared for coconut palm plantations.

At the turn of the 19th century, cloves were introduced from other islands in the Indian Ocean, and they soon became a major export crop. Other spices, such as vanilla and cardamom, were also grown and yet more forest was cleared for plantations.

Throughout the 19th century, the powerful nations of Europe put pressure on the sultans of Zanzibar to restrict the trade in slaves. As this was reduced, the trade in cloves and other spices became even more important. During the colonial period, plantations continued to be developed and the natural forest continued to be reduced. A department of forestry was established to exploit the forests' timber supplies, but apparently it was not until the 1950s that it came to the attention of the Forestry Department that there was very little indigenous forest left on the island of Zanzibar. The largest remaining area, Jozani Forest, to the southeast of Zanzibar Town, was purchased from an Arab landowner by the department and the felling of trees was restricted. In 1960, Jozani was declared a protected nature reserve and in 2004 it became the heart of Zanzibar's first national park: Jozani-Chwaka Bay National Park.

Their debt wiped, with the African Development Bank cancelling a balance in excess of US$640 million, the economy gained new buoyancy. According to accountancy powerhouse PricewaterhouseCoopers, approximately 20% of government revenue was spent in paying external debt prior to HIPC; whilst afterwards less than 8% of revenue will be spent on debt service leading up to 2010. Under the HIPC, resources saved from debt service are allocated to key anti-poverty programmes, including education, health and infrastructure. With fewer draining economic pressures, the people of Zanzibar should benefit. It remains to be seen whether the Zanzibari government can follow the successful lead of its mainland counterpart.

SEAWEED FARMING In 1989, seaweed farming was introduced on the east coast of Unguja (Zanzibar Island) and has since become a vital source of income for coastal villagers. The seaweed is planted and tended on beach areas between the high- and low-water marks (see box, *Sustainable seaweed farming*, page 290). It is harvested and dried, collected in Zanzibar Town, and then exported to several countries in Europe and Asia for use as a food thickener or stabiliser. Seaweed is now a valuable addition to Zanzibar's traditional exports of coconuts, cloves and other spices (see boxes, *Coconuts*, page 53, and *Cloves*, page 54).

Despite the success with seaweed, exports are limited, and Zanzibar imports many basic foodstuffs, including rice (from Pakistan, Thailand, Vietnam, Indonesia, India, China and the USA), maize (from mainland Tanzania), cooking oil (from Kenya, Tanzania, Singapore and Dubai), sugar (from Brazil), plus wheat and flour (from France, Germany and the USA). Other imports include mineral water (from the Gulf States) and beer (from Denmark).

TOURISM Whilst tourism remains relatively marginal to life in Pemba and Mafia, it has grown rapidly on Zanzibar Island over the last 25 years. Investment here has been significant and some of the wealth has stayed on the islands, but as well as providing opportunities, this has created many new problems.

Jobs in the tourism sector have developed skills in many islanders, and there is a class of local entrepreneurs who wouldn't have existed without tourism. Popular festivals have been introduced, several traditional handicraft techniques have been restored, and some villagers, especially women, have had the chance to earn income and better their lifestyle as a direct result of growing tourism.

The benefits are easy to find, but the tourism boom has not been universally good. Pragmatic observers agree that it's not tourism which is the problem per se; it's the sensitivity and sustainability of the individual tourism developments. It's all about how responsible the tourism enterprises are with the resources and culture of the islands. This issue of 'responsible tourism' is moving up the agenda, as evidenced by the rise of consciously responsible lodges like Chumbe Island and Michamvi Sunset Bay. However, there's a long way to go before all of the hotels and lodges match the high standards set by these.

Officially, the government recognises this problem, and back in 1992 introduced a National Environmental Policy for Zanzibar. This stressed that the quality of life of the Zanzibaris should not be harmed by the destruction of their environment, and that cultural and biological diversity should be preserved. In the words of President Salmin Amour, 'unchecked development could soon become unsustainable for our people and our small islands'. Sadly, in spite of the policies and well-intentioned sentiment, the speed and scale of the current growth in tourism developments continue unabated, and the local population is increasingly questioning its benefits.

There are signs that some of the more ethical elements of the tour operator community are starting to take these issues seriously. In 2008, the independent UK-based charity Tourism Concern (*www.tourismconcern.org.uk*) conducted a review of tourism on Zanzibar on behalf of the UK members of its Ethical Tour Operators Group (ETOG). This involved analysing and inspecting some of the hotels most popularly featured and spending time with island-based industry bodies, local and international NGOs, tourists, community groups and local residents. ETOG started this project to establish the most critical issues affecting tourism businesses and communities, and to highlight examples of best practice. Armed with this information, ETOG's members aim to find a practical way to raise ethical standards.

This is a positive step by a few overseas tour operators, but to have a substantial impact on Zanzibar's tourism issues requires the Zanzibari government to engage fully in the issue, and to work for long-term sustainability.

Sadly, there is little sign of this happening in any real form. The government is doing little in the way of fairly regulating the pace of development, or trying to upgrade the island's basic water supplies, communications, rubbish collections or other island infrastructure. Despite this, as visitors, we should do our best to act responsibly towards Zanzibar's environment and cultures, and to travel as responsibly as possible.

Visitor numbers and the tourism economy

The Zanzibar Commission for Tourism was founded in 1987 to promote Zanzibar as a tourist destination, and in 1992, the Zanzibar Investment Promotion Agency was created to encourage overseas investment, particularly in tourism projects. Buoyed by their presence, the first half of the 1990s saw a dramatic rise in the development of tourism, but the last few years have seen a truly staggering increase.

In 1995, over 56,000 visitors were arriving in Zanzibar each year; earnings derived from the tourism sector are said to have contributed an estimated US$1,971 million to the economy (see the Tanzanian government website, www.tanzania. go.tz/zanzibar, although we are unsure how these stats were derived, as this means that each visitor effectively contributes over US$35,000!).

By the end of 2005, numbers had exceeded 100,000 visitors per year for the first time, and by 2008 official tourism figures were sitting at 140,000 arrivals, with real figures estimating visitor numbers to be closer to 160,000. Zanzibar Association of Tourism Investors (ZATI) show arrivals hit a record high in 2011, peaking at 220,000

There are often some discrepancies in tourism arrival figures on account of official figures only including travellers arriving directly from abroad and not tourists coming in from Dar es Salaam or from safaris on the Tanzanian mainland. In descending order, the majority of visitors come from Italy, the UK, Germany, the Netherlands and the US, all lured by images of pristine beaches, swaying palms and exotic island life. Tourist arrivals to Pemba and the Mafia Archipelago remain insignificant by comparison.

The government recently announced a target of half a million tourists to Zanzibar annually by 2013. In a similar vein, the Zanzibar Commission for Tourism's projection figures currently estimate close to 450,000 annual visitors by 2020. While far below the figures recorded by larger countries like Kenya, these ever-increasing visitor numbers clearly show that Zanzibar's tourism industry has changed gear since the early 1980s. If the projected growth is achieved, it is hard to see how the islands will cope, socially or environmentally, with what would equate to about a 700% increase in visitors in 25 years.

Tourism currently represents about 22% of Zanzibar's gross domestic product (GDP) and 77% of foreign direct investment (FDI), which contrasts with cloves, which account for around 45% of GDP. Whilst export earnings from this traditional commodity fall (see box *Cloves*, page 54), the income from tourism is rising to plug the gap. Some observers expect tourism to be Zanzibar's largest generator of foreign exchange within a decade.

National tourism policies The Zanzibari government's current policies and development plans consistently emphasise tourism which benefits the local population, protects and conserves the natural environment and maximises local employment and locally produced goods and services. All very admirable aims, but in reality, few of these guiding principles seem to be translated into laws to regulate development.

Large developments, often European all-inclusive resorts, seem to be being built on every available plot of land on the north and east coasts, container-loads of goods are continually imported from China, and in most hotels significant numbers of employees are from mainland Tanzania and overseas. It is hard not to reach the conclusion that the government is doing its people a gross disservice by only paying lip service to these issues.

In spite of this, there are some stalwart hoteliers and tour operators doing the utmost to be socially and environmentally aware; throughout this book we have highlighted their achievements and ambitions, so that travellers can vote with their feet.

Issue awareness With huge question marks hanging over the sustainability of the current level of tourism to Zanzibar, and the islands' leaders exhibiting only myopia on many of the issues, alarm bells are ringing for responsible travellers. Being aware of what the issues are is a crucial step towards travelling responsibly, and some of the main issues include the following.

Fresh water depletion Fresh water is very precious on low-lying islands like these, and there is mounting evidence of groundwater depletion: water levels in wells used by villagers for generations have dropped and, in a few areas, old wells that were once fresh are now becoming brackish.

Zanzibar Town draws its water from a freshwater aquifer flowing under the centre of the island; a pipe network pumps water to the main coastal communities outside the capital. The demand from hotels is rising, sometimes leaving the volume of piped fresh water for the villagers as both inadequate and unreliable. Some communities have sunk wells to directly access the groundwater, as have some hotels (whilst others ferry their water in by truck), but the pressure on this critical resource is growing. One survey claimed that, on average, tourists use 180 litres of water per day (this of course includes all use – washing, laundry, hotel cleaning, etc) compared with the average local Zanzibari's consumption of less than 40 litres.

Nungwi and Kendwa are at the end of the pipe network, and here the problem is most acute. Villagers are increasingly experiencing serious problems getting access to fresh water. With the island's mushrooming hotels drawing more water from the pipe, in addition to all of the communities along its route north, there is rarely much water left by the time it gets to Nungwi. This has led to conflict between the villagers and the hotels and, with further development under way and no real solution in place, things are set to get increasingly difficult. For recent

1

observations, Tourism Concern's WET report (*www.tourismconcern.org.uk*) looks at these specific community water problems, though with less emphasis on the role of good governance than many believe central to the issue.

Rubbish Rubbish is a major problem on Zanzibar Island. There is minimal municipal waste collection, and that which does exist focuses almost exclusively on Zanzibar Town. At the end of 2006, the statement from the governmental Environment Department declared that 'out of about 200 tonnes of solid waste produced daily in Stone Town, the Zanzibar Municipal Council workers are only able to collect about 60 tonnes'. This situation is visibly worsening every year with little state investment or significant effort to manage the problem.

The main problem, however, is that there is only a single stinking landfill site for the whole of Zanzibar Island to use. This is totally inadequate. The result is that much rubbish is dumped around the island, or at sea, by both local residents and irresponsible hotels and tourists. It's often noted that, as much of the island is made of coral rock, digging more landfill sites may not be easy, but despite this there are a number of active rock quarries around the island.

Several of the better hotels now have efficient waste-management plans, and separate glass for a recycling NGO, while some pay for an official collection and hope the waste is not dumped before it reaches the landfill site. Some investment comes from overseas governments, and in Jambiani and Kendwa, small NGOs and concerned residents are trying hard to address the problem on a local level. However, with large-scale developments mushrooming, a formal government strategy and serious financial backing are critical to curb the problem.

Social vices Most local people on Zanzibar regard tourism as a broadly positive industry in terms of its potential to earn money. However, increasingly there is resentment felt about the behaviour of tourists. You only need to watch bikini-clad women walking through a village, or see beer bottles piled high at a beach barbecue, to realise how inconsiderate some visitors are to local values.

Unsurprisingly, as with many traditional, reserved communities faced with a dramatic influx of international tourists, cultural erosion can also be observed on Zanzibar. As a predominantly (95%) Muslim country, alcohol and drugs have had little place in society in the past. Now, with the Western influence of tourists and growing wealth from ad hoc guiding, souvenir selling and prostitution, exposure and addiction to both is starting to become a problem among young local men, especially in Stone Town and Nungwi. This often evolves to cause problems like opportunist theft for money, and it increases village tensions with traditional elders appalled at the behaviour of the youths.

Similarly, prostitution is another fairly recent island issue, within both the tourist and local communities. Female sex workers are now travelling from the mainland in search of tourist dollars, local men are offering their services to foreign girls in beach bars, and local women are selling their bodies to other villagers flush with new-found wealth.

Many hotels and NGOs are acutely aware of these tensions and are working hard, directly or through local charities, to address social and environmental issues in their area. Many more in the tourism sector appear oblivious to the issues.

Overfishing There is growing concern about overfishing, particularly for crab, lobster, squid and octopus, to supply restaurants catering for tourists. Fishermen on all coasts are reporting difficulties in finding fish big enough to sell and, in spite of legal restrictions, fishing on the coral reef is increasing as a direct result. A secondary consequence of the voracious tourist appetite for fresh seafood has been to inflate the price of fish and shellfish beyond the means of many local villagers. Demand in some areas is making the ingredients for traditional meals, such as octopus, too expensive for purchase by the fishing communities from where they come.

Construction materials For years, beach sand, coral rock and native trees have been used for construction, leading to accelerated coastal erosion. As just one example, mangrove poles are a particularly good construction material; they are very strong, often straight and highly resistant to termites (see box, *Mangrove forest depletion*, page 276). However, these have seldom been sustainably harvested. This has depleted Zanzibar's original mangrove forests, which are vital to the marine ecosystems as a nursery for many small fish as well as a buffer for the coast against the ocean.

2

People and Culture

PEOPLE

POPULATION AND SETTLEMENT The population of Zanzibar was 984,625 in 2002, the date of the last published census results, with an annual growth rate of 3.1%. This growth has remained fairly steady for some years, though the general feeling of Zanzibari residents today is that recent years have seen a more significant increase. Of the total residents, around two-thirds of the people (622,459) live on Zanzibar Island (Unguja), with the greatest proportion settled in the densely populated west. Zanzibar's largest settlement is Zanzibar Town (sometimes called Zanzibar City), on Zanzibar Island, with 205,870 inhabitants. Other towns on Zanzibar Island include Chaani, Bambi, Mahonda and Makunduchi, but these are small by comparison. Outside these towns, most people live in small, traditional villages and are engaged in farming, fishing or tourism-related industries.

On Pemba the overall settlement pattern is similar. The largest town is Chake Chake, with a population of 19,283; other smaller towns are Wete and Mkoani. Mafia's total population was 40,801 in 2002, the last reported census year.

There is considerable disparity in the standard of living between the inhabitants of Mafia, Pemba and Unguja and between urban and rural populations, which are split roughly equally. The average annual income of just US$250 hides the fact that about half the population lives below the poverty line on less than US$1 per day. Despite a reasonable standard of primary health care and education, infant mortality is still 83 in 1,000 live births, and it is estimated that malnutrition affects one in three of the islands' people; life expectancy at birth is 48.

While the incidence of HIV/AIDS is considerably less in Zanzibar than in Tanzania as a whole (0.6% of the population, as against the national average of around 8%), it is a growing problem. The Zanzibar AIDS Commission reports that women show HIV prevalence rates that are higher than their male counterparts (0.7% and 0.5% respectively), and that understanding of infection transmission is still poor in many communities. Projections from observations of two population surveys suggest 7,200 Zanzibaris are living with HIV, and this number is disturbingly three times higher in young females than in their male counterparts. In late 2006, the government unanimously adopted its first National HIV/AIDS Policy with plans for a door-to-door awareness campaign, HIV prevention education in school curricula and the promotion of condom use (the screening of visitors for HIV on arrival was omitted). This has been a positive step, but sadly trends such as the simultaneous increase in drug and alcohol usage, the rise in prostitution, and mounting numbers of mainland Tanzanians seeking work on the island, are still likely to increase the infection rate in the long term.

ORIGINS It is thought that Zanzibar's original inhabitants came from the African mainland around 3,000 to 4,000 years ago, although this is not certain and no descendants of these early people remain, having been completely absorbed by later arrivals.

Over the last 2,000 years, the records have become a little clearer. Historians know that Bantu-speaking people migrated from central Africa and settled across east and southern Africa during the 1st millennium AD (for more details see *Chapter 1, History*, page 3). Those who settled on the east African coast and offshore islands, including Zanzibar, came into contact with Arab traders who had sailed southwards from the Red Sea region. The Bantu adopted some customs of the Arabs and gradually established a language and culture which became known as Swahili.

From the 10th century, small groups of immigrants from Shiraz (Persia) also settled at various places along the east African coast, and especially in Zanzibar, and mingled with the local people. Over the following centuries, small groups of Arab and Persian peoples continued to settle here and intermarry with the Swahili and Shirazi. The largest influx occurred in the 18th and 19th centuries, when Omani Arabs settled on Zanzibar as rulers and landowners, forming an elite group. At about the same time, Indian settlers formed a merchant class.

Today, most of the people in Zanzibar are Shirazi or Swahili, although clear distinctions are not always possible. They fall into three groups: the Wahadimu (mainly in the southern and central parts of Zanzibar Island), the Watumbatu (on Tumbatu Island and in the northern part of Zanzibar Island) and the Wapemba (on Pemba Island), although again distinctions are hard to draw, and in fact, often not made by the people of Zanzibar themselves. The islands' long history of receiving (if not always welcoming) immigrants from Africa and Arabia has created a more relaxed attitude to matters of tribe or clan than is found in some parts of Africa.

Zanzibar is also home to groups of people of African origin who are descendants of freed slaves, dating from the 18th and 19th centuries. In more recent times, a large number of Africans have immigrated from mainland Tanzania. Additionally, some Arabs who were expelled after the 1964 Revolution have returned to Zanzibar.

Other people on Zanzibar include small populations from Goa, India and Pakistan, mainly involved in trade or tourism, and a growing number of European expatriates and volunteers, many working in the tour industry, with others employed as teachers, doctors and engineers.

LANGUAGE *with thanks to Said el-Gheithy*

The indigenous language spoken throughout Zanzibar is Swahili (called Kiswahili locally). This language is also spoken as a first language by Swahili people along the east African coast, particularly in Kenya and mainland Tanzania, and as a second or third language by many other people throughout east Africa (including Kenya, Tanzania and Uganda, and in parts of several other countries such as Rwanda, Mozambique and Congo), making Swahili the common tongue of the region. Although there are many forms and dialects found in different areas, visitors with a basic grasp of Swahili will be understood anywhere.

Swahili is an African language, and includes many words and phrases of Arabic origin, plus words from other languages such as Persian, English and Portuguese. Over the centuries Swahili has developed into a rich language, lending itself especially to poetry. Zanzibar is regarded as the home of Swahili – it is spoken in its purest form here and in pockets on the coast of Tanzania and Kenya. In fact, in these areas, tradition dictates that ordinary conversation should approximate the elegance of poetry. Generally, as you travel further inland on the east African mainland, the Swahili becomes increasingly more basic and simplified.

For visitors, English and several other European languages, such as French and Italian, are spoken in Zanzibar Town and most tourist areas. However, if you get off the beaten track, a few words of Swahili will be useful to ask directions, to greet people or even to begin a simple conversation. Even in the tourist areas, using a few Swahili words (for example, to ask the price of a souvenir or order a meal in a restaurant) can add to the enjoyment of your visit. Arabic is also spoken. For basic words and phrases, see *Appendix 1, Language*, page 413.

RELIGION Most of the people in Zanzibar are Muslims (followers of the Islamic faith) and all towns and villages on Zanzibar Island and Pemba have mosques. Visitors to Zanzibar Town cannot fail to hear the evocative sound of the muezzins calling people to prayer from the minarets, especially for the evening session at sunset. And visitors cannot fail to notice the effects of the holy month of Ramadan, when most people fast during the day, and the pace of life slows down considerably (see also *Public holidays*, page 109). There are also small populations of Christians and Hindus.

Islam Islam was founded by the Prophet Muhammad, who was born around AD570 in Arabia. He received messages from God during solitary vigils on Mount Hira, outside his home town of Mecca. When driven out of Mecca by his enemies, he migrated to Medina. Here, at the age of about 53, he started to convert the world to Islam, and his message spread rapidly through the Arab world and beyond.

Muhammad died in AD632, but fired by evangelist zeal, Arab Muslims had conquered all of northern Africa by the early 8th century, and introduced the new religion there. By AD1100, Islam had spread from Arabia and the Horn of Africa along the east African coast, through the current countries of Kenya and Tanzania, all the way down to Sofala (in present-day Mozambique). Today, Islam is the dominant religion of these coastal areas, which include the islands of Zanzibar.

The five main tenets of Islam are prayer (five times a day), testimony of the faith, fasting (the period of Ramadan), almsgiving, and the pilgrimage to Mecca (the hajj). The Muslim calendar dates from the Hejira, the flight of Muhammad from Mecca to Medina, which corresponds to 16 July AD622 in the Christian calendar. The Muslim year consists of 12 lunar months of 29 or 30 days each, making 354 days. Eleven times in every cycle of 30 years a day is added to the year. This means that Muslim festivals fall 11 or 12 days earlier every year, according to the Western calendar.

Other religions There are small populations of Christians and Hindus living on the islands. The two most notable churches are the Anglican Cathedral Church of Christ and the Catholic Church of St Joseph in Zanzibar Town; Hindu temples are also present to serve the local community.

Alongside the established world faiths, traditional African beliefs are still held by most local people, and there is often considerable crossover between aspects of Islam and local custom (for more details, see box, *The Shetani of Zanzibar*, page 40).

CULTURE

ARTS AND CRAFTS
Music and dance As you wander around Zanzibar Town, you will hear calls to prayer from the many mosques as well as the sounds of American rap music

and Jamaican reggae. Around the next corner, however, you are also likely to hear film music from India or the latest chart-toppers from Egypt and the Gulf States. Thankfully the islands have not entirely lost their own cultural traditions, and equally popular in Zanzibar are local musical forms, in particular the style known as *taarab*.

Taarab Zanzibar has been at the crossroads of trade routes for thousands of years as peoples of Africa, India, Iran, China and other parts of Asia and the Arab world have all played their parts in influencing the music, architecture, food and culture of the region. In its origins, *taarab* was court music, played in the palace of Sultan

THE SHETANI OF ZANZIBAR
Gemma Pitcher

Throughout the centuries Zanzibar Island (Unguja) and, to a greater extent, Pemba Island have been famous as centres of traditional religion and witchcraft, alongside their better-known role as centres of the spice and slave trades. Today the cult of the *shetani* (meaning a spirit or spirits, the word is singular or plural) is still going strong in Zanzibar and Pemba – a dark undercurrent unseen and unknown by the majority of visitors.

According to local traditional beliefs, shetani are creatures from another world, living on earth alongside animals and humans, but invisible most of the time and generally ill-intentioned. Many of the ebony carvings on sale in Zanzibar's curio shops depict the various forms a shetani can take – for example, a hunched and hideously twisted old woman, a man–dog hybrid, or a young girl with the legs of a donkey.

There is no real way, say the locals, of protecting yourself from the possibility of being haunted or attacked by a shetani. The best thing is simply to keep out of their way and try to make sure they keep out of yours – for example by hanging a piece of paper, inscribed with special Arabic verses, from the ceiling of the house. Almost every home or shop in Zanzibar has one of these brown, mottled scraps, attached to a roof beam by a piece of cotton.

Should the worst happen in spite of these precautions and a shetani decide to take up residence in your home – or even, in the worst-case scenario, your body – the only thing to do is to visit a *mganga* (sorcerer). To be a mganga is a trade that generally runs in families, with secrets and charms passed on from father to son or mother to daughter. *Waganga* (the plural of mganga) meet periodically in large numbers to discuss their business (patients must pay handsomely for their services) and initiate new recruits. A committee of elderly, experienced practitioners will vet a younger, untested mganga before declaring him or her fit to practise.

Each mganga is in contact with ten or so shetani, who can be instructed to drive out other shetani from someone who is possessed, or to work their power in favour of the customer. The waganga are also herbalists, preparing healing medicines where spirit possession is not indicated, or combining both physical and occult treatment in severe cases.

But there are some shetani, goes the current thinking, which even a mganga cannot control. The latest and most famous of these was (or is) Popo Bawa – a phenomenon of far greater significance than just a run-of-the-mill shetani, which gripped Zanzibar's population in a wave of mass hysteria in 1995.

Popo Bawa (the name comes from the Swahili words for 'bat' and 'wing') began on the island of Pemba, where he terrorised the local population to such an extent

Barghash. The sounds of Arabic musical traditions and those from India, Indonesia and other countries of the 'Dhow region' (the Indian Ocean basin) are clearly distinguishable even today, mingling to form a unique flavour and providing the frame for the Swahili poetry which makes up the heart of taarab music.

Currently, two major taarab groups exist in Zanzibar: Nadi Ikhwan Safaa and Mila na Utamaduni (also called Culture Musical Club, or just Culture). Of the two, Culture are the more professional and have become quite well known internationally, not only through CD releases such as *Spices of Zanzibar* or the more recent *Bashraf* albums, but also because they have successfully toured Belgium, France, Germany, Switzerland, the United Arab Emirates, Réunion and many other countries. Nadi

that they called upon their most powerful sorcerers to drive him across the sea to Zanzibar. There the reign of terror of the 'shetani-above-all-shetani' continued.

The experiences of those who claimed to be visited by the demon were terrifying. They awoke in the middle of the night to find themselves paralysed and with the feeling of being suffocated. They then saw a squat, winged figure, around 1m tall, or slightly smaller, and with a single eye in the middle of its forehead, approaching the bed. Helpless, they were powerless to move or cry out as the demon raped them, men and women alike. Only when Popo Bawa had departed were they able to raise the alarm.

During the height of the Popo Bawa hysteria, people took to the rooftops and village squares, following a rumour that safety could only be had by those who slept outside, in a group. Despite precautions like these, tales of the demon's progress around the island spread, until the government was forced to broadcast announcements on the radio pleading for calm. Despite this, a helpless, mentally handicapped young man was beaten to death by a mob that had become convinced he was the demon. This seemed to be the climax of the whole affair – after that, the hysteria abated somewhat and Popo Bawa retreated. He is widely expected to return, however, and when local people talk of him, it's with a nervous laugh.

American psychologists came to Zanzibar to study the events and write papers, and stated that the case of Popo Bawa is simply a Zanzibari version of a phenomenon known as a 'waking dream'. One of the characteristics of such a dream is a feeling of being weighted down or even paralysed. Other characteristics include extreme vividness of the dream and bizarre or terrifying content. It is this same phenomenon that is used by sceptics in the USA to explain the stories of those who claim to have been abducted by aliens.

Nevertheless, to the people of Zanzibar, Popo Bawa was very real and proof that shetani exist. Of course, they are not all as horrific as Popo Bawa; the lesser shetani come in all shapes, sizes and colours – beautiful Arabic women, hideous Ethiopian hags, or tall, handsome white men. Shetani can be forced to work for humans, but it's a risky business. Some successful businessmen are said to keep a whole room of shetani in their houses to promote material success and make mischief on their adversaries. But the price of such supernatural intervention is high – a goat, a chicken or a cow must be sacrificed regularly and its blood sprinkled in the four corners of the room. If this sacrifice is not faithfully and regularly made, the shetani will take a terrible substitute – it will demand instead one of its master's male children …

BI KIDUDE

A description of the music of Zanzibar would not be complete without mentioning Bi Kidude – now well into her nineties, and still one of the island's most famous singers. She used to perform with Siti binti Saad, has toured the world and has sold thousands of cassettes. When she is performing, she claims to feel like a 14 year old, and for once, seeing is believing. Her voice is raw and unfiltered, and her singing and drumming with a large drum strapped to her hips is an exhibition of sheer energy. With the agility of a teenager and the sly wisdom of a thoroughly experienced performer, her stage presence is absolute and intense. She is most famous for her performance of unyago ngoma, which is played at all-female initiation rituals for brides to prepare them for their wedding night, featuring explicit lyrics as well as movements.

Ikhwan Safaa, affectionately known by local people as Malindi Music Club, are Zanzibar's oldest group, who trace their roots back to 1905. The group plays a style of taarab in which the distant Middle Eastern origins are still very much to the fore.

Different theories abound about the real origins of taarab in Zanzibar. Legend has it that in the 1870s Sultan Barghash sent a Zanzibari to Cairo to learn to play the *qanun*, a kind of zither, common to the Arab-speaking world. Among the first singers to record taarab music in the Swahili language was the legendary Siti binti Saad, who was taken to India by a film director. Siti stopped performing in the 1940s, but her records – solo and in duet with Sheikh Mbaruk – continued to be issued on 78rpm throughout the 1950s and are still much in demand. Besides the qanun, other instruments that came to feature in the taarab groups (or orchestras) include the oud, violins, *ney*, accordion, cello and a variety of percussion. Thus, much of the traditional taarab music sounds like a more Africanised version of some of the great Egyptian popular classical orchestras that played alongside singers like Oum Kulthoum, who is still played on Radio Zanzibar to this day.

The best way to experience taarab is at a local concert, but visitors to Zanzibar are also welcome at the orchestras' rehearsals in Malindi or at Vuga Clubhouse in the evening. What Andy Morgan (*Roots* magazine) says in an article on Zanzibari music definitely holds true: 'There's hardly anything in the whole of Africa as uplifting as the swelling sounds of a full taarab orchestra in full sail.'

Kidumbak The suburb of Ng'ambo – the 'other side' of Zanzibar Town, where the lower-class living areas spread out and where poorer families and more recent arrivals to the city live – is the home of *kidumbak*. This music style, which is less refined and more upbeat than taarab, could be located musically somewhere between Stone Town big-orchestra taarab and the rural *ngoma* music. It is most often performed at weddings and other celebrations and is closely related to taarab. In fact, contemporary kidumbak often makes use of the latest taarab hit songs and is sometimes called *kitaarab*, which means 'a diminutive type of taarab' or 'derived from taarab'. Historical evidence suggests that Swahili taarab was originally performed in a very similar way to kidumbak and only later changed to resemble court orchestra music.

The kidumbak ensemble consists of a single melodic instrument, customarily a violin (played in frantic fiddle-style), a *sanduku*, or tea-chest-bass, two small clay drums (*ki-dumbak*), which form the rhythmic core of every such ensemble, and other rhythm instruments, such as *cherewa*, a kind of maracas manufactured from coconut shells filled with seeds, or *mkwasa*, short wooden sticks played like claves. In contrast to taarab, kidumbak is much more rhythmic and the lyrics more drastic than the poetic settings of the taarab songs, often criticising other people's social behaviour. At wedding performances, the singer has to be able to string together a well-timed medley of ngoma songs, and she or he must have the ability to compose lyrics on the spot. At a Zanzibari wedding, one kidumbak set usually lasts for an hour; as one song joins the next, the intensity heats up, with the main attraction being the interplay between the music and song of the players and the dancing and chorus response of the wedding guests.

Beni This brass band music originated around the end the 19th century as a mockery of colonial-style military bands. It was soon incorporated into the competitive song-and-dance exchanges so popular on the Swahili coast and spread from there all over east Africa. *Beni* (from the English 'band') is a popular wedding entertainment with a strong focus on rhythm and dance and audience participation.

Beni borrows choruses from the latest taarab hits and arranges them in extended medleys with the female wedding audience joining in for the chorus and as dancers. It is funny music, vivacious, raucous and lively. If you can imagine a deranged military marching band playing as loud as possible on half-broken trumpets, trombones, drums – only vaguely in tune with each other, but having a great time – then you will get the idea!

In Zanzibar, beni is performed both as a street parade and, stationary, for a wedding dance. The band Beni ya Kingi usually kicks off the opening parade for the Festival of the Dhow Countries (see *Festivals*, page 49), which winds its way slowly with a great crowd through the narrow streets of Stone Town before reaching Forodhani Gardens at the waterfront, which then turns into a wild and lively party.

Ngoma Ngoma, literally translated, means 'drum' and is a term used to encompass all local African traditional forms of dancing, drumming and singing. There are literally hundreds of different ngoma styles throughout Tanzania, variations often being so slight that untrained eyes and ears can hardly notice the difference. A number of these originate from Zanzibar and Pemba and all are spectacular to watch. The often-elaborate native costumes emphasise the unity of the dancers' steps and the rhythm section, which usually consists of several handmade drums and percussion instruments (such as oil tins beaten with a stick). *Ngoma ya kibati* from Pemba, for example, consists of a very rapid declamatory style of singing which is an improvised dialogue to drum accompaniment with singers/dancers coming in for a chorus every so often. Even if you can't follow a single word of the firework-like exchange between the two main singers, *kibati* is hilarious; if you understand all of the references and hints implied, it is of course even more so. Another example is *msewe*, supporting the rhythm section, and named after the material which is strapped to the ankles of the male dancers.

Each ngoma style has its own special costume. In *kyaso*, men dance dressed in shirts and *kikois* (special woven cloth from the east African coast) with a long, narrow stick in their hand, all movements beautifully co-ordinated. In *ndege*, women in colourful dresses all hold bright umbrellas, moving forwards with slightly rotating steps and movements of the hips. In *bomu*, the women dress up like men and in other funny costumes and dance around in a circle.

The variations are endless and performances are never dull. According to Abdalla R Mdoe, choreographer for Imani Ngoma Troupe, a privately initiated performance ensemble that specialises in all kinds of ngoma, three different types can be differentiated: ceremonial ngomas, which are performed at weddings, circumcision and other festivities; ritual ngomas (eg: *kisomali* to cure a sick person, or *pungwa* to avert evil); and religious ngomas, which in Zanzibar are closely related to the Muslim festivities of Zikri, Duffu, Maulidi and Hom.

Modern taarab Undoubtedly a pop-phenomenon (and therefore ephemeral) is a modern style of taarab, called *rusha roho*, which translates literally as 'to make the spirit fly' and has some untranslatable meaning approximating to 'upsetting someone' or 'making the other one jealous'. Modern taarab is also the first style of taarab designed to be accompanied by dance, and features direct lyrics, bypassing the unwritten laws of lyrical subtlety of the older groups. Much of modern taarab music is composed and played on keyboards, increasing portability; hence the group is much smaller in number than 'real taarab' orchestras and therefore more readily available to tour and play shows throughout the region. This fact has led to its enormous popularity in Zanzibar, boosted by the prolific output of cassette recordings, which, though not up to European studio quality standards, still outsell tapes by any other artist local or international.

Visual arts
Tingatinga paintings Among the visual arts, by far the best-known contemporary Zanzibari style is *Tingatinga* (or *tinga-tinga*). Paintings in this distinctive style can be found for sale at souvenir stalls and shops all over Zanzibar, as well as at tourist centres on the Tanzanian mainland and in Kenya. The subjects

of Tingatinga paintings are usually African animals, especially elephants, leopards, hippos, crocodiles and gazelles, as well as guineafowl, hornbills and other birds. The main characteristics of the style include images which are both simplified and fantastical, bold colours, solid outlines and the frequent use of dots and small circles in the design.

The style was founded by Edward Saidi Tingatinga, who was born in southern Tanzania in 1937 and came to Dar es Salaam looking for work in the 1950s. After doing various jobs, in the early 1960s Tingatinga became unemployed and looked around for a way to earn money. At that time, carvers and sculptors, notably Makonde people, were producing some indigenous work, but most local painters favoured pictures based on European representational styles or Congolese styles from central Africa (in fact, in the 1950s and 1960s many painters from Congo and Zaire, now the DRC, came to Kenya and Tanzania to sell their work to tourists and well-off residents). Legend has it that Saidi Tingatinga decided he could do what the Congolese artists did – paint pictures and sell them for money.

With no training, he produced pictures that were initially simple and straightforward. Subjects were the animals and people he remembered from his home in southern Tanzania. He used just four or five different colours (actually house paint – and the only colours available) and painted on wooden boards. But despite this humble beginning, Tingatinga quickly sold his early paintings, mainly to local European residents who admired the original, 'naïve' style.

Within a few months, Tingatinga's paintings were in high demand. He couldn't keep up with the orders which flooded in, so he employed several fellow painters

ZANZIBAR DOORS

Around Zanzibar and particularly in Stone Town, you'll come across massive, carved and decorated doorways, some on imposing frontages and others tucked incongruously down narrow alleys.

When a house was built in Zanzibar, the door was traditionally the first part to be erected. The greater the wealth and status of the house's owner, the larger and more elaborately carved his front door. Symbolic designs and quotations from the Koran were added to exert a benign influence: a kind of hand-crafted insurance policy. Waves of the sea climbing up the doorpost represent the livelihood of the Arab merchant to whom the house belonged, while frankincense and date-palms symbolise wealth and plenty. From a darker side of history, chains carved at the side indicate that slaves were held in the house. Some designs are thought to pre-date the Koran: the stylised lotuses could relate to Egyptian fertility symbols, and the fish may possibly represent the protective Syrian goddess Atargatis or the ancient Egyptian fish god.

Many doors are studded with brass spikes and bosses, which may stem from the Indian practice of studding doors of medieval castles with sharp iron spikes to prevent their being battered in by war elephants. In AD915, an Arab traveller recorded that Zanzibar Island abounded in elephants, and around 1295, Marco Polo wrote that Zanzibar had 'elephants in plenty'. But they must have been extinct long before the Arabs built houses in Stone Town, and the studs and bosses seen today are purely decorative.

The oldest carved door in Zanzibar, which dates from 1694, is now the front door of the Peace Memorial Museum.

Gemma Pitcher

Baraza benches, often simply called *barazas*, have been a focal point of community life in Zanzibar for centuries. These thick benches of solid stone are built into the walls around courtyards or flank the heavy doors of distinctive Arab-style townhouses. The houses which line the long, narrow streets of Stone Town often have barazas outside – and you will also see barazas on the verandas outside traditional Swahili homes, while in the villages a palm-leaf shelter, flanked by wooden seats, fulfils the same function.

Barazas evolved as a way for Islamic men to receive visitors in their homes without compromising the privacy of their womenfolk. Coffee and sweetmeats would be served on the baraza to anyone who arrived, with only the closest friends or family members being invited into the house. The Omani sultans held public meetings, also known as barazas, outside their palaces to receive petitioners or give visiting dignitaries a public audience.

Today, barazas are still a meeting point for all sections of Zanzibari society. Every urban baraza area is lined with people lolling on the warm, smooth cement benches, gossiping, playing games of *bao* or cards, drinking sweet, thick Arabic coffee or simply idling away a long afternoon with a nap. Draughts boards are scratched in chalk on the stone surfaces, ladies sit comfortably to plait each other's hair, and for traders with no market stall of their own, a baraza provides a flat surface on which to pile their tiny pyramids of oranges, tomatoes and mangoes.

In the rainy season, when torrents of water, sometimes laced with rubbish, make walking down the streets of Stone Town uncomfortable and even hazardous, the barazas outside the houses provide a useful elevated pavement, and pedestrians jump from one to the next in an attempt to keep their feet dry.

The baraza as an architectural feature is an idea that seems to have caught on in a big way among the designers of Zanzibar's smarter hotels; almost every courtyard, nook and cranny – and even bathroom – now boasts its own baraza bench, often whitewashed to match the coral walls or inlaid with mosaic tiles.

to help him produce more. There was no concept of copyright, and Tingatinga encouraged his colleagues to base their works on his style. As their success grew, soon the artists were able to afford to use bright enamel paints (the type used for touching up paintwork on cars and bicycles) and painted on canvas so tourists could take home pictures more easily. By the end of the 1960s, Tingatinga painting had become recognised as truly original contemporary African art.

In 1972, Saidi Tingatinga died, but the artists he'd encouraged formed a group named in his honour, and continued to produce and sell works in his style. Today, demand from tourists is still high, and vast numbers of Tingatinga artists produce paintings on cloth, wooden boards and other objects such as trays, plates and model wooden cars. There's even an aeroplane at Zanzibar Airport with its tail decorated in Tingatinga style.

With so many Tingatinga paintings available in Zanzibar and around east Africa, the quality of the work varies considerably; many pictures for sale in the streets have been bashed out quickly with little care or attention to detail. But if you search hard among the dross, or visit a shop where the trader has an interest in stocking better-quality stuff, you can often find real works of art (and still at reasonable prices) which do justice to the memory of Saidi Tingatinga – the founder of a fascinating, entertaining and quintessentially African style.

TRADITIONAL GAMES Stroll casually around any village or town on the islands of Zanzibar, and eventually you'll be sure to come across two hunched, intent figures seated on a baraza bench – their grunts of satisfaction or derision accompanied by the click of counters on wood. Sometimes a crowd of spectators will have gathered, pointing and shouting garbled instructions. Look closer and you'll make out the object of all this excitement – a flat wooden board, 32 little round holes and a lot of brown polished seeds. This is *bao* – Zanzibar's favourite pastime.

Games of bao – the name simply means 'wood' in Swahili – can go on for hours or even days at a time. Experienced players develop little flourishes, scattering the counters (known as *kete* – usually seeds, or pebbles or shells) expertly into holes or slapping handfuls down triumphantly at the end of a turn. Bao is played, under various different names and with many rule variations, across Africa, western India and the Caribbean. Swahili people are proud of their version, known as 'king' bao, and claim it as the original and purest form of the game. Tournaments are held periodically in Zanzibar and on the coast of the mainland – as in chess, one grandmaster eventually emerges.

The object of the game is simple: to secure as many of your opponent's counters as possible. Bao masters (usually old men) are said to be able to think strategically five to seven moves ahead, a level comparable to professional chess players. Children learn bao as soon as they can count, scratching little holes in the ground in lieu of a board and using chips of wood or stones as counters.

The African love of carving has produced a proliferation of bao boards of many different sizes, shapes and forms – the board can be represented as resting on the back of a mythical beast, grows human heads from either end, or is smoothed into the shape of a fish. Bao boards make excellent souvenirs and are sold in almost every curio shop, often along with a badly photocopied set of printed instructions that are guaranteed to bamboozle even a maths professor. Far better to find a friendly local to teach you – the game is actually surprisingly simple to pick up.

Keram is the second most popular game in Zanzibar, and probably first arrived here from India. It's a fast-paced, raucous game played on a piece of wood carefully shaped into a small, square snooker table with cloth pockets at each corner. The game is similar to pool, with nine black disks, nine white disks, one red 'queen' disk and one larger white striker. Players flick the striker from their side of the board in an effort to get their own-colour disks into the pockets. Boards are kept smooth and speedy by liberal applications of talcum powder.

Bao and keram, like their Western equivalents chess and pool, have very different characters. While bao is traditionally a daytime game, played in shady village squares by elderly, dignified men, keram is popularly played at night in bars, often in the midst of a noisy and tipsy crowd of Jack the Lads.

FESTIVALS
Sauti za Busara Music Festival (February)
The 'Sounds of Wisdom' annual festival, occasionally called the Zanzibar Music Festival, is a fabulous fiesta celebrating the best of African music. Held every February in key venues across Zanizbar, with the biggest stars performing in Stone Town's Old Fort amphitheatre and Forodhani Gardens, it is a great opportunity to see live performances from a range of regional artists. For three days, the beats of jazz, taarab, pop and a host of

The word 'dhow', commonly applied by Europeans to any traditional seafaring vessel used off the coast of east Africa, is generally assumed to be Arabic in origin. There is, however, no historical evidence to back up this notion, nor does it appear to be an established Swahili name for any specific type of boat. Caroline Sassoon, writing in *Tanganyika Notes & Records* in 1970, suggests that the word 'dhow' is a corruption of *não*, used by the first Portuguese navigators in the Indian Ocean to refer to any small local seafaring vessel, or of the Swahili *kidau*, a specific type of small boat.

The largest traditional sailing vessel in wide use off the coast of east Africa is the *jahazi*, which measures up to 20m long and whose large billowing sails are a characteristic sight off Zanzibar and other traditional ports. With a capacity of about 100 passengers, the jahazi is used mainly for transporting cargo and passengers over relatively long distances or in open water, for instance between Dar es Salaam and Zanzibar. Minor modifications in the Portuguese and Omani eras notwithstanding, the design of the modern jahazi is pretty much identical to that of similar seafaring vessels used in medieval times and before. The name *jahazi* is generally applied to boats with cutaway bows and square sterns built on Zanzibar and nearby parts of the mainland. Similar boats built in Lamu and nearby ports in Kenya are called *jalbut* (possibly derived from the English 'jolly boat' or Indian *gallevat*) and have a vertical bow and wineglass-shaped stern. Smaller but essentially similar in design, the *mashua* measures up to 10m long, has a capacity of about 25 passengers, and is mostly used for fishing close to the shore or as local transport.

The most rudimentary and smallest type of boat used on the Swahili coast is the *mtumbwi*, which is basically a dugout canoe made by hollowing out the trunk of a large tree – the mango tree is favoured today – and used for fishing in mangrove creeks and other still-water environments. The *mtumbwi* is certainly the oldest type of boat used in east Africa, and its simple design probably replicates that of the very first boats crafted by humans. A more elaborate and distinctive variation on the mtumbwi is the *ngalawa*, a 5–6m-long dugout supported by a narrow outrigger on each side, making it sufficiently stable to be propelled by a sail. The ngalawa is generally used for fishing close to shore as well as for transporting passengers across protected channels such as the one between Mafia and Chole islands in the Mafia Archipelago.

The largest traditional boats of the Indian Ocean, the ocean-going dhows that were once used to transport cargo between east Africa, Asia and Arabia, have become increasingly scarce in recent decades due to the advent of foreign ships and other, faster modes of intercontinental transport. Several distinct types of ocean-going dhow are recognised, ranging from the 60-ton *sambuk* from Persia to 250-ton boats originating from India. Oddly, one of the larger of these vessels, the Indian *dengiya*, is thought to be the root of the English word 'dinghy'. Although a few large dhows still ply the old maritime trade routes of the Indian Ocean, they are now powered almost exclusively with motors rather than by sails.

There's an excellent small exhibition on boats in the Pemba Museum in Chake Chake, and in the House of Wonders in Zanzibar Town. Don't miss the fascinating examples of traditional 'stitched dhows', with their timbers 'sewn' tightly together.

other ethnic genres fill the evening air (17.00–01.00), as hundreds of artists and thousands of revellers descend on the capital. It's a joyous, fun-filled time to be in town … just be sure to book accommodation well in advance!

A three-day festival pass will cost around US$105 for international visitors (online booking available); all children under 12 years are admitted free of charge (**m** 024 223 2423; **m** 0773 822294; **e** busara@busara.or.tz; www.busaramusic.org/, www.facebook.com/sautizabusara).

Festival of the Dhow Countries – Film Festival (July) Without a doubt, the highlight of Zanzibar's artistic and cultural calendar is the Festival of the Dhow Countries – a 16-day event usually held in early July every year, and touted as east Africa's premier cultural event and among the most significant cultural events in all of Africa. The 'dhow countries' are those of Africa and the Indian Ocean basin, and so include east and southern Africa, northern east Africa, west and central Africa, the Horn of Africa, Arabia, Iraq, Iran, the subcontinent of India, Madagascar and the Indian Ocean islands, plus what the organisers call 'their global diaspora'.

The festival has grown from strength to strength since its humble beginnings at the Zanzibar International Film Festival (ZIFF) back in 1998, and now includes theatre, performances of traditional and contemporary music and dance, plus exhibitions of paintings, sculptures, craftwork and photography. However, the central part of this event is still the film festival, with its large, interesting and eclectic mix of films from all of the dhow countries and places further afield. Several film-makers are also present, there are prestigious awards for new films (short and long features and documentaries) and the festival also includes workshops, talks and discussions, as well as an energetic series of entertainments called the Children's Panorama.

On the more serious side, film- and media-related workshops have included Women Film-makers, Making Current Affairs Programmes for African Audiences, Constructing African History in the Cinema, and Creative Journalism.

The main venue for the festival is the open-air theatre at the Arab Fort, with films and performances on the main stage of the amphitheatre and live music in the adjoining Mambo Club, while other events are held at the Palace Museum, the House of Wonders and the Old Dispensary (Stone Town Cultural Centre). The Old Customs House, which became the home of the Dhow Countries Music Academy in 2002, is the venue for musical masterclasses. There's also a series of free shows in Forodhani Gardens, just outside the Fort.

Many events are free and admission charges are kept to a minimum (around US$0.50 for Tanzanian residents, US$5 for non-residents) to encourage local participation. The festival's directors have always aimed to deliver an event which is accessible to the local population; pricing them out would fail their objective. There's also an ambitious (but highly successful) programme of 'Village Events', which transports a selection of everything the festival offers in Zanzibar Town (film, music, theatre, women's workshops, children's shows, etc) out to the rural areas of Unguja and Pemba islands. The Festival of the Dhow Countries' organisers are keen to promote July as 'culture month' on Zanzibar, and this is undoubtedly an excellent time to visit the islands, although of course it's likely to be busy at this time. You can get more information from ZIFF, the festival organisers, who are based at the Old Fort in Zanzibar Stone Town (**m** 0777 411499; **e** ziff@ziff.or.tz; www.ziff.or.tz).

Mwaka Kogwa – Shirazi New Year (July) In a very different vein, the festival of Mwaka Kogwa is held every year in several villages around Zanzibar, but most

famously and most flamboyantly at the village of Makunduchi, in the south of Zanzibar Island. The traditional festival originated in Persia and celebrates the arrival of the New Year according to the Shirazi calendar. This one-day festival normally occurs during July, but it would be better to check the dates locally as changes are possible (for more details on the festival itself, see box, *The Mwaka Kogwa festival at Makunduchi*, page 319).

3

Natural Environment

PHYSICAL ENVIRONMENT

This place, for the goodness of the harbour and watering and plentiful refreshing with fish, and for sending sorts of fruits of the country, as cows ... and oxen and hens, is carefully to be sought for by such of all ships as shall hereafter pass that way.

James Lancaster, captain of the Edward Bonaventure,
first English ship to visit Zanzibar (1592)

LOCATION AND SIZE Zanzibar consists of two large islands, plus several smaller ones, about 40km off the coast of east Africa, in the Indian Ocean, about 6°S of the Equator. The two large islands are Unguja (usually called Zanzibar Island) and Pemba. Zanzibar Island is about 85km long and between 20km and 30km wide, with an area of 1,660km². The smaller Pemba Island, at around 985km², is some 67km long and between 15km and 20km wide.

The islands are generally flat and low lying, surrounded by coasts of rocky inlets or sandy beaches, with lagoons and mangrove swamps, and coral reefs beyond the shoreline. The western and central parts of Zanzibar Island have some low hills, where the highest point is about 120m above sea level. Pemba Island has a central ridge, cut by several small valleys, and appears more hilly than Zanzibar Island, although the highest point on Pemba is only 95m above sea level.

CLIMATE

February 19th. We anchored off Zanzibar at dawn. A day of fierce heat. The island is said to enjoy a cool season. I have never struck it. An hour's stroll ashore sufficed to revive old memories, then I retired to the ship for a cold bath and an afternoon under the electric fans.

Evelyn Waugh, Tourist in Africa *(1959)*

The climate of Zanzibar is dominated by the movements of the Indian Ocean monsoons, and characterised by wet and dry seasons. The northeast monsoon winds (known locally as the *kaskazi*) blow from November/December to February/March, and the southwest monsoon winds (the *kusi*) blow from June to September/October. The main rains (the *masika*) fall from mid March to the end of May, and there is a short rainy season (the *vuli*) in November.

Throughout the year, humidity is generally quite high (less so in the rainy season), although this can be relieved by winds and sea breezes. Temperatures do not vary greatly throughout the year, with daytime averages around 26°C (80°F) on Zanzibar Island from June to October, and around 28°C from December to February, although in this latter period the humidity is often higher, so temperatures feel hotter. Pemba tends to be cooler and gets slightly more rain than Zanzibar Island.

WILDLIFE

Unlike on the African mainland, there are no large wild animals on Zanzibar. Forest areas are inhabited by monkeys and small antelopes, while civets and various species of mongoose are found all over the islands. Birdlife is varied and interesting, with over 200 species being recorded, although bird populations are not as high as in other parts of the east African region. The marine wildlife, in the coral reefs that surround the islands, is particularly rich.

FLORA The islands of Pemba and Unguja (usually called Zanzibar Island) were originally forested, but human habitation has resulted in widespread clearing, although a few isolated pockets of indigenous forest remain. Formed about 27 million years ago and seven million years ago respectively, both islands were originally coral reefs which became exposed as sea levels dropped, so the main rock type is a coralline limestone, known locally as 'coral rag'.

On the eastern side of Zanzibar Island, and in parts of the northern and southern areas, the landscape is very flat where coralline rock is exposed or covered by a thin layer of a calcareous sandstone soil, which supports low scrubby bush, known as coral rag thicket, quite dense in some areas. The western and central parts of the island are slightly more undulating, with a deeper soil cover: red, iron-rich and more fertile. Additionally, the western sides receive more rain than the eastern sides of the islands. Thus the western parts of Zanzibar Island were once covered in forest, similar in most respects to the low coastal forest which existed on the east African mainland, but today very little of Zanzibar's indigenous natural forest remains, as it has mostly been cleared and used for agriculture. Local people grow crops on a subsistence basis, and this area is also where most of Zanzibar Island's commercial farms and spice and fruit plantations have been established.

The only significant areas of natural forest remaining in Zanzibar are at Jozani, a forest reserve on the south-central part of Zanzibar Island, and at Ngezi, a forest reserve in the north of Pemba Island, although smaller patches do exist elsewhere. The water table around Jozani is particularly high (during the rainy season the water can be over 1m above the ground) and the trees are mainly moisture-loving species.

Trees and deforestation Despite the establishment of forest reserves such as Jozani and Ngezi, Zanzibar's forests continue to be cut down at an unsustainable rate. A lack of definitive boundaries, ignorance and need prevailing. Timber is used for construction, boatbuilding and furniture-making, and as fuel, both for domestic purposes and to burn coral to produce lime for building works. This last use has grown particularly quickly as the number of hotels in Zanzibar has increased.

Mangrove wood from coastal areas is also being cut at an alarming rate. Forestry Department figures show that in 1992, about ten million poles were cut in Chwaka Bay Forest, compared with 2.5 million in 1990. This wood is used for fuel and furniture, and in the construction and repair of buildings, but unfortunately the cutting of poles in the mangrove swamps leads to beach erosion and the destruction of habitats for fish and other marine life.

To replace some of the disappearing forest, through the 1990s, the Zanzibar Forestry Department planted acacia, casuarina and eucalyptus trees in Unguja and Pemba, as well as orange, coffee and cinnamon plants in Pemba. Another scheme,

Coconuts are the second most important crop on Zanzibar after cloves. They grow on a certain species of palm tree which are generally planted where clove trees cannot survive, although as diversification is encouraged, it is not uncommon today to see coconut palms and clove trees on the same plantation.

Coconuts are picked throughout the year, and large quantities are consumed locally as food, with the milk used for cooking. The pickers skilfully climb up the palm trunks using only a short loop of rope, then drop the nuts to the ground. The outer husks of the coconuts are removed by striking them on a sharp stick or metal bar fixed in the ground.

Coconut products – mainly the 'kernel' (the white edible parts) – are also exported. The process involves splitting the coconuts in two and leaving them to dry so that the white fleshy kernels can be easily removed from the shells. The kernels are then dried for a few more days in the sun or in a special kiln. Gangs of workers separating the husks and kernels, and small coconut kilns, can be seen in the plantation areas outside Zanzibar Town.

When the kernels are properly dried, the resulting substance is called 'copra', which is widely used in the food industry as a flavouring, or for decoration. Copra is also processed into an oil that is used in some foods and in the production of soap, candles and hair oils. In the days before aerosol foam, copra was particularly good for making shaving soap as it helped produce a good lather.

The coconut husks are not wasted: they are buried under sand on the beach for several months, which helps to soften the fibres and make them separate from the rest of the husk. They are periodically dug up and beaten on rocks to help this process, and then buried again for another few months. The fibre is called 'coir', and is used for mats and rope-making. In the areas outside the towns you will often see local women working with coir in this way.

called the Zanzibar Cash Crop Farming System Project (ZCCFSP), discouraged farmers from cutting clove trees for firewood. All logging, and even the removal of dead wood, has officially been stopped in the Jozani and Ngezi reserves, although how carefully this new rule will be policed remains to be seen.

A relatively new project outside Zanzibar Town is engaged in the use of timber from coconut palm trees, which are found all over Zanzibar and Pemba islands. Traditionally, palm has not been used as a timber because it is very hard to cut or plane. However, modern high-quality joinery tools mean coconut wood can now be turned into beautiful furniture and fittings such as doors and window frames. The aim of the project is to use the local palm trees after they have come to the end of their natural fruit-producing life. By using this local source of timber, it is hoped that other trees will not be cut down or imported to Zanzibar from the mainland. Several of the hotels and tour companies around Zanzibar are now using coconut-wood items.

Other trees occurring on Zanzibar include mango (*mwembe*), which is used for its fruit and as timber for boatbuilding, kapok (*capoc*), and *Bombax rhodographalon*, which is used in light construction, and also produces a substance similar to cotton, traditionally used to make stuffing for mattresses and pillows. Other fruit-producing trees, grown in plantations or singly around local villages include guava, breadfruit, orange and pomegranate.

Natural Environment   WILDLIFE

3

Cloves are the buds of a tree which, when dried, produce a unique flavour and aroma that is beloved of chefs the world over. The name comes from the French word *clou* meaning 'nail', which the buds resemble.

Cloves were introduced to Zanzibar from the end of the 18th century from the French colonies of the Seychelles, Ile de France (now Mauritius) and Réunion, where they had earlier been introduced from the Moluccas in Indonesia by French sailors. Sultan Said (sultan between 1804 and 1856) recognised their value and encouraged the setting up of plantations on Zanzibar and Pemba. When the plantations were established, it was found that growing conditions on Pemba Island were superior to those on Zanzibar, and the bulk of the clove crop actually came from there.

At the height of the clove trade, in the second half of the 19th century and the early 20th century, the islands of Zanzibar produced more than 90% of the world's supply of cloves, and the power and wealth of Zanzibar were based largely on this trade. Today, about 75% of the islands' total produce comes from Pemba.

Clove trees (*Eugenia aromatica* or *Eugenia caryophyllata*) grow to a height of around 10–15m and can produce crops for over 50 years. In the first eight years of growth, the buds are left to turn into colourful pink flowers. When a tree reaches maturity, however, the buds are painstakingly picked by hand before they open, when they are still white, then separated from their stems. Buds and stems are dried in the sun on palm-leaf mats or on a special stone platform called a *sakufu*, during which time they turn brown. During the harvest season, between July and January, with a break during the November rainy season, the scent of cloves is carried on the breeze right across Pemba in particular, where you can often see sacks of cloves being loaded at Mkoani for shipping to Zanzibar Island. Here, they

Spice trees and food plants The main crops grown in Zanzibar are coconuts and cloves. Bananas, citrus fruits and other spices are also grown commercially. As well as the famous clove trees, other spice plants found on Zanzibar and Pemba include black pepper, cinnamon, cardamom, jasmine, chilli and henna, whose small leaves are dried, ground and mixed with lemon to give the paste familiar to Eastern beauticians. The main crops grown by local people for their own consumption include maize, cassava, yams, bananas and pumpkins (see box, *History of Zanzibari agriculture*, page 30).

MAMMALS As described above, much of Zanzibar's indigenous forested area has been cleared, so natural habitats for all wild animals are severely restricted. Probably the best places to see indigenous mammals are the Jozani Forest Reserve on Zanzibar Island and the Ngezi Forest Reserve on Pemba.

In this section, scientific names of species are given according to information provided by the Jozani Forest Reserve and Ngezi Forest Reserve. Other authorities disagree on some classifications and nomenclature, especially regarding subspecies, but this is unlikely to be important for most visitors.

The Jozani Forest Reserve is well known for its population of **red colobus monkeys** (see colour section, page 4). This animal is found elsewhere in Africa, but those on Zanzibar form a distinct species, called Zanzibar red colobus or Kirk's red colobus (*Procolobus kirkii*), endemic to the island and one of the rarest primates in Africa.

are offloaded at the port, or on the beach near the Tembo Hotel, and carried by truck to the nearby distillery.

All cloves in Zanzibar have to be sold to the government, which buys at fixed rates, then sells on at market rates to the users and producers. So important is the crop that, on Pemba, vehicles have to stop as they pass police checkpoints to give the opportunity for vehicles to be checked for smuggled cloves. Sometimes, however, the government rates paid to the clove growers are so low that a harvest is not economically viable, and the cloves are left on the trees. As a result, some plantations have been completely abandoned in recent years, creating anger and resentment among the local farmers.

Most of the cloves that are harvested are processed into oil at the distillery on Zanzibar Island. This oil is used mainly as a flavouring device in foods such as cakes, pickles, cooked meats and ready-made mixes. It is also used in some antiseptic solutions, such as mouthwashes, and in mild painkillers for toothache. Its other major use is in cosmetics, where it gives a sweet-spicy note to many different kinds of perfumes.

The best-quality dried buds are kept separate and used whole in cooking, pickling or the making of spiced wines and liqueurs. These buds are also distilled into a high-grade oil for use in particularly fine perfumes. In the cosmetics industry, the oil from good Zanzibar clove buds is reckoned to be the best in the world.

Today, Zanzibar is still a major exporter of cloves and clove products, representing about 75% of foreign-exchange earnings – although these are highly dependent on the fluctuating world market price. Agriculture's contribution to Zanzibar's gross domestic product (GDP) currently stands at around 32%, although this has been falling over recent years.

Although hard to see in the forest canopy, one group of red colobus in Jozani is partly habituated to human presence, so you are quite likely to spot some if you visit. These monkeys are mainly reddish-brown in colour, with a darker back and 'cap', and a paler forehead-patch, but their most striking and unusual feature is the male's white crest on the forehead. On closer inspection, particularly of facial areas, you will notice that each monkey has slightly different coat patterns and colourings.

In Jozani and some other patches of forest, you are likely to see the **blue monkey**, also called Sykes' monkey, the mitis monkey or the Zanzibar white-throated guenon (*Cercopithecus mitis albgularis*), which on Zanzibar is bluish-grey, or even a greenish-grey, with a distinct white throat-patch. Although the two types of monkey compete for some food items, they are often seen foraging peacefully in mixed groups. The Swahili word for monkey is *kima*. On Zanzibar, the blue monkey is more commonly given this name. When

Blue monkey

distinguishing between the two, the blue monkey is called *kima mweusi*, and the red colobus *kima punju* – 'poison monkey' (probably because the colobus has a stronger smell than other monkeys, and is reputed to have an evil influence on trees where it feeds).

A local subspecies of **vervet monkey** (*Cercopithecus aethiops nesiotes*) occurs on Pemba, but it is thought not to be on Zanzibar Island. This monkey is smaller than

The Zanzibar leopard (*Panthera pardus adersi*), is a local subspecies. Two different types have been recorded: the *kisutu*, which is similar to the mainland leopard, but with a more compact spot pattern and lighter background; and the *konge*, which is larger than the kisutu with dark fur and faint spot pattern.

Leopard tend to be shy and mainly active at night. Perhaps because of their elusive, nocturnal habits, they have traditionally been considered unlucky by local people, and are often associated with witchcraft, so have been actively hunted. They are also hunted because they are seen as vermin by farmers, and for their skins which can be sold to dealers. The leopard has been further pushed to the edge of extinction by an ever-growing loss of suitable habitat, as forest areas are cleared, and by a loss of prey, as Zanzibar's small antelopes are also hunted unsustainably.

By the 1980s, the leopard was believed to be extinct in Zanzibar, but in 1994, an American researcher called Scott Marshall found evidence of three leopards on Unguja (Zanzibar Island), including prints, droppings and a suspected den near Chwaka. In his report, Marshall suggested that these leopards were trapped and 'domesticated' at a young age, to be used in ceremonies by local witchdoctors or traditional healers. He also suggested that there may be several more leopards similarly kept in captivity at other villages in Zanzibar, although this assumption was based on local anecdotal evidence, rather than on positive sightings.

However, in 1998, the South African wildlife experts Chris and Tilde Stuart published a report describing their exhaustive methods to locate any signs of leopard on Zanzibar Island, and concluded that none existed in a wild state. They also looked into the possibility of a few 'kept' leopards remaining in existence but found no hard evidence. They further concluded that even if a small number of 'kept' leopards were being held in secret, there was no hope at all for long-term survival of this species on Zanzibar.

Leopard

the red colobus and the blue monkey, generally greyish with a dark, rusty-brown back and black feet.

Other mammals found on Zanzibar, mainly in forested areas, include the **bush pig** (*Potamochoerus porcus*), although its numbers are reported to be greatly reduced; **Zanzibar tree hyrax** (*Dendrohyrax arboreus neumanni*), a rodent-like animal the size of a rabbit (this subspecies is endemic), with hoofed feet and rounded ears, and a loud piercing scream when threatened; **Ader's duiker** (*Cephalophus adersi*), a species of small antelope found only on Zanzibar and, until recently, the Kenyan coast; and **Zanzibar suni** (*Nesotragus moschatu moschatus*), another endemic subspecies of antelope which is even smaller than the duiker. The endemic **Pemba blue duiker** (*Cephalophus monticola pembae*) occurs at Ngezi Forest. All of these animals are nocturnal or extremely shy and are unlikely to be seen.

Ader's duiker

Leopard (*Panthera pardus adersi*), or *chui* in Swahili, have been recorded in Jozani, and elsewhere in Zanzibar. Again, this is an endemic subspecies, smaller than the mainland version and with finer markings, and also very unlikely to be sighted. Recent studies have concluded that this animal is now extinct on Zanzibar (see box, *Leopards in Zanzibar*, opposite).

The small-eared **greater galago** or **bushbaby** (*Otolemur garnettii*) and the Zanzibar **lesser galago** (*Galagoides zanzibaricus*) both occur on Zanzibar, the latter listed as vulnerable by the IUCN. The **small-eared galago** (*komba* in Swahili) is about the size of a rabbit, generally brown, with very distinctive large ears and eyes, and a large bushy tail. The **Zanzibar galago** (*komba ndogo*) also has large eyes and ears, but it is smaller (about half the size of the greater galago) and grey in colour. Both animals are nocturnal, especially active at dawn and dusk, and have distinctive cries – sometimes like a child crying (hence their name), other times loud and shrill, and positively spine-chilling. They are known to be inquisitive and will forage around huts and villages at night. They are attracted to bowls of locally brewed palm wine, and often get captured when intoxicated and incapable of escape. A local saying, *mlevi kama komba*, means 'as drunk as a bushbaby'!

Also found in Zanzibar is the **African civet** (*Viverra civetta schwarzi*; *orngawa* in Swahili); it looks like a very large cat with a stocky body, thick tail, and black, white and grey markings which form rough stripes. The **Javan civet** (*Viverricula indica rasse*) occurs on Pemba and Unguja, probably introduced by southeast Asian traders.

Smaller mammals include the **Zanzibar slender mongoose** (*Herpestes sanguineus rufescens*), most often seen running across roads with its tail vertical, and the **bushy-tailed mongoose** (*Bdeogale crassicauda tenuis*) – rarely seen anywhere. The **marsh mongoose** (*Atilax paludinosus rubescens*) occurs only on Pemba and may be seen at Ngezi Forest. The banded mongoose is a non-indigenous species, introduced to Zanzibar Island.

Populations of rats, mice and shrews (plus 14 species of bat) occur on both Zanzibar and Pemba islands. Those worthy of note include the **Zanzibar four-toed elephant shrew** (*Petrodromus tetradactylus zanzibaricus*) with distinctive long slender legs and a trunk-like snout for eating insects, and the **Pemba flying fox** (*Pteropus voeltzkowi*), a large fruit bat with distinctive rufous colouring and fox-like face, found only on Pemba Island (see *Chapter 12*, page 343).

REPTILES, AMPHIBIANS AND INVERTEBRATES
Of all of the reptiles on Zanzibar, undoubtedly the easiest to spot is the **giant tortoise** (*Geochelone gigantea*) that inhabit Prison Island, a few kilometres offshore from Zanzibar Town. They were introduced here from the island of Aldabra, in the Seychelles archipelago, in the 18th century.

If you visit Jozani, you'll probably see some of the forest's population of tiny black and gold **frogs**. In the rainy season, when the ground floods, you'll see their tadpoles too. **Chameleons** can also be seen in Jozani and other parts of the island. Like the mongoose they are often seen crossing roads, but often very slowly, and very precariously. Other reptiles include **snakes** (rarely seen) and **geckos** (frequently seen on the inside walls of buildings – particularly the budget hotels in Zanzibar Town – although this is no cause for worry as they're small, timid and harmless).

The long black **millipedes** which you'll see on paths, especially after rains, are also harmless, and will curl up in a ball if you disturb them. Smaller still, though much more dangerous, is the **mosquito**. These are relatively common on Zanzibar, so see *Chapter 4*, *Malaria*, page 86 before you arrive.

One of the best places to see some of Zanzibar's reptiles (among other animals) is at the Zanzibar Land Animals Park (ZALA) a few kilometres west of Jozani Forest on the road to Kizimkazi (see *Chapter 11*, page 321)

BIRDS *Dudley Iles*

Zanzibar is not noted as a major birdwatching area, but over 200 species of bird have been recorded on the islands of the archipelago. The avifauna of Zanzibar includes the resident birds, plus visitors – migrants and seabirds. For any keen birdwatcher travelling on the east African mainland, polishing off the holiday with at least a few days in Zanzibar can make the trip-list even more impressive – the islands boast several species and races which are unique. Even for the more casual birdwatcher, Zanzibar provides some fine opportunities. Knowing the name of the bird that flew over the beach, or sings from a bush in your hotel garden, will make your time in Zanzibar even more rewarding and enjoyable.

Overview Like the majority of offshore islands, Unguja and Pemba have a smaller avifauna than the mainland of east Africa. Unguja can claim about 220 species, and Pemba slightly fewer. Of these, about 35 have been added since 1994, an indication of increasing tourist interest and observations. On Zanzibar, visitors are able to make a larger contribution to natural history records than on the mainland, since there have been fewer observers until recently.

Although Unguja and Pemba are similar in size, geography and position, they provide an interesting avifauna comparison. Unguja has woodpeckers, shrikes, cuckoo-shrikes and bulbuls, while Pemba has none of these. But Pemba has its own species of green pigeon, scops owl, white-eye and sunbird found nowhere else in the world.

As well as the resident birds, migrants from Eurasia, the Middle East and southern Africa pass through or remain to winter on the islands. Those from the north arrive in September/October and leave again in February/March. For European visitors it is a delight to see a familiar spotted flycatcher in the hotel garden, or hear the sound of a curlew calling from the shore at low tide.

Habitats The main bird habitats on Zanzibar, and some of the species found there, are described below. If the name of a bird is singular (eg: golden weaver), it refers to one species. If the name is plural (eg: bee-eaters, kingfishers), it refers to several species of the same or similar genus.

Parks and gardens Perhaps surprisingly, some of the best places to see birds are the parks and public gardens of Zanzibar Town, or the gardens of the many hotels situated along the coasts of Unguja and Pemba. The seed- and fruit-bearing trees, and the insects they attract, in turn attract many mannikins, warblers, coucals, sunbirds and swifts.

A bird you cannot miss in towns and around the big hotels on the coast is the Indian house crow (see box, *The Indian house crow*, opposite).

Farmland The more fertile areas of Zanzibar, mostly the centre and west of Unguja and much of Pemba, are occupied by the majority of the rural population. Over the centuries natural coastal scrub and forest have been cleared and turned over to agriculture, either for small-scale subsistence farming or for commercial plantations growing fruit and spices. The plentiful supplies of seeds, fruits and insects here attract many birds, including the beautiful long-tailed paradise

THE INDIAN HOUSE CROW

From information provided by Dudley Iles, updated by Helen de Jode, Zanzibar Ecotourism Association

The Indian house crow (*Corvus splendens*) was introduced to Zanzibar in 1891. The bird is a scavenger and 50 crows were sent by the Indian government to help clear domestic waste building up in Stone Town at the time. Although the Indian house crow did consume some of this rubbish, it is by nature an aggressive bird and it began to attack many of the island's small birds and their eggs. As early as 1917 it was realised that the crows had become a pest, and they were subject to various control efforts including trapping, shooting and poisoning, but to little effect. By the 1940s, the Indian house crow had spread throughout Zanzibar Island, and by the 1970s its population had increased to such an extent in Zanzibar Town that many small bird species were rarely seen.

The crow population continued to grow, and by 1990 their impact on the indigenous bird population was considerable, with the town becoming virtually devoid of all other species. In addition, the Indian house crow was affecting agricultural and livestock production: feeding on germinating maize, sorghum and soft fruits, eating young chicks and ducklings and attacking calves and sometimes even cattle.

Between 1990 and 1995, the Finnish International Development Agency funded a control programme organised by wildlife expert Tony Archer and a team from the Zanzibar Commission for Lands and Environment. They used firstly a Malaysian-designed crow trap, and later a poison which was developed in the USA to control starlings as agricultural pests. The trapping and poisoning strategies were combined with a bounty on the collection of Indian house crow eggs and chicks during the breeding season. According to a report issued by Tony Archer, almost 45,000 crows were killed between 1993 and 1995. An estimated 95% of the crow population was killed in Stone Town and 75% across the island as a whole, allowing the small bird populations to return.

Unfortunately, since 1995, as funding dried up, there has been little continued effort to control the numbers of crows in Zanzibar. Increasing amounts of rubbish generated by a growing human population in Zanzibar Town, and a growth in tourism in coastal areas, are partly to blame for the rise in the number of crows. Current levels are having a serious impact on the indigenous bird population and are becoming an environmental health hazard.

In Dar es Salaam, where a similar crow problem exists, the Wildlife Conservation Society of Tanzania (WCST) has succeeded in killing over 43,000 crows using crow traps paid for by hotel owners and with some limited funding from the Canadian Fund for Local Initiatives.

In Zanzibar, a small voluntary organisation, registered as the Zanzibar Ecotourism Association, or ZEA (e *ecotourism-znz@twiga.com*), has since 1999 been encouraging hotels to become part of a similar sustainable programme for Zanzibar, but it lacks financial support. Under ZEA co-ordination, several hotels and individuals around Unguja have now established their own crow traps, but many more are needed if the island is to be rid of the Indian house crow.

flycatcher and parties of golden weaver (the only widespread weaver in Zanzibar). You may also see green wood-hoopoe, crested guineafowl (although these are now rare) and the diminutive emerald-spotted wood dove.

The telegraph wires along the roads provide vantage points for lilac-breasted roller and occasionally for the rufous-coloured broad-billed roller, and in winter for the blue-cheeked bee-eater.

Lesser-striped swallow hunt for flying insects over the countryside, and visit pools to collect mud for nest building. In areas where there are coconut palms you will see palm swift.

Freshwater ponds and grasslands   Some farming areas consist of grassland, grazed by cattle, and often flooded after rain. Some of these wet areas are used to grow rice. Here you will see black-winged bishop, a small bright red weaver, plus herons and egrets, especially cattle egret, and maybe even a goshawk or harrier.

Where undisturbed, ponds and marshes support breeding jacana (or lilytrotter) and black crake, and possibly Allen's gallinule. You may also see small parties of pygmy goose, white-faced whistling duck and occasionally the rare white-backed duck. In winter months, purple heron and yellow wagtails (from Eurasia) feed in the rushes along pond edges.

Other birds seen in these areas include little grebe, red-billed teal and moorhen.

Bush   Many areas of Zanzibar, especially the north and east of Unguja (Zanzibar Island), are not fertile and have not been cleared. They are covered in low scrubby vegetation called coral rag bush. It grows on well-drained rock which was once a coral reef, but was exposed when sea levels dropped many millions of years ago. The poor vegetation here does not attract great numbers of birds, but a few exciting species can be seen, especially in the early morning or late evening, including the pale-eyed sombre bulbul, eastern bearded scrub robin, crowned hornbill and collared sunbird. You might also see birds of prey such as African goshawk or black kite, plus rollers and shrikes. With luck a Gabon nightjar may rise suddenly from near your feet.

Forests and woodland   Only a small percentage of Zanzibar's indigenous forest remains, following centuries of clearing for farms and plantations. The main areas are Jozani Forest on Unguja and Ngezi Forest and Kiyuu Forest on Pemba, characterised by tall trees with buttressed roots and a convergent canopy, interspersed with ferns and smaller bushes. Masingini Forest near Bububu north of Zanzibar Town can also be rewarding. The forest birds of Zanzibar are shy and hard to spot, but your chances are better in the early morning, when you might see Fischer's turaco, wood owl, crested guineafowl or tambourine dove, plus swifts, hornbills, woodpeckers and weavers.

In patches of woodland, on the edge of areas which have been cleared for farming, you may see more weavers, plus coucals, sunbirds, flycatchers and bulbuls.

Mangroves   Mangroves occur on small offshore islands or around estuaries, in or near areas which are covered by water at high tide. Individual mangroves can grow to 5m in height, and close together, which creates a forest-like atmosphere (the mangrove vegetation of Zanzibar is discussed in *The seas and shores of Zanzibar,* page 63). This habitat is rich in marine life, which is exploited by humans as well as resident and migrant shore birds including herons and kingfishers. Other species you are likely to see include mouse-coloured sunbird and blue-cheeked bee-eater.

Seashore and sandbars Naturally, as a group of islands, Zanzibar is surrounded by seashores, made up of beaches, low cliffs, creeks and tidal coral-mud flats. On the beaches you will find various wading birds, including plovers, whimbrels and sandpipers; many of these will be familiar to European naturalists, as Zanzibar becomes an increasingly important wintering ground for these northern species.

Also look out for the greater sand plover (which comes from central Asia) and the striking crab plover, which breeds along the Somali coast. Another notable shore bird is the dimorphic heron, which feeds along the tide line: about 49% of these birds are mouse grey, and another 49% are pure white, while the rest show intermediate plumages. Perhaps the most striking seashore bird is the African fish eagle, which may be seen in some areas.

On the numerous sandbars off the west coast of Zanzibar you can see more waders, plus flocks of terns, gulls and cormorants. The sooty gull often seen here is a visitor from the Red Sea.

Open sea Some birds spend most of their time at sea, in (or above) deeper water, and rarely come to the shore. You will see these only if you are out on a boat, possibly diving or fishing, or crossing to Zanzibar Town on a ship from Pemba or Dar es Salaam. Oceanic birds are rare, but you may occasionally see frigatebirds or a roseate tern, or a masked booby from the breeding colony on Latham Island, south of Zanzibar.

Birdwatching areas
There are many places where you can watch birds on Zanzibar, and we list just a few recommended areas here.

Victoria Gardens Also known as the People's Gardens (see page 194), this small park in Zanzibar Town has flowers and flowering trees and attracts a good range of birds. Here you might see scarlet-breasted sunbird, the Indian race of house sparrow, bronze mannikin, black-and-white mannikin, and the neat but skulking green-backed camaroptera, a complex name for Zanzibar's only widespread resident warbler. Overhead, parties of little swift hawk for insects.

Mbweni Ruins Hotel garden On the outskirts of Zanzibar Town (see page 199), this good hotel has a beautiful garden, and is an excellent birdwatching area. You don't have to be a guest to come here for lunch and a walk around their nature trail. At least 50 species have been recorded here by the hotel management, who are very knowledgeable on local wildlife and can advise on good birdwatching places on Zanzibar. The hotel's dining veranda overlooks a beach where many shore birds, including oystercatchers, whimbrels, sooty gull and lesser crested tern, await the retreat of the tide. Nearby is an area of mangrove. In the hotel gardens you'll see bronze mannikin, mangrove kingfisher, little swift and scarlet-chested sunbird, plus Eurasian golden oriole and blue-cheeked bee-eater in winter. During the heat of the day, the hotel pond is beloved by black-breasted glossy starling, dark-capped bulbul (more widely known as common, black-eyed or yellow-vented bulbul), golden weaver and as many as 50 Java sparrows (introduced around 1857 but now resident).

Bwawani Marsh Situated near the port on the edge of Zanzibar Town, this is the largest reed swamp on Unguja, although it was formed by accident when the Bwawani Hotel was built. Some 20% of Unguja's birds have been recorded here including a few, like the hottentot teal and purple gallinule, which have not been recorded elsewhere on the island.

Other species to look out for are lesser swamp warbler, Allen's gallinule, jacana, wood sandpiper, night heron, purple heron and the African race of the little bittern. The best viewing spots are on the Bububu road and on the smaller road leading to the hotel. Unfortunately, the swamp has become a dumping ground for local rubbish. Beware!

Jozani Forest A good area for keen birders, particularly if you visit early or late in the day, is Jozani Forest Reserve, although the birds here typically hide themselves in the undergrowth or high canopies. The area south of Jozani Forest itself, on the other side of the main road, where the semi-habituated monkeys are found, is also good for birding (for more details, see page 329). Birds occurring here include the olive sunbird, the little greenbul (a racial endemic), dark-backed weaver, paradise flycatcher, east coast batis (a neat black-and-white flycatcher), crowned hornbill and cardinal woodpecker. Local specials include the east coast akalat and Fischer's turaco. At dawn or dusk you may also see African wood owl.

In the nearby mangrove forest, where a walkway has been constructed, you can see mangrove kingfisher, mouse-coloured sunbird and maybe tropical boubou.

Chwaka Bay This is the largest and most complex area of mud and sand on Zanzibar. It is an important area for local fishing, seaweed production, and for wintering shore birds, most notably the crab plover. Much of the east coast, from Chwaka to Nungwe, can offer good birdwatching along the shore – and even beyond the reef at low tide. Birds occurring here include waders, terns and gulls, plus herons such as the green-backed heron and dimorphic heron.

Matemwe This is a small village about halfway between Chwaka and Nungwi – with typical east coast conditions. There is a wide beach here, backed by palm groves and coral rag bush, and each habitat attracts typical species. The Matemwe Lodge's gardens (see *Chapter 9*, page 253) are typical of many carefully planted and well-watered lodge gardens; they attract sombre greenbul, collared sunbird and paradise flycatcher, among others.

Chumbe Island This small island lies off the west coast, within easy reach of Zanzibar Town. About 63 bird species have been recorded here since 1992, but these are mostly sea and shore birds. The resident land birds are limited to about six common species, including African reed warbler, and most notably the small colony of mouse-coloured sunbird.

Perhaps Chumbe's main avian interest lies in the vagrants which occasionally appear, such as a wood warbler (only the third recorded sighting in all Tanzania) and, in 1999, a peregrine falcon. In 1994, around 750 pairs of roseate tern bred on two islets off Chumbe, but, although some 500 young were reared, the birds have not returned. House crows, fish eagles, rats (now eliminated) and bad weather were the probable reasons for their staying away (for more details on visiting the island, see *Chapter 11*, page 329).

Misali and Panza islands Misali Island lies close to Pemba Island while Panza Island lies off Unguja. Each has coastal forest and typical shore habitats. Like all small islands they are limited in bird species but are attractive for migrants. Misali is noted for a small population of Fischer's turaco, while on Panza brown-necked parrot occur. Panza also has large colonies of fruit bat and white-winged bat which attract bat hawks.

Ngezi Forest On Pemba Island, Ngezi Forest (see *Chapter 12*, page 369) is a good birding destination. Birds recorded here include palm-nut vulture, African goshawk, and four endemics: Pemba scops owl, Pemba white-eye, Pemba green pigeon and Pemba violet-breasted sunbird. Ngezi is also home to a good population of fruit bats.

THE SEAS AND SHORES OF ZANZIBAR *Matt Richmond PhD*

For anyone visiting the islands of Zanzibar, Mafia Island or the coast of mainland Tanzania, the diversity of marine life in the surrounding shallow waters may not be immediately obvious. However, the main marine habitats (mangroves, coral reefs and seagrass beds) are part of an extremely diverse, productive and vitally important marine ecosystem. Other marine habitats include the beaches and cliffs fringing the shore, and the vast areas of open water. The species of plants and animals which make up these habitats around Zanzibar and off mainland Tanzania are mostly the same as those found elsewhere in the western Indian Ocean (eg: Mozambique, Madagascar, Mauritius and the Seychelles), though slightly different from those in similar habitats as far away as southeast Asia, Australia and the South Pacific islands. Some species of fish and other creatures do, however, span this entire Indo-Pacific region.

MARINE HABITATS
Beaches and cliffs Around the main islands of Zanzibar (ie: Unguja and Pemba), many shores are fringed by either coconut-lined coral-sand beaches, where ghost crabs scamper, or rocky limestone cliffs – remains of ancient reefs once below the sea (over 100,000 million years ago), then exposed as sea levels dropped, now undercut and battered by high-tide waves. The cliffs provide a home to the brilliant red-yellow grapsid rock crabs and the bizarre eight-plated chiton snail, plus numerous other small snails, rock oysters and rock-skipper fish.

Mangroves In sheltered bays and inlets, where wave action is reduced, mangrove stands and forests are commonplace. Mangrove trees are specially adapted to survive in the sea, and all ten species found in the western Indian Ocean occur in Zanzibar. At high tide mangroves attract numerous species of fish, crabs and shrimps which depend on the forests as nursery grounds for their young. At low tide, red-clawed fiddler crabs carry out their formal challenges when not sifting the mud for food, while mud-skippers flip from pool to pool or from branch to branch when the tide is in. One of the best places to experience these fascinating marine forests is the mangrove boardwalk at Jozani Forest – especially when the tide is in. You can also snorkel around a mangrove forest on Misali Island, off Pemba, or in many other inlets around the main islands.

Seagrass beds and lagoons The intertidal areas or zones lie between the high- and low-tide marks. Where beaches slope sharply, this is a narrow strip. Where old coral beds slope imperceptibly and are almost flat, this area may extend 2km or more. Intertidal zones provide a habitat for thousands of molluscs, crabs, sea-cucumbers, seaweeds and several species of seagrasses, which are themselves food for fish at high tide.

Seagrass (*Cymodocea rotundata*)

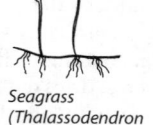

Seagrass (*Thalassodendron ciliastumm*)

Along the east coast of Unguja (and the east coasts of the other islands and the mainland) shallow lagoons occur, extending to the reef crest. The lagoons support assorted coral, seagrass and seaweed communities and often great selections of starfish and beautiful nudibranch (sea hares and their relatives).

Blue starfish

Coral reefs Corals are not plants, but animals belonging to the *Coelenterata* group (which also includes sea anemones and jellyfish). Corals exist in clean, clear, shallow, warm water, and so are found only in tropical regions. A coral begins life as a soft, many-tentacled 'polyp' around 1mm in size, and then produces a hard calcium carbonate skeleton around itself for protection. These types of coral are called **hard corals**. A coral colony develops from a single polyp by a process called 'budding' (where a new polyp grows out of an existing one). When polyps die, their hard skeletons remain, and the colony expands as new polyps form on the skeletons of old dead polyps. In this way colonies grow, and the growth rate varies from about 1cm to 5cm per year depending on species, depth

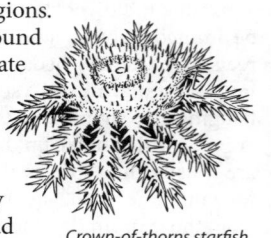
Crown-of-thorns starfish feeding on brain coral

and water conditions. Groups of colonies together make up the coral reefs found fringing the islands. Different types of hard coral form their colonies in different shapes; the commonly known varieties include staghorn coral, plate coral, mushroom coral, table corals and brain corals – all abundant in shallow water.

Staghorn coral

Coral also uses a form of sexual reproduction where sperm and eggs are mixed (either internally with a coral embryo or larvae later being released, or by 'spawning' where eggs and sperm are released by polyps to mix in the water). In both ways the corals can colonise new areas.

Within the polyps exist microscopic algae-type organisms called *zooxanthellae*, which trap the sunlight needed to power the chemical reactions that produce the coral's hard calcium skeleton. It is the *zooxanthellae* which give the coral its colour – usually pink or pale brown in a variety of shades – as the coral polyps themselves are virtually transparent. Thus when coral is picked, and taken out of the water, the corals and the *zooxanthellae* die and lose colour, leaving only the pale 'bleached' chalky-white skeletons.

During daylight hours, the coral colonies use sunlight in much the same way as plants do, but at night-time on a reef, most hard coral species are busy, with polyps extending their tentacles to catch planktonic foods.

Soft corals, on the other hand, do not have a hard external skeleton and do not form reefs. They are far more colourful than hard corals, although they also require light to build the tiny crystal fibres embedded in their soft pink, lilac or cream-coloured tissues. The daytime feeding of the eight-tentacled polyps, a feature of this group, is clearly visible on soft corals which can, in places, dominate underwater scenes.

On the east coasts of Unguja and Pemba, typical fringing reefs are marked by a continuous line of surf resulting from Indian Ocean swells. At low tide the reef crest dries out revealing pink algal-rock and boulders – the coral itself usually only becoming prolific on the seaward slope below 5m. On Unguja, the coral-covered reef slopes dip down to about 20m, after which a fairly bare sandy seabed continues down a further 4km to the ocean bottom. On the more sheltered west coasts of the Zanzibar Channel, smaller, isolated patch reefs with sandbars, and island reefs (around Chapwani, Changuu, Bawe and Chumbi islands), provide coral gardens in the relatively shallow waters. In contrast, parts of the reef around Pemba Island drop down over 50m or more offering spectacular vertical coral walls. Some of the most dramatic dive sites along the Tanzanian coast are found on the steep slopes of Pemba Island.

On any of these coral reefs you will immediately note the amazing variety of colourful fish of all sizes and shapes, incredible in their patterns and forms: butterflyfish, parrotfish, surgeonfish, damselfish, emperors, goatfish, pufferfish, angelfish, triggerfish, groupers and grunts to name a few. Most of these typical coral reef fish

Emperor fish

are territorial and reside over small areas of reef, rarely leaving their patch and aggressively protecting it from others of their own species.

Grouper

Some, like the butterflyfish, pair up for life and occupy a patch the size of a tennis court; others, such as the blue-lined yellow snappers, roam around the reefs in schools of a few hundred.

Because of the rich diversity of life forms, coral reefs have been compared to tropical rainforests. With Zanzibar's waters containing more than 700 fish species associated with coral reefs, over 100 species of hard corals, 150-odd species of seaweed and 300-plus species of seashells, to mention just a few of the more obvious sea creatures, the comparison is certainly a valid one. Then there are sponges, anemones, brittlestars, sea cucumbers, sea-squirts, feather-stars and crustaceans, all forming a seemingly chaotic, mind-boggling complexity which has fascinated scientists since Darwin's time.

The loss of the microscopic *zooxanthellae* from the coral, resulting in bleaching, was a major feature of the reefs around Zanzibar and elsewhere in the tropics in 1998, as the region experienced increased seawater temperatures (up to 32°C) associated with a severe, and much-publicised, shift in global climate conditions called El Niño. Although coral bleaching had occurred in the past, this event was on a scale not witnessed before. Much coral (both hard and soft) bleached and failed to regain its *zooxanthellae*. Within about five months vast areas of previously rich and diverse coral communities died. In many reef areas since then, new, small colonies have begun to emerge from settlement of coral larvae, and the coral component of these reefs is beginning to return to that prior to 1998. In other areas, total recovery to pre-1998 conditions may take decades or centuries. For reasons that are still unclear, much more coral around Pemba eventually died, whereas on Unguja corals recovered after bleaching.

Open waters The open waters, though mostly empty at first glance, can be very busy at times. They are home to vast schools of small, plankton-feeding, pelagic fish species such as sardines, silversides and Indian mackerel, continuously on the move and relentlessly pursued by larger pelagic fish, like skipjack, yellowfin tuna, kingfish, sailfish and marlin.

Sailfish

Yellowfin tuna

Out at sea, in the Pemba Channel or off the east coast, flocks of hundreds of white terns identify tuna feeding frenzies as they dart into the shoals of small pelagic fish forced up to the surface by the tuna below.

Also feeding out at sea for most of their lives are turtles, coming into shallow waters when looking for a mate. Green and hawksbill turtles are the most common (for more details, see page 69).

Both the friendly bottlenose dolphin and the less bold humpback dolphin can be seen in small groups, or pods, quite close to the shore (see box, *The Kizimkazi dolphins*, page 326). Around Unguja there appear to be a few pods of 10–15 members, each with its own territory. One area where they are commonly seen is off Kizimkazi in southwest Unguja (viewing is easily arranged with a local boat), or around Mnemba Island in the northeast, or, with a bit of luck, even off Zanzibar Town. Watching dolphins is especially enjoyable if you're also sipping a cool beer on the Africa House Hotel terrace at sunset. At Kizimkazi and Mnemba it's also sometimes possible to see groups of spinner dolphins, providing an unforgettable memory.

Less common are whales, though humpback whales have been spotted several times around October/November in the Zanzibar Channel and off Nungwi in the north, leading their recently born young back to the summer feeding grounds in Antarctica.

Tides and weather Tides, the daily rise and fall of sea level, are a noticeable feature along the east coast of Africa. They are dictated mostly by the moon (and to a lesser extent the sun) and there are two main types. The smaller tides, known as neap tides, occur during the half-moon phases and result in a tidal range (the difference between high and low water) of only 1.5m. From this period onwards the tidal range increases until a full or new moon (ie: every two weeks), when spring tides occur. These result in the largest tidal range, of about 4m between high tide and low tide. Spring tide low water always occurs at around 10.00–11.00, for about three days, twice every lunar cycle (at full moon and new moon). Through the rest of the lunar cycle, the time of each tide changes from one day to the next by an average of 50 minutes (about 30 minutes during spring). So if high tide is at 15.00 on one day it will be about 15.50 on the following day.

During spring low tides the low-water mark can be a couple of kilometres out, and these days are ideal for walking out on the intertidal flats and reef crest to explore the kaleidoscope of life. Take care to avoid trampling on living coral and on sea urchins or blue-spotted stingrays. Good footwear (trainers, plastic sandals or neoprene booties) is strongly recommended. Even the tiniest cut or graze can flare up into a nasty tropical ulcer which will keep you out of the sea for days recovering. Also be aware of the speed with which the tide comes in and don't be caught out on the reef crest of the east coast with the incoming tide around your waist – you'll have an exhausting swim back to the beach if you do. And remember, tidal currents are strongest during spring tides so be careful not to swim too far out, or into tidal channels.

Needle spine urchin

Prevailing weather also greatly influences sea conditions and travellers should be aware of the main seasons (these are described in more detail in *Chapter 4, When to visit*, page 73).

LOCAL PEOPLE AND MARINE LIFE It won't take you long to realise that a great number of Zanzibaris are dependent on the surrounding seas and shallows for their variety of foods. Various fishing methods are used to catch this vital source of protein which contributes over 70% of the needs of the local population. On dark new-moon nights in the Zanzibar Channel, sardine boats with lights attract and net vast shoals; on the same nights gill-netting boats, with 15cm-mesh nets, are after the large pelagic species (tuna, kingfish and billfish) in the southern Pemba Channel, operating mostly from Nungwi. Conventional hook-and-line fishing and passive fish-trapping using baited basket-traps (*madema*) are still practised all around the islands.

Kingfish

During the low spring tides thousands of women and children collect octopus, shells, sea cucumbers and moray eels from the intertidal flats, whilst other women tend to their seaweed (*mwani*) farm patches in the lagoons on the east coast. The lines of sticks protruding out of the water at low tide can't be missed (for more details see box, *Sustainable seaweed farming*, page 290).

Mangroves are also harvested: the wood has been used for building poles for centuries because of its resistance to rotting and insect infestation. However, the rapid increase in demand over the last few years, with overcutting in places, has led to deterioration of the forests and the marine life which relies on them. Recently, the felling of planted *Casuarina* (Australian pine, though not actually a true pine) has produced, so far, acceptable insect-resistant poles, easing some of the pressure on the mangroves.

Octopus

CONSERVATION Owing to the rapid increase in human population (at present doubling every 20 years), the availability of new fishing materials, the development of a number of destructive fishing methods and the inability of the government to enforce fisheries regulations, the delicate balance of life in the shallow seas (and therefore this vital source of food) is beginning to be destroyed. Spear-fishing is on the increase and because of its effectiveness can quickly strip the reefs of the larger fish, and even of small species such as butterflyfish. Not only does it reduce fish numbers and make them wary of snorkellers, such as around the shallow reefs close to Zanzibar Town or in the lagoon on the east, but by removing these vital predators the balance within the ecosystem is being lost. Netting around reefs, and the type of fishing known locally as *kigumi*, where corals are broken deliberately to force fish out into the surrounding net, are also practised and extremely destructive. Dynamite-fishing is also very destructive, but mostly restricted to the mainland coast. Also restricted to the mainland and Mafia coasts, fortunately for Zanzibar, is the collecting of shallow live coral (mainly of the genus *Porites*) for baking on open kilns into lime. On Unguja at least, quarried coral rock is used instead.

Careless anchoring of boats on coral reefs can also, over a short time, cause considerable localised damage. In 1994, a project funded by the Dutch embassy of Dar es Salaam through the Institute of Marine Sciences established, in conjunction with the tourist boat operators who use the reefs, 15 permanent moorings for the islands and reefs close to Zanzibar Town, thus reducing tourism-related damage. Although these have since deteriorated and are no longer functional, the project did serve to increase the awareness of the importance and needs of living coral reefs, and in general boat operators around Zanzibar Town are careful when dropping anchor, attempting to set it in sand or rubble. Perhaps in the future the shallow coral gardens around Bawe Island and the sandbanks off Stone Town will come under some form of management to conserve their productivity and attractiveness to visitors. The main threat to these shallow coral reefs, some of which have superb hard coral communities, remain the *kigumi* fishermen.

The local demand for marine curios (shells, dead coral and turtle products) has increased with the growing number of tourists, further adding to the overexploitation of the marine resources. The collection of large, colourful, attractive mollusc shells like the giant triton (*Charonia tritonis*) and the bull-mouth helmet shell (*Cypraecassis rufa*) have secondary effects which are not that obvious. These feed on the crown-of-thorns starfish (*Acanthaster planci*) and sea urchins respectively. Absence of the molluscs again upsets the balance, and populations of these echinoderms can increase alarmingly, furthering the destruction of the coral reefs. Collection of live hard corals is, of course, extremely damaging to the reef ecosystem. A colony the size of a football can take over 20 years to grow and the implications of mass removal for sale to tourists or export need no further explanation. Don't buy the stuff!

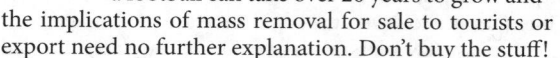

Giant triton shell

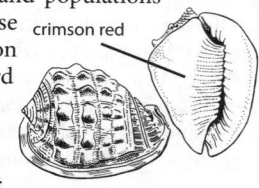

crimson red

Bull-mouth helmet shell

Some steps are being taken to try and address the problems. With the involvement of donor organisations and conservation bodies such as the Worldwide Fund for Nature, private enterprise, the Institute of Marine Sciences, and the Zanzibar authorities (Department of Fisheries, Commission of Environment and Department of Tourism), plans to create marine protected areas have made some progress. On Pemba the only marine protected area is Misali Island Conservation Area, which involves local fishermen in conservation and charges fees to visiting divers and snorkellers. On Unguja, a few miles south of Zanzibar Town, Chumbe Island Coral Park (CHICOP), a private investment, includes a protected forest and coral reef on its western shores. Chumbe (see page 339) can be visited for a day, or you can stay overnight, and funds generated contribute to raising awareness of marine issues through the educational centre used by local school pupils. Further south, the Menai Bay Conservation Area brings fisheries and mangrove issues to local community groups supported by the government in an attempt to manage the resources for the long term. The only other marine protected area is a zone 200m wide around Mnemba Island, an exclusive private island resort off the northeast coast. However, the spectacular turquoise waters around Mnemba Island extend beyond this boundary and the 20km of fringing reefs are accessible to divers and snorkellers from several beach hotels operating from the north and east coasts of Unguja.

Tourism development, now a rapidly growing industry, also has a role to play in marine conservation. By acknowledging that the marine resources on which it depends are finite and also vital to the neighbouring coastal villages, and by attempting to come up with methods which assist all of the users, tourism can contribute to a healthy future for all concerned. Survival of both may be in the balance.

So, when bobbing around over a coral garden, or simply sitting on the seabed, 10m down, watching the coral reef world around you, or wading through the dark mud in a mangrove forest, think about it ... and enjoy it. There's a whole lot going on: between individuals, between species, between habitats and between the ecosystem and the people who use it. This section has touched upon some of the more salient issues and examples of life in the seas and on the shores of Zanzibar.

Many more exist to be discovered and pondered; while doing so, the following are a few points to remember:

- Don't touch living coral. There's no need to and it is more sensitive than it looks. Be careful when reef walking and snorkelling or diving. Be aware of what your flippers are doing and avoid landing on coral when entering into the water. Maintain good buoyancy control at all times.
- Help prevent anchor damage. Insist on the use of permanent moorings, if available, or anchor only in sand.
- Don't buy shells, turtle products or corals.
- Spread the word. Explain what you now know about the local marine ecosystems to other visitors and locals.

SEA TURTLES Original text by Fiona Clark, updated by Lorna Slade, ecologist, Zanzibar Sea Turtle Survival Project

Five types of sea turtle occur in the western Indian Ocean: the **green turtle** (*Chelonia mydas*), the **hawksbill turtle** (*Eretmochelys imbricata*), the **loggerhead turtle** (*Caretta caretta*), the **Olive Ridley turtle** (*Lepidochelys olivacea*) and the **leatherback turtle** (*Dermochelys coriacea*). All are endangered species. The most commonly found turtle in Zanzibar is the green turtle, followed by the hawksbill. Both nest in Zanzibar. Leatherback and loggerhead are sometimes seen, but don't nest. There have been no records of the Olive Ridley since 1975.

Zanzibar is not a major turtle nesting site, but appears to be a feeding ground for sea turtles from other areas; nesting is more prolific on Pemba. Conservationists have recovered tags from captured turtles showing that green turtles come to Zanzibar from Aldabra Island, in the Seychelles, and from Europa and Tromelin islands. Loggerheads that nest in KwaZulu-Natal (South Africa) also feed in Tanzania – one loggerhead was captured in Tanzania just 66 days after being tagged in South Africa.

The current turtle scene The IOSEA (Indian Ocean and South-East Asian) Marine Turtle policy is an intergovernmental agreement that aims to protect, conserve, replenish and recover marine turtles through partnership organisations. According to its 2008 country report on Tanzania, there remain a number of challenges to sea turtles, including artisanal/subsistence fishing using gill nets, illegal harvesting, mangrove depletion, coastal (especially tourism) development, human and light disturbance, pollution, coral destruction, limited knowledge of genetics and population dynamics, and other inherent threatening factors. All of this occurs in spite of a number of protection and conservation initiatives being spearheaded by the government in collaboration with local communities, NGOs, the National Turtle Committee and development partners.

Zanzibar's turtle conservation work has so far centred on working with communities to raise general awareness about surveillance, nesting activities, monitoring, beach cleaning and potential ecotourism benefits. This community education and involvement is critical but it must be matched with workable solutions to help the traditional fishing industry better adapt to the necessary conservation goals.

The number of turtles caught in the nets of bottom trawlers has declined steadily from the mid 1990s, though it remains at approximately 70–80 turtles annually at present (many of these survive capture only to be later slaughtered for their shells). In addition, almost 600 turtles annually become trapped in the long, curtain-like gill nets used in traditional fishing methods (85% of fish in Tanzanian waters are caught in this way). Illegal and unregulated turtle fishing also continues with dynamite-fishing, the use of spear guns and lethal entanglement in monofilament fishing lines. The future is not entirely bleak though. A dedicated government committee has been formed to address all of these problems and there are a number of techniques and devices which can yet be employed to protect the turtles. We must only hope that adequate financial and human resources will back up the new policies and protect these graceful sea creatures.

The bad news The sea turtle population is decreasing in Zanzibar. This is bad because turtles are part of a food web which includes seagrasses, sponges, jellyfish and tiger sharks, and also because living turtles are attractive to tourists and (like dolphins) can sometimes be a way for local people to earn money.

The number of nesting sites has been reduced dramatically, and turtles are hunted and trapped by more efficient means than previously. Local fishermen tell how, 20 or 30 years ago, some beaches would contain 100 or more turtle nests every year. But these days the same beaches contain only two or three nests. Places where nests can still be found include Mnemba Island, the beaches north of Matemwe Bungalows, and around Kizimkazi. Pemba is home to the most important nesting beaches; turtles nest on Misali Island, at Ras Kiuyu and on the beaches near Ngezi Forest – especially Vumawimbi. Unfortunately, except for the island sites, few of these nests are successful: many eggs are taken by people, while others are lost to the sea when erosion has formed steps on some beaches forcing turtles to nest in places that are vulnerable to the high tide.

The burgeoning tourist industry also has its costs. In the last ten years, many hotels have been built on turtle-nesting beaches. Buildings often extend right to the beach, vegetation is cleared and the beach lit up at night, disturbing any turtles coming up to nest and disorientating any hatchlings. For example, Nungwi on the north coast and Kiwengwa Beach on the east coast of Unguja (Zanzibar Island) are now wall-to-wall hotel with no space or peace for turtles.

Turtle-hunting in Zanzibar only became illegal in October 1993. Although penalties are quite severe (a large fine, or two years in prison, or both) enforcement of the new law is unlikely. The Fisheries Department is under-resourced and has many other problems to deal with (such as dynamite-fishing).

Turtles are usually captured with gill nets, which are set on the seabed, while others are caught with spear guns. They are brought ashore and have their flippers and shell removed, often while still alive. The number of turtles caught increased dramatically in the 1960s when gill nets, snorkelling gear and spear guns were introduced. Some local fishermen claim that their increased catch proves the population is increasing too, but the same fishermen also agree that nesting turtles have all but disappeared. Uroa on the east coast of Unguja is a renowned area for turtle-hunting and the beach sometimes looks like a turtle graveyard.

In March 1996, there were two incidents of poisoning in Pemba through the consumption of turtle meat, resulting in the deaths of 37 people. Hawksbill turtles, in particular, are known on occasion to harbour toxins thought to originate from toxic algae in the food chain. These toxins do not harm the turtle, but have disastrous effects on any humans eating the meat. These unfortunate incidents helped reduce turtle slaughter, but apparently only for a short while.

The good news Since 1992, there have been several small-scale turtle-protection projects run with volunteer help through the government of Zanzibar's Department of the Environment. These include the following:

- A Swahili-language education package for schools and other youth groups, emphasising the plight of sea turtles and their need to be protected. A poster carrying the same message has also been produced both in English, aimed at visitors, and in Swahili, aimed at locals.
- A nest protection scheme, run by Matemwe Bungalows, a hotel on the east coast. Local villagers are paid a small fee if they report an intact nest, and a further bonus for each successful hatching. To avoid the problems of beach erosion, some nests are moved to safer sites.
- A survey and protection scheme carried out by the management of the exclusive lodge on the private Mnemba Island. This is an ideal site for turtles, with safe beaches (no local fishermen are allowed to land) and deep-water access.
- A nest protection and monitoring scheme on the protected Misali Island, off Pemba, now a marine conservation area, patrolled by local rangers and still one of the best turtle-nesting areas in Zanzibar.
- Community education and involvement in nest-recording and monitoring in both Pemba and Unguja, including the successful production of an educational drama and video, has played a key role in reducing threats to turtles. Through active inclusion of local community members in conservation activities, the role of turtle security has become a source of employment and social status, reinforcing the benefits of protecting the creatures.
- There are plans afoot to try and introduce the use of turtle excluder devices (TED) in the country's fisheries legislation. In essence, the TED is a metal grid of bars that attaches to trawling nets and allows larger animals, like turtles and sharks, to escape whilst still keeping prawns, shrimp and the like inside. With a hatch opening at either the top or the bottom, the heavy weight of the sea turtles, sharks and larger fish causes the hatch to open on impact, providing them with an escape route. The success of the TED has varied around the world, but it is a start at further regulating fishing methods, and may help a few more adult turtles to escape in the future.
- In areas where turtle mortality is critically high through animal and egg poaching, cash rewards for conservation have been used. This is clearly not financially sustainable and has had mixed results in the archipelago. On Zanzibar Island, incentive-driven conservation has proven to be counter-productive in obtaining committed public participation; however, on Mafia, modest incentives have been highly effective in involving local communities and in protecting nests. This is a short-term solution though and it is generally agreed that generating revenue to fund turtle conservation through turtle tourism and park entry fees is a far more positive and sustainable method. Mnarani Aquarium below is one successful example.
- Mnarani Aquarium (see page 240) in Nungwi is a local conservation initiative to protect turtles and educate villagers and tourists. Managed by a group of local fishermen, in a large tidal-fed rock pool, the water has been stocked with several species of fish and around ten green and hawksbill turtles. The Department of the Environment has allowed this group (only) to keep a maximum of eight turtles for educational purposes and any excess brought in by fishermen are periodically tagged and released. Although generally keeping turtles in captivity is not to be encouraged, in this case the local community benefit, and the educational value to locals (school children are allowed in free) and tourists are judged to be worth it. The aquarium does not keep mature female turtles.

- Both green and hawksbill turtles are now being tagged for monitoring on Pemba and Mafia islands, with the latter project also undertaking genetic studies.

Turtle-shell products

Zanzibar used to be a major centre for turtle-shell, usually called 'tortoiseshell', and at the height of the trade (the early 20th century) some 3,300kg were exported every year from the islands and nearby mainland coast. Demand dropped, but has recently been revived by the growth of tourism. A survey showed that the amount of turtle-shell jewellery went up five times between early 1993 and late 1994. Less than half the tourists who bought turtle-shell items knew what it was, or that turtles were endangered. However, local conservationists and aware tourists complained to such a degree that many shops now refuse to stock turtle-shell products. Tourists are asked by conservation organisations to boycott any shops that continue to sell turtle products.

Local police and customs officials are now also aware that turtle-shell products are illegal. Tourists buying whole shells from hawkers should be aware that conservationists and hoteliers will report them to the police for possession of turtle shells, and if caught they will be reprimanded and the shell confiscated.

Local perspectives

Lest we get too self-righteous about all of this, we should perhaps remember that Zanzibar is a poor country and that a large sea turtle is worth about a month's wages for an office worker, and considerably more than that to a fisherman or farmer. Turtle meat is also held traditionally to have healing properties. Stopping the local people from catching turtles will inevitably make some of them poorer, yet if the turtle-hunting continues, there will soon be none left anyway. But many Zanzibaris can't afford the luxury of thinking ahead. Life is hand to mouth and the 'if I don't catch it someone else will' attitude is of course understandable.

Having said that, there does need to be a halt to turtle killing as populations are in danger of extinction. In addition to finding alternative food and income sources for local communities, it is also essential that continued education, improved law enforcement and government protection for important nesting beaches are maintained, to ensure that the turtle has a place in Zanzibar's future.

4

Planning and Preparation

Truly prepossessing was our first view … of Zanzibar. Earth, sea and sky all seemed wrapped in a soft and sensuous repose … The sea of purest sapphire… lay basking … under a blaze of sunshine.

Richard Burton, British explorer (1856)

WHEN TO VISIT

The best time to visit these islands is during the dry seasons – December to February and June to October (see *Climate*, page 51, for more details) – but generally speaking, from December to February any wind comes from the northeast, so beaches on the southern and western parts of the islands are more sheltered. Conversely, from June to October it tends to come from the southwest, so northern and eastern coasts are best. Ultimately, however, these islands are at the mercy of the ocean, and their weather patterns can be unpredictable at any time of year. Even during the 'dry' seasons, afternoon showers are not unknown, although they tend to be short and pleasantly cooling (for more details, see box, *Climate chart*, below).

It is also possible to visit the islands during the rainy season. Then there are fewer visitors and you are more likely to get good bargains from lodges and hotels (the ones that remain open) and trips. The rain can be heavy, but is not usually constant; the sunsets can be particularly magnificent; and pineapples are in season! Travel can be more difficult at this time, with roads damaged and buses delayed, but you'll get there eventually.

At holiday times, such as Christmas and Easter, the islands are popular with expatriate workers from Dar es Salaam and Nairobi as well as overseas visitors. Expect full flights and higher hotel rates. Conversely, during the Islamic fasting period of Ramadan (see page 39), many restaurants and shops are closed during the day, and life runs at a generally slower pace.

If you're going scuba diving or game fishing, see box, *Zanzibar diving and fishing seasons*, page 113. If local festivals appeal, then see *Festivals*, page 47. Sports fans

CLIMATE CHART

	Jan	Feb	Mar	Apr	May	Jun	Jul	Aug	Sep	Oct	Nov	Dec
Temp (°C): av min	25	25	24	23	22	20	19	19	19	21	22	24
av max	31	31	31	30	29	29	28	28	28	29	30	31
Hrs of sun/day	8	8	7	5	6	8	7	8	8	8	8	8
Rainfall (mm)	80	70	140	390	250	60	45	40	50	90	220	160
Av days of rain	7	6	12	19	14	4	5	6	6	7	14	12

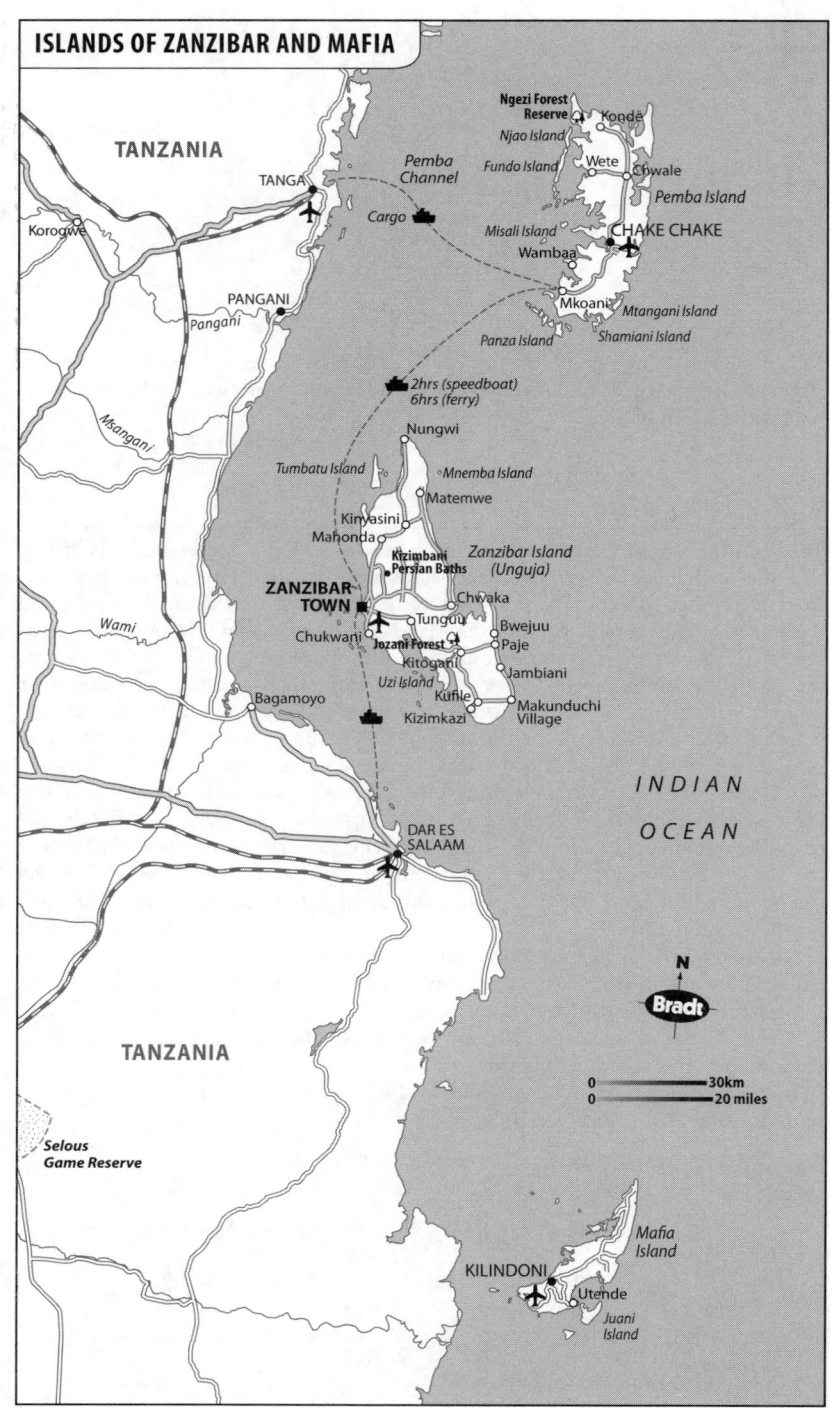

ISLANDS OF ZANZIBAR AND MAFIA

TANZANIA

Korogwe

TANGA

PANGANI

Pangani

Msangani

Wami

Bagamoyo

DAR ES
SALAAM

TANZANIA

Selous
Game Reserve

Pemba
Channel

Cargo

Ngezi Forest
Reserve   Konde

Njao Island

Fundo Island   Wete   Chwale

Misali Island   Pemba Island

Wambaa   CHAKE CHAKE

Mkoani   Mtangani Island

Panza Island   Shamiani Island

2hrs (speedboat)
6hrs (ferry)

Nungwi

Tumbatu Island   Mnemba Island

Matemwe

Kinyasini

Mahonda

Kizimbani   Zanzibar Island
Persian Baths   (Unguja)

ZANZIBAR   Chwaka
TOWN   Tunguu

Chukwani   Bwejuu
Jozani Forest   Paje
Kitogani   Jambiani
Uzi Island   Kufile
Kizimkazi   Makunduchi
Village

INDIAN

OCEAN

N

Bradt

0 ————— 30km
0 ————— 20 miles

KILINDONI   Mafia
Island

Utende

Juani
Island

may like to tie in their visit with the Zanzibar International Marathon, held every year in early November.

HIGHLIGHTS

Read this book's introduction to understand why we think the real highlights of these islands are often away from the resorts and obvious places – and in the unscheduled interactions with the local people that you meet and the unspoilt areas you stumble across whilst exploring. That said, we recognise that a little initial direction can help to make the best of a trip, so we'll try to give you a few pointers here.

WHERE TO STAY The choice of places to stay is endless – but a few really stand out. Top of the list, and most budgets, is **Mnemba Island** (page 260). It's very expensive, but it's also exceedingly good, and remains the best by far in the archipelago. We approached it fully expecting to comment that it was overpriced, but the reality is that it is in a different league from the other places in this guide. It's very polished, yet also very simple; the ultimate in barefoot luxury. More recently, the arrival of **Kilindi** (page 242) in Kendwa, has opened up a fabulous island alternative at a significantly reduced (relative) cost. Its understated elegance, impressive space and super service quite possibly make this Zanzibar island's premium property for escapists.

For small, high-quality beach lodges with more reasonable price tags, our top tips would be the trio of spacious villas at **Matemwe Retreat** (page 253); its more relaxed sister property, **Matemwe Lodge** (page 253); and the fabulous new hotel sharing its beach, **Green & Blue** (page 255). **Ras Nungwi Beach Hotel** (page 227) in Nungwi; **Shooting Star** (page 267) in Pwani Mchangani; social **Sunshine Hotel** (page 258) in Matemwe; bijoux **Anna of Zanzibar** (page 286) and **Fumba Beach Lodge** (page 337) in the quiet southwest of Zanzibar. All offer consistently high levels of service, individually styled accommodation and access to stunning beaches and watersports. The reopening of old-time favourite the **Sultan Palace** (page 286) on the Michamvi Peninsula means a delightful return of elegance, personal service and a terrific cliff-top pool to the area.

Whilst looking at these, compare them with the three main lodges on Mafia Island: **Pole Pole** (page 382), **Kinasi** (page 383) and **Chole Mjini** (page 384). Mafia doesn't offer the extensive beaches of Zanzibar, but it's much quieter and in many ways gives a great deal of exclusivity for your money, with the added bonus of some superb diving and snorkelling. It's a great favourite of ours, and very undervalued.

For small, secluded beach retreats which cost even less, have a look at **Mchanga Beach Lodge** (page 262) and **Pongwe Beach Hotel** (page 270). **Michamvi Sunset Bay** (page 283) also merits a mention, and operates impressive community initiatives alongside its personal service.

Budget travellers might want to check out **Sunset Bungalows** (page 244) in Kendwa, which offers good-value bungalows on the beach, the delightful **Bellevue Bungalows** (page 295) on the Michamvi Peninsula, which has neat rooms, good food and a thoroughly chilled vibe, **Karamba** (page 323) in KIzimkazi, **Blue Oyster** in Jambiani (page 310), or **Nyota Beach Bunglows** (page 259), both in Matemwe. Meanwhile, **Santa Maria Coral Reef** (page 272) is a small and simple place in a coconut grove beside a sweeping bay; it's proof that you can still find magical places to match tight budgets.

If you're looking specifically at the busy Nungwi area, then at the top end, **Z Hotel** (page 219) claims 'boutique on the beach', and has tried hard to raise the hospitality bar in the area. The mid-range **Flame Tree Cottages** (page 224) offers a more laid-back, great-value place to stay a few minutes' walk from the buzzing heart of town, and a little further away, **Mnarani Beach Cottages** (page 228) is very friendly and reasonably priced, with one of Zanzibar Island's best views.

If you're taking a family, lack mobility, or are simply seeking the extensive facilities of a larger resort, then good-value **Breezes** (page 288), **Karafuu Resort** (page 285) in Michamvi, **La Gemma dell'Est** (page 245) in Kendwa are worth considering. We feel all of these are a step above most of the island's other big resort offerings. They are well managed and the facilities and beach locations are excellent.

For something completely different, those interested in ecology or conservation shouldn't miss a few days at **Chumbe Island** (page 339) for a terrific all-round experience!

The best hotels in Stone Town change quite fast, as new ones start up and often raise the bar, but currently **Beyt al Chai** (page 148), and several newcomers – theatrical **Emerson Spice** (page 149), central **Jafferji House & Spa** (page 144) and **Zanzibar Palace** (page 152), treasure-filled **Kholle House** (page 149) – are our pick of the finest upmarket, boutique guesthouses. The large and efficient **Serena Inn** (page 148) remains the undisputed best hotel in town, whilst for something less expensive, but still with a pool, **Dhow Palace** (page 154) is a good choice. Slightly cheaper in price, but brimming with character, central **Maru Maru** (page 149) intimate **Kisiwa House** (page 151) and **Zanzibar Coffee House** (page 156) are excellent, as is the **Clove Hotel** (page 153).

For backpackers and the budget-conscious, funky **Rumaisa Hotel** (page 155), ethical **Zenji Hotel** (page 157) and the renovated **St Monica's Hostel** (page 160) should be top of the list.

If you are keen to stay by the beach just outside Zanzibar Town, **Mtoni Marine** (page 202) is idyllic and excellent for families, whilst **Maruhubi Beach Villas** (page 201) has some good sea-view rooms. Equally, if a villa stay is more your thing, there are now some excellent options: Che Che Vule (page 255), Upendo Beach Villa (page 286) and Matemwe Beach Village (page 257).

WHERE TO EAT If you enjoy good food, then Zanzibar can be a great place to visit – though choose your lodges and restaurants carefully or you may be disappointed in the lack of culinary variety and quality. Most of the top lodges have good food and you can expect to eat well; but only a few stand out. In Stone Town, the roofop tea house at **Emerson Spice** (page 149) is hard to beat for its five-course degustation and atmospheric panorama, whilst **Beyt al Chai** and the reliable **Terrace at the Serena Inn** (pages 145 and 148) come right at the top of the chart for cuisine. **Kilindi** (page 242), **Ras Nungwi Beach Hotel** (page 227) and **Green & Blue** (page 255) offer excellent seaside dining in top-end settings, whilst **Pongwe Beach Hotel** (page 270), **Sunshine Hotel** (page 258) and **Mtoni Marine** (page 163) all pride themselves on delivering fine food with an affordable price tag. They share this with the vastly cheaper, superb village cuisine served in **Okala Restaurant's** (page 316) implausibly simple *makuti banda*, tasty tapas at Bellevue Bungalows (page 295), and super sharing platters and fresh cocktails in the beach chic surroundings of **Upendo Bar & Restaurant** (page 289). For a tasty meal with a worthy cause, students at the Jambiani Tourism Training Institute offer dinner every Friday night at **Albi's Well** (page 315) as part of their course.

For up-to-date advice on Stone Town's best independent restaurants, we'd always suggest that you ask locally; things change quickly and some of our recommendations in the main listings are likely to be out of date sooner than they're printed. However, a clutch of newcomers have been added to our list of all-time favourites, to make for a much more varied and exciting culinary collection in the city. Our current top tips by day: the **Stone Town Café** for filling breakfasts, cheerful **Lazuli** for fresh wraps and smoothies, and **Zanzibar Coffee House** or **Zenji** for coffee pick-me-ups (page 167). Appetisers and sundowners on **Tatu**'s top floor (or a nightcap from its extensive whisky collection if you visit later) are fun before dinner at **Loulou**, known for its refined, contemporary cusine (page 164), or try **Abyssinian Maritim** for authentic Ethiopian (page 162) or **La Taverna** for a friendly, family-run Italian (page 164). **Rendezvous Les Spices** (page 165) is perfect for delicious, fresh Indian dishes, or **Nyumbani** or **Two Tables** for truly authentic Zanzibari dinners (pages 163 and 164).

WHAT TO SEE AND DO Whilst lazing on the beach can be very relaxing, if this is the limit of your activities then you will miss out on a lot. At least accept the offer of a local beach masseuse if there is one; they can be surprisingly good.

A highlight of many trips to Zanzibar and Mafia is the **diving**, which is good at many places around these islands. The best diving spots would certainly include the reef around Mnemba Island (page 260), those in Mafia's marine park (page 380), and for advanced divers, the challenging waters around Pemba (page 343). The less aquatic might prefer to go **snorkelling**, and if so they should add Chumbe Island to this short list of reefs. Chumbe has world-class, pristine coral, and no scuba diving is allowed there. Chumbe's also worth visiting for its guided **forest and intertidal walks** (page 339), which are both attractions in their own right, especially for nocturnal sightings of huge coconut crabs.

A sunset dhow cruise can be magical and romantic, but better still is a **dhow trip to a remote sandbar**: lie on a deserted beach, snorkel on the reef, eat fresh seafood and look out to nothing but tropical ocean. The upmarket lodges on Mafia (page 382) all arrange these trips from Chole Bay, whilst on Zanzibar Island, Fumba Beach Lodge (page 337), Unguja Lodge (page 323) and ethical operator Eco+Culture (page 338) all run similar trips in the Menai Bay Conservation Area.

If you're in the Nungwi area, then do wander along to see the turtles at the **Mnarani Natural Aquarium** (page 240). It's a great conservation project and a rare chance to see hatchling turtles at very close quarters.

More generally, any trip to Zanzibar Island should include a **spice tour**: ask around to make sure you will have a knowledgeable guide. The trip idea may seem clichéd, but plucking everyday spices from what seems like a tangled bit of unruly forest can be fascinating. For something slightly different, combine the spices with some Zanzibari history on the acclaimed **Princess Salme tour** (page 206). Starting at Mtoni Palace, the day trip takes in the palace ruins, a traditional coffee ceremony, the Kidichi plantations and a delicious Swahili lunch, and even helps fund the palace conservation initiatives.

For animal lovers, visit the colobus monkey colony in **Jozani-Chwaka Bay National Park** (page 329), and maybe even drop into the **Zanzibar Butterfly Centre** (page 333) next door. Meanwhile, those in search of a much more original, albeit less predictable, experience should consider visiting the community beside **Ufufuma Forest** (page 277).

For some genuine community insight and interaction, the **Jambiani Cultural Tour** (page 318) is really very good. Tailored to the particular interests of the visitor, it offers some hands-on entertainment and enlightening insights into the lives of the rural population, and ensures a percentage of the tour is reinvested into necessary village development. Equally, the newly opened **Seaweed Center** in Paje (page 305) offers tours and valuable insight into the importance of this marine agriculture to local villagers.

No trip to Zanzibar is really complete without a night or two in **Stone Town**. Whilst here, take a walk around the narrow alleys, venture into the bustling market on Creek Road, stroll through Forodhani Gardens, relax in Mrembo Traditional Spa (page 187), and treat yourself to a rooftop meal on a balmy evening. For more insight, most of the local tour operators (see *Chapter 5*, page 134) can arrange guides for half- and full-day excursions.

TOURIST INFORMATION

⟨i⟩ Tanzania Tourist Board IPS Bldg, Dar es Salaam, Tanzania; ☎+255 022 2111244; e info@ tanzaniatourism.go.tz; www.tanzaniatouristboard. com

⟨i⟩ Tanzania Trade Centre (UK) 3 Stratford Pl, London W1C 1AS; ☎+44 207 758 8070; e info@ tanzatrade.co.uk; www.tanzatrade.co.uk

ORGANISED TOURS

If you're staying on a low budget (eg: US$20-per-night bungalows) or want to travel without a fixed schedule, then it'll be best to arrange your own accommodation and flights, booking things as you go or a few days in advance during high season – then you can just travel where and when the mood takes you.

The advantages of such a trip hinge on the freedom that you have to make and change your arrangements, as well as from the increased choice of lower-budget options available to you. The disadvantages mainly arise from the problems you may have when places are full, and you are forced to spend time and energy finding somewhere different to stay.

However, if you're planning to book your trip in advance, and you want to stay in more comfortable places (eg: US$75 per night or more), then you will probably find it easier, and also cheaper, to arrange your trip through a specialist tour operator. Few tour operators will deal with low-budget accommodation.

A few tour operators offer scheduled trips to Zanzibar (ie: you join a group on fixed dates and with a pre-determined itinerary). However, most will work on a tailor-made basis (ie: they design a trip for you, around your dates and what you want to do).

The main advantage of such trips is that using a specialist, you have their experience and knowledge of the island, and its various options, at your command. You should discuss your preferences with them in detail, and then a good tour operator will be able to plan a trip that will suit you well – discussing all the pros and cons of the various choices, and answering all of your questions along the way. Hence you're much more likely to get a trip that will really suit you well!

A very good secondary reason is if you're visiting top-end lodges and camps, then it will almost certainly be cheaper to book your trip through a good specialist than it would be to arrange the trip for yourself. And, of course, you pay one price upfront which includes most things (flights, transfers, accommodation, etc), so you simply sit back, relax and enjoy the trip, knowing you don't need to worry about the logistics of it.

The main disadvantage of using a tour operator is the fixed itinerary: you cannot change your plans on a whim (or at least not without a cost), say to spend more or less time at a particular place.

The best way to find a trip that suits your own interest and pocket is to phone a knowledgeable tour operator direct (for a list of tour operators, see pages 79–81). Ask for their brochure, study their website, and then discuss your ideas with them.

An important part of your preparation for a visit is learning about the history, geography and culture of Zanzibar before you arrive. If textbooks and encyclopaedias put you off, read a few novels or travelogues to get yourself in the mood, or dip into some of the early explorers' accounts (see the books listed in *Appendix 2, Further Information*, page 416). Also, scan the foreign pages of newspapers, or magazines specialising in developing countries, to familiarise yourself with politics and current affairs. You should certainly try to learn a few phrases of Swahili. All of this will make your trip much more rewarding.

You'll often find tour operators featured in the editorial or advertising section of the Sunday travel supplements of major newspapers and specialist travel magazines.

TOUR OPERATORS Finding a good tour operator for a trip to Zanzibar and the islands isn't always easy. Endless operators can send you there, but you will get the best trip if you work with one who really knows the area and has visited all of the islands and lodges.

Don't let anyone convince you that there are only half a dozen decent beach lodges here: it's simply not true. If the operator that you're speaking to doesn't know most of the places in this book and offer a wide choice to suit you – then use one that does.

Here I (Chris McIntyre) must admit a personal interest in the tour-operating business. I run the specialist UK tour operator Expert Africa (020 8232 9777; e info@expertafrica.com; www.expertafrica.com). We organise trips to Tanzania and these islands for travellers from all over the world. Booking your trip with us will always cost you the same as, or less than, booking the safari camps and beach lodges directly.

We advise our travellers from personal experience, and then allow them to make up their own minds. None of our team works on commission – so unlike many companies, we'll never push you into buying anything. Similarly, we have no financial ties to anywhere in Africa, so can offer truly independent advice on the full range of the choices available. Our only aim in advising you is to arrive at a trip that suits you perfectly.

Our trips are completely flexible, and they start from about US$750/£500 per person sharing for a week, including transfers, accommodation and most meals. I believe that Expert Africa has the best-value programme to Zanzibar and the islands – and the most extensive and comprehensive website. I'll happily send you a detailed colour brochure and start to help you plan your trip. However, for a comparison, some of the specialist African tour operators who also feature Zanzibar and the islands include the companies listed below. If you're looking for a pure diving trip, perhaps including a live-aboard, then you should consider one of the UK's specialist diving operators (see page 81).

In the UK

Aardvark Safaris RBL Hse, Ordnance Rd, Tidworth, Hants SP9 7QD; 01980 849160; e mail@aardvarksafaris.com; www. aardvarksafaris.com. Small, reliable upmarket safari specialist to Africa & Madagascar.

Abercrombie and Kent St George's Hse, Ambrose St, Cheltenham, Glos GL50 3LG; 0845 4851529; www.abercrombiekent.co.uk. Worldwide holidays for groups & individuals to upmarket destinations with upmarket price tags.

4

Acacia Expeditions 23a Craven Terrace, London W2 3QH; ☏020 7706 4700; www.acacia-africa. com. Adventure holidays & overland/camping safaris throughout Africa.

Africa Travel Resource Westcott Rd, Dorking, Surrey RH4 3NB; ☏01306 880770; www. africatravelresource.com. Web-based tour operator selling its own Zanzibar favourites.

Cazenove and Loyd 9 Imperial Studios, 3–11 Imperial Rd, London SW6 2AG; ☏020 7384 2332; info@cazloyd.com; www.caz-loyd.com. Top-end tailor-made specialists to Africa, the Indian Ocean islands, Latin America & the Indian subcontinent.

Expert Africa (see advertisements on pages i & 320) 9/10 Upper Sq, Old Isleworth, Middx TW7 7BJ; ☏020 8232 9777; info@expertafrica.com; www. expertafrica.com. Specialist team including Chris McIntyre, this book's co-author, offering a wide range of unbiased tailor-made choices.

Gane and Marshall Aldenham, 2 Deer Park Lane, Tavistock, Devon PL19 9HD; ☏01822 600600; e holidays@ganeandmarshall.com; www. ganeandmarshall.co.uk. Worldwide operator with a Zanzibar programme.

Hartley Safaris The Old Chapel, Chapel Lane, Hackthorn, Lincs LN2 3PN; ☏01673 861600; info@ hartleys-safaris.co.uk; www.hartleys-safaris.co.uk. Long-established tailor-made holiday specialists to east & southern Africa & the Indian Ocean islands.

Imagine Africa 1a Salcott Rd, London SW11 6DQ; ☏020 7622 5114; e info@imagineafrica. co.uk; www.imagineafrica.co.uk. Small, motivated tour operator with wide coverage including Africa, Asia, India, Latin America & riding holidays

Natural High 5 Chaldicott Barns, Semley, Shaftesbury, Dorset SP7 9AW; ☏01747 898104; e enquiries@ naturalhighsafaris.com; www. naturalhighsafaris.com. Small tailor-made trip specialists to Africa, run by old African hands, focusing on Tanzania.

Okavango Tours and Safaris White Lion Hse, 64a Highgate High St, London N6 5HX; ☏020 8347 4030; e info@okavango.com; www.okavango.com. Tailor-made trip specialists to Africa & the Indian Ocean islands, with a good knowledge of Tanzania.

Pulse Africa ☏020 8995 5909; info@ pulseafrica. com; www.pulseafrica.com. Specialist operator featuring Egypt, Gabon & southern & east Africa, including Zanzibar.

Rainbow Tours Layden Hse, 2nd floor, 76–78 Turnmill St, London; ☏020 7666 1250; e info@ rainbowtours.co.uk; www.rainbowtours. co.uk. Established specialists to South Africa & Madagascar, plus Latin America & the rest of Africa, including Tanzania's islands.

Safari Consultants Africa Hse, 2 Cornard Mills, Cornard Tye, Great Cornard, Suffolk CO10 0GW; ☏01787 888590; www.safari-consultants.co.uk. Long-established tailor-made trip specialists to east & southern Africa, & the Indian Ocean islands, with a very good knowledge.

Scott Dunn World 116 Putney Bridge Rd, London SW15 2NQ; ☏020 8682 5400; e africa@ scottdunn.com; www.scottdunn.com. Worldwide coverage (everywhere except North America), with a tailor-made programme to Tanzania.

Steppes Travel (formerly Art of Travel) 51 Castle St, Cirencester, Glos GL7 1QD; ☏01285 880980; e africa@steppestravel.co.uk; www. steppestravel.co.uk. Upmarket tailor-made specialists to Latin America, Asia, Africa & the Indian Ocean islands, including Tanzania.

Tim Best Travel 1b The Village, 101 Amies Street, London SW11 2JW; ☏020 7591 0300; e info@timbesttravel.com; www.timbesttravel. com. Upmarket holidays to Africa, the Indian Ocean islands & Latin America, inc Tanzania.

Tribes Travel (see advertisement on page 72) The Old Dairy, Wood Farm, Ipswich Rd, Otley, Suffolk IP6 9JW; ☏01473 890499; www. tribes.co.uk. Small, highly responsible operator, particularly strong on cultural trips, offering holidays worldwide on fair-trade principles.

Zanzibar Travel Reynards Hse, Selkirk Gdns, Cheltenham, Glos GL52 5LY; ☏01242 222027; e info@zanzibartravel.co.uk; www.zanzibartravel. co.uk. Small tailor-made tour operator focused on Kenya, Tanzania & Tanzania's islands.

In France

Wild Spirit Safari ☏+33 1 45 74 11 14; +33 1 47 49 91 50; e infos@wild-spirit-safari.com; www. wild-spirit-safari.com. Kenya & Tanzania specialists offering add-on trips to Zanzibar, with offices in Paris & Arusha (Tanzania).

Zanzibar Voyage ☏+33 1 53 34 92 71; e contact@zanzibar-voyage.com; www. zanzibar-voyage.com. Paris-based Zanzibar specialist with a good range of hotels & Tanzanian safari add-ons.

Dive specialists

Dive Tours 46 Watergate St, Chester CH1 2LA; ☎01244 401177; e info@divetours.co.uk; www. divetours.co.uk

Dive Worldwide Capitol Hse, 12–13 Bridge St, Winchester, Hants SO23 0HL; ☎0845 130 6980, 01962 302087; e info@diveworldwide.com; www. diveworldwide.com

RED TAPE

Most foreigners entering the country need a visa for Tanzania or a visitor's pass, depending on their own nationality. Whether you first arrive in Dar or Zanzibar, you will be asked how long you want to stay. Up to three months is usually not a problem, and you'll receive a stamp in your passport. Currently, most visas can be obtained on arrival in Tanzania – although the airport queues can be long and they must be paid for in hard currency cash, so it's often best to get them in advance. A visa will often take several weeks to issue, so apply well in advance of your trip. The charge for issuing a single-entry (90-day) visa ranges from US$20 to US$100, depending on your nationality. At the time of writing, it is US$60 for UK citizens and US$100 for US passport holders, but do check the latest charges with your local embassy. Visa applications by researchers and journalists will need to be cleared by the Commission for Science and Technology (COSTECH) before being granted.

If you are planning to come via Nairobi or Mombasa, you may also need a visa or visitor's pass for Kenya. You may also need a return ticket out of Tanzania or Kenya, or be required to show that you have sufficient funds to cover your stay (for other currency matters, see page 101).

Tanzanian regulations, which also cover Zanzibar, forbid the import or export of Tanzanian shillings worth more than US$100 without a permit. Similarly, if you wish to import or export more than US$10,000 in foreign currency, you should also seek advice from your local Tanzanian embassy or high commission.

There is no longer any legal requirement for a yellow fever vaccination certificate, unless you have come from a country where yellow fever is endemic. That said, the vaccination is strongly advised (see *Health*, page 84). In theory you might also be asked for a cholera-exemption certificate; in practice we've never experienced this.

If you intend to hire a car or motorbike, then it's best to bring an International Driving Permit (IDP), which is easy to obtain from your national motoring association (in Britain contact the AA or RAC), and also a few spare passport-size photos. Entry regulations do change, so double-check the above with your nearest Tanzanian embassy, high commission or tourist office before you leave.

EMBASSIES AND CONSULATES

TANZANIAN EMBASSIES ABROAD

🟢 **UK** 3 Stratford Pl, Bond St, London W1C 1AS; ☎020 7569 1470; www.tanzania-online.gov.uk. You can download a visa application form from this website & send it off to the high commission along with your passport, the visa fee (currently £38 for a single-entry visa), 2 passport photos, & an SAE for return. The process takes up to 10 days by post. If you want to visit the high commission in London in person, you need to pay in cash; cards, cheques or postal orders are not accepted. Alternatively, visas can be organised upon arrival.

🟢 **US** 2139 R St, NW, Washington, DC 20008; ☎+1 202 939 6125; www.tanzaniaembassy-us.org

🟢 **Belgium** 363 Av Louise, 11050 Brussels; ☎+32 2 640 6500; e tanzania@skynet.be; http://tanzania.visahq.com/embassy/Belgium/

🟢 **Canada** 50 Range Rd, Ottawa, Ontario K1N 8J4; ☎+1 613 232 1500/1509; f +1 613 232 5184; www.vec.ca

🟢 **Germany** Botschaft der Vereinigte Republik von Tansania, Eschenallee 11 Charlottenburg,

Westend, 14050 Berlin; ☏ +49 30 303 0800; f +49
030 303 08020; www.tanzania-gov.de

⊖ South Africa 822 George Av, Arcadia, Pretoria;
☏ +27 12 342 4371; www.tanzania.org.za

FOREIGN CONSULATES IN ZANZIBAR Most countries have embassies or high commissions in Dar es Salaam or Nairobi, but a couple, including Britain and Germany, also have limited diplomatic representation on Zanzibar:

⊖ UK British Consular Correspondent, Mr Christian Chilcott; Scuba Do; m 0777 417157; Dar 022 229 0000 (24 hrs)

⊖ Germany Honorary Consul, Mrs Angelika Sepetu, Kiembe Samaki Kijijini, Zanzibar; ☏ 024 2233691; m 0777 410045 (pm); e sepetu_family@yahoo.com; www.daressalam.diplo.de

Consulates are generally unable to assist with visas or with simple problems such as illness or theft of belongings, but they will try to help in more serious cases such as wrongful arrest or imprisonment.

If you lose your passport, you can get an Emergency Travel Document from the Ministry of the Interior in Zanzibar. This will allow you to leave Zanzibar and either go directly back to your own country, or reach Dar where most countries have representation and you should be able to get a replacement.

GETTING TO ZANZIBAR

BY AIR Most visitors to these islands fly first to Dar es Salaam, on mainland Tanzania, and then take a short regional service to Zanzibar. Small Tanzanian carriers (particularly Coastal Airways and ZanAir – see page 124) offer a frequent schedule of flights that hop back and forth across the Zanzibar Channel, and this is by far the quickest and easiest way to reach the islands from mainland Tanzania.

There are a handful of direct flights between Zanzibar and Nairobi, in Kenya, with Kenya Airways; these are very convenient when combining Zanzibar with a safari itinerary in Kenya. There are also direct flights between Europe and Zanzibar, but currently all of these are charter flights run by mass-market tour operators based in Italy, France and Spain.

From Europe
Scheduled flights The main international scheduled airlines serving Tanzania are:

✈ **Air Tanzania** www.airtanzania.com. To Dar from Johannesburg daily, with good connections to Zanzibar.

✈ **British Airways** www.ba.com. From London to Dar direct, 3 flights a week (9hrs 35mins).

✈ **Emirates** www.emirates.com. From most major European cities, via Dubai, to Dar daily.

✈ **Ethiopian Airlines** www.flyethiopian.com. From Addis Ababa daily except Thu, with connections to most European & several American cities.

✈ **Kenya Airways** www.kenya-airways.com. At least 2 flights daily between Nairobi & Dar (1hr 15mins), plus 2 between Nairobi & Zanzibar (1hr 40mins), with good connections to Europe & around Africa.

✈ **KLM** www.klm.com. From Amsterdam to Dar daily (10hrs 35mins), via Kilimanjaro International Airport.

✈ **South African Airlines** www.flysaa.com. To Dar from Johannesburg daily (3hrs 30mins), plus direct flights between Johannesburg & Zanzibar 3 times a week.

Britain is one of the cheapest places in Europe to buy scheduled flights to Zanzibar, Dar, Mombasa or Nairobi. Specialist African agencies can also arrange regional flights to/from Zanzibar, and whole trips, including safari-and-beach combinations. The cheapest direct flights from London to Zanzibar start from around £400 (US$630) in the low season, and rise to around £750 (US$1,200) in the high season – plus an additional amount for airport and departure taxes and fuel surcharges, which is currently about £400–430. The relatively high taxes and surcharges are direct reflections of both the price of aviation fuel (oil) and also the increasingly high taxes levied by many governments on air travel.

The best deals are usually found by buying a long time (9–12 months) in advance; tickets for travel in the near future almost always command a premium. To buy just flights, you should talk to the 'seat-only' travel agents. To find them, look through the advertisements in the travel supplements of the Sunday newspapers. Be prepared to shop around, and to find that many of the bargain fares offered in ads are unavailable when you phone.

Flights bought as part of a whole trip which includes accommodation (known as 'Inclusive Tour fares', or 'IT fares' in the trade) will usually be the lowest. To buy an IT fare as part of a whole trip, seek out a tour operator who specialises in Africa, perhaps starting with the list of specialist tour operators, on pages 79–81.

Charter flights For visitors from mainland Europe, another option to consider may be holiday charter flights. Increasing numbers of charter flights from Europe (and particularly Italy, France and Spain) fly direct to Zanzibar; currently there are none from the UK. These are usually sold only as part of a week or two-week package visiting one of Zanzibar's larger 'resorts'. However, if the planes are not full then tour operators will sometimes sell 'flight only' deals, which are good value. Again, see advertisements in national newspapers.

From the USA There are no direct flights to any of the islands, or even to Dar es Salaam, from the USA. You must fly to Europe or another African capital, such as Johannesburg or Nairobi, and then connect through to Dar es Salaam or Zanzibar.

From Kenya Kenya Airways and Precision Air fly between Nairobi and Zanzibar daily, often code-sharing. Currently, there are daily flights at 08.10 and 18.40, taking approximately 90 minutes.

The fare is about US$250 one-way, including taxes. Agents in Nairobi or Mombasa can arrange these flights. More details of airlines are given in *Chapter 6, Other practicalities*, page 177.

From South Africa and elsewhere From South Africa, Air Tanzania and South African Airways run a code-share flight between Johannesburg and Dar es Salaam daily, departing at 13.50 and arriving in Dar at 18.30. There is a connection to Zanzibar (at no extra cost if you book through Air Tanzania). South African Airways has also started daily direct flights between Johannesburg and Dar, departing at 09.50 (arriving 14.35), and two additional flights on Sundays and Fridays at 14.55 (arriving 19.25). Alternatively, a low-cost carrier, 1time, operates three weekly (Tuesday and Saturday) direct flights from Johannesburg to Zanzibar.

If you want to reach Zanzibar from somewhere else in the world other than the countries mentioned above, it is usual to fly to Europe, Nairobi or the Gulf States and pick up a connecting flight from there. For example, from many parts of Asia you could fly on Gulf Air to Muscat then take another plane to Dar es Salaam.

Departure taxes There is a departure tax in US dollars (currently US$30) when flying out of a mainland Tanzanian or Zanzibar airport on an international flight. This is payable in US dollars, either in cash or, increasingly, included in the cost of pre-paid airline tickets. If you do need to pay in cash, then travellers' cheques, other currencies and even Tanzanian shillings are not accepted for this; you must have US dollars. You can change whatever you have into US dollars at an airport bureau de change, but often the exchange rates given are very poor. However you carry your money, it's always worth carrying some dollars in cash to cover costs like this. For domestic flights, the airport tax is US$5.

Before you pay anything, especially if you've come to Zanzibar on an international return flight, check that the departure tax isn't already included in your ticket price (even better, check what taxes are included when you buy your ticket). If you are flying to Dar to pick up an international flight, you need only pay the international departure tax once (probably at Dar), although you will still pay the domestic departure tax for your flight out of Zanzibar.

Even ship passengers cannot escape departure taxes! Tourists leaving by boat from Zanzibar are charged a US$5 'seaport departure service charge'. This also is payable in dollars only, but many of the ship companies include this tax in the ticket price. Check this carefully to avoid paying twice.

BY SEA

From Kenya We're not aware of any passenger ships currently running between Zanzibar and Mombasa. Dhows taking tourists from Kenya to Zanzibar Island are very rare; they're more frequent, though still irregular, between Mombasa and Pemba (see page 346) but do read the warnings in *Chapter 5*, page 127, carefully before deciding on this form of transport. If you ask around in the old port area of Mombasa you can usually find a boat going about twice a week to Wete or Mkoani on Pemba, although times and days are variable and seaworthiness often highly questionable. A one-way trip costs about US$10 to US$15, payable in Kenyan shillings or hard currency.

From mainland Tanzania Several large passenger ships run daily between Dar es Salaam, Zanzibar and Pemba, and less frequently to other points on the mainland (for details of these, see *Chapter 5*, page 125).

HEALTH   *with Dr Felicity Nicholson*

People new to exotic travel often worry about tropical diseases, but it is accidents that are most likely to carry you off. Road accidents are very common in many parts of Zanzibar so be aware and do what you can to reduce risks: try to travel during daylight hours, always wear a seatbelt and refuse to be driven by anyone who has been drinking. Listen to local advice about any areas where crime is an issue.

BEFORE YOU GO

Travel insurance Visitors to Zanzibar must take out a comprehensive **medical insurance policy** to cover them for emergencies, including the cost of evacuation to another country within the region. Such policies come with an emergency number (often on a reverse-charge/call-collect basis). You would be wise to memorise this – or indelibly tattoo it in as many places as possible on your baggage. Note that many policies exclude diving as an activity, so do check this.

Personal effects insurance is also a sensible precaution, but check the policy's fine print before you leave home. Often, in even the best policies, you will find a limit per item, or per claim – which can be well below the cost of a replacement. If you need to list your valuables separately, then do so comprehensively. Check that receipts are not required for claims, and that the excess that you have to pay on every claim is reasonable.

Annual travel policies can be excellent value if you travel a lot, and some of the larger credit-card companies offer good deals. However, often it is better to get your valuables named and insured for travel using your home contents insurance. Insurers who offer these year-round policies will try harder to settle your claim fairly as they want your business in the long term.

Immunisations and medication
Preparations to ensure a healthy trip require checks on your immunisation status: it is wise to be up to date on tetanus, polio and diphtheria (now given as an all-in-one vaccine, Revaxis, that lasts for ten years), and hepatitis A. Immunisations against meningococcus and rabies may also be recommended.

Legal requirements
Officially, proof of vaccination against yellow fever is only needed for entry into Zanzibar if you are coming from another yellow fever endemic area, but for some time the Zanzibari authorities have been asking for proof of vaccination for visitors coming from Tanzania – which effectively incorporates most visitors. The decision to vaccinate or not is a complex one as the actual risk of yellow fever in Tanzania, including Zanzibar, is considered to be very low indeed. Having the vaccine, assuming that there were no contraindications, would only be warranted if you were spending time in another country where there is active disease. If the vaccine is not suitable for you and you are not at risk of disease then most health-care professionals would issue an exemption certificate instead.

Recommended precautions
Hepatitis A vaccine (Havrix Monodose or Avaxim) comprises two injections given about a year apart. The course costs about £100, but may be available on the NHS; it protects for 25 years and can be administered even close to the time of departure. **Hepatitis B vaccination** should be considered for longer trips (two months or more) or for those working with children or in situations where contact with blood is likely. Three injections are needed for the best protection and can be given over a three-week period if time is short. Longer schedules give more sustained protection and are therefore preferred if time allows. Hepatitis A vaccine can also be given as a combination with hepatitis B as 'Twinrix', though two doses are needed at least seven days apart to be effective for the hepatitis A component, and three doses are needed for the hepatitis B.

The newer injectable **typhoid** vaccines (eg: Typhim Vi) last for three years and are about 85% effective. A dose of three capsules over five days lasts for approximately three years, although in the UK it is only licensed for one year, but may be less effective than the injectable forms. They should be encouraged unless the traveller is leaving within a few days for a trip of a week or less, when the vaccine would not be effective in time. **Meningitis** vaccine (ideally containing strains A, C, W and Y), is recommended for all travellers, especially those who will be in close contact with local people (see *Meningitis*, page 94). Vaccinations for **rabies** are ideally advised for everyone, but are especially important for travellers visiting more remote areas, especially if you are more than 24 hours from medical help and definitely if you will be working with animals (see *Rabies*, page 95).

Experts differ over whether a BCG vaccination against **tuberculosis** (TB) is useful in adults: discuss this with your travel clinic.

In addition to the various vaccinations recommended above, it is important that travellers should be properly protected against **malaria**. For detailed advice, see below.

Ideally you should visit your own doctor or a specialist travel clinic (see opposite) to discuss your requirements, if possible at least eight weeks before you plan to travel.

Malaria Along with road accidents, malaria is the greatest health risk to travellers in Tanzania, Zanzibar included.

There is no vaccine against malaria, but using prophylactic drugs and preventing mosquito bites will considerably reduce the risk of contracting it. Seek professional advice to ascertain the preferred anti-malarial drugs for the country you are visiting at the time you travel. If mefloquine (Lariam) is suggested, start this 2½ weeks (three doses) before departure to check that it suits you; stop it immediately if it seems to cause depression or anxiety, visual or hearing disturbances, severe headaches, fits or changes in heart rhythm. Side effects such as nightmares or dizziness are not medical reasons for stopping unless they are sufficiently debilitating or annoying. Anyone who has been treated for depression or psychiatric problems, has diabetes controlled by oral therapy or who is epileptic (or who has suffered fits in the past) or has a close blood relative who is epileptic, should probably avoid mefloquine.

In the past doctors were nervous about prescribing mefloquine to pregnant women, but experience has shown that it is relatively safe and certainly safer than the risk of malaria. That said, there are other issues, so if you are travelling to Zanzibar whilst pregnant, seek expert advice before departure.

Malarone (proguanil and atovaquone) is as effective as mefloquine. It has the advantage of having few side effects and need only be continued for one week after returning. However, it is expensive and because of this tends to be reserved for shorter trips. Malarone may not be suitable for everybody, so advice should be taken from a doctor. The licence in the UK has been extended for up to three months' use and a paediatric form of tablet is also available, prescribed on a weight basis.

Another alternative is the antibiotic doxycycline (100mg daily). Like Malarone it can be started one day before arrival. Unlike mefloquine, it may also be used in travellers with epilepsy, although certain anti-epileptic medication may make it less effective. In perhaps 1–3% of people there is the possibility of allergic skin reactions developing in sunlight; the drug should be stopped if this happens.

Chloroquine and proguanil are no longer considered to be effective enough for Zanzibar but may be considered as a last resort if nothing else is deemed suitable.

All tablets should be taken with or after the evening meal, washed down with plenty of fluid and, with the exception of Malarone (see above), continued for four weeks after leaving.

In addition to prophylactic drugs, there is a case for carrying a treatment for malaria, in case you develop malarial symptoms when medical assistance is unavailable. The longer you are spending in Africa, the more the case for this strengthens, and it would certainly be recommended to anybody undertaking a long overland trip, or volunteering or working in a remote area, or who travels in Africa regularly. Whatever you decide, you should seek up-to-date advice to find out the most appropriate medication.

In addition to taking anti-malarial medicines, it is important to avoid mosquito bites between dusk and dawn, which is when the *Anopheles* (malaria-carrying) mosquito is most active. Pack a **DEET-based insect repellent** (ideally containing 50–55% DEET), such as one of the Repel range, and take either a **permethrin-impregnated bednet** or a **permethrin spray** so that you can treat bednets in hotels. Permethrin treatment makes even very tatty nets protective and mosquitoes are also unable to bite through the impregnated net when you roll against it. Putting on socks and long clothes (including long-sleeved shirts or blouses) at dusk reduces the risk of bites and the amount of repellent needed. Be aware, however, that malaria mosquitoes usually hunt at ankle level and their bite can penetrate through socks, so apply repellent to your feet and ankles whether or not you wear socks. Travel clinics usually sell a good range of nets, treatment kits and repellents. See *Avoiding insect bites* on page 96 for more information on how to avoid mosquito bites.

Despite all of these precautions, it is important to be aware that no anti-malarial drug is 100% protective, although those on prophylactics who are unlucky enough to catch malaria are less likely to get rapidly into serious trouble. Travellers to Africa cannot acquire any effective resistance to malaria as it takes at least 18 months in holoendemic areas to gain any meaningful protection. There is no scientific evidence that homeopathic remedies are effective in either preventing or treating malaria. In addition, the Faculty of Homeopathy does not promote the use of homeopathic remedies for the prevention of malaria.

Travel clinics and health information A full list of current travel clinic websites worldwide is available from the International Society of Travel Medicine on www. istm.org. For other journey preparation information, consult www.tripprep.com. Information about various medications may be found on www.emedicine.com. For information on malaria prevention, see www.preventingmalaria.info.

UK

✚ **Berkeley Travel Clinic** 32 Berkeley St, London W1J 8EL (near Green Park tube station); ☎020 7629 6233

✚ **Cambridge Travel Clinic** 48a Mill Rd, Cambridge CB1 2AS; ☎01223 367362; e enquiries@travelcliniccambridge.co.uk; www. travelcliniccambridge.co.uk; ⏱ noon–19.00 Tue–Fri, 10.00–16.00 Sat

✚ **Edinburgh Travel Clinic** Regional Infectious Diseases Unit, Ward 41 OPD, Western General Hospital, Crewe Rd South, Edinburgh EH4 2UX; ☎0131 537 2822; www.mvm.ed.ac.uk; Travel helpline (☎0906 589 0380); ⏱ 09.00–noon Mon–Fri. Provides inoculations & antimalarial prophylaxis, & advises on travel-related health risks.

✚ **Fleet Street Travel Clinic** 29 Fleet St, London EC4Y 1AA; ☎020 7353 5678; www. fleetstreetclinic.com. Vaccinations, travel products & latest advice.

✚ **Hospital for Tropical Diseases Travel Clinic** Mortimer Market Bldg, Capper St (off Tottenham Ct Rd), London WC1E 6AU; ☎020 7388 9600; www.thehtd.org. Offers consultations &

advice, & is able to provide all necessary drugs & vaccines for travellers. Runs a healthline (☎ *0906 133 7733*) for country-specific information & health hazards. Also stocks nets, water-purification equipment & personal protection measures.

✚ **Interhealth Worldwide** Partnership Hse, 157 Waterloo Rd, London SE1 8US; ☎020 7902 9000; www.interhealth.org.uk. Competitively priced, 1-stop travel health service. All profits go to their affiliated company, InterHealth, which provides health care for overseas workers on Christian projects.

✚ **Liverpool School of Medicine** Pembroke Pl, Liverpool L3 5QA; ☎0151 708 9393; www.liv. ac.uk/lstm

✚ **MASTA** (Medical Advisory Service for Travellers Abroad) Moorfield Rd, Yeadon, Leeds, West Yorks LS19 7BN; ☎0113 238 7500; www.masta-travel-health.com. Provides travel health advice, antimalarials & vaccinations. There are over 25 MASTA pre-travel clinics in Britain; call or check online for the nearest. Clinics also sell mosquito nets, medical kits, insect protection & travel hygiene products.

MALARIA SYMPTOMS

Malaria usually begins with a fever, the first symptoms of which are often a general flu-like feeling of slight disorientation in the head or weakness in the legs. You may then feel cold, shivery, shaky and very sweaty. Headache, feeling sick and vomiting are common with malaria and you are also likely to experience muscle aches. The cycle of fever and sweating is repeated at intervals from daily to alternate days to around three days with a fever-free period between. Some people develop jaundice (yellowing of the eyes and/ or skin). However, it is not necessary for all of these symptoms to be present before suspecting malaria. The only consistent symptom is a fever of 38°C or more which lasts for more than a few hours.

While you are away, assume that any high fever lasting more than a few hours is malaria, regardless of other symptoms. Although the progression of malaria is variable and unpredictable, early diagnosis and treatment will greatly increase the likelihood that it doesn't develop into a life-threatening condition, so seek medical help as soon as possible, or – if this is not possible – be prepared to self-diagnose and medicate. Remember that the symptoms of malaria may develop anywhere from seven days after entering a malarious area to up to one year after leaving, so if symptoms appear after your return home tell a doctor immediately and mention that you have been in a malarious area.

➕ **NHS travel website** www.fitfortravel. scot.nhs.uk. Provides country-by-country advice on immunisation & malaria, plus details of recent developments, & a list of relevant health organisations.

➕ **Nomad Travel Store/Clinic** 3–4 Wellington Terrace, Turnpike Lane, London N8 0PX; ✆020 8889 7014; travel-health line (office hrs only) ✆0906 863 3414; e sales@nomadtravel.co.uk; www.nomadtravel.co.uk. Also at 40 Bernard St, London WC1N 1LJ; ✆020 7833 4114; 52 Grosvenor Gdns, London SW1W 0AG; ✆020 7823 5823; & 43 Queens Rd, Bristol BS8 1QH; ✆0117 922 6567. For health advice, equipment such as mosquito nets & other anti-bug devices, & an excellent range of adventure travel gear. Clinic also in Southampton.

➕ **Trailfinders Travel Clinic** 194 Kensington High St, London W8 7RG; ✆020 7938 3999; www. trailfinders.com/travelessentials/travelclinic.htm

➕ **Travelpharm** The Travelpharm website (*www. travelpharm.com*) offers up-to-date guidance on travel-related health & has a range of medications available through their online mini pharmacy.

Irish Republic

➕ **Tropical Medical Bureau** Grafton St Medical Centre, Grafton Bldgs, 34 Grafton St, Dublin 2; ✆1

671 9200; www.tmb.ie. A useful website specific to tropical destinations. Also check website for other bureaux locations throughout Ireland.

USA

➕ **Centers for Disease Control** 1600 Clifton Rd, Atlanta, GA 30333; ✆800 311 3435; travellers' health hotline (fax service) 888 232 3299; www. cdc.gov/travel. The central source of travel information in the USA. The invaluable *Health Information for International Travel*, published annually, is available from the Division of Quarantine at this address.

➕ **Connaught Laboratories** Pasteur Merieux Connaught, Route 611, PO Box 187, Swiftwater, PA 18370; ✆800 822 2463. They will send a free list of specialist tropical-medicine physicians in your state.

➕ **IAMAT** (International Association for Medical Assistance to Travelers) 1623 Military Rd, 279, Niagara Falls, NY 14304-1745; ✆716 754 4883; e info@iamat.org; www.iamat.org. A non-profit organisation that provides lists of English-speaking doctors abroad.

➕ **International Medicine Center** 915 Gessner Rd, Suite 525, Houston, TX 77024; ✆713 550 2000; www.traveldoc.com

Canada

➕ **IAMAT** Suite 1, 1287 St Clair Av W, Toronto, Ontario M6E 1B8; ☎ 416 652 0137; www.iamat.org

➕ **TMVC** Suite 314, 1030 W Georgia St, Vancouver, BC V6E 2Y3; ☎ 888 288 8682; www.tmvc.com. Private clinic with several outlets in Canada.

Australia, New Zealand, Singapore

➕ **IAMAT** PO Box 5049, Christchurch 5, New Zealand; www.iamat.org

➕ **TMVC** ☎ 1300 65 88 44; www.tmvc.com.au. Clinics in Australia, New Zealand & Singapore, including: *Auckland* Canterbury Arcade, 170 Queen St, Auckland; ☎ 9 373 3531 *Brisbane* 75a Astor Terrace, Spring Hill, QLD 4000; ☎ 7 3815 6900 *Melbourne* 393 Little Bourke St, 2nd floor,

Melbourne, VIC 3000; ☎ 3 9602 5788 *Sydney* Dymocks Bldg, 7th floor, 428 George St, Sydney, NSW 2000; ☎ 2 9221 7133

South Africa and Namibia

➕ **SAA-Netcare Travel Clinics** Sanlam Bldg, 19 Fredman Dr, Sandton, P Bag X34, Benmore, JHB, Gauteng, 2010; www.travelclinic.co.za. Clinics throughout South Africa.

➕ **TMVC** NHC Health Centre, cnr Beyers Naude & Waugh Northcliff; PO Box 48499, Roosevelt Park, 2129 (postal address); ☎ 011 888 7488; www.tmvc.com.au. Consult website for details of other clinics in South Africa & Namibia.

Switzerland

➕ **IAMAT** 57 Chemin des Voirets, 1212 Grand Lancy, Geneva; www.iamat.org

Personal first-aid kit Pharmacies in the main towns in Zanzibar generally have good supplies of medicines, but away from these you will find very little, so it's wise to take a small first aid and medical kit. More elaborate medicines, if you need them, are available from the private hospitals in Zanzibar. A few travellers choose to carry an 'anti-AIDS kit' (a pack of needles, syringes and other items which come into contact with blood) for use in an emergency; your doctor or a vaccination centre can provide more information. A minimal first-aid kit contains:

- A digital thermometer
- A good drying antiseptic, eg: iodine or potassium permanganate (wipes are better than cream)
- A few small dressings and plasters (including some waterproof)
- Tubigrip bandages
- Suncream
- Insect repellent
- Anti-malarial tablets
- Impregnated mosquito net or permethrin spray
- Antihistamine tablets and cream (good for insect bites)
- Aspirin or paracetamol
- Antifungal cream (eg: Canesten)
- Ciprofloxacin or norfloxacin, for severe diarrhoea
- Tinidazole for giardia or amoebic dysentery
- Antibiotic eye drops, for sore, 'gritty', stuck-together eyes (conjunctivitis)
- A pair of fine-pointed tweezers (to remove hairy caterpillar hairs, thorns, splinters, coral, etc)
- Alcohol-based hand wash or bar of soap in plastic box
- Condoms or femidoms
- Adequate supplies of any personal medication

IN ZANZIBAR When travelling around Zanzibar or east Africa, the different climatic and social conditions mean visitors are exposed to diseases not normally encountered at home. Although you will have received all the vaccinations recommended in the *Before you go* section, this does not mean you will be free of all illness during your travels: certain precautions still have to be taken.

You should read a good book on travel medicine (see *Appendix 2, Further information*, page 416) and be aware of the causes, symptoms and treatments of the more serious diseases. But don't let these colourful descriptions put you off – with a little care and attention most of these illnesses can be avoided.

Staying healthy

Food and storage Throughout the world, most health problems encountered by travellers are contracted by eating contaminated food or drinking unclean water. If you are staying in the better camps or lodges, or eating in restaurants, then you are unlikely to have problems in Zanzibar.

However, if you are backpacking and cooking for yourself, or relying on local food, then you need to take more care. Tins, packets and fresh green vegetables (when you can find them) are least likely to cause problems – provided that clean water has been used in preparing the meal. In Zanzibar's hot climate, keeping meat and other animal products unrefrigerated for more than a few hours is asking for trouble.

Water purification It is less common to get sick from drinking contaminated water, but it happens, so try to drink from safe sources. At good hotels, clean bottled drinking water will always be available. You can now buy bottled water widely throughout these islands, although if you venture very far from the beaten track, then supplies are not always reliable so carry bottles with you.

When buying bottled water, check the seal as it is not unknown for discarded bottles to be filled with tap water and sold again. That said, don't become nervous and avoid drinking altogether; such scams are very rare. It is vital to keep up your liquid intake in the hot climate to avoid dehydration.

If heading far from civilisation, then prepare to purify your own water with chlorine dioxide tablets, which are available from outdoor/camping shops. Bring these with you; you may not be able to buy them in Zanzibar. These will work more effectively if you filter out any larger, suspended particles from the water before adding them. Several manufacturers in Europe and USA produce filter pumps designed to do this whole process quickly and easily, eg: Aquapur.

Medical facilities
If you need medical attention, there are several hospitals and medical centres in Zanzibar Town, and the larger and more upmarket hotels have on-call European doctors who can be called out for a fee. Pharmacies in Zanzibar Town have a basic range of medicines, but specific brands are often unavailable, so bring with you all that you will need. For details, see page 179.

Common medical problems

Heat and sun Heatstroke, heat exhaustion and sunburn are often problems for travellers to Zanzibar, despite being easy to prevent. To avoid them, you need to remember that your body is under stress and make allowances for it. First, take things gently; you are on holiday, after all. Next, keep your fluid and salt levels high: lots of water and soft drinks, but go easy on the caffeine and alcohol. Third, dress to keep cool with loose-fitting, thin garments – preferably of cotton, linen or silk. Finally, beware of the sun. Hats and long-sleeved shirts are essential. If you must expose your skin to the sun, then use sunblocks and high-factor sunscreens (the sun is so strong that you will still get a tan). Be especially careful of exposure in the middle of the day and of sun reflected off water, and wear a T-shirt and lots of waterproof suncream (at least SPF25) when swimming. The glare and the dust can be hard on the eyes, too, so bring UV-protection sunglasses and, perhaps, a soothing eyebath.

Travellers' diarrhoea At least half of those travelling to the tropics/developing world will experience a bout of travellers' diarrhoea during their trip; the newer you are to exotic travel, the more likely you will be to suffer. By taking precautions against travellers' diarrhoea you will also avoid typhoid, paratyphoid, cholera, hepatitis, dysentery, worms, etc. Travellers' diarrhoea and the other faecal-oral diseases come from getting other peoples' faeces in your mouth. This most often happens from cooks not washing their hands after a trip to the toilet, but even if

LONG-HAUL FLIGHTS, CLOTS AND DVT   *Dr Felicity Nicholson*

Any prolonged immobility, including travel by land or air, can result in deep-vein thrombosis (DVT) with the risk of embolus to the lungs. Certain factors can increase the risk and these include:

- Having a previous clot or a close relative with a history
- Being over 40, with increased risk in over 80s
- Recent major operation or varicose-veins surgery
- Cancer
- Stroke
- Heart disease
- Obesity
- Pregnancy
- Hormone therapy
- Heavy smoking
- Severe varicose veins
- Being tall (over 6ft/1.8m) or short (under 5ft/1.5m)

A deep-vein thrombosis causes painful swelling and redness of the calf or sometimes the thigh. It is only dangerous if a clot travels to the lungs (pulmonary embolus). Symptoms of a pulmonary embolus (PE) – which commonly start three to ten days after a long flight – include chest pain, shortness of breath, and sometimes coughing up small amounts of blood. Anyone who thinks that they might have a DVT needs to see a doctor immediately.

PREVENTION OF DVT
- Keep mobile both before and during the flight; move around every couple of hours
- Drink plenty of fluids during the flight
- Avoid taking sleeping pills and excessive tea, coffee and alcohol
- Consider wearing flight socks or support stockings (see *www.legshealth. com*)

If you think you are at increased risk of a clot, ask your doctor if it is safe to travel.

the restaurant cook does not understand basic hygiene you will be safe if your food has been properly cooked and arrives piping hot. The most important prevention strategy is to wash your hands before eating anything. The maxim to remind you what you can safely eat is:

PEEL IT, BOIL IT, COOK IT OR FORGET IT.

This means that fruit you have washed and peeled yourself, and hot foods, should be safe but raw foods, cold cooked foods, salads, fruit salads which have been prepared by others, ice cream and ice are all risky, as are foods kept lukewarm in restaurant or hotel buffets. Self-service or buffet meals are safest to eat when the food is hot and freshly cooked – for example, a late buffet lunch eaten in the mid-afternoon will have been sitting around a long while. If you do get travellers' diarrhoea, see box *Treating travellers' diarrhoea*, opposite, for treatment.

From water It is also possible to get sick from drinking contaminated water, so try to drink from safe sources. You must assume that tap water is risky wherever you are in Tanzania. To make risky water safe, it should be brought to a boil (even at altitude it only needs to be brought to a boil), passed through a good bacteriological filter or purified with chlorine dioxide tablets. If you buy bottled water (which is widely available) make sure the seal is intact. Iodine is no longer recommended for anyone to use for purifying water.

Eye problems Bacterial conjunctivitis (pink eye) is a common infection in Africa; people who wear contact lenses are most open to this irritating problem. The eyes feel sore and gritty and they will often be stuck together in the mornings. They will need treatment with antibiotic drops or ointment. Lesser eye irritation should settle with bathing in salt water and keeping the eyes shaded. If an insect flies into your eye, extract it with great care, ensuring you do not crush or damage it otherwise you may get a nastily inflamed eye from toxins secreted by the creature. Small, elongated red-and-black blister beetles carry warning colouration to tell you not to crush them anywhere against your skin.

Prickly heat A fine pimply rash on the trunk is likely to be heat rash; cool showers, dabbing dry, and talc will help. Treat the problem by slowing down to a relaxed schedule, wearing only loose, baggy, 100%-cotton clothes and sleeping naked under a fan; if it's bad you may need to check into an air-conditioned hotel room for a while.

Skin infections Any mosquito bite or small nick in the skin gives an opportunity for bacteria to foil the body's usually excellent defences; it will surprise many travellers how quickly skin infections start in warm humid climates and it is essential to clean and cover even the slightest wound. Creams are not as effective as a good drying antiseptic such as dilute iodine, potassium permanganate (a few crystals in half a cup of water) or crystal (or gentian) violet. One of these should be available in most towns. If the wound starts to throb, or becomes red and the redness starts to spread, or the wound oozes, and especially if you develop a fever, antibiotics will probably be needed: flucloxacillin (250mg four times a day) or cloxacillin (500mg four times a day). For those allergic to penicillin, erythromycin (500mg twice a day) for five days should help. See a doctor if the symptoms do not start to improve within 48 hours.

Fungal infections also get a hold easily in hot, moist climates, so wear 100%-cotton socks and underwear and shower frequently. An itchy rash in the groin or flaking between the toes is likely to be a fungal infection. This needs treatment with an antifungal cream such as Canesten (clotrimazole); if this is not available try Whitfield's ointment (compound benzoic acid ointment) or crystal violet (although this will turn you purple!).

Diseases

Bilharzia or schistosomiasis with thanks to Dr Vaughan Southgate of the Natural History Museum, London, and Dr Dick Stockley, The Surgery, Kampala

Bilharzia or schistosomiasis is a disease that commonly afflicts the rural poor of the tropics. Two types exist in sub-Saharan Africa – *Schistosoma mansoni* and *Schistosoma haematobium*. It is an unpleasant problem that is worth avoiding, though can be treated if you do get it.

It is easier to understand how to diagnose it, treat it and prevent it if you know a little about its cause. Contaminated faeces are washed into the lake, the eggs hatch and the larva infects certain species of snail. The snails then produce about 10,000 cercariae a day for the rest of their lives. The parasites can digest their way through your skin when you wade or bathe in infested fresh water.

Winds disperse the snails and cercariae. The snails in particular can drift a long way, especially on windblown weed, so nowhere is really safe. However, deep water

TREATING TRAVELLERS' DIARRHOEA

It is dehydration that makes you feel awful during a bout of diarrhoea and the most important part of treatment is drinking lots of clear fluids. Sachets of oral rehydration salts give the perfect biochemical mix to replace all that is pouring out of your bottom, but other recipes taste nicer. Any diluted mixture of sugar and salt in water will do you good: try Coke or orange squash with a three-finger pinch of salt added to each glass (if you are salt-depleted, you won't taste the salt). Otherwise make a solution of a four-finger scoop of sugar with a three-finger pinch of salt in a 500ml glass. Or add eight level teaspoons of sugar (18g) and one level teaspoon of salt (3g) to one litre (five cups) of safe water. A squeeze of lemon or orange juice improves the taste and adds potassium, which is also lost in diarrhoea. Drink two large glasses after every bowel action, and more if you are thirsty. These solutions are still absorbed well if you are vomiting, but you will need to take sips at a time. If you are not eating you need to drink three litres a day plus whatever is pouring into the toilet. If you feel like eating, take a bland, high-carbohydrate diet. Heavy greasy foods will probably give you cramps.

If the diarrhoea is bad, if you are passing blood or slime, or if you have a fever, you will probably need antibiotics in addition to fluid replacement. You should always seek medical treatment but if you are not near help then you may want to start some treatment *en route*. A three-day course of ciprofloxacin (500mg) twice daily (or Norfloxacin) may be appropriate for dysentery. If you are planning to take an antibiotic with you, note that both norfloxacin and ciprofloxacin are available only by prescription in the UK. If the diarrhoea is greasy and bulky and is accompanied by sulphurous (eggy) burps, one likely cause is giardia. This is best treated with tinidazole (four x 500mg in one dose, repeated seven days later if symptoms persist).

and running water are safer, while shallow water presents the greatest risk. The cercariae penetrate intact skin, and find their way to the liver. There male and female meet and spend the rest of their lives in permanent copulation. No wonder you feel tired! Most finish up in the wall of the lower bowel, but others can get lost and can cause damage to many different organs. *Schistosoma haematobium* goes mostly to the bladder.

Although the adults do not cause any harm in themselves, after about four to six weeks they start to lay eggs, which cause an intense but usually ineffective immune reaction, including fever, cough, abdominal pain, and a fleeting, itching rash called 'safari itch'. The absence of early symptoms does not necessarily mean there is no infection. Later symptoms can be more localised and more severe, but the general symptoms settle down fairly quickly and eventually you are just tired. 'Tired all the time' is one of the most common symptoms among expats in Africa, and bilharzia, giardia, amoeba and intestinal yeast are the most common culprits.

Although bilharzia is difficult to diagnose, it can be tested at specialist travel clinics. Ideally tests need to be done at least six weeks after likely exposure and will determine whether you need treatment. Fortunately it is easy to treat at present.

Avoiding bilharzia If you are bathing, swimming, paddling or wading in fresh water which you think may carry a bilharzia risk, try to get out of the water within ten minutes.

- Avoid bathing or paddling on shores within 200m of villages or places where people use the water a great deal, especially reedy shores or where there is lots of water weed.
- Dry off thoroughly with a towel; rub vigorously.
- If your bathing water comes from a risky source try to ensure that the water is taken from the lake in the early morning and stored snail-free, otherwise it should be filtered or Dettol or Cresol added.
- Bathing early in the morning is safer than bathing in the last half of the day.
- Cover yourself with DEET insect repellent before swimming: it may offer some protection.

HIV/AIDS The risks of sexually transmitted infection are extremely high in Zanzibar, whether you sleep with fellow travellers or locals. About 80% of HIV infections in British heterosexuals are acquired abroad. If you must indulge, use condoms or femidoms, which help reduce the risk of transmission. If you notice any genital ulcers or discharge, get treatment promptly since these increase the risk of acquiring HIV. If you do have unprotected sex, visit a clinic as soon as possible; this should be within 24 hours, or no later than 72 hours, for post-exposure prophylaxis.

Ebola Visitors to Africa often express concern about this deadly, very contagious and highly publicised disease. However, Ebola has never been diagnosed in Tanzania, and while outbreaks have occurred in neighbouring Uganda and Congo, these were highly localised and occurred a long distance from the border. In the unlikely event of an outbreak, protective measures will be taken and you should follow whatever local advice is given.

Meningitis This is a particularly nasty disease as it can kill within hours of the first symptoms appearing. The telltale symptoms are a combination of a blinding headache (light sensitivity), a blotchy rash and a high fever. Immunisation with the newer tetravalent vaccine ACWY protects against the most serious bacterial form of meningitis and is usually recommended for longer-stay trips or if you are working closely with the local population – in particular with children. A single injection gives good protection for three years and also prevents carriage and therefore the possibility of bringing home the disease and giving it to family and friends. Other forms of meningitis exist (usually viral) but there are no vaccines for these. Local papers normally report outbreaks. If you show symptoms go to a doctor immediately.

Dengue fever This mosquito-borne disease – and other similar arboviruses – may mimic malaria but there is no prophylactic medication available to deal with it. The mosquitoes that carry this virus bite during the daytime, so it is worth applying repellent if you see any mosquitoes around. Symptoms include strong headaches, rashes, excruciating joint and muscle pains and high fever. Dengue fever lasts only for a week or so and is not usually fatal. Complete rest and paracetamol are the usual treatment. Plenty of fluids also help. Some patients are given an intravenous drip to keep them from dehydrating. It is especially important to protect yourself if you have had dengue fever before. A second infection with a different strain can result in the potentially fatal dengue haemorrhagic fever.

Sleeping sickness African trypanosomiasis, or sleeping sickness, is a parasitic infection transmitted by the tsetse fly. There are two subspecies; one predominates in east Africa and usually causes an acute infection, whereas the other predominates in central and west Africa and causes a slower progressive, chronic infection. Tsetse flies are a common pest in many Tanzanian game reserves, but fewer than 100 new cases of sleeping sickness are recorded in the country annually, even though millions of Tanzanians live in tsetse areas.

Tickbite fever African ticks are not the rampant disease transmitters they are in the Americas, but they may spread tickbite fever and a few dangerous rarities. Tickbite fever is a flu-like illness that can easily be treated with doxycycline, but as there can be some serious complications it is important to visit a doctor.

Ticks should ideally be removed as soon as possible as leaving them on the body increases the chance of infection. They should be removed with special tick tweezers that can be bought in good travel shops. Failing that you can use your finger nails: grasp the tick as close to your body as possible and pull steadily and firmly away at right angles to your skin. The tick will then come away complete, as long as you do not jerk or twist. If possible douse the wound with alcohol (any spirit will do) or iodine. Irritants (eg: Olbas oil) or lit cigarettes are to be discouraged since they can cause the ticks to regurgitate and therefore increase the risk of disease. It is best to get a travelling companion to check you for ticks; if you are travelling with small children, remember to check their heads, and particularly behind the ears.

Spreading redness around the bite, fever and/or aching joints after a tickbite imply that you have an infection that requires antibiotic treatment, so seek advice.

Rabies Rabies can be carried by all mammals (beware the village dogs and small monkeys in the parks) and is passed on to man through a bite, scratch or a lick of an open wound. You must always assume any animal is rabid, and seek medical

AVOIDING INSECT BITES

The prevalence of malaria in Zanzibar means it is crucial to avoid mosquito bites between dusk and dawn, even if you are taking prophylactic drugs as nothing is 100% effective. Pay particular attention to your ankles, since malaria-carrying mosquitoes often hunt at ground level. As the sun is going down, don long clothes and socks, and apply repellent to your ankles (under or over your socks) and to any other exposed flesh. Ideally, sleep under a permethrin-treated bednet or in an air-conditioned room. If that is not possible, burning a mosquito coil or mat will hugely reduce mosquito activity, as will putting on a fan (mosquitoes dislike turbulent air). In areas where mosquitoes seem common, it is advisable to close all windows at night, or any time you have the lights on, to prevent them from infiltrating the room from outside.

Many budget hotels make no effort to control mosquito numbers, so rooms are often infested. If you suspect this to be the case, spray the room with a suitable aerosol insecticide before you go out for dinner, paying special attention to the dark corners where they rest by day (under the bed or behind curtains or cupboards) and any en-suite bathroom. If you didn't bring an aerosol room spray with you, you should be able to buy one at larger supermarkets in most towns. Mosquitoes and many other insects are attracted to light. If you are camping, never put a lamp near the opening of your tent.

By day it is wise to wear long, loose (preferably 100% cotton) clothes if you are pushing through scrubby country; this will deter ticks as well as tsetse flies and day-biting *Aedes* mosquitoes which may spread dengue fever. Tsetse flies hurt when they bite and are attracted to the colour blue; locals will know where they are a problem and where they transmit sleeping sickness.

help as soon as possible. Meanwhile scrub the wound with soap under a running tap or while pouring water from a jug. Find a reasonably clear-looking source of water (but at this stage the quality of the water is not important), then pour on a strong iodine or alcohol solution of gin, whisky or rum. This helps stop the rabies virus entering the body and will guard against wound infections, including tetanus.

Pre-exposure vaccinations for rabies are ideally advised for everyone, but are particularly important if you intend to have contact with animals and/or are likely to be more than 24 hours away from medical help. Ideally three doses should be taken over a minimum of 21 days as this will change and simplify the treatment course. Contrary to popular belief these vaccinations are relatively painless.

If you are bitten, scratched or licked over an open wound by any warm-blooded animal, then you should seek medical help as soon as possible. It is not possible to tell by looking at an animal if they are infectious for rabies as they can look well. Post-exposure prophylaxis should be given as soon as possible, though it is never too late to seek help, as the incubation period for rabies can be very long. Those who have not been immunised will need a full course of injections and in most cases the first dose of vaccine is given with a weight-determined injection of rabies immunoglobulin (RIG). This is expensive (around US$800) and may be very hard to come by, but if you have had the full course of pre-exposure vaccination then it is not needed. This is a good reason to vaccinate travellers before they go if they have time.

And remember that, if you develop rabies, then mortality is virtually 100% and death from rabies is probably one of the worst ways to go.

Snakebite Snakes rarely attack unless provoked, and bites in travellers are unusual. You are less likely to get bitten if you wear stout shoes and long trousers when in the bush. Most snakes are harmless and even venomous species will dispense venom in only about half of their bites. If bitten, you are unlikely to have received venom; keeping this fact in mind may help you to stay calm. Many so-called first-aid techniques do more harm than good: cutting into the wound is harmful; tourniquets are dangerous; suction and electrical inactivation devices do not work. The only treatment is antivenom. In case of a bite that you fear may have been from a venomous snake:

- Try to keep calm – it is likely that no venom has been dispensed.
- Prevent movement of the bitten limb by applying a splint.
- Keep the bitten limb BELOW heart height to slow the spread of any venom.
- If you have a crêpe bandage, wrap it around the whole limb (eg: all the way from the toes to the thigh), as tight as you would for a sprained ankle or a muscle pull.
- Evacuate to a hospital that has antivenom.

And remember:

- NEVER give aspirin; you may take paracetamol, which is safe.
- NEVER cut or suck the wound.
- DO NOT apply ice packs.
- DO NOT apply potassium permanganate.

If the offending snake can be captured without risk of someone else being bitten, take this to show the doctor – but beware since even a decapitated head is able to bite.

CRIME AND SAFETY

As in most countries, crime in these islands is gradually on the increase. Similarly, problems tend to occur with greater frequency in the cities and tourist heartlands than in the rural areas. Perhaps inevitably, the juxtaposition of relatively wealthy tourists and a high density of relatively poor local people causes envy and leads to the occasional crime.

Zanzibar Town is notorious for opportunist pickpockets, and occasionally tourists do have bags and cameras snatched while walking around the narrow streets of the Old Town (for more specific details on places to be careful, see box, *Safety in and around Zanzibar Town*, page 145). There have also been robberies on some of the beaches around Zanzibar Town; it is better not to go there alone, especially at night. The authors have yet to hear of any crime problems on Mafia Island – but then this is a small, rural island with a low population density.

You can reduce the chances of having anything stolen by not displaying your wealth. Don't bring valuable jewellery to these islands; leave it at home. Keep your valuables secure, out of sight and preferably back in the safe at your hotel. Keep most of your money there too, and do not peel off notes from a huge wad for every small purchase. Wandering around the town with a camera casually slung over your shoulder or a state-of-the-art MP3 player is insensitive and simply asking for trouble. A simple, dull-looking bag is much safer than something smart or fashionable.

Theft from hotel rooms is unusual, though not unheard of. Most hotels have safes, where valuables can be stored, although reports of stuff disappearing from the safes of more basic budget hotels are not unknown (for more details, see box, *Safety in and around Zanzibar Town*, page 145).

In contrast to the comments above, there have in recent years been some very serious incidents indeed. On a few occasions, an organised, armed gang has attacked and robbed a remote beach lodge or resort. These incidents are thankfully

ADVICE FOR DISABLED TRAVELLERS

Gordon Rattray, www.able-travel.com

Zanzibar might sound like the last place you'd want to venture to if you have difficulties walking. Wheelchairs and sandy beaches don't agree, and its island status provides more logistical problems, forcing you to ask if the getting there is actually worth it.

It is. A Zanzibar experience is unique, and with some preparation, patience, and the innate helpfulness of the local people, you will be surprised by just how possible it is.

GETTING THERE AND AWAY The ferries from Dar es Salaam are not an easy option. Boarding on Zanzibar is via a gangplank, which is steep at low tide and can be difficult even for able-bodied people with luggage. On board there are various decks with stairways between them and there are no facilities to make mobility easier.

A quicker, more comfortable and more practical (albeit more expensive) option is to fly. The airport staff cope very well with disabled passengers, although you will need to be manually lifted in and out of the small 13-seater planes which are used for many flights from Dar to Zanzibar. Zanzibar Airport has standard bathroom facilities only.

LOCAL OPERATORS Sama Tours (page 135) and Fernandes Tours (page 134) are particularly open to requests from less-mobile travellers. Sama Tours have a guide/driver who is also an experienced personal assistant.

TRANSPORT Buses and dala dalas (small converted trucks) have no facilities for wheelchairs. Help will always be available, but be aware that they may run only as far as the dirt track leading to some coastal resorts, leaving you to walk a short distance. Taxis might be your easiest way of getting around, and drivers are usually happy to assist with transfers, but you must be assertive and explain clearly what help you need. It is always advisable for people prone to skin damage to sit on their wheelchair cushion in the vehicle as it may be old, meaning the seating won't give as much support as it once did.

ACCOMMODATION Although most buildings' entrances are at least one step up from street level, the majority are ground floor and might be construed as being 'accessible', depending on your abilities. Unless you are going to have the time and energy to look for accommodation on arrival, the best advice rare – but they do happen. In response, some of the more upmarket resorts now have armed security teams or armed policemen patrolling at night. Whilst these cannot guarantee the safety of visitors, it does give some reassurance that such serious crime is being tackled by the Zanzibari police.

TERRORISM Islamic terrorist groups are present in east Africa, and to varying degree, pose a threat across the entire region. In August 1998, al-Qaeda simultaneously bombed the US embassies in Nairobi and Dar es Salaam, killing 244 people (of whom only 12 were Americans) and injuring more than 5,000. In July 2010, terrorist group al-Shabaab, based in Somalia, killed 70 in bomb attacks

is to research your options in advance. Specialist tour operators will normally take time to listen to your needs or, if you prefer, many hotels can be found directly on the internet. If photos aren't available, the owners are easily contacted and can describe their facilities by email. Bradt's guidebook, *Access Africa* (see *Appendix 2, Further information*, page 416), includes a section on Zanzibar, where access in properties all around the island is described.

RESTAURANTS Many eateries are on the ground floor, with one or two steps at the entrance. The proprietors will want your custom, so if you fancy eating there, you can be sure they will quickly organise a couple of waiters to help you in.

HEALTH Doctors will know about 'everyday' illnesses, but you must understand and be able to explain your own particular medical requirements. If possible, take all necessary medication and equipment with you and pack this in your hand luggage during flights in case your main luggage gets lost. Zanzibar is humid, so feels hot all year. If this is a problem for you, a plant-spray bottle is an ideal cooling aid.

SECURITY The advice given elsewhere in this book (see page 97) applies to all travellers, but it is worthwhile remembering that, as a disabled person, you might appear more vulnerable. My experience, however, is that the opposite is true; Zanzibaris will sooner help and protect someone who is obviously less able, than take advantage of the situation.

ACTIVITIES The streets around Stone Town are generally smooth and step-free, and many of the highlights are ground floor with only one or two steps. Where ancient stairways do exist, help is easily found. Several spice farms are on level ground, and if you cannot follow the tour group then guides are usually happy to bring the spices to you – even in your vehicle – and explain their uses. Inform your guide or tour company in advance of your capabilities and they will make an appropriate itinerary.

Beaches will always be naturally difficult for wheelchair users. I've still not heard of anyone on Zanzibar using a beach wheelchair (with massive tyres to ride on soft sand), but I have no doubt this will come. Until then, we'll need to be content with sipping a cool drink in the shade with a good book. Is that so bad?

on Kampala, Uganda. Ever since, some travellers have looked nervously towards east Africa, citing Islamic influences, porous borders, long coastlines and a relative availability of arms as reasons to be wary of terrorism there.

The truth is that there are large Islamic communities on the islands, especially on Pemba and Zanzibar. These communities probably have their extremist elements, very much like the extremists who live in communities in the UK, Europe and the USA. So whilst Zanzibar (and, to a lesser extent, Pemba) has many factors which may cause concern, at the time of writing the British Foreign and Commonwealth Office terrorism rating is low, citing only 'an underlying threat from terrorism'.

That said, the nature of these incidents means that attacks could be indiscriminate, including in places frequented by expatriates and foreign travellers, so vigilance is always recommended.

WHAT TO TAKE

CLOTHING You are unlikely to experience great extremes of temperature on Zanzibar, although days can be very warm and some nights chilly. Clothing should be light and loose-fitting for daytime, and you may need something slightly more substantial for evenings. Even in the dry seasons, a rain jacket is a good idea (though you may not need it). Umbrellas (should you need them) are available locally. You'll need a good pair of shoes for sightseeing, and a pair of sandals for relaxing. A hat to keep off sun and rain completes the outfit.

Plastic beach shoes, rafting sandals or something similar to avoid the spiky sea urchins, are useful for walking out into the sea across old coral beds. Remember, though, never to tread on live coral. In a few seconds you can break off chunks which will take several decades to re-grow.

Dress codes are very relaxed, even in the smartest hotels and restaurants, so you won't need black tie or a ball gown. However, it's important to be sensitive towards local customs. When wandering around towns and villages you should be aware of local Muslim sensibilities: dress modestly and do not expose too much bare flesh. Remember that a woman walking around a Zanzibar town with bare shoulders and a short skirt, or a man without a shirt, is as unacceptable as someone parading naked on your local high street.

Of course, tourists don't need to don robes, veils and turbans, but around town it is important for women to have knees and shoulders covered. This is recommended for men, too. Therefore, for men and women, long trousers are better than shorts, although baggy surf-shorts or culottes are acceptable. Many women find skirts more comfortable than trousers. For men and women, long-sleeved shirts and blouses are better than vests and skimpy T-shirts. For the beach, normal swimming gear is fine, although going into local fishing villages in briefs or bikinis shows a complete lack of sensitivity.

EQUIPMENT If you're planning to base yourself in one place during your stay, or if your transfers are pre-arranged, then carrying your stuff in a suitcase or kitbag is absolutely fine. However, if you're likely to have to carry your own luggage, particularly if you're travelling around and visiting the islands as part of a longer trip, then it is usually easier to carry all your clothing and equipment in a rucksack.

Most rucksacks have internal frames, whilst some turn neatly into travel bags, with a zipped flap to enclose the straps and waist-belt. Both are fine, although if the straps can be zipped away then they are less likely to be damaged on bus roof-racks or airport carousels.

If you're staying in the cheaper hotels, sheets are not always very clean, so a light sheet sleeping bag is useful. It's unlikely you'll need a full sleeping bag; if you do hit the islands in a cold snap, most smaller hotels provide blankets. The better hotels and lodges have good facilities including towels and clean bed linen.

To avoid getting malaria, it is important to protect yourself from mosquitoes. Most hotels provide nets over the beds, but in the smaller cheaper hotels these are often in bad condition and riddled with holes. Either take your own **mosquito net** (visit a good camping shop before you travel), or take a needle and cotton to make running repairs. For added protection, bring a roll-on **insect repellent** and use mosquito coils (available locally) in your room at night. Remember: it takes only one mosquito to give you malaria.

Free-camping, outside an organised campsite, is illegal on the islands and there are no official campsites, so it is not worth bringing a tent. Fortunately, basic beach hotels and hostels can be very cheap.

All but the cheapest hotels provide towels. Personal items to bring include **toiletries, lipsalve, sun protection cream** and **sunglasses**. Soap, toothpaste and some medicines can be bought locally if you run out. Suncream is available in some hotel shops, but it's expensive, so it's advisable to bring all you need. Equally, condoms can be extremely difficult to buy on the islands, so bring your own supply if you are likely to need them.

You'll almost certainly bring a **camera**; make sure you bring spare batteries and enough film, if you use it (although basic print film can be bought in Zanzibar Town, and from some hotels and beach lodges). For more information on cameras and photography, see box, *Photographic tips*, page 104.

A **first-aid and medical kit** is recommended, and suggested content is discussed under *Health*, page 84, but what you need depends on your type of holiday, the amount of travel, and how far you plan to get off the beaten track. Whatever, you should include the basics:

If you're staying in the smaller, cheaper hotels, the following items will be useful:

- **Torch/flashlight** Power cuts are frequent. Most of the larger hotels and more upmarket places have generators, but some do not; some places only have power for a few hours at night, if at all. If you are looking to invest in a new torch, we cannot but praise the excellent *LED Lenser* products: high-quality metal torches with powerful LED lights. Check out something like the P7 for a robust, bright, hand-held option (*www.ledlenser.com*).
- **Pocket multi-tool** A Swiss Army knife or one of the more serious 'Leatherman' tools will always come in handy: from preparing fresh fruit to making minor repairs, these are an essential element of many travellers' kit.
- **Water bottle and purification tablets** If you're heading into the most remote areas, then water supplies may not always be drinkable.
- **Universal sink plug** Plugs always seem to be missing from the more basic hotels.

Finally, if you're keen on snorkelling, it is worth taking your own **mask, snorkel and fins**. Hiring these is usually easy and cheap, but hired kit from all but the best operators can fit poorly, spoiling the whole experience.

MONEY AND BANKING

CURRENCY Tanzania's unit of currency, used throughout these islands, is the Tanzania shilling (TSh). However, as non-Tanzanians have to pay for some items,

A *kanga*, the traditional coloured wrap worn by local women, makes an ideal souvenir. You can wear it, use it as a beach mat on the coast or a sheet to cover bare mattresses if you're in cheap hotels, and then hang it on your wall, throw it over your sofa or turn it into cushion covers when you get home. A kanga normally comes as a large rectangle which the women then cut into two pieces, each about a metre square. One half is worn as a wrapover skirt and the other is worn as a headscarf (a knot is usually tied in one corner and used for keeping money). Prices for a kanga, from the market or a local cloth shop, start at about US$5.

On Zanzibar and elsewhere on the coast, men traditionally wear a *kikoi*, a wraparound 'kilt' of woven cotton, usually striped and thicker than a kanga. Once again, a kikoi also has many practical travel uses before you take it home to use as a seat cover. Prices start at US$8.

If you want to combine African and Western clothing, you could even have a local tailor make up a shirt or pair of baggy shorts from a kikoi. For more ideas see the excellent little book *101 Uses for a Kanga*, by David Bygott, available in Zanzibar bookshops.

such as flights, ferry tickets and hotels, in foreign currency, the US dollar has effectively become an unofficial second currency. The prices of many other items, such as tours or rental cars, are also often quoted in US dollars, although these may be paid in TSh at the current rate. All of the watersports and dive operators currently quote prices in US dollars, though this trend has been known to switch to euros as they strengthen.

Prices in TSh, and exchange rates against hard currencies, are likely to vary considerably in the future, but prices in US dollars tend to remain more constant. As much as is possible, we have tried to quote in US dollars in this book to allow for sensible cross-comparisons.

At the time of going to press, the rate of exchange was as follows:

£1 = TSh 2,547
US$1 = TSh 1,611
€1 = TSh 2,156

For visitors to the islands, the most convenient currency to use is US dollars. Ideally, it should be carried in cash, in a mix of high and low denominations; this is handy as it can be used almost anywhere. Although travellers' cheques are a more secure form of money to carry (as they can be replaced if stolen), here they attract very poor rates of exchange and are simply not accepted by a large number of hotels. Hence, unless you're bringing a great deal, cash is much easier to carry.

CHANGING MONEY On the islands, the easiest place to change money is Zanzibar Town, where there are banks and many bureaux de change (see *Chapter 6*, page 177). It is also possible to change money in Chake Chake on Pemba (see page 350). Around Zanzibar Island, money can also be changed at most large and medium-sized hotels – although often the rates are poor. Several tour companies are also licensed to change money. For those travelling via Dar es Salaam Airport, there are a couple of convenient bureaux de change just outside the international terminal; the domestic terminal has no change facility.

Both banks and bureaux de change offer tourists free-floating market rates; there is no black market in currency in Tanzania. Generally, the banks offer better rates for travellers' cheques and the private bureaux offer better rates for cash, particularly for large denomination bills. The bureaux also tend to have a faster service. Banks and bureaux accept most foreign currencies, but staff are most familiar with US dollars and euros, and these get relatively better rates than other currencies.

Try not to change more than you will need into Tanzanian shillings (TSh); it can be difficult to get a good rate when changing this back. When calculating the amount of money you need to change into TSh, remember that under Tanzanian law, visitors from overseas must pay for many items, such as the larger hotels, car hire and air tickets, in foreign currency (usually US dollars). Most other large purchases, like boat trips and costly souvenirs, can also be paid for with US dollars.

CREDIT CARDS You can use your credit card (or debit card) at most larger souvenir shops, travel agents, and better hotels and lodges (even just to settle the bill for 'extras'); however, you may be charged as much as a 10–15% handling fee. This will seem unreasonable, until you talk to owners of businesses about their difficulties in dealing with the banks in Zanzibar, then you'll understand!

There are a scattering of automated teller machines (ATMs) in Stone Town, and we'd be surprised if these don't gradually multiply with time. Generally situated at banks or larger hotels, with the machines themselves in a secure ante-room, they all have a permanent security guard on the door and tend to operate a one in/one out policy to card holders.

In theory, drawing cash may also be possible through larger hotels or tour companies, but again, expect high commissions (more information on using credit cards is given in *Payments and reservations*, page 108) For Visa cardholders there's an assistance point at the office of Coastal Travels and Mtoni Marine, near the Serena Inn in Zanzibar Town. This is not a bank or bureau, though: it issues only relatively small amounts of cash against a card in cases of emergency, and the exchange rates are still poor compared with cash or travellers' cheques.

COSTS AND BUDGETING The cost of a visit to the islands depends very much on your standard of travel. Zanzibar Town has the most choice and, in many ways, the lowest prices for the quality that you get.

At the bottom end, the very cheapest hotels cost between US$10 and US$25 per person per night and will be extremely basic. If you have meals in local eating-houses and small restaurants (snacks US$2–3; curry US$5–6; grilled seafood US$4–10; pizza US$5–8), supplemented by lunches of fruit and bread from the market, plus tea or soft drinks (US$1–3) or the occasional alcoholic sundowner (US$3–6), then your food and drink budget will be around US$15–20 a day.

Hotels in the expansive middle range cost between about US$75–150 for a double, and meals in smarter restaurants cost the equivalent of around US$15 per person. Towards the top of the range, good-quality hotels are US$150–300 for a double, with meals in the best establishments from around US$25 per person.

Outside Zanzibar Town, most places are beach lodges. The cheapest of these, supplying little more than a (sometimes clean) room, will again be around US$20–30 per person per night. Pay between about US$40–75 per person per night and you can find clean and pleasant places by the dozen. US$75–150 per person per night buys you somewhere smart – usually places that need booking in advance, whilst you can pay up to US$1,250 per person sharing for the exclusive delights of Mnemba – but then this is one of Africa's top lodges.

You also need to take into account the costs of getting around. Buses are very cheap, costing the equivalent of only a few dollars to cross the island. For

PHOTOGRAPHIC TIPS   *Ariadne Van Zandbergen*

Zanzibar doesn't offer the possibilities for wildlife photography that exist on mainland Tanzania (although the red colobus monkeys at Jozani Forest can be an excellent subject), but the Swahili culture combined with the idyllic Indian Ocean beach scenes create some stunning photographic opportunities.

EQUIPMENT Although with some thought and an eye for composition you can take reasonable photos with a 'point-and-shoot' camera, you need an SLR camera if you are at all serious about photography. Modern SLRs tend to be very clever, with automatic programmes for almost every possible situation, but remember that these programmes are limited in the sense that the camera cannot think, but only make calculations. Every starting amateur photographer should read a photographic manual for beginners and get to grips with such basics as the relationship between aperture and shutter speed.

Always buy the best lens you can afford. The lens determines the quality of your photo more than the camera body. Fixed fast lenses are ideal, but very costly. A zoom lens makes it easier to change composition without changing lenses the whole time. If you carry only one lens, a 28–70mm (digital 17–55mm) or similar zoom should be ideal. For a second lens, a lightweight 80–200mm or 70–300mm (digital 55–200mm) or similar will be excellent for candid shots and varying your composition. Wildlife photography will be very frustrating if you don't have at least a 300mm lens. For a small loss of quality, tele-converters are a cheap and compact way to increase magnification: a 300 lens with a 1.4x converter becomes 420mm, and with a 2x it becomes 600mm. Note, however, that 1.4x and 2x tele-converters reduce the speed of your lens by 1.4 and 2 stops respectively.

For wildlife photography from a safari vehicle, a solid beanbag, which you can make yourself very cheaply, will be necessary to avoid blurred images, and is more useful than a tripod. A clamp with a tripod head screwed on to it can be attached to the vehicle as well. Modern dedicated flash units are easy to use; aside from the obvious need to flash when you photograph at night, you can improve a lot of photos in difficult 'high contrast' or very dull light with some fill-in flash. It pays to have a proper flash unit as opposed to a built-in camera flash.

DIGITAL/FILM Digital photography is now the preference of most amateur and professional photographers, with the resolution of digital cameras improving the whole time. For ordinary prints a six-megapixel camera is fine. For better results and the possibility to enlarge images and for professional reproduction, higher resolution is available up to 16 megapixels.

Memory space is important. The number of pictures you can fit on a memory card depends on the quality you choose. Calculate how many pictures you can fit on a card and either take enough cards for your trip, or take a storage drive onto which you can download the content. A laptop gives the advantage that you can see your pictures properly at the end of each day and edit and delete rejects, but a storage device is lighter and less bulky. These drives come in different capacities up to 80GB.

independent travel, you can hire bicycles for around US$5 per day, motor-scooters for US$25 or cars from around US$40.

Organised tours of the spice plantations, Jozani Forest or boat trips out to the smaller islands start from about US$25 per person for a small group. If you

Bear in mind that digital camera batteries, computers and other storage devices need charging, so make sure you have all the chargers, cables and converters with you. Most hotels have charging points, but do enquire about this in advance. When camping you might have to rely on charging from the car battery; a spare battery is invaluable.

If you are shooting film, 100 to 200 ISO print film and 50 to 100 ISO slide film are ideal. Low ISO film is slow but fine grained and gives the best colour saturation, but will need more light, so support in the form of a tripod or monopod is important. You can also bring a few 'fast' 400 ISO films for low-light situations where a tripod or flash is no option.

DUST AND HEAT Dust and heat are often a problem. Keep your equipment in a sealed bag, stow films in an airtight container (eg: a small cooler bag) and avoid exposing equipment and film to the sun. Digital cameras are prone to collecting dust particles on the sensor which results in spots on the image. The dirt mostly enters the camera when changing lenses, so be careful when doing this. To some extent photos can be 'cleaned' up afterwards in Photoshop, but this is time-consuming. You can have your camera sensor professionally cleaned, or you can do this yourself with special brushes and swabs made for the purpose, but note that touching the sensor might cause damage and should only be done with the greatest care.

LIGHT The most striking outdoor photographs are often taken during the hour or two of 'golden light' after dawn and before sunset. Shooting in low light may enforce the use of very low shutter speeds, in which case a tripod will be required to avoid camera shake.

With careful handling, side lighting and back lighting can produce stunning effects, especially in soft light and at sunrise or sunset. Generally, however, it is best to shoot with the sun behind you. When photographing animals or people in the harsh midday sun, images taken in light but even shade are likely to be more effective than those taken in direct sunlight or patchy shade, since the latter conditions create too much contrast.

PROTOCOL In some countries, it is unacceptable to photograph local people without permission, and many people will refuse to pose or will ask for a donation. In such circumstances, don't try to sneak photographs as you might get yourself into trouble. Even the most willing subject will often pose stiffly when a camera is pointed at them; relax them by making a joke, and take a few shots in quick succession to improve the odds of capturing a natural pose.

Ariadne Van Zandbergen is a professional travel and wildlife photographer specialising in Africa. She runs the Africa Image Library. For photo requests, visit www. africaimagelibrary.co.za or contact her on ariadne@hixnet.co.za.

want a vehicle or boat to yourself, this can go up to about US$75 for a day's outing. Snorkelling trips are around US$30 whilst a single dive to local reefs starts at US$35; both activities command a supplement if conducted on the reefs off Mnemba Island, which ranges from US$15–60. PADI Open Water dive certification courses range from US$450–700; centres are now obliged to sell the teaching material (around US$50) for these courses, but this is not always included in the price. Game-fishing trips are notoriously costly with a half-day coming in at around US$500. Entry to most of the historical sites and ruins on the island is free, as is lying on the beach!

ACCOMMODATION

For visitors to Zanzibar, the accommodation and food available are amongst the most important aspects of a visit. This section describes briefly what you can expect, but these things do change with time and you should be ready for this.

Aside from style, throughout the guide, the accommodation listings have been subdivided into six price brackets to help you choose something best suited to your budget. The price code is based on the nightly cost of a standard double room.

Hotels offering full-board (FB) or all-inclusive stays have details of their rates at the time of going to print, to help with budget planning.

HOTELS AND GUESTHOUSES

Zanzibar Town At the upper end of the range, Zanzibar Town has had only one large, international-standard hotel for decades: the Serena Inn, part of a chain of other properties in Tanzania and Kenya. Double rooms cost around US$265. In 2013, Hilton will open in this bracket and, quite possibly, Four Seasons too. There is little else in Stone Town of the same quality and size, although several grand old buildings have been renovated and opened as quite lovely, smaller boutique hotels. They combine good quality with local flavour and often some style, although they lack some of the extensive facilities of the Serena. Prices range from US$125–300 for a double room.

Zanzibar Town has a wide choice of mid-range hotels, costing between US$50 and US$120 for a double, where rooms are en suite, clean and comfortable, perhaps with air conditioning at the upper end of the scale.

At the lower end of the price range there are many small hotels and guesthouses which offer a basic room for US$10–20 per person. Rooms may not be spotless, and facilities are likely to be shared, but these are generally popular with budget travellers and it's worth looking around for the better places. All hotels in Zanzibar include breakfast in the room price, unless otherwise stated.

Zanzibar Island Around Zanzibar Island, away from Zanzibar Town, nearly all of the hotels and guesthouses are built on, or very near, idyllic tropical beaches, complete with palm trees, white sand and warm blue waters. Some travellers come here for a couple of days, just to relax; others linger for weeks. Places to stay range from large hotels and resorts with many facilities to small but comfortable lodges and bungalows to very basic local-style guesthouses. More recently, this range includes private villa rentals.

At the top end are a dozen or so fairly stylish, **smaller beach lodges** which cater to individual visitors, usually on pre-arranged trips. Typically they'll have between about ten and 30 rooms. Staying here you can expect good food, very comfortable accommodation and a fairly exclusive atmosphere. Expect to pay around US$75–

Rates for a standard double room

Exclusive	♛	US$300 plus
Luxury	$$$$$	US$200–300
Upmarket	$$$$	US$100–200
Mid range	$$$	US$50–100
Budget	$$	US$25–50
Shoestring	$	Below US$25

250 per person per night for somewhere smart – or considerably more in the case of Mnemba.

Next there are a number of **large beach resorts**, with upwards of 50 rooms each. These are generally used by pre-booked package tourists who fly in and spend most or all of their time on Zanzibar within the resort. Some focus so clearly on packages bought overseas (typically in Italy) that their rates are in euros, and they will not even accept 'walk-in' guests.

At the **lower end of the market**, US$10–60 will give you a night at one of a diverse range of places. These have little in common except that they normally deal largely with walk-in guests. At the better places, reservations are recommended during the busy season. There's a huge choice, ranging from places that are aspiring to be the next exclusive beach lodge, down to basic bungalows beside a beach where even if you did succeed in reserving a room (if they had a phone, and if it was working), it would be a very unusual thing to do.

As the number of tourists visiting Zanzibar continues to grow, the number of places on Zanzibar's coast – and the range of places – increases also. Expect to find more new places when you arrive, and expect a few old places to have disappeared or been renamed.

Pemba and Mafia Visitor numbers to Pemba and Mafia are absolutely minuscule compared with Zanzibar; these islands therefore offer far less choice. Mafia's clutch of small beach lodges represents particularly good value if you value a fairly high degree of exclusivity without wanting anything that is too luxurious or expensive. Pemba has only a few real beach lodges, all very different.

SELF-CATERING Cooking for yourself is not common at all. A few budget hotels and guesthouses might allow you to use the kitchen, but this would be very unusual. For places that do allow self-catering, this is always noted in our listings. Perhaps the obvious candidates are Flame Tree Cottages and Mnarani Beach Cottages, both in Nungwi, and the trio of Zi Villa properties or Che Che Vule in Matemwe.

In a relatively recent trend, there are several private villas for rent, based all across the island. Whilst these in theory would allow for self-catering, they invariably come fully staffed with a chef prepared to shop and cater to your party's needs.

CAMPING Informal camping on Zanzibar is illegal and, as yet, there are no official campsites on the islands. Camping is permitted in the grounds of some budget hotels on the coast, but this is far from usual as the hotels are so cheap anyway.

PAYMENTS AND RESERVATIONS Officially, all non-Tanzanian visitors must pay hotel bills in foreign currency, usually US dollars, so all prices are quoted in this currency. Residents and citizens are sometimes charged lower rates (typically 50–80% of the visitor rate), and can usually pay in Tanzanian shillings (TSh). In many places foreigners can also pay in TSh – at the current rate of exchange so it makes no difference to the price – but US dollars are usually easier to carry and deal with. Smaller hotels often accept only cash. Larger and smarter hotels (typically over the 'US$50 per night' bracket) will usually accept credit cards, and sometimes accept US dollar travellers' cheques – although many will add a surcharge of 5–15% for the privilege. To avoid surprises, always check a hotel's policy on payments before reserving a room.

Hotels and lodges which remain open during the low season (March to early June) often have substantially lower prices then. Conversely, many places will charge additional premiums (over and above their normal high-season rates) for accommodation over Christmas and the New Year. At any time of year, rates may be negotiable if you're in a small group (six people or more), or plan to stay for a long time (more than about five or six nights); this is especially true of the smaller, lower-budget lodges and hotels.

If you intend to stay in budget hotels and lodges, then it is usually possible simply to arrive and get a room on the spot; there's normally lots of choice. However, the smartest hotels and lodges on these islands are generally the busiest, and for them, advance reservations are always wise, if not essential. Unless you book at least three to four months in advance, it can be difficult to secure consecutive nights at any of the island's top 20 or so beach lodges between July and October.

Communications by phone, fax and email are all possible, but allow between three and five weeks for a reply by normal mail!

EATING AND DRINKING

RESTAURANTS In **Zanzibar Town** there are several good restaurants catering specifically for visitors, specialising in local dishes, seafood or curries; meals usually cost between US$7 and US$20 per person. There are also smarter restaurants, where prices are a little higher.

Zanzibar Town also has restaurants where meals and snacks are less elaborate and prices are around US$5–7. There are also some small eating-houses catering mainly for local people where you can eat for around US$2–3. They usually only have one or two types of food available, such as stew and rice, but they also serve chapattis, samosas and other snacks.

Outside Zanzibar Town, in the smaller towns and villages on Zanzibar, Pemba and Mafia, there are relatively few places to eat. Local people tend to eat in their

RESTAURANT PRICE CODES		
Average prices for a single main meal		
Gastronomic	$$$$$	US$15 plus
Creative cooking	$$$$	US$10–15
Mid range	$$$	US$5–10
Cheap & cheerful	$$	US$3–5
Rock bottom	$	US$1–3

Between December and March is the main mango time on Zanzibar, and the markets are full of these tasty green-to-yellow fruits. From March to mid June it's the wet season (*masika*), when pineapples are plentiful, and July to September is when oranges are in abundance.

own houses and there are not enough tourists around yet to create a substantial market for cafés and restaurants. On the coast, hotels and guesthouses usually have restaurants attached, where food and service generally reflect the overall standard of the accommodation. A few small restaurants have opened by the most popular beaches, catering for the growing influx of visitors.

You have to try hard to really splash out on food in Zanzibar, but throughout this book listed restaurants are accompanied with a price code to give an indication of expense.

CAFÉS AND BARS In Zanzibar Town, many places serve drinks as well as food, although at busy times you may be required to buy a meal rather than have a drink on its own. You can buy international and Tanzanian brands of fizzy drink, plus local and imported beers. Prices vary greatly according to where you drink: a bottle of Coke from a shop or small backstreet café costs US$1, and may cost four times this in a smarter café or restaurant. A bottle of local beer (including Safari, Tusker or Kilimanjaro) costs US$1.50 in a local bar, and at least double this in smarter places.

At larger hotels and restaurants in Zanzibar Town or on the coast you can also buy imported beers, wines (mostly from South Africa) and spirits.

SELF-CATERING If you plan to provide for yourself in Zanzibar Town, there are several shops selling locally produced bread and cakes, plus a reasonable choice of food in tins and packets imported from Kenya and beyond. Zanzibar Town has a market that's good for fruit and vegetables, plus fresh meat and fish if you have a means of cooking it. Other towns have small markets where you can buy meat, fish, fruit and vegetables, and shops with a limited but adequate supply of tinned food.

PUBLIC HOLIDAYS

The islands share most public holidays with the rest of Tanzania. Offices and businesses are usually closed on these days, although some tour companies remain open. Public holidays with fixed dates include:

1 January	New Year
12 January	Mapinduzi 'Revolution' Day
7 April	Sheikh Abeid Amani Karume Day
26 April	Union Day: Zanzibar and Tanganyika
1 May	Workers' Day
7 July	*Saba Saba* (Seven Seven)
8 August	Peasants' and Farmers' Day
14 October	Nyerere Day
9 December	Independence Day
25 December	Christmas Day
26 December	Boxing Day

Christmas Day, Boxing Day, New Year's Day and Easter are public holidays, although many tour companies stay open, and celebrations are low key on this largely Muslim island.

The Muslim feasts of Idd il Fitri – the end of Ramadan – and Idd il Maulidi (also called Maulidi ya Mfunguo Sita) – Muhammad's birthday – are celebrated by many people and are effectively public holidays. Dates of these holidays depend on the lunar calendar, and fall 11 or 12 days earlier every year. Approximate dates for Ramadan for the next few years are as follows:

2013   9 July–7 August
2014   28 June–27 July
2015   18 June–16 July

On Revolution Day (12 January), don't be surprised if you hear live gunfire from the army barracks or even heavy anti-aircraft artillery fire (also live!) from warships moored off Zanzibar Town, particularly at night (when the tracer makes a nice arc through the sky). It's just the military celebrating – not another revolution!

WATERSPORTS

These islands have some superb destinations for divers, fishermen (and women) and watersports enthusiasts, and even if you're only a casual snorkeller or angler, there's plenty to attract you. Some diving and fishing companies are based in Zanzibar Town, but most operate from the coastal hotels around the islands (for details on the best seasons for diving and fishing, see box, *Zanzibar diving and fishing seasons*, page 113).

DIVING Diving is an important element of an increasing number of people's trips, so here are some general comments on the various areas for diving around the islands. See individual sections for more details.

Dive sites The seas around these islands offer some of the best diving conditions in the Indian Ocean. As well as coral reefs, the marine life is also a major attraction. All around the islands you'll find coral and colourful reef fish, while encounters with larger fish such as groupers, barracudas, sharks, rays and mantas, plus turtles, dolphins and even whales, are possible at the better dive sites.

Off the west coast of Zanzibar Island, and within easy reach of Zanzibar Town, are numerous small islands, sandbanks and reefs where divers can experience good corals with slopes and drop-offs. There are also some good sites for experienced divers, including a couple of wrecks (there are no wrecks on the east coast).

Off the north coast and northern part of the east coast are many more reefs. There's also Mnemba Island (sometimes more fancifully termed Mnemba Atoll). This tiny island stands on the edge of a much larger circular coral reef upon which you'll find some of the finest dive sites on this stretch of the east African coast. These days it is popular though, and so you'll find many dive boats floating above different sites on this reef; all come from around Nungwi and Zanzibar's northeast coast. Tumbatu Island also has some good reefs, used by one or two of the operations in Kendwa and Nungwi.

One long barrier reef runs along virtually the whole of the **east coast of Zanzibar Island**. Although this is seldom quite as colourful as the Mnemba reef, it does offer good variation between its different sites, and many are good. You are much more likely to be on your own here, especially towards the south, than anywhere around the northern tip of Zanzibar.

Southwest Zanzibar has long been ignored with few divers being able to dive here, but the relatively new dive centres at Fumba Beach Lodge (page 000) and Unguja Lodge (page 323) are changing this. On the evidence so far, the diving here is a match for anywhere around Zanzibar, with the possible exception of some of the best Mnemba reefs. However, with usually no other divers or boats around, the whole experience here is arguably much better.

Pemba Island, and the numerous smaller islands nearby, has some spectacular diving spots. A number of Pemba's wall and drift dives are notable for variable and strong currents, and so are really more suitable for very experienced divers – hence the island is a favourite amongst live-aboard operations.

Mafia Island, by contrast, has a real mix. Inside Chole Bay is generally sheltered and shallow; an ideal place for novice divers to learn with some lovely, gentle diving. Outside the bay is more dramatic fare, capable of surprising even experienced divers with big ocean fish and breathtaking sights, including a particularly spectacular ocean-facing coral wall. The corals here probably aren't generally as lush as Mnemba's – but larger fish are much more common.

Dive companies The main diving seasons are outlined in the box, *Zanzibar diving and fishing seasons*, page 113, but it's worth noting that at any time of year, the east coast areas are exposed to the Indian Ocean swell, while the west coast tends to be more sheltered.

LICENCE TO DIVE

PADI International recognises that there can be issues with some unlicensed dive centres and instructors passing themselves off as registered centres, particularly in remote locations. Their advice to all divers is 'don't take anything at face value – certificates, flags and branding can be forged and obtained outside official channels'. In a bid to combat these unscrupulous operations and individuals, PADI has set up a searchable database of licensed members and resorts so that divers can access reliable, up-to-date information (*www.padi.com/english/common/search/dcnr*). It is equally possible to search by location for instructors and companies that are under investigation or have been suspended. It may be wise to check both before donning any sub-aqua kit.

With all dive centres, PADI registered or not, divers are well advised to talk with the staff (and management where possible) to ascertain their commitment to providing a quality service. Are they eager to listen? Do they understand the kind of dive experience sought? Are they willing, perhaps even eager, to prove their credentials? Are they willing to demonstrate the quality of their equipment before requiring a commitment to hire or dive with it? Can they demonstrate that the air in the cylinders is from a reputable source, and is recently certified as clean (air quality should be sampled and checked quarterly)? Is there a sense of pride among the staff that they are working for a trustworthy and reputable company?

There are many operations on Zanzibar, Pemba and Mafia offering safe, enjoyable diving, with well-maintained modern equipment, clean air and a keen eye for customer service, but asking questions and getting a feel for an operation is critical before taking the decision to venture underwater.

The diving operators on the island are detailed within the individual chapters of this book, under the relevant area section. Prices for dives vary slightly between them, but of the main, and arguably best, centres, there is little difference between them. Pricing is invariably in US dollars, with good reductions available for multi-dive packages.

Diving is a dangerous sport and some of the better operators will insist on divers doing a formal refresher course if they have not been underwater within the previous six months. Treat this as a valuable reintroduction, and a testament that the dive centre takes safety seriously; it's a sensible precaution.

Nearly all the dive centres on the islands are based at hotels and beach lodges, and can be contacted either directly or through the hotel/lodge. With the exception of Mnemba, you rarely need to be staying at a hotel to use the dive centre facilities, although some places give a discount to guests. The individual dive operations are listed in the relevant areas in which they operate, but there are a few centres on Zanzibar Island (as well as on Pemba and Mafia) that are worthy of mention for appearing to us (we're divers, although we're not specialist dive-centre inspectors) to offer especially high-quality trips, and for displaying a responsible attitude towards safety and their community.

On Zanzibar Island, listed clockwise by location from Zanzibar Town, our pick from the sub-aqua scene: the largest of the dive chains, **One Ocean** with centres in Stone Town and several on the east coast; **Scuba Do Diving** in the heart of Kendwa Beach; long-established **East Africa Diving & Watersport Centre** on Nungwi's West Beach; **Zanzibar Watersports** at Ras Nungwi Beach Hotel and Paradise Bungalows in Nungwi and Kendwa Rocks; **Mnemba Island Lodge Dive Centre** (for guest use only); **Rising Sun Dive Centre** at Breezes Beach Club and Royal Zanzibar; and **Fumba Beach Lodge Dive Centre** in the island's southwest.

Courses Most – but not all – of Zanzibar's dive operators are affiliated with PADI, and offer at least the introductory courses. Of these, the most popular is Discover Scuba which, for around US$90 per person, incorporates a theory session, usually based in a pool, followed by a boat dive to around 40ft (12m). The course may be completed in half a day, but is sometimes spread out over a day with a break for lunch.

The first of PADI's certification courses is the Open Water, which includes tuition in both diving theory and practical skills, and four open-water dives. Prices for this start at around US$450, rising to over US$700. Rates for the Advanced course, which incorporates five dives, are slightly lower than those for the Open Water, which is a prerequisite. As a rule, all of these 'entry' courses include equipment; for more advanced courses, equipment hire may incur an additional charge.

The equivalent Open Water referral (where the classroom element has been completed in advance) comes in at nearer US$400. PADI (*www.padi.com*) has recently introduced **PADI eLearning**, a new way in which prospective divers can take the Open Water course. Applicants nominate a dive operator, then complete all the paperwork online while still at home. They then print out the results, and take them down to their chosen operator, who will conduct the practical part of the course, and pose an 18-question review. While costs are the same as for taking the course in the more traditional way, the benefits are significant in terms of convenience at home, as well as time saved when on holiday. Several dive centres have signed up to this scheme and highly encourage clients to make use of the system.

Nitrox diving is gaining popularity for the extended bottom time it can give at shallow depths. By adjusting the mix of air in a tank to 32/68 oxygen/nitrogen

If you are coming to Zanzibar specifically for scuba diving, there are some points you need to know. Diving is possible at any time of year, and divers visit different parts of the archipelago according to conditions. Having said that, most people avoid the main rainy season from March/April to May, even though during this period there can be some very good days. The weather is especially changeable at this time, and in less than an hour can switch from beautifully calm and sunny conditions to a full-blown tropical rainstorm, reducing visibility on the surface to a few hundred metres and churning up the water.

Generally speaking, from June/July to October, when the winds come from the south, the northern coasts of Zanzibar Island and Pemba Island are better, although during August some days can offer perfect conditions, while on other days the sea may be rough. September to December is usually the calmest time, and from November to February/March, the southern coasts are preferred, as the winds come from the north. Pemba enjoys some of its best visibility of the year in February.

At any time of year the western sides are more sheltered, while the eastern sides (the ocean side) are more prone to swells and rough days. As in many other parts of the world, the weather and sea conditions on Zanzibar are unpredictable and there's always a chance of a bad day during the 'good' times, and perfect conditions at the heart of the 'bad' times.

If you're seriously into game fishing, the best time is from August to March, although conditions are also reasonable from July to September. August to November boasts excellent sport fishing for yellowfin tuna, sailfish and marlin. Marlin are even more prevalent between November and March during the billfish season, when striped marlin are positively prolific (schools of up to ten recorded) and blue and black marlin are common.

(the norm is 21/79), divers can dive to a maximum of 30m (100ft) but can stay at that depth for up to 30 minutes on a first dive. On 50/50 oxygen/nitrogen, divers are limited to 9–12m (30–40 ft) but bottom time is increased by up to 50%. Nitrox certification is offered by only a handful of companies on Zanzibar. It takes two days for an initial course, and costs around US$300.

SNORKELLING Most of the dive centres mentioned above will also cater for snorkellers, by hiring out snorkels and fins. You'll have to take a boat from virtually all the lodges and hotels throughout the islands in order to reach decent reefs for snorkelling. Some places will offer excursions of an hour, at other places snorkelling is a half-day trip and you'll share the boat with divers.

Off the west coast of Zanzibar Island, Chumbe Island stands out as having some of the best-preserved and most easily accessible coral in the region; it really is in pristine condition, outshining any of the coral gardens known elsewhere near the islands.

Off the northeast coast, the house reef close to the shore on the western side of Mnemba Island is used by many lodges from Nungwi and the northeast coast. Residents of Mnemba have the relaxing luxury of being able to walk into the water rather than sail for several hours to get there, but they share the same reef. Further south, on **Zanzibar's southeast coast**, snorkelling is along the main barrier reef.

Planning and Preparation WATERSPORTS

4

The **southwest of Zanzibar** has been explored relatively little compared with most of Zanzibar's other areas, although it's perhaps worth noting that the teams from Safari Blue and Eco+Culture (see page 338) offer snorkelling on the tiny islands south of Fumba.

The place most often used for snorkelling off **Pemba** is known as Misali Island. After a speedboat ride here from Fundu Lagoon, you can snorkel from the beach (often while the boat takes divers elsewhere to dive). Live-aboards obviously have more scope, although they tend to concentrate on the diving rather than snorkelling.

From the lodges on **Mafia Island**, snorkelling is usually an hour or two's gentle dhow ride away. The reefs around the mouth of Chole Bay are interesting and quite tidal; the sandbanks exposed by the ocean around low tide are idyllic – magical empty places to laze around, beachcomb and snorkel from the beach.

FISHING The waters around Zanzibar and Pemba islands offer some of the best fishing in the world, especially the Pemba Channel, between Zanzibar and Pemba islands, or around Mafia Island, south of Zanzibar. Big-game fish include barracuda, kingfish, sailfish, billfish, wahoo, dorado and blue marlin.

Fishing companies There are several fishing companies based on Zanzibar: some are experienced and reputable, others seem less so. When making bookings or enquiries you should ask about the equipment they use: what type is it? How suitable is it for big-game fishing? How old is it? How often is it serviced? Ask about safety equipment too: are the boats fitted with radios? Do they carry spare outboard motors, life jackets and so on? You may also feel it important to assess their 'catch and release' ethos; with numbers of big-game fish dwindling, 'catch and release' really should be the norm.

A few of the dive centres listed above can also organise fishing trips on request, or Mtoni Marine (page 202) can also put you in touch with game-fishing operators on the north and east coasts. Serious game-fishermen may be best starting their enquiries with **Zanzibar Watersports**, **Fishing Zanzibar** and **Game Fish Lodge**, all in Nungwi (pages 228 and 236–7).

SHOPPING

If you're looking for souvenirs, collectables or gifts to take home, then the islands have a lot to offer. Most of the shops and stalls are in Zanzibar Town (see *Chapter 6, Shopping*, page 171), but you can also buy things at many of the lodges and hotels elsewhere. The villages do not tend to have much in the way of curios visibly displayed as in other African countries, though some beaches now have Maasai market stalls.

Zanzibar Town market is particularly good for the aromatic spices that make Zanzibar so famous. Wander around the Old Town to find endless shops and stalls selling wooden carvings; paintings in the Tingatinga (see page 44) style and others; jewellery in stone, gold and silver; models or mobiles made from coconut shells; and a plethora of other souvenirs. Carved boxes inlaid with shells, or decorated with hammered brass, are very popular.

Several curio shops sell antiques and original hand-crafted pieces; very many more sell genuine junk. Some antiques have been brought to the islands by Arab or Indian traders in the last couple of centuries; virtually all are now reproductions. The Zanzibar clocks, originally used by Zanzibari merchants, are unique. Carpets, rugs and mats, made in the Persian or Arab style, are easy to carry home. Traditional

Zanzibar furniture, such as tables, beds and wardrobes decorated with stained glass and mirrors, can be found but these are less easy to get back!

Some shops still sell shells and coral, taken from the reefs and beaches around the islands. They wouldn't do this if thoughtless visitors didn't buy them. This trade encourages people to catch and collect live molluscs, and to break off live coral. Reefs take decades to grow, and if you buy these items, then you are helping to degrade, and eventually destroy, the islands' fascinating marine life.

You may also see turtle shells, or items made from turtle-shell such as bracelets or earrings. Again, turtles are an endangered species in Zanzibar and you should not buy these things (for more details, see *Sea turtles*, page 69). Similarly, in this part of the world, anything made from ivory is likely to have come from a poached elephant: avoid it. All of the above marine objects are illegal to export, so beware if you do try to take anything through the airport.

For the very best in quality and ethics, visit some of the 'Made in Zanzibar' suppliers detailed under *Made in Zanzibar*, page 171.

MEDIA AND COMMUNICATIONS

MEDIA Unlike mainland Tanzania's vibrant and diverse media scene, Zanzibar's independent press has had a rough ride. In November 2003, *Dira*, the island's first post-revolution, independent newspaper, was forced to cease publication after the Zanzibar government alleged that it had violated registration procedures and professional ethics. The popular private paper had been previously almost bankrupted by a huge libel fine of TSh660 million (about US$500,000) following the publication of 'false and harmful' reports about the Zanzibar president's family: namely two articles that accused his children of using their father's influence to buy up state-owned companies.

Following this, a period ensued where, in spite of international pressure to allow free expression, the media scene was wholly government-run; private broadcasters and newspaper publishers were banned. Then, at the end of 2005, 13 new private publications were granted licences, including four newspapers: *Zanzibar Wiki Hii*, *Marhaba*, *ZIFF* and *Fahari*. However, it must be noted that their content is far from independent and impartial. State-operated TV Zanzibar and its radio counterpart, Voice of Tanzania-Zanzibar, still dominate, and continue to act as a channel for government opinion, with little, if any, room for political criticism of those in power. The current media environment may be private but it is far from wholly independent, with strict laws effectively leading to some censorship.

That said, things are improving, with the media opening up with the advent of the coalition government. International media rights organisation Reporters Without Borders, who campaign for global press freedom and the right to be informed, see real improvements on the island. Press laws may be stricter than on the mainland, with rigorous local government monitoring, but the situation has visibly eased. Censorship and harassment have declined, and access to the mainland media has increased for the local population.

Many Zanzibaris now receive local and mainland (independent) broadcast channels, and satellite television is increasingly widespread. The BBC World Service is also available on FM in both Zanzibar and Pemba.

Looking to the future, it is possible that the combination of allowing a private press to operate, and the creation of a revised Freedom of Information Act, will continue to improve press freedom on the islands.

Changes to telephone codes are a frequent occurrence in Tanzania, Zanzibar and the other archipelago islands. Every effort has been made to ensure this book is accurate; however, further numeric variations are inevitable in the future. The key dialling codes and most significant recent changes are detailed here.

CALLS TO ZANZIBAR The area code for all of Zanzibar (Zanzibar Island and Pemba Island) is 024, if you are calling from elsewhere in Tanzania, Kenya or Uganda. For calls from other countries, individual numbers must be prefixed with the international code for Tanzania +255, then 24 for Zanzibar (minus the first 0).

CALLS WITHIN ZANZIBAR Calling within Zanzibar, you simply dial the number you want, without the 024 area code. For emergency calls dial 112, and for directory enquiries dial 118.

CALLS FROM ZANZIBAR Phoning out of Zanzibar to mainland Tanzania, Kenya or Uganda, you will need the city or area code, followed by the individual number. For all other countries, it is necessary to dial the international access code (000), plus the country code (eg: 1 for USA, 44 for Britain, 27 for South Africa), followed by the city or area code (minus the first 0), then the individual number.

Area codes on the Tanzanian mainland that have changed include:

Area	Code	Area	Code
Dar es Salaam	022	Mtwara	023
Tanga	027	Dodoma	026
Arusha	027	Tabora	026
Kilimanjaro	027	Mwanza	028

POST Most towns and large villages on these islands have post offices, or at the least a postal collection, but it's best to send all your mail from Zanzibar Town. The main poste restante service for Zanzibar is also in Zanzibar Town (see page 178). The post service is reliable, with letters taking about a week to ten days to reach destinations in Europe and North America (Australia takes a bit longer). Letters to destinations inside Tanzania cost about US$0.20, while postcards to countries outside Africa are about US$0.50 (slightly more for letters).

TELEPHONE AND FAX The best place on the islands for calling from a landline is the public call office, next to the old post office in Zanzibar Town. There are several private phone bureaux around here also. International calls to Europe or the USA cost between US$2.50 and US$5 per minute, depending on where you go. Note that most places charge per full minute; go over by one second and you might as well speak for the next 59 (more details are given in *Chapter 6, Zanzibar Town*, page 178). Elsewhere on the islands the better hotels and lodges will usually allow guests to make international calls, although rates are high.

There are now a handful of mobile phone (cell phone) networks and increasingly good signal coverage in the islands. These work around most larger towns and main arteries, and increasingly in more isolated spots too. You'll get a signal in most parts of Zanzibar Island, in the busier areas of Pemba Island and Mafia and even in the lodges on Mafia Island, and the exclusive Mnemba Island.

If you're bringing a mobile phone from home, those with GSM capability should work here; check with your own service provider before you depart.

For longer stays, consider picking up a Tanzanian SIM card to cut costs; details of how best to do this are given in the Zanzibar Town section (see *Chapter 6*, page 178).

INTERNET Most of the phone bureaux in Zanzibar Town also offer internet services, and there are an ever-increasing number of dedicated internet bureaux. More details and specific locations are given in *Chapter 6, Zanzibar Town*, page 179.

BUSINESS HOURS

Most shops and travel company offices in Zanzibar Town are open every day, although some close on Fridays, the Muslim holy day, or on Sundays, the official day off. Normal business hours are from between 08.00 and 09.00 until noon, then from 13.00 or 14.00 until 17.00 or 18.00. Some private shops and tour agencies take a longer break at midday and stay open later in the evening. In the low season, some souvenir shops stay closed, while others open mornings only. Government offices and banks are closed on Saturdays and Sundays; post offices are closed Saturday afternoons and Sundays. Opening hours on Pemba and Mafia are similar, but less predictable.

TRAVELLING RESPONSIBLY

CULTURAL ETIQUETTE

- Dress and act sensitively: locals consider revealing clothing or public displays of affection offensive. Keep swimwear for the beach, and in towns or villages keep your upper legs and shoulders covered. Sporting bare chests or bikini tops as you stroll around the market is the height of rudeness and arrogance.
- Support locally owned, small-scale shops and businesses. This is the best way for your money to benefit the grass-roots economy.

STUFF YOUR RUCKSACK – AND MAKE A DIFFERENCE

www.stuffyourrucksack.com is a website set up by TV's Kate Humble which enables travellers to give direct help to small charities, schools or other organisations in the country they are visiting. Maybe a local school needs books, a map or pencils, or an orphanage needs children's clothes or toys – all things that can easily be 'stuffed in a rucksack' before departure. The charities get exactly what they need and travellers have the chance to meet local people and see how and where their gifts will be used.

The website describes organisations that need your help and lists the items they most need. Check what's needed in Zanzibar, contact the organisation to say you're coming and bring not only the much-needed goods but an extra dimension to your travels and the knowledge that in a small way you have made a difference.

- Buy locally made crafts, but avoid wildlife products, such as ivory, skins, coral, shells from turtles or any other kind of marine animal, and even wooden carvings, unless the material comes from a sustainable renewable source.
- Always ask permission before photographing local people. And accept refusals.
- Non-Muslims should not enter mosques without permission.
- During the holy month of Ramadan, local people fast, and you can show understanding for this tradition by not eating or drinking in public places (eating in tourist restaurants is fine).

GIVING SOMETHING BACK Shopping in some of the fair-trade shops listed in the *Made in Zanzibar* section, page 171, booking through an ethical tour operator and donating money to lodge-sponsored community projects are all ways in which visitors to Zanzibar are able to actively contribute to the social and environmental development of the island and its poorest communities. For those who would like to take that a step further, we have listed a few local NGOs (Non-Governmental Organisations) on the island which seem to be doing excellent charity and development work, and very much need sustained support.

During our research, we visited and contacted a number of possible NGOs, but we know from experience that they're not always good at responding to enquiries – perhaps partly due to the pressures that they're under, and partly due to the limitations of their communications. A few stood out for not only doing some great work, but also for having a clear mission, good leadership and relatively easy communication channels. We have listed them here for travellers keen to 'give something back' in a real sense when they visit or return from a trip to Zanzibar.

Hands Across Borders Society (HABS) PO Box 210, Jambiani or c/o Dr Stan Marcus, 3831 Blenkinsop Rd, Victoria, BC V8P 3P6, Canada; ☎ +1 250 721 9009; e habszanzibar@yahoo.ca; www.handsacrossborderssociety.org. HABS was established in 1999 in British Columbia. Its main priority is to provide complementary health & education services to communities in need within the developing world, including from its excellent base in Jambiani on Zanzibar Island. In addition to providing complementary health-care services & education to the villagers at its Chiropractic Wellness Centre, HABS is also involved in assisting & funding a number of other village projects & amenities, with the most recent being the construction of the Jambiani Tourism Institute where local people are now trained to help them secure employment in the burgeoning hotel scene.

Health-care practitioners are welcome to volunteer here for placements of 1 month & over, financial contributions are gratefully received to fund everything from electricity to supplies, & unlike many charities, the Jambiani base is happy to receive material donations from walk-in visitors. The most useful supplies to donate are orthopaedic supports, straps, bandages, Deep Cold & antibiotic creams.

Health Improvement Project: Zanzibar (HIPZ) Rosehill, Broomfield, Bridgwater, Somerset TA5 2EL, UK; ☎ 01823 451 510; e team@ makunduchi.com; www.makunduchiproject. com. Registered as a charity in 2006, HIPZ is an ambitious health-care development scheme, being spearheaded by 2 British consultant surgeons. It aims to establish a unique public/ private partnership with the Zanzibar government to improve health care in Zanzibar through fundraising & professional support. Their original & flagship project, is to renovate, equip & run the district hospital in Makunduchi (southern Zanzibar), where many of the 60,000 locals currently have little or no access to health care. Such is their current success that HIPZ have recently taken on another hospital.

Makunduchi Hospital is 1 of only 2 district Hospitals on Zanzibar, but its facilities have been neglected for years. HIPZ aim to build a new hospital, train local staff, provide medical & IT equipment, offer high standards of clinical care, & expand medical services to include everything from A&E to maternity & dental care. A significant recent success is the newly constructed maternity unit, which is now delivering comprehensive obstetric care free of charge, as well as operating an ambulance retrieval service to bring labouring women from remote communities to deliver safely in the unit. Hot on its heels, the children's ward is the next target for improvement. The hope is that the hospital will become a model for the introduction of similar facilities across the island, & that a sustainable, locally managed facility can vastly improve access to high-quality community healthcare.

SOS Children's Village Zanzibar St Andrew's Hse, 59 St Andrew's St, Cambridge CB2 3BZ, UK; ☎01223 365589; e info@sos-uk.org.uk; www. soschildrensvillages.org.uk. The Zanzibar SOS Children's Village was built in 1988, in a residential district near the airport. 11 family houses are now home to 120 orphaned & abandoned children, providing them with a safe place to live, a 'mother', love & care. The construction of a nursery school, primary & secondary school, health-care centre, sports fields & mosque, has led the village to become a real neighbourhood centre, serving the local community as well as the orphans. Away from the village, 3 youth houses are home to older children & young people taking their first steps towards independence. The orphanage is doing excellent work but it relies on the continued charity of many people: for financial donations to fund school books, desks, a generator, construction & renovation; gifts from footballs to pens; & child sponsorship. If you are interested in helping, they have a clear website which can accept donations & arrange child sponsorship. They're trying to provide as normal an environment as possible for their children & this understandably precludes impromptu visits from curious visitors, although existing sponsors are warmly welcomed.

Umoja wa Walemavu Zanzibar (UWZ) – Organisation of People with Disabilities in Zanzibar ☎024 2233719; e uwz@zanzinet. com; www.uwz.or.tz. Established in 1985, UWZ is a cross-disability organisation operating on Pemba & Unguja (Zanzibar Island). Their aim is to assist disabled people within the community in practical ways as well as championing their human rights. The group's stated vision: a society in which people with disabilities have equal rights, opportunities, respect & dignity. They are actively involved in training on disabled rights, policy & legislation, in addition to community work to provide support, rehabilitation, skills training (eg: sign language) & education to people with disabilities & their local communities.

Zanzibar Action Project (ZAP) The Old Buck, Church Lane, Sedgeford, Norfolk PE36 5NA, UK; ☎01485 570905; e (via website); www. zanzibaraction.co.uk. ZAP is a small UK-based charity, run by its founders Pat & Janie Preece. Dividing their time between England & Zanzibar, their aim with ZAP is to work in close partnership with the local community to provide sustainable medical, educational & vocational aid, concentrating on the area around Jambiani. It's a very community-driven organisation striving to ensure over 80% of its funding goes directly to diverse projects in the village. Current ZAP projects include a scheme to provide basic drugs, equipment & health-care education to the local government clinic; enabling volunteer teachers & retired doctors from the UK to work with the community on 3-month placements; running English, sewing & IT classes for women & teenagers; providing porridge for the nursery school; sponsoring vocational training for young people; & securing a grant to construct a much-needed concrete water tank.

Part Two

THE GUIDE

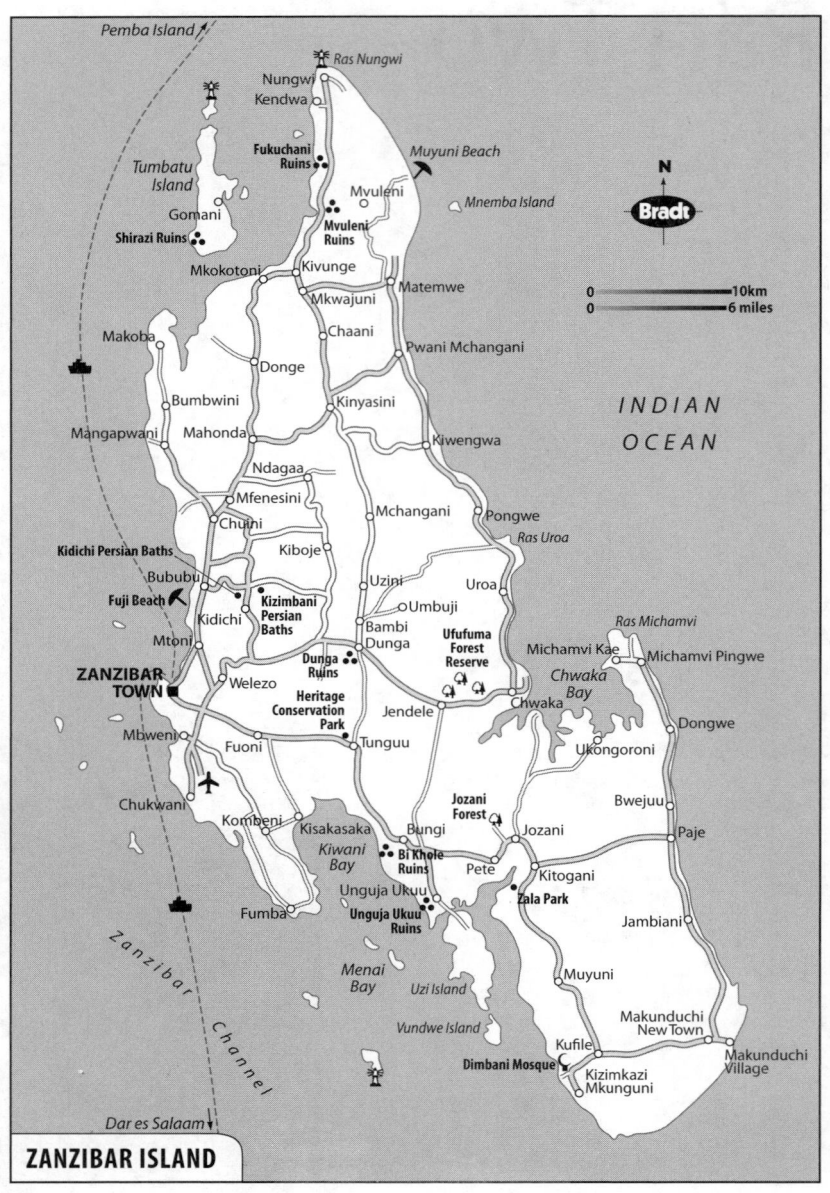

Pemba Island

Ras Nungwi
Nungwi
Kendwa
Muyuni Beach
Fukuchani Ruins
Tumbatu Island
Mvuleni
Mnemba Island
Gomani
Mvuleni Ruins
Shirazi Ruins
Mkokotoni
Kivunge
Matemwe
Mkwajuni
Makoba
Chaani
Pwani Mchangani
Donge
Bumbwini
Kinyasini
Mangapwani
Mahonda
Kiwengwa
Ndagaa
Mfenesini
Mchangani
Pongwe
Chuini
Ras Uroa
Kidichi Persian Baths
Kiboje
Bububu
Uzini
Uroa
Fuji Beach
Kizimbani Persian Baths
Umbuji
Kidichi
Bambi Dunga
Ufufuma Forest Reserve
Ras Michamvi
Mtoni
Michamvi Kae
Michamvi Pingwe
ZANZIBAR TOWN
Dunga Ruins
Welezo
Heritage Conservation Park
Chwaka Bay
Jendele
Chwaka
Dongwe
Mbweni
Fuoni
Tunguu
Ukongoroni
Chukwani
Jozani Forest
Bwejuu
Kombeni
Kisakasaka
Bungi
Jozani
Paje
Kiwani Bay
Bi Khole Ruins
Pete
Kitogani
Unguja Ukuu
Zala Park
Fumba
Unguja Ukuu Ruins
Jambiani
Menai Bay
Uzi Island
Muyuni
Vundwe Island
Makunduchi New Town
Kufile
Makunduchi Village
Dimbani Mosque
Kizimkazi Mkunguni

Zanzibar Channel

Dar es Salaam

INDIAN OCEAN

Bradt

N

0 ——————— 10km
0 ——————— 6 miles

ZANZIBAR ISLAND

5

Zanzibar Island Essentials

GETTING TO ZANZIBAR

International flights to Tanzania are covered in *Chapter 4*, pages 82–4. From mainland Tanzania, there are two main ways of reaching Zanzibar: plane or boat.

The gruelling and slightly cheaper option is by sea, using one of several boat services that cross daily between Zanzibar and Dar es Salaam. However, the vast majority of people arrive by air on one of the many reasonably priced, direct daily flights from Dar es Salaam, Arusha or Kilimanjaro International Airport (the last named lies roughly midway along the 80km road connecting the towns of Arusha and Moshi). Light aircraft flights (often via Dar) also link Zanzibar to Pemba and Mafia, as well as the more popular national parks and game reserves in northern and southern Tanzania.

BY AIR

Zanzibar's airport Located about 7km inland from the capital, the recently renamed Abeid Karume International Airport has not traditionally offered the best island welcome. Architecturally challenged, woefully small, ill-equipped and disorganised, it was not the greeting to 'paradise' one might hope.

However, after much neglect, recent years have seen Zanzibar's airport finally getting some attention and investment. In the first phase of work, 2010 saw the single runway extended and renovated to allow larger aircraft to land, paving the way for increased direct flights from long-haul destinations. Arguably, a more significant development has been the addressing of dire terminal facilities.

Funded by the Chinese, construction is now under way on an additional, modern international terminal building, with completion dates imminent, though not confirmed. This should certainly improve the waiting times and experience for long-haul, predominantly charter, passengers, and may even serve to ease pressure on the crumbling existing terminal for the Dar arrivals, though sadly any actual upgrades here seem unlikely.

International air arrivals If you are arriving or leaving Zanzibar on a large international flight (as is the case with most European charters), you will traditionally have queued outside for some time under the beating African sun. Long, slow, muddled queues necessitate a cool hat, some water and lots of patience. That said, hopefully by the time you arrive, the new terminal will be completed and the experience vastly improved. Be prepared for the worst until then though, especially if travelling with young children.

Tanzanian air arrivals Dar es Salaam's domestic terminal is a five-minute drive from the international terminal. If you already have a connection to Zanzibar booked you will be met at the international terminal and transferred in a small minibus. If you haven't arranged anything, take a taxi for a few dollars and seek out the next flight with space. Facilities are limited: there is no bureau de change, but a small souvenir shop has a good range of books, and you'll be able to get a decent coffee in the tiny Italian-owned café. Here – and for all internal flights – you will be asked to pay a departure tax of US$9 – made up of US$8 airport tax, and a further US$1 safety tax.

If you have arranged a tailor-made trip with a good tour company, then they will usually arrange for a member of staff to guide you through the check-in process and will often help you to circumvent any long queues for charter planes.

Scheduled flights
There are a number of scheduled flights from Dar es Salaam to Zanzibar, and although airfares vary slightly you should expect to pay around US$80 one-way from Dar es Salaam. Flights between Zanzibar and Pemba are US$105; Zanzibar and Mafia cost around US$160; Zanzibar to Selous are US$200; to Ruaha US$360; and up to Arusha (gateway to the parks of the northern circuit) US$250.

The main carriers on these routes are:

✈ **Air Tanzania (ATC)** ATC Bldg, Ohio St/Garden St, Dar es Salaam; ☎022 2118411, 0782 737 732 (Dar Airport); e info@airtanzania.com; www.airtanzania. co.tz. The national carrier flies daily between Dar es Salaam & Zanzibar, with same-day connection to flights to & from Johannesburg. In addition to their main office, they have a base at Dar Airport & within the Tembo Hotel, Zanzibar Town.

✈ **Coastal Aviation** 107 Upanga Rd, Dar es Salaam; ☎022 2117959 or 022 2842700/1 (Dar Airport) or 024 2233112, m 0713 670815 (Zanzibar Airport); e safari@coastal.cc; www. coastal.cc. A reliable small operator with a good reputation & strong network of scheduled flights connecting Zanzibar daily to Dar es Salaam, Arusha, Tanga, Pemba, Selous Game Reserve, Ruaha National Park, Mwanza, Serengeti, Ngorongoro & Manyara. In addition to Dar es Salaam, they have an office beside the Serena Hotel in Zanzibar's Kelele Sq.

✈ **Precision Air Flight Services** NIC Bldg, Samora/Pamba Rd, Dar es Salaam; ☎022 281211718; m 0748 550022 (Dar) or ☎024 2235126 (Zanzibar); e contactcentre@ precisionairtz.com; www.precisionairtz.com. This company has a few daily flights between Zanzibar & Dar, as well as connections to several other destinations in east Africa. There is an office in Dar as well as the desk at the Mazsons Hotel in Zanzibar Town.

✈ **ZanAir Limited** Malawi Rd, Zanzibar Town; ☎024 2233670/3768; branch office, Zanzibar Airport; ☎024 2233670; e reservations@zanair. com; www.zanair.com. Based on Zanzibar, with offices in Zanzibar Town & at the airport. There are 7 flights from Dar es Salaam to Zanzibar every day, & these usually tie in with the timetables of long-haul flights to/from Europe. There are also connecting flights to Selous, Arusha & Pemba.

Private charter flights
If you're in a hurry, or need to connect to another flight at a difficult time, then you can charter your own aircraft to get from Zanzibar to almost anywhere in east Africa. The charter planes are small, from three to eight seats, and best arranged well in advance. Private charters can be arranged with Precision, Coastal or ZanAir (listed above).

Customs and immigration
The island's customs and immigration officials used to have a reputation for being tough and corrupt, but today they're by and large polite, if somewhat disorganised. These days, most people arriving from Europe, Kenya or elsewhere, will fly via Dar es Salaam and clear Tanzanian customs and immigration there.

Some shoestring travellers have been approached by baggage porters at the ferry port, and been tempted into buying ferry tickets at the (cheaper) residents' rate, rather than the foreigners' rate. The porter offers to buy the ticket for you, then accompanies you onto the boat, explaining to 'their friend' the ticket collector about your temporary residential status. Then, once you're on board, the porter asks for (or demands) a tip – which is often more than the foreigners' ticket price. If you resist, you get reported to the no-longer-friendly ticket collector, who demands that you pay a costly fine. Resist that, and they'll call the police, who will no doubt be keen to extract their own, even more costly, fine. So you end up paying the porter more than the normal ferry price, and feeling cheap and embarrassed into the bargain. Now it's our turn for a tip: always pay the correct fare.

BY SEA

Zanzibar's port Zanzibar's main port is at the heart of Zanzibar Town's waterfront, towards the northern end of Mizingani Road. Several large passenger ships run daily between Dar es Salaam, Zanzibar and Pemba, and – more rarely – to other points on the mainland. As the number of flights between Dar and Zanzibar has increased, and their airfares have become more competitive, the number of passenger boat services has declined.

Ships that are used by occasional tourists are listed below. In both Dar es Salaam and Zanzibar Town, all the ship booking offices are at the main passenger port, very near the city centre. Schedules and prices are chalked up on boards outside each office and you can easily buy tickets on the spot. Reservations are not essential but if at all possible you should buy a ticket in advance (a few hours to a couple of days) to make sure. Non-Tanzanians usually have to pay in US dollars and prices are quoted in this currency; Tanzanian residents enjoy cheaper rates, and can pay in Tanzanian shillings.

Note that all non-Tanzanian passengers leaving Dar must pay a port departure tax of US$5. The departure tax office is near the ship booking offices, and tickets are carefully checked before you board. Most of the shipping companies include this charge in the ticket price, so check very carefully whether this is included to avoid unnecessarily paying again at the port tax office.

In Zanzibar, in particular, many touts and hustlers hang around the boat ticket offices, encouraging you to go to one company instead of another. This can be time-consuming, irritating and disconcerting, so as an alternative you can buy your ticket through one of the reliable tour companies listed on pages 134–7. This will often save time and hassle, and it usually does not cost you any more money (the tour company gets a commission from the shipping company). Some tour companies do charge extra for this service, however, so check before you make arrangements. At Dar es Salaam, there are fewer hustlers, but still it's best to decline assistance politely.

Travellers at the port have also reported problems from over-zealous porters. If you drive into the port by taxi, you might want to ask your taxi driver to carry your bags for an extra tip, simply to avoid hassle.

Passenger ships and ferries The main passenger ships used by visitors between Dar es Salaam and Zanzibar are:

⛴ Fast Ferries (*Sea Express I* & *Sea Express II*)
📞 024 2234690; m 0754 278692 (Zanzibar);
📞 022 2137049 (Dar); e info@fastferriestz.com;
www.fastferriestz.com. *Sea Express I* is a large
hydrofoil, with a capacity of 150 passengers,
which travels between Dar & Zanzibar twice daily
in each direction. The journey takes 2–2.5hrs.
Departures from Dar are at 09.00 & 11.30, arriving
Zanzibar around 11.30 & 14.00; departing Zanzibar
at 07.00 & 15.00 to head back to Dar. This boat
looks significantly more attractive than some that
ply the waters, though it is sometimes reported
to be unsteady in rough seas, & seasick bags are
not provided! There is limited deck space but
comfortable airline-style seating is provided inside.
Sea Express II, the company's newest vessel,
commenced operations between Dar, Zanzibar
Island & Pemba in Nov 2005. Travelling in a circuit
between the ports, it's worth checking locally
or online for the current schedule. At the time
of writing, Fast Ferries were departing Zanzibar
at noon daily for the 3hr crossing to Pemba, &
returning from Pemba to Zanzibar at 11.00 daily.
The office for Fast Ferries is on the right at the
far end of the parade between the port gates
& the water. One-way fares for non-residents:
Dar–Zanzibar US$35/40 economy/first; Zanzibar–
Pemba US$45/50 economy/first; Dar–Pemba
US$60/65 economy/first; child fares are reduced
by 30% on the Dar–Zanzibar route. They have an
excellent & clear website, which has timetables,
tariffs & an online booking facility.
⛴ *Mapinduzi* 📞 024 2230302/2857; www.
zanzibarshipping.com. Zanzibar Shipping
Corporation (ZSC), the state-owned line, runs the
Mapinduzi ('Revolution'), an old cargo-passenger
ship, between Dar & Zanzibar, & also between
Zanzibar & Pemba, & Dar & Mtwara on the southern
coast of mainland Tanzania. These services are used
by local people because they are cheap, & some
travellers on a tight budget also travel this way.
Although the boats are slow, the cabins are quite
airy & comfortable, & this is a pleasant way to travel
if you're in no hurry. The official schedule follows a
2-week pattern, although it is notoriously unreliable.
Fares: on the deck, around US$5; shared cabin
US$10; private cabin US$12
⛴ MV *Flying Horse* 📞 022 2124507 (Dar);
m 0784 472497/606177 (Zanzibar); e asc@raha.
com. This large catamaran, run by the African
Shipping Corporation, has a capacity of more

than 400 passengers. The daytime service from
Dar to Zanzibar departs at 12.30 daily & arrives
at 15.30. The return trip from Zanzibar departs at
21.00 daily, but does not arrive in Dar until 06.00
the following day. The boat runs deliberately
slowly, stopping at sea for a time on this overnight
journey so passengers don't have to disembark in
the middle of the night. The seating areas have
AC & an 'in-flight' video is usually shown. The ship
also has a small bar & restaurant. It's possible to
travel on the deck, which has a few seats & an
awning to keep off the sun, but little else. Some
travellers view this as a very pleasant way to travel,
especially when leaving Zanzibar port at sunset, &
for budget travellers it is a good way to save on a
night's accommodation. In Zanzibar, the booking
office is the first on the left inside the port gates.
Fares: US$25pp including a mattress for overnight
⛴ *Sea Bus* & *Kilimanjaro* 📞 024 2231655
(Zanzibar)/022 2123324 (Dar); m 0777 334347;
e azam@cats-net.com; www.azammarine.
com. The 2 large Sea Bus vessels are Australian-
built high-speed boats, owned by Azam Marine
Company, & both run once daily in either direction
between Zanzibar & Dar es Salaam, taking about
2hrs to make the crossing. *Sea Bus I* departs from
Dar at 10.30 & starts the return trip from Zanzibar
at 13.00. *Sea Bus II* departs from Zanzibar at
10.00 & starts the return trip from Dar at 16.00.
In addition there are a trio of catamarans named
Kilimanjaro I, *II* & *III*, & a new state-of-the-art
catamaran, *The Pride of Tanzania*, currently under
construction, & is expected in service by mid 2013.
Between them, the Kilimanjaro ferries sail 4 times
daily each way between Dar & Zanzibar (07.00,
09.30, 12.30, 15.30). On Mon, Thu & Sat there's
also a service running from Dar to Pemba, with
a 30min transit in Zanzibar. It departs Zanzibar
at 09.30 & 16.00 respectively. First-class tickets
US$40; second class US$35; children US$20, & all
can be booked online as well as portside.
⛴ Sea Star Services Ltd 📞 024 2234768;
m 0777 411505. This large catamaran is also
among the most efficient services between Dar es
Salaam & Zanzibar. With a grand-looking green
marble booking office at the port (relative to the
beach hut-style office occupied by others), tickets
can be bought for the once-daily departure to Dar
es Salaam. *Sea Star* departs Zanzibar for Dar at
07.00 for a 2hr crossing. Fares: first class US$35;
second class US$45

2011 SPICE ISLANDER FERRY DISASTER

On 10 September 2011, the MV *Spice Islander I*, a passenger and cargo ferry carrying around 3,500 people and goods from Zanzibar Town to Pemba, capsized and sank off the northern coast of Unguja. The carrying capacity of the ferry was 690, including crew, yet officially 2,967 people were reported missing or dead, 203 bodies were recovered from the sea and 619 passengers, many infured, were rescued. The ferry was woefully overloaded, and the consequences utterly tragic. The harrowing details recounted by rescue teams, made up of dive operators and fast ferries, are horrific: dead bodies afloat, desperate and drowning people clawing at crammed dive boats, and picturesque beaches littered with body bags and the injured. An official investigation into the sinking took place, and further accidents have happened since, so whether ferry operators genuinely address the issues of poor maintenance and overloading remains to be seen. What is abundantly clear though, is the need to be highly cautious in choosing to travel by local ferry. If it looks too busy – do not board the boat!

Traditional dhows Dhows do operate between Dar es Salaam, Zanzibar and the ports along the Swahili coast, but – following a spate of incidents in which tourists drowned – the government imposed strict safety standards on any dhows wanting to carry tourists. They now need to have radios, lifejackets and various other fairly standard pieces of marine safety equipment – which are notably lacking from most dhows!

We advise strongly against travelling illegally on any dhow unless the captain is very clearly aware of these regulations, and working within them. Not only is it illegal, but many 'normal' working dhows are dangerously overloaded, and quite frightening and unpleasant vessels in which to cross a busy stretch of open ocean.

GETTING AROUND ZANZIBAR ISLAND

You can travel around Zanzibar Island in several different ways: by hire car, motorbike, scooter, bicycle, tourist minibus, *dala dala*, bus, taxi, organised tour, walking, hitchhiking, or a combination of all of these. Outside Zanzibar Town, the main roads are predominantly tar these days, whilst minor routes are dirt or graded gravel. All are highly variable in quality, from smooth, newly resurfaced tar to appallingly rutted gravel, where travel can be slow and uncomfortable. Happily, there are increasingly fewer of the latter. As in the rest of east and southern Africa, traffic drives on the left in Zanzibar, although in many ways the greatest risk on the road is the other drivers: be very aware.

HIRED VEHICLES

Car hire Car hire is possible on Zanzibar Island, although whether it's wise for most visitors is a real question. There are no international car-hire companies on the island, so vehicle quality is highly variable. Driving standards are not good and roads can be in poor condition, so accidents are frequent. We do not generally recommend that visitors hire cars here, but if you choose to do so exercise great caution and never drive at night: it can be exceedingly dangerous.

If you do want a car, it's probably best arranged through one of the tour companies (see *Tour companies*, pages 134–7). A few have their own vehicles, while others will make arrangements on your behalf. Rates vary but are generally between US$50 and US$60 per day for a small car (eg: a Suzuki 'jeep') and around US$100 per day for a larger car (eg: a Toyota Land Cruiser). However, quality is more variable than price, and standards on Zanzibar are often low; check your car *very* carefully for defects and even go for a short test drive before accepting it. The price usually includes unlimited distance, but you pay for the fuel. Be aware that there is likely to be none in the tank on collection!

Insurance is normally included in the rental, although some companies are vague about this. It's always important to check your exact legal position should you be unfortunate enough to have an accident involving another car or person. Get this in writing, which may be harder than you realise. A deposit, proof of identity and your driving licence are usually required, and you will need a local driving permit, which must be arranged in advance (at least 24 hours prior to car collection). The police road blocks around the island will fine you without this paperwork, so do not leave without it (see *Driving licences*, page 132). It is not a bad idea to also carry a valid International Driving Permit (IDP).

Motorbike and scooter hire It is possible to hire motorbikes (almost all are Honda 125cc or 250cc trail bikes or similar) or scooters (mostly Vespas and Piaggios) from many of the tour companies (see pages 134–7). Prices vary, but are generally around US$25–30 per day for a scooter, US$35–40 per day for a motorbike.

For a cheaper deal, try Nasor Aly Mussa's Scooter Service, usually shortened to Fundi Nasor, a small garage just off New Mkunazini Road in Zanzibar Town, near the Anglican cathedral. As with cars, you should take your scooter for a test drive to make sure everything works before agreeing to hire.

Some tourists to Zanzibar hire scooters, imagining them to be similar to Greek island-style mopeds. However, scooters have larger engines and are harder to handle than mopeds, and there have been a number of accidents and injuries. You should not hire a scooter if you have never ridden one before; the dirt tracks and pot-holed roads of Zanzibar are not ideal places to start learning.

If you're keen, however, do check beforehand that your travel insurance policy covers you for using this type of transport, as not all do.

Bicycle hire For getting around Zanzibar Town, or going further afield around the island, fit and adventurous visitors will find bicycles ideal. Most bikes are heavy steel Chinese-built roadsters, so you shouldn't plan on covering too many miles (it's generally too hot to cycle fast anyway). You can also hire mountain bikes, but most of these are pretty basic all-steel models, and only slightly lighter than the Chinese roadsters. They do have gears, however, which makes them easier to ride.

Bikes can be hired through several of the tour companies listed (see pages 134–7) and daily rates start at US$10 for the Chinese roadsters, and US$15 for mountain bikes. Take your bike for a short test ride before hiring to make sure everything works. Unless you plan extensive off-road forays, make sure your tyres are pumped up fairly hard, especially on the mountain bikes, where semi-flat fat tyres can make for hard going. Your bike should come with a puncture outfit and pump, but if it doesn't these can be bought from the bicycle *fundi* (mechanic) in the market in Zanzibar Town.

Roads can be rough, but are generally flat, and traffic is very light once you get away from Zanzibar Town. If you get tired, you can put your bike on top of a bus or *dala dala* and come home the easy way.

Keen cyclists might like to contact Mreh Tours (see page 135) – the only company as far as we know to offer specific cycle tours of Zanzibar.

Taxis The saloon-car taxis which are available around Zanzibar Town can be hired to take you further afield, but some drivers do not like to go off the tar roads as the rocky dirt roads are liable to damage the undersides of their beloved vehicles (the minibuses have higher clearance, or at least the bus drivers seem not to worry).

A short ride through town will cost just over US$3, a trip further afield to Mbweni Ruins or Mtoni Marine Centre around US$7–10 (one-way), and an airport transfer to/from Zanzibar Town US$10–15. A taxi to Jozani Forest is US$20–25 one-way, or around US$30–35 return, possibly more if you plan to spend all day in the forest. To Nungwi or Bwejuu is around US$40–50 one-way. If you're going this far, then it's probably best to arrange for a proper minibus and guide to take you.

Tourist minibuses On Zanzibar Island, most travellers will get between Zanzibar Town and one of the beaches using a minibus. These can be arranged by the *papaasi* (touts) (see box, *Guides and the 'papaasi'*, page 142) who lurk at budget hotels looking for custom. A ride in one of these vehicles can cost as little as US$5, although often the *papaasi* will have their own favourite beach places, which pay them a commission for each visitor who stays; make sure you are very clear about your destination, the timings and the cost before getting on board.

If haggling with the *papaasi* is not for you, most local travel agents can arrange a reliable private minibus from Zanzibar Town to any beach lodge for about US$50 per vehicle. For most people this is the preferred way of getting around.

Alternatively, if you know which lodge you want to go to, call them and ask them to arrange a minibus for you; they will often do this through a reliable travel agent with whom they work and at a reasonable rate.

If you have pre-arranged your trip, then you'll probably be met at the airport by a driver with a vehicle who will transfer you to your chosen lodge. Sometimes it's easy, especially for short trips, to incorporate a visit to a spice farm on the way, as part of these transfers.

PUBLIC TRANSPORT

Buses It is possible to reach many parts of Zanzibar Island by public bus, although few visitors use their services – most use tourist minibuses or *dala dalas*. All buses leave from Darajani Bus Station, on Creek Road in Zanzibar Town. Fares are very cheap: for example, it costs only a few dollars to travel half the length of the island between Zanzibar Town and Bwejuu. Note, however, that prices can rise suddenly if there is a fuel shortage.

On most routes, especially the longer ones, there is only one bus each day. They usually leave Zanzibar Town around midday to take people back to their villages after visiting the market. They reach their destinations in the evening, and 'sleep' there before returning to Zanzibar Town very early in the morning (between 02.00 and 04.00) in time for the start of that day's market. Some of the longer journeys can be very slow. For example, Zanzibar Town to Nungwi takes three to five hours, Zanzibar Town to Makunduchi between four and six hours.

Buses do not always go to their final destination. For example, bus No 1 (the route for Nungwi) may only go as far as Mkokotoni. Therefore, always check that the bus is going to the destination you think it should be.

Some of the bus routes listed below are also covered by public minibuses or *dala dalas*, which fill the gaps in the bus service 'timetables'. These are usually slightly more expensive than the buses, but also tend to be quicker.

Route number	To	No per day	First	Last
NORTH				
1	Mkokotoni (occasionally continuing to Nungwi)	15	05.30	20.00
2	Bumbwini & Makoba, via Mangapwani	3	05.30	18.00
14	Nungwi, via Mahonda, Kinyasini & Chaani	7	07.00	18.00
NORTHEAST				
6	Chwaka (some continue to Uroa & Pongwe)	5	07.00	16.00
13	Uroa	5	08.00	16.00
15	Kiwengwa	5	08.00	18.00
16	Matemwe	6	07.00	18.00
SOUTHEAST				
9	Paje, sometimes to Bwejuu & Jambiani	7	06.00	17.00
10	Makunduchi, via Tunguu, Pete & Munyuni	4	07.00	16.00
SOUTHWEST				
7	Fumba, via Kombeni	4	06.00	16.00
8	Unguja Ukuu	4	06.00	16.00
CENTRAL				
3	Kidichi & Kizimbani, via Welezo	7	06.00	18.00
4	Mchangani, via Dunga, Bambi & Uzini	5	06.00	17.00
5	Ndagaa, via Kiboje	4	06.00	16.00
11	Fuoni, via Tungu & Binguni	10	07.00	18.00
12	Dunga, then north to Bambi	5	07.00	17.00

Public minibuses and *dala dalas* For independent travellers, local minibuses and small converted trucks called *dala dalas* cover many routes around Zanzibar Island. On Pemba, minibuses and *dala dalas* link Chake Chake to the towns of Wete and Mkoani, and also serve outlying villages. Minibuses and *dala dalas* are faster than buses, and are gradually replacing them on the roads. Fares are cheap: typically about US$0.50 around Zanzibar Town and a few dollars to cross the island.

Buses and *dala dalas* from outlying villages heading for Zanzibar Town tend to leave very early in the morning but, apart from that, there are no truly fixed timetables: most vehicles simply leave when they're full. At any bus or *dala dala* station, don't expect an information board: you will need to ask around to find the transport you need. Be aware that the last buses to some coastal villages will leave Zanzibar Town by mid afternoon.

Dala dala journeys are invariably an experience, with time to interact with local people, but comfort is limited. Seating is on hard timber benches along the sides of the vehicle, and it's quite likely that parcels and packages of all shapes and sizes will be packed in around you.

In spite of their erratic appearance, *dala dalas* do have standardised route numbers and destinations. There are three main terminals in Zanzibar Town: Darajani Bus Station on Creek Road (opposite the market), Mwembe Ladu and

Mwana Kwerekwe. The latter two stations are a few kilometres from town and are best accessed by a short hop on a *dala dala* from Darajani.

The most useful *dala dala* routes and times are listed in the box below; the name in brackets is the destination as written on the front of the vehicle.

Hitchhiking Hitching around Zanzibar Island is possible, but traffic can be light so you will need patience. However, a combination of public transport, walking and hitching is sometimes the only way to travel for budget travellers – and simply a

DALA DALA ROUTES AND FREQUENCY

Dala dala number	Departs	To	No per day	First	Last
AROUND ZNZ TOWN					
502	Darajani	Bububu, via Marahubi & Mtoni	Lots	06.00	21.00
505	Darajani	Airport (U/Ndege)	Lots	06.00	21.00
510	Darajani	Mwana Kwerekwe (m/Kwerekwe)	Lots	06.00	21.00
511	Darajani	Kidichi Spice (K/Spice), via Kidichi Persian baths	Lots	06.00	21.00
NORTH					
101	Creek Rd	Mkokotoni	15	05.30	21.00
102	Darajani	Bumbwini, via Mangapwani	5	10.00	16.00
116	Creek Rd	Nungwi	25	05.30	21.00
121	Darajani	Donge & Mahonda	5	10.00	18.00
NORTHEAST					
117	Creek Rd	Kiwengwa, some continue to Pwani Mchangani	9	06.00	19.00
118	Creek Rd	Matemwe	10	06.00	19.00
206	Darajani or Mwembe Ladu	Chwaka, via Dunga Palace	10	06.00	18.00
209	Mwembe Ladu	Pongwe	3	07.00	16.00
214	Mwembe Ladu	Uroa, via Dunga Palace	7	06.00	18.00
SOUTHEAST					
309	Darajani or Mwana Kwerekwe	Jambiani, via Jozani	5	07.30	16.00
310	Darajani	Makunduchi, via Jozani	10	06.30	21.00
324	Darajani	Bwejuu, via Jozani, Paje & Kae Michamvi	Lots	09.00	14.00
SOUTHWEST					
308	Mwembe Ladu or Mwana Kwerekwe	Unguja Ukuu	4	08.00	15.00
336	Darajani or Mwana Kwerekwe	Kibondeni	Lots	06.00	20.00
326	Darajani or Mwana Kwerekwe	Kizimkazi, via Zala Park	5	07.00	16.00

matter of taking the first vehicle which will give you a lift. You should usually expect to pay a few dollars for a lift.

PRACTICALITIES

Driving licences Unlike mainland Tanzania, you need an International Driving Permit (IDP) or a 'local driving permit' to drive either cars or motorcycles legally on Zanzibar.

An IDP is easy to obtain from your national motoring association – eg: in Britain contact the AA (*www.theaa.com*), or the RAC (*www.rac.co.uk*), provided that you have a standard driving licence at home. If applying by post, the process takes time, so order one well in advance of your trip. In the UK, it is also possible to apply for an IDP in person at major post offices.

The alternative is a local driving permit, which can be issued for you in Zanzibar. The rental company can usually organise this for you with minimal fuss for about US$10, and we would recommend that you do this for smooth passage at police encounters.

It is essential that you have either this or an IDP if you drive a car or a motorcycle on the islands; your own national driving licence is not enough. Enforcing this, the traffic police on Zanzibar routinely stop any tourist they see behind a wheel. There are several checkpoints on the roads between Zanzibar Town and the north and east coasts. If you do not have either an IDP or a local driving permit then you'll have to repeatedly pay small bribes or a heftier official fine.

Beware of eager tour companies who are keen to rent you a car and say that IDPs are not essential. Also watch out for a scam where local *papaasi* rent you a motorbike claiming that an IDP is not needed, before informing the police, who then find and fine you.

Petrol and diesel Petrol is now widely available (usually, but not with total reliability) in Zanzibar Town and across the island, notably at *en route* to Nungwi, and at Kinyasini, Chwaka, and at Kitogani, near the junction where the road turns off to Paje.

Petrol costs are increasing on the island, as in the rest of the world, with costs currently about US$1.31 per litre for petrol and US$1.34/litre for diesel. Occasional fuel shortages in outlying parts of the island mean it is generally worth filling up as and when you see a petrol station, but certainly prior to leaving Zanzibar Town. In an emergency, however, it is normally possible to locate 'black market' fuel at about 20% above the standard pump price.

Maps The most up-to-date area maps you will find are likely to be within this book. We spend a great deal of time plotting all of the listings and roads using GPS co-ordinates and tracks that we generate whilst researching. Many of the larger, more colourful maps available are sadly out of date as development on Zanzibar far outstrips the time between reprints. However, for those keen to get hold of some larger island maps than we are able to include here, there are a few possibilities.

A straightforward tourist map of Zanzibar Town and Zanzibar Island is available from the Zanzibar Tourist Corporation offices, and from some bookshops and hotels in the town. It costs around US$2. Far better than this is the attractive, hand-drawn map of Zanzibar Stone Town and Zanzibar Island produced by local artist Giovanni Tombazzi, which is widely available for around US$8, and highlights landmarks and a little of their historical background. This is part of a wider series of maps, including many of the national parks and mountains of mainland Tanzania.

The *Gallery Map of Zanzibar* is available in the Gallery bookshop. The map of Zanzibar Island is not as easy to read or detailed as Giovanni's map, but the map of Stone Town is clear and useful.

A map called *Pemba: The Clove Island* is available in some book and gift shops, and is well researched, again at a scale of 1:100,000. There are two versions, however: one from 1992 and a better one from 1995. The date is on the back cover.

Most commercially produced maps of Tanzania also include Zanzibar. One of the best is the *Tanzania Travellers Map* published by Macmillan, which shows the mainland at a scale of 1:2,000,000 and has more detailed maps of Zanzibar Island (1:500,000) and Pemba Island (1:830,000) on the back, although even these contain a few errors.

Good-quality maps of Zanzibar and Pemba islands (produced by the British Directorate of Overseas Surveys at scales of 1:50,000 and 1:10,000) are available in Zanzibar Town from the Map Office in the Commission of Lands and Planning, part of the Ministry of Environment, near the People's Bank of Zanzibar and the Fort. Maps cost about US$2.

ORGANISED TOURS

In Zanzibar Town, it seems that every other shop or office is a tour company, and it's always easy to find someone to arrange and organise tours within Zanzibar. The problem is finding a good tour company. This section is designed to help you locate something suitable for your needs and budget.

The most popular tours organised from Zanzibar Town are boat excursions to Prison Island and the trips around the plantations called 'spice tours' (see box, *Spices and spice tours*, page 136). Most companies also arrange tours to Jozani-Chwaka Bay National Park to see the colobus monkeys (page 329), trips to Kizimkazi to see the dolphins (page 326), and visits to old palaces and other ruins in the Zanzibar Town area (pages 197–215) or elsewhere on the island. You can also usually arrange transport to the beaches on the north or east coasts and other parts of Zanzibar with a tour company.

Many companies can also make hotel and ship reservations, flight bookings, car-hire arrangements, and so on. Check the arrangement before organising this: some make no charge for the service (instead getting commission from the transport company or hotel), whilst others charge a small fee. Watch out for those charging a hefty fee for the service, which can sometimes be no more than a couple of phone calls on your behalf.

Tour prices are usually quoted in US dollars (although they can be paid for in TSh or other currencies), and tend to vary considerably between the different companies. A lot depends on the quality you're looking for. At one end of the scale, budget outfits offer cheap and cheerful tours, where you'll be sharing a basic minibus or *dala dala* with several other tourists, the quality or knowledge of your guide may be poor, and their social and environmental ethics highly questionable. At the other end of the scale, you can arrange a private tour for just a couple of people, in a good-quality vehicle, often with air conditioning, and a knowledgeable, responsible guide. Good companies can provide guides who speak English, French, German, Italian and often other languages.

This is not to knock the cheaper outfits: many tourists go on budget tours and have an excellent time. In the same way, some of the so-called upmarket companies may rest on their laurels a bit and not be up to scratch. It is therefore worth comparing a few tour companies before finally arranging your tour, and when comparing prices it is also very important to compare exactly what you get for your money. Your best source of recommendations (good or bad) is always other tourists and travellers, so talk to some of them if you can before signing up for anything. All the companies listed here have been recommended by the authors or readers of previous editions of this book.

To get an idea of prices, companies running tours which you share with (four–eight) other people offer the following rates:

City Tour	US$20	**Dolphin Tour**	US$35
Prison Island Tour	US$25	**Spice Tour**	US$25
Jozani Forest Tour	US$25		

All these rates are per person, but for the tour only, and do not include extras like entrance fees (ie: for the Palace Museum this is US$2, for Prison Island US$4, for Jozani Forest US$4).

If you want a private tour, with a mid-range or top-quality tour company, the rates are more likely to be around US$15–30 more expensive per person, for a minimum of two passengers, and usually include all entrance fees, although you should check this when booking or comparing prices.

While in Zanzibar you can also use tour companies to set you up with tours to Pemba, the Tanzanian mainland, Kenya and even further afield. In recent years there's been significant growth in the number of companies offering fly-in safaris to the national parks of Selous and Ruaha in southern Tanzania. Logistically it's easier to get there than to the northern parks of Serengeti and Ngorongoro, although many companies offer this option, too.

All tour companies have to be licensed by the government of Zanzibar and, if you have a reason to be dissatisfied, you can complain to the Ministry of Tourism who may take action against the company on your behalf. In reality, there's little control but it's still best to use only registered companies. If you decide to use unofficial operators, take care.

Most of the companies listed here can arrange tours on the spot (or with a day's notice), but you can also make prior arrangements by phoning, faxing or emailing in advance.

TOUR COMPANIES Tour companies based in Zanzibar Town include the following (listed alphabetically):

Eco+Culture Tours ✆024 2233731; m 0777 410873; e ecoculture@gmx.net; www. ecoculture-zanzibar.org. This tour company (situated on Hurumzi St opposite 236 Hurumzi Hotel) is deliberately not trying to do what all the other companies do. For example, instead of the ubiquitous 'standard' spice tour, it takes guests to plantations & gardens guided by a local herbalist, & as well as a visit to Jozani Forest, walks in the community forest at Ufufuma are arranged. Well-guided, insightful village tours are another great option – a genuine opportunity to meet local people in the company of respected local guides. Trips are sometimes slightly more expensive than those arranged by some other tour companies but they are refreshingly different, ethically minded & well guided. A percentage of all tour revenue is returned into funding solid community projects, telling of the organisation's origins as an NGO. Robert & Haji in the Zanzibar office are gentle & very friendly, & we highly recommend them as an island operator. See also page 318.

Fernandes Tours & Safaris ✆024 2230666; m 0777 413352/474344; e fts@zanlink.com; www.fernandestoursznz.com. This small, friendly & well-connected company on Vuga Rd used to work mainly with incoming tour groups from Britain, South Africa & elsewhere, but is now branching out to provide good-quality tailor-made trips around Zanzibar for groups & individuals in the mid-range price bracket. You can arrange things on the spot, or in advance.

Fisherman Tours & Travel ✆024 2238791/2; m 0777 440044/441144/412677; e reservations@ fishermantours.com; www.fishermantours.com. This well-established & experienced company on Vuga Rd has skilled & efficient staff, & caters for overseas tour groups, as well as individuals & small parties. Offering a complete guide & escort service, they have their own fleet of vehicles, & most drivers are equipped with mobile phones. Other services include the organisation of wildlife safaris on mainland Tanzania, as well as the usual tours around Zanzibar, plus car hire, hotel bookings, ground transfers & so on. In the past, Fisherman Tours received quality awards from business organisations in Europe & America, & do (fairly) consistently deliver a good service. The office is near Air Tanzania & they have full credit-card facilities.

Gallery Tours & Safaris ✆024 2232088; m 0777 853824; e info@gallerytours.net; www. gallerytours.net. In 2007, Gallery Tours & Safaris was opened by local businessman Javed Jafferji, owner of Gallery Bookshop, Jafferji House & author of several coffee-table books on the Swahili coast. Positioned as a high-end tour operation, it is hoping to raise the standard of guiding, vehicles & customer service found amongst the ground handlers. Catering for both groups & individuals, the team here is geared up to deal with everything from standard spice tours to weddings. Smart branding & attention to detail make this one of the best operations around. In conjunction with Zanzibar Serena Inn, Gallery Tours also owns the company Original Dhow Safaris. Its fleet of 3 traditional dhows departs every sundown from the Serena Hotel for a luxury sundowner trip, complete with a well-stocked bar & tasty canapés. This trip must be booked at least 1 full day in advance & is highly recommended as a pre-dinner holiday treat.

Island Express Safaris & Tours ✆024 2234375/64; m 0774 111222/111888; e info@ islandexpress.co.tz; www.islandexpress.co.tz. Established in 1998, Island Express is a smart, efficient operation with offices in central Stone Town on Kajificheni St, as well as beside the airport. Offering a more personal service than most other tour operators on the island, tours & transfers with Island Express are never for groups, but are only ever

arranged on a private basis. This does make them slightly more expensive, though not prohibitively so, & of course gives complete flexibility on your trip. Staff are friendly & professional with fluent English, Spanish, French & German guides available. A recommended operation.

Mreh Tours ✆024 2233476; e mrehtours@ zanzinet.com. This company offers all the usual tours, & is especially keen on bicycle hire & tours by bike. One itinerary is a 9-day cycling trip around the island (no doddle even on Zanzibar's flat roads, as the bikes are the traditional steel Chinese models, not tip-top lightweight jobs), though shorter, more manageable variations are possible. Costs are around US$50 a day including bike, food, drink & backup vehicle. Basically, if you have the slightest interest in cycling, call in at their office on Baghani St, near the Chavda Hotel, & discuss the options with Saleh Mreh Salum, the energetic & friendly owner.

Pristine Trails (see advertisement on page 119) ✆027 275446; m 0767 100788; e info@ pristinetrails.com; www.pristinetrails.com. An independent travel company wholly owned by Tanzanians & offering tailor-made trips all over the country.

Sama Tours (see advertisement on page 36) m 0713 608576/0777 430385/431665; e samatours@zitec.org; www.samatours.com. As well as spice tours, boat trips & all the usual services, the helpful team at Sama Tours on Gizenga St (behind the House of Wonders) arranges cultural tours, giving visitors an opportunity to meet local people: recommended by clients as a great opportunity for photos. Guides speak English, French, German & Italian. Sama Tours also offers 'special' spice tours, organised by one of the knowledgeable, multi-lingual owners, Salim Abdullah. Sama Tours caters for both groups (anything from cruise ships to overland trucks) & individuals seeking tailor-made tours, airport & port collection, hotels, excursions, transfers, car hire, & so on. They are friendly & recommended. Prices depend on the length of the tour, the services required & the number in the group.

Sun N Fun Safaris ✆024 2237381/7665; m 0741 600206; e zanzibarsun@hotmail.com. In the same building on the waterfront as Sea View Indian Restaurant, & with the same enthusiastic management, this company can set you up with absolutely anything, usually at a very reasonable price. It runs tours of Zanzibar Town & the island, provides transfer services to the airport or east coast, & can help with general tourist information on the island & beyond. It can also assist with visas, car & bike hire, boat trips, flight tickets & bus tickets in Zanzibar & on the mainland. The office sells postcards, stamps (it has a mailbox), maps & souvenirs of the 'I love Zanzibar' variety. Students carrying an ISIC card are eligible for a 5% discount on all their services.

Suna Tours ☎024 2237344. Suna is run by the formidable Naila Majid Jiddawi, a former Zanzibari MP & bastion of Zanzibar tourism promotion. The company represents some mid-range hotels on the east coast & can assist with reservations for any other hotel on the coast, as well as arranging transport, good-quality spice tours & trips to the islands. The company office is in a small white building at the end of Forodhani Gardens, near the Arab Fort, & the staff here are very happy to provide general tourist information, even if you don't take one of their tours.

Tropical Tours & Safaris ☎024 2236794; m 0777 413454/0773 663396;

e info@tropicaltoursandsafari.com; www.tropicaltoursandsafari.com. From a small but highly efficient office, this straightforward & friendly budget company has been recommended by several travellers, & offers the usual range of tours (a spice tour, dolphins, Jozani Forest, Nungwi & Prison Island trips), plus car hire, & ferry & air ticket reservations. More recently it's started handling everything from mainland safaris to beach weddings. It's on Kenyatta Rd, opposite Mazsons Hotel.

ZanTours ☎024 2233042/3116; m 0777 417279; e zantoursinfo@zitec.org; www.zantours.com. This company confidently entered the tourist scene in 1997 & is now the largest operator on Zanzibar. It has a large office in the Malindi area, efficient staff, a fleet of clean vehicles & an impressive range of tours, transfers, excursions & safaris. They cater for groups of any size (from several hundred to just a few) including individuals wanting tailor-made services. You can walk in & they'll set something up on the spot, although most of their clients arrange things in advance by email. ZanTours is closely

SPICES AND SPICE TOURS   *Gemma Pitcher*

Sooner or later every visitor to Zanzibar Island (Unguja) will be offered a 'spice tour' – a trip to the farmlands just outside Stone Town to see aromatic plants and herbs growing wild or cultivated in kitchen gardens. Even if you decline a tour, the array of spices on offer in the souvenir shops or heaped in baskets in the local markets will tell you that spice is central to Zanzibar's history and economy.

The history of spices in Zanzibar begins early in the 16th century, when the 'spice race' between the major European powers to control the lucrative trading routes to the Far East was at its height. Portuguese traders gained a toehold on Zanzibar as part of their plan to rule the coast of east Africa and imported various plants, including spices, from their colonies in South America and India. Some land was cleared for plantations, but the Portuguese never really developed their presence on Zanzibar beyond a military one.

It was left to the Omani Arabs, who ruled Zanzibar from the early 19th century, to develop Zanzibar economically as a spice-producing entity. Sultan Seyyid Said, the first Omani sultan to govern Zanzibar, quickly realised the potential of his new dominion, with its hot climate and regular rainfall, as a location for spice farming. With the demise of the slave trade in the late 19th century, spices became Zanzibar's main source of income.

When the era of the sultans ended and the long arm of the British Empire reached Zanzibar, the island's new colonial administrators encouraged the farming of spices and other useful plants, bringing European scientists to establish experimental agricultural stations and government farms such as those at Kizimbani and Kindichi. Today these areas still contain spice plantations controlled by the modern Tanzanian government.

allied to ZanAir (see page 124) & some tours utilise their fleet of planes. One of their most popular tours is a short fly-in excursion from Zanzibar direct to the Selous National Park in southern Tanzania, which many other agents sell too.

Zanzibar Different m 0777 430 177/0779 226966; e info@zanzibardifferent.com; www. zanzibardifferent.com. Owned by the delightful Stefanie Schoetz of Mrembo Traditional Spa (see page 187) & creator of the Princess Salme Tour (see page 206), this small, deliberately different (as it's name suggests) company is a great addition to the ever-expanding selection of island operators. Small & personal, they have put a new spin on some classic Zanzibari tours, as well as adding original offerings in music, cookery & the arts, some fabulously atmospheric dinner concerts at Mtoni Palace (usually Fri), & now even mainland add-ons. They are very flexible with all tours being specially adapted for children if necessary. Ethical & responsible in their outlook, a percentage of profits goes to the Mtoni Palace Conservation Project. This is a little operation, well worth seeking out.

Zenith Tours ☏ 024 2232320; m 0777 413084/0774 413084; e info@zenithtours.com; www.zenithtours.com. This very professional & efficient organisation, situated behind the Old Fort, offers transfers, accommodation & excursions in the mid-range price bracket, including safaris to the mainland. They are also linked to World Unite, a German-based international volunteering organisation, with details of internships & volunteer opportunities across a range of sectors (nursery schools to medical & environmental placements) in Tanzania & Zanzibar. They have an office in Dar es Salaam in the Clocktower Bldg on Uhuru St, or their website details tour & travel information in 4 European languages for those wishing to plan in advance.

INDEPENDENT GUIDES If you prefer not to use a tour company, it is possible to arrange a tour of the spice plantations, a boat trip to the islands or transport to the

But spices in Zanzibar today are by no means simply the preserve of governments keen to produce cash-rich export products or a useful tourist attraction. For the ordinary people of Zanzibar, spices and useful plants are a vital part of everyday life and a rich element in the island's strong and vibrant culture. The spices grown in village kitchen-gardens give their flavour to the distinctive cuisine of Zanzibar, provide innumerable cures for everyday ailments, and yield the dyes and cosmetic products needed to celebrate weddings and festivals.

A spice tour is probably the best way of seeing the countryside around Stone Town and meeting rural communities. Guides take you on a walking tour of the villages and plantations at Kizimbani or Kindichi, picking bunches of leaves, fruit and twigs from bushes and inviting you to smell or taste them to guess what they are. Pretty much all the ingredients of the average kitchen spice rack are represented – cinnamon, turmeric, ginger, garlic, chillies, black pepper, nutmeg and vanilla among many others. Local children follow you all the way round, making baskets of palm leaves and filling them with flowers to give to you. At lunchtime, you'll stop in a local house for a meal of pilau rice and curry, followed by sweet Arabic coffee and perhaps a slice of lemongrass cake. Many spice tours include a visit to the Persian baths built by Sultan Said for his harem, and stop at Fuji or Mangapwani beaches just outside Stone Town for a swim on the way back.

All in all, even if horticulture isn't one of your interests, a spice tour is still an excellent way of gaining an insight into one of the most important aspects of rural life in Zanzibar.

east coast with an independent guide. Many double as taxi drivers; in fact many are taxi drivers first, and guides second. One driver, a Mr Mitu, has been doing these tours for many years and has been recommended by many visitors, although sometimes he subcontracts work to other drivers. These days he's so popular that instead of Mr Mitu in his taxi you might find yourself joining a large group touring the island in a fleet of minibuses. He's even got his own office (\ *024 2234636;* m *0777 418098*) – a tiny room tucked away behind the old Ciné Afrique with the walls covered in photos. Mr Mitu's tours leave from outside the Ciné Afrique every morning at 09.30, returning about 15.00, cost around US$15 per person and are still highly recommended by those who have been.

There are several other taxi drivers who also organise their own spice tours. Most will undercut the tour companies (about US$35 for the car seems average), although you may not get the same degree of information that you'd get with a specialist guide.

You are almost certain to meet some of the local independent 'guides' who are in fact just hustlers (see box, *Guides and the 'papaasi'*, page 142) who tout for business outside hotels and restaurants, or along the streets of Stone Town. For spice tours, *papaasi* prices are often cheaper than those offered by regular companies, but the tours are usually shorter, the vehicles out of condition, and without a proper guide, which usually makes the whole thing pointless unless you are a fairly skilled botanist.

For short boat trips, it doesn't usually make much difference if you go with the *papaasi* or a regular company, although if you deal with the *papaasi* be aware that safety equipment is likely to be inadequate, if available at all, and if things go wrong, it is very difficult to complain or get your money back.

6

Zanzibar Town

> The streets are, as they should be under such a sky, deep and winding alleys, hardly twenty feet broad, and travellers compare them to the threads of a tangled skein.
>
> *Richard Burton, British explorer (1857)*

Zanzibar Town, sometimes called Zanzibar City, is situated about halfway along the west coast of Zanzibar Island. It has a population estimated at 205,870 in the 2002 national census, which makes it by far the largest settlement on the Zanzibar Archipelago, and the sixth largest in Tanzania. During the colonial period, before the development of towns such as Dar es Salaam, Nairobi and Mombasa, Zanzibar Town was the largest settlement in the whole of east Africa.

Zanzibar Town is divided into two sections by Creek Road, though the creek itself has now been reclaimed. On the west side is the 'heart' of Zanzibar Town: the evocative old quarter, usually called Stone Town. This is the more interesting section for visitors: many of the buildings were constructed during the 19th century (although some date from before this time), when Zanzibar was a major trading centre and at the height of its power. The trade created wealth which in turn led to the construction of palaces, mosques and many fine houses. Discovering the architectural gems hidden along the tortuous maze of narrow streets and alleyways that wind through Stone Town is part of the island's magic for many visitors. Aside from the souvenir Tingatinga paintings and beaded jewellery, it's a scene virtually unchanged since the mid 19th century (see Burton's description above).

On the east side of Creek Road is Michenzani, or the 'New City', though this part of town used to be called Ng'ambo (literally 'the other side') and is still often referred to by its unofficial name. It's a sprawling area of mainly single-storey houses, local shops and offices, covering a much wider area than Stone Town. This used to be where the poorer African and Swahili people lived, while wealthier Arabs, Indians and Europeans lived in Stone Town. To a large extent this rich–poor division still exists today. Some attempt has been made to 'modernise' this area: at the centre of Michenzani are some dreary, uninviting blocks of flats (apartment buildings) which were built in the late 1960s by East German engineers as part of an international aid scheme. Few visitors go to this eastern part of Zanzibar Town, as there is little in the way of 'sights', though a visit here certainly helps to broaden your understanding: you'll realise that beside Stone Town is a city where thousands of real people live and work in less exotic, but no less authentic, surroundings.

The best way to explore Stone Town is on foot, but the maze of lanes and alleys can be very disorientating. To help you get your bearings, it is useful to think of Stone Town as a triangle, bounded on two sides by sea, and along the third by Creek Road (see map, Zanzibar Stone Town, pages 140–1). If you get lost, it is always

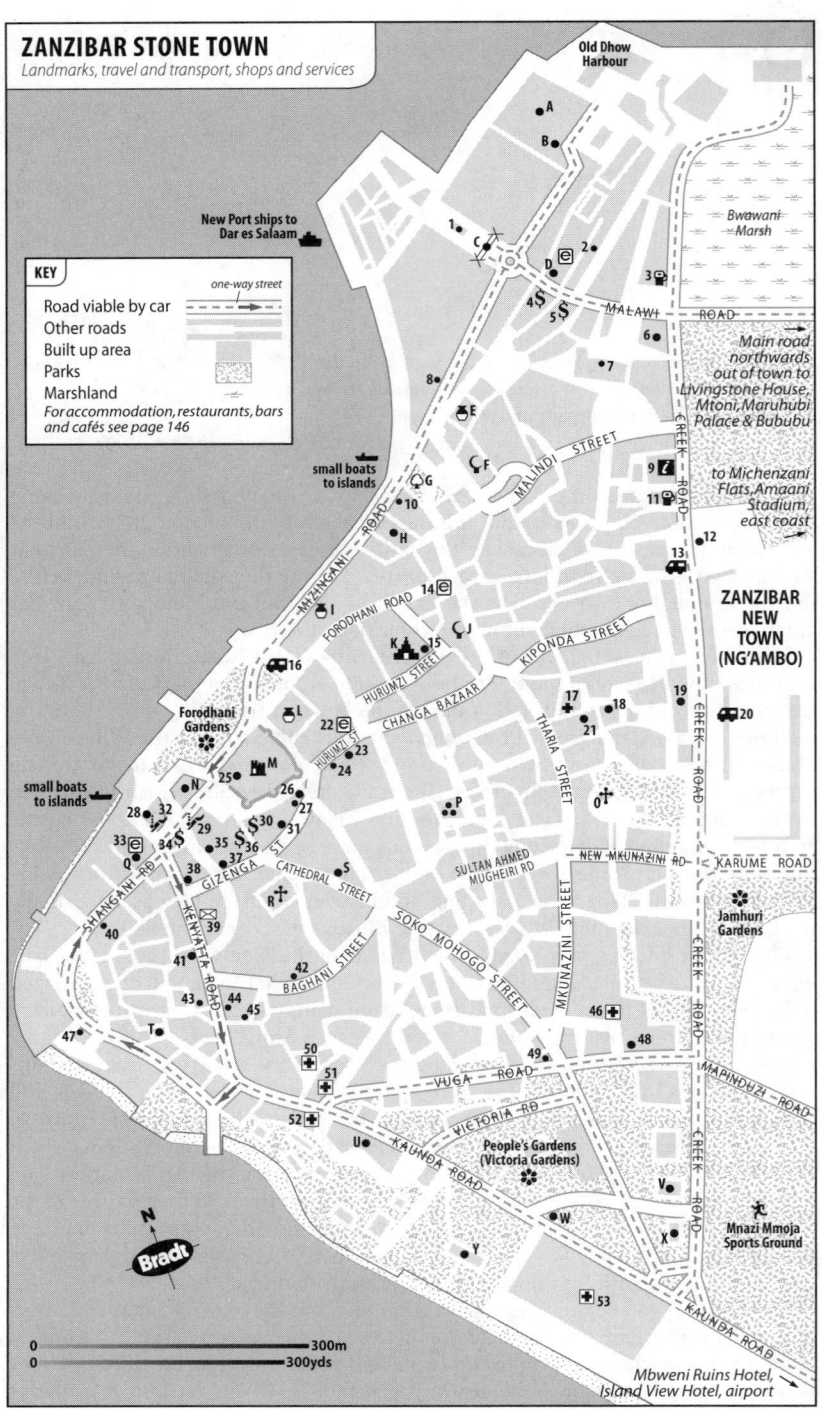

ZANZIBAR STONE TOWN

Landmarks, travel and transport, shops and services

Old Dhow Harbour

New Port ships to Dar es Salaam

KEY

one-way street	
Road viable by car	
Other roads	
Built up area	
Parks	
Marshland	

For accommodation, restaurants, bars and cafés see page 146

small boats to islands

Bwawani Marsh

Main road northwards out of town to Livingstone House, Mtoni, Maruhubi Palace & Bububu

to Michenzani Flats, Amaani Stadium, east coast

MALAWI ROAD

MALINDI STREET

MZINGANI ROAD

FORODHANI ROAD

Forodhani Gardens

small boats to islands

HURUMZI STREET

CHANGA BAZAAR

KIPONDA STREET

ZANZIBAR NEW TOWN (NG'AMBO)

THARIA STREET

CREEK ROAD

HURUMZI ST

SHANGANI RD

KENYATTA ROAD

GIZENGA ST

CATHEDRAL STREET

SULTAN AHMED MUGHEIRI RD

SOKO MOHOGO STREET

NEW MKUNAZINI RD

MKUNAZINI STREET

KARUME ROAD

Jamhuri Gardens

BAGHANI STREET

VUGA ROAD

VICTORIA RD

KAUNDA ROAD

MAPINDUZI ROAD

CREEK ROAD

People's Gardens (Victoria Gardens)

Mnazi Mmoja Sports Ground

KAUNDA ROAD

Mbweni Ruins Hotel, Island View Hotel, airport

N

Bradt

0	300m
0	300yds

LANDMARKS AND ATTRACTIONS

A   Clove Distillery
B   Fish market
C   Port gates
D   Ciné Afrique (closed)
E   Old Dispensary
      (Stone Town Cultural Centre)
F   Ijumaa Mosque
G   The Big Tree
H   Old Customs House
I   Palace Museum
J   Aga Khan Mosque
K   Hindu Temple
L   House of Wonders
M   Old Arab Fort
N   Orphanage
O   Anglican Cathedral
P   Hamamni Baths
Q   Old British Embassy
R   St Joseph's Catholic Cathedral
S   Mrembo Traditional Spa
T   Tippu Tip's House
U   High Court
V   Museum Annexe
W   Zanzibar Milestone
X   Peace Memorial Museum
Y   State House

TRANSPORT AND TOUR OPERATORS

1   Shipping company ticket offices
2   Mitu Tours
7   Zan Tours and ZanAir
8   New Passenger Terminal
10   Sun N Fun Tours
13   Taxi rank
15   Eco+Culture
16   Taxi rank
20   Bus & *dala-dala* station
24   Sama Tours
27   Gallery Tours
29   Bahari Dive Centre
32   One Ocean Dive Centre
40   Air Tanzania
42   Mreh Tours
43   Kenya Airlines
43   Precision Air

44   Tropical Tours
45   Madeira Tours
47   Coastal Travel & Aviation
49   Fernandes Tours
49   Fisherman Tours

SHOPS

12   Vodacom shop
17   Pharmacy
18   Masumo Bookshop
19   Market
21   Shamshuddin Cash & Carry
        Supermarket
23   Moto
25   Keramica shop
26   Sasik
28   Zawadi Chest
31   Gallery Bookshop
35   Upendo
37   Supermarket
38   Zanzibar Gallery
41   Memories of Zanzibar

LOCAL SERVICES

3   Petrol station (Gapco)
4   Malindi Bureau de Change
5   Star Bureau de Change
6   Police station (main)
9   Zanzibar Tourism Corporation (ZTC)
11   Petrol station (Gapco)
14   Palace Internet Café
22   Microwaves Internet
30   People's Bank of Zanzibar
33   National Bank of Commerce
34   Too Short Internet Café
36   People's Bank of Zanzibar
        (Foreign Exchange)
39   Post Office & Telephone Centre
46   Zanzibar Medical & Diagnostic Centre
48   Kiswahili Language Institute
50   Afya Medical Hospital
51   Dr Mehta's Hospital
52   Zanzibar Medical Group
53   Mnazi Mmoja Hospital

Zanzibar Town

6

possible to aim in one direction until you reach the outer edge of the town where you should find a landmark.

Although many of the thoroughfares in Stone Town are too narrow for cars, when walking you should watch out for bikes and scooters being ridden at breakneck speed! It's also useful to realise that paths wide enough for cars are usually called roads while narrower ones are generally referred to as streets. Hence, you can drive along New Mkunazini Road or Kenyatta Road, but to visit a place on Kiponda Street or Mkunazini Street you have to walk. When looking for hotels or places of interest, you should also note that most areas of Stone Town are named after the main street in that area: the area being referred to as Kiponda Street or Malindi Street, instead of simply Kiponda or Malindi. This can be confusing, as you may not be on the street of that name. But don't worry: at least you're near!

TRAVEL AROUND ZANZIBAR TOWN

Most visitors and locals get around the town on foot, and in Stone Town this is the best and often the only way, but there are other means of transport available. Note that if there is a petrol shortage, as periodically happens, taxi fares automatically go up and petrol prices can increase exponentially.

TAXI Private taxis for hire wait at taxi ranks around town; they do not usually cruise for business, although if you see a taxi in the street it is always possible to

GUIDES AND THE 'PAPAASI'

Nearly all tourists who come to Zanzibar Town use the services of a guide at some stage during their visit. If your trip was arranged from outside Zanzibar, it will sometimes include the services of a guide. Even if you organise something simple through a tour company in Zanzibar, like a visit to the spice plantations, the price usually includes a guide to show you around. Guides from reputable companies have to be registered with the Tourism Commission, and will carry identity cards, which they receive on completion of a short instruction course.

There are also many other guides in Zanzibar who are not registered. Most of these are not really guides at all, but touts and hustlers who make their money showing tourists to hotels and souvenir shops, arranging transport or getting groups together to share boat rides. These touts are known locally as beach-boys or *papaasi* – literally meaning 'ticks', ie: parasites or irritating bloodsuckers.

When a ship comes into Zanzibar from Dar es Salaam, there is usually a group of papaasi on the dockside. Some can be quite aggressive, but a few are not too unpleasant and will help you find a place to stay (which may be useful, as the labyrinth of alleys in Stone Town is disorientating at first). Tell them exactly what you want in terms of standard and price. In theory, it should not cost you any more money and could save you a lot of walking but in practice it does not always work so well. The papaasi will usually expect a commission from the hotel for bringing them a guest. Some hotels pay more commission than others, and some do not pay at all, so the papaasi will only take you to the places where they get a decent cut. Hence their hotel recommendations are usually far from impartial.

We have heard from several travellers who arrived on Zanzibar, aiming to stay in a certain hotel, only to be told by the welcome party of papaasi that it was 'full', 'closed' or even 'burnt down'. If you're in any doubt, it is best to be polite but firm flag it down. The main taxi ranks are near the Gapco petrol station on Creek Road, outside the ZanAir office just east of the Port Gates, beside the House of Wonders, in front of the Serena Inn, and at the northern end of Kenyatta Road.

There are no meters. Wherever you go, you should agree the fare with the driver before starting your journey. A short ride through town costs US$3–4; all the way across town costs around US$5–6. A longer ride, from town out to Mtoni Marine Centre or Mbweni Ruins Hotel, will be about US$6–8. From town to the airport is around US$10–15, and it should be the same the other way, but from the airport into town taxi drivers may quote fares of US$20 or higher.

DALA DALA Converted small lorries with two rows of wooden seats at the back, called dala dalas (or dalas for short), carry passengers on local runs around town and to outlying suburbs. There are several routes, all starting at the Darajani Bus Station on Creek Road. The most useful routes for visitors are detailed in *Chapter 5*, page 131. Fares rise from pennies up to a maximum of US$1.50–2 for trans-island journeys.

BICYCLE A bike is very handy for getting around Zanzibar Town and the surrounding area. Bikes can be hired from several of the tour companies listed in this chapter (see also *Chapter 5*, page 134). They are either sturdy steel Chinese-made models, or more modern-looking (though almost as heavy) mountain bikes. Prices for Chinese bikes are about US$10 per day; mountain bikes are US$15 per day. A deposit of around US$50 may be required.

(or simply ignore them completely), and find your own hotel. Even better, make a phone call or send an email to reserve a room in advance; some hotels even give discounts for advance bookings.

After arranging your hotel, most papaasi will want to be your 'guide', offering to show you around the sights or souvenir shops of Stone Town, find companions for dive trips or boat excursions, or arrange transport to the east coast. Use these services if you need them but be prepared to pay if necessary. Always be aware that the owners of the souvenir shops, boats and dive centres will usually pay commission to the papaasi, a charge which will, of course, be effectively passed on to you.

Some papaasi are outright crooks, and involved in robberies and other crimes like drug dealing. Others are conmen, and some travellers have been stung arranging budget hire cars where a papaasi has taken a deposit then simply disappeared. Changing money is another potentially expensive operation, where initially tempting good rates precede sleight-of-hand tricks or simply snatch-and-run theft. Budget travellers have also reported having drugs planted on them by papaasi they befriended, who then reported them to the police; any fines (official or unofficial) paid out included a kickback to the informant.

If you deal only with reputable tour companies (whether low or high budget) you'll have none of these problems. Although trustworthy guides have identity cards, some papaasi have managed to get some too (they could be fakes, or simply stolen – it's hard to tell). This of course is confusing for tourists. There is a need for legitimate guides on Zanzibar, who can help tourists without hassling them, and it is hoped that the government will apply itself to this matter in the near future.

CAR AND MOTORBIKE A car or motorbike is not really necessary or practical for getting around Zanzibar Town as distances are short and parking is often difficult. There are no international car-hire companies on the island; however, both can be hired from various tour companies listed in *Chapter 5*, page 134. Prices vary, but are generally around US$25 to US$30 per day for a scooter, US$35 to US$40 per day for a motorbike, between US$50 and US$60 per day for a small car (eg: Suzuki 'jeep') and around US$100 per day for a larger 4x4 (eg: a Toyota Land Cruiser).

WHERE TO STAY

The following selection of places to stay in and around Zanzibar Town is not exhaustive, as new places continually open and existing ones change name, location and ownership; however, it is as comprehensive as we could make it, and it does aim to highlight the best accommodation in each price bracket. In addition to those listed below, notable new city hotels are likely to be opened by Melia and Four Seasons, one possibly on the prime waterfront property neighbouring the Serena.

If you are coming from the airport (or elsewhere on the island) by taxi, and don't have a reservation, be firm about which hotel you want to go to, otherwise the driver will most likely take you to wherever offers him the best commission, not you the best quality or value. Do also remember that many hotels in the older part of Zanzibar Town cannot be reached by vehicle because of the narrow maze of lanes, and you may have to walk a few hundred metres through the streets to reach it. If the driver shows you the way, and this is advisable if you haven't been before, then he'll probably help with your luggage, in which case it's usual to give a fair tip for this extra service.

Much of the accommodation is in, or very near, Stone Town, which is the best area for atmosphere and ease of getting around. Several of the places do not have exact street addresses, or if they do these are not used. Also, many lanes and house numbers, even if they exist, are unmarked. For ease, we have tried hard to mark the lanes, landmarks and all listed properties on the Zanzibar Stone Town maps, pages 140 and 146.

Unless stated otherwise, hotels listed below offer air conditioning and en-suite bathrooms as standard, For details of price categories, see page 107.

EXCLUSIVE

Jafferji House & Spa (see advertisement on the inside back cover) (8 suites & 2 rooms) 170 Gizenga St; m 0774 078442/1; e info@ jafferjihouse.net; www.jafferjihouse.net. In early 2012, Javed Jafferji opened up his childhood home as an elaborately crafted boutique hotel. Resident publisher, shopkeeper & tour operator, Javed is well known in Zanzibar for his photographs, & here a selection of them can be found adorning the walls. This hotel seriously has the wow factor: an artistic blend of old & new combining with the sumptuous deep red & gold colour scheme to create an extravagant & theatrical spectacle perfumed with spices. Zanzibari doors, old wall clocks & gramophones are reminiscent of days gone by, while warm colours & a top-quality finish

give a modern feel. The 8 suites & 2 standard rooms all have baths, & are overflowing with exquisite furniture & traditional fabrics. Bedrooms are named after important figures in Zanzibar's history, such as the Princess Salme suite with its large ornately carved bed, stained-glass windows, old-fashioned telephone & terracotta walls. The Jafferji suite, on the top floor, is the best of all, with an enormous copper bath, a varnished wooden floor & traditional Zanzibari wooden frontage, plus, of course, fabulous views. Up on the rooftop is a tiny but gorgeous outpost of Cinnamon Spa, with Zanzibari therapists offering massages in an open-sided treatment room with a stand-alone bath & shower & the best spa views in town. Downstairs, the Mistress of Spices restaurant (see *Where to eat and drink*, page 163) offers freshly prepared

Theft from hotel rooms is very unusual, but we'd always recommend that you pack away your things in a locked bag when you leave your room for any length of time, and that you store any valuables in the hotel's safe, preferably within a sealed, lockable bag or pouch, to prevent tampering. This is not really an issue at hotels in the middle and upper price ranges because many offer individual safety-deposit boxes, either at reception or in the rooms, and several budget hotels in Zanzibar Town now run an organised system with a book for guests to write in exactly what they leave.

More serious robberies (sometimes with violence) have occurred on some of the beaches in and around Zanzibar Town. You should not walk here alone, particularly after dark. Other notorious parts of town include the port, and the area around the old Garage Club on Shangani Road, especially late at night when drunken youths wander the streets looking for kicks (just as they do in many other parts of the world). Another time to be wary is the hour or two just after sunset during the period of Ramadan, when everybody is inside breaking their fast, and the streets are deserted.

international food from an à la carte menu & there's also a useful internet café & TV room. Despite all the opulence, the hotel still feels warm & welcoming, like a home, albeit a stylish one. ⚑

⌂ **Zanzibar Serena Inn** (51 rooms) ☎024 2232306; e zserena@zanzinet.com; www. serenahotels.com. Part of the efficient Serena chain, which has lodges all over east Africa, this large, impressive hotel is in the Shangani area of Stone Town, overlooking the sea. Converted from 2 historic buildings, & restored at great expense (see box, *The Serena Inn*, page 148), the staff here are consistently excellent, in part due to the hotel's very good training scheme, & will actively go out of their way to engage & assist. Every room boasts all the in-room & public facilities visitors expect of an international-class hotel, including an inviting seafront swimming pool, 2 excellent restaurants, a coffee shop, rather pricey Wi-Fi, satellite TV & reasonably priced, in-house massage treatments. If you happen not to be on holiday here, there's a business centre & conference facilities. In addition to its standard rooms, the hotel also has state, executive, honeymoon & business rooms. In the next couple of years, the Serena may expand into the neighbouring property to generate an additional 20–30 rooms & a larger conference facility, though plans for this seem to have stalled somewhat. Generous discounts are available in the low season & sometimes also during quiet midweek periods; it's also worth noting that here,

like many of the top end hotels, cheaper rates are often available if you book through an overseas tour operator. ⚑

LUXURY

⌂ **Mashariki Palace Hotel** (18 rooms) ☎024 2237232/3; m 0776 775774; e info@masharikipalacehotel.com; www. masharikipalacehotel.com. Once the home of the religious counsellor to the sultan, Mashariki Palace was completely renovated before opening as a fashionable boutique hotel in early 2011. While some original features remain, the décor leans towards a more modern style, with soaring ceilings & bare white walls bringing a sense of space & calm. The rooms are furnished in shades of brown & cream, & offer very little in the way of decoration apart from a couple of beautiful hand-carved ceilings. Rooms here are named after areas of Stone Town & are divided into 3 categories – Darajani, the smallest, Shangani & Forodhani. Shangani rooms are slightly larger & some have a balcony, while Forodhani are the largest, with higher ceilings, sea views & a terrace. Whatever the category, each offers tea & coffee facilities, a TV & a fridge, although drinks must be ordered to fill it. Somewhat strangely, due to government planning regulations the rooms also offer cooking facilities, which are covered by a large wooden box in the corner. Outside is a pretty little courtyard with a couple of photos of the hotel's restoration,

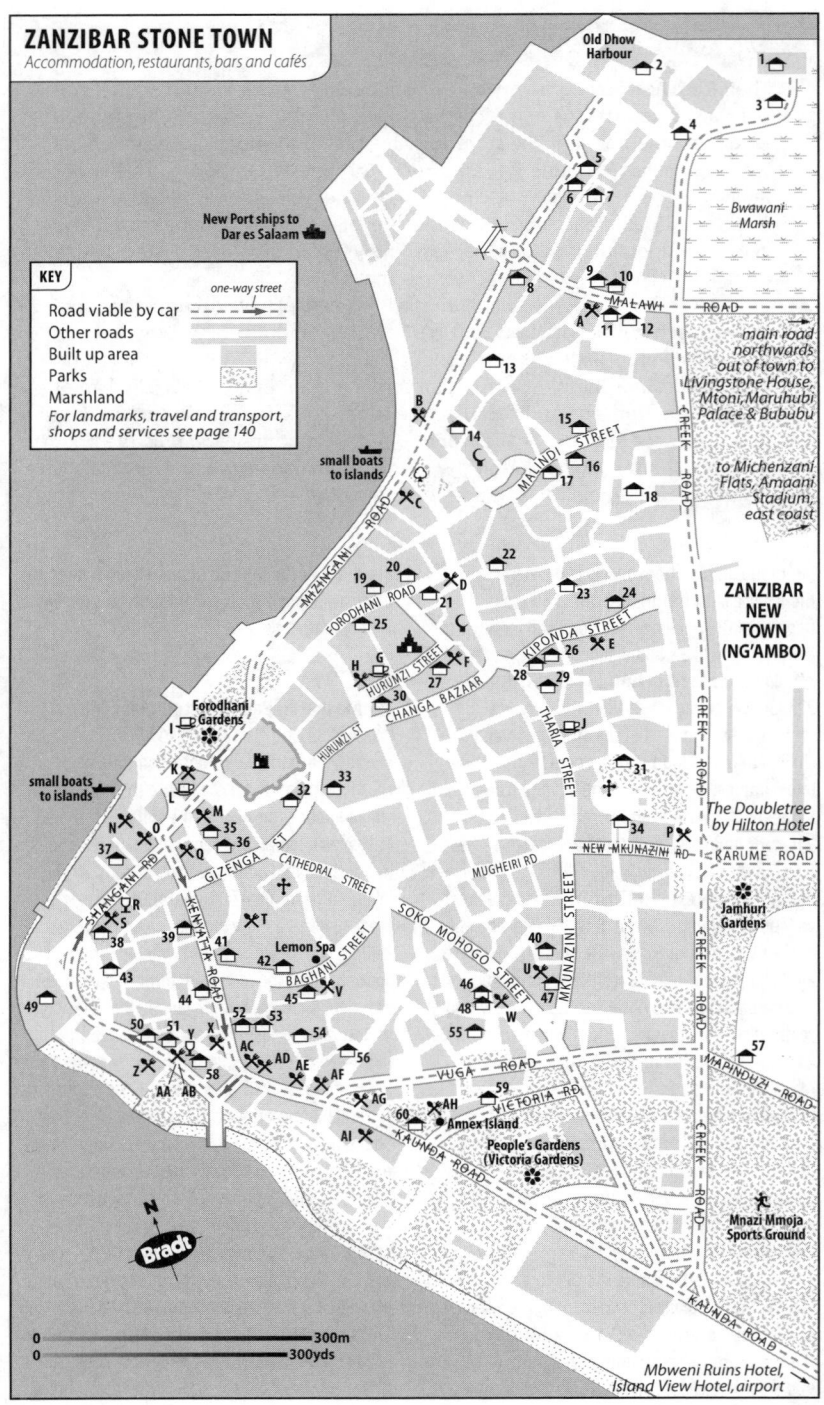

HOTELS AND GUESTHOUSES

1. Bwawani Hotel
2. Funguni Palace
3. Rumaisa Hotel
4. Sealand Hotel
5. Bandari Lodge
6. Princess Salme Inn
7. Warere Town House
8. Hotel Marine
9. Malindi Lodge
10. Mzuri Guest House
11. 1001 Nights
12. Zenji Hotel
13. Zanzibar Grand Palace
14. Kholle House
15. Safari Lodge
16. Narrow Street Hotel
17. Pyramid Hotel
18. Kokoni Hotel
19. The Seyyida
20. Kiponda Hotel
21. Asmini Palace
22. Zanzibar Palace Hotel
23. Annex II of Narrow Street Hotel
24. Pearl Guesthouse
25. Mashariki Palace Hotel
26. The Swahili House
27. 236 Hurumzi
28. Emerson Spice
29. Zanzibar Coffee House
30. Clove Hotel
31. Riverman Hotel
32. Jafferji House
33. Maru Maru
34. St Monica's Hostel
35. Karibu Inn
36. Coco de Mer Hotel
37. Tembo House Hotel
38. Abuso Inn
39. Shangani Hotel
40. Jambo Guesthouse
41. Stone Town Café & B&B
42. Chavda Hotel
43. Beyt al Chai
44. Mazsons Hotel
45. Pearl of Zanzibar
46. Manch Lodge
47. Flamingo Guest House
48. Haven Hotel
49. Zanzibar Serena Inn
50. Karibu Zanzibar
51. Al Johari
52. Dhow Palace Hotel
53. Kisiwa House Hotel
54. Zanzibar Hotel
55. Florida Guest House
56. Mauwani Inn

KEY TO ZANZIBAR STONE TOWN
Accommodation, restaurants, bars and cafés

57. Mnazi House
58. Africa House Hotel
59. Victoria House
60. Garden Lodge

RESTAURANTS, BARS AND CAFÉS

A. Passing Show Restaurant
B. Mercury's Bar & Restaurant
C. Sea View Indian Restaurant
D. Pal
E. House of Spices
F. Kidude
G. Tunda Café
H. Clove Restaurant
I. Cafés of Forodhani
J. Kaya Tea Room
K. Monsoon Restaurant
L. Buni Café
M. New Radha Vegetarian Restaurant
N. Livingstone Beach Restaurant
O. Archipelago Restaurant
P. La Taverna
Q. The Silk Route
R. Dharma Lounge
S. Wings Fast Food
T. Lazuli
U. Green Garden Restaurant
V. Freddie M's
W. Nyumbani Restaurant
X. Pagoda Chinese Restaurant
Y. New Happy Club 2000
Z. Amore Mio Restaurant
AA. La Fenice
AB. Tatu
AC. Casablanca Restaurant
AD. Camlur's Restaurant
AE. Rendezvous Les Spices
AF. Loulou
AG. Abyssinian Maritim
AH. Sambusa Two Tables Restaurant
AI. Tropicana
27. Two Top Restaurant
    (236 Hurumzi)
29. Zanzibar Coffee House Café
    (Zanzibar Coffee House)
43. Beyt al Chai Restaurant
    (Beyt al Chai)
49. Baharia Restaurant
    (Zanzibar Serena Inn)
51. Fusion
    (Al Johari)
59. Bustani
    (Victoria House)

The Zanzibar Serena Inn is in the Shangani part of Stone Town. The main building was originally the External Communications ('Extelcoms') headquarters, built in the early 20th century by the British colonial administration. The next-door house is much older and was originally known as the Chinese Doctor's Residence. The explorer David Livingstone stayed here before one of his journeys to the African mainland. It later became the private home of the British consul.

The Extelcoms building had been empty for many years, and the Chinese Doctor's Residence had fallen into a bad state of repair before restoration began. Their conversion into today's Serena Inn hotel was sensitively handled, the design reflecting Zanzibar's Indian, Arabic and colonial heritage. The regeneration was completed in 1997, and the architects and local craftsmen must be congratulated on the quality of their work and the retention of the building's original character. The walls of the hotel are decorated with historic prints and contemporary paintings, but perhaps the most interesting 'decorations' are the old telecommunications equipment that was discovered in the basement. Abandoned and forgotten by the colonial staff 100 years before, most of the apparatus was handmade in wood and brass. Several items have now been restored to their original condition.

The Serena's restoration goes beyond façades and decorations. It is the first hotel in Zanzibar to install a sewage plant, so that waste discharges are treated to international standards. (Most other waste from Stone Town gets pumped out to sea in its raw state.) Although dumping sewage at sea, in whatever state, is never an ideal solution, the hotel owners should be commended for this positive step.

while upstairs the breezy terrace offers rooftop & distant sea views from the well-stocked bar & restaurant. **$$$$$–**☂

⌂ **Kisiwa House** (11 rooms) ☏ 024 2235654; m 0772 789272; e info@kisiwahouse.com; www.kisiwahouse.com. Right next door to the Dhow Palace, the former Baghani House Hotel has been lovingly upgraded to this elegant & welcoming hotel, which opened in 2009. Rooms are divided into 3 categories – Burdani, Malkia & Sulaima – all decorated in pure white with splashes of sea blue. Burdani suites are the only ones without sitting rooms, while Suliama rooms are simply huge & have stand-alone baths. All 3 are kitted out with fans, safes, TV, AC & silk-edged mosquito nets. Little touches & accessories such as kangas, water glasses & bolsters, fill in the gaps, all of which continue the blue colour scheme. Spacious bathrooms contain both baths & showers, plus 2 sinks & various sweet-smelling lotions & potions. With a cheery, light-filled reception, filled with potted plants & vases of anthuriums, this place

shows a touch of imagination throughout. Darini, the sunny rooftop restaurant & bar, has both an indoor & outdoor section with the hint of a sea view. Easy listening music accompanies meals of local-style seafood with an international twist. **$$$$$**

⌂ **The Doubletree by Hilton** (58 rooms & 4 suites) ☏ 024 2240476; e znzdt_reservations@hilton.com; www.doubletree.com. Opened in early 2013, Doubletree by Hilton, Stone Town is only the 2nd international hotel chain to make its mark on the city, the Serena Inn being the other. Located 2.5km out of the old town, this is a modern hotel with traditional touches. Its rooms & suites boast abundant facilities, as well as numerous guest services. The hotel bar serves drinks & snacks (⊕ *10.00–midnight*), while lunch & dinner are à la carte in the restaurant. The 5th-floor terrace is geared for relaxation with shisha pipes & distant sea views. Business travellers here benefit from a 24hr business centre, 6 conference venues, Wi-Fi & ease of access to the airport. **$$$$$**

236 Hurumzi (22 rooms) 📞 024 2232784 m 0777 423266; e 236hurumzibookings@zanlink.com; www.236hurumzi.com. An offshoot of the defunct Emerson's House, & formerly Emerson & Green Hotel until its namesake owners parted company, 236 Hurumzi is a Stone Town institution. The hotel itself sprawls across 3 venerable buildings dating from 1840–70, one of which was originally the home of Tharia Topan, a prominent Ismaili Indian merchant who also built the Old Dispensary (see page 184), & Zanzibar Coffee House (see page 156). The house has been completely restored & tastefully decorated with antique Zanzibari furniture & carpets, & has a distinctly bohemian atmosphere. Each of the 16 rooms in the main building is different in character, including the open-sided Pavilion Room, the vast Crystal Room with its intricately carved balcony & the airy island South Room – reached by a small bridge. Each room, very deliberately, has no TV & no fridge. Some rooms have AC, others rely on natural cooling – shutters, shades, deep balconies & a sea breeze. Next door, 240 Hurumzi has recently been converted into a further 6 rooms, which all have shared kitchens & are aimed at long-term visitors, but are sometimes booked on a per-night basis. These newer rooms are all on the top 2 floors of the building & are brimming with antiques & Zanzibari furniture. For those not self-catering, b/fast is taken in the hotel's Tower Top Restaurant, the 2nd-highest building in Zanzibar Town, with some of the finest skyline views to boot. Daily dinners (US$25pp) with traditional entertainment are also served here, see *Where to eat and drink*, page 162. **$$$$–$$$$$**

Africa House Hotel (15 rooms) m 0777 212621; e frontdesk@africahouse.com; www. africahousehotel.com. This sea-facing hotel was once among the most popular places to stay in Zanzibar Town. Situated along the Shangani waterfront, Africa House served as the English Club from 1888 until the end of the colonial era, but is perhaps best known for its expansive balcony bar, which, if you don't mind forking out, remains an ever-popular sundowner venue offering a winning combination of fruity cocktails & frothy coffees, a cracking ocean view & tasty bar food. The spacious rooms are a mix of stylish traditional décor & modern facilities. The tiled floors may seem incongruous with the antique beds & heavy velvet curtains, but the rooms are cool, clean &

functional. With some great new accommodation options in the city, the unattractive, shopping-centre style frontage, variable service & steep bar prices perhaps make this less attractive an option than it once was but it's a good low-season deal. **$$$$–$$$$$**

Beyt al Chai (5 rooms) m 0777 444111; e reservations@stonetowninn.com; www.stonetowninn.com. Behind thick walls & antique shuttered windows, Beyt al Chai is a relaxed & peaceful haven. Standing across Kelele Square from the Serena, it was originally built by an Arab merchant & its name, literally meaning 'house of tea', bears testament to its past use as a place where the local nobility came to indulge in the house speciality, spiced tea. Until its opening as a boutique hotel in 2005, the building had always been someone's home, & its friendly Zanzibari team continues to offer relaxed hospitality & home comforts. The rooms are spread over 3 floors & each has an individual name & style. They are light & airy & full of character with high ceilings, authentic Zanzibari furniture & vibrant silk & organza fabrics covering the windows & beds. The 2 room categories, Sultan & Prince, are distinguished largely by the size & opulence of the rooms, as well as their view. On the 1st floor, a large landing leads out onto a small courtyard, whilst inside, the front corner of the house was turned into a bright & cool bar in 2012. Filled with stylish furniture & spice tables covered in sumptuous, azure & gold-thread cushions, this makes for a chilled place to read, chat & watch the world go by. Opposite the bar, a fabulous restaurant serves b/fasts, light lunches & delicious dinners to guests & city visitors; it's very much a current culinary hot spot. (see *Where to eat and drink*, page 162). **$$$$–$$$$$**

Emerson Spice (6 rooms) 📞 024 2232776; m 0774 483483; e reservation@emersonspice.com; www.emersonspice.com. This exotic, newly opened hotel is the brainchild of Emerson, former part-owner of the renowned Emerson & Green Hotel, now 236 Hurumzi. At the time of visiting there were 6 striking theatrical rooms, each with a colourful twist on traditional Swahili design. There are plans for further rooms in the adjoining building, which will no doubt continue Emerson's unique style. Ceilings are immense, vibrant colours adorn the walls, & potted plants, stained-glass windows & intricately carved wooden doors add to the atmosphere. Rooms are kitted out with fans

& AC, fridges & bright mosquito nets, & eclectic curtain fabrics & dark wooden furniture. Some rooms even have hand-painted murals on the wall, such as the Ancient Eqyptian scene in the Aida room, & all come with a dramatic tale attached to their interior design. Open-plan bathrooms feature Arabic baths & twin sinks, bordered with decorative painted ceramic tiles. The attention to detail continues throughout the communal areas of the property where the interior courtyard & its twinkling blue pool are reminiscent of a Moroccan riad. In time, the hotel will open out into a cool, palm-filled walled garden. Culinary creativity is worth noting here, too: enter the heavy wooden doors through the cool blue entrance hall & take the twisting wooden staircase up to the rooftop restaurant (see page 161) which serves inventive internationally & locally influenced food. B/fast can be served in the entrance hall, on the rooftop or on your own balcony. With its exciting design, beautiful rooms & impressive food, the Emerson Spice looks set to become one of the most popular choices for an atmospheric stay in Stone Town. **$$$$–$$$$$**

🏠 **Maru Maru** (44 rooms) 📞024 2238516/7/8; e info@marumaruzanzibar.com; www. marumaruzanzibar.com. In Jan 2012, after an impressive 6-year renovation, Maru Maru opened in a prime spot just behind the Old Fort & the House of Wonders. On the site of an old Hindu temple, Maru Maru means marble tile in Swahili, & it's easy to see why this name was chosen. Gleaming tiles are found all over the interior of this modern hotel, which has been created from 2 adjoining buildings, with the older side having more of a Zanzibar touch & therefore more character than the new one. The result is a spotless, well-finished & bright hotel with lots of dazzling white walls. Enthusiastic & organised manager Paolo is well-practised in dealing with tourists, having previously managed a safari camp in Tanzania's Selous Game Reserve, & he has brought his expertise to give Maru Maru a head start. This is obviously paying off with the well-trained & incredibly polite staff. The modern rooms are sensibly classified into twin, queen & king, with the only difference between the 3 being the bed size. In addition, room 6 is a family room sleeping 4. All the rooms offer Wi-Fi, a safe, in-room tea & coffee facilities & a flat-screen TV. Furniture such as the wooden desk, wardrobe &

mosquito-netted bed are crafted locally, while newer rooms have blue lamps, making them feel a tad dark. The rooms are all en suite, 6 in the old building have traditional hammam baths & the rest have showers. There's a choice of 2 dining areas – the Fountain Restaurant, found in the courtyard by a twinkling fountain & more suited to snacks & afternoon teas, & the Terrace Restaurant up on the roof. Here, the fabulous harbour view across town & the cathedral spires make this a popular choice for laughter & cocktails at sunset, followed by spicy Indian suppers made from locally sourced produce. On a more practical note, Maru Maru is one of few hotels in Stone Town to have a lift, while for anyone who wishes to self-drive, there's parking provided. **$$$$–$$$$$**

UPMARKET

🏠 **Al Johari** (15 rooms) 📞024 2236779; e info@al-johari.com; www.al-johari.com. Flanked by 2 golden lions, the heavily carved door of Al Johari brings a touch of boutique bling to Stone Town's upmarket hotel scene. The Mauritian owners carefully refurbished the 2 old buildings, which now combine to make up the hotel, & the interiors try hard to strike a balance between traditional Zanzibari influences & modern amenities. Meaning 'jewel' in Swahili, there is certainly a good degree of opulence in this property: 2 gold lions at the entrance, a multi-storey cascading waterfall, fine wines & an impeccable array of antiques. Rooms are tastefully furnished with crisp white linen on beautiful Zanzibari beds, marble floors, thick Persian carpets & minibars; the rooms have massage showers (plus jacuzzis in suites), glass sinks & organic herbal products. The downside is a recurring leaking shower issue, which hopefully the management will address soon. There is a lovely rooftop bar where guests enjoy whiskies & flavoured shisha pipes amid a décor & ambience distinctly reminiscent of a bygone era: gentle music, Tiffany lamps, a brass sea-facing telescope, a cabinet of well-thumbed books, whirring fans & chivalrous staff. Adjoining the bar, in a glass AC area, is the fine dining restaurant, Fusion (see *Where to eat and drink*, page 162). Al Johari is most easily found by following the Shangani Road to Tatu, then taking the signed alleyway away from the sea. **$$$$**

🏠 **Chavda Hotel** (43 rooms) 📞024 2232115; e chavdahotel@zanlink.com; www.chavdahotel.

co.tz. Situated in Baghani Street, just off Kenyatta Road in the Shangani area, Chavda is pretty soulless despite its antique-style Indian furniture & Persian carpets. The generally spacious bedrooms are adequate, if uninspiring, with tiled floors, white walls & lacquered timber ceilings. Zanzibari beds, minibar, safe, TV, phone, mosquito nets & a spacious pink bathroom are standard, whilst some also have a tiny concrete balcony (not big enough to sit on). Upstairs is a restaurant & a very pleasant rooftop bar with Wi-Fi, offering one of the best skyline views of St Joseph's Cathedral & the city beyond. There are 2 conference centres & free collections from the port or airport for pre-booked guests. $$$$

🏠 **Kholle House** (10 rooms) m 0779 898200; e info@khollehouse.com; www.khollehouse. com. After 3 years of restoration work, Kholle House opened its carved wooden doors in Feb 2011 & is set to become a hit with those seeking a traditionally inspired boutique bolt-hole. Named after Princess Kholle, who once used the rooms to display her most treasured possessions of artwork & ceramics, the house makes the most of its fascinating past by including many original historic features. It's beautiful, & much thought has gone into the high-quality furnishings, with antique chests, French ceramics, glass lanterns & Zanzibari beds complementing a warm & welcoming ochre colour scheme. Rooms are split into 3 categories, with Classic Rooms, Deluxe Rooms & Prestige Suites varying in size but all boasting Zanzibari beds, mosquito nets, fans & AC, as well as a selection of bathroom products infused with local spices. B/fast is, unusually, à la carte & is served in the downstairs b/fast room, which overlooks the garden. Here, various loungers & cushions are scattered about for whiling away a hot afternoon, plus there's the added bonus of an inviting pool, a precious rarity in Stone Town & welcome relief after a hot day's sightseeing or shopping. One point to note if arriving by taxi – ask your driver for 'Holy House' (the Swahili pronunciation) otherwise you may be met by a rather bemused look! $$$$

🏠 **Tembo House Hotel** (40 rooms) 024 2233005/2069; e tembo@zitec.org; www. tembohotel.com. This hotel has a great location on Shangani Road, just west of Forodhani Gardens, leading right down to the sea. Easily identified by its grey elephant sculpture at the entrance (*tembo* means 'elephant' in Swahili), Tembo has long been a popular option. Part of the hotel was the 1834 American consulate, & there's also a more recent extension, creating a new wing & old wing, both overlooking the ocean & both quite Indian in décor. The bedrooms are all off chequerboard-tiled corridors, lined with Arabesque arches & plants in colourful ceramic pots. All have a mosaic Turkish bath, heavily carved furniture, mosquito nets, fridge & TV. Most have a sea view or overlook the large courtyard swimming pool, but choose carefully or pay the US$10 view supplement on booking. The 2 large corner rooms are fabulous for a trpl or couple wanting space, as they have huge private terraces with amazing sea views; sadly the plastic sun loungers are a little out of character. Due to a high demand for interconnecting family rooms, Tembo recently added 4 Mercury House apts, each consisting of 2 adjoining en-suite rooms – 1 dbl, 1 twin – a lounge with a flat-screen TV & a kitchenette. Obviously aimed at the self-catering market, these can also be booked on a B&B basis, with guests heading to the main hotel for b/fast. The public spaces are good & varied at Tembo, with a lounge on the upper floor of the old building, boasting a huge stained-glass window which fills the room with coloured light from its bold diamond pattern, & a beachfront restaurant with neat tables on decking under a row of sweet almond trees (non-residents welcome). Whilst the hotel is on the beach & deckchairs are laid out, it's not really a beach hotel, but rather a city hotel with a seafront location. There is a reasonable amount of passing local trade on the shoreline, so expect some hassle to buy cashews & sunglasses if you choose to sit out. Equally, the water is relatively polluted this close to the harbour & city so swimming is not advisable. It's also worth noting that, as with its sister property, the Dhow Palace, the Muslim owners of Tembo do not serve any alcohol. $$$$

🏠 **The Seyyida** (17 rooms) 024 2235462; m 0776 247744; e info@theseyyida-zanzibar. com; www.theseyyida-zanzibar.com. The Seyyida, which means 'lady of the manor' in Swahili, is relatively new on the scene, but is a welcome addition. It offers a cool & quiet haven from the heat & bustle of Stone Town outside. The spacious rooms are set around a verdant linear courtyard, & vary in size & views. All are equipped with various mod cons including a flat-screen satellite TV, minibar fridge, an internet connection &

very effective AC. The tasteful décor is a mixture of modern & Zanzibari style, with attractive wooden furniture & billowing gold curtains, while patterned cushions & throws add a hint of colour. At the top of the building, Lulu is a cheerful rooftop bar & restaurant (see *Where to eat and drink*, page 162) whose sweeping sea & harbour views are some of the best in town, making this a popular sundowner spot, even if you're not staying the night. **$$$$**

⌂ **The Swahili House** (20 rooms) m 0777 510209; e info@theswahilihouse.com; www. theswahilihouse.com. In 2008, Moivaro Lodges (behind Unguja Lodge & Fumba Beach Lodge, pages 323 & 337) acquired what was an unloved, dilapidated hotel & embarked on a serious regeneration project. They've since taken this towering 19th-century Indian merchant's house, built around a central roofed courtyard, & converted it into the elegant Swahili House. It is now a traditional hotel with an authentic Zanzibari feel & good management. The rooms are decked out in locally produced furniture & antiques, with polished stone floors, narrow wooden balconies (some rooms) & a touch of modernity thrown in in the form of AC & fans. There are 3 room types – Deluxe Rooms, Suites & Sultan Suites – of increasing size, some with balconies. Rooms are spread over 4 floors, with those nearest the top offering excellent views of Stone Town's alleyways. For the best view, however, head for the rooftop restaurant, where you'll find a long wooden-topped bar surrounded by relaxing benches on which to lie back with a cool drink & admire the panorama. There's even a jacuzzi up there! **$$$$**

⌂ **Zanzibar Grand Palace Hotel** (34 rooms) ☎024 2235368/9; e info@zanzibargrandpalace. com. Just opposite the port gates, on Turky's Square, stands this rather unremarkable new hotel. The rooms & 2 suites have a drab décor but are well finished & clean; the suites have the added bonus of a spacious lounge. Alcohol-free minibars & safes are the norm, while cable TV, free Wi-Fi & room service suggest that this hotel is aimed firmly at the business market. This is backed up by the presence of the Busara Convention Centre, Stone Town's largest conference room, seating 150. The hotel is one of few in town to have a lift, which whisks guests up to Banrama, the rooftop restaurant, where chefs rustle up a selection of largely seafood dishes made with organic ingredients (main course US$6). Although the air is fresh up here, the view is unappealing, with container ships & the ugly dock being the main sight. Downstairs & out on the square the Dock Café doles out strong espressos & quick snacks to weary businessmen. **$$$$**

⌂ **Zanzibar Hotel** (11 rooms) m 0778 717800; e frontdesk@zanzibarhotel.co.tz; www. zanzibarhotel.co.tz. Under the same ownership as Africa House Hotel & with a large garden plot in Stone Town, this grand hotel should be buzzing. But more often than not its fading public spaces, dilapidated garden & spacious rooms are empty & its staff hard to find. There is some promise here – the high-ceilinged rooms have been carefully furnished with antiques, including a wonderfully ornate carved wooden clock in the foyer, island artwork & crisp, colourful linens giving it an old-fashioned feel. Mosquito nets, TV & tea-/coffee-making facilities are standard throughout. The Royal Deluxe rooms have king-size beds whilst the Twin Deluxe have queen-size; the latter can be found in rooms with lovely views over the fountain courtyard. There's a compact b/fast room in the main foyer, while in the garden stands the independently run Lemon Spa. Sadly, on our most recent visit we found a lonely pet dik dik wandering the garden, & a collection of dejected caged vervet monkeys in a corner. Hopefully, good management in the future can find these a better home & turn this hotel into the success story it should be. **$$$$**

⌂ **Zanzibar Palace Hotel** (see advertisement on page 196) (9 rooms) ☎024 2232230; m 0773 079222; e info@zanzibarpalacehotel.com; www. zanzibarpalacehotel.com. Renovated & opened in Jul 2006, Zanzibar Palace Hotel quickly gained a reputation as one of the best boutique hotels in Stone Town. The hotel's interiors have a distinctly Zanzibari feel: steep staircases, a central atrium, handcrafted wooden furniture, antique Arab *objets d'art*, rich fabrics & atmospheric glass lanterns. Yet for all the historic furnishings, modern creature comforts abound: AC throughout the public areas & bedrooms, a DVD library & in-room player & even Wi-Fi. Each bedroom is individually named & has its own particular décor, but all are beautifully finished to a high standard with ornate chairs & sumptuous fabrics, & boast impressive bathrooms (the standard rooms have a shower & no bath, whereas the deluxe & suites have both). The 2 suites, Sherali & Dunia, & the deluxe room, Arabica, all on the 3rd floor, are particularly luxurious & would make wonderfully romantic honeymoon hideaways. That said, juicy mango wedges or sugared French toast may lure you to b/fast (both continental & cooked) in the ground-floor dining room, where calming instrumental music & chatter about the day's activities set the tone. Helpful staff are on hand for travel tips, the small bar serves cold drinks throughout the day & board games are available for when you tire of city explorations or the heat. Alternatively, you could head for the tranquil new spa that recently opened next door. With state-of-the-art equipment & a continuation of the opulent interiors of the main hotel, this is a great place to spoil yourself. **$$$$**

MID RANGE

🏠 **Asmini Palace** (12 rooms) m 0774 276464/5; e asminipalace@zanlink.com; www. asminipalace.com. Asmini Palace is located on Forodhani Road in the Kiponda area, between Palace Restaurant & Kiponda Hotel. Asmini is a new white building, constructed with traditional architecture in mind: an arched entrance, central courtyard & carved timber doors, shutters & balconies from every bedroom. The staff are delightful & its rooms are clean & uncluttered, with king-size Zanzibari beds, crisp embroidered linen & a small seating area. Mosquito nets, cable TV & fridge are provided in every room. There is a sunny rooftop restaurant for lunch & dinner & a large b/fast area on the ground floor filled with fresh flowers, while free Wi-Fi is available on the 1st & 2nd floors. Unusually for Stone Town, this hotel has a lift to the rooftop – a real bonus for those with limited mobility or weary legs. A good-value option in this price range. **$$$–$$$$**

🏠 **Abuso Inn** (23 rooms) ☎ 024 2235886; m 0777 425565. Set back from the Shangani Road, almost opposite the Tembo Hotel, this convenient family-run hotel is much better than first impressions imply. Its spick & span rooms are pretty good: polished timber floors, comfy king-size & twin Zanzibari beds, fresh linen, good-quality furniture & even some sea views. Fans, AC, mosquito nets, hot water & attractive traditional furnishings are standard. Guests can relax with a cold drink (no alcohol is served) in the sofa-filled TV & lounge area, while b/fast is served on the recently opened rooftop restaurant. The spacious

rooms & central location continue to make this one of the best deals in this range. **$$$**

🏠 **Bwawani Hotel** (100 rooms) ☎ 024 2235006; m 0777 416039/0773 139916; e hotelbwani@hotmail.com; www.bwawani. com. Built in 1972 on the outskirts of town, this 4-storey, government-owned monolith is a drab monstrosity on the outside & abysmal inside. The timber reception area houses a number of oversized presidential portraits watching over the hapless staff, whilst the adjoining lounge has a blaring TV broadcasting images of scantily clad women in low-budget movies. The trademark long, dark corridors exude the institutional feel of a 19th-century asylum, whilst the spacious rooms are frankly disgusting: mouldy, cigarette-burnt carpets, chipped baths, dripping toilets, collapsing drawers & bedding emblazoned with marker-pen stencilling of the hotel's initials. The main 'facilities' are located in separate buildings around the grounds & include the basic Marruna Fitness Centre, the 'Komba Discotheque' (⏱ 23.30–04.30 Tue–Sun) & 4 crumbling conference rooms. The Café Changu Restaurant, garishly decorated, produces simple meat & rice dishes 19.00–22.00 daily. There is a crumbling swimming pool but it is not in use, & by the looks of things, has not been swum in for a while. Unverifiable rumours have long circulated that the hotel will one day be privatised & rebuilt by an international hotel chain, but for now it remains in desperate disrepair & is best avoided. **$$$**

🏠 **Clove Hotel** (8 rooms) m 0777 484567; e clovehotel@zanlink.com; www.zanzibarhotel. nl. Transformed by its Dutch owner-manager, Lisette, in 2004. Clove's service, reliability & fresh décor have made it into one of the best mid-range options in the city. It's well located, at the kink halfway along Hurumzi Street, opposite a palm-filled café corner. This lends a sense of space to the hotel, in spite of the atmospheric warren of alleyways which surround it. Behind its white walls & mint-green shutters, the hand-painted lilac & pink corridors lead to rooms with lovely coconut wood furniture, Swahili batik bedcovers & large apricot bathrooms. There are safes, mosquito nets & fans in every room & the beds are specifically designed for taller visitors (they're over 2m in length, unusual in Zanzibar). All except 2 of the rooms are dbls, those remaining being specifically designed for families of 4. There's a lovely, sea-view rooftop terrace – one of the city's best – where local artwork & homemade African jam are sold to guests. It's shady & enjoys a cool afternoon breeze which, along with its honesty bar, book exchange, free Wi-Fi & cushion-strewn sofas make it a perfect hangout. Min 2-night stay. **$$$**

⌂ **Coco de Mer Hotel** (13 rooms) ☎024 2230852; m 0785 099123/0718 060807; e cocodemer_znz@yahoo.com; www.cocodemer-zanzibar.com. Behind the NBC bank in Shangani, this is a straightforward but friendly place with rooms set around an airy courtyard, decorated with potted plants. All of the rooms are different & it's well worth looking at a few on arrival. The rooms downstairs are a bit dark, but those upstairs are bright & cheerful with stripy red blankets. All of the rooms have ceiling fans & hot-water showers; 3 have a small TV & there are pie-in-the-sky plans to add AC to the downstairs rooms. The restaurant does good-value food around main meal times & there's an adjacent ground-floor bar which serves a variety of snacks & sandwiches. US$10 per car transfers are available from the port/airport but be sure that you have a confirmed reservation at the hotel in Shangani as there have been rumours of people being taken to a less salubrious annex. **$$$**

⌂ **Dhow Palace Hotel** (30 rooms) ☎024 2233012/0304; m 0777 878088; e dhowpalace@zanlink.com; www.dhowpalace-hotel.com. In the Shangani area, just off Kenyatta Road, this is an excellent & frequently recommended hotel. It's a renovated old house built in 1559 around 2 cool central courtyards, complete with a tinkling fountain & swimming pool respectively. From the blue mosaic pool & its adjacent juice bar, the distinctive harlequin stained-glass windows of the newer rooms & their balconies rise upwards. By contrast, the original rooms all access a private section of shared balcony & boast more space, & a less kitsch interior. All of the rooms are nicely furnished with Zanzibari beds, vibrantly edged mosquito nets, genuine antiques, a refreshing amount of space & bathrooms complete with Persian baths. All mod cons are provided, including fridge, cable TV & Wi-Fi. The whole place is spotlessly clean, the staff are friendly & the atmosphere is very tranquil. B/fast & other meals are served in the à la carte restaurant downstairs, while upstairs is a lovely sundowner lounge & snooker table, overlooking the city's rooftops. It

lacks only a seafront location, although if it had this the rates would be significantly higher, so instead you get real comfort & a heat-busting pool at an excellent price. **$$$**

⌂ **Hotel Marine** (24 rooms) ☎024 236069; m 0777 411102; e hotelmarinestar3@hotmail.com. This stand-alone hotel is in a large house opposite the port gates & overlooking the Mizingani Road roundabout. Inside, a grand staircase winds around an inner courtyard to rooms on 3 upper floors. Once dim & gloomy, it has been brightened up with a fresh coat of yellow & green paint, although the b/fast room remains dull & dingy. The rooms are of fair quality, with dark beds & apparently clean linen, but they feel run-down & fans do little more than blow the dust around. Assumed essentials, such as fridge & small TV, as well as the 2 guest computers in reception, simply make things cramped. In addition, the general hustle of the port & the incessant din of motorbikes below make this a far from relaxing retreat. At the time of researching, we were left in no doubt that guests were a great inconvenience to the staff, which perhaps goes some way to explain why there were none. **$$$**

⌂ **Karibu Zanzibar Hotel** (9 rooms) ☎024 2230932; m 0777 223309; e karibuznzhotel@zanlink.com; www.karibuzanzibarhotel.co.tz. This former private house was converted to a rather characterless hotel in 2009. The rooms all feel fairly cramped, & the bathrooms are tiny. Impractically, bathers are required to sit on the toilet in order to use the shower, thereby drenching the entire room, including the already soggy toilet paper. Fraying seats & crackling TVs fill the rooms at this simple hotel, which also contain AC & fans, while green lighting gives the corridors a radioactive glow. There are plans to build a new restaurant to replace the teeny b/fast room, but the chances of this having opened by the time you visit are slim. For the price you can do better than this basic & sterile place. **$$$**

⌂ **Mauwani Inn** (7 rooms) m 0777 475748; e reservations@mauwaniinn.com; www.mauwaniinn.com. Mauwani, meaning 'flowers' in Swahili, is situated just off Kenyatta Road, opposite Afya Medical Centre & behind the Rendezvous Les Spices Restaurant. The change of ownership in Jan 2012 has brought increased staff friendliness along with plans for expansion. While the hotel is still a little rough around the edges, it offers small &

simple but very clean rooms with tiled floors, a fan, TV, mosquito net & AC, with some rooms sharing a lemon-fresh bathroom. Currently b/fast is the only meal offered, & in good weather can be eaten outside where the compact seating area is shared with a family of clucking chickens. Being popular with students, they do free pick-ups from the port & airport. **$$$**

🏠 **Mazsons Hotel** (36 rooms) 📞024 2233062/3694; m 0741 340042; e reservationmazsonshotel@zanlink.com; www. mazsonshotel.net. This hotel on Kenyatta Road has an interesting history: old records show it was built in the mid 19th century by Said bin Dhanin, who is thought to have settled here about the time that Sultan Said moved his court to Zanzibar from Muscat. Ownership changed hands several times, & during the early part of the 20th century the building was a Greek-run hotel before becoming a private dwelling once again. After the revolution, the house, along with many others, fell into disrepair. Today, it is a hotel & once again beginning to look a little tired. The reception area is large & dated in décor: a heavily carved reception desk, chandeliers, plastic flowers & velour sofas. The slightly soulless bedrooms have white tiled floors with beige linen & walls hung with tacky plastic 'flowing' waterfalls. Large TVs, safes, small fridges & functional bathrooms feature in all. There's an overpowering smell of insect repellent, but at least the mosquitoes should stay away. Some rooms have access to the shared balcony at the front of the hotel, overlooking the square & Kenyatta Road. The hotel has a reasonable restaurant, Yungi Yungi, serving à la carte international food, which is popular with locals, as well as a business centre & 3 conference rooms. Although power supplies are pretty good on Zanzibar these days, this hotel has its own large generator in case of cuts – in fact, it's so big it supplies many surrounding buildings as well. **$$$**

🏠 **Pearl of Zanzibar Hotel** (10 rooms) 📞024 2231435; m 0777 576755; e salimjaffer@gmail.com. The former Ahlan Palace has been spruced up by a new Canadian owner, who took over in 2011. The century-old building has been sensitively renovated to modernise & brighten up the style. The sizeable bedrooms are spread over 3 floors, with upstairs rooms having balconies. There are no TVs in the rooms, because as the owner states, 'you are not on holiday to watch TV'. Each

room is furnished with a Zanzibari bed, while the top-floor 'penthouse suite' has an extra large 6ft bed. Light bathrooms are larger than expected, & toiletries are provided. There is a dearth of wall decoration, but this is made up for by the colourful rugs & bedspreads in the rooms, as well as the chequerboard floor & sunny yellow walls. Wi-Fi & spare laptops are available for guests. Downstairs there's a bright covered courtyard; b/fast is the only meal served, but guests are welcome to use the kitchen or visit Freddie M's Café next door. The knowledgeable owner can also help with bookings at the Lemon Spa, which is directly opposite. Note: Pearl of Zanzibar is not to be confused with the far more basic, Pearl Guesthouse, despite what your taxi driver may tell you! **$$$**

🏠 **Rumaisa Hotel** (7 rooms) 📞042 239024; m 0777 410695; e inforumaisa@yahoo.com; www.rumaisahotel.blogspot.com. This funky little place opened in Nov 2011 & trendy travellers & 'flashpackers' have been recommending it ever since. Rumaisa is located in the Funguni area of Stone Town, quite a walk from the centre but allowing for lower prices than there would otherwise be for the standard of room. All rooms are well finished & furnished in different vivid colours in Zanzibar style with TV, hot water, Wi-Fi, fans, a fridge, & a solar emergency light. The decoration here is very pretty, with Indian furniture giving a homely feel to ensure guests feel like they're staying over with a friend. Rooms are simple, but an effort has been made to brighten them up, with cheerful touches from stained glass to tropical fish shower curtains. Staff are helpful & friendly, & there's a lovely clean smell pervading the air. The blustery rooftop bar is filled with music in the evenings, when the owner's father plays the guitar & drums for guests. At the front, a communal balcony has a sea view with Prison Island in the distance. There are plans to add a further 14 rooms at some point in the future, but hopefully the hotel will retain its cosy feel. **$$$**

🏠 **Shangani Hotel** (28 rooms) 📞024 2236363/3688; m 0777 411703; e shanganihotel@hotmail.com; www.shanganihotel.com. On busy Kenyatta Road, opposite the old post office, this hotel is an adequate mid-range choice. Enter reception by passing through the bureau de change, in the knowledge that the rooms are better than this

1st impression may give. They are little more than simple & functional, but they are all clean & uncluttered with distinctive flowery bedspreads. AC, fan, fridge & satellite TV are standard, though the ambient noise level is definitely less towards the back of the hotel. B/fast & other meals are taken in the rooftop restaurant & a consistently reliable internet café is attached. **$$$**

🏠 **Stone Town Café & Bed & Breakfast** (8 rooms) m 0778 373737; e baraka@zanlink.com; www.stonetowncafe.com. Above the bustling Stone Town Café (see page 167) on Kenyatta Road, the family-owned & run Stone Town B&B offers delightful modern rooms with dbl polished wooden Zanzibari beds, AC, fans & fridges. Each room has a small seating area with a TV & en-suite shower rooms with hot water as standard. Cool floors & warm colours make this a cosy place to spend a night or 2, while high-quality accessories & sturdy furniture raise the standard above the average Stone Town B&B. B/fast is included at the popular Stone Town Café downstairs, where guests can order what they want from the menu up to a value of US$7, with anything over this costing extra. **$$$**

🏠 **Zanzibar Coffee House** (8 rooms) 024 2239319; m 0773 061532; e coffeehouse@zanlink.com; www.riftvalley-zanzibar.com. Housed in an 1885 Arabic home, originally built by Sir Tharia Topan, wazir (high-ranking advisor) to Sultan Said Barghash & described by Stanley in *Through the Dark Continent* as 'one of the richest merchants in town', Zanzibar Coffee House is by contrast an understated, unpretentious haven. Tucked in the maze of streets behind the Creek Road market, & with only pedestrian access, its individually styled bedrooms, each named after a type of coffee, sit above the excellent café of the same name, which uses its own home-ground beans. Well proportioned & modestly furnished, the rooms are simple & atmospheric, with traditional Zanzibari 4-poster beds, antique dressers & glass lamps. Most are en suite, whilst a few share bathroom facilities; there are few modern trappings except AC, & no telephones, TVs or gadgets. A stay here is in fact made all the more pleasurable for its simplicity. Coffee aromas permeate the building, the gracious staff provide a very friendly service & the stunning tower-top terrace offers one of Stone Town's most appealing b/fast views. **$$$**

🏠 **Safari Lodge** (28 rooms) 024 2236523; m 0784 606177; e info@safarilodgetz.com; www.safarilodgetz.com. Constructed from 2 adjoining houses, Safari Lodge is a well-signed, 3-storey building with impressive carved timber balconies spanning the width of its upper floors. One half is older than the other, & the hotel's spacious rooms vary in standard depending on which side you're in. All of them are impressively bright & immaculately clean, with the 3 good-value suites on the newer side being bang up to date, with soft white & brown furnishings. Inside each has a large Zanzibari bed or 2, AC & fan, & cable TV. It has a convenient location for exploring the Old Town, a decent rooftop restaurant for skyline b/fasts. Have no hesitation in ordering dinner here (in advance – it's all fresh ingredients), as this was the only place in Stone Town to offer to show us their pristine kitchen. Dbl **$$$**; **$** dorm

🏠 **Princess Salme Inn** (10 rooms) 024 2236588; m 0777 435303; e info@princesssalmeinn.com; www.princesssalmeinn.com. At the northern end of town, in a building with distinctive turquoise shutters, the Princess Salme Inn is set back a little from the Mizingani Road, beside Bandari Lodge & Warere Town House. In keeping with the name, a framed photo of Princess Salme greets guests in reception, where they are offered a warm welcome, bijou bedrooms & an airy rooftop complete with self-catering facilities (fridge, cooker & crockery). There are pastel-shaded walls, white bedding & fluffy towels, mosquito nets over the beds & windows, & efficient fans. The majority of the rooms share 2 central bathrooms, whilst the en-suite dbl, complete with a Zanzibari bed, is best used by people who know each other well as the only divider to the bathroom is a plastic shower curtain adorned with leaping dolphins. The rule here is simple: the more you pay, the more facilities you get. **$$–$$$**

🏠 **Warere Town House** (12 rooms) 024 2233835; m 0782 234564; e warere_townhouse@hotmail.com; www.warere.com. Situated in a leafy corner neighbouring the Princess Salme Inn, this pleasant 3-storey lodge has been popular for many years with travellers on a tight budget. Located in an early 20th-century homestead, it is a simple, comfortable haunt, slightly tatty around the edges, with rooms offering traditional Zanzibari furnishings, kanga curtains & sparkling bathrooms with hammam baths. 4 rooms boast breezy flower-filled balconies, albeit overlooking the unattractive back of Bandari Lodge, & all guests can access the basic rooftop terrace. **$$–$$$**

🏠 **Zenji Hotel** (see advertisement on page 138) (9 rooms) m 0774 276468/0776 705592; e info@zenjihotel.com; www.zenjihotel.com. Opposite the now defunct Ciné Afrique, this Dutch–Zanzibari hotel is a haven of calm with the hustle & bustle of Malawi Road literally on its doorstep. In fact, it is only the noisy location that lets down this quirky little place, a real find among the shabbier options near the port. The rooms have been given poetic & exotic-sounding names such as Spirit of Nature & Room of Wonder, each of which is priced differently depending on facilities. All have AC, fans & hot water, but 2 share a bathroom, only some have balconies & 1 has a private toilet in the corridor, rather than in the room. Kitted out in locally handcrafted furniture, with colour-trim mosquito nets, pastel shades on the walls & tie-dye sheets, the rooms are full of charm & light. A tasty buffet b/fast served up on the roof includes homemade bread & cake, while caffeine fiends will be happy to note that cappuccinos & espressos from the Zenji Café (see *Where to eat and drink*, page 167), made with coffee from the Zanzibar Coffee House (see opposite) are included in the room price. Wi-Fi is free, & the hotel has laptops that guests can borrow. While maintaining high standards, Zenji is also conscious of giving back to the community. All staff here are local & many are uneducated. The hotel gives them free English lessons twice a week, & this must be working, as they are some of the friendliest staff in any Stone Town hotel. There's a small curio shop in reception where quality local crafts are sold, & the hotel has a strong involvement in women's aid projects. **$$–$$$**

🏠 **1001 Nights** (10 rooms) m 0777 435303; e info@1001nightszanzibar.com; www.1001NightsZanzibar.com. Just down the road from the port in the Malindi area of town, the former Adam's Inn is now the rather lacklustre 1001 Nights, with the same management as the nearby Princess Salme Inn (see opposite). Walking through the purple reception, there can be an uneasy air, with lingering shady characters, but upstairs the rooms are clean & simply equipped with a fan, a chair & a mirror. Higher-priced rooms

have their own bathroom & even a rickety TV. However, for safety & hospitality, Zenji Hotel next door is a far superior option. **$$**

🏠 **Annex II of Narrow Street Hotel** (10 rooms) ✆ 024 2235659; m 0717 784125/0776 251557; e favourboy@hotmail.com. Between the Big Tree & Creek Road market, in a warren of narrow alleys, this place is something of a mission to locate. In spite of its name, it is not directly connected to Narrow Street Hotel. Manned by a team of laid-back, friendly locals, Annex II is a somewhat ramshackle arrangement of neat but tired rooms, at the top of some quite steep stairs (help is willingly offered to tourists with heavy bags). The rooms do vary considerably in size & configuration so it's worth looking at a few on arrival: Room 303 is a good choice for a trip of 3 singletons; Room 304 is a large suite of 2 dbl beds. Although perceived luxuries aren't up to much (small TVs crackle loudly & the baths are badly chipped), there are fridges & AC & the basic package is perfectly reasonable for the price. There's also an expansive breezy rooftop terrace, where b/fast is served to the gentle tune of children playing & bicycle bells from the street below. **$$**

🏠 **Bandari Lodge** (5 rooms) ✆ 024 2237969; m 0777 423638; e bandarilodge@hotmail.com. Just 100m north of the port gates, Bandari's entrance is easily identified by 2 towering palm trees & a walled entrance. One of a clutch of affordable hotels in Malindi, it offers good-value, no-frills accommodation. Zanzibari beds, indigo mosquito nets, simple furniture & fans are the norm, with only room 5 having a slightly tired-looking en-suite bathroom with flip-flops provided. 2 rooms on the 2nd floor are particularly spacious trpls (3 dbl beds). There's a book exchange, seemingly popular with Mills & Boon readers, & a good selection of multi-lingual magazines available. B/fast is served in the central atrium & a basic, concrete kitchen is available for guest use. The very friendly owner is always on hand to help with Stone Town advice & onward plans. **$$**

🏠 **Funguni Palace Hotel** (13 rooms) ✆ 024 2233525; m 0777 411842; e fungunipalace@yahoo.com; www.fungunipalace.com. New in 2011, the rooms are clean & comfy if a little soulless, with chunky polished wooden beds, yellow walls & gold-trim mosquito nets. Fans, AC, phones & TV are found in all rooms, while some have balconies. Giant sofas are crammed in to the reception room where vases of flowers brighten the place up a bit, while up on the roof is the unremarkable b/fast room. **$$**

⌂ **Garden Lodge** (18 rooms) ☏ 024 2233298; e gardenlodge@zanlink.com. Situated in a house on the busy Kaunda Road, near Victoria Gardens & the main hospital, this place is simple but neat & very friendly. The vehicle entrance is surrounded by a small garden terrace of tropical flowers & palms, whilst the building is clad in cerise bougainvillea, making this feel like a pretty lush retreat for Zanzibar Town. Catering primarily to students, tour groups & backpackers, the bright yet shabby rooms here all have dbl beds in twin configuration, with good-quality furniture & linen, fans, mosquito nets & reliable hot water. Upstairs rooms are brighter & airier; try to get one at the back to avoid traffic noise disturbance. There are small balconies at the front of the hotel laid out with deckchairs & a cool 1st-floor lounge with crimson Zanzibari chairs. There is a vivid orange rooftop terrace for b/fast & a few good restaurants within easy walking distance. This is a good choice for the price. **$$**

⌂ **Haven Lodge** (9 rooms) ☏ 024 2235677; m 0777 437132; e thehaven@yahoo.com. This is a friendly & good-value place, in the southern part of Stone Town between Soko Mohogo Street & Vuga Road. Makame, the manager, aims to offer simple bedrooms & separate bathrooms, hot water, a big b/fast & as much tea & coffee as you like, & broadly he succeeds. There's a good deal of space for the price, cheerful embroidered bedspreads, fans, a generator in case of power cuts, an organised safe-deposit system, luggage storage, a kitchen for self-catering (free) & cheap transfers to the coast, boat trips & tours; they even have bikes for hire. If you do stay, look out for the distinctive reception desk covered in coins & be sure to visit nearby Nyambuni Restaurant for great Swahili fare. **$$**

⌂ **Island View Hotel** (18 rooms) ☏ 024 2234605/5222; e islandview@africamail.com, sadrumitha@hotmail.com. About 2km south of Zanzibar Town, at Kilimani, this is a small & welcoming B&B, run by the friendly Mitha family. All rooms are spacious with dbl/twin bed, mosquito net, fan, TV & fridge. 5 of the rooms are now available with AC, too. Meals can be ordered,

tea or coffee is available all day free of charge, & there's internet access. This hotel is very handy for the airport, & only a few mins' drive from town (transport can be provided). **$$**

⌂ **Jambo Guesthouse** (9 rooms) ☏ 024 2233779; m 0777 496571; e info@ jamboguest.com; www.zanzibar.net/hotels/ jambo_guest_house. In a quiet & peaceful quarter of the Mkunazini area, 5mins from the Anglican cathedral & opposite the pleasant outdoor Green Garden Restaurant, this straightforward little hotel has a range of room sizes, all of which share bathroom facilities. Most of the simple, yellow rooms are on the wood-panelled 1st floor, & all have coconut-wood beds, neatly edged mosquito nets & ceiling fans, while decoration comes in the form of plastic sunflowers. The rooms are looking a little scuffed but they do have AC & this helps with the heat & humidity. Bathrooms are small & unremarkable but the water is always hot. B/fast is served beside reception & is usually accompanied by Sky News. It's a good-value budget place, offering thoughtful little extras such as a free luggage store & tea & coffee, all of which have made it justifiably popular with backpackers for many years. With advance bookings, it's also possible to arrange a free pick-up from the port or airport. **$$**

⌂ **Karibu Inn** (25 rooms) ☏ 024 2233058; m 0777 417392; e karibuinnhotel@yahoo.com. On a narrow street, parallel with Kenyatta Road, in the Shangani part of town, this hostel-like place caters mainly for young travellers, budget tour groups or people on overland truck expeditions. There is a laissez-faire vibe here, a consistent crowd of braided backpackers hanging around the reception & a very basic lounge. Rooms are dispersed around a warren of levels & corridors; they are clean but basic & primarily sgl/dbl en suites. Dormitories are available, each of which sleeps between 5–8 people with sgl beds, plenty of space, ceiling fans & an en-suite bathroom. The friendly management can set you up with budget tours, & also run a safe-deposit scheme. They will not tolerate stains from henna tattoos on sheets or towels & will charge for any damage. Dbl **$$**; Dorm **$**

⌂ **Kiponda Hotel** (15 rooms) ☏ 024 2233052; m 0777 431665; e info@kiponda.com; www. kiponda.com. On Nyumba ya Moto Street in the Kiponda area, not far from the main seafront, this is a small, quiet hotel in a building which used to house part of a sultan's harem. It has been renovated in local style & still has an original carved wooden entrance door. The Zanzibari management team, headed up by the very helpful Salma, give the place a relaxed & friendly atmosphere, & although it's a touch more expensive than the budget hotels to which it is sometimes compared, it is also a lot quieter & better value. The older rooms are looking somewhat forlorn, but the newer ones are cleaner & much more colourful with simple furnishings & efficient fans; there is even a deep sink for washing laundry. Some rooms have AC, & 2 have their own bathroom located outside the room. Good b/fasts are available in the airy restaurant, although unfortunately what was once a clear sea view is now obscured by the Seyyida Hotel (see page 150).This area mutates into a casual coffee bar from 11.00 to 18.00, serving cold drinks, including beer, making it a nice place to hang out in the heat of the day. The hotel has good connections with Sama Tours & can help with flights & ferry reservations. Discounts are available for long stays & for groups, with extra reductions in low season. **$$**

🏠 **Kokoni's Hotel** (14 rooms) PO Box 3257, Zanzibar; ☏024 2230239; m 0745 863817; e kokonishotel@hotmail.com. In the Kokoni area, between Malindi Street & Creek Road, a short walk behind the Gapco petrol station, this is the former Hotel Karwan Sarai. It's a big old house with a distinctive red, wraparound baraza bench outside, & a range of very basic rooms; some are large & airy with old wooden shutters leading onto a small balcony overlooking the square, while others are small & dark with no view & pretty tatty furnishings. Most rooms have en-suite shower rooms, all have fans, & some also have TV, while the rooftop lounge has good views across Stone Town. It's a quiet place & good value, but veering towards the soulless. **$$**

🏠 **Malindi Lodge** (8 rooms) ☏024 2232359; e malindilodge2007@yahoo.com. On Malawi Road, close to the port gates & next to Ciné Afrique, Malindi Lodge is in a convenient location if you're arriving or departing by boat. 2 rooms boast a fridge & en-suite shower, whilst the remaining ones share 2 central bathrooms. Rooms are all fairly small & some overlook the busy road below, making them a less quiet option. However, with simple Zanzibari beds, bright turquoise linen

& floors to match which are consistently kept spotlessly clean, this is a good choice within its price range. B/fasts are served at the banquet table on the ground floor & offer a good time to chat to the staff about directions & onward plans. **$$**

🏠 **Manch Lodge** (23 rooms) ☏024 2231918; m 0778 202038; e manchtime_72@hotmail.co.uk; www.manchlodge-zanzibar.net. A stone's throw from Haven Lodge, this is another budget place on Vuga Road. A friendly bunch of locals usually hang out on the veranda & lend this place its relaxed air. The interiors here are unusual: large posters showing worldwide scenes, chintzy sofas on the balcony, & a crazy patterned floor seeming particularly curious choices. Rooms are quite cramped with heavy brown furniture, while the en suites are unventilated concrete cubes literally within the bedrooms (take a shower before bed & it won't be amorous gestures making the place steamy!). To escape the heat there's a breezy balcony on the 1st floor &, unusually for Stone Town, at least a few trees to break the view. B/fast is in the flower-filled garden & is an indulgent affair including pancakes & eggs for those staying for 4 nights or more. British visitors may smile at Heinz baked beans on the menu, while for lunch & dinner there's an array of burgers, pizzas, samosas & salads for US$5–7. It's just about acceptable for the price but phone in advance for a free pick-up from the port, or 1 from the airport for US$2. **$$**

🏠 **Mnazi House** (10 rooms) m 0778881213; e info@mnazihouse.com; www.mnazihouse. com. Constructed entirely using the skills of local carpenters, painters, craftsmen & suppliers, this gleaming new property is located in the Kikwajuni residential area of Stone Town, allowing visitors to watch everyday life passing by right on the doorstep. Rooms are Zanzibari in style & fresh flowers make guests feel at home. The hotel is opposite a football field, so there is a possibility of watching or even joining in a friendly local game. Due to the location, guests are asked to be quiet after 22.00 so as to not disturb local residents. **$$**

🏠 **Pyramid Hotel** (11 rooms) ☏024 2233000; m 0777 461451/0748 255525; e pyramidhotel@ yahoo.com; www.pyramidhotel.co.tz. On Kokoni Street, between the Malindi & Kiponda areas, this old hotel is just behind the Ijumaa Mosque, a short walk back from the seafront. A budget travellers' favourite for many years, & deservedly so, it gets its name from the very steep & narrow staircases (almost ladders) that lead to the upper floors. The rooms have nets, AC, fan & hot water, yet vary in atmosphere: some are large & bright, others small & dark, so choose carefully. The manager Ibrahim & his staff are very friendly & the rooftop restaurant does great b/fasts. Overall, it's a good budget choice, offering a US$10/car pick-up from the airport or port, free use of a rather slow computer in reception, as well as a book-swap service. **$$**

🏠 **Sealand Hotel** (14 rooms) 📞024 2232621; 📱 0774 282020; e sealandhotel@gmail.com. This backstreet hotel is tricky to locate, especially as the name is not prominently displayed & reception is on the 2nd floor. Once inside, the décor is straight out of the 1970s but the staff are helpful & friendly, even though the TV blaring in reception is rather offputting. Not many foreigners stay here, but should you choose to, you'll find large rooms, which although dusty in the corners are perfectly acceptable. All have ceiling fans, TV, hot water, AC, & clean but slightly chipped bathrooms. Sealand is owned by the same people as the Narrow Street Hotel, & is of a similar standard, but with a less advantageous location. **$$**

🏠 **St Monica's Hostel** (16 rooms) 📞024 2230773; e monicaszanzibar@hotmail.com; www.stmonicahostelzanzibar.s5.com. Beside the Anglican cathedral, St Monica's whitewashed walls sit behind its lush front garden. Built in the 1890s to house teachers, nurses & nuns working at the UMCA mission, it now offers a warm welcome to both church guests & younger backpackers. A recent programme of major renovations & enthusiastic Isaac, the new manager, have rejuvenated the hostel's buildings & soft furnishings. There is a pleasant, reverential atmosphere, largely emanating from the bold architecture: cool thick walls, wide staircases, Arabesque arches, traditional wooden shutters & rooms with wide balconies overlooking the cathedral or pretty palm gardens. Rooms – 7 en suite, 9 with shared bathrooms – are clean & simple with mosquito nets. There is a restaurant, run by the parish's Mothers' Union, offering fresh Swahili cuisine for b/fast, lunch & dinner (no alcohol); a long-standing art shop selling vibrant paintings & hand-printed T-shirts; & there's a new airy lounge area for games & gossip. A great-value, friendly place in this price range. **$$**

SHOESTRING

🏠 **Flamingo Guest House** (15 rooms) 📞024 2232850; 📱 0777 491252; e flamingoguesthouse@hotmail.com, flamingoguesthouse@yahoo.com. In a fairly noisy area of Mkunazini Street, this no-frills place has all the charm of a multi-storey car park. Behind reception, an external concrete staircase ascends to an array of en-suite & shared-facilities rooms. The beds are basic & all rooms have a sink & ceiling fan, though several smell of damp & the shared showers & toilets are grim. The roof terrace once had great views of the Anglican cathedral, but it is now obscured by curtains & a washing line, making it a generally less than pleasant place. **$**

🏠 **Mzuri Guest House** (11 rooms) PO Box 4118, Zanzibar; 📞024 2230463; 📱 0713 774261/0777 488344. On the busy Malawi Road (50m east of the port), Mzuri's inconspicuous entrance, opposite the Passing Show Restaurant, is easily missed. Once found, head upstairs to the 1st-floor reception desk & rooms. Catering primarily to the low-end Tanzanian market & a few cash-strapped backpackers, Mzuri's small, en-suite bedrooms are all pretty grim: a mishmash of patterned lino flooring with grubby walls & basic bathroom facilities. There is a TV & a noisy AC unit in every room, along with various ceiling holes. B/fast is included in the room rate & is served on the landing; soft drinks are available all day at reception. **$**

🏠 **Narrow Street Hotel** (8 rooms) 📞024 2232620; 📱 0774 281010; e narrowstreethotel@ymail.com. In an interesting bit of town, this old hotel is in the maze of narrow alleys off Malindi Street. The Zanzibari-styled rooms are all neat & tidy with carved furnishings, TVs, AC & pretty pink mosquito nets. They are quite small though, so ideally you should know your room-mate well before checking in. The en-suite bathrooms are also bijou but they are simple & clean & the water is always hot. The staff are a bit sleepy, & don't be surprised to find them all gawping at the TV in the lounge area, but this is a fair low-budget choice for in a central location. **$**

🏠 **Pearl Guesthouse** (13 rooms) 📞024 2237611; 📱 0741 40004; e pghzanzibar@rogers.com; http://members.rogers.com/pghzanzibar. Not to be confused with the far superior Pearl of Zanzibar, this dark & dingy place opened in 1992 & appears to have remained in the same state ever since. Pale yellow interiors match the fading sheets

& it needs a good clean but is otherwise fine. Some of the rooms have an outside bathroom, & all have a separate toilet. All rooms have fans & 2 also have AC, which costs an extra US$5/room. Guests also have the option of b/fast for an extra US$2pp, or they can use the somewhat dubious kitchen. You'll have to carry your food upstairs to the roof to eat, where high walls & drying laundry obscure what would be a decent view. Pearl is cheap as chips, but you get what you pay for. **$**

✖ WHERE TO EAT AND DRINK

This section lists restaurants, cafés, snack bars, eating-houses and all other places that serve primarily food – or food and drink in equal measures. Bars, and other places which mainly serve drinks, are listed along with music venues in *Bars, clubs and entertainment*, pages 169–71.

Some restaurants and cafés in Zanzibar Town are simple and aimed at locals, and their prices reflect this; others are smarter and cater specifically for tourists, expatriates and wealthier residents.

The dining experience in the city has recently taken a dramatic turn for the better, with some stylish evening eateries opening, a burgeoning selection of cool cafés, and even a great new street food area for Forodhani Gardens' traditional night dining. Several hotel restaurants in Zanzibar Town, such as those at **Emerson Spice**, **Beyt al Chai** and the **Serena Inn**, deserve a special mention for their cuisine, and are listed below (though most of the upper- and mid-range hotels welcome residents and visitors to their dining rooms). At the other end of the scale, there are many, seemingly nameless, basic eating-houses which you may just stumble across as you walk around the streets of Zanzibar Town. Menus are rare in these establishments, and some of the very small places may only have one meal available These places are harder to keep track of, so look for the longest queues to spot the current best bets.

The following list, arranged very loosely into categories of quality and price (for codes, see page 108), cannot hope to be complete given the current pace of change, but it indicates the type and range of places available. Nearly all those included are open in the evenings for dinner, and most also open for lunch; some are open all day. At busy times reservations may be necessary in some of the smarter and better-known restaurants.

RESTAURANTS
Gastronomic
✖ **Abyssinian Maritim** m 0772 940556/0713 359054/0752 940556; ⏰ 11.00–14.00 & 18.00–23.00 daily. In 2011 this great little place opened on the corner opposite the High Court in Vuga. Abyssinian Maritim is a traditional Ethiopian restaurant, serving authentic cuisine, great coffee & shisha pipes amid a north African décor. Already gaining popularity with Zanzibari expats & visitors who've stumbled across its entrance, this culinary departure from Swahili curries is a very welcome addition to the restaurant scene. **$$$$$**

✖ **Emerson Spice Rooftop Tea House**
☎ 024 2232776; m 0775 046395; e reservation@ emersonspice.com; www.emersonspice.com; ⏰ 17.30–23.00 daily. On the rooftop of the Emerson Spice (see page 149), this intimate, open-sided dining experience offers a lovely bird's-eye vista over town, a buzzing atmosphere & an impressive 5-course degustation menu. Open every night for a single sitting (cocktails from 17.30; dinner 19.00), the US$25pp set menu is excellent value, consistently delicious & worth booking to avoid disappointment. Accommodating only 25 diners a night at individual tables under the central rooftop canopy, it's highly personal & often overseen by the charismatic owner. Be sure to arrive in time for sundowners to take full advantage of the evening breeze & sunset atmosphere: hear muezzins call the faithful to prayer, look down on traders heading home & watch warm pinks fill the sky before nightfall.

Cocktails (US$5) are made to order & aromatic food is cooked by a small smiling team in the corner of the terrace. Presented beautifully, the food is also quite delicious, with inventive ingredients & Swahili fusion flavours. The tempting menu changes daily based on seasonally available produce & freshly landed seafood: calamari ceviche, lobster on green papaya salad, black pepper-seared tuna, Tambi prawns with grilled mango, & coconut chilli kingfish, to name but a few. Desserts such as baked bananas or plum tart round off the seafood feast, & are happily washed down by reasonably priced bottles of imported wine. (Note: The fixed menu means any food allergies should be mentioned at the time of booking). For special occasions, traditional music or dancing may also be arranged, & is a real treat for diners! $$$$$

✕ Livingstone Beach Restaurant m 0773 164939. Livingstone consists of a large, uncluttered & attractively decorated dining room leading out to a private beach where you can dine with your toes trailing in the sand. Situated opposite Zawadi Chest, the restaurant has a decidedly upmarket ambience & the (mostly seafood) menu is priced accordingly, with most main courses falling into the US$14–20 range, although there's also a children's menu, & shisha pipes for those so inclined. $$$$$

✕ Lulu Restaurant & Lounge ✆024 2235462; m 0776 247744; e info@theseyyida-zanzibar. com; www.theseyyida-zanzibar.com. Up on the roof of the Seyyida Hotel (see *Where to stay*, page 151), Lulu is a peaceful light lunch or evening retreat serving a tempting selection of dishes such as king prawns with dry martini sauce & lyonnaise potatoes (US$20) or fruity flavoured shisha pipes (US$5). But Lulu is most popular for late-afternoon sundowners where hotel guests & passers-by alike can enjoy a cocktail of the day (US$8) under the shade of giant umbrellas. This place has an enviable view of the sea from its sunny terrace & is worth a pit stop for that alone. $$$$$

✕ Tower Top Restaurant 236 Hurumzi, Hurumzi St; ✆024 2230171; m 0777 423266. Up on the roof of 236 Hurumzi (see page 145), this restaurant has a superb view, which the management modestly claims to be the 'best on the island'. Meals (US$25pp) are relaxed affairs, starting with sunset drinks & cocktails, against the sound of the muezzins calling from the minarets

around town. Guests sit on carved chairs looking out over the bay, working slowly through starters & several courses of an Arabic–Swahili meal & ending with Arabic coffee, all to the tune of the traditional musicians. Space means numbers are limited & sustained marketing & PR efforts mean reservations are essential. That said, the diners' high expectations are rarely matched these days & complaints about slapdash service & food quality are on the rise. Whilst the view is great, there are far better places in Stone Town for culinary delights. $$$$$

✕ Baharia Restaurant Serena Hotel, Shangani Rd; ✆024 2233587. Not as flamboyant as the Tower Top Restaurant at the 236 Hurumzi, this is a good-quality place nonetheless. The food is a mix of Asian, African & European, with a popular Swahili night every Sat, which includes live band music. Starters like salads or mini kebabs are US$5, while main courses include curries for around US$10, fish in garlic & ginger for US$12.50, & lobster for US$25. In the Mdele Coffee Shop & patisserie, snacks & light meals start from around US$5, & you can have coffee & cakes for US$4. $$$$–$$$$$

✕ Beyt al Chai Kelele Sq; m 0777 444111; e reservations@stonetowninn.com; www. stonetowninn.com. Overlooking peaceful Kelele Square, this fabulous little restaurant serves light lunches & delicious dinners, the quality of which has made this one of Zanzibar Town's assured culinary hot spots. Diners are seated at neatly laid tables amid twinkling candles & dine to the sounds of classical music; service is friendly & polite, if sometimes a little slow. Imaginative dishes such as crab *mille feuille* & grouper medallions with bacon are matched with a tempting wine list & although prices may be relatively high, the ingredients, flavours & sophisticated atmosphere combine to make it all good value for money & highly recommended. $$$$–$$$$$

✕ Fusion Al Johari Hotel; ✆024 2236779; e info@al-johari.com; www.al-johari.com. Fusion is a fine dining, glass-enclosed restaurant on the top floor of the Al Johari Hotel. Adjoining the chic colonial bar, it serves an eclectic menu at b/fast, lunch & dinner, with tastes from Italian to Indian being equally well catered for. Seafood starters are complemented with summer soups, pastas, marinated meats & totally tropical desserts, not to mention a lengthy wine & cocktail list. Meals are regularly rounded off with one of the 13 whiskies in stock, or a flavoured shisha pipe. Staff are well dressed, polite & friendly, & the food has received reasonably good reviews. $$$$–$$$$$

✗ **Mtoni Marine restaurants** ☎ 024 2250117. At Mtoni Marine, just a few km north of Zanzibar Town, the 3 restaurants are too far to reach on foot (& not a pleasant walk anyway) but well worth the short taxi ride. The food in the main restaurant is an imaginative mix of European & Swahili techniques & ingredients, whilst the beachfront sushi bar & sports café are established local institutions. All receive consistently good reports for being both high quality & good value. More details are given in *Chapter 7*, page 202. $$$$–$$$$$

✗ **Mistress of Spices** Jafferji Hse; m 0773 740888; e info@jafferjihouse.net. Adjacent to & part of the same building as Jafferji House (see *Where to stay*, page 144), Mistress of Spices is a wonderfully atmospheric dining room, with silk-covered ceilings, antique mirrors & Moroccan lamps casting their unique shadows across the tables. B/fasts, lunches & dinners are created using high-quality, fresh local ingredients & of course the spices that pervade the air. Try the 'Signature Jafferji House Juicy Meaty Beefburger' which comes with avocado salsa & potato wedges (US$10). No alcohol is served here, but there are ample spice-infused coffees & fresh juices to quench your thirst. $$$$

✗ **Sambusa Two Tables Restaurant** Victoria St; ☎ 024 2231979; m 0777 416601. Usually just called Two Tables, this place is particularly worthy of mention, because it's good & because for a long time there was nothing else quite like it on Zanzibar. This is a small place (it really does have only 2 tables – although 1 seats about 8 people), on the balcony of a private house. It's set back off Victoria Street, between the junction of Kaunda Road & Beit al Amaan, but is clearly signposted on a roadside tree. The entrance is tucked around the back of the building, in a leafy corner past dozing cats & well-tended chickens. Food is cooked by husband-&-wife team Salim & Hidaya in their own home, with help from the rest of the family. Phone or visit in the afternoon to make a reservation. A full meal of spiced rice, curries & innumerable tasty local delicacies costs about US$10. The food is highly rated, but do pace yourself: if you fill up on the delicious snacks & starters you may

not do justice to the main course when it arrives! BYOB. $$$$

Mid range

✗ **House of Spices** Kiponda Str; ☎ 0242231264; m 0773 573727; e info@houseofspiceszanzibar. com; www.houseofspiceszanzibar.com. Offering tempting fusions of local & Mediterranean cuisine from the top floor of an attentively renovated Zanzibari house, House of Spices is justifiably popular with both expats & tourists. Most diners sit on the lantern-lit roof terrace, where there's also a bar, while on the ground floor is a small spice shop selling tea & coffee. The friendly waiters can help you choose from the varied menu, which includes a range of curries & salads, as well as tapas & pizza. Alternatively, the fresh seafood plates come with a choice of 5 tasty sauces, each made with a different aromatic spice. To accompany the meal, there's a choice of beers, a long list of spirits & a couple of wines. $$$–$$$$

✗ **Monsoon Restaurant** Forodhani Gdns; m 0777 410410; e monsoon@zanzinet.com. Near the Fort & the seafront, beside the tunnel, this is a smart French-run place serving a good selection of Mediterranean & spicy Zanzibari food, accompanied by live *taarab* music on Wed & Sat nights. There are 2 parts to Monsoon: 1 is a bar, while the other is a massive open space covered in rugs & cushions. You leave your shoes at the door & lounge around kasbah-style. Thick walls & good ventilation mean it's always cool, & so are most of the clients. If you want to relax even more there is also a very pleasant & shady terrace with about 10 tables facing Forodhani Gardens. Main courses cost US$7 upwards, while 3-course dinners cost US$12–15. $$$–$$$$

✗ **Amore Mio** Shangani Rd; ☎ 024 2233666; e e_walzl2yahoo.it. Rated by many as the best Italian eatery on the island, this long-standing, unfussy 'Cafeteria Italiano' has an attractively breezy waterfront location & offers the alternatives of eating inside or outdoors. Pasta dishes & pizzas cost around US$7, hot paninis are in the US$3–4 range, & it serves a good strong coffee as well as a range of ice creams. For a late-night bite, after drinks at Africa House, it's a great choice. $$$

✗ **Archipelago Restaurant** ☎ 024 2235668. Opposite the National Bank of Commerce on Kenyatta Road, this excellent 1st-floor restaurant has rapidly established itself as one of the most popular lunch spots in Stone Town, thanks in large part to its bright décor & elevated balcony overlooking the beach. The other chief ingredient in its success is that the food – curries, fish dishes, burgers (US$6–8) – is excellent, very reasonably priced, & the product of a sustainable fishing policy. No alcohol is served but the fresh juices more than make up for this. Archipelago has the same great Aussie–Zanzibari owners as the Stone Town Café, Café Foro (in the gardens) & Parachute Café (at the airport). $$$

✕ Green Garden Restaurant Off Mkunazini St; ⏱ 11.00–22.00 daily. In the southern part of town, opposite Jambo Guesthouse, this appropriately named restaurant is a delightfully chilled, open-air eatery, set on raised terraces under tall palms. Behind its timber wall, neat concrete paths meander between well-tended gardens, to shady tables & a cool makuti-thatched bar/lounge, complete with fans. It's a friendly, unpretentious place to relax or write postcards home. Food ranges from tapas-style dishes (hoummous & warm pitta, US$3) to the more substantial (king prawn platter, US$10), with refreshing snacks (tropical fruit salad, US$1.50) & wood-fired pizza (US$7). Free Wi-Fi for paying customers. $$$

✕ La Taverna ✆0776650301; ⏱ 11.00–23.00 daily. A little off the main tourist trail, towards the market, this is a gem of a restaurant with a host of happy regular customers, delightful young Italian owners & consistently tasty, homemade pasta/pizza. In a brilliantly whitewashed single-storey house, food is served under broad umbrellas on the terrace: delicious handmade ravioli, myriad pasta shapes with tempting seafood & fresh vegetable sauces & crisp pizzas (far superior to most you'll experience on the island). Wine is inexpensive & free flowing, which all adds to the relaxed, casual vibe. $$$

✕ Loulou ✆024 2240170; e info@loulouzanzibar.com; www.loulouzanzibar.com; ⏱ daily 11.00–22.00. Lou Lou is the swish, contemporary restaurant that follows in the catering footsteps of the now defunct Sunrise Hotel & Restaurant in Bwejuu. Owner Georges Noel is a professional Belgian chef & long-time Zanzibar resident, so it is no surprise that this place is already a success. In the sleek white & orange interior, tantalise your taste buds with such delights as puffed crab pancake with béchamel sauce (US$9) or handmade *bilingani* (pasta with aubergine, plum tomato, cashew nuts, olive oil & herbs (US$8), but do leave room for the signature decadent Belgian chocolate mousse (US$6). Loulou's strapline is 'refined Belgian cuisine', but it's really Belgian cuisine with a Zanzibari twist, & is very highly recommended. (Do not confuse this restaurant with the similar-sounding Lulu at the Seyyida Hotel.) Cash only. $$$

✕ Mercury's Bar and Restaurant Mizingani Rd; ✆024 2233076; m 0777 416666; e mercurys@zanlink.com; ⏱ daily. Named after Zanzibar's most famous son (see box, *Freddie Mercury*, page 166), this place has a fine setting on the bay, overlooking a small beach, the bobbing fishing & pleasure boats of the new port, & the historic seafront buildings of Mizingani Road. It's a real Stone Town institution: perennially popular & always with a relaxed, island atmosphere. Wooden tables & chairs are set out on the large wooden deck under broad sunshades & a huge almond tree (growing through the roof). You can sip thirst-quenching spiced ice tea, choose from the extensive cocktail list & a menu which unashamedly cashes in on the former Queen singer's apparent dietary preferences – Freddie's Favourite Salad (US$6.50), anyone? Despite this corniness, the food is reliably good: pizzas fresh from the open oven (Margaritas from US$6.50 up to prawn, fish & octopus for US$8.50), Oriental-inspired stir-fries (Thai stir fry with steamed rice, US$14.50), & for friends a Seafood Extravaganza sharing platter (lobster, squid, prawns, crab, octopus & catch of the day US$24) & a baffling range of cocktails around US$3–5. Happy 'hour' is 17.00–20.00, & there's live music Fri–Sun nights (20.30–23.00), ranging from traditional *bashraf* & *kidumbak* to reggae & pop. $$$

✕ Nyumbani Between Soko Mohogo St & Vuga Rd; e amir@artlover.com; ⏱ evenings only from 19.30. Nyumbani is similar to Sambusa Two Tables (see page 163), in that you eat in someone's house, although the dining room here is a bit larger. Nyumbani means 'at home', & it's most appropriate here, as you're welcomed into the home of Amir, a local artist, & his wife Khadija. They do the cooking, helped by Amir's sister Moulid. We think this place is wonderful, but if you need any more persuading, have a look at the visitors' book. For US$6 you get a set menu of Swahili specialities, with soup & spicy snacks as starters, a main course with local styles of rice, fish & vegetables, & a dessert of dates, fruit & numerous sweets made from nuts, sugar & spices. (Don't forget to check out the works of art while you're there, too.) This place is in the backstreets behind Haven Lodge, in the southern part of Stone Town, & can be difficult to find, but someone at Haven will be happy to direct you. You need to make arrangements by around noon if you want to eat later that day. You can also book a few days in advance. Unfortunately in the past some people have made reservations then not turned up, so Amir quite understandably asks for a deposit. Reservations are most easily made by visiting the house, though you can also speak to Amir on the phone (📞024 2238170, office – he has a day job!) or leave a message at Manch Lodge (📞024 2231918). $$$

✗ **Old Fort Restaurant** Mizingani Rd; m 0744 278737/0741 630206; e hamoup@yahoo.com; ⏱ for lunch & dinner 08.00–20.00 daily. Opposite the Forodhani Gardens, Zanzibar's old Arab Fort (known locally as Ngome Kongwe) has been here for centuries, but was renovated in the early 1990s. As well as a historical landmark it's now an impressive cultural centre, with a semicircular open-air theatre, several souvenir shops, & this shady outdoor café-restaurant – a very good place to meet friends or take a break from sightseeing, especially as it keeps unusually long hours. There's a good selection of snacks for around US$4, local dishes such as chicken & ugali (maize meal) or fish curry & chapatti for around US$5, plus coffees, beers & chilled wine. Every Tue, Thu & Sat, there's an evening of entertainment (*taarab* music, African dance, etc) & a BBQ – you may need to book ahead. $$$

✗ **Pagoda Chinese Restaurant** Off Kenyatta Rd; 📞024 2234688; e pagoda888@hotmail.com; ⏱ 11.30–14.30 & 18.00–23.00 daily. The Pagoda, just off Kenyatta Road near the Africa House Hotel, is run by Mr Chung, who has lived on Zanzibar for many years. They proudly & justifiably claim to serve the only genuine Chinese food in Zanzibar. The restaurant is highly rated, with good service, immaculate tables, slightly kitsch surrounds, generous servings & fresh food. Chinese agricultural technicians from projects around the island often come here, so it must be good! Starters range from 5 spring rolls for US$2 to crispy deep-fried squid for US$4, & main courses include sweet & sour fish, prawns piripiri, chicken in oyster

sauce & satay beef, all around US$7. Roast duck is US$10, & the menu also includes a few specialities, such as Chinese curried crab, for US$8. There are also a lot of vegetarian options, & meals include crisp, fresh vegetables specially flown in from Kenya. Rice & noodles are around US$2.50. $$$

✗ **Palace Restaurant and Internet Café** Forodhani Rd, Kiponda; m 0777 410004; e alyealtamimu@hotmail.com; ⏱ 09.00–21.00 (restaurant). Next door to the offices of the Aga Khan Foundation, the Palace Restaurant & Internet Café is about the best signposted place in Stone Town, with A4 directions plastered to walls at nearly every alley junction. Its owner, Mr Altamimi, is a gentle, well-informed gentleman who offers fresh food & fast internet. The restaurant is in a large, open atrium with a refreshingly breezy orientation & blue & cream furnishings. Helpful staff serve an eclectic selection of food that varies according to seasonal availability (lobster salad US$5; coconut noodle soup US$6; chicken masala with rice US$7; beef medallions with potatoes US$8) & 13 excellent freshly squeezed juices (US$2) – try the delicious mango with ginger. Alongside the restaurant are the reliable internet café (see page 179) & a delightfully pretty spa with 2 treatment rooms & an Arabic bath. $$$

✗ **Rendezvous Les Spices** Kenyatta Rd; m 0777 410707. This French-owned restaurant serves what is arguably the best Indian food on the island. Easily located on Kenyatta Road, the restaurant buzzes most evenings & the vibrant murals give the place tremendous colour & atmosphere. It's reasonably priced too, with starters around US$3–4, & main courses such as crab masala, chicken tikka, lamb biriyani or various tandooris for US$7–8. Vegetarian dishes are available, & specials, such as prawn curry, are around US$8.50. Cash only. $$$

✗ **Sea View Indian Restaurant** Mizingani Rd; 📞024 2232132; ⏱ 07.00–22.00 or later. On the seafront near the People's Palace, this is one of the oldest tourist-orientated restaurants in Zanzibar Town, founded back in the 1980s & still going strong. With tables on an upstairs balcony & a beautiful view across the bay, it's ideal for b/fasts, lunches & evening meals. During the day (until 18.00) you can enjoy spicy snacks with your drinks – a plate of spring rolls, samosas & bhajis is about US$2 – plus toasted sandwiches for US$2.50, & omelette & chips from US$4. For larger lunches or evening meals the choice is very small, but the quality consistently good. Vegetarian thalis (a mixture of dishes) cost US$7.50, & fish, chicken, squid or octopus in coconut sauce with popadums, plus snacks for starter, a fruit dessert & tea or coffee costs US$7. $$$

✖ **Tatu** m 0778 672772; e info@tatuzanzibar. com; www.tatuzanzibar.com; ⊕ 11.00 until the last customer leaves; kitchen ⊕ noon–22.00. Meaning 3 in Swahili, 'tatu' is a reference to the 3-storey building that's home to this bar/ restaurant. The 1st floor is a social little pub area, complete with free Wi-Fi & a satellite TV enjoyed by sports fans & expats; the 2nd floor is a reasonably good restaurant open for lunch & dinner; whilst the top floor is a fine, open-sided cigar & whisky bar serving super snacks by day (try the excellent prawn tempura), sea view sundowners,& serious nightcaps. Open from noon until the wee hours, there are 85+ single malts to sample here – allegedly east Africa's largest collection of the 'water of life'. Tatu is currently a hit with social residents & tourists alike. $$$

✖ **The Hot Spot Bistro** Kenyatta Rd; ☏0774164866; e info@bistrohotspot.net. With the strap line 'For Food & Beverage Lovers', this 2012 arrival aims to please – & doesn't fail. In a beautifully restored building on Kenyatta Rd, the Jafferji family have added another quality organisation to their collection: see page Jafferji House (page 144) & Gallery Tours (page 135). Here, the menu boasts tasty 'upscale comfort food' - spicy fish goujons, balsamic chicken,

burgers, pies & sweet treats like jam roly-poly & Black Forest cake. Come for the acoustic music nights (18.00–20.00, Tue & Thu); movie nights (18.00; children's films 15.00 Sat); a coffee & chat with prominent local historian, John da Silva (Sun brunch); or to make use of the free Wi-Fi over a fresh pastry. Food is made fresh & takes time, but the boutique & excursion desk will keep you busy if simply sitting isn't enough. $$$

✖ **The Silk Route** ☏024 2232624; ⊕ 11.00– 15.00 & 18.00–23.00. Just around the corner from Forodhani Gardens, this Indian fusion restaurant rustles up a range of hot & fiery curries served with freshly baked naans & spiced rices. Fresh prawns & fish feature in many of the dishes, but beef, chicken & vegetable versions are also available. The restaurant is spread over 3 floors, with the most prized dining spots being on the top floor balcony overlooking the gardens & the sea. This fresh & breezy setting also helps overly ambitious chilli eaters to cool themselves down! Prices are reasonable, starting at US$5 for a seafood curry, rising to US$10 for a meat-based dish, while 3-course lunches are a steal at US$8pp. $$$

✖ **Lazuli** Off Kenyatta Rd; ☏07762 666679; e bonita_zanzibar@yahoo.com; ⊕ 11.00–21.00 Mon–Sat. Under South African–Zanzibari ownership, this small, cheerful café is a Stone Town highlight for casual dining. With a simple, unassuming exterior, Lazuli's little whitewashed room, azure shutters & jaunty coloured tablecloths give it a somewhat Mediterranean air. Its calm is certainly a very welcome find amid the dust &

FREDDIE MERCURY

The late Freddie Mercury, former lead singer and front man for the rock band Queen, was born on Zanzibar on 5 September 1946. His name then was Farouk Bulsara, and his father was an accountant working for the British government in the House of Wonders. His family had emigrated to Zanzibar from India but were originally of Persian extraction. When he was nine, Farouk was sent to boarding school in India, and never returned to Zanzibar. He later went to a college in London, and in the 1970s formed Queen with three other former students.

The current inhabitants of various houses around Zanzibar Town will tell visitors 'Freddie lived here'; his father moved house several times so the claims could all be genuine. Local historians confirm that the Bulsara family lived in the house now occupied by Camlur's Restaurant, and in at least one other house near the post office, either on Kenyatta Road or the small square just behind the post office.

heat of a sightseeing day. In addition, the menu boasts probably the most refreshing drinks in town & a consistently excellent selection of light meals. Imaginative, vitamin-packed smoothies (US$2), fresh fruity cocktails (non-alcoholic) & spiced iced coffees are simply delicious & ingredients are impeccably fresh in the tempting selection of fruit-syrup pancakes, chapati wraps, tempura, burgers & creative salads. Understandably, Lazuli is becoming popular. The only downside is speed: service here *is* slow, so don't come in a rush; instead appreciate that everything is made to order & will be delicious when it eventually arrives. $$–$$$

Cheap and cheerful

Cafés of Forodhani Gardens In the revamped Forodhani Gardens, there are now 3 small waterfront cafes, including the recommended **Café Foro** (nearest the children's playground) & **Zenji Forodhani Garden Café** (www.zenjiforodhani. com). Each has an identical pavilion building by the sea & shaded outdoor seating. Selling a selection of cold drinks & with varying menus of fish, burgers, wraps, salads & sweet treats, they are all open for b/fast, lunch & snacks, & offer a very pleasant sense of calm & green space. $$–$$$

Camlur's Kenyatta Rd; 024 2231919; ⊕ evenings Mon–Sat. A long-standing favourite, this small & friendly place serves delicious Goan specialities, such as fish & coconut curry, starting from about US$3. (See box, *Freddie Mercury*, opposite.) $$

Freddie M's 024 2231435. This funky little café is adjacent to Pearl of Zanzibar hotel & run by the same people. Serving mainly drinks & ice cream within its tangerine walls, it's a great place to unwind with a book & while away the afternoon with a latte or a fresh fruit juice. $$

Kaya Shop & Tearoom Mkunazini St; m 0748 901937/0744 526459. Tucked away on a quiet alley behind Creek Road market is a small shop selling pan-African crafts: Kaya Shop. Duck behind the market, go straight ahead, turn right at the small walled garden & you've arrived, or ask anyone in the vicinity & they'll direct you to this well-known little place. Opened in late 2004, as the dream of Dutch tour leader Suzanne & local painter Boblee, Kaya has a tiny tea room, serving fresh juices, spiced teas & tasty cakes. It's a thoroughly friendly café for a midday or afternoon break: simple, unhurried & consistently good. $$

New Radha Vegetarian Restaurant Off Kenyatta Rd; 024 2234808. Tucked away up the narrow street which runs parallel to Kenyatta Road near the Karibu Inn, Radha Vegetarian Restaurant is a very reasonably priced place, proudly serving pure vegetarian Indian food. With consistently delicious food, this place is deservedly popular & at busy times it's wise to book a table in advance. A thali consisting of dhal, rice, lentil & vegetable curries, okra, roti, popadum & lassi costs US$5. You can also get savoury snacks such as samosas & spring rolls, cakes & sweets, fresh juices & beers. $$

Parachute Café Zanzibar Airport. If you're leaving Zanzibar by air, the enterprising owners of Stone Town Café have opened this small sister café next to the airport. Serving surprisingly good drinks, snacks & meals, it's by far the best option in the area. $$

Stone Town Café Off Kenyatta Rd; 0773 861313; www.stonetowncafe.com; ⊕ 08.00–22.00. In a quiet spot just off Kenyatta Road, below the popular B&B of the same name (see *Where to stay*, page 156), the scents of spiced tea & falafel waft from this buzzing Aussie–Zanzibari-run café. Marked out by lush potted plants, passers-by queue for unfussy, tasty dishes served by friendly staff. Busy in the morning, when hungry tourists & B&B guests pop in for the all-day b/fast, but popular all day for its cheesy pizzas (US$6), fresh fruit shakes & smoothies & tasty teatime treats like sticky date pudding with caramel sauce (US$3). A thoroughly recommended stop for foot-weary sightseers. $$

Zanzibar Coffee House Café ⊕ 08.00–18.00 daily. This friendly café on Mkunazini Street, behind the main Creek Road market, is an excellent place to break a morning of sightseeing with a cold soda, fresh juice, milkshake or strong cup of freshly ground coffee & a light snack – the glass cabinet boasts a deliciously tempting array of fresh cakes, pies, pastries, croissants & sandwiches. Good accommodation is also available (see *Where to stay*, page 156). The café is filled with heavy wooden kitchen-style tables that are perfect for gossiping groups, as well as intimate tables for 2. Its solid, polished stone walls keep the place cool. As its name suggests, the coffee here is excellent; all of the beans are grown by the café's owners on fair-trade estates in Zanzibar & in the Southern Highlands, & there's an in-house roasting & grinding room adjoining the café. The resulting serving options are varied – from creamy cappuccinos to iced delights. $$

⛄**Zenji Café** m 0777 247243; www. zenjicafeboutique.com. Just below the friendly Zenji Hotel (see *Where to stay*, page 157) is this great café, whipping up a selection of milkshakes, velvety ice creams, fruity smoothies & revitalising coffees. The Dutch–Zanzibari owners claim to bake the best brownies in Zanzibar, a claim well worth testing – the brownies are rich, decadent & wickedly good. Community is the key here with a local project providing the raw ingredients & a small boutique on the side of the café selling gifts made by Tanzanian projects such as the Sewing Enterprise for Women (SEW), based in Arusha, who have crafted batik cushions & remarkable bags made from unopened condoms. The only drawback here is the location, right on busy Malawi Road, but strategic planting around the terrace at least partially shields the view of the traffic, & watching the world go by is arguably something of its city charm. $$

Rock bottom

⛄**Buni Café** Kenyatta Rd; ⏰ 08.00–18.00. With a prime central location, opposite the National Bank of Commerce, this small café serves great fresh coffee (iced for hot days) along with cakes & a selection of sandwiches & other snacks for around

US$3 – the raised terrace is an excellent spot for people-watching over a late b/fast or light lunch. $

✗ **Clove Restaurant** Hurumzi St; ⏰ lunchtime only. Run by a friendly group of Swahili women, this is an open-air place in a small & shady garden square opposite the Clove Hotel. Their busiest time seems to be lunch, so you should check in advance if you plan on eating here in the evening. Local dishes such as meat & ugali (maize meal), rice & fish, or curry & chapatti cost around US$4. $

✗ **Passing Show Hotel** Malindi Rd; ⏰ lunchtime only. Despite the name, this is not a hotel, but a Zanzibar institution nonetheless. Serving generous bowls of rice with an assortment of meats, vegetable sauce or beans for around US$2, or larger plates of rice & meat or chicken for up to US$3; the food is good, cheap & the service quick. This place caters mainly for local people, although visitors are always welcome. Lunchtimes can be very busy but turnover is reasonably quick & tables are available both inside & streetside. $

✗ **Tropicana Restaurant** Next to the High Court, this little place caters for nearby office workers, & serves cheap meals of fish & rice for around US$2. Swahili only spoken. $

✗ **Forodhani Night Market** Forodhani Gardens. Read more about this nightly food fiesta under *Street food*, below. $

STREET FOOD For very cheap eats, and a wonderful taste of the local atmosphere, by far the best place to eat in the evening is at the nightly food market. Once a ramshackle collection of waterfront stalls, the renovation of **Forodhani Gardens** has led to the creation of a purpose-built, hard standing area for the food market, just opposite the House of Wonders. The smarter surroundings, organised litter collection and arrival of chefs' hats for the traders have certainly improved the market's hygiene and image, although in many ways the experience is unchanged.

The food stalls remain a social gathering place for both local people and tourists, and as the sun goes down the stallholders fire up their braziers and hurricane lamps, and serve food such as fish and meat kebabs (*mishkaki*), grilled squid and octopus, chips, fishcakes, samosas, chapattis and 'Zanzibar pizzas' – akin to a filled savoury pancake. Or try the nutritionally challenged *chipsi mai yai*: an omelette filled with

DAFU

Young coconuts, known locally as *dafu*, are a delicious Zanzibari snack. When in season, piles of these rough, light brown 'footballs' can be found adorning street stalls and markets all over the island. Simply choose a coconut, watch the salesman chop off its top with a knife, and sit back to drink the refreshing milk inside, while the purveyor carves a makeshift spoon from the coconut shell, allowing you to scoop out the tender 'meat'.

chips, sometimes served with shredded cabbage. Most of the food is grilled on hot coals in front of you, and served on a paper plate. Prices are very reasonable, and a filling plate will cost between US$2 and US$4. You can simply stroll along the line of stalls, seeing what takes your fancy, asking the price and buying a few items at each, or get a whole plate put together at one stall. The food is invariably highly regarded but it is worth choosing from a stall doing brisk trade to ensure fresh ingredients.

Other stalls sell water, sugar-cane juice, ice cream and cold drinks – look for the refreshing local pineapple drink named Zed. The sweet-toothed could seek out *haluwa*, made from tamarind, oil and sugar: it's so sweet and sticky that a little goes a long way. Coupled with the souvenir sellers touting their wares, an evening at the food stalls is often one of the cuisine highlights of a trip to Zanzibar.

Another place for snacks is **Malawi Road** in the Malindi area, in front of the old Ciné Afrique, or outside the Majestic Cinema on Vuga Road. As crowds gather for the evening films, stalls do a brisk trade in peanuts, crisps, chips, cakes, chapattis and samosas.

FOOD SHOPPING If you are self-catering or just going on a picnic for the day, Zanzibar Town has a large market selling many types of fruit and vegetables, plus fresh fish and meat. You can also buy fresh bread in the market from the salesmen who ride in from the bakeries in the suburbs with large baskets on the backs of their bicycles. Dotted around the town are many small shops with a supply of basics, such as bread, biscuits, some fruit and vegetables, and maybe a few tinned items. As these foods are mainly for local people, prices are low. For more choice go to the 'container stores' (they're built in converted shipping containers) along Creek Road or to the shops in the street near the Ciné Afrique, where you'll find a good range of food in tins and packets, imported mainly from Kenya, but also from other parts of the Indian Ocean. Most items are reasonably priced, only slightly more than if bought in Dar or Mombasa. The best supermarket with the widest stock in Stone Town is the Shamshuddin Cash & Carry Supermarket, off Creek Road, near the market.

BARS, CLUBS AND ENTERTAINMENT

The number of bars in Zanzibar Town grows steadily each year. Some bars cater almost exclusively to tourists, others mainly to local Tanzanians who have migrated to Zanzibar from the mainland (indigenous Zanzibaris are generally Muslim so don't drink alcohol). Tanzanian, Kenyan, South African and a selection of international beers are usually available, as are soft drinks and a smattering of local and imported spirits. Wines are mostly South African, with international fine wines really only available at a couple of the top-end restaurants affiliated with hotels, like the Serena or Beyt al Chai, and a few of the newer bars. In addition, many of the larger hotels have separate bars, open to non-guests, and many of the restaurants and cafés mentioned in the section above also serve drinks. Once upon a time, no visit to Zanzibar would have been complete without a visit to the **Sunset Bar** at the Africa House Hotel (see *Where to stay*, page 148). Over recent years though, prices here have risen and standards fallen, and there are better options for sundowners with a sea view: notably **Mercury's** (see below), **Tatu** (page 166), **Lulu** (page 162) and the **Forodhani Gardens' cafés** (page 166).

BARS AND CLUBS

☆ **Bwawani Disco** Bwawani Hotel. There is a disco most nights at the dire Bwawani Hotel (see *Where* *to stay*, page 153), in a dark & equally seedy room under the dry swimming pool. W/ends are the most popular, entry is cheap (US$2) & evenings don't usually warm up until about midnight.

☆ **Dharma Lounge** Vuga Rd; 024 2233626; m 0777 416374/413031. Once the favourite after-dinner hangout for island expats & hip locals, Dharma Lounge has a well-stocked bar, dance floor & extended opening hours (until approx 04.00). Under the same ownership as Mercury's on the waterfront, this is a reasonable option for those who hit Stone Town in party spirit.

♀ **Mercury's** Mizingani Rd. Aside from its all-day meals, Mercury's is a good spot for sundowners & long evenings by the waterfront. This place is noted for its happy hour – out of high season running generously from 17.00 to 20.00 – & its excellent range of cocktails. Ever-popular shisha pipes are also available & there's live evening music to keep you entertained. If you're here for the scenery more than the booze, in the May–Sep period the angle of the sun means the sunsets are easier to appreciate at Mercury's than at Africa House or Tatu.

♀ **Sunset Bar Africa House Hotel** Shangani; m 0774 432340/0777 212621; www. africahousehotel.com. Despite what is said above, for the history & wide terrace, there is still appeal here. Cocktails are *de rigueur*, with an extensive menu to tempt you, & especially popular among locals & the more adventurous visitors are the traditional pipes, also known as hubble-bubble pipes, water pipes or, correctly, as shisha pipes. The sun usually sets around 18.30, so try to get there in good time (say an hour before) if you want the best terrace seats. You can order snacks & meals (*US$4–10*) to enjoy on the veranda, or head upstairs for something more formal in the Tradewinds Restaurant or Sunset Grill (see page 148).

LIVE MUSIC There is live *taarab* music at the **Monsoon Restaurant** (see *Where to eat and drink*, page 164) on Wednesday and Saturday nights. Otherwise, there is no one particular venue in Zanzibar Town for live music, but local artists – from traditional taarab to Afro-pop and rap – often perform at bars such as **Mercury's** or the **Starehe Club**. To find out what's going on, ask at your hotel or look for posters around town advertising special events. The **Arab Fort** is another good venue for live music – mostly traditional musicians and dancers, but sometimes contemporary performances, too, plus of course the annual **Sauti za Busara festival** (see box below). A couple of times each week a 'night at the fort' evening is organised, which includes at least two performances plus a barbecue dinner. There are often performances on other nights, too. The best thing to do is call in at the Fort during the day, and ask the staff at the desk what's happening in the evening.

CINEMAS In the 1920s, Zanzibar boasted the first cinema in east Africa: the Majestic Cinema (not to be confused with the Majestic now on Vuga Road). It was designed by British resident and architect John H Sinclair. Sadly it burned down as the result of a projector fire and the island's film lovers have suffered a series of

SAUTI ZA BUSARA – ZANZIBAR'S ANNUAL MUSIC FESTIVAL

If you're heading to Stone Town in early February, be sure to buy tickets for Sauti Za Busara. Centred on Stone Town's atmospheric Old Fort, this four-day extravaganza celebrates the best of African music, traditional and modern. Over 200 musicians and artists take to the stage during this highly successful festival, which also includes screenings of documentaries and music videos. An electric atmosphere of African beats and friendly festival-goers from all over the world, plus a variety of souvenirs and street food, make this eclectic festival one of Africa's best. Tickets can be purchased through the festival's website, www.busaramusic.org, or bought on the door, but expect to queue. Do bear in mind that city accommodation sells out fast around festival time, so book early for a guaranteed room.

setbacks since, the most recent being the closure of the Ciné Afrique on Malawi Road and its conversion into a supermarket and offices.

Currently the only options for big-screen films are the rare showings in the atmospheric **Old Fort amphitheatre** (the annual Zanzibar International Film Festival – ZIFF – showcases films here in June/July) and the very tired **Majestic Cinema** on Vuga Road, where kung fu flicks and Hindi melodramas predominate, with mainstream Hollywood movies shown to die-hard fans. In spite of its missing roof and broken chairs, old faithful movie-goers continue their cinematic pilgrimage.

There is hope that things will improve in the future though. In 2007, the Zanzibar International Film Festival (ZIFF) committee vowed to pull out all the stops in seeking permission to renovate the Majestic Cinema and turning it into a decent, contemporary venue. These things can take time to materialise on Zanzibar, but ZIFF must be commended for trying, and with recent backing from the likes of Nick Broomfield, an award-winning British film-maker, there's hope that the Majestic will be saved from conversion to offices and one day returned to its former glory.

SHOPPING

Zanzibar Town is something of an Aladdin's Cave for visiting shoppers, with a vast array of shops, large and small, catering for the ever-growing tourist influx. Even die-hard deal-hunters will be hard pushed to visit them all, and there are bound to be even more by the time you visit. A selection of both favourites and perennials are listed here, though particularly worth checking out are those mentioned below; aside from their positive credentials, their products are without question some of the best quality and most original around. For a long time, quality and variety were an issue for visiting shoppers, with cheap, mass-produced, imported tat almost all that was available. The last few years have seen real and positive change, however. A handful of international designers have set up in Stone Town, raising the bar not only in terms of the shopping experience, presentation, quality and originality of goods, but also in training up local Zanzibari and Tanzanians in the value of creating and selling better goods. Prices for these items are understandably considerably higher, but it is very much the case that you get what you pay for.

In the larger tourist shops and boutiques listed, prices are fixed and you can pay in US dollars or by credit card (surcharges are usual), whilst in the market and at smaller locally run outlets, cash (Tanzanian shillings) is necessary and bargaining is part of the experience. There are no hard and fast rules to the latter, and sensible judgement is required, but a basic rule of thumb is to start negotiations at half the asking price and if you ultimately pay around 75% of the initial price, then it's likely both parties will walk away happy.

MADE IN ZANZIBAR – FAIR-TRADE AND HIGH QUALITY In recent years, there has been a welcome trend towards training the local community, especially women, to produce high-quality, well-designed clothing and accessories. These are then sold to delighted tourists through some of the better hotel gift shops and a growing number of stylish boutiques, whilst the individual Zanzibaris benefit from a new skill and a fair price for their efforts. In all of these places, prices are fixed; save bargaining for the markets.

Several of the brands below belong to the 'Made in Zanzibar' producers' network. Founded in 2008, the collective hopes to cross-promote quality products from Zanzibar to support the local 'eco-nomy', and provide an identifiable brand for visitors. A little more information is available online at www.madeinzanzibar.com, but do look out for the logo when shopping. Currently, the best projects, products and shopping outlets are:

Fahari Opposite the Stone Town Café, Fahari's beautiful boutique showcases its well-made, stylish products: leather bags, accessories and jewellery. Established by an experienced British accessories designer, Julie Lawrence, it's a relatively recent arrival making a big impact as both a super social enterprise and NGO, and as an excellent addition to the high-end shopping scene.

Fahari means 'to have a sense of pride' in Swahili, and that's exactly what's instilled in the Zanzibari women trained here. Since its inception, 54 local ladies have been trained in the fields of creative design, manufacture, marketing and sales, with 14 now working full-time, with profit share, in the shop. Other trained staff benefit from new and improved skills, experience and occasional work. All this means purchases here genuinely support local women in building a sustainable future. In addition, a fusion of traditional Zanzibari skills (woodcarving, henna painting, kitenge design and palm weaving), locally sourced Indian Ocean products, international expertise and cutting-edge designs, ensure the products are genuinely appealing to visitors, especially those with a keen eye for originality and quality. All design and manufacture is done on Zanzibar, to exacting standards, with traditional concepts and techniques given a modern twist to ensure consistency and quality. Items are not cheap, but neither should they be; these are ethically produced, handmade and high-quality goods. A great place to treat yourself or take back some impressive souvenirs. Items can be bought at the shop or if suitcase space is tight, buy online from the extensive web catalogue www.fahari-zanzibar.com.

Kanga Kabisa (✆ 024 2232100; e Marianne@kangakabisa.com; www.kangakabisa. com) Founded in 2004 by Lotta Gillving, Kanga Kabisa produces women's, men's and children's clothes, as well as a few accessories, made exclusively from vibrant locally produced cotton kanga cloth. Colourful fabrics, cool cotton and functional Nordic designs courtesy of its Swedish initiator – often with a nod to '60s and '70s fashion – are perfect attire for summer- or beachwear. With locally-sourced materials and a strong desire to minimise environmental impact in island production, Kanga Kabisa is a real model for simple, ethical businesses in the region. Available for purchase in their Shangani shop (beside Africa House Hotel), as well as some hotel gift shops. The 'Made in Zanzibar' network is also the brainchild of the Kanga Kabisa team (see page 171).

Moto (to make a booking ✆ 0773 031178/0777 466304; e moto@madeinzanzibar. com; www.motozanzibar.wordpress.com) Initiated in 1997 by Antje Förstle, Moto is an island-wide handicraft co-operative which aims to work as a competitive small industry to better develop the rural economy, ensure the continuation of traditional crafts, and further train Zanzibari artisans. Impressively, it is as environmentally responsible as it is socially aware: soil, roots and barks provide the products' striking natural dye colours and solar cookers are used exclusively in their production. The latter significantly save on valuable natural resources, whilst educating its members about alternative energies and giving them a competitive edge on final sales. The finely made array of vibrant palm basketry (US$11 for a bag), wide-brimmed straw hats (US$17), household decorations and woven fabrics are striking and immediately appealing in both design and quality. They may be slightly more costly than some on the market, but the craftsmanship is significantly better and Moto currently operates in nine Zanzibari villages, providing an umbrella for 19 co-operatives, totalling over 100 men and women, all of whom benefit from the supportive structure, work ethic, shared business opportunities and established route to market, through its shops on Hurumzi Street in Stone Town and in Pete, just outside Jozani Forest.

For a greater insight into this project and the traditional skills involved, hands-on tours are now available too. The three-hour **Zanzibar Crafts & Culture Tour** takes place at the community workshop and small museum in Pete, to which transport can be arranged from Stone Town. Try your hand at painstaking *ukili* plaiting, marvel at the large fabric hand-looms or even join the batik workshop, before enjoying a tasty Swahili lunch whilst chatting to the friendly staff.

Dada (e *dada@madeinzanzibar.com; dadazanzibar.wordpress.com*) Initiated by the same environmentally and socially aware team behind Moto, Dada began in 2007 as a 'wholesome food and e-cosmetics' network. Meaning 'sister' in Swahili, Dada offers training and employment for women in the Matemwe area, whilst producing some delicious homemade foodie treats and spiced cosmetics.

Using seasonal ingredients (often organic), locally sourced, produced on a small scale with solar equipment, and then beautifully packaged, the women here take great pride in their lovely wares. Packets of dried spices and tropical fruits, bottled Swahili cooking sauces, jams, tropical mustards (try the sweet date mustard with cognac) and chutneys (take home some tasty baobab chutney for your next ploughman's lunch!), imaginative snacks (from chilli 'n' cashew date balls to coconut crusted ginger), spice teas, island muesli, organic honey, and even pasta (from traditional varieties to the likes of beetroot and wholegrain tagliatelle) certainly tempt the taste buds, and make excellent souvenirs. Or for something more personal, cleansing, moisturising and exfoliating soaps are also handmade in their workshop, alongside natural mosquito repellent, solid shampoo, body oils and a dedicated men's grooming range, 'Jambo Bwana'.

In addition to creating these fabulous products and Dada's own product training, the parent NGO goes far beyond this remit and is involved in everything from rainwater harvesting and the promotion of accessible alternative energy to hygiene and training in sustainability and business skills. It is a project supported by many of the forward-thinking hotels, and products can be purchased in the MOTO shops, several hotel gift shops and now even in some Zanzibar Town supermarkets.

Malkia (*www.malkia.dk*) In 2003, Iben Djuraas, a Danish designer on Zanzibar, established a women's co-operative in Bwejuu, making clothing for women and children. Named Malkia, the Swahili word for 'queen', Iben's project was one of the first on the island to mix chic Scandinavian fashion design with vibrant ethnic textiles. Made entirely from Swahili kanga fabrics, the wrap skirts, summer dresses and tunic tops are fun and flattering attire. Training and improving the women's sewing skills, creating simple, stylish patterns and providing a route to market, Iben sought to ensure that the Malkia women learnt valuable skills and an income to better the lives of themselves and their children.

Iben no longer lives on the island, so the operations of the project have been handed over to the women whom she trained. For now, they continue to produce contemporary, stylish clothing at reasonable rates, and we sincerely hope that they will maintain their current quality in the years to come. Malkia purchases can be made at several hotel shops on the island, including Matemwe Beach Village and Mtoni Marine Centre, as well as at Mrembo Spa (see page 187) in Stone Town or by asking in Bwejuu village for the Malkia ladies.

Saifa (*https://sites.google.com/site/saifashop*) Originally established as a hand screen-printing T-shirt company, Saifa opened its current shop just off Kelele Square in early 2007. Owned by tailor Omar Mrisho, its emphasis has shifted and alongside its screen-printed T-shirts it now sells a variety of handmade hats, bags, wallets and accessories. Everything is made from vibrant African fabric, be it locally sourced kanga and kitenge, or Tanzanian batik, and it's a good place to pick up souvenirs from some of the island's best fair-trade producers.

Sasik Sasik, an acronym formed in part from its initiator's name (Saada Abdulla Suleiman Industry Karibuni), began in 1994 when Saada taught herself the art of appliqué and encouraged friends and family to learn too. Seeing a potential market for the colourful products they made, she applied for and received a grant from the UK-based Tanzania Gatsby Trust to set up a local women's co-operative. Initially, the funds were used for the simple workshop at the back of their current shop on Gizenga Street. Here, 12 local women were taught the fine hand-stitched technique and their distinctive Swahili–Arabic soft furnishings began to emerge. Now, 45 women are employed (there are plans to triple this in time), many earning an income for the first time and actively improving their standard of living and the education of their children. The intricate appliqué cushion covers, bedspreads and wall hangings are made on the spot and you can buy off the shelf or order bespoke colour schemes and designs.

Surti & Sons In a small unassuming shop on Gizenga Street, the family craftsmen at Surti & Sons have been handmaking leather sandals and bags since 1976. Three decades on, their beautiful, durable footwear is made under the careful supervision of Pravin Surti, a softly spoken man with a genuine desire for customer satisfaction. Well known for quality within the community, and favoured footwear supplier of expats and more affluent Zanzibaris, the sandals here are made with good leather, finely stitched for comfort, and are available in a variety of lovely colours and styles. Men and women are equally well catered for, with leather belts and bags available in addition to shoes (sandals US$25–35). This family are true artisans and a purchase here is certainly an enduring souvenir.

Upendo In a lovely little shop, next door to the Coco de Mer Hotel, Upendo sells gorgeous cotton children's clothing and some stylish ladies' summerwear. Initiated by Dorthe Davidsen Langås, a Danish resident on the island, Upendo operates a multi-faith sewing school and workshop on site, and seeks to empower local women through education, employment and economic independence. Every year, 30 Zanzibari ladies are given vocational training to Tanzanian national diploma level, invited to seminars on business skills, and are offered interest-free loans to purchase their own sewing machines. Many go back to set up their own small businesses and ten are employed in the Stone Town workshop to make the beautifully cut, colourful clothes which are for sale in the shop. As cool, stylish, easy-to-wear outfits for travelling women and children or gifts to take home, the clothes are ideal for summer, and importantly, all of the profits are ploughed back into sustaining and developing the project. More details and the designs can be seen at www.upendomeanslove.com.

Zenji Boutique On the frenetic Malawi Road, this little boutique (within Zenji Hotel & Café, page 157) makes excellent browsing after one of the café's famously gooey chocolate brownies. A real treasure trove of eclectic Zanzibari and Tanzanian arts and crafts, lovingly displayed with impressively detailed descriptions of all of the products, their production and ethical pedigree.

By encouraging local artisans, promoting and selling their products, Zenji hopes to ensure artisans are able to make a sustainable income and that traditional handicrafts are kept alive, and their production even stimulated.

The boutique sells products made by both talented individuals and several inspiring groups: women's co-operatives, the disabled and environmentally conscious. There are rice and flour sacks transformed into attractive bags, lovely dishes and cutlery produced from recycled metal, hand-dyed fabrics, glass and beaded jewellery and a host of other enticing gifts. In addition, there is a small workshop where local women create delightfully decorative and original paper beads; buy something ready-made or join a workshop to learn and create your own. Worth a stop for a wide selection of original souvenirs in a range of budgets.

TOURIST SHOPS One of the best places to start any shopping trip is the **Zanzibar Gallery** on Kenyatta Road. This shop sells a range of carvings, paintings, jewellery, materials, maps, clothes, rugs, postcards, antiques and real pieces of art from all over Africa. You can also buy local spices, herbs, pickles and honey, and locally made oils such as pineapple bath oil or banana-scented bubble bath – all made naturally from Zanzibar fruit. It also has a very good selection of books (see page 176). The Zanzibar Gallery is run by local photographer and publisher Javed Jafferji; his own books (signed) are also for sale, including some beautiful large-format photo books, plus illustrated diaries and address books featuring photos from Zanzibar and Tanzania.

Another all-round place on Kenyatta Road is **Memories of Zanzibar**, opposite the post office. This shop sells everything from beaded flip-flops and silver bracelets to carpets and gourd-lamps, as well as a good selection of books about Zanzibar, and African music CDs. At the seafront end of the same road is **Zawadi Chest;** it's neatly laid out and has a particularly good display of kikois (see page 102), metalwork from the Dar es Salaam charity foundry, Wonder Welders, and an excellent selection of imported swimwear.

There are many more shops on Kenyatta Road and along Gizenga Street, as well as its continuations Hurumzi Street and Changa Bazaar. In addition, these streets are lined with pavement traders offering carvings, paintings and beaded trinkets. Most of the shops and stalls stock contemporary carvings as well as older, traditional statues and artefacts from mainland Tanzania and elsewhere in Africa. Tingatinga paintings on canvas or wooden trays, assorted gold, silver and stone jewellery, packets of spices, and mobiles made from coconut shells in the shapes of dolphins, dhows or tropical fish are readily available at every turn. Some of the paintings and craftwork stocked in the souvenir and craft shops is bashed out and of very poor quality, but occasionally, if you search hard enough, you'll find real works of art which have been more carefully made. It's worth spending a bit more time and money (if indeed the stallholder charges more for better quality – some don't seem to) to get something that will still look good when you get it home.

For Tanzanian designer chic, check out **Doreen Mashika**'s fashionista fare at 267–8 Hurumzi Street (www.doreenmashika.com). The expensive shoes and handbags are stylish and offer a taste of African design talent. Meanwhile, **ZAYAA Gallery** (Zanzibar Young Artist Association) at the eastern end of Hurumzi Street showcases young artists and has some especially lovely women's art, inspired by henna patterns. **Real Art** on Gizenga Street offers a good, if more expensive, selection of Tanzanian and Zanzibari art. Paintings and sculptures are organised by style and artist, with quality works selected by the knowledgeable owner, Anita. Inside the **Old Fort**, seek out the small art shop beside the restaurant for original watercolours, oil paintings and well-observed pen-and-ink drawings. The friendly artists are on site and many of their works are impressive. Alternatively, a few doors down, **Keramica** sells original, slightly more contemporary products, in the shadow of the amphitheatre.

Local craftwork can also be found in the **Orphanage Shop**, near the Fort. The orphanage is a large building on Mizingani Road, notable for a tunnel passing right through the middle of it. The shop is on the side nearest the sea. Here, blind craftworkers weave a good range of baskets, rugs and other items.

ANTIQUES Around Zanzibar Town there are also several shops selling antiques from Arabia and India, dating from Omani and British colonial times. **Coast Antique Shop** on Gizenga Street has a particularly good selection of Zanzibar clocks. There are several more antique shops on the street between St Joseph's Cathedral and Soko Mohogo crossroads.

TAILORS On Gizenga Street, the **tailor** at **Mnazi Boutique** can copy any shirt, skirt or trousers you like, from material you buy in the shop or elsewhere in town. Prices start at US$10, and go up to US$25 for a complicated dress. If you prefer traditional African clothing, consider a kanga or a kikoi (see box, *Kangas and kikois*, page 102). Alternatively, **Osman**, the tailor opposite ZAYAA Gallery at the end of Hurumzi Street, is highly recommended (in spite of his tiny, fabric-strewn workplace). He'll happily assist in fabric purchase and will sew mock-ups of bespoke clothing before committing to your chosen material. On Kenyatta Road, the smarter **One Way** boutique also sells piles of T-shirts embroidered with giraffes and elephants or emblazoned with Kenyan and Tanzanian slogans and logos.

POSTCARDS For **postcards** you can't go wrong at **Angi's Postcards & Maps**, on Mizingani Road, near the Big Tree; there's a truly massive selection here, all at good prices.

JEWELLERY **Hassan Jewellers** on Mkunazini Street, close to the market, is reliable and reputable. They stock a good range of tanzanite and will be able to supply authentication certificates showing the stone's size, cut and clarity (☏ *024 2231242*). Be aware when making your purchase that tanzanite is a soft stone which scratches easily; better to have it set as earrings or in a necklace than as a daywear ring.

NEWSPAPER AND BOOKSHOPS Newspapers from Kenya and mainland Tanzania, some international magazines and a reasonable range of books are available from the **Masumo Bookshop**, off Creek Road, and from some of the souvenir shops along Kenyatta Road near the old post office. Coffee-table books fact and fiction can all be purchased from the well-stocked **Gallery Bookshop** on Gizenga Street, which is open from 09.00 daily, though shuts at lunchtime on a Sunday.

The best bookshop is the **Zanzibar Gallery** on Kenyatta Road (see page 175). It has a good selection of guidebooks and coffee-table books on Zanzibar and other parts of Africa, animal and bird field guides, maps, histories and a range of general novels for those seeking some beach reading material.

CAMERA SUPPLIES Slide and print film for cameras is available in several souvenir shops in Zanzibar Town (the ones along Kenyatta Road have the best stock). The **Shamshuddin Cash & Carry Supermarket**, near the Masumo Bookshop, also has a good stock. The best place to buy film is Majestic Quick Foto, on the east side of

Creek Road, opposite the BP petrol station. Be sure to check the expiry dates if you buy film from more offbeat establishments.

For pictures from a different era, visit the Capital Art Studio on Kenyatta Road, near the Dolphin Restaurant. The shop itself gives the impression that it has been unchanged since colonial times, with a good selection of old photographic prints from the 1950s and 1960s, and a few earlier ones, all taken by the owner's father. They also sell camera film and batteries, and offer a one-day developing service.

OTHER PRACTICALITIES

This section covers local services that visitors may require during their time in Zanzibar Town. For more general matters covering Pemba and Mafia islands, see pages 343 and 373 respectively.

AIRLINES For details of international and domestic flights to and from Zanzibar, see *Chapter 4, Getting to Zanzibar*, page 82. If you do need to book or reconfirm a ticket while you are on Zanzibar, this is most easily done through one of the tour operators recommended in *Chapter 5*. For further details of the airlines represented on Zanzibar, see *Chapter 4*, page 82.

✈ **Air Tanzania** Tembo Hotel; ✆ 024 2230213; m 0784 737508; e airtanzania@zanlink.com; www.airtanzania.com

✈ **Coastal Travel Offices** Zanzibar Airport: ✆024 2233112; m 0785 500009; & Stone Town: Kelele Sq, Shangani (close to the Serena Hotel); ✆024 2239664; e aviation@coastal.cc, safari@coastal.cc; www.coastal.cc

✈ **Precision Air Flight Services** Kenyatta Rd (next to Mazsons Hotel); ✆024 2234521; e pwznz@precisionairtz.com, pwreservations@precisionairtz.com; www.precisionairtz.com

✈ **ZanAir Offices** Zanzibar Airport: ✆024 232993; m 0777 413240; & Stone Town: Malawi Rd, Malindi; ✆024 2233670/3788; e reservations@zanair.com; www.zanair.com

BANKS AND MONEY CHANGING Some general points on banks and bureaux de change are given in *Chapter 4*, page 101. Hard-currency cash can be changed into local currency at most banks as well as at a number of private bureaux de change dotted around Stone Town. These days, there isn't much to choose between the rates offered by banks and the private 'forex bureaux'; indeed some of the private bureaux offer an inferior rate to the banks, but you'll generally find the transaction takes a minute or two at a private bureau whereas changing money at banks often involves long queues and plenty of paperwork. Good private bureaux de change include the **Shangani Bureau de Change** (at the northern end of Kenyatta Road, near the Tembo Hotel), **Malindi Bureau de Change** (east of the port gates) and **Morning Star Bureau de Change** on Gizenga Street opposite United Travel Agents. Most large hotels will also change money, although some deal only with their own guests, and they often offer poor rates. There are also currency bureaux at the port and airport. The only place that exchanges travellers' cheques is the first-floor 'Foreign Trade Dept' at the National Bank of Commerce on Kenyatta Road. The rate here is pretty good and the commission (0.5%) is negligible. You can draw cash against Visa cards at the security-guarded ATM outside the same bank, but the only place where you can draw against MasterCard is at the excellent Barclays Bank headquarters and ATM a couple of kilometres out of town along the road towards the north coast.

Elsewhere, getting cash on a debit or credit card is virtually impossible, although most upmarket hotels will accept major credit cards.

COMMUNICATIONS

Post Some general points on postal services and costs are given in *Chapter 4*, page 116. Although letters can be sent from other post offices around Zanzibar Island, it's best to send all your mail from Zanzibar Town. The service is reliable, with letters taking about a week to ten days to reach destinations in Europe and North America (Australia takes a bit longer).

✉ **General Post Office (GPO)** ⏰ 08.00–12.30 & 14.00–16.30 Mon–Sat, 08.00–12.30 Sun. Zanzibar Town's main post office is a large building in the new part of town on the road towards the Amaani Stadium.

✉ **The Old Post Office** Kenyatta Rd, Shangani; ⏰ 08.00–13.00 & 14.00–16.30 Mon–Thu, 08.00–noon & 14.00–17.00 Fri, 09.00–noon Sat. This post office is much more convenient for tourists. It's possible to buy stamps here, & this is also the place to collect letters sent by poste restante (although some items may get sent to the main post office by mistake – so make sure anyone writing to you addresses the envelope: 'Old Post Office, Kenyatta Road, Shangani').

Telephone Zanzibar Town has a wide choice of places where you can make calls. Some are properly equipped, others are just a dusty phone in the corner of someone's shop which is nevertheless proudly touted as an 'international communication centre'.

One of the best phone centres is **Tanzanian Telecommunications (TTCL) international telephone office** (⏰ *08.00–21.00 daily*), next to the Old Post Office on Kenyatta Road. Calls cost US$1 for ten minutes inside Zanzibar, US$1 for three minutes elsewhere in Tanzania, and US$1–3 for other international destinations. The office is large, cool and quiet, and the staff members are very friendly and helpful.

Another option for international calls is to buy a phonecard from the international telephone office (they are also sold at some shops and hotels) and use this in the direct-dial phone booth outside. A 150-unit card costs US$10 and gives you two minutes to Europe or the USA. A 500-unit card costs US$25. For local calls a 10-unit card is US$4, and a 100-unit card is US$8.

If the international telephone office is closed, local boys loiter by the phone booths outside with cards and will charge you per unit to use them. There will probably even be a few young entrepreneurs with mobile phones, who allow international calls at negotiable rates. It makes you wonder who is really paying the bill.

At the private phone bureaux around Zanzibar Town, international calls are about the same price as those charged by the TTCL, although a few places manage to undercut this rate, and some can be considerably more, so it's worth checking if you've got a lot of calls to make.

For cheaper international calls, it's also worth seeking out some of the better **internet cafés** for 'Voice over Internet Protocol' options, such as Skype. There's a delay of a second or two while you're speaking, but once you're used to that, it's fine and significantly cheaper.

For current codes, see box, *Zanzibar telecommunications*, page 116.

Mobile phones If you bring a mobile phone from home, it's emphatically worth the minor investment in a Tanzanian SIM card (which costs around US$1 and gives you a local number) and airtime cards (available in units of TSh1,000 to 5,000). International text messages and calls out of Tanzania are seriously cheap: at the time of writing, a few dollars will buy you around 20 text messages to anywhere in the world, and international calls work out at around US$0.50/minute.

By contrast, you can expect to rack up a hefty bill very quickly by using your home SIM for calls and/or messages, since in most instances these are charged at international rates out of your home country, even when you are phoning home. SIM and airtime cards can be bought at a specialist Vodacom outlet (there's one opposite the taxi rank on Creek Road) or at numerous other small shops displaying the ubiquitous Vodacom sticker.

Email and internet

In the last decade, internet cafés have sprung up everywhere. Like the phone offices (indeed, many are also phone offices), some are large and air conditioned with several terminals, while others are in the corner of someone's shop and you connect to the outside world crammed between boxes of soap and tinned meat. In general, most hotels do not offer public email services, though there are increasing numbers with Wi-Fi and a pay-to-play PC.

The cost of internet use from a PC is a pretty standard US$1 per hour across town, and there are several dozen cafés to choose from. Most charge per 30-minute increment, starting at a few dollars, and if you go over this by a few seconds you'll be charged for the next 30 minutes.

Some of the more reliable and well-equipped internet cafés include:

Asad Secretarial Services Near the Clove Hotel is this small place with good connections, charging US$1/hr.

Palace Internet m 0777 410004. Part of the Palace Restaurant complex (see *Where to eat and drink*, page 165) on Forodhani Road, this AC internet café has 10 flat-screen, up-to-date PCs from which you can surf the net (US$1/hr), print (b/w US$0.40; colour US$50), burn CDs (US$1.50) and DVDs (US$2.50), download memory cards (US$3–4 depending on size), & even laminate your favourite prints.

Sanjay Internet Café Just off Gizenga St, behind the House of Wonders, this small place has

about 5 terminals, & normally charges US$1/hr, but sometimes offers special rates of half this price.

Shangani Internet Café Kenyatta Rd; 024 2232925. This is one of the best places in Zanzibar Town. It has long opening hours, fast connections, about 15 computers, a fridge full of ice cream & cold drinks, & charges US$1/hr.

Too Short Internet ⏱ 08.00–23.00. Opposite the National Bank of Commerce, this is centrally located with long hours, & around 8 quick machines at the standard rate of US$0.50/30mins. If you're travelling with a laptop & fancy a night in, for US$2 you can also rent DVDs here (US$10 refundable deposit).

HOSPITALS, DOCTORS AND PHARMACIES

Zanzibar's main public hospital is Mnazi Mmoja General Hospital, on the south side of Stone Town. During the island's revolutionary heyday it was called the Lenin Hospital, but this title has now been dropped. Like many hospitals in developing countries, the staff are dedicated but the wards are badly underfunded, undersupplied and in very poor condition. Equally distressing is the pile of rubbish (including drip-feeds and needles) simply dumped on the beach behind the hospital.

Most tourists in need of urgent medical attention should go to one of Zanzibar's **private medical clinics** where the staff speak English and the service is usually better. Of course, this has to be paid for, and costs around US$50 per consultation, but all fees should be covered by your travel insurance. The medical centres also have pharmacies selling medicines and other supplies.

Private medical clinics

Zanzibar Medical and Diagnostic Centre 024 2231071, 24hr emergency m 0777 750040/413714. Just off Vuga Road, near the Majestic Cinema, this clinic is recommended by most expats. It's a fully equipped facility, run to

European standards, & the staff members speak several European languages.

Zanzibar Medical Group 024 2233134. Another good-quality private clinic, on Kenyatta Road, charging US$30 per consultation.

Serious medical emergencies

In case of a real emergency, it's likely that you'll want to be flown to one of the private clinics in Dar es Salaam. The **IST Clinic** (m *0754 783393; www.istclinic.com*) there comes highly recommended, and the **Aga Khan Hospital** (+255 *(0)22 2115151/53; www.agakhanhospitals.org/dar/ index.asp*) is also reputed to be of a high standard. However, by the time you need one of these, you should be calling your insurance company – who will make the decisions and organise this for you.

In a case of major complications or complex surgery, it's likely that they would need to air-evacuate you to Nairobi or Johannesburg.

Other medical centres

If your insurance covers only major medical problems, and you want to keep costs down for something minor, you could go to one of Zanzibar's other medical centres:

Afya Medical Hospital 024 2231228; m 0777 411934. Off Vuga Rd at the southern end of Stone Town, Afya is large & well stocked, with friendly staff. Consultations cost US$2, blood or urine tests are available, & there's also a pharmacy.

Dr Mehta's Hospital 024 2230194; m 0741 612889. On Vuga Rd.

Fahaud Health Centre Near St Joseph's Cathedral. This very basic centre offers consultations for US$3 whilst a malaria blood test is US$2. Should your test prove positive, they also sell Fansidar at US$1 per tablet.

Pharmacies

If you need to buy medicines, Zanzibar Town has several pharmacies stocking drugs which are mostly imported from Europe and India. Stocks are not always reliable, so if you know you're likely to need a specific drug during your visit, then it's best to bring a full supply with you. There are pharmacies near the A Novel Idea bookshop, next to 236 Hurumzi Hotel, and another highly recommended outfit opposite the Shamshuddin Cash & Carry Supermarket near the market (the pharmacist here is excellent if you are in need of medical advice). Straightforward medicines, toiletries and tampons are also available at the 'container stores' on Creek Road.

POLICE

In case of emergency in Zanzibar Town, the **main police station** (*999 or 024 2230772*) is in the Malindi area, on the north side of Stone Town. This is also the central police station for the whole of the island. Robberies can be reported here (travel insurance companies usually require you to provide a copy of the basic report on the incident from the local police if you are making a claim), but you should not expect any real action to be taken as the police are not particularly well motivated and corruption is rife.

Zanzibar also has a platoon of **Tourist Police**, supposedly to assist and protect the island's foreign visitors, although many people question their effectiveness. They are mostly seen driving around town in fancy new patrol cars, while touts continue to hassle tourists unimpeded.

SWAHILI LESSONS

If you would like to learn a few words (or even more) of the local language, Kiswahili, there are options with formal classes as well as a number of local people willing to assist. For experienced teachers and structured learning, the best place to start is the **Institute of Kiswahili and Foreign Languages** (*024 2230724/3337;* e *takiluki@zanlink.com; www.glcom.com/hassan/takiluki.html*). Inside the State University on Vuga Road, the institute offers individual lessons and courses. Classes are normally 08.00–noon and cost US$4 per hour, or US$80 for a week's course. Single lessons away from the institute and longer courses, which include lodgings in the house of a teacher or local family, are also available.

SWIMMING

SWIMMING The hotel swimming pools at the Serena and Tembo are no longer open to non-guests; however, Dhow Palace (see *Where to stay*, page 154) will allow visitors to use their pool for TSh3,000 per person (approximately US$2.50). If it's hot and you're desperate for some aquatic relief, **Maruhubi Beach Villas** (see *Where to stay*, page 201) slightly out of town, also allows non-residents to swim in its large beachside pool for US$5 per day, while children of guests at **Mtoni Marine Restaurant** (see *Where to stay*, page 163) will certainly enjoy the lush gardens and refreshing pool.

TOURIST INFORMATION

TOURIST INFORMATION The **Zanzibar Tourist Corporation** (**ZTC**) is the state travel service. It has offices in Livingstone House, on the northeast side of town on the main road towards Bububu, where you can make reservations for the exceedingly basic ZTC bungalows on the east coast. For general tourist enquiries, you're better off asking at the ZTC office on Creek Road, where the members of staff are a bit more helpful, and there are postcards and maps for sale.

For general information, hotel staff and some tour companies are happy to help, even if you don't end up buying a tour from them. Try **Eco+Culture**, **Sama Tours**, **Suna Tours** or **Gallery Tours**, listed in *Chapter 5, Tour operators,* pages 134–7. Also worth visiting is the information desk at the **Arab Fort**, which has details of local musical, cultural and sporting events.

For less formalised (but equally useful) information, check the noticeboard at the open-air restaurant inside the Fort. Local events are advertised here, alongside details of companies selling tours, spare seats on charter flights and local residents selling cars or motorbikes. This is also a good place to leave messages for those people you last saw in Cairo or Cape Town and are trying to contact again.

WHAT TO SEE AND DO

One writer has compared the old Stone Town of Zanzibar to a tropical forest where tall houses stretch to the sky instead of trees, and the sun filters through a network of overhanging balconies instead of foliage. Its labyrinth of twisting streets and alleys is a stroller's paradise, with new sights, sounds or smells to catch the imagination at every turn: massive carved doors, ancient walls, tiny tempting shops with colourful wares and bustling shoppers, old men hunched over a traditional game, kids with homemade toys, ghetto-blasters at full volume, little boys hawking cashews or postcards or fresh bread, the sound of the muezzin calling from the mosque and the scent of cloves or ginger or lemongrass – and everywhere the echoes of Zanzibar's rich and fascinating history, the sultans, shipbuilders, explorers, slave markets, merchants and exotic spice trade.

Stone Town was originally built on a peninsula which has probably been inhabited since the first people arrived on Zanzibar (although the creek that separated its eastern edge from the rest of the island has now been reclaimed). Ras Shangani, at the western tip of the peninsula, is thought to have been the site of a fishing village for many centuries, and at least one of Zanzibar's early Swahili rulers, the Mwinyi Mkuu, had a palace here.

In the 16th century, Portuguese navigators built a church and trading station on the peninsula as it had a good harbour and was easy to defend. When the Omani Arabs began to settle on the island in the 18th century, they built a fort on the site of the church, and today's Stone Town grew up around the Fort.

6

Although the narrow streets of Zanzibar are like a labyrinth, Stone Town is not very large, and getting seriously lost is unlikely. (If you don't know where you are, just keep walking and you'll soon come out onto Creek Road or one of the streets alongside the sea.) In fact, for many visitors getting lost in the maze of narrow streets and alleys is all part of the fun.

However, if your time is limited, you prefer not to become disorientated, or you want to find some specific sites of interest, it's possible to hire a knowledgeable guide from most local tour companies.

If you don't want a formal tour, but would still like to be accompanied by a local, you could engage the services of the papaasi (see box, *Guides and the 'papaasi'*, page 142), although generally they will be more interested in taking you to souvenir shops (where they might earn a commission from your purchases) than museums. It might be wiser to ask your hotel or a reputable tour company to put you in touch with someone who will happily walk with you through the streets, and show you the way if you get lost. We have heard from readers who employed a local schoolboy, who was also very happy to practise his English, and this seems an excellent idea. About US$5 (in Tanzanian shillings) for a day's work would be a suitable fee.

A few local individuals worth contacting, who are both reliable and knowledgeable are cultural radio presenter **Farid Himid** (m *0777 484734*), who gives cultural/historical tours for US$15 per person, or for serious historians, Goan-born **John da Silva**, a local artist with an encyclopaedic knowledge of every public building and house (and literally every balcony and door) in the town. He is very occasionally available and can be contacted through Sama Tours (see *Tour operators*, page 135).

Most of the houses you see today were built in the 19th century, when Zanzibar was one of the most important trading centres in the Indian Ocean region. The coralline rock of Zanzibar Island was easy to quarry for use as a construction material, so that many of the houses were built in grand style with three or four storeys. Previously most of the houses on Zanzibar had been much smaller, built of mangrove poles and palm thatch, making the fine white buildings in Stone Town even more exceptional.

Today, nearly all of these old houses are still inhabited, although many are in a very bad state of repair. The coralline rock was a good building material but it is also soft, and easily eroded if not maintained. Crumbling masonry, along with dilapidated woodwork, is sadly an all too familiar sight in Stone Town – and in some places where the surface has disintegrated it reveals the rough blocks of ancient coral beneath.

However, since the end of the 1980s and through the 1990s, several buildings in Stone Town have been renovated. The Zanzibar government, with assistance from the United Nations Centre for Human Settlements (the Habitat Fund), plans to preserve many more, eventually restoring the whole of Stone Town to something like its original magnificence. The Stone Town Conservation and Development Authority has been established to co-ordinate this work, although it is sometimes hampered by a lack of co-ordination with the local government authorities.

During the 19th century, many of Stone Town's inhabitants were wealthy Arabs and Indians. Consequently the houses were built in two main styles: the Arab style, with plain outer walls and a large front door leading to an inner courtyard; and the Indian style, with a more open façade and large balconies decorated with ornate railings and balustrades, designed to catch sea breezes and dispel the humid atmosphere.

Many of the buildings have doors with elaborately carved frames and panels, decorated with brass studs and heavy locks. The size of the door and the intricacies of its decoration were signs of the family's wealth and status. Today, the Zanzibar door has become a well-recognised symbol of the town and island's historic and cultural background, and many new buildings incorporate one into their design – either a genuine one removed from an old building, or a reproduction (see box, *Zanzibar doors*, page 45).

Among the houses and tucked away in the narrow streets you will come across mosques, churches and other public buildings, almost hidden in the maze. Stone Town also has a few streets of shops, some of them still called bazaars. Some shops are very small, no more than a kiosk, with a few dusty food tins or a couple of jars of sweets on the shelf; others are larger, catering for locals and visitors, with a wider range of goods. There are also antique and curio shops (bargain hard here), and an increasing number of places selling a wide and inventive selection of locally produced arts and crafts, aimed specifically at the growing tourist market.

As you explore the narrow streets with all their historic links, remember that Zanzibar Town today is very much a real community, where people live and work. It is not a museum piece created for tourists. You should not enter any private house or courtyard unless expressly invited to do so, and before you peer through a window or doorway, stop and ask yourself – would you appreciate a stranger doing the same in your home? You should also show respect for local sensibilities (see *Clothing*, page 100). Mosques are not usually open to non-Muslim visitors. Taking photos of buildings is generally acceptable, but you should never photograph people without their permission (see box, *Mosques of Zanzibar Town*, page 196).

THE MARKET The market is about halfway along Creek Road and a good place to visit even if you don't want to buy anything. The long market hall is surrounded by traders selling from stalls, or with their wares simply spread out on the ground. It's a very vibrant place where everything, from fish and bread to sewing machines and secondhand car spares, is bought and sold. People bring their produce here from all over the island, and others come to buy things they can't get in their own villages. You could spot dog-eared schoolbooks, anonymous tangles of metal being soldered into usefulness, rough wooden chairs, suitcases, shoes, baskets, kitchenware, clocks and watches, CDs, mobile phones and doubtless the occasional kitchen sink. Some food displays may be best avoided by the squeamish: the massive deep-sea fish heads, jaws agape; dark haunches of beef and slabs of less identifiable meat; pearly squid tentacles; grubby recycled bottles and jars containing oil, honey, pickle and goodness knows what else … and the inevitable accompanying buzz of flies. Don't miss the swathes of multi-patterned cotton fabrics, the fragrant spices and mound after mound of exotic fruit and vegetables though – and just enjoy people-watching and being part of a Zanzibar experience which hasn't yet become especially touristy.

Towards the end of the 19th century, the town's marketplace was inside the Old Fort. Today's market hall was built in 1904, and some very early photographs of the market displayed in the museum show that very little has changed since then.

On occasional evenings, a public auction is held in the street behind the market where furniture, household goods, old bikes, and all sorts of junk are sold. It is very entertaining to watch, but make sure you don't bid for anything by mistake: keep your hands still!

LIVINGSTONE HOUSE On the northeast side of the town, this old building is now the main office of the Zanzibar Tourist Corporation (ZTC). It was built around 1860 for Sultan Majid (sultan from 1856 to 1870). At this time Zanzibar was used as a starting point by many of the European missionaries and pioneers who explored eastern and central Africa during the second half of the 19th century. David Livingstone, probably the most famous explorer of them all (see box, *David Livingstone*, page 192), stayed in this house before sailing to the mainland to begin his last expedition in 1866. Other explorers, such as Burton, Speke, Cameron and Stanley, also stayed here while preparing for their own expeditions. The house was later used by members of the island's Indian community, and in 1947 it was bought by the colonial government for use as a scientific laboratory for research into clove diseases. After independence and the revolution it became the Zanzibar headquarters of the Tanzania Friendship Tourist Bureau, the forerunner of today's ZTC.

THE OLD DISPENSARY Opposite the new port buildings, on Mizingani Road, this is a grand four-storey building with a set of particularly decorative balconies. It is also called the Ithnasheri Dispensary, and lettering at the top of the front wall reads 'Khoja Haji Nasser Nur Mohammed Charitable Dispensary'. It was originally built in the 1890s as a private house for a prominent Ismaili Indian merchant called Tharia Topan, who was a customs advisor to the sultans, and one of the wealthiest individuals on Zanzibar at the time. In 1899, he gave the house up to be used as a dispensary, also funding the medicine and other services. Topan also provided money (with the Aga Khan and Sultan Ali) for a non-denominational school which opened in Zanzibar in 1891. The dispensary fell into disrepair during the 1970s and 1980s, but was renovated in 1995 with funding from the Aga Khan Charitable Trust. A few years later it opened as the Stone Town Cultural Centre with a small exhibition (free) of historical photographs. The building has largely been taken over by offices now but the Aga Khan Trust for Culture is hopeful that the building will one day become the Indian Ocean Maritime Museum. We wait in anticipation for more news of this impressive building's future.

THE OLD CUSTOMS HOUSE On Mizingani Road (the main seafront), overlooking the sea, this large building has a plain façade and is fairly featureless apart from the beautiful set of carved wooden doors. These have been decorated in the Arab style with fish, lotus and anchor-chain motifs. Hamoud, grandson of Sultan Said, was proclaimed sultan here in 1896. In 1995, the Customs House was renovated with funds provided by UNESCO, the United Nations' cultural organisation.

The equally large building next door to the Customs House was formerly Le Grand Hotel and then became a private house before being abandoned. A group of developers has long-term plans to convert it into a hotel once again but there are no signs of this materialising yet.

THE PALACE MUSEUM (☉ *09.00–18.00 daily; admission adult/child US$3/1*) This is a large white building with castellated battlements situated on Mizingani Road, where the latter runs very close to the sea. Originally called the Sultan's Palace, it was built in the late 1890s for members of the sultan's family. From 1911, it was used as the Sultan of Zanzibar's official residence, but was renamed the People's Palace after the 1964 Revolution, when Sultan Jamshid was overthrown. It continued to be used as government offices until 1994 when the palace was turned into a museum dedicated to the history of the sultans of Zanzibar.

Remarkably, much of their furniture and other possessions survived the revolutionary years and can now be seen by the public for the first time. In spite of the uninspiring, dishevelled reception area, the museum itself is well organised and informative: the ground floor is dedicated to the early years of the sultanate (1828 to 1870), while the upper floors contain exhibits from the later, more affluent period of 1870 to 1896. These include thrones, banqueting tables and ceremonial furniture, and also more personal items such as beds and the sultan's personal water closet. There is also a room devoted to Princess Salme, the daughter of Sultan Said, who eloped to Hamburg with a German merchant in 1866. It's a fascinating story, told by the princess herself in her book *Memoirs of an Arabian Princess*, which you can buy in the museum in English, French, German and Italian (see also the box, *Princess Salme*, pages 208–9). Outside in the palace garden are the graves of Sultans Said, Barghash, Majid, Khaled, Khalifa and Abdullah.

An excellent little leaflet is available containing a clear, concise historical background with plans and descriptions of all the palace rooms. Guides are also available from the ticket desk to show you around and describe the exhibits in detail; their fee is open to negotiation, but should be agreed beforehand (approx US$5 is fair).

BEIT AL AJAIB (HOUSE OF WONDERS) (*Admission US$3.50; photography permitted*)

This large building dominates the waterfront area of Zanzibar Town, and is one of its best-known landmarks. A perfect rectangle, it is one of the largest buildings on the island even today, rising over several storeys, surrounded by tiers of pillars and balconies, and topped by a large clock tower. After more than a century of use as a palace and government offices, it opened in 2002 as the Museum of History and Culture and contains some fascinating exhibits and displays. It's a pity to rush your visit: allow yourself enough time to browse.

Built in 1883 as a ceremonial palace for Sultan Barghash, Beit al Ajaib was designed by a marine engineer, hence the great use of steel pillars and girders in the construction, and located on the site of an older palace used by Queen Fatuma, the Mwinyi Mkuu (ruler of Zanzibar) in the 17th century.

In its heyday, the interior of the new palace had fine marble floors and panelled walls. It was the first building on Zanzibar to be installed with electric lighting, and one of the first in east Africa to have an electric lift – which is why, not surprisingly, the local people called it 'Beit al Ajaib', meaning 'House of Wonders'.

In 1896, the building was slightly damaged by naval bombardment during an attempted palace coup, started when Sultan Hamad died suddenly and his cousin Khaled tried to seize the throne (see box, *The shortest war in history*, page 26). From 1911, it was used as offices by the British colonial government and after the 1964 Revolution it was used by the ASP, the ruling political party of Zanzibar. In 1977, it became the headquarters of the CCM (Chama Cha Mapinduzi, the Party of the Revolution), the sole political party of Tanzania at the time. In the early 1990s, Beit al Ajaib was virtually abandoned by the government and the party and stood empty for some years, slowly falling into disrepair, despite short-lived plans, which never materialised, to turn it into a hotel.

Four years after it originally opened to the public, the museum is still under development, with about half the planned displays now completed. Those already finished cover a variety of subjects relating to Zanzibari and Swahili culture and history, including dhow-building (one of the amazing traditional 'stitched dhows' is there, its timbers literally 'sewn' together), the maritime history of the Swahili coast, and the early history of Stone Town and the Swahili trading empire of the

19th century. Further displays covering the Portuguese period and Omani and British colonial times are planned, as is a library and conference centre. Among the many items recently transferred here from the now closed Peace Memorial Museum, though they may not yet be in their final locations, you should be able to find Dr Livingstone's medical chest, a section of track from the short-lived Zanzibar Railroad, some old bicycle lamps customised to run on coconut oil, and the old lighthouse lamp.

As well as the items on show, the House of Wonders building itself is a fascinating exhibit, to which the museum now allows public access. The ground floor offers great views up through the central courtyard to the top of the building. On the next level, the floor is covered with marble tiles. On each floor are four massive carved wooden doors. On the next floor up from the exhibition room you can go out onto the upper balcony and walk all the way around the outside of the House of Wonders. Needless to say, the views over Stone Town and the bay are spectacular.

Outside the House of Wonders are two old bronze cannons which have Portuguese inscriptions. It is thought that these cannons were made in Portugal sometime in the early 16th century, but the Omanis probably brought them to Zanzibar, after taking them from Persian forces who had originally captured the guns from the Portuguese in 1622.

THE ARAB FORT (*Donation on entrance; photography permitted*) The Arab Fort (also called the Old Fort, and by its local name Ngome Kongwe) is next to the House of Wonders. It is a large building, with high, dark brown walls topped by castellated battlements. It was built between 1698 and 1701 by the Busaidi group of Omani Arabs, who had gained control of Zanzibar in 1698, following almost two centuries of Portuguese occupation. The Old Fort was used as a defence against the Portuguese and against a rival Omani group, the Mazrui, who occupied Mombasa at that time.

The Fort was constructed by the Busaidi Omani Arabs on the site of a Portuguese church which had been built between 1598 and 1612. In the main courtyard, remnants of the old church can still be seen built into the inside wall. In the 19th century, the Fort was used as a prison, and criminals were executed or punished here, at a place just outside the east wall. The Swahili word *gereza*, meaning 'prison', is thought to be derived from the Portuguese word *igreja*, meaning 'church'.

In the early 20th century, the Fort was also used as a depot for the railway line that ran from Zanzibar Town to Bububu. In 1949 it was rebuilt and the main courtyard used as a ladies' tennis club, but after the 1964 Revolution it fell into disuse.

Today, the Fort has been renovated, and is open to visitors. It is possible to reach the top of the battlements and go onto the towers on the western side. In 1994, a section was turned into an open-air theatre. The development was imaginative yet sympathetic to the overall design and feel of the original building: seating is in amphitheatre style, and the Fort's outer walls and the House of Wonders form a natural backdrop. The theatre is used for performances of contemporary and traditional music, drama and dance. The Fort also houses a tourist information desk, with details on performances in the amphitheatre and other events around town, plus a selection of books for sale and a range of tour company leaflets to browse. There are also several spice and craft shops, a pleasant café, and remarkably some very clean public toilets. And don't miss the Tower Workshop in the west tower, where local artists create and display their works. (More details are given in *Shopping*, page 171.) Even if historical ruins don't interest you, the Fort is well worth a visit. With so many attractions and facilities, it's easy to spend quite a few hours here.

FORODHANI GARDENS The Forodhani Gardens (Jamituri Gardens on some maps) are between the Arab Fort and the sea, overlooked by the House of Wonders. Forodhani means 'customs' and this is close to the site of the original Customs House. The gardens were first laid out in 1936 to commemorate the Silver Jubilee of Sultan Khalifa (sultan from 1911 to 1960), and were called Jubilee Gardens until the 1964 Revolution. In the centre of the gardens stands a podium where the band

MREMBO TRADITIONAL SPA

(Telephone or visit to book appointments; m *0777 430117;* e *mrembozanzibar@ yahoo.co.uk)*

Recently, a number of 'spas' have sprung up around Zanzibar as the Western craze for 'wellness' treatments has descended on the island. Many are little more than a massage table, some lemongrass oil and a friendly, if untrained, local masseuse; a few, in the larger hotels, are more sophisticated and professional with Far Eastern therapists and imported lotions and potions. All can prove a thoroughly enjoyable distraction, but the most engaging and original by far is Mrembo Traditional Spa.

In an old antique store halfway along Cathedral Street, close to St Joseph's Cathedral, Mrembo is a small, wonderfully unassuming place offering the finest traditional treatments from Zanzibar and Pemba. Their flagship treatment, singo, is a natural exfoliating scrub traditionally used when preparing Zanzibari girls for marriage. Prepared by hand with a pestle and mortar (*kinu*), the fresh jasmine, ylang ylang, rose petals, *mpompia* (geranium), *mrehani* (sweet basil) and *liwa* (sandalwood) combine to create the most wonderfully aromatic blend. Perfuming the skin for days after treatment and leaving it soft as silk, it's equally popular with honeymoon brides today. For men, the clove-based scrub vidonge is said by Pembans to increase libido and stamina, and is even offered in souvenir packages. Hot sand massages, authentic henna painting and beauty treatments are available too, with all of the herbal products coming fresh from the owner's garden and skilfully prepared in front of you. The treatment rooms are cool and candlelit, with simple kanga-covered massage tables and sweet-smelling incense. There is a cold-water shower for post-scrub rinsing and a very chilled *taarab* music room for relaxing before and afterwards.

Although not their *raison d'être*, Mrembo is also an impressively inclusive community project. Two of the four local therapists are disabled: one deaf, Ali, and one blind, Asha. Trained in therapeutic massage by professional therapists from the African Touch (a Canadian-funded, community-based organisation in Kenya), they have both benefited enormously in confidence and social standing from their practical education and employment. Each has an able-bodied assistant at Mrembo to ease understanding, though Ali will cheerfully encourage you to try a little Kiswahili sign language, using the alphabet poster for guidance.

For a lazy afternoon of complete beauty pampering or a simple massage or manicure whilst the sun's at its peak, Mrembo Traditional Spa is a great place to while away the time with a cup of refreshing ginger tea and friendly staff. It is a true oasis of calm in the centre of Stone Town, and an experience not to be hurried.

of the sultan's army used to play for the public. Nearer the sea is a white concrete arabesque arch which was built in 1956 for the visit of Princess Margaret (sister of Queen Elizabeth II of Britain), although this was never officially used, as the princess arrived at the dhow harbour instead. She did visit the gardens, however, and planted a large tree, which can still be seen today.

Forodhani has long been a popular place for local people and visitors in the evenings, lured by the waterfront gathering of stalls serving drinks and hot snacks. Years of excessive overuse and poor maintenance had taken their toll, however, and for several years the 'gardens' were a euphemism for an unattractive, parched wasteland.

Wonderfully, things have changed. On 17 January 2008, the Aga Khan Trust for Culture, with approval from the Zanzibar government, finally began a major rehabilitation of the gardens. They had been in discussion about the project with the government since 2002 when the organisation first proposed comprehensive seafront rehabilitation. The aims of the project were to improve the infrastructure and to restore and preserve the civic components of the gardens, none of which had happened in the past as a result of overuse, disrepair and limited private refurbishment.

The project was completed in 2010, and the changes are plain to see. Everyone agrees that the new Forodhani Gardens are a vast improvement, with the practical introduction of wheelie bins, lighting and waste collections, a new sea wall of salvaged stone, an organised food court for the evening stallholders (see *Where to eat and drink*, page 168), three inviting cafés, a bandstand, a dhow-shaped adventure playground and tropical planting amid manicured lawns. We, like the Aga Khan, hope that this project will prove a catalyst for urban upgrading and economic opportunity, as well as aesthetically improving the remaining waterfront area.

ST JOSEPH'S CATHOLIC CATHEDRAL This large cathedral, with prominent twin spires, is off Kenyatta Road in the Baghani part of town. Although its spires are a major landmark from a distance, the cathedral can be surprisingly hard to find in the narrow streets, and it's best to follow the small sign off Gizenga Street. The cathedral was built between 1893 and 1897 by French missionaries and local converts, who had originally founded a mission here in 1860. The plans were drawn by the same French architect who designed the cathedral in Marseilles, France. The tiles and the stained-glass windows were imported from France, and the murals on the inside walls, painted just after the cathedral was completed, also show a clear French influence. Unfortunately, some of the murals have been badly restored.

The cathedral is in regular use by the town's Catholic community, a mixture of Zanzibaris, Tanzanians from the mainland, Goans and Europeans. There are several masses each Sunday, and one or two on weekdays too. Outside mass times, the main cathedral doors may be locked, and entrance is via the back door reached through the courtyard of the adjoining convent.

THE HAMAMNI BATHS In the centre of Stone Town, east of St Joseph's Cathedral and northwest of Sultan Ahmed Mugheiri Road (formerly New Mkunazini Road), are the Hamamni Baths. The area is called Hamamni, which means simply 'the place of the baths' from the Arabic *hammam* (bathhouse).

This was the first public bathhouse in Zanzibar, commissioned by Sultan Barghash and built by an architect called Haji Gulam Hussein. It is one of the most elaborate on Zanzibar, and is constructed in the Persian style. (Such baths are found in many Arab and Islamic countries, and are commonly known by Europeans as 'Turkish baths'.) Today the baths are no longer functioning, but it is still possible to go in and look around. Inside, the bathhouse is surprisingly large, with several sections including the steam room, the cool room and the cool-water pool.

The caretaker lives opposite: he will unlock the door, make a small entrance charge, give you a guided tour and sell you an informative leaflet about the baths' history and function.

TIPPU TIP'S HOUSE Tippu Tip (also spelt Tippoo Tib and Toppu Tob) was a slave trader, whose real name was Hamed bin Mohammed el Marjebi. He was born in the 1840s and began to participate in the slave trade at the age of 18. His nickname is thought to come either from a local word meaning 'to blink', as he apparently had a nervous twitch affecting his eyes, or because his eyes resembled those of a type of bird called Tippu Tib locally because it had characteristic blinking eyes.

During the mid 19th century, Tippu Tip travelled for many years across the east African mainland, trading in slaves and ivory. He also helped some of the European explorers such as Livingstone and Stanley with their supplies and route planning.

Contemporary records describe him as tall, bearded, fit and strong, with dark skin, an intelligent face and the 'air of a well-bred Arab'. He reportedly visited his concubines twice a day, and is said to have argued with missionaries that Abraham and Jacob (men of God, who appear in the Bible and the Koran) had both been slave owners themselves. Tippu Tip became very wealthy and by 1895, after many years of trading on the mainland, he owned seven plantations on Zanzibar and 10,000 slaves. He died in 1905.

The house where Tippu Tip lived is near the Africa House Hotel, behind the offices of Jasfa Tours. Until the 1960s it was a private residence, but after the revolution it was turned into a block of flats and is now occupied by several families. The house has not been maintained since its transformation, and one writer has called it 'the most magnificent squat in all of Africa'. It is not open to visitors. However, the huge carved front door (a sign of Tippu Tip's great wealth) leading into the courtyard can still be seen.

THE ANGLICAN CATHEDRAL (*US$3 during the day (except at service times), payable at a small kiosk & including the cathedral, surrounding area & a guide*). The Cathedral Church of Christ, also called the Cathedral of the Universities' Mission to Central Africa (UMCA), is near the junction of Creek Road and Sultan Ahmed Mugheiri Road (formerly New Mkunazini Road) on the eastern side of Stone Town. It stands on the site of the slave market, used in the 18th and 19th centuries when Zanzibar was a large slaving centre.

A group of UMCA missionaries had originally come to east Africa in 1861, following the call of the explorer David Livingstone to oppose the slave trade and spread Christianity across Africa. In 1864, they settled in Zanzibar, after a number of earlier sites proved unsuccessful. When the slave market was closed by Sultan Barghash in 1873 the missionaries bought the site and almost immediately started building the cathedral. Some adjoining land was donated to the mission by a wealthy Indian merchant called Jairam Senji. Today, nothing of the old slave market remains (but see *St Monica's Hostel*, pages 191–3).

When the first service was held in the cathedral, on Christmas Day 1877, the roof was not finished. It was finally completed in 1880. Tradition has it that the cathedral's altar stands on the site of a tree to which the slaves were tied and then whipped to show their strength and hardiness. Those who cried out the least during the whipping were considered the strongest, and sold for higher prices.

The man who was the force and inspiration behind the building of the cathedral was Bishop Edward Steere, who was Bishop of Zanzibar from 1874 to 1882. (He was also the first compiler of an English–Swahili dictionary, using the Roman alphabet; until then Swahili had been written using Arabic script.) He trained local people as masons and used coral stone and cement for building materials. Sultan Barghash is reputed to have asked Bishop Steere not to build the cathedral tower higher than the House of Wonders. When the bishop agreed, the sultan presented the cathedral with its clock. The tower was finished in 1883.

The legacy of David Livingstone lives on in the cathedral: a window is dedicated to his memory, and the church's crucifix is made from the tree that marked the place where his heart was buried at the village of Chitambo, in Zambia.

The mosaic decorations on the altar were given to the cathedral by Miss Caroline Thackeray (a cousin of the English novelist William Makepeace Thackeray), who was a teacher at the mission here from 1877 to 1902.

Behind the altar are the bishop's throne and 12 other seats for the canons. They are decorated with copper panels and show the names of several biblical figures, written

THE EAST AFRICAN SLAVE TRADE

From the earliest times, slaves were one of the many 'commodities' exported from Africa to Arabia, Persia, India and beyond. In the 18th century, the demand increased considerably and Arab trading caravans from Zanzibar penetrated mainland Africa in search of suitable slaves. Various contemporary accounts describe all aspects of the trade, from the initial capture of the slaves to their sale in the infamous market of Zanzibar Town.

In the interior, the Arab traders would often take advantage of local rivalries and encourage powerful African tribes to capture their enemies and sell them into slavery. In this way, men, women and children were exchanged for beads, corn and lengths of cloth.

When the Arab traders had gathered enough slaves, sometimes up to 1,000, they returned to the coast. Although the Koran forbade cruelty to slaves, this was frequently ignored on the long journey to Zanzibar: the slaves were tied together in long lines, with heavy wooden yokes at their necks or iron chains around their ankles which remained in place day and night until they reached the coast.

The trade in slaves was closely linked to the trade in ivory: the Arab traders also bought tusks from the Africans and some of the captured slaves may have had to carry these on their heads as they marched towards the coast. If a woman carrying a baby on her back became too weak to carry both child and ivory, the child would be killed or abandoned to make the ivory load easier to carry. Any slaves unable to march were also killed and left behind for the vultures and hyenas. The passage of a slave caravan was marked by a long line of decaying corpses.

After many weeks or months of marching, the slave caravans reached the coast at ports such as Kilwa and Bagamoyo. Here, the slaves were loaded onto dhows, seldom more than 30–35m long, and taken to Zanzibar. Each dhow carried between 200 and 600 slaves, all crammed below decks on specially constructed bamboo shelves with about 1m of headroom. There was not enough room to sit, or to kneel or squat, just a crippling combination of the three. Sometimes slaves were closely packed in open boats, their bodies exposed day and night to the sea and the rain. They were thirsty, hungry and seasick and many died of exhaustion. Meals consisted of a daily handful of rice and a cup of stagnant water. Sanitation in Swahili. The window behind the altar has been decorated with pictures of African saints, from Egypt, Carthage and Ethiopia. Around the church are many plaques, dedicated to the memory of missionaries who died here, and to the sailors and airmen who were killed in action during the East Africa Campaign of World War I.

Today, services are held every Sunday (in Swahili), and an English service is held on the first Sunday of the month. The cathedral is also open to visitors.

Outside the cathedral, in a small garden next to the school, is a sculpture of four slaves chained in a pit – an understated yet powerfully emotive work of art that is well worth seeing.

ST MONICA'S HOSTEL This is an impressive old stone building in its own right. Apart from its hostel accommodation (see *Where to stay*, page 160) and its gallery and craft shop, its basement provides one of Zanzibar's simplest, but arguably most moving and evocative, reminders of the dehumanising horrors of the slave trade. A stone staircase leads down from the entrance hallway to what is reputed to be the dungeon where slaves were kept before being taken to market.

was non-existent and disease spread rapidly. When any illness was discovered, infected slaves were simply thrown overboard.

By the time the slaves reached Zanzibar, they were suffering from starvation and the effects of torturously cramped conditions: it was sometimes a week after landing before they could straighten their legs. The slave traders paid customs duty on all slaves who landed, so any considered too weak to live were thrown overboard as the ship approached the port. Even so, many more slaves died in the Customs House or on the streets between the port and the market.

Before being put on sale, the slaves who did survive were cleaned so that they would fetch a better price. Men and boys had their skins oiled and were given a strip of material to put around their waist. Women and girls were draped in cloth, and sometimes even adorned with necklaces, earrings and bracelets. Generous layers of henna and kohl were smeared onto their foreheads and eyebrows.

The slaves were put on sale in the market in the late afternoon. They were arranged in lines, with the youngest and smallest at the front and the tallest at the rear, and paraded through the market by their owner, who would call out the selling prices. The owner would assure potential buyers that the slaves had no defects in speech or hearing, and that there was no disease present. Buyers would examine the arms, mouths, teeth and eyes of the slaves, and the slaves were often made to walk or run, to prove they were capable of work. Once their suitability had been established, they were sold to the highest bidder.

After being sold to a new owner, slaves were either put to work in the houses and plantations of Zanzibar or else transported again, on a much longer sea voyage, to Oman or elsewhere in the Indian Ocean. However, the slaves were relatively well treated when they arrived at their new homes. They were fed, housed and clothed, and given small plots of land, with time off to tend them. Young mothers were rarely separated from their children, and good slaves were often freed after a few years. Many took paid jobs, such as gardeners and farmers, for their previous masters: some even became leaders of slave caravans or masters of slave ships.

Source: Charles Miller, The Lunatic Express, *Macmillan, 1971*

DAVID LIVINGSTONE

David Livingstone is the best known of all the European explorers who travelled in 19th-century Africa, and many of his journeys began and ended in Zanzibar.

He was born on 19 March 1813 in the village of Blantyre, near Glasgow, in Scotland. In 1841, at the age of 28, he went to South Africa as a missionary doctor. There he married Mary Moffat, a missionary's daughter. On his early expeditions in southern Africa he crossed the Kalahari Desert and, in November 1855, became the first European to see Mosi oa Tunya ('the smoke that thunders'), which he renamed the Victoria Falls. Livingstone made his fourth major expedition from 1858 to 1864 in the area around the Lower Zambezi and Lake Nyasa (present-day Lake Malawi). He was accompanied by Dr John Kirk, another Scot, who joined the expedition as a medical officer and naturalist. After the expedition, in April 1864, Livingstone spent a week in Zanzibar before travelling back to Britain.

Livingstone returned to Zanzibar in January 1866 as he had been asked by the Royal Geographical Society to explore the country between Lake Nyasa and Lake Tanganyika, to solve the dispute over the location of the source of the Nile. He left for the mainland on 19 March 1866 and travelled around the southern end of Lake Nyasa.

After several years of exploring the region, during which time little news of his travels had reached the outside world, Livingstone met with journalist Henry Stanley at Ujiji on Lake Tanganyika on 10 November 1871 – the famous 'Dr Livingstone, I presume' incident (described in more detail in the box, *Henry Morton Stanley*, page 20). At this meeting, Livingstone was suffering terribly from foot ulcers, fever and dysentery, and had only a few days' supply of cotton with which to buy food. But two weeks later his strength had returned sufficiently for him to set out on a small expedition with Stanley. They explored the northern shores of Lake Tanganyika, establishing that the River Ruzizi flowed into (not out of) the lake, and could not therefore be a headwater of the Nile.

Livingstone and Stanley left Ujiji on 27 December 1871 and reached Kazeh, halfway to the coast, in February the following year. Livingstone was in good health, so Stanley continued on alone and arrived in Zanzibar in May 1872.

Livingstone stayed at Kazeh until August 1872, then set out on a short expedition around the southern shores of Lake Tanganyika. He was still looking for the source of the Nile when he became ill again with dysentery. He died at the village of Chitambo, a few miles south of Lake Bangweulu (Zambia) on 2 May 1873. Two of his loyal companions, Susi and Chumah, removed his heart and buried it under a tree at the spot where he died. They dried his body in the sun for two weeks, then carried it to Zanzibar, wrapped in bark and cloth, where it was identified by a broken bone in the left arm, once crushed in the jaws of a lion. Livingstone's body rested at the British consulate before being taken to London for burial. Stanley and Kirk were among the pall bearers at his funeral in Westminster Abbey on 18 April 1874.

The tree under which Livingstone's heart was buried eventually fell down, and a stone monument now stands in its place. However, some of the wood from the tree was made into a cross, and this now hangs in the Anglican cathedral in Zanzibar Town (see page 189).

Try to go there with a local person or competent guide who can set the scene and recount the history while you are there. It's chilling. The dank rooms – more like tombs – are cramped and airless, with low doorways and tiny windows. Even today it's a sombre place – but imagine it crowded with slaves in their hundreds, men, women and children together, sick and exhausted after their gruelling sea voyage (see box, *The East African slave trade*, pages 190–1), crammed five deep on the narrow stone slabs and shackled with chains which still lie there today.

THE PEACE MEMORIAL MUSEUM This is at the southern end of Stone Town, near the junction of Creek Road and Kaunda Road in the area called Mnazi Mmoja. It is also known by its local title: Beit al Amaan (House of Peace). With its distinctive dome, arabesque windows and whitewashed walls, the building looks like a mosque or basilica church. It was designed by the British architect J H Sinclair, who also designed the High Court, the British residency and several other public buildings around Zanzibar Town.

'Museum' is a misnomer nowadays, as virtually all its viewable exhibits have been shifted to the rapidly developing museum in the House of Wonders (see page 185) and the place now serves as a library. Its well-known giant tortoises have been transferred to Prison Island.

THE ZANZIBAR ARCHIVES (⏰ *07.30–15.30 Mon–Fri, 07.30–14.00 Sat; free admission*) For real aficionados, the Zanzibar Archives (Nyaraka za Taifa in Swahili) contain some fascinating material. This includes many books and manuscripts in Arabic dating from the 17th century, when the Omani sultans took control of Zanzibar; consular and protectorate records from the British colonial times; papers and documents relating to the various European expeditions that started from Zanzibar in the second half of the 19th century; plus a lot of contemporary material such as stamps, newspapers, maps and photographs. If there is something of special interest, the staff on duty can help you search through the collections. If you just want to browse, there is an exhibition room with some items of interest on display.

The archives are situated outside the main town, about 2km along Nyerere Road from the Mnazi Mmoja Hospital, in an area called Kilimani. To get there take a dala dala on Route U and ask to be dropped at Nyaraka za Taifa, or at the prison. The dala dala will stop at the bottom of Kinuamiguu Hill (the only hill on this road); turn left (north) off Nyerere Road, then take the first road on the right.

OTHER PLACES OF INTEREST IN ZANZIBAR TOWN Although the following places aren't major sights in themselves, you'll probably find yourself walking nearby as you visit some of the more important palaces and museums, and the following background information will be useful.

Mnazi Mmoja sports field Opposite the museum, on the other side of Creek Road, is Mnazi Mmoja sports field (Mnazi Mmoja means 'one coconut tree'). This area used to be a swamp at the end of the creek that separated the Stone Town peninsula from the rest of the island. The land was reclaimed and converted to a sports field during the colonial period, hence the English-style cricket pavilion in the corner. In the 1920s, part of the sports ground was set aside for exclusive use by members of the English Club; it contained tennis courts, a croquet lawn and the only golf course on the island. Today, Mnazi Mmoja is used mainly for informal football matches and, although the creek itself has been reclaimed, the sports field is still prone to flooding in the rainy season.

Nyerere Road The road leading southeast out of the town (now called Nyerere Road) was originally built by Bishop Steere of the Universities Mission in Central Africa as a causeway across the swamp. Today, it is a pleasant avenue lined with giant casuarina trees.

The People's Gardens The People's Gardens are on Kaunda Road, at the southern end of Stone Town, near the main hospital. They were originally laid out by Sultan Barghash for use by his harem. Many of the trees and bushes in the garden, including eucalyptus, coffee, tea and cocoa, were added by Sir John Kirk, the British consul on Zanzibar from 1873 to 1887. The gardens were given to the people of Zanzibar by Sultan Hamoud on the occasion of Queen Victoria's Jubilee in 1897 and they were renamed Victoria Gardens. The building in the centre of the gardens was called Victoria Hall. It was built over the baths of the harem and used as the Chamber of the Legislative Council from 1926 to 1964. After the revolution, the hall and gardens fell into disrepair. They were renovated in 1996, with help from the German government, and Victoria Hall is now rather ignominiously the offices of the Zanzibar Sewerage and Sanitation Project.

The large house opposite the gardens, on the south side of Kaunda Road, was built in 1903 as the official British Residency. After the 1964 Revolution, when the Victoria Gardens were renamed the People's Gardens, the old British Residency became the State House – the official residence of the president. The building next door to the State House was the embassy of the Soviet Union, but is now the offices

THE PALACES AT MIZINGANI

The Palace Museum (formerly the People's Palace, and before that the Sultan's Palace) was constructed on part of the site of an even older palace called Beit el Sahel, the House of the Coast, which was originally built for Sultan Said between 1827 and 1834. Contemporary accounts describe Beit el Sahel as a two-storey whitewashed palace, with a roof of green and red tiles, separated from the beach by a high wall, with a grove of pomegranates behind. The accounts go on to describe how Sultan Said spent three days of each week at Beit el Sahel, and the rest of the time at his country palace at Mtoni, about 5km north of Zanzibar Town. He often walked from the town to Mtoni even though his stables were full of Arabian horses. Every morning, the best horses were brought out from the stables and fastened to the seaward side of the wall with long ropes, to roam about and wade in the soft sand at low tide.

Another palace, called Beit el Hukm (the House of Government), was built later behind Beit el Sahel. Then, in 1883, Beit al Ajaib (the House of Wonders) was built. These three palaces were connected by a series of covered passages. A lighthouse at the front was nicknamed the 'Sultan's Christmas tree' by British navy officers, on account of its many rows of lamps.

Beit el Sahel, Beit el Hukm and the lighthouse were all destroyed in the bombardment of 1896 (see box, page 26). The palace that exists today (now the museum) was constructed partly on the site of Beit el Sahel. On the site of Beit el Hukm a private house was built, which is now the offices of Stone Town Conservation and Development Authority, easily seen between the Palace Museum and the House of Wonders, set back from the road. The building has a well-maintained garden with palm trees and shrubs. Outside the main entrance is a pair of cannons, made in Boston, Massachusetts, in 1868.

of the Zanzibar Investment Promotions Agency (ZIPA), a government agency set up to attract foreign business capital to Zanzibar.

The Big Tree Just west of the Old Dispensary, about 100m along Mizingani Road, is a large tree originally planted by Sultan Khalifa in 1911. Known simply as the Big Tree (or in Swahili as Mtini – 'the place of the tree'), it has been a major landmark for many years. It can be seen on numerous old photos and etchings of Zanzibar Town and is still clearly visible on the seafront from ships approaching the port. Today, traditional dhow builders use the tree as a shady 'roof' for their open-air workshop and taxi drivers congregate around the makeshift car park.

The Orphanage Next to the Fort, the road runs through a tunnel under a large building that is the island's orphanage. Built in the late 19th century, it was used as a club for English residents until 1896, and then as an Indian school until 1950. There is a small craft shop on the ground floor opposite the gardens selling pictures and curios made by the orphans and other local artisans (see *Shopping*, page 171).

The Upimaji building Between the Orphanage and the People's Bank of Zanzibar, this building is now the Commission for Lands and Environment. In the 1860s, it was the offices and home of Heinrich Ruete, the German merchant who eloped with Princess Salme (see box, *Princess Salme*, page 208).

The old British consulate This fine old house was used as the British consulate from 1841 to 1874, after which the consulate was moved to the Mambo Msiige building (see below). The first consul was Lieutenant Colonel Atkins Hamerton, posted here to represent the interests of Britain after Sultan Said moved his capital from Oman to Zanzibar.

Later consuls played host to several well-known British explorers, including Speke, Burton, Grant and Stanley (see page 15), before they set out for their expeditions on the east African mainland. In 1874, the body of Livingstone was brought here before being taken back to Britain for burial at Westminster Abbey.

From 1874 to 1974 the building was used as offices by the trading company Smith Mackenzie, but it was taken over by the government in the late 1970s. It is still used as government offices today, and visitors cannot enter, but there is not much to see on the inside; most of the building's interest lies in its grand exterior.

The Mambo Msiige building The name of this grand house means 'look but do not imitate'. Incorporating a variety of architectural styles, it overlooks the open 'square' at the far western end of Shangani Road. It was originally built around 1850 for a wealthy Arab, but the building was sold to the British Foreign Office in 1875 and used as the British consulate until 1913. From 1918 to 1924, it was the European hospital, after which it became government offices. Today, the Zanzibar Shipping Corporation is based here.

The Zanzibar Milestone Near the People's Gardens is this octagonal pillar, built with marble taken from the palace at Chukwani, showing the distances from Zanzibar Town to other settlements on the island. For complete accuracy, the distances were measured from this exact point. The distance to London is also shown: 8,064 miles. This is the distance by sea. (By 1870, ships between Zanzibar and London travelled via the Suez Canal. Before this all voyages were much longer, via the Cape of Good Hope.)

MOSQUES OF ZANZIBAR TOWN

Most of Zanzibar's population is Muslim; consequently Zanzibar Town has several mosques. The oldest is the Malindi Mosque, a small, inconspicuous building near the port, with a minaret which is thought to be several hundred years old. Three of the larger mosques are in the northern part of Stone Town: the Ijumaa Mosque (Sunni), the Ithnasheri Mosque (Shia) and the Aga Khan Mosque (Ismaili). These were all built in the 19th century. Compared with the large mosques of other Islamic cities, often decorated with domes and tall minarets, the mosques of Zanzibar are relatively unpretentious. However, in 1994 the Ijumaa Mosque (near the Big Tree) was renovated in a modern arabesque style, and the other large mosques may follow this trend.

Non-Muslims are not normally allowed to enter any mosque in Zanzibar Town, but if you have a genuine interest a good local guide might be able to speak to the mosque's elders on your behalf and arrange an invitation. Men will find this easier than women. There are usually no restrictions on non-Muslims (men or women) visiting the area around a mosque, although photos of local people praying or simply congregating should not be taken without permission.

7

Around Zanzibar Town

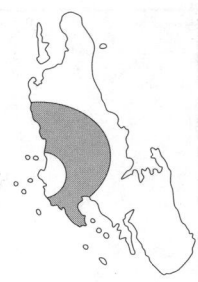

All the places listed in this chapter lie within 20km of Zanzibar Town, the majority being very close. Most can be reached easily as a day trip, by taxi, hired scooter, bike or a combination of foot and public transport. Equally, visits can be arranged with a tour company, with some of the palaces and bathhouses included in standard spice tours. Of the palaces, Mbweni lies south of Zanzibar Town, whilst Maruhubi and Mtoni, and the Persian Baths of Kidichi and Kizimbani, lie to the north.

SOUTH OF ZANZIBAR TOWN

The main attraction on the coast immediately south of Zanzibar is the Mbweni area, which is 3km from the town centre and hosts a number of ruined and extant buildings dating to the late 19th century. There are a few hotels dotted around these southern suburbs of Zanzibar Town, and while they are not as convenient for sightseeing, shopping or visiting restaurants as their more central counterparts, they lie close to the airport, making them useful for very early departures or late arrivals. Most also run free shuttle services for guests to and from the centre. The hotels outside town are generally quieter, and many are used by those on business trips, as some government and NGO offices are also in this area.

MBWENI AND ENVIRONS The coastal area of Mbweni is almost directly south of Zanzibar Town and is a historically and botanically important area. Receiving relatively little settlement by the 7th-century Arabs, 12th-century Persians or 16th-century Portuguese, it was the site of a wealthy Omani family retreat in September 1871 when Bishop Tozer (Bishop of Zanzibar from 1863–73) purchased 30 acres of land, then called Mbweni Point Shamba, for the UMCA (Universities' Mission to Central Africa). The stated intention was to create a village for freed slaves and an Anglican mission. Tozer's successor, Bishop Steere (Bishop of Zanzibar from 1874–82) oversaw the building of the church and other coral-rock mission buildings in what was the first large-scale missionary settlement in east Africa. The initial plot was extended over time to cover about 150 acres and developed to build schools, workshops, homes and a market, as well as sugar, coconut and maize plantations. Several of the buildings are still standing today.

At Mbweni Ruins Hotel and good bookshops in town you will be able to find an informative book called *Zanzibar: History of the Ruins at Mbweni* by Flo Liebst, which provides great insight into what's around, as well as the UMCA missionaries of east Africa and a general history of Zanzibar.

Getting there and away To reach Mbweni, take the main road out of town towards the airport. Go uphill through the area called Kinuamiguu ('lift your legs')

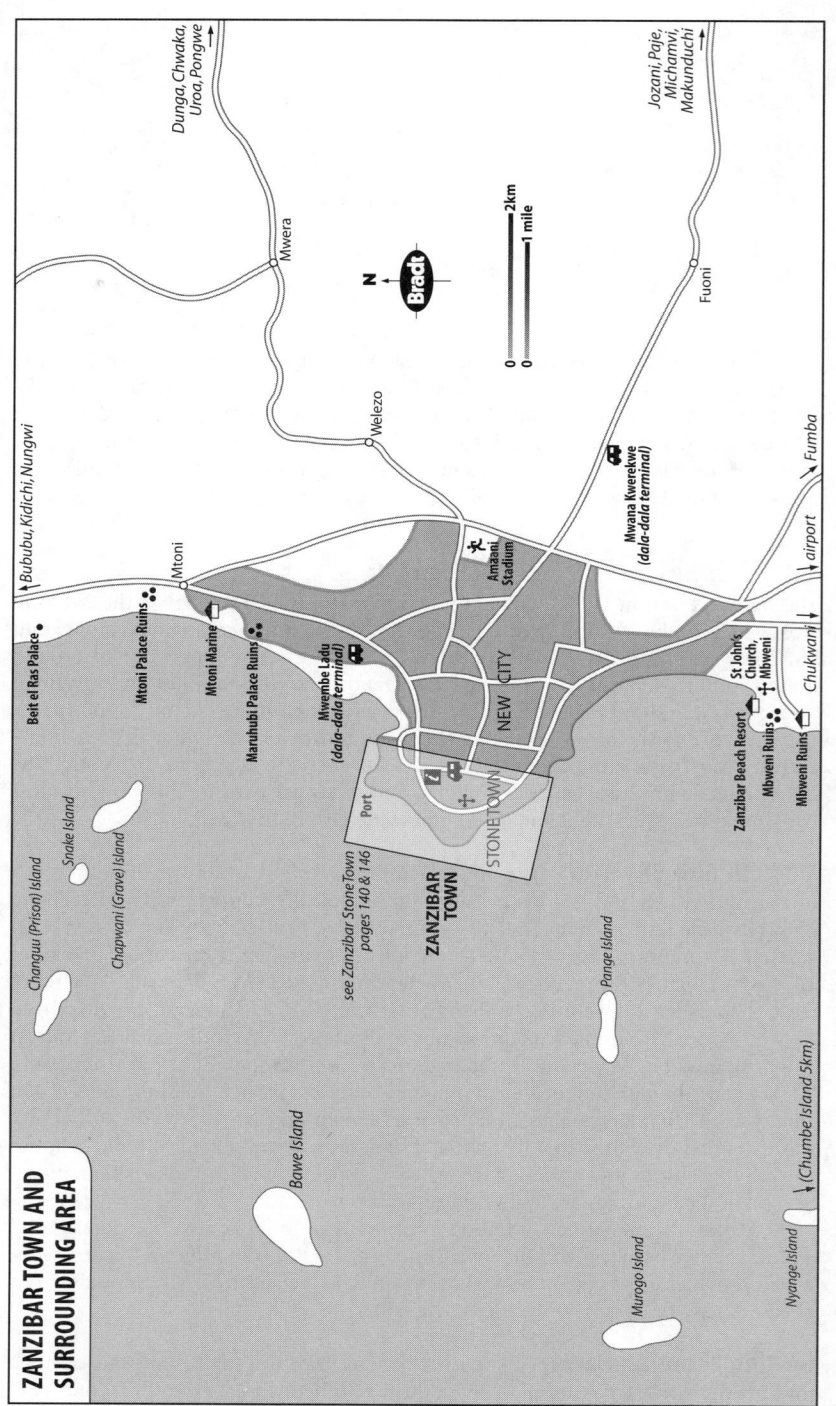

ZANZIBAR TOWN AND SURROUNDING AREA

Dunga, Chwaka, Uroa, Pongwe

Jozani, Paje, Michamvi, Makunduchi

Bububu, Kidichi, Nungwi

Mwera

Welezo

Fuoni

Mtoni

Beit el Ras Palace

Mtoni Palace Ruins

Mtoni Marine

Maruhubi Palace Ruins

Mwembe Ladu (dala-dala terminal)

Amaani Stadium

NEW CITY

Mwana kwerekwe (dala-dala terminal)

Fumba

airport

Chukwani

St John's Church, Mbweni

Zanzibar Beach Resort

Mbweni Ruins

Mbweni Ruins

Port

STONE TOWN

ZANZIBAR TOWN

see Zanzibar Stone Town pages 140 & 146

Changuu (Prison) Island

Snake Island

Chapwani (Gravel Island)

Bawe Island

Pange Island

Murogo Island

Nyange Island

(Chumbe Island 5km)

N

Bradt

2km
1 mile
0
0

198

and then Mazizini. After a few kilometres, at a signpost to Mbweni and Chukwani, fork right, then after 500m turn right again onto a smaller road. Continue down this road towards the sea to reach Mbweni. **Dala dala** number 505 runs between the town and the airport, going past the main Mbweni and Chukwani junction.

Where to stay

Zanzibar Beach Resort (84 rooms) \024 2236033/44; m 0788 410297; e znzbeachresort@zanlink.com, zbr@zanlink. com; www.zanzibarbeachresort.net. About 7km from Zanzibar Town & 3km from the airport, between the areas of Mazizini & Mbweni. At the time of researching, the overpowering stench of rubbish on arrival & the surly reception staff did not make for a good first impression. The hotel is set in large, open grounds, the front section of which overlooks the sea, & has en-suite rooms catering primarily to conference groups. Accessed along neat paths through gardens lined with conical cairns, the rooms are in 2-storey chalets with whitewashed walls & thatched roofs, some with a sea view from the balcony. All have dark furniture, AC, mini fridge, TV & safe. The hotel's Spice Restaurant serves local food, while the Jahazi Resturant cooks seafood. There's also the Discovery Bar & disco, a squash court, gym, massage parlour, 100-person conference room, & facilities for fishing & watersports. Zanzibar Beach Resort has one of the island's largest swimming pools, which has a separate pool bar. **$$$$$**

Mbweni Ruins Hotel (13 rooms) \024 223 5478/9; e hotel@mbweni.com/mbweni@zanlink. com; www.mbweni.com. In the grounds of the Mbweni Ruins, this small hotel is often rated as one of the best of its type in & around Zanzibar Town. The botanically named bedrooms are bright & comfortable, each with a large bathroom, canopy bed, tasteful bureau & practical additions like a kettle. For the personal touch, look carefully at the in-room artwork, the handiwork of one of the owners, Flo Montgomery. Every room has a small private balcony, a mere hop, skip & jump to the pool or beach. Room 14, Ylang Ylang, has arguably the best view over the palm oasis to the sea beyond, & the Baobab honeymoon suite boasts its own lovely rooftop terrace. The lodge is in the early stages of building further rooms amid the ruins themselves, so by the time you travel 1 or more of these may be complete. Food at the Raintree Restaurant (lunch US$10–20; dinner US$10–35) is made to order with fresh ingredients & it's a popular lunchtime spot for a few doting cats & visitors. The ruins are open to visitors & sometimes the hotel arranges atmospheric weddings or open-air dinners amongst the pillars & arches of the school chapel. Al fresco yoga classes are held here 3 nights a week. The hotel is set in extensive well-maintained grounds with a lush botanical garden (inspired by botanist John Kirk) & nature trail through its shady terraces. Nearby mangroves provide good birding, & the hotel has its own list of birds & butterflies. The staff are keen naturalists, & can advise visitors on all aspects of local natural history. From the beachfront swimming pool to the new Bustani Spa or the waterside Mangrove Bar, Mbweni is a relaxing spot & a good choice for those who want to experience Stone Town but escape the bustle. A free shuttle service runs to/from town 3 times a day; transfers to/from the port or airport cost US$15 for 4 people. **$$$$–$$$$$**

What to see and do

St John's Church At the heart of Mbweni, on a small road lined with large old 'rain trees' (should you visit in a shower, you'll find the leaves all closed), is the English-style St John's Church, complete with a tower and surrounding cemetery. Nearby is the old clergy house, which was more recently the Inn by the Sea Hotel (now closed).

St John's was opened in 1882 by UMCA missionaries and converts, and consecrated in 1904. The church has a marble altar inlaid with colourful mother-of-pearl shell and a wooden chair made for Bishop Tozer by the sailors of HMS *London*, the British naval ship famous for its slave-dhow captures. In the interesting cemetery there are also a number of very prickly cycads, naturally endemic on the east coast of Zanzibar, and thought to have been planted here by the Mbweni missionaries.

A number of descendants of freed slaves continue to live in the area and today you can visit the church and cemetery with the help of the church sexton, Peter Sudi. He is a direct descendant of John Swedi, the first African deacon of the UMCA and one of the first five slave boys to be freed and taken in by Bishop Tozer at the mission.

There are Anglican services at 08.00 every Sunday.

St Mary's School for Girls Past St John's Church towards the sea, a dirt road leads to Mbweni Ruins Hotel (see *Where to stay*, page 199), whose grounds house the remains of the St Mary's School for Girls. This Victorian school was constructed by missionaries, under the guidance of bishops Tozer and Steere, on a property known as Mbweni Point Shamba. Constructed between 1871 and 1874, the school was a large square building, based around a central courtyard, and incorporating the old Arab house on the property into its entrance.

The school educated orphaned girls who had been freed from captured slave-dhows and the daughters of freed slaves who lived at the mission, each with their own house and small garden. Most of the girls were trained as teachers, and were taught reading, writing, arithmetic, geography and sewing. The headmistress from 1877 until 1902 was Caroline Thackeray (a cousin of the English novelist William Thackeray). In 1877, Ms Thackeray paid for the construction of an 'Industrial Wing' in which her less academically inclined pupils were given vocational training in basketry, stitching, laundry and cooking to enable them to run a home and seek employment. In 1906, the school became a convent and in 1920 the buildings were sold by the church to a consortium including the Bank of India. Over the following years, they slowly became ruined and were never used or lived in until the present time.

St Mary's also had its own chapel which, in spite of its lack of roof, is still in good condition today and makes a lovely spot for romantic dinners if you're celebrating a special occasion at the hotel.

Sir John Kirk's House Along the road which passes northwards in front of St John's Church is the house of Sir John Kirk, British consul-general in Zanzibar from 1873 to 1887. Kirk first came to Africa in the 1850s as the medical officer and naturalist on Livingstone's Zambezi expedition. As consul-general he was very active in the suppression of the slave trade and he is often regarded as the 'power behind the throne' during the rule of his close friend, Sultan Seyyid Barghash. Some historical records claim that this house was in fact a gift from Barghash, built as a country retreat for Kirk and his family when he was promoted from vice-consul to consul-general. It is certainly known that Kirk used the house frequently and that as a keen and experienced botanist he established a large experimental garden here, which later provided the core species of all the botanical gardens of Zanzibar and mainland Tanzania. He imported many new plant species to the islands from the Royal Botanic Gardens at Kew as well as from India, the Far East and South America, and worked on improving varieties of useful and edible crops. He established spices such as nutmeg, cardamom, cinnamon, vanilla, black pepper and ginger, as well as exotic fruit trees from avocado to lychee, palms and cycads, and even rubber vines, both endemic and imported. He also planted cinchona, the source of quinine, along with other known medicinal plants. Kirk collected trees and flowers from the mainland of Africa which formed the basis of the then standard work, *Flora of Tropical Africa*.

In 1887, Kirk left Zanzibar and sold his house to Caroline Thackeray (see page 190), and each subsequent year she opened the impressive grounds to the public for an annual garden party. Although Thackeray retired as headmistress of St Mary's in 1902, she inhabited the house until her death aged 83 in 1926. She was buried in the cemetery at St John's Church and bequeathed the property to the UMCA. The house was subsequently sold to a wealthy Arab, who used it until the early 1960s. Today the property remains privately owned and is not open to the public, and although the gardens are somewhat wild and overgrown Kirk's rare and exotic species stand strong.

NORTH OF ZANZIBAR TOWN

Along the coast north of Zanzibar Town, stretching over a distance of about 5km, are several palaces dating from the 19th century. Built for the various sultans who ruled Zanzibar during this period, it was commonplace for these wealthy families to retreat from the heat, smell and disease of the city in the hotter months to less populated corners. Some of the palaces and homes are in good condition and worth a visit; others will appeal only to keen fans of historical ruins and those with exceptionally good imaginations.

For the palaces that are open, the entrance price is very low and the ticket you buy at the first place you visit will also allow you access to many other historical sites on the same day. This includes the baths at Kidichi, the caves at Mangapwani and several other sites around the island.

The main settlement in this area, the amusingly named Bububu, is approximately 10km north of the Stone Town and is known for the attractive Fuji Beach and a number of small coastal hotels which are strung along the water's edge.

GETTING THERE AND AWAY Many of this area's historical sites are included in spice tours, and all are easily accessed with a hire car or private vehicle. On public transport, the Route 2 bus which heads north to Mangapwani village will often continue to the coast and coral cave with a little persuasion.

For Bububu, Fuji Beach and Mtoni, take dala dala No 502 from Zanzibar Town, a route which can also be used for the Persian Baths at Kidichi, alighting at Bububu and continuing on foot in a westerly direction for 3km. Kidichi is also the final stop on dala dala 511 and public bus route 3.

WHERE TO STAY AND EAT The hotels below all lie alongside or within a few hundred metres of the main tar road between Stone Town and Bububu/Fuji Beach. They are listed in the order you would pass them coming from the direction of Zanzibar Town.

Unless stated otherwise, hotels listed below offer air conditioning and en-suite bathrooms as standard,

Maruhubi Beach Villas (12 rooms) m 0777 451188; e maruhubi@zanlink. com; www.maruhubibeachvillas.com, www. zanzibarmaruhubi.com. Situated close to the eponymous ruins some 3km north of Stone Town, this attractive, low-key resort is clearly signposted off the main road. It has a superb location on a sandy beach offering views back to the House of Wonders on the Zanzibar waterfront as well as to Mtoni Beach. Accommodation is in airy & spacious semi-detached bungalows, running in a single row perpendicular to the sea. The majority are set in beautiful tropical gardens, but rooms 1–4 are set on a coral rock pier with wonderful panoramic views up & down the coast. Interiors are lovely in their simplicity with large, coconut wood Zanzibari beds, subtle apricot walls, sparkling bathrooms & wide verandas, complete with mattress-covered sun loungers. The huge makuti Sunset Restaurant offers lunch & dinner at neat tables, around which are turquoise director's chairs. Menu options are varied & reasonably priced – vegetarian pancake US$5; calamari tempura US$7; beef kebab US$10 – & it is licensed to serve alcohol. The new pool above the beach is a big asset & non-residents can pay US$5/day to indulge. **$$$–$$$$**

🏠 **Mtoni Marine** (43 rooms) ☎024 2250140; **m** 0777 486214; **e** mtoni@zanzibar.cc; www. mtoni.com. Located between the palaces of Maruhubi & Mtoni, about 5mins' drive north of Zanzibar Town, Mtoni Marine is a highly recommended, friendly hotel set in exceptional tropical gardens overlooking the bay & a large, private stretch of sandy beach. The management style, a mix of Zanzibari & Italian, is relaxed & efficient – a perfect combination. There's a broad range of accommodation from the spacious Palm Court dbls to 2-bedroom family apts. The rooms are all cool & comfortable with high ceilings & cleverly incorporated Omani features. Each is tastefully decorated with beautiful colours, quality fabrics & a raft of mod cons. Within the grounds, there are 2 restaurants & the sushi is particularly well regarded. Snacks start at US$3–5 & you can enjoy an excellent meal for US$12–20. For casual dining, there are weekly buffet BBQs (US$35) & the ever-popular Mcheza Bar & Bistro serving oven-baked pizzas, sandwiches & burgers whilst broadcasting international sport to residents & tourists. For something more romantic, candlelit dinners & imported wines are available in the main restaurant, or there is a sunset dhow cruise for great views of Stone Town (US$35pp, inc snacks & soft drinks). All-day dhow cruises are also arranged, US$40 including lunch, drinks & snorkel gear, with discounts for hotel guests. The hotel also has a spa, a pleasant 25m pool & a great playhouse/climbing frame for energetic children. Staff can arrange tours (for something local, see box, *The Princess Salme tour*, page 206), car hire, boat trips & taxis (US$6 to Stone Town; US$15 to the airport). With lovely rooms at fantastic value,

THE WIVES AND CHILDREN OF SULTAN SAID

During his lifetime, Sultan Sayyid Said (Sultan of Oman and Zanzibar from 1804 to 1856) had three legitimate wives, or *harino* (singular *horme*). Under Islamic law, at any one time, he was allowed up to four harino.

In 1827, he married his cousin Azze Binte Seif bin Ahmed, daughter of Seif bin Ahmed and grandchild of Sultan Ahmed. Azze was considered to have equal status with her husband. She was reported to be strong-willed and to rule the royal household with a firm hand. Apparently, no act of state was carried out without her advice and approval.

In 1847, Said married his second wife, Binte Irich Mirza, nicknamed Schesade (or Scheherazade), a beautiful, extravagant princess, and the granddaughter of the Shah of Persia. She came to Zanzibar in 1849 and Said built the baths at Kidichi for her in 1850, using stonemasons and plasterers from her homeland. Schesade had no children so Said divorced her and sent her back to Persia. By the late 1850s, Schesade had become a prominent member of the Persian army, fighting against her former husband with the hellish fury of a woman scorned.

Said's third wife was Binte Seif bin Ali, of whom little is known. He also possessed a great many pan-African concubines and once these women had given birth, they were known as *sarari* (singular *surie*), immediately freed and given equal status with the legal wives.

During his lifetime, Said is credited with fathering 120 children (99 daughters and 21 sons) and when he died in 1856, he left a single widow, his first wife Azze Binte Seif, and 75 sarari. Of his children, only 36 were still alive: 18 sons and 18 daughters. Two of his sons, Thuwaini and Turki, became sultans of Oman; four more sons, Majid, Barghash, Khalifa and Ali, became sultans of Zanzibar.

particularly for families or those wanting a little space for their Stone Town explorations, Mtoni continues to build on its strong reputation as a good-quality hotel. **$$$–$$$$**

⌂ **Via Via** (5 rooms) m 0744 286369; e zanzibar. tanzania@viaviacafe.com. Also known as Kalinge's Garden Bungalows, after its European owner Mama Kalinge, this is an affiliate of the well-known Belgian café in Arusha. Set in a shady green oasis about 7km from Stone Town along the Bububu road, & within 5mins' walk of Fuji Beach, it's a relaxed set-up, offering uncluttered accommodation in rustic 4-bed bungalows suitable for budget travellers & families. Each room has a dbl & 2 sgl coir-rope beds & mosquito nets. In the terraced makuti lounge, there are comfortable chairs, a lovely coconut-wood bar & even a hutch of cute white bunnies. Facilities include free airport pick-ups & transport to & from Stone Town, as well as a home-cooked *plat du jour* for around US$5. **$$**

⌂ **Imani Beach Villa** (9 rooms) ☏024 2250050; m 0773 903983; e info@imani-zanzibar. com; www.imani-zanzibar.com. About 9km from Stone Town, Imani Beach Villa is clearly signposted off the main road at Bububu. From here, a bumpy coral-rock track meanders downhill towards the sea & Imani's beachfront plot. Tucked away in a mass of cerise bougainvillea & banana trees, it is a small & delightful home-from-home hotel. From clearing up the beach to creating some of the island's most original cocktails, managers Simon & Kristen Bennett have a hands-on attitude & strong service ethic. Under their guidance, Imani has been re-energised & revamped into a gem of a hidden hideaway. All rooms feature enormous Zanzibari beds & clean bathrooms. Centred on the villa's small, antique-filled lounge/entrance, the ocean view from the daybed, the sound of rolling waves & the constant breeze all create a distinctly exotic air. Outside, billowing orange & monochrome fabric panels conceal a cool Arab-style bar & restaurant in the tropical garden. Tasty meals are served at low tables, seating is on piles of cushions & Persian carpets, & cost around US$20. Check out the treehouse for sundowner drinks. A taxi to/from town is around US$10 & the hotel also has bikes which are free for guest use. **$$$**

⌂ **Bububu Beach Guesthouses** (6 rooms) m 0777 422747; e kilupyomar@hotmail.com; www.bububu-zanzibar.com. Set in Bububu village, these 2 guesthouses are simple but clean, friendly & very relaxed. Each can sleep up to 8 people (2 dbls; 1 quad) in adequate rooms & seem reasonably good value. There's a living room, dining room & kitchen. Although mainly geared to longer-stay visitors & family groups, the rooms can be rented individually, with self-catering or FB options available. Meals can be taken at nearby Fuji Beach (see *What to see and do*, page 210), which has a bar & restaurant. The owner Omar Kilupi can arrange spice tours, rental cars & motorbikes, or challenge you to a game of chess as he's one of the island's master players! There's a free transfer service to/from town twice a day or you can catch one of the frequent dala dalas running between Bububu village & Zanzibar Town. From the dala dala stop on the main road in Bububu village, it's a short walk down a dirt track towards the beach to reach the hotel. **$$**

⌂ **Ngalawa Lodge** (18 rooms) m 073 644621; e ngalawa.lodge@yahoo.com. Ngalawa is marketed primarily as a business-orientated hotel, & the arresting entrance gates don't give the best first impression, though some holidaymakers might enjoy this place. It's set on a large plot of land, far back from the beach (with no access), & uses a fraction of its available space. The unused land looks unloved & overgrown, & though earmarked for various sports' courts, suspicion is that accommodation expansion is more likely. The airy dbl rooms are simple & clean, with coconut wood furniture, large beds covered in starched white linen & all with a TV, fan & safe; the bathrooms unusually contain both a bath & a shower. In the gardens, a pool, surrounded by shaded chairs & tables, is an attractive spot to lounge among the flowers. There is a battered tennis court (rackets & balls provided), but it's a prickly trek through long grasses to reach it. There's no official lounge but guests can relax in front of the TV in the Mbudya bar & restaurant boma, where pizzas (US$5), steaks (US$9) & pot roast (US$8) are made to order. A few more guests would improve the hotel's atmosphere significantly. **$$$**

⌂ **Hakuna Matata Beach Lodge & Spa** (13 rooms) 0756 144605; e info@zanzibar-resort. com; www.hakuna-matata-beach-lodge.com. 12km north of Zanzibar Town, Hakuna Matata is built amid the ruins of Sultan Barghash's Chuini Palace (see *What to see and do*, page 210), lending it a crumbling, historic charm. The 13 thatched stone cottages are divided into 3 categories, the difference being the increasing size of the room & bed. Brightly patterned blue sofas, lamps carved into elephants & wooden Maasai figures all seem a bit gaudy, but the standard of finish is high, with carved queen- or king-sized beds, hot water & sunlit terraces. Being raised up on a cliff, many cottages have a wonderful view out to sea or of the secluded bay below. Pretty, well-tended gardens have been designed to complement the ruins rather than hide them, & the 2-tier pool even has an aqueduct guarded by lion statues. Previous diners have highly recommended the seafood restaurant, which also serves up produce from the lodge's own gardens. Down on the sand, beached dhows, sunloungers & a sheltered lagoon await. As the name suggests, there is a spa – it's particularly popular with brides-to-be beautifying before their big day. Hakuna Matata is a peaceful place with a lot of history, only really let down by scarce staff. **$$$$**

🏠 **Mangrove Lodge** (10 rooms) m 0777 436954; e info@mangrovelodge.com; www.mangrovelodge.com. Just north of Hakuna Matata, Mangrove Lodge is a relaxed seaside retreat on a pretty slice of mangrove beach. The Zanzibari owner, manager & former guide Haji & his Italian business partner Paolo have admirably taken a variety of measures to try to reduce the environmental impact of the lodge. There's purposely no energy-devouring AC, & most cooking is done over fire. Locally sourced materials, brought in by cart, were used to construct the buildings; local carpenters built the furniture & carved the door frames; & the furnishings were sewn by local tailors. Now, pathways through gardens & lawns link the pretty thatched bungalows, each with either a dbl or a sgl bed & a kitchenette. Inside, the simple rooms with net-draped beds are brightened by local touches: traditional ceilings & kanga-covered chairs, Zanzibari doors & hand-stitched mats. The restaurant looks out over the fishing boats bobbing in the bay & in keeping with the eco policy, ingredients for the Italian–Swahili food are purchased locally, all leftovers are composted & no plastic bottles or bags are used. Sunbathers can choose between 2 secluded beaches: Mangroves, which surrounds a small lagoon, & Mawimbini, also home to the Mangrove bar & Haji's trinket shop. Haji arranges hygiene & language classes for his staff, & guests are welcome to join in should

they wish to improve their Swahili. Mangrove plans to further improve its eco-credentials with rainwater collection & solar power in the future. **$$$**

🏠 **Zanzi Resort** (7 villas) m 0777 111333; e office@zanziresort.com; www.zanziresort.com. Zanzi Resort is a Polish-owned hotel complex 20mins' drive north of Stone Town. With sweeping clifftop views, luxurious villas offer peace & seclusion in tropical gardens spread over 6ha. Sleeping up to 4 in each, they are well appointed with king-size beds, a lounge & a bathroom. Each has a huge private garden, swimming pool with a current machine & an outdoor shower. Those with adventure-seeking children might like to request a villa where rooms are nestled into the surrounding trees, giving the impression of sleeping in a treehouse. Villa exteriors are painted in hues of terracotta & orange with modern designs by artist Szymon Adamczyk. Next to each villa is a path leading down to a secluded beach. The resort offers a personal concierge service, 1 per villa, & on request private meals are rustled up by the imaginative chef & served in your villa or on the beach; budding cooks can even join chef Rafal for personal cookery classes. Alternatively, a range of massages & treatments are offered by resident Thai therapists. **$$$–$$$$**

🏠 **Sea Cliff Resort & Spa** (120 rooms) ☎ 0767 702241; e reservations@seacliffzanzibar.com; www.seacliffzanzibar.com. Despite being an enormous international-standard resort offering a plethora of holiday activities, Sea Cliff just about manages to retain some Zanzibari flavour. A 20min drive from Stone Town, the high-quality rooms follow a muted colour scheme of creams & golds, with antique Zanzibari furniture & elegant lanterns. With the resort's enviable clifftop location, all but the garden rooms have private balconies with ocean views. Each room has a high-quality finish, mod cons from LCD satellite TV to iPod docking, & an outdoor seating area. Sea-view & deluxe rooms contain jacuzzis & twin basin bathrooms, whilst deluxe also boasts a balcony & patio over 2 levels. Guests at Sea Cliff have an exhaustive list of activities on offer – from darts to football – plus a modern gym containing a squash court, 2 tennis courts (rackets & balls free) & a mini climbing wall, whilst the watersports centre has a plethora of options including sailing, waterskiing, windsurfing, pedalos & even deep-sea fishing; all non-motorised activities are free. The more sedate can drift off on a sunset cruise or explore the area by bicycle. The 80m kidney-shaped pool is split over 2 levels & consists of 2 infinity pools, a children's pool & an artificial beach. Surrounding the pool, the impressive gardens have manicured bright green lawns splashed with the deep pink of bougainvillea. At the Shwari Spa, treatments including facials & scrubs are on offer from Balinese therapists & there's also a sauna & pool. There's also a very well-equipped gym where yoga classes take place, & while you're there, the kids club will keep the little ones entertained. Remarkably, at the far north of the property is a paddock with a number of horses, & rides can be tailored for all levels. Recharge at one of 3 restaurants — Mangapwani, with local & international buffets, Terrace Restaurant, offering casual outdoor dining, & Kobe Restaurant, for light lunches by the pool — or at the 4 bars. The lounge is a popular place for a spot of afternoon tea & cake, & there's a weekly entertainment programme which includes acrobats & the 'Coconut Band'. The business market is equally catered for, with the 3 conference rooms & a separate dining area for delegates. 1 free transfer to Stone Town is offered for every 3 nights stayed. ♔

WHAT TO SEE AND DO
Palaces

Maruhubi Palace The Maruhubi Palace is on the coast, about 4km north of Zanzibar Town. Named after the original landowner, the palace itself was built in 1882 for Sultan Barghash (sultan from 1870–88) and at one time he reputedly kept 100 women here: one official wife and 99 concubines. (The sultan himself lived at the palace in Zanzibar Town.)

The palace was built with coral stone and wood, and was reported to have been one of the most ornate on the island. Large walls were built around the palace grounds, thought to have been inspired by the park walls seen by Sultan Barghash on his visit to England in 1875. Unfortunately, the palace was destroyed by fire in 1899 and all that remain today are the great pillars, which supported the upper storey, and the Persian-style bathhouse, where the separate bathrooms for the women, and the large bath for the sultan's own use, can still be seen. The original water tanks, now overgrown with water lilies, can still be seen in the grounds. To the north of the pillars, at the back of the beach, is a small set of arches and steps; this was part of the palace's reception area. (The House of Wonders in Zanzibar Town, see page 185, contains a photo of the palace taken at the end of the 19th century when it was still in use.)

To reach the palace, take the main road north out of Zanzibar Town towards Bububu. Pass Livingstone House on your right and, after a few kilometres, the Maruhubi Palace is signposted on your left. Dala dalas on route B run between the town and Bububu village, past the palace entrance gate.

Beit el Mtoni or Mtoni Palace About 2km north of Maruhubi is Mtoni Palace. Built for Sultan Seyyid Said in 1828, as he moved his court from Oman to Zanzibar, it is said that the land previously belonged to Saleh bin Haramil al Abray, the Arab trader who first imported cloves to Zanzibar (see *Chapter 1*, page 10).

Mtoni, which means 'place by the river', is the oldest palace on Zanzibar and was the largest during Sultan Said's reign. It was home to his first and only legitimate wife, many of his secondary wives, their children and the hundreds of slaves that tended to them. It is well worth a visit, either combined with lunch at the adjoining Mtoni Marine Hotel or as part of the Princess Salme tour (see page 206).

One of the palace's most notable residents, Princess Sayyida Salme, was one of Sultan Said's many daughters. Born at Beit el Mtoni, she became well known as the Arabian princess who fell in love with a German merchant, Rudolph Heinrich Ruete, and eloped to Hamburg (see box, *Princess Salme*, page 208).

In her very readable 1888 chronicle about life on Zanzibar, *Memoirs of an Arabian Princess from Zanzibar*, Salme recalls her paradisiacal childhood home:

Beit il Mtoni, distant about five miles from the city of Zanzibar, lies on the sea coast, surrounded by most beautiful scenery, and quite hidden in a grove of palm and mango trees, and other gigantic specimens of tropical vegetation. The house of my birth is called 'Mtoni house', after the little river Mtoni, which rises only a few miles inland, runs through the whole palace into numerous fountains, and flows directly behind the palace walls into the splendid and animated inlet which severs the island from the African continent.

Of the building itself, she states:

It had a large courtyard where gazelles, peacocks, ostriches and flamingos wandered around, a large bath-house at one end and the sultan's quarters at the other, where he lived with his principal wife, an Omani princess whose name was Azze.

Salme records that over 1,000 people were attached to the sultan's court in the palace. She describes how her father, the sultan, would pace up and down on a

THE PRINCESS SALME TOUR

(*Bookings must be made at least one day in advance* ✆ 024 2250140; m 0777 430117; e mtoni@zanzibar.cc; www.mtoni.com)

In mid 2008, the dedicated team at Mtoni Palace Conservation Project created a lovely new tour combining a number of historical palaces and traditional ceremonies, as well as an informative spice tour and delicious Swahili lunch.

Escorted by a guide from the conservation project, small groups (approx 4–6) are taken around the evocative ruins of Mtoni Palace, Princess Salme's birthplace, in a colourful, thatched cart pulled by Henrika the friendly donkey. Then it's off by dhow, which sails to Bububu for a traditional coffee ceremony with tasty local treats (*kashata* – peanut brittle – and candy-like *halua*). After a short walk, perhaps into the grounds of Salme's cousin's home, the group visits the lush Kidichi plantation area. Here, there's a guided tour of Mzee Yussuf's spice farm before he and his wife serve a deliciously fresh, homemade meal. Expect pilau rice, coconut curry, fish masala, roasted meats, stewed beans, *kachumbari* salad (east African coleslaw), an array of tropical fruits and spice tea.

Heading back down the hillside after lunch in a private dala dala, there are great views towards the Indian Ocean and Stone Town before the vehicle arrives at the Persian Baths (see box, *The wives and children of Sultan Said*, page 202). Henrika gets her break here and satisfied guests are whisked back to Mtoni Marine by minibus, where a chilled drink in the bar is the perfect end to the excursion.

The Princess Salme tour leaves Mtoni Marine reception (see *Where to stay and eat*, page 202) at 08.30, returning at 14.00 and costs US$55 (US$5pp supplement for fewer than 3 people), including all entrance fees and lunch. It's an original and varied way to see these sites and enjoy traditional Zanzibari cuisine, and US$5 of the charge is donated to the valuable work of the Mtoni Palace Conservation Project.

large round tower overlooking the sea, where he could see his fleet anchored off the shore. If visitors came by boat, he would greet them on the steps of his palace as there was no landing pier, whilst Salme and the other princesses were carried out to their boats on chairs.

Sadly, she also goes on to describe her return visit to Zanzibar in 1885, after the death of Sultan Said, and the abandoned, decaying palace that she found at Mtoni. The palace was then turned into a warehouse during World War I and today only the main walls, arches, parts of the roof and bathhouse remain. Yet although severely deteriorated, Mtoni Palace still offers a glimpse into the world of the Arabian royalty that once lived there. With only a little imagination and one of the conservation team guides, the impressive scale of the vast inner courtyard, individual bathing complex and palace gardens can still be appreciated and enjoyed.

In the early 1990s, the Zanzibar Directorate of Archives, Museums and Antiquities (DAMA), in collaboration with Mtoni Marine Centre, initiated a project aimed at conserving the Mtoni Palace ruins and the surrounding gardens. Archaeological survey drawings and historical research have been commissioned and undertaken, excavations of the reservoir and impressive aqueduct in front of the palace have been completed, and substantial progress has been made in clearing the gardens, replanting original species, restoring walls using original techniques and providing visitors with some insight into the palace's history and importance. There is still a tremendous amount to be done but this work is set to continue with involvement of students from the local archives and archaeology institutes.

It is a slow, careful and expensive process, but the Mtoni Palace Conservation Project is working hard to generate the necessary funds through a number of special events and tours (see box, *The Princess Salme tour*, opposite), though visitor donations are obviously welcomed. With more resources, it may just be possible to restore significant sections of Mtoni Palace and its gardens to their former splendour and to save any further dilapidation to the parts of the palace that are now beyond repair. For Zanzibaris, this is vital work to preserve a tangible memento of their past, on an island where so many historical buildings have been destroyed.

Beit el Ras Palace Further north along the coast, the construction of this palace was commissioned by Sultan Said as an 'overflow' house for his children and their servants, when Mtoni Palace became too crowded. Building started in 1847 but was not completed by the time of Said's death in 1856. Sultan Majid (Said's successor) did not continue the project and much of the stone from the palace was used during the construction of the Zanzibar railroad (described on page 210). The remaining ruins were abandoned and finally demolished in 1947 to make room for a school and teacher training centre. Today, the palace is within the grounds of the Nkrumah Teacher Training College (Chuo Cha Ualimu Nkrumah) and only the giant porch of the original palace remains, with high arches and steps leading up one side. Beit el Ras means 'the palace on the headland' and from the porch you get good views over this part of the coast and out towards the group of small islands off Zanzibar Town. It is reached by turning off the main road a few kilometres beyond Mtoni.

Kibweni Palace North of Beit el Ras, this 'palace' was built in Arabic style by the British authorities in 1915. In the village of Kibweni, its official title was Beit el Kassrusaada (Palace of Happiness), although this name seems to have been long forgotten. Sultan Khalifa II (sultan from 1911–60) used the palace as a country residence but after the revolution it was taken over by the government and is still used as an official residence. It is not open to the public.

PRINCESS SALME

The daughter of Sultan Said and a *surie* (secondary wife) from Circassia, in southern Russia, Salme was born at Mtoni Palace in August 1844, and resident there for her first seven years. Describing her early childhood at Mtoni Palace, she tells of learning sewing, embroidery and lacemaking from her mother. She and her brothers and sisters had a private teacher and lessons were conducted in an open gallery containing a single large mat and a Koran on a stand. The royal children were taught the Arabic alphabet, reading and a little arithmetic. The boys were also taught to write, using homemade ink, and the well-bleached shoulder blade of a camel for a slate. But Salme was rebellious and taught herself to write in secret.

Twice a day, early in the morning and in the evening, all children over five had riding lessons. When they had made sufficient progress, the boys received Arabian horses, while the girls received white donkeys from Muscat. When the princesses rode their donkeys to the clove plantations, slaves ran by the side of each animal with a large parasol to protect the riders from the sun. The children also learnt to swim in the sea at an early age.

Salme was given her own African slaves as personal attendants. At bedtime, one slave would massage her, while another fanned gently, until the princess fell asleep, still fully dressed. Slaves fanned the princess all through the night. In the morning, her slaves massaged her gently until she awoke. Her bath was filled with fresh spring water. Slaves laid out the day's clothes, on which jasmine and orange blossoms had been strewn overnight, and which were scented with amber and musk before they were worn. Windows and doors were left open throughout the year, even in colder, wetter weather when a charcoal fire was burning. The fresh air helped to disperse the strong scents. Slaves washed the linen daily. Due to the heat, it dried in little more than half an hour, was smoothed flat (not ironed) and put away.

As a child, Salme was allowed to mix freely with boys of her own age. After she was nine years old, the only men allowed to see her were her father, close male relatives, and her slaves. She wore trousers, a shirt reaching to her ankles, and a handkerchief on her head. The shirt and trousers were always of a different pattern. On her walks, she wore a *schele*, a large shawl of black silk. When she appeared before a stranger, the law required her to be veiled; part of her face, her neck and chin had to be completely covered. Most importantly her ankles also had to be hidden.

In October 1859, Salme became involved in family intrigue between her elder brothers, Barghash and Majid. She helped Barghash escape to the Marseilles clove plantation after his attempt to overthrow Majid failed (see box, *The Escape to Marseilles*, page 16). Majid never punished Salme for her part in the plot but by siding with Barghash she lost the friendship of many of her other brothers and sisters. When she renewed her friendship with Majid, she isolated herself from her fellow conspirators.

By 1866, Salme was living in Zanzibar Town. Although 22 years old, she was still unmarried. Rejected by her family, she began socialising regularly with many of the foreigners on the island. She became friendly with a young German merchant from Hamburg, called Heinrich Ruete, who was living in a house next to hers. They began a covert relationship, speaking to each other from their balconies across the narrow street, and meeting secretly in the countryside.

In July 1866, Salme discovered she was pregnant. Some historians have suggested that she was forced to leave Zanzibar in a hurry, as an illegitimate pregnancy would have brought disgrace to her family and the whole Busaidi dynasty and could have resulted in her death; others have described her romantic 'elopement' with Heinrich Ruete. However, an analysis by Said el-Gheithy of the Princess Salme Institute presents events in a slightly different light:

No doubt, her pregnancy sent shock waves through her clan and threatened the position of the European traders, reliant on the goodwill of the sultan. Yet following extensive research, and through a knowledge of her personality from at least one person who knew her, it seems Salme was a very organised and stable individual, with a strength of personality which made her adverse to irrational movements. We must not overlook or underestimate her ability to choose rationally from the options available. The concept of an 'elopement' represents her as somewhat flighty. Rather, the move to Germany should be understood as a planned emigration and her departure could be described, to use a Swahili phrase, as 'leaving without saying goodbye'.

Salme left Zanzibar on a British warship, and for several months after her departure a wave of anti-European feeling spread through Zanzibar Town. Another British warship was sent to suppress any possible reprisals against Europeans. When Salme reached Aden, she stayed with some European friends, renounced Islam and was baptised into the Anglican Church, with the name Emily. In Zanzibar, Heinrich wound up his affairs, and then travelled to join Salme in Aden. They were married immediately and travelled to Heinrich's home in Hamburg.

In the following three years Salme and Heinrich had two daughters and a son. Tragically, in August 1871, Heinrich fell while jumping from a tram, and was run over; he died three days later. No longer welcome in Zanzibar, Salme remained in Germany, making one short visit to London in 1875, and two brief returns to Zanzibar in 1885 and 1888, but her attempts at reconciliation with her family were unsuccessful. She lived in exile in Syria until 1914 and died in Germany in 1924. Among the possessions found after her death was a bag of sand from the beach at Zanzibar.

In Zanzibar Town, Princess Salme is remembered at the Palace Museum (see *What to see and do*, page 184), which has a room devoted to her life and writings. This was set in place by Said el-Gheithy in collaboration with the Museums of Zanzibar.

In London, the Princess Salme Institute was established in 1994 to raise awareness about the life and writings of this remarkable woman, and to promote training and research relevant to Zanzibar. The Institute is based at the Africa Centre (*38 King St, London WC2E 8JT;* +44 (0) 207 836 1973; e *sayyidasalme@ hotmail.com*). The director of the Princess Salme Institute is Said el-Gheithy, who kindly checked the accuracy of the text in the *The Escape to Marseilles* box on page 16, and provided some of the information.

For cultural events in Zanzibar, such as the Zanzibar International Film Festival (ZIFF), the Princess Salme Institute acts as a contact point in Europe, as well as providing practical help to academics and professionals working in and around Zanzibar.

Chuini Palace About 10km north of Zanzibar Town, on the coast near the village of Chuini, lie the ruins of Chuini Palace. Meaning 'place of the leopard', it was built for Sultan Barghash, added to by Sultan Ali bin Said, and destroyed by fire in 1914. The ruins are on private land and can only be visited by those dining or staying at Hakuna Matata Lodge (see *Where to stay and eat*, page 203), which is built among a section of them.

The Zanzibar railroad

In the early 1900s, a light railway (36-inch gauge) was built and operated by an American company. Running from a point outside the Arab Fort in Zanzibar Town, it travelled along the seafront and up the coast to the village of Bububu. Construction began in 1904 and ended in 1905, the service was used mainly by locals but a special first-class coach was joined to the train so that passengers from the steamers could get a brief glimpse of the island. The line was closed in 1928, but railway buffs can still see the remains of bridges and embankments, as today's main road between Zanzibar Town and Bububu runs parallel to the line (and in some cases over it). Bits of the original track can be seen at Bububu.

In his book *Sketches in Mafeking and East Africa* (published in 1907), Lord Robert Baden-Powell quotes from a description of the Zanzibar train by an American writer called Miss Kirkland. 'Have you ever been to Bu Bu Bu? If not, do not call yourself a travelled person', she wrote. 'Bu Bu Bu is a settlement in a shady grove on the island of Zanzibar, and is the terminus of a new and important railroad – six and a half miles long.'

It has been suggested that the name Bububu comes from the sound made by the train's hooter, but maps dating from before the building of the railway show the village already had this title. It is more likely that the name was inspired by the sound of the freshwater springs which bubble to the surface just outside the village. Most of Zanzibar Town's water supply still comes from here.

Bububu Bububu is a small, rural village with a police station and checkpoint. The main road continues north from here towards Mahonda and Nungwi, and a new minor tar road branches off east to reach the agricultural area of Kidichi, where most visitors on spice tours arranged in Zanzibar Town are taken. If you stay on the main road for a few more kilometres, near the village of Chuini (about 10km north of Zanzibar Town) a wide dirt road forks off left, signposted to Bumbwini, and this leads to Mangapwani.

Fuji Beach Fuji Beach, near Bububu village, is a pleasant place to pause during or after some energetic sightseeing. A small dirt road leads down to the beach from near the police station in the centre of Bububu. This is the nearest beach to the town where swimming is safe and it makes a reasonable day-trip destination in its own right if you are staying in Zanzibar Town, short of time and fancy some seaside relaxing.

Local legend has it that the beach's name was due to one Mr Honda, a Japanese engineer who came to Zanzibar to build roads, but fell in love with a local girl and decided to stay. He built a 'taverna' called Fuji Beach Bar, at the time the best on the island, and the name stuck. Even though Mr Honda is no longer around, his legacy remains. The bar still sells beers and snacks, and the staff will look after your gear while you are swimming. (There have been reports of robberies here, so this is worth arranging carefully.) If you want to stay for more than a day, see the list of accommodation on page 201.

Kidichi Persian Baths The Persian Baths at Kidichi lie to the northeast of Zanzibar Town, about 4km inland from the main coast road, in the island's main clove and coconut plantation area. The baths were built in 1850 for Sultan Said. He owned land in this part of the island, and he and his second wife, Binte Irich Mirza (also called Schesade, more often written Scheherazade), would come here for hunting or to oversee the work being done on their plantations. The bathhouse was constructed so that they could refresh themselves after the journey from town. Schesade was a granddaughter of the Shah of Persia, so the baths were built in the Persian style, with decorative stucco work. An underground furnace kept the water warm. A small resthouse was also built nearby, but none of this remains.

Today, you can enter the bathhouse, and see the changing room, bathing pool and massage tables. Unfortunately, the bathhouse has not been especially well maintained over the years, and there is mould growing on much of the stucco. A colony of bats seems to have taken up residence as well. At the top of the domed ceiling is a circle of small windows: these used to be stained glass, which cast patterns of coloured light over the white walls. The conservation team from Mtoni are already looking at ways to repair and preserve the baths, and teams of specialists have been to investigate. With funding to match their care and enthusiasm, there is hope that further decay can be averted.

To reach Kidichi, continue up the main road northwards from Zanzibar Town to Bububu. At the police station, turn right onto a new tar road that leads through coconut palms and clove plantations, and past a long row of souvenir stalls selling spices and other goods. After about 4km the bathhouse, a domed white building, is seen on the right, just a few metres off the dirt road. There are several more spice–souvenir stalls here, and in the surrounding area houses where tour groups go for lunch.

Kizimbani Persian Baths Near Kidichi, these baths were also built in the Persian style for Sultan Said, at about the same time as the baths at Kidichi. They are similar in style though there is no interior decoration here. The surrounding plantations originally belonged to Saleh bin Haramil, the Arab trader who imported the first cloves to Zanzibar (they were confiscated by Sultan Said on the grounds that Saleh was a slave smuggler, see *Chapter 1*, page 10). Today the experimental station here is the island's centre for agricultural research.

To reach the baths from Kidichi, continue eastwards along the tar road. After about 2km, at a crossroads, there are roads left (north) to Mfenesini and Selem, and right (south) to Mwendo and Mwera. Go straight on, along a dirt road, passing through plantations, to reach the Kizimbani Experimental Station headquarters. The baths are on the right side of the track.

Mangapwani

Mangapwani Coral Cave Mangapwani (meaning 'Arab shore') lies on the coast, about 20km north of Zanzibar Town. The Coral Cave is a deep natural cavern in the coralline rock with a narrow entrance and a pool of fresh water at its lowest point. Water was probably collected from here by early inhabitants of this part of the island but at some point in the past vegetation grew across the entrance and the exact position of the cavern was forgotten.

Later, the area became the property of a wealthy Arab landowner called Hamed Salim el Hathy who had many slaves working on his plantations. During this time, the cavern was rediscovered by a young boy searching for a lost goat. Local people were able to use the water again, and Hamed Salim arranged for his slaves to collect the water regularly for his own use. It has been suggested by historians that the cave may have been used as a hiding place for slaves after the trade was officially abolished in 1873.

Most people come here on an organised tour, or by privately hired car or bike. Buses on Route 2 link Zanzibar Town with Mangapwani village, as do dala dalas No 102, but services are not frequent. To reach the cavern from Zanzibar Town, take the main road through Bububu to Chuini, then fork left towards Bumbwini. After 6km, in Mangapwani village, fork left again and head westwards towards the coast (the Serena Restaurant and Watersports Centre, due to be the site of the new Serena Hotel, is also signposted this way). About 1km from the junction, a narrow dirt road leads off to the left (there's a small signpost). Follow this to reach the cavern. A flight of stone steps leads through the entrance down into the cave itself.

Mangapwani Slave Chamber The Mangapwani Slave Chamber is a few kilometres further up the coast from the Coral Cave. Although sometimes called the Slave Cave, it is a square-shaped cell that has been cut out of the coralline rock, with a roof on top. It was originally built for storing slaves, and its construction is attributed to one Mohammed bin Nassor Al-Alwi, an important slave trader. Boats from the mainland would unload their human cargo on the nearby beach, and the slaves would be kept here before being taken to Zanzibar Town for re-sale, or to plantations on the island. It is thought that sometime after 1873, when Sultan Barghash signed the Anglo–Zanzibari treaty which officially abolished the slave trade, the cave was used as a place to hide slaves, as an illicit trade continued for many years.

To reach the Slave Chamber from Zanzibar Town, follow the directions to the Mangapwani Coral Cave. Instead of turning into the Coral Cave, continue on the dirt road for another 1km to reach the entrance to the Serena Restaurant and Watersports Centre. Just before you reach the Serena's 'beach club', a small dirt track branches off to the right. Follow this for 1km through palm trees and bushes to reach the Slave Chamber. With care, you can reach the steps that lead down onto the chamber floor. Nearby a small path leads to a secluded beach, separated from the main Mangapwani Beach (described below) by some coral-rock outcrops.

Mangapwani Beach Mangapwani Beach lies a few kilometres west of Mangapwani village. This has long been the planned site of a new Serena Hotel and the island's first golf club, but for now it remains the location of the accommodation-free Mangapwani Serena Beach Club. You can come here for a seafood lunch (US$30 for three courses) or something less gargantuan like lobster or prawns for US$9, or a pasta dish for US$4. There's also a nice little bar beneath the trees and a scattering of loungers on the sand. The beach is exceptionally beautiful at high tide and a great place to swim or relax. Free transfers by boat and road are arranged by the Serena Inn in Zanzibar Town (see page 145; daily trips depart 10.00, return 15.00), or you can pay to travel here any time with local tour companies or taxis.

ISLANDS NEAR ZANZIBAR TOWN

A few kilometres from Zanzibar Town are several small islands; some are good destinations for a relaxing day's outing. Boat trips to the islands can be arranged with a tour company, with one of the papaasi (touts) who look for business around town and along the seafront, or direct with one of the boat captains. Costs range from US$15 to US$70 for the boat, or from US$5 to US$25 per person, depending on who you deal with, the number of hours you want, the quality of the boat and whether you're prepared to share with other people or want a boat to yourself. Other factors might be lunch or snorkelling gear included in the price. You can hire a boat for yourself, or reduce costs by getting your own small group together. If you're alone, it's usually easy to link up with other travellers. Boats go across to the islands every morning from the beach by the Big Tree on Mizingani Road (the seafront), from the beach near the Tembo Hotel and the beach opposite the Africa House Hotel (see *Chapter 6*).

When staying on the islands overnight, check that security is provided by the hotel, and do bear in mind that these islands are isolated, without mains electricity and most of Zanzibar's boats do not have lights, making travel by sea highly treacherous after dark. There has been at least one serious 'pirate' raid on a hotel in the past, albeit some time ago now, so exercise caution after dark and consider a stay here carefully if you have small children or any existing medical conditions.

CHANGUU ISLAND Lying in the Zanzibar Channel, 6km northwest of Zanzibar Town, Changuu is a coral-rag islet, also known as Prison Island and at one time Kibandiko Island. It was originally owned by a wealthy Arab trader who used Changuu as a detention centre for disobedient slaves. After the abolition of slavery, in 1873, the island was bought by General Lloyd Mathews, commander of the sultan's army, who built a house here (see box, *William Lloyd Mathews*, page 213). In 1893, a prison (recently converted into a café, library and boutique) was built on the island but it was used instead as a quarantine station for the whole east African region. In the 1920s, passengers arriving from India had to spend between one and two weeks on Changuu before proceeding to Zanzibar Town.

Today, it is most famous for providing sanctuary to a creep of giant tortoises (*Geochelone gigantea*), descendants of four gifted from the Seychellois governor to his opposite number in Zanzibar in the 18th century. Shipped from their home on the island of Aldabra in the Seychelles, they started to breed and by 1955 there were 200 tortoises. Sadly, their numbers began to drop after independence, partly because people started to steal them to sell abroad, either as unusual pets or as food for 'exotic restaurants'. Numbering 100 in 1988, 50 in 1990 and only seven by late 1996, measures were taken to protect them and in the same year 80 hatchlings were moved to Zanzibar for protection – ironically, 40 of them still disappeared. Today the tortoises are protected in a large sanctuary compound provided by the Zanzibar government with help from the World Society for the Protection of Animals. In 2000, there were 17 adults, 50 juveniles and 90 hatchlings, all individually identified and protected by microchips injected under the skin. Since then, many more have been brought in, mostly juveniles. You can go into the sanctuary to see the tortoises close up and even feed them (they delight in fresh mango peel), but please do obey the signs and do not lift or sit on the tortoises.

Changuu Island has a small beach and there's reasonable snorkelling on the nearby reef. A secluded beach hotel has recently opened, too, and daily tours to see the historical ruins and tortoises are organised by many of Stone Town's operators (see *Tour companies*, pages 134–7), invariably making the 20-minute crossing by dhow under sail.

🏠 Where to stay

🏠 Changuu Private Island Paradise
(27 rooms) 📱 0773 333241/2; 📧 info.changuu@ privateislands-zanzibar.com; www.privateislands-zanzibar.com. The team here has restored & converted many of the crumbling Arab & colonial buildings on the island, built 15 individual beachfront cottages & introduced a host of guest facilities from a pool to a floodlit tennis court in the forest. 'Deluxe' thatched cottages in the northwest of the island offer the most privacy & boast outdoor showers & baths, whilst the 'standard' rooms to the southwest are in the former 1931 Quarantine

The house on Changuu Island, a short distance offshore from Zanzibar Town, once belonged to William Lloyd Mathews, a military officer and later a government official in Zanzibar in the latter part of the 19th century.

Mathews was a Welshman born in Madeira in 1850. He entered the British Navy in 1864, and from 1870 served in the slave-patrolling boats of HMS *London*. In August 1877, Mathews was seconded from the navy and appointed to command and organise a European-style army for Sultan Barghash, who wanted to enforce his sovereignty over the interior. Until then, the sultan's army had been composed of Arabs and Persians only, but the new army contained 500 Africans, with a uniform of red caps, short black jackets and white trousers. The Arab officers wore dark-blue frock coats and trousers, with gold or silver lace, possibly modelled on the uniforms of the British Royal Navy. The British government donated 500 rifles and by the beginning of the 1880s Mathews had about 1,300 men under his command.

One of the new army's first tasks was to stop the slave smuggling between Pemba and Pangani on the mainland and they were soon successful, capturing several slave smugglers and hindering the illicit trade. Mathews was released from the navy and became Brigadier-General Mathews, commander-in-chief of Zanzibar's army.

In 1891, when a constitutional government was established in Zanzibar, Brigadier-General Mathews was appointed as His Highness's First Minister and he was awarded a knighthood on 3 March 1894. On 11 October 1901, Sir William Lloyd Mathews died in Zanzibar, of malaria, at the age of 51. He was buried with full naval and military honours in the English cemetery outside Zanzibar Town.

Area & have good views across to Stone Town's waterfront. The décor in all is bright & cheerful with vibrant paint & fabrics, a good amount of space & veranda deckchairs for soaking up the sun. There is no mains electricity, & whilst there is generator power from 18.00–23.00, there is no AC & it's worth remembering to bring a good torch for evening beach walks. In a restored 19th-century home, Mathews' Restaurant serves extensive 4-course dinners & a good, predominantly seafood, lunch menu. There's a pleasant little beach & whilst swimming & snorkelling in the sea is possible, serious caution is advised as these are busy shipping waters. On land, guests have free run of the island nature trails, whilst day visitors are confined to the ruins & Aldabra tortoise sanctuary. For all the pleasures of privacy though, island life is not for those who plan on several excursions or for those seeking lively evenings – the 20–30min boat transfers to Zanzibar Town soon mount up (US$60 boat/return – unless you hitch with the touring day trippers). It is very isolated here, & remember it's not possible to travel to/from the island after dark as few boats out of Stone Town will have lights. ♛

CHAPWANI ISLAND This is also called Grave Island as a small section of it has been used as a Christian cemetery since 1879. Most of the graves belong to British sailors who were killed fighting against Arab slave ships, including Captain Brownrigg, who died with most of his men at the hands of the notorious slave-trafficker Hindi bin Hattam as he attempted to rescue 100 slaves on board Hattam's dhow to Pemba. A number of graves belong to crew of the World War I British ship *Pegasus*, which was bombarded and sunk by the German *Königsberg* in Zanzibar Town harbour. (This latter event is described in detail in the book *Königsberg: A German East African Raider*, listed in *Appendix 2*.)

top left Blue monkey (*Cercopithecus mitis albgularis*) (AZ) page 55

top right Flap-necked chameleon (*Chamaeleo dilepis*) (AZ) page 57

above left Pupae at the Zanzibar Butterfly Centre (AZ) page 333

above right Coconut crab (*Birgus latro*) (AZ) page 339

below Suni antelope (*Nesotragus moschatu moschatus*) (CM) page 260

top left   **Lychee** (AZ)

top right   **Pineapple** (AZ)

above   **Nutmeg** (AZ) page 136

right   **Jackfruit** (AZ)

below   **Frangipani flower** (AZ)

left Tall houses line the labyrinthine alleyways of Stone Town (CM) page 139

below left and right Zanzibar Town's Market Hall is the place to track down everything from fish to sewing machines, fragrant spices and multi-patterned cotton fabrics (both CM) page 183

bottom The Anglican Cathedral was built on the site of the former slave market in Zanzibar Town (AZ) page 189

above left Unlike the mosques of other major Islamic cities, those of Zanzibar are relatively unassuming in design (AZ) page 196

above right Forodhani Gardens in Stone Town is a popular eating spot in the evening (AZ) page 186

below The Old Dispensary was originally built in the late 19th century as the private home of an Indian merchant who was one of the wealthiest individuals on Zanzibar at the time (CM) page 184

left   Fishermen fixing their nets, Nungwi
(AZ) page 217

below left
and right   Stone Town's market is a hive of activity,
with refreshments such as pineapple and
freshly pressed sugarcane juice on sale
(both AZ) page 183

bottom   Seaweed has been farmed by coastal
dwellers for centuries (AZ) page 180

above   *Dala-dala* at Jambiani post office (CM) page 305

below   *Tingatinga* paintings and curios on sale in Nungwi (SM) page 217

There is a small beach on the island, and a lovely patch of indigenous forest, with a population of small duikers, some massive coconut crabs and a colony of fruit bats, which every evening do a few circuits of the island then zoom off to Zanzibar Town in a dark cloud. There are about 100 species of bird in the area, including a small population of black heron in the northeast, whose presence the new lodge is trying hard to encourage.

Where to stay

Chapwani Private Island (10 rooms) 0777 433102; e chapwani@zitec.org; www. chapwaniisland-zanzibar.com; ⊕ mid Jun–mid Apr. Simple rooms in small, semi-detached bungalows open onto the sandy beach. All are en suite with Zanzibari beds, mosquito nets & a timber-decked terrace, complete with a lounger & chairs. There is generator power most of the day, but it goes off at midnight, so don't elect to stay here if AC is a must, & certainly don't forget your torch. Activities are limited, but there's a nice pool tucked in the trees or, for a more natural dip, a tidal outlet in a coral crevasse on the northeast of the island, which is a pleasant place to swim at high tide. At low tide, the exposed reef offers interesting exploration, with coral, starfish & barnacle-clad rock pools around the island, & a pleasant wooded interior (watch out for little dik-dik antelope). Food has recently had an injection of pizzazz with the arrival of French chef & a free shuttle boat allows for a daily excursion to Zanzibar Town if shopping & sightseeing are on your agenda. The environment & the multi-lingual management make this a pleasant place to stay but like the other islands in the channel off Zanzibar Town, it lacks the feeling of real 'desert island' isolation by being so close to the main shipping routes, & yet doesn't benefit from the evening buzz of Stone Town. **$$$$$**

SNAKE ISLAND Sometimes known by its Swahili name, Nyoka, this is a very small island between Changuu and Chapwani. Tourist boats rarely land here as there is no beach, and local legend claims it was once infested by snakes which has long kept the local community away from its shores.

BAWE ISLAND About 6km due west of Zanzibar Town, Bawe is a beautiful little island with broad sandy beaches and a densely vegetated centre. In 1879, the island was given to the Eastern Telegraph Company by Sultan Barghash to be used as the operations station for the underwater telegraphic cable linking Cape Town with Zanzibar, the Seychelles and Aden in Yemen. A second line was run from Bawe Island to the External Telecommunications building in the Shangani area of Zanzibar Town. The old 'Extelcoms' building has now been converted into the Serena Inn, but the original phone line is largely redundant.

Lovely as the beach may be, it is firmly on the busy shipping route to Zanzibar Town and isn't visited as frequently as Changuu. In theory, it's possible to combine trips here with the tortoise excursions or simply arrange an out-and-back voyage with a boat captain in Zanzibar Town, though access prices do tend to be higher than those to Changuu.

Where to stay

Bawe Tropical Island (15 rooms) m 0773 333241/2; e info.bawe@privateislands-zanzibar. com; www.privateislands-zanzibar.com. Ochre, thatched cottages line the sand here, & like its sister hotel on Changuu Island (see page 213), the interior colour schemes are vibrant & the en-suite bathrooms feature moulded-concrete baths. There are spacious, pole-shaded terraces & it's nice to be merely a stone's throw from the warm, shallow sea, though a good awareness of the shipping traffic is important. There is little more to do than sit on the beach, & access to Stone Town is possible only on short day trips (sea journeys in unlit boats are dangerous after sunset), making a stay less attractive to those keen to experience Stone Town by night.

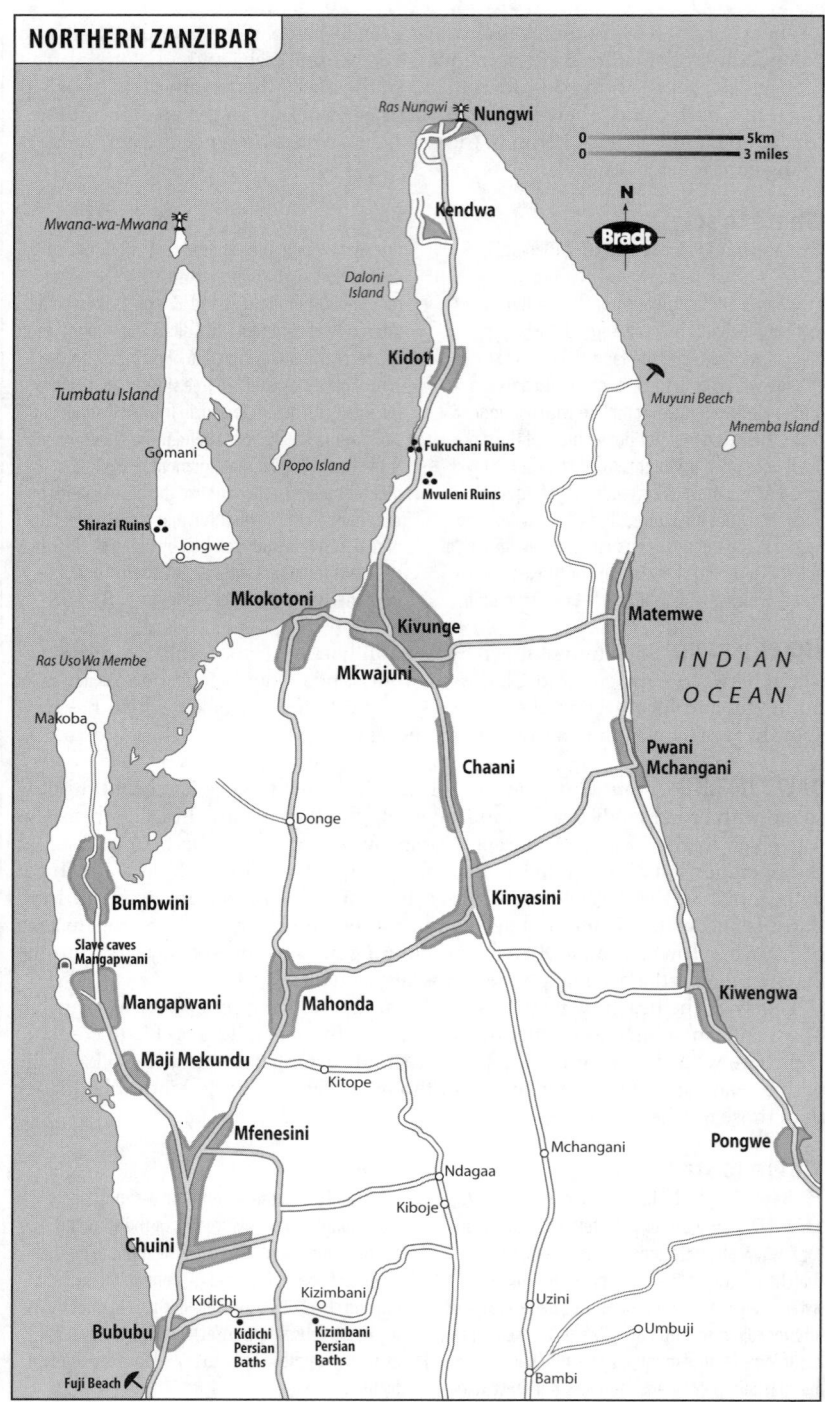

NORTHERN ZANZIBAR

Ras Nungwi �֎ **Nungwi**

0 ——————— 5km
0 ——————— 3 miles

N

Bradt

Mwana-wa-Mwana �֎

Kendwa

Daloni
Island

Kidoti

Tumbatu Island

Muyuni Beach

Mnemba Island

Gomani

Popo Island

⛏ Fukuchani Ruins

Shirazi Ruins ⛏

⛏ Mvuleni Ruins

Jongwe

Mkokotoni

Kivunge

Matemwe

Ras Uso Wa Membe

Mkwajuni

INDIAN
OCEAN

Makoba

Chaani

Pwani
Mchangani

Donge

Bumbwini

Kinyasini

Slave caves
Mangapwani

Kiwengwa

Mangapwani

Mahonda

Kitope

Maji Mekundu

Mchangani

Pongwe

Mfenesini

Ndagaa

Kiboje

Chuini

Uzini

Kidichi

Kizimbani

Umbuji

Bububu

Kidichi
Persian
Baths

Kizimbani
Persian
Baths

Bambi

Fuji Beach ⚓

8

Northern Zanzibar

Burgeoning guesthouses, vibrant nightlife and pressure on its community and natural resources now characterise northern Zanzibar above its pleasant, white-sand beaches, warm sea, nautical heritage and good diving opportunities. Less than two hours' drive from Stone Town on the fast tar road past increasingly rural villages, this is the heart of the island's budget tourism industry, as well as home to an increasing number of luxurious resorts. Focused around Nungwi village on the northernmost tip, and spreading with increasing momentum towards the golden sands of Kendwa, on the northwest coast, this bustling centre initially appears to offer every component of the perfect holiday: a wide range of accommodation, watersports galore, fresh seafood washed down with daily cocktails, and a lovely outlook. Sadly, however, there are some serious social and environmental problems bubbling in this area and many visitors, and a good number of the foreign and local investors, appear to be blind to the spiralling situation.

The alarming growth in the number and scale of developments is quite staggering. Once-small backpackers' bolt-holes have grown from a handful of rooms to mid-size hotels, mid-range places have added literally dozens of rooms to their original quota, whilst large-scale luxury or all-inclusive resorts now sit cheek-by-jowl on vast tracts of land around the north coast. Quite literally every beachfront plot from Ras Nungwi to Kendwa now has some tourist accommodation, either operational or under construction. Every single property listed in this chapter has expanded either up or out, or has been newly built since the last edition of this book, a continuation of the trend seen in the previous edition too. It is crowded and the development not always attractive: high breeze-block walls now block the once-stunning views along the northeast coast and ever-taller hotels jostle for a spot on the low coral cliffs at the seaside. It's still just about possible, however, to escape the 'Nungwi Strip' to seek out the quieter, more spectacular beaches of the northeast coast and Kendwa, but it's getting more challenging with every month that passes, and even once-quiet Kendwa is succumbing to the developers as long-standing backpacker haunts are bought up with a view to increasing and upgrading their offering.

NUNGWI

Nungwi is traditionally the centre of Zanzibar's dhow-building industry, and over the last decade the coastline here has rocketed in popularity to become the island's busiest beach destination. The ramshackle fishing village has been sidelined by an ever-increasing number of guesthouses, bars, shops, restaurants and bikini-clad Europeans. Ageing hippies, cool dudes, gap-year students and bright young things escaping European city jobs are all drawn to its white sand, stage-set palm trees, turquoise sea and sparkling sunshine.

By day, the beach sees sunbathing tourists slumber, swim and indulge in lemongrass massages, whilst local guys tout their 'tours' and sell a range of mediocre paintings, sunglasses and replica football shirts; then, as the sun sets, the visitors arise and the whole place buzzes with party spirit. Beach bonfires blaze, cocktails flow and the music rocks till dawn; this is not a location for those seeking silence or solitude. The setting may be beautiful, but the number of people, the constant noise and the seemingly uncontrolled levels of development all take the edge off its charm.

In the last five years, the number of hotel rooms in Nungwi has rocketed from 405 to 931– a staggering 129% increase! It is shocking to see and for anyone who has visited this area before, the village and beachfront are totally unrecognisable: hotels have grown into a sprawling mass in literally every direction, roads have been re-routed and costs have escalated. With the exception of the World Bank-funded tar road to Stone Town, and the police post paid for by local hoteliers, there has been no significant thought given to how the natural resources, specifically fresh water, or basic utilities will cope with this vast increase in visitor numbers. The local population are suffering the consequences, which is in danger of further alienating them from those who come to enjoy their 'island paradise'.

Ironically, given its current state, Nungwi was one of the last coastal settlements on Zanzibar to have a hotel, or any tourist facilities. As recently as the mid 1990s, proposals for large developments in the area were fiercely opposed by local people. Today, in spite of the influx of tourists, Nungwi remains a fairly traditional, conservative place and the proudly independent villagers give the impression that the visitors are here on sufferance. They are not unfriendly, however, and most visitors find that a little bit of cultural respect, politeness and a few words of Swahili go a long way. It is very important to behave and dress appropriately in the village (see also *Cultural etiquette*, page 117).

Some visitors, particularly backpackers, find themselves torn between either coming to Nungwi and the north coast, or going to Paje, Bwejuu and Jambiani on the east coast. For some thoughts on the differences between these two areas, see page 251.

GETTING THERE AND AWAY
Nungwi can be reached by **bus, tourist minibus** or **hired vehicle**. From Zanzibar Town the main road to Nungwi goes via Mtoni, Mahonda, Kinyasini and Kivunge. There is a more scenic route directly north of Mahonda to Mkokotoni, which, once the preserve of 4x4s only, is now wonderfully accessible on the new tar road.

As you enter Nungwi, a conglomeration of signs advertising accommodation and activities marks a fork in the road and the end of the tar. Head right for Nungwi's east coast hotels and the village, or straight on for the beachfront properties of North, South and West beaches.

If you are travelling by public transport, there are daily **dala dalas** (No 116) leaving Creek Road in Zanzibar Town for Nungwi, roughly every 30 minutes between 05.30 and 21.00. Alternatively, between 07.00 and 18.00 there are half-hourly public buses (Route 14) departing Darajani Terminal, Zanzibar Town. On arrival in Nungwi, the main stop is opposite a large football pitch inland of the village, from where it's a 15-minute walk through the village to the heart of the tourist throng. The shared tourist minibuses, a more popular option, will stop in the centre of the action, beside Amaan Bungalows. Departures south leave from the same locations.

It has also been known for onward travellers to pay local fishermen to take them by **boat** to their next destination, even as far as Matemwe on the northeast coast.

Ask around to ensure reliability and safety, make sure people know where you're going, and do check that there's a decent motor and safety equipment (like life jackets and working radios or mobile phones) for longer trips.

GETTING AROUND Most places in and around Nungwi are within walking distance, but if you're staying on the slightly more upmarket east side of the peninsula, and fancy letting your hair down on the lively west side, the local **taxi** service charges US$8–10 each way. Ask your hotel to put you in touch with a responsible driver, or contact the reliable brothers at **One Stop Tours & Safaris** (m *0777 433652/461517*).

If you want to tour this part of the island, for example to visit Fukuchani and Mvuleni Ruins (see *Regional excursions*, page 248), then it's possible to hire **motorbikes**, **jeeps** and **bicycles**. Ask your hotel or a reputable ground operator to help you arrange this.

WHERE TO STAY For simplicity, the following hotels and guesthouses are listed roughly in clockwise order, from the southwest of the peninsula, round the headland and down the eastern coast. All those slightly inland from the coast are classed as 'village' properties.

Unless stated otherwise, hotels listed below offer air conditioning and en-suite bathrooms as standard,

South Beach The road into Nungwi from Zanzibar Town comes to a fork on the village outskirts. To reach places at the southern end of the west side of the peninsula, go left here, along a dusty track, towards the sea. This area has become unofficially known as South Beach, but it's a handy name, and might just stick.

Just west of the village, South Beach is effectively the busiest beach. There is no reef in front of the shore here, so the water is deep enough for swimming, whatever the state of the tide. As the beach faces west, it is also a great spot for watching the sun go down. A number of the cheaper places to stay are located here, but more recently it has become home to the imposing, contemporary Z Hotel, so its 'budget basics' image is beginning to change. Whatever the accommodation, this remains the liveliest part of Nungwi.

Z Hotel (35 rooms) m 0774 266266; e info@thezhotel.com/reservations@thezhotel.com; www.thezhotel.com; ⊕ Jun–mid Apr. One of the swankiest hotels here, Z Hotel opened its heavy designer doors in 2008. It is the seaside dream of London property developers, Keith & Julian, & brings an amount of city-boy bling previously unseen on the Nungwi beach scene. Billed as 'boutique on the beach', the rooms are divided into 6 levels of luxury with sophisticated interiors featuring billowing voile curtains, striking wallpapers, bespoke coconut-wood beds & cool travertine stone floors. In each, there are iPod docking stations & plasma TVs, & the White Company toiletries & stocked minibars complete the indulgent feel. Every room has a balcony & the sea can be seen, to varying degrees, from each one; for real ocean lovers the cantilevered decks in the cottages & the 3rd-floor jacuzzi terrace of the Z Suite are favourite lookouts. Elsewhere in the compact complex, the natural stone pool above the beach is a crowded hangout, surrounded with parasols & even a few 4-poster daybeds, each with their own integrated plasma TV. After sundown, the adjacent Cinnamon Bar (see *Where to eat and drink*, page 230) with its multi-coloured ceiling fans & Saruche Restaurant (see *Where to eat and drink*, page 230) are evening hot spots for cocktails & seafront dining. A great deal of money has been spent on sourcing high-end, branded fixtures, fittings & fabrics, & on trying to present a quality product. The hotel has had its issues – the salt-infused air is not kind to modern technology & the searing sun soon bleaches fabrics – but lessons have been learnt & changes are being made, & Z has established itself as Nungwi's chic heart. Its

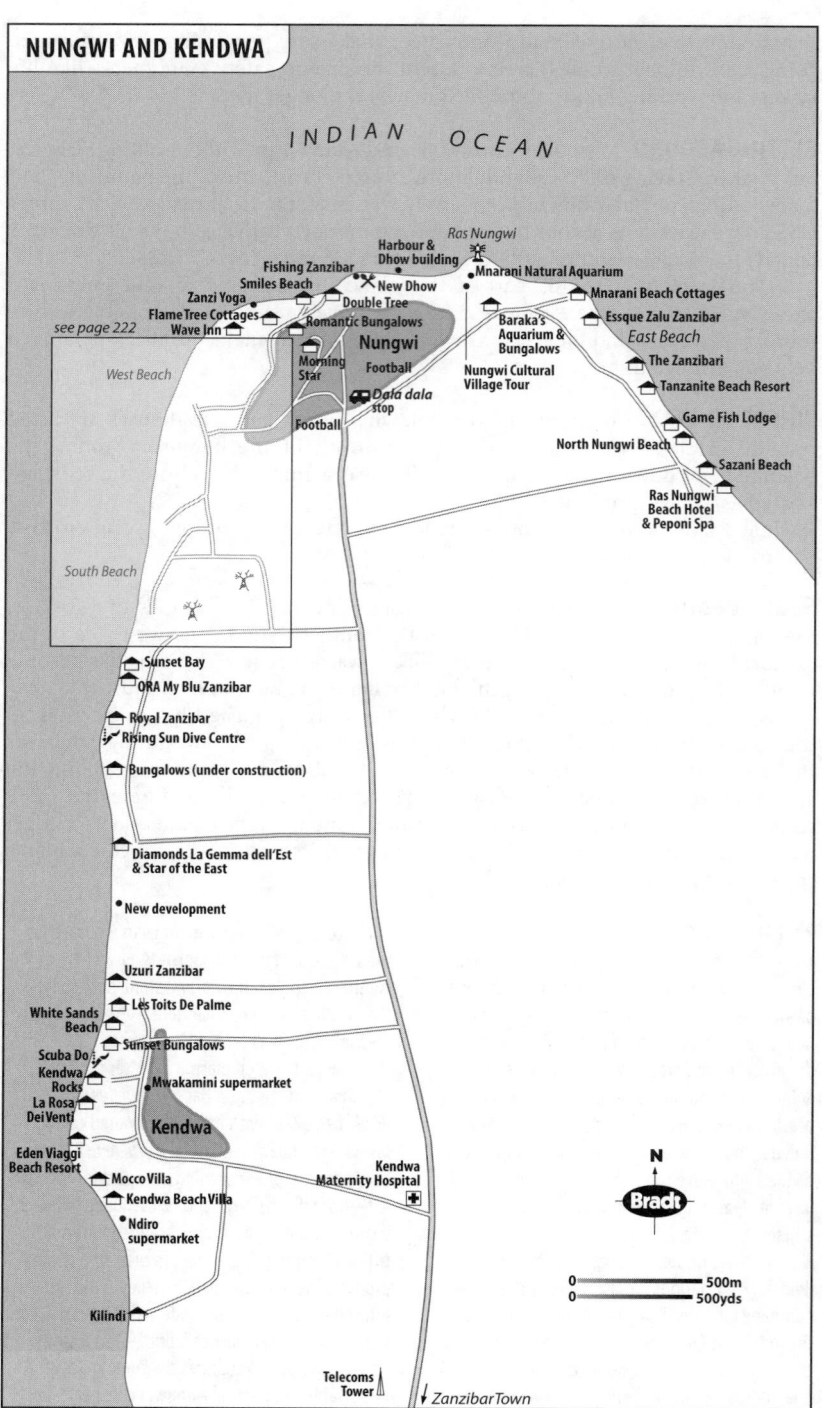

NUNGWI AND KENDWA

INDIAN OCEAN

Ras Nungwi

Harbour &
Dhow building

Mnarani Natural Aquarium

Fishing Zanzibar
Smiles Beach
Zanzi Yoga
Flame Tree Cottages
Wave Inn

New Dhow
Double Tree

Mnarani Beach Cottages
Essque Zalu Zanzibar
East Beach

Romantic Bungalows

Nungwi

The Zanzibari

see page 222

West Beach

Morning
Star

Football

Baraka's
Aquarium &
Bungalows

Nungwi Cultural
Village Tour

Tanzanite Beach Resort

Dala dala
stop

Game Fish Lodge

Football

North Nungwi Beach

Sazani Beach

South Beach

Ras Nungwi
Beach Hotel
& Peponi Spa

Sunset Bay

ORA My Blu Zanzibar

Royal Zanzibar
Rising Sun Dive Centre

Bungalows (under construction)

Diamonds La Gemma dell'Est
& Star of the East

New development

Uzuri Zanzibar

Les Toits De Palme

White Sands
Beach

Sunset Bungalows

Scuba Do
Kendwa
Rocks

Mwakamini supermarket

La Rosa
Dei Venti

Kendwa

Eden Viaggi
Beach Resort

Kendwa
Maternity Hospital

Mocco Villa

Kendwa Beach Villa

Ndiro
supermarket

N

Bradt

Kilindi

0   500m
0   500yds

Telecoms
Tower

Zanzibar Town

biggest issue may prove to be the less salubrious surrounding sprawl. **$$$$$–☕**

🏠 Royal Zanzibar Beach Resort (96 rooms) 📞0242240512/2526; e info@royalzanzibar. com, reservations@royalzanzibar.com; www. royalzanzibar.com. The large, castellated accommodation blocks of this resort occupy a substantial plot between Nungwi & Kendwa. Planted with tropical gardens & above a pleasant sandy cove, Royal Zanzibar is owned by the same family as Southern Palms Beach Resort in Kenya & operates in a similar all-inclusive, entertainment-focused vein. Eating & drinking are heavily emphasised with a staggering 8 restaurants & bars, from à la carte Samaki with its oriental dining to the swim-up Upendo pool bar. For those who want to work off the calories, there's an on-site subsidiary of the east coast's Rising Sun Dive Centre, & both residents & passers-by can organise dive excursions (other watersports equipment is for guest use only). For younger guests, the kids' club is open daily 10.00–18.00 or there are 4 free-form pools, games & racket sports. **$$$$$**

🏠 ORA My Blu Hotel (87 rooms) 📞+39 0521 1917481; e info@orahotelsgroup.eu; www. mybluehotel.com. Sandwiched between Royal Zanzibar & Sunset Bay, My Blu is part of the ORA portfolio, & as such is another Italian-owned & managed all-inclusive resort, attracting a young, social crowd on reasonable FB packages. The accommodation blocks have a slightly Mediterranean feel & surround the free-form swimming pools. Rooms are divided into categories based on terrace, sea view & overall size (2–4 people), & all have fairly simple interiors with dark timber furniture offsetting brilliant white walls & beamed ceilings. Flat-screen satellite TVs, Wi-Fi & minibar are standard. There is a poolside bar & an open-sided, buffet-style restaurant serving adequate food. Atop the seafront coral cliff, a large area of thatched umbrellas, & loungers sit on a manmade raised beach, with lovely sea views, & there's direct access to the beach for walks linking Kendwa & Nungwi when the tide is low. FB. **$$$$**

🏠 Veraclub Sunset Beach (44 rooms) www. veratour.it. Sunset Beach is currently being managed by Italian all-inclusive tour operator, Veraclub. The hotel is still reasonably small by this coast's standards, & rooms are divided among 11 slightly crude, 2-storey buildings (more vegetation would certainly be beneficial to their appearance).

Inside, rooms are spacious, if soulless, with a tiled shower room & balcony. There are Zanzibari beds & an array of mod cons such as cable TV & mini fridge. For a sea view, request a room towards the front of the complex or your balcony may look at little more than the block in front. Landscaping is primarily lawn, leaving the place feeling a little stark, but there is an 'imported' beach above the coral cliff to ensure guests can sunbathe with their toes in the sand at any time of day, & a lovely swimming pool. The buffet restaurant & bar is in a canvas-sided makuti structure by the sea, & sitting on its comfy sofas, cocktail in hand, there's a distinctly tropical feel. Practise your Italian if you want to make small talk though, as guests & staff will be primarily Mediterranean. It is also worth knowing that without written confirmation of your reservation, gaining access to the hotel in the first place is virtually impossible. **$$$$$ – ☕**

🏠 Baobab Beach Bungalows (85 rooms) m 0776 014164; e fo.baobab@gmail.com; www. baobabbeachbungalows.com. Remarkably, this resort has actually reduced its room numbers in the last 2 years. It remains one of the larger establishments on this stretch of coast though, & is still marketed exclusively to Italians through the all-inclusive operator 'Phone & Go. If you are not Italian, the banners emblazoned with Italian slogans, restaurant 'pasta station', & Italian-speaking staff may well put you off staying here. At the southernmost end of South Beach, Baobab does boast its own small sandy cove, but the rise in visitor numbers & bead-selling Maasai make it busier than ideal. Above this enclave, the hotel has moved sand onto the coral rock to create a raised 'beach', for scores of loungers & makuti parasols. From here, the blocks of pleasant rooms stretch back inland & are all spotlessly clean with a private balcony. They are set back from the sea, amid neatly manicured gardens; some with a reasonable view of the water & all close to the central swimming pool. The buffet-only Baobab Restaurant serves passable Italian cuisine & there's a sea-view bar. Based in an open-sided beachfront centre, which arguably enjoys the resort's premium position, Diving Ocean (www.divingocean.it) is open to non-residents. PADI courses & the usual ½- & full-day Mnemba snorkelling & diving excursions are available, using 2 speedboats, with dhow trips & kayak rental for those who prefer a slower ride. Bungalow **$$$$**; lodge/deluxe **$$$$$**

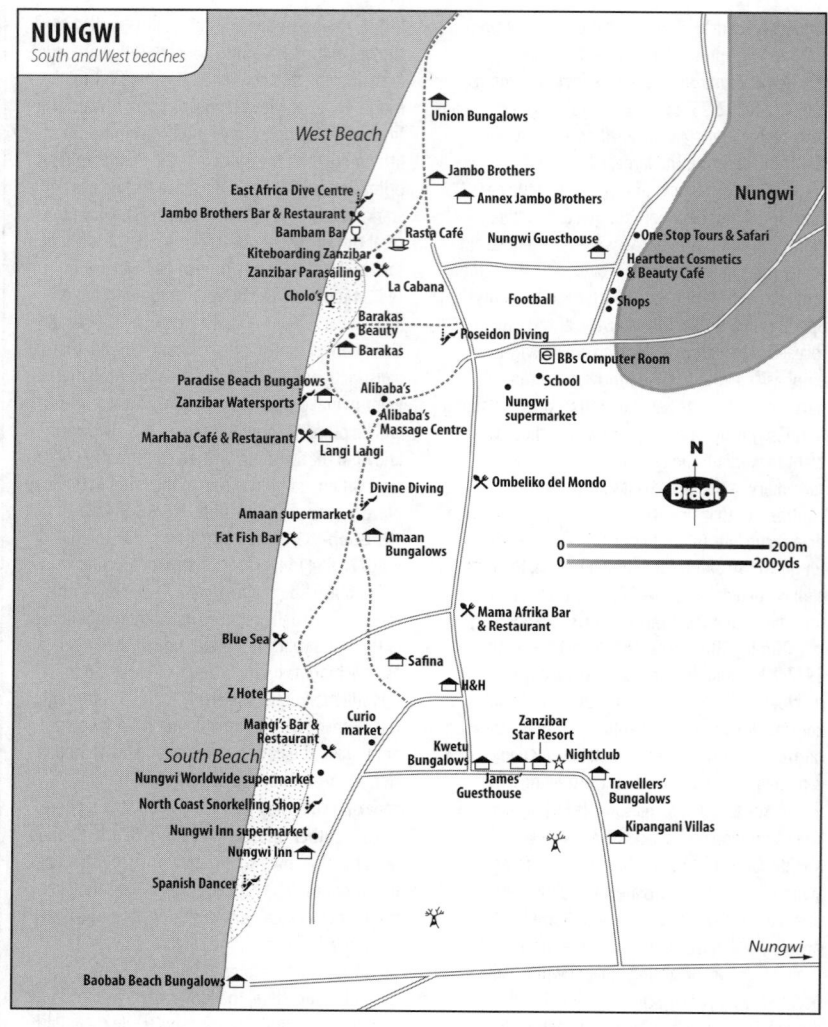

NUNGWI
South and West beaches

West Beach

Union Bungalows

Jambo Brothers

East Africa Dive Centre
Jambo Brothers Bar & Restaurant
Bambam Bar
Kiteboarding Zanzibar
Zanzibar Parasailing
Cholo's

Annex Jambo Brothers

Rasta Café

Nungwi Guesthouse

La Cabana

Barakas Beauty
Barakas

Paradise Beach Bungalows
Zanzibar Watersports

Marhaba Café & Restaurant

Langi Langi

Alibaba's
Alibaba's Massage Centre

Divine Diving

Amaan supermarket
Fat Fish Bar

Amaan Bungalows

Blue Sea

Z Hotel

Mangi's Bar & Restaurant
South Beach
Nungwi Worldwide supermarket
North Coast Snorkelling Shop
Nungwi Inn supermarket
Nungwi Inn

Spanish Dancer

Baobab Beach Bungalows

Nungwi

One Stop Tours & Safari
Heartbeat Cosmetics & Beauty Café
Shops

Football

Poseidon Diving

BBs Computer Room

School

Nungwi supermarket

Ombeliko del Mondo

N

Bradt

0 ——— 200m
0 ——— 200yds

Mama Afrika Bar & Restaurant

Safina

H&H

Curio market

Kwetu Bungalows

Zanzibar Star Resort

Nightclub

James' Guesthouse

Travellers' Bungalows

Kipangani Villas

Nungwi

⌂ **The Nungwi Inn Hotel** (24 rooms) ☎024 2240091; m 0777 432833; e thenungwi_inn@ hotmail.com; www.nungwiinnhotel.co.tz. The sea-view rooms here are right on the beach, just behind the dive centre, whilst the other rooms are set in gardens, without sea views, across the dirt road. The reception is roughly between the 2, at the back of the beachfront restaurant. Rooms are bright & airy, & have starched white bedding, mosquito nets, 24hr electricity (generator for night-time power cuts only) & hot water (electricity dependent). The hotel's newest rooms are in semi-detached thatched cottages which offer slightly more space. If a true sea

view is your priority, opt for rooms 1–4 or 7/8. The restaurant (see *Where to eat and drink*, page 231) is on the sand & offers nice, simple food. Rooms can be booked directly or through the Spanish Dancer Dive Centre website (www.spanishdancerdivers.com), & confirming the agreed rate is recommended. Garden room & sea-view room. **$$$**

⌂ **Safina Bungalows** (30 rooms) m 0777 415726; e newsafina@hotmail.com. Under the enthusiastic management of Ali Omar, Safina continues to be renovated to a good standard. In spite of the lack of sea view, it's a comfortable & spotlessly clean bedtime retreat, & has benefited enormously from the main village road moving away from its front garden. The staff remain as accommodating as ever & the garden continues to flourish. All rooms benefit from 24hr electricity (inc backup generator) & hot water. Dbls have duvets in addition to the standard sheets, & the basket of plastic flowers in each room shows care & effort, if not contemporary taste. B/fast is served upstairs in the half-finished building overlooking the central garden & marooned, & increasingly weather-worn, 'Welcome Safina' dhow. If post-beach chilling on the veranda isn't enough, there is a small massage room, the Malaika Spa, where Conchesta offers spiced oil massages (US$25–30/hr), basic beauty therapies & henna painting. **$$**

🏠 **H&H Beach Bungalows** (20 rooms) ☎024 2250630; **m** 0777 416937/413769; **e** bububu@ zanzinet.com. Tucked behind Safina, Hamim & Hamida Abdallah's bungalows are a basic but great-value option. Dbl, twin & trpl rooms are set out around a small, sandy quad, where fruit & eggs are served each morning. Rooms (US$20–30pp) are clean, if in need of airing, & there are small newly tiled terraces, & the bathrooms have hot water & good-quality fittings. There are ceiling fans, mosquito nets & mains electricity (no generator, so susceptible to power cuts). Hamim is a tour operator in Stone Town, so transfers & excursions can be arranged with ease. **$$**

West Beach

Northwards from Paradise Beach Bungalows, still on the west side of the peninsula, is another stretch of beach which, for the purposes of this book, we'll call West Beach. The places to stay here are described south to north.

🏠 **Paradise Beach Bungalows** (18 rooms) ☎024 2240050; **m** 0777 416308; **e** shaabani_ makame@hotmail.com. Accessed beside the high gate at Langi Langi, Paradise Beach Bungalows no longer has any bungalows. Following sustained, albeit fairly slow, redevelopment, it now offers virtually identical rooms & a dormitory in a concrete accommodation block. Whilst the building is aesthetically challenged & the landscaping sparse, the rooms are clean & all have fans, 24hr electricity & large, tiled bathrooms. The dorm sleeps 7 in 3 bunk beds & a sgl shrouded in mosquito nets, & has its own bathroom, though the lighting & an unsightly green carpet are both poor. Equally, decent bedding has not yet reached this corner of Nungwi. That said, all rooms benefit from being positioned in front of a stepped access point to the beach – a broad sandy stretch at high tide & a small cove at low: perfect for a quick dip in the heat of the afternoon sun. The affiliated restaurant (food noon–21.00; drinks 10.30–23.00) has an extensive shaded deck overlooking the sea & West Beach. It serves an array of pizzas (US$4.50–9.50) fresh from its stone oven, & fresh 'n' fruity cocktails (US$3–4). The Zanzibar Watersports (see *What to see and do*, page 236) dive & activity centre at the entrance to this little complex has certainly had a positive impact on the place & makes it a convenient location for those who are travelling on a budget but are keen on sub-aqua activities. **$$**

🏠 **Baraka Beach Bungalows** (9 rooms) **m** 0777 422910/415569; **e** barakabungalow@ hotmail.com; http://barakabungalow.atspace. com. In the shadow of Paradise Beach Bungalows, these solid, makuti-thatched bungalows surround a small garden beside West Beach. The rooms have fans, electricity & hot water, & the interiors are simple with unpolished concrete floors, basic furniture & fairly thin mattresses on the beds. The small terraces overlooking the palms, fuchsias & hibiscus make this a perfectly pleasant corner. There's a selection of room sizes, accommodating 2–6 people, so small groups of friends may be comfortable here, & being a mere coconut's throw from the pleasant West Beach, it's also well placed for sun worshippers. However, this proximity does also mean that the music from Cholo's (see *Where to eat and drink*, page 232) is likely to drift towards the rooms until around midnight, though the days of really wild parties appear to be in the past. For those who are up early or late, the beachfront restaurant is open all hours & serves stir-fries, pasta, grilled seafood (all US$6.50) & frothy cappuccinos (US$4). **$$**

🏠 **Jambo Brothers Bungalows** (14 rooms) **m** 0777 473901. Razed to the ground by a neighbouring electrical fire in 2010, long-standing Jambo Brothers has since been rebuilt & expanded into a new building slightly further away from the beach. The split locations have led to a somewhat disjointed feel, to add to an already erratic management, but another 10 rooms are planned & this may serve to unite the 2 areas. Reception & 7 simple bungalows are located immediately behind East Africa Diving Centre, whilst the 7 additional rooms, in the imaginatively titled Annex Jambo Brothers, are in a whitewashed building perpendicular to the sea & on a not particularly attractive side street. The bungalows are very simple with timber beds, lino floors & beach views; all have fans, mosquito nets & hot-water showers. The Annex rooms are better, & in fact a good option if you're watching your budget. Green concrete floors, floral purple kanga curtains, *mkeke* mats & Zanzibari beds are thoughtfully chosen, whilst the whole place is spotless. AC is available in these rooms, too. There is an open-sided makuti restaurant, Waves, next to the Union Bungalows reception, whilst (confusingly) the similarly named Jambo Restaurant on the beach is of no affiliation. If you want to book in advance, Delene Kutz at the neighbouring dive centre (e *eadc@zitec.org*) will kindly pass on any messages & translate as necessary. Bungalows **$$**; new rooms **$$$**

🏠 **Union Bungalows** (13 rooms) m 0773 176923/0777 432908; e unionbungalow@ hotmail.com; http://unionbungalow.atspace.com. A few steps along the beach from Jambo Brothers, Union Bungalows has a new rock-top reception building, complete with small shop & internet point. Check in here or at the friendly Blue Wimbi restaurant in front of the neat little cottages. All rooms have hot water, fans, electricity & mosquito nets; bed linen is colourful & mkeke mats adorn the tiled floors. Mid 2011 saw the addition of 4 dbl rooms; here, fans, AC, mini fridges & even a hat stand come as standard. This is certainly a budget option, & a little tired, but it's all perfectly acceptable. Dbl **$$**; new room **$$$**

🏠 **Wave Inn** (10 rooms) At the time of researching this edition, Wave Inn was closed & being guarded by some unusually unhelpful Swahili ladies. It appears to have a large pale pink, unfurnished restaurant area overlooking the harbour, behind which are 10 neat, flat-roofed terraced rooms & a small pool; we await opening news.

🏠 **Flame Tree Cottages** (16 rooms) ☎ 024 2240100; m 0773 353753; e etgl@zanlink.com; www.flametreecottages.com. This fabulous little place on the edge of Nungwi village is owned by a delightful Zanzibari–Scottish couple, Seif &

Elizabeth. Flame Tree Cottages has a new house (inc a large honeymoon/family suite on the 1st floor) & 15 red-roofed, whitewashed bungalows spread out in extensive gardens beside the beach. Inside, the rooms are immaculate with lovely linen, beautifully finished wardrobes made by the local carpenters, & wide, shady verandas. There's even a thoughtfully placed mini-hose for washing the sand off your feet. Rooms have electricity & constant hot water. 3 share a kitchenette, while some have their own; they are compact but well kitted out, & for a small surcharge housekeeping will supply pans & crockery though almost no-one self-caters, especially with freshly prepared meals being served in the restaurant or garden. Chef Christopher's delicious dishes (fish goujons with tartare US$5.50; beef goulash US$8; steamed chilli crab claws US$9) make this one of Nungwi's best dining experiences, especially when enjoyed overlooking the dhows in the harbour. The recent addition of a pool has enhanced the feeling of space & peace – something increasingly difficult to find in Nungwi. Lounging around in one of many hammocks around the garden, just reading & relaxing, is lovely & the staff are genuinely happy to help. The existing gentle activities range from lemongrass oil massage (US$12/30mins) to snorkelling trips aboard the owner's dhow, & there's now a Zanzi Yoga pavilion on site (*www.yogazanzibar.com*; see page 240) offering beachside classes. Boules & badminton are also available. Flame Tree's website is as clear & organised as the place itself, & is well worth a look. **$$$$**

🏠 **Smiles Beach Hotel** (16 rooms) ☎ 024 2240472; m 0774 444334; e info@ smilesbeachhotel.com; www.smilesbeachhotel. com. An architectural medley has produced Smiles' appearance. Spaced in an arc around a flower-filled, semicircular garden, the 4 striking villas are pale yellow, with tiled pagoda roofs & elaborate exterior spiral staircases. Smiles is Zanzibari-owned & is one of the best-quality, quieter options in Nungwi, & a firm favourite with passing overland groups & repeat visitors. The rooms are good quality & Indian in flavour. All are immaculate, bright & airy. Each has a sliding mosquito net, high-quality security locks, satellite TV & beach towels; some also have minibars. The spacious trpl, which could fit 6 people, is made up with 3 large Zanzibari beds. The 'Honeymoon Sweet' [sic] features a giant corner bed as its centrepiece &, like the others, offers indulgent b/fasts in bed. For those who can drag themselves the few metres to the beach, there's a seafront restaurant (no alcohol), complete with a mosaic mirrored wall, & beach BBQs (US$15–20pp) if a crowd of 15 or more can be mustered. **$$$–$$$$**

🏠 **Doubletree by Hilton Resort**
(103 rooms) 📞 024 2240476; m 0779 999056; e znzdt_reservations@hilton.com; www. doubletree.com. Set in spacious grounds on the northernmost stretch of West Beach, this accommodation has a touch more character than you might expect from an international hotel chain. The well-kept standard rooms come with showers or baths, a kettle, safe, mosquito nets & depending on location, have either a pool or a sea view. Larger suites are found in houses built in a diagonal line towards the beach. At the front of each level is a narrow balcony, with red concrete floors & a neat balustrade, which leads to 2 rooms. These have high ceilings, Zanzibari beds, good-quality furniture & the usual mod cons. At the other end of the beach is the 2-level restaurant, where Moroccan lanterns hang from the ceiling & half an old dhow is mounted on the wall. Here, themed evenings with local musicians entertain, while grilled meats & creamy desserts grace the table. The other, more informal all-day restaurant is found on the beach & serves a selection of freshly caught seafood & light snacks. The usual array of watersports is available, along with table tennis, pool & volleyball, plus a wonderfully cool gym, with state-of-the-art equipment. **$$$$**

Nungwi village
Away from the beaches, in Nungwi village itself, there are a number of options.

🏠 **Amaan Bungalows** (58 rooms)
📞 024 5501152; m 0775044719; e info@ amaanbungalows.com; www.amaanbungalows. com. Heralded by rows of fluttering international flags, Amaan Bungalows is a sprawling, whitewashed, castellated complex in the heart of Nungwi's accommodation cluster. A Nungwi scene stalwart, Amaan's rooms are divided into 3 broad categories: deluxe, garden & sea view. The last perch on a coral-rock cliff above the sea, within easy earshot of the sound of rolling waves; the large picture windows & cantilevered decks more than justifies the upgrade cost for this category. However, all the rooms are clean & well cared for with en-suite tiled bathrooms, hot & cold water, ceiling fans (AC in deluxe & sea view), mosquito nets, mains electricity, UK-style 3-pin sockets & a private terrace throughout the complex. Most rooms can be made up for sgl to trpl occupancy, & 3 are interconnecting for groups & families. This is an ever-developing complex, popular with a young crowd seeking to be at the very centre of the action & older visitors on a budget. Bordering the main footpath through town, Amaan also has a practical grocery shop for forgotten essentials & replenishing suncream supplies, a souvenir shop & a reliable internet café, Infusion. The bureau de change inside reception will convert virtually any major currency into Tanzanian shillings & a safety deposit system is in operation. Marina Grill & Infusion, immediately opposite on the seafront, are affiliated with Amaan & are good places to eat pizza & seafood, drink virtually anything & be merry at any hour of the day (HB & FB rates include meals at either place). Guests staying here for 3 nights are eligible for a 25% discount at Pemba Misali Beach, on Pemba island, & the staff can assist in arranging necessary ferry transfers. **$$–$$$$**

🏠 **Baraka's Aquarium Bunglows** (4 rooms)
m 0777484165; e barakabungalow@hotmail. com; http://barakabungalow.atspace.com. Adjacent to the tidal pools at Baraka's Turtle Aquarium, there are now 2 bungalows, each housing 2 dbl rooms. The rooms are spacious, with built-in concrete beds, timber-framed mosquito nets, a table & chairs, & a curtain screening the toilet & shower. They are clean & functional, but not very inspiring. There are wide verandas, staggered to offer guests some privacy, & a number of free-range chickens around. There are also 4 rather sad rock pythons in a concrete cage, who for a few thousand shillings can be draped around your neck; just hope they've had their allowance of rats for the day! **$$**

🏠 **Romantic Bungalows** (6 rooms)
m 0773354112; e h_ellen_85@hotmail. com, pierogentile47@msn.com; www. romanticbungalows-nungwi.com. Behind its high gates are thatched terraced rooms set around a small, green open courtyard, which is the only real

view given Romantic Bungalows' location between the beachfront properties & the village. The rooms are basic, with concrete floors, simple Zanzibari furniture & dim lighting; b/fasts are served in the small open-sided dining area, with fresh fruits, eggs & toast on offer. **$$**

⌂ **James' Guest House** m 0772 525484/0785 091255; e bookings@jamesguesthouse.com; www.jamesguesthouse.com. Through a red gate opposite a baobab tree, James' proclaims to be 'Backpacker Paradise Nungwi'; a fact disputed by some who stay. Walking up the access road between 2 high block walls, you pass through the messy back-of-house before arriving in a reasonably pleasant leafy courtyard, around which the L-shaped terraced accommodation sits. The accommodation blocks are festooned with large flags from an eclectic selection of countries, & spacious, tiled rooms offer 1 or 2 dbl beds each, with crude timber frames to support mossie nets (inc a few holes), clean if dark bathrooms, & a fan (no generator, so subject to electricity cuts). The plot boasts a central tree, strung with bottles of gin & Jameson's, a small raised bar with cushioned chairs & a precariously balanced TV (free satellite channels only). The restaurant, overlooking a rather bleak concrete area, was not functioning at the time of our last visit (no fixtures, fittings or chef) though b/fasts of eggs, fresh fruits & chapati are included in the rates. **$$**

⌂ **Zanzibar Star Resort** (10 rooms) ☎024 2230233; m 0773 663503/ 0779 790089; e info@ zanzibarstarresort.com, munaarich@yahoo.com; www.zanzibarstarresort.com. Managed by Munaa, an astute young woman from Arusha, Zanzibar Star Resort opened the doors to its immaculate rooms in Nov 2011. Behind its perimeter wall, well-tended gardens filled with bananas, flowering shrubs & some of Nungwi's most verdant lawns, lead to the Arabesque reception, & 2-storey accommodation block. Rooms are arranged in a staggered diagonal to create a little terrace privacy, whilst inside they are clean & modern with pale tiled floors, dark timber furniture, smart en suites, & an array of mod cons. Currently it's B&B only, though restaurant access is relatively easy, & a small pool is under construction. However nice Zanzibar Star Resort proves to be, it is impossible to escape its location issues: not only distanced from the beach but immediately neighbouring the new 'Nungwi Nightclub' – the structure may be

soundproofed but the departing guests are not! **$$$–$$$$**

⌂ **Nungwi Guesthouse** (10 rooms) m 0777 494899; e nungwiguesthouse@yahoo. com. Located at the western edge of the village behind the nursery school, close to the football pitch & shops, Nungwi Guesthouse (formerly Ruma Guesthouse) is easily identified by the Bushman-esque paintings on its ochre walls. Zanzibari-owned, this place offers very basic rooms with striking wraparound murals, in a simple concrete building. There's a central chill-out courtyard under makuti thatch with hammocks, cushioned coir-rope sofas & a few playful kittens, & the atmosphere is decidedly relaxed. Free-spirited backpackers are most warmly welcomed. **$–$$**

⌂ **Travellers Bungalows** (10 rooms) m 0774 132828. Travellers' semi-detached bungalows house equally dire rooms. Primarily used by visiting Zanzibaris & local fisherman coming for the evening, the dirty sheets, rusty fans, peeling plaster walls & bucket of water in lieu of a dysfunctional shower should be enough to dissuade most other visitors. The bar blares music & lunch/dinner can be made with notice, though a glance at the food-encrusted hob is likely to put you off ordering. It is anticipated that the new neighbouring nightclub will increase business here, & sadly this is probably true. The presence of burglar bars surrounding the bar & provocatively dressed ladies hanging around day & night add a distinctly seedy air to an already unpleasant place. **$**

⌂ **Kipangani Villas** ☎0777 971776; e info@ kipanganivilla.com; http://kipanganivilla.com. About 10mins' walk from the beach & local amenities, Kipangani is a trio of self-catering villas, marketed to urban escapists & international volunteers. Using very simple timber & thatch constructions & with distinctly ethnic-influenced interiors (mkeke matting, kanga trimmed mossie nets, rustic timber beds), this place offers the more adventurous a spacious place of their own. Villas have simple bedrooms, moulded concrete or stone-clad bathrooms, a small open-plan kitchen (inc fridge), a shaded balcony & *baraza*-based lounge areas. The villas are set back from the road behind a shared garden filled with bananas, papayas, suitably tropical flowering trees, chickens & a dhow bar. Although children are welcome, the rustic nature of the buildings & garden, & relative isolation may not suit all families; equally, the proximity to the new nightclub may become an issue. Discounted rates are available for volunteers & families. **$$$**

⌂ **Kwetu Bungalows** (10 rooms) m 0784 780464. Scheduled to open in 2013, Kwetu Bungalows is a clutch of 6 promising 2-storey, octagonal buildings occupying the corner plot on the main road into South Beach. Whitewashed with ruby red staircases & solid coconut doors to the rooms, this place may be worth a look when it opens, if you are content to pass on a sea view.

East Beach
At the tip of the Nungwi Peninsula is the lighthouse; from here, the coast curves back sharply to the south. This eastern side of the peninsula has developed significantly more slowly than the South and West beaches, but in the last five years tourism development has started with a vengeance and every plot from Mnarani to Ras Nungwi is now under construction or operational as a hotel. It still offers some great accommodation choices set on low cliffs of coral rock above sandy beaches, but the exclusivity is fast diminishing.

⌂ **Essque Zalu Zanzibar** (40 rooms, 9 villas) m 0778 683960; e reservations@essquehotels. com; www.essquehotels.com. The imposing makuti construction that makes up Essque Zalu's reception area & restaurant is visible from quite a distance, while up close it's reminiscent of Sydney Opera House. The suites are set in lush landscaped gardens & have a spacious bedroom, a separate lounge with flat-screen TV & a desk filled with branded notepaper, a walk-in wardrobe & an enormous bathroom. All boast an electronic safe, which ingeniously has a plug socket inside it so you can charge your laptop while it's locked away. The rooms differ only in their view, which is of either the sea or the garden, although some rooms have views of both from their balcony. The resort is centred on the huge, saltwater pool, which comes complete with a whirlpool, water jets & multi-coloured lighting – ecological awareness is obviously not a priority here. Looking out over the pool are the 2 restaurants: the casual, deli-style Market Kitchen downstairs, & the more upmarket A La Carte restaurant upstairs (7 courses US$55), which doubles as a gallery for showcasing worldwide artists. A further, laid-back lunchtime restaurant is at the end of the long wooden jetty, a somewhat controversial structure given it's siting on the seasonal Kaskazi dhow path. On the other side of the pool are the vast villas, which contain 3–4 bedrooms, a lounge, kitchen (self-cater or arrange a private chef), bathroom with stand-alone bath, outdoor plunge pool & private massage room where the masseuses from the adjacent Zalu Zanzibar spa can offer a personal pampering session. The spa (see *What to see and do*, page 240) itself is an oasis of calm, with treatment rooms, a steam room, a gym & sauna, & a range of therapies on offer. There's no need to worry about the little ones, as they can head off to the Petit VIP kids' club (*www.petitvip.com*), where a range of supervised crafts, games & activities will keep them amused. Although facilities abound & the rooms are top-notch, Essque Zalu prioritises style over sensitivity to its environment. **$$$$$–**

⌂ **Ras Nungwi Beach Hotel** (33 rooms) ☏ 024 2233767/2512; e info@rasnungwi.com; www.rasnungwi.com. A perennially popular choice for high-end honeymooners, Ras Nungwi Beach Hotel is by far one of the most reliable upmarket places to stay in Nungwi & retains a calm, low-key atmosphere. Its rooms are set in compact, well-tended gardens & all have good electronic safes. Broadly speaking, the higher the room category here, the closer the room is to the sea & the more it has to offer. The lodge or garden rooms sit in a row above the central area & car park & only a couple of these have distant sea views but each has a traditional Zanzibari bed with mosquito net & a veranda, & any can be made up for sgl, dbl or trpl occupancy. The rondavels of the superior deluxe chalets all enjoy sea views, but only the latter offer dressing gowns & stereos. In addition, set slightly away from the rondavels, the Ocean Suite operates as a private, separate villa & has a private plunge pool & sundeck; this is Ras Nungwi's premium accommodation. Alongside the hotel's large central bar & split-level dining room, there's an internet point (although Wi-Fi is available in all public areas), satellite TV room & a games area with a pool table, table tennis, board games & darts. The exceptional food & a great wine list are highlights of any stay here. Delicious fresh, often organic, dishes served in the Ubora

Restaurant are the norm. With all guests staying on a HB basis there's an extensive b/fast buffet laid out every morning, an à la carte lunch menu & 4-course table d'hôte dinner. Weekly tasty seafood BBQs with Swahili cuisine classics also feature, often accompanied by some gentle live music. In front of the main restaurant area is a small freshwater swimming pool & sundeck with paths radiating down to the beach & secluded reading areas. There's an excellent PADI dive centre (see Zanzibar Watersports, page 236), offering courses & recreational dives as well as a range of other watersports. Big-game fishing has long been one of the manager's passions & the hotel has use of 3 specialist boats through its subsidiary, Zanzibar Big Game Fishing (see *What to see and do*, page 237). Alternatively, play tennis, or for something more gentle, the Peponi Spa is a highly professional operation with superb treatments: try the Sandalwood & Sugarcane Safari Scrub (US$75/hr) or a cooling Zanzibar Sun Therapy (US$60/40mins). $$$$$-🛏

🏠 **The Zanzibari** (11 rooms) 📞024 5500590; **m**; 0772 222919; **e** info@thezanzibari.com; www.thezanzibari.com. Formerly the Chinese-owned Golden Dragon Lodge, the Zanzibari has undergone significant transformation under its new owners, & is far better for it. The original angular accommodation blocks have a Mediterranean holiday apt appearance, but have been improved with extensive tropical climbers & flowering shrub borders. The interiors of these dbl rooms are cool & clean: smart 4-poster beds made up with crisp white sheets with vibrant turquoise accents, large en suites with a bath & separate shower, a handy sofa & sliding glass doors onto wide coconut-wood verandas (book the 1st floor for better views), private balcony or terrace. Mini fridges, AC & fan are standard throughout, & the rooms' only real negative is they are a reasonable distance from the sea & pool area. The 2 new family suites are right above the raised beach. Complete with their own plunge pool, they are a good option for families who want some private space alongside regular hotel facilities. Inside, there's a dbl bedroom downstairs & a lounge, complete with satellite TV, which opens onto a private terrace. Upstairs is 1 large room with open-fronted makuti thatch to keep the place cool. It usually comprises a dbl & sgl bed, & a lounge area. There's a large pool

with loungers dotted around the surrounding stone patio & a pole & bougainvillea shade for sunbathers. All guests can enjoy the 3 cliff-top jacuzzi pools for dhow-spotting dips $$$$-🛏
🏠 **Game Fish Lodge** (4 rooms) **m** 0753 451919; **e** gamefish@zanlink.com. On the site of the old Mkadi Guesthouse, this small, laid-back South African-owned lodge specialises in fishing trips (see *What to see and do*, page 237), as its name suggests. It is very much a family-run operation, with Colin & Lesley providing most of the necessary services themselves – transfers & tours – & doing the catering. Guests often drink & dine together too, lending this place a slightly house-party vibe. The original guesthouse rooms remain, though they have been renovated, & sit on a terrace beside the road looking down the steep hill towards the cliff edge & sparkling sea. It is a cracking view. The rooms all have pine furniture, appliqué bedspreads & a cheerful kanga-clad coir sofa; a small ceiling-mounted fan, TV, CD & DVD player are also included. Down the rocky hill, past the chicken coop, is an impressive open-sided restaurant/bar with some particularly good map murals of Zanzibar & Pemba; chill out here in a fishing-net hammock, stroke the friendly cats or have a game of pool. Advance notice of arrival is recommended, as the gates are not always manned. $$$$
🏠 **Mnarani Beach Cottages** (see advertisement on the 1st page of the 2nd colour insert) (37 rooms) 📞024 2240494; **m** 0777 415551; **e** mnarani@zanlink.com; www.lighthouseZanzibar.com. Mnarani means 'at or near the lighthouse' in Swahili, & aptly describes this resort's situation. Close to the northernmost tip of the island, from where it is possible to see the sun rise & set, this is a delightful place. Neat sand paths, bordered by masses of established pink hibiscus, lead between the rooms & to the beachfront bar/restaurant area. Here, overlooking a stunning stretch of beach, the deck provides a perfect spot for sunbathing, sundowners or simply chilling on the swings. This is a very civilised place to recharge your batteries. In small, melon-coloured cottages, rooms 1–8 have perfect sea views, interrupted only by an occasional coconut palm, whilst rooms 9–12 are set in lush gardens close to the pool. The rooms are relatively small but spotlessly clean, tastefully decorated & with good en-suite facilities. Coconut-wood furniture sits on broad terraces at the front of each one, whilst loungers & inviting rope hammocks

There's ocean on both sides, but Nungwi often suffers shortages of fresh water. Nearby wells are shallow and, as an increasing number of tourist developments tap into the natural water table, the local people justifiably fear their supply will run dry. For many existing guesthouses, the flow is already erratic, and at most larger hotels the water has to be trucked in for bathroom and kitchen use. For drinking, you can buy bottled water. Nevertheless, Nungwi is a place to seriously watch your water consumption – that is, go easy on the lingering showers, not the rehydration!

hang between palms & shady fir trees. There is even a raised, manmade beach for relaxing during high tide. There are also 4 family cottages with large galleried interiors, a lounge, kitchen & useful information pack – plus some 2- & 3-bed family flats. The sizeable Zanzibar House contains spacious rooms (all named after islands), each filled with good-quality furniture, fridge & large, sea view balcony complete with hammock (opt for the 1st & 2nd floors for the finest views). Alternatively, honeymooners on the 2nd floor can escape up the spiral stairs to the roof terrace for some of the area's best panoramic views. Dhow snorkelling trips can be arranged (US$35/4 people inc soft drinks, snack & equipment), or it's possible to hire watersports equipment (hourly rental costs US$5/10 sgl/dbl kayak & US$10 surfboard). Kayaks are free for those on snorkelling trips. The lagoon immediately in front of the hotel is also a great place for kitesurfers. The beachfront Cinnamon Spa is a simple affair under thatch & resident Kenyan therapist offers local scrubs (US$30), massage (US$30/hr) & a popular sunburn treatment (US$25). For alternative relaxation, the bar has a relaxed vibe, daily cocktails & very handy tide timetables, & Mnarani's staff are some of the friendliest on the north coast. Among Mnarani's real assets is the dense vegetation that separates it from the lighthouse, for unlike any other plot on this coast, it does not feel boxed in by development. Another positive is its environmental consciousness – rainwater is collected, leftovers are composted, all materials are local, & solar panels provide the power. On top of this, owner Nassor is active in the local community & is involved in various much-needed projects supporting Nungwi village. All rates are HB; FB also available. **$$$$**

🏠 **Sazani Beach Hotel** (11 rooms) ☎024 2240014; m 0741 324744; e bookings@ sazanibeach.com; www.sazanibeach.com. Adjacent to Ras Nungwi Beach Hotel, Sazani Beach has been in its current form since the new millennium. Having gained some new American shareholders in 2008, there have been rumours of luxury renovations here for some time, but for now it retains its slightly offbeat & laid-back character, & is very much in need of good management. Set high up on coral rock, there are 2 very simple dbl rooms in the main house, 2 large rooms suitable for dbl or trpl occupancy, which run perpendicular to the sea in a semi-detached block, standard dbls in semi-detached bungalows, & a beach banda. All are basic but clean, & have 24hr electricity, mosquito nets, fans, hot water & a stunning sea view. Early-morning tea can be brought to your room, before b/fast is served on the small patio area. Homemade jams & freshly brewed coffee feature alongside traditional eggs & bacon. A new restaurant area is tucked behind billowing cotton panels, or BBQs can be organised for successful game-fishing guests. Sazani has traditionally been a hangout for kitesurfers, keen to catch the shore trade winds (up to Force 6) in the clear lagoon immediately in front of the hotel, & has recently also become a base for 'Two Can Fly' paragliding. Free Wi-Fi for guests. **$$$$**

🏠 **Tanzanite Beach Resort** (17 rooms) m 0777 485022; e info@tanzanitebeachresort. com; www.tanzanitebeachresort.com. If you can ignore the huge, rusting satellite dish at the entrance & the immature gardens, Tanzanite has a stunning ocean outlook from its raised location. It caters mainly to German & Italian visitors & delivers a reasonably good level of accommodation. Large rooms, 2 of which are classed as seafront, are in semi-detached thatched bungalows with sparse furnishings, standard dbl beds (crazy given the size of room), small fans, mosquito nets, small bathrooms & a shaded terrace. There is a restaurant (🕐 to non-residents

Northern Zanzibar NUNGWI

8

12.30–22.00) serving a fairly limited 'fish 'n' mash' menu, a popular pool table, & a lovely kidney-shaped swimming pool, complete with token coconut palm & raised stone decking. There is no beach in front of the hotel as the coral-rock shelf extends below the property, but a faux beach festooned with hammocks has been engineered on the cliff top, with sea swimming possible at high tide & coastal walking at low. **$$$$**

⌂ North Nungwi Beach Hotel (10 rooms) **e** vugahotel@yahoo.com. Framed by the main door as you approach this hotel, the picture-perfect view of paths leading down to the Indian Ocean, with cerulean waves breaking on the distant reef, is as good as it gets. Step inside, & a once idyllic retreat is now run-down & poorly managed. The main terrace of rooms by the road offers simple accommodation with ceiling fans & a broad shared veranda. In addition, there are 2 further rooms closer to the beach, beside the restaurant, which may have a better outward appearance, but are truly dismal inside: ripped mattresses, a security screen that appears to have been used as a BBQ grill in a former life, & desperately dim lighting. It is a shame that there is such an obvious lack of care & investment here, but for now this hotel's fabulous outlook is the only possible reason to stay here. **$$$**

✖ WHERE TO EAT AND DRINK

Nearly all the hotels and guesthouses in Nungwi have attached restaurants, many of which are open to guests and non-guests alike (see the *Where to stay* section for more details of these). Along South Beach a number of casual restaurants, cafés and bars serve seafood dishes for around US$10, and snacks, pizzas and burgers for around US$6, all washed down with fresh fruit juices, milkshakes, ubiquitous Coca-Cola and African beer, whilst Z Hotel's Saruche lords over them with its fusion feasts. Between South and West beaches, a band of more structured restaurants perch on the coral cliff above the sea, All have similar menus of fresh seafood, oven-fired pizzas and local curries, and many do happy hours and backpacker meal-and-beer specials. North of Paradise Beach Bungalows is a clutch of funky, sand-between-your-toes bars, offering cocktails and music on the beachfront. For a more grass-roots flavour, deep in the village you are likely to find cheap local fare from around US$2–3, though venues are highly changeable.

With little building regulation apparent, beachfront bars, restaurants and guesthouses tend to close and spring up again virtually overnight as land is sold on to ever-higher bidders. For many years, simply setting up a barbecue beside a few chairs, tables or logs on the sand signalled being in business, but things are changing and more substantial restaurant structures are slowly replacing these ad hoc eateries. Here, we've listed only some of the more reliable, long-running establishments, some perhaps better avoided, and those that are new but showing promising signs of staying the course, at least for a few years. You should accept that you're quite likely to find more newcomers on arrival, so do also ask around for current culinary hot spots.

✖ Saruche Restaurant **m** 0773 535808; ⊕ dinner only, daily. The formal restaurant at Z Hotel, Saruche serves an à la carte menu of African–European fusion food with a heavy emphasis on local seafood. Accompanied by an international wine list, ocean views & island antiques, it's a pleasant place to dine & one of the smartest options currently in Nungwi. Peruse the menu from the lavish daybeds & couches in the lounge, then pick a table on the deck overlooking the beach or high-tide waves. There are traditional music & entertainment nights throughout the week, featuring everything from belly dancers to troops of drummers, & after-dinner nightcaps in upstairs bar Cinnamon (see below) are very much de rigueur. **$$$$**

♀ Cinnamon Cocktail Bar **m** 0773 535808; ⊕ 07.00–late, daily. At the northern end of South Beach, on top of the coral cliff, Cinnamon is part of the Z Hotel complex but welcomes non-residents, too. With its 1st-floor location, overlooking the South Beach scene & the sea, the young & beautiful are attracted by its contemporary décor & fabulous tropical cocktails. Sipped at cushion-clad baraza benches, surrounded by ever-changing mood lights & chilled tunes, this is a great pre-dinner drinks spot & is certainly one of Nungwi's most stylish drinking dens to date. Stay for sushi & tempting tasting platters at lunch or dinner, or just work your way through the extensive cocktail list. There is a cool vibe here & it's the only place by the beach where fashionable ladies won't feel out of place in high heels. **$$$**

✕ Infusion (formerly Blue Sea Restaurant) m 0775 044719; ⏱ 09.00–late, daily. Approached from South Beach, this is the first of this coast's clutch of raised seafront restaurants. The friendly staff serve a range of popular seafood dishes, including octopus, calamari, prawns & cigale (rock lobster), which is amusingly spelt 'seagull' on the menu. For something a bit different try the seafood coconut curry (US$9.50) or if you're really hungry go for the seafood platter (US$19). Lobster is reasonably priced at US$16, whilst those tired of fish can sample delights from the pizza oven (US$5–8) or a spicy satay kebab (US$10). Meals can be accompanied by a choice of fresh juices or a hot & frothy cappuccino from the restaurant's Italian espresso machine. **$$$**

✕ Langi Langi m 0773 911000; ⏱ 07.00–22.00 daily. On a large cantilevered deck of the hotel of the same name, Langi Langi is a relaxed coffee shop by day & a Swahili restaurant by night. Serving super cappuccinos & cake at b/fast & fresh curries for dinner it's a popular place & worth booking to guarantee a table for dinner. Service is friendly & menu variations always possible, whilst the breeze & rolling waves add to the casual vibe. Dine inside amid the monochrome photos of Stone Town & antique *objets d'art*, or out on the vast deck. Alcohol is not sold, but beer & wine can be chilled & served if you bring your own along. Couples, families & large groups are all equally well accommodated. If you like the food, ask about the cookery classes here. **$$$**

♀ Mangi's Bar & Restaurant m 0777 417042; ⏱ 08.00–22.00 daily. Relocated as part of the Z Hotel pool area expansion, long-running Mangi's is now back on the sandy beach where it first started out as Dolphin Restaurant. A shaded spot beside Nungwi Inn Hotel, it's a relaxed hangout serving fresh juices, US$4 cocktails (the Zanzibar Mzungu concoction of banana, rum, milk & vodka appearing popular), & snacks like samosas, chapattis & baked potatoes. **$$$**

✕ Marina Grill m 0775 044719; ⏱ 07.00–23.00 daily. Bright & breezy Marina Grill is relaxed by day but livens up during the 17.00–19.00 happy hour, when a selection of cocktails is offered. The expansive, mangrove-pole terrace affords diners uninterrupted views out to sea & a welcome breeze. The speciality here is fish, which features in a range of salads, sandwiches & pasta dishes (US$7). Fresh seafood is served freshly grilled or fried, & the piri piri prawns with chips are a popular choice (US$13). Although the staff could be friendlier, it's a welcoming enough place & there's also a satellite TV for catching up on international sports. **$$$**

✕ Ombeliko del Mondo m 0773 604265; ⏱ 09.00–22.00 daily. This pleasant *cucina italiana* is unusually located: tucked behind Amaan Bungalows, on the far side of the dusty access road, with precious little in the way of a nice view. The place was opened in 2007 by Lella, a lovely Mantovan who only speaks Italian, & the menu (in English & Italian) is full of traditional Italian delicacies: seafood antipasti, pastas, risottos & tempting *dolcis*. Good coffees are available. There's an open kitchen, smart lounge & a neat restaurant area, buzzing with Mediterranean chatter, all under a huge makuti roof. Starters cost around US$5.50 & main courses US$5–10, & whilst quality & reviews are consistently good, portions are a little on the small side for some diners. **$$$**

✕ Nungwi Inn Restaurant ☎024 2240091; m 0777 418769; ⏱ from 06.00; last food orders taken 22.00. On South Beach, in front of the hotel with the same name, this restaurant receives consistently good reviews for its simple, traditional fare, which is listed in technicolour on a wall that doubles as a backboard. Guests can sink their feet in the sand, watch the beach volleyball & peruse the menu whilst seated under neat pole shading. Order a 'Nungwi Killer' cocktail (Bacardi, vodka, Cointreau, tequila, lime & Coke) & little is likely to be on the agenda for the afternoon, though more popular are the open-oven pizzas (US$5–9), burgers (US$6–9) & grilled lobster (US$13–50), plus the regular beach BBQ. But before making your choice, look out for the amusing 'absent menu' – a list of dishes that the restaurant doesn't serve! **$$–$$$**

♀ Bam Bam Bar ⏱ 11.00–late, daily. At the northerly end of West Beach, Bam Bam is a dilapidated hangout for some slightly disillusioned locals & resident Rastafarians. Western tourists rarely venture inside this open-sided bar, in part because of aesthetics & in part because there is no obvious welcome; women especially may feel uncomfortable. It is open from 09.00 until the last person leaves, & judging by the state of some of the occupants, that seems to be never. There are plenty of other drinking establishments to try before this one. **$$**

♀**Cholo's Bar** m 0777 505434; ⏰ 10.00–late, daily. For all-day drinking & wild nights, Cholo's is a perennial favourite. Tucked under palms at the back of West Beach, this eccentric establishment is well known for its 24hr music, crowd of local Rastas & backpackers, & free-flowing alcohol. The bar is a piece of living art composed of 2 marooned dhows with suspended dugout canoes acting as seats & an array of motorbikes, sanitary ware & various other salvaged items used for structure, storage & décor. Beach bonfires are a periodic evening attraction along with ad hoc BBQs & dining at upturned dhow tables. Once the place to drink when everywhere else had shut, this long-standing bar has relatively recently been taken over & given a facelift. Its late-night opening & idiosyncrasies have been retained but it's smartened up a little & added daytime appeal with a raft of 4-poster timber daybeds on the beach in front. Good spot if you like a mojito whilst sunbathing, though expect a reasonable amount of attention. Weekly beach parties & 'ladies' nights' draw crowds, & you'll likely see the expat hotel staff jostling for bar space, though it's a tamer hangout than it once was. **$$**

♀**Kizuri** ⏰ 11.30–late, daily. This 2012 addition to the Nungwi bar scene is a bijou place, with thatched shade, cushioned concrete baraza booths & chilled music. Offering a range of cocktails & cool drinks, it also has a restaurant serving pan-African/European fusion food. Tall coconut trunk tables encourage stand-up drinking, or settle down for a longer stay to watch the sunset & while away a pleasant beachfront evening. Success has come quickly & upward expansion is likely if things continue, but hopefully the quality & laid-back vibe will remain. **$$$**

✖ **Mama Africa Restaurant & Bar**
⏰ 10.00–late, daily. Mama Africa caters very much to a local clientele. The open courtyard

within its imposing walls is a popular hangout for the Maasai & mainland immigrants working in Nungwi. Here, red Coca-Cola chairs are set out in rows in front of a white wall for nighttime TV & film projections, there's a variety of pool & table football games around, & a food counter. B/fast, lunch & dinner are served from 08.00–22.00, but the awful stench & sight of the fly-covered goat carcass hung in front of the serving counter is likely to kill most visitors' appetites. **$–$$**

✖ **Morning Star Restaurant** ⏰ lunch & dinner, daily. A very local establishment in the heart of the village, Morning Star is signposted off the main dust road through the village between the BBS Computer Room & the dala dala stop. It is allegedly open daily for b/fast, lunch & dinner. However, it does seem to close regularly for 'maintenance', so best not to rely on it if you're starving. If by chance it is open, expect a set meal of Swahili seafood dishes in a basic setting & some curious villagers for company. Outside seems to be the hub of local *bao* games, so you may even be able to join the crowd for a heated match after your meal. **$$**

✖ **New Dhow Restaurant** ⏰ lunch & dinner, daily. This restaurant is a locally owned & run little place that's been around since the start of the millennium. Operating from a small makuti hut immediately behind the harbour, Khamis prepares tasty pilau rice & daily 'catch of the day' seafood dishes: BBQ octopus (US$4.50) to grilled ginger & garlic lobster (US$16). Round off a meal with bananas in coconut milk (US$4.50) & watch the dhows & fishing ladies. **$$–$$$**

♀**Rastacafe** ⏰ 17.00–early morning. Behind a low timber garden fence next to Kiteboarding Zanzibar, this tiny makuti thatched bar serves fresh coffee, from spiced Zanzibari style to Italian cappuccinos. Run by a friendly Rastafarian, Girasole, it's open from early evening until the last of the beach party revellers head home in the wee hours. **$–$$**

SHOPPING There are several small shops in Nungwi village, where you'll find an array of cheap souvenirs, including carvings, paintings and jewellery, as well as essential items. Head inland across the football pitch behind Cholo's, and you'll first come to a neat building on your right, one half of which is the well-equipped Nungwi School computer room (see *Other practicalities*, opposite), while the other half is **Choices**, a souvenir shop which also sells swimwear. A few steps further on, there is a small parade of shops. Here, there's an ever-changing array of beauticians, barbers, local cafés, and the long-standing **Nungwi Supermarket**: a veritable Aladdin's den of imported luxuries from toothpaste and toiletries to chocolate and Pringles.

Taking the road deeper into the village, there's another internet access point, the **California Foto Store** for film processing (we cannot vouch for the quality of your prints!), the New Nungwi Salon where the brave can have a bikini wax, and the local-style Jambo Mixed Shop, behind which is the Ahsanna Dispensary for villagers.

Amaan Bungalows Supermarket has a reasonable selection of knick-knacks and food/drink basics, whilst behind Paradise Beach Bungalows, **Mr Alibaba** and his sons, Abdul and Suleiman, sell everything from kangas to cold drinks, postcards and tours.

Alternatively, if you just need to grab a few essentials and don't want to stray too far from sunbathing, there are a couple of places on South Beach. **Nungwi Inn Supermarket**, next to its namesake hotel, is very well laid out, clearly priced and stocks a good selection of snacks, drinks, toiletries and beach requisites such as sunscreen. Between the curio market and North Coast Snorkelling, up some very steep and irregular coral-rock steps, **New Worldwide Supermarket** sells a similar range of goods, but is not nearly as nicely laid out. There's a good selection of known-brand suncreams for US$10–15 (various SPFs), a reasonable variety of US$3 alcopops and beers, some warm white wine for US$10 and even some carrot cake mix. Alternatively, stay on the beach and wait for the beach traders to parade the sand with boards covered in mirrored sunglasses, beaded jewellery and cold drinks.

For artwork and souvenirs, a fairly contained **curio market** has steadily grown on the alley running perpendicular to South Beach, alongside Z Hotel. Known locally as the Masaai Market, on account of the traders' tribal background, you'll find some entertainingly named shacks – IKEA Zanzibar – alongside those with delusions of grandeur: 'Leonardo da Vinci' for paintings and 'Gucci' for accessories. Joking aside, this organised approach to displaying the carvings and beadwork is to be commended, though there is still some way to go to reduce the sustained mobbing of fair-skinned passers-by.

OTHER PRACTICALITIES

Internet Most of the larger or smarter hotels have internet facilities, and a reasonable number of the smaller backpacker places will let you use an office PC to check email. Amaan Bungalows has three PCs available for general use in a small internet café off reception. Wi-Fi is becoming more widely available, though connections remain somewhat erratic and bandwidth fairly low.

If you do need a PC or internet access, we would recommend the reliable Nungwi School IT centre as a first choice, as income here is used to reinvest in the school's excellent computer initiative. Founded in 2002 by Bibi Biorg, a generous 75-year-old lady who first visited Nungwi as a tourist, the **BBs Computer Room** (⊕ 08.00–20.00 Mon–Fri & 08.30–19.30 on holidays & w/ends; rates are very low at US$0.60/30mins & US$1/hr) was designed to offer computer lessons to all Nungwi School's pupils as well as IT training for local adults. Four computers at the back of the class have Wi-Fi and paying customers, mostly tourists, can access these at any time during opening hours, regardless of whether classes are present. Though heavily supported by pupils and parents, and proving sustainable from its commercial activities, the centre is still heavily reliant on donations and visitors' dollars, so even if a few dollars to email home is all you can manage, the cause is a good one. If you are in a position to give more support, the headmaster can be contacted on e bbs@zanlink.com. The centre is clearly signposted beside the football field, on the right as you approach from the beach.

Post The postbox outside Mr Alibaba's shop (see *Shopping*, above) offers a twice-daily mail collection for those all-important postcards home.

WHAT TO SEE AND DO Most visitors come to this area to relax on the beach, swim in the sea, and perhaps to party at night. For local attractions, the small turtle sanctuary, terrific local coral reefs and growing array of watersports are still a draw. If you want a more cultural experience, check out the village tour, head down the coast to the 16th-century Swahili ruins at Fukuchani and Mvuleni, the bustling and ramshackle market at Mkokotoni, or venture across the water to Tumbatu Island.

If you want peace, quiet and fewer people, you will probably need to visit a different corner of the island.

Watersports The sweeping cape on which Nungwi is sited is surrounded by warm, turquoise seas, making it a perfect spot to engage in countless water activities. On the west side of the peninsula, especially on South Beach, locals offer boat rides, Mnemba picnic excursions, sunset booze cruises and snorkelling trips, whilst a growing number of Europeans are setting up motorised watersports operations. Prices are all very similar; quality is highly variable. Listen to your instinct and other travellers' advice carefully when deciding who is currently offering the best trip.

Snorkelling

Captain Mau m 0777 415496; e mauZanzibar@ yahoo.com. Next to Bam Bam Bar on West Beach, Captain Mau is a lovely local lad hiring out mask & fin sets (US$5/1/2 day; US$10/day) & arranging local excursions in his small wooden boat, complete with shade cloth. He will happily take visitors to Mnemba, Tumbatu & Kendwa Reef for snorkelling, but do be aware of safety considerations if you opt to go to the further destinations: he has only 1 motor & it's a long paddle back if it breaks.
North Coast Snorkelling Shop ⊕ 06.00–18.00. With a prime location on the coral rock

above South Beach, at the entrance to the curio market, the entrepreneurial Hamadi Ali has established a small hire shop for masks, snorkels, fins & fishing rods. He buys kit from tourists in Stone Town, & rents it out here. The quality is variable but you are free to try things on & select the best for you, & there is a range of good brands available (Cressi, Mares, Tribord) as well as adult & child sizes. Rates are US$5 snorkelling kit/day; US$10 fishing rod/day. If you would like him to take you out fishing, it's US$200 for a half day on his boat, complete with sunshade.

Diving Diving is especially popular here and many of the hotels offer dives and dive courses: you can visit the local reef, or go further afield to reefs such as Leven Bank and Mnemba. Over recent years several dive operations have come, gone or changed their name or location; at the beginning of 2012, six dive operations were in operation in Nungwi. Listed in alphabetical order, the centres are very different in feel and ethos, and divers are advised to talk seriously to the individual operators about safety and experience before signing up for courses or underwater excursions.

✦ Divine Diving m 0777 771914/0772 299395; e info@scubazanzibar.com; www. scubazanzibar.com. Based at Amaan Bungalows, Divine Diving is a newcomer on the northern diving scene, offering both yoga & scuba. Breathing technique classes to improve underwater air consumption sit alongside a range of PADI specialist courses (night diving, fish ID, enriched air, deep diving, search & recovery, drift & navigation). The well-qualified, experienced

expat team hail from South Africa, UK, Spain & Israel, so can teach in several languages. They regularly dive 25 local sites & encourage attention to detail: small groups, new Mares equipment, safety procedures & a link with the island's DAN hyperbaric chamber. This centre is affiliated with Zanzi Yoga (see page 240). US$55/95/175/385 (plus US$30 to Mnemba Atoll) for 1/2/4/10 dives; Discover Scuba US$85; Open Water US$450; Advanced US$365; Night Dive US$75.

Diving Poseidon m 0777 720270; www. divingposeidon.com. Owned by Austrian couple Ilse & Bernhard Kotlar (dive master & PADI Master Scuba Diver Trainer respectively), this relatively new dive PADI centre is located away from the shoreline, between Baraka Beach Bungalows & Nungwi village. The small bungalow base is clearly painted with the sea god himself, & houses the dive equipment: Mares BCDs, Dacor/Cressi regulators & shortie suits. They operate 1 covered fibreglass boat, taking 10 divers on 2-tank dives to sites around the north coast, Mnemba and Leven Bank (advanced divers only). Dives are usually led by local dive masters. US$60/95/180/390 for 1/2/4/10 dives; Discover Scuba US$75; Open Water US$360; Advanced US$270.

East Africa Diving & Watersport Centre m 0777 416425/420588; e EADC@zitec.org; www.diving-Zanzibar.com. Owned & operated by an experienced, straight-talking German–South African couple, Michael & Delene Kutz, this is the oldest dive centre on the north coast. On the beach in front of Jambo Brothers Guesthouse, this efficient PADI 5* Gold Palm Resort offers very well-priced courses to Dive Master & a host of scuba trips. Dive sites are reached by dhow, or 2, 14-person RIBS, & each boat has 2 experienced captains, with power of veto over any potentially unsafe dive. Safety appears to be taken seriously here, with all boats equipped with first aid & oxygen; dive leaders carry permanent surface marker buoys; steel tanks are continually quality tested using a new Bauer Pure Air Station, & the whole centre actively contributes to the DAN Decompression Chamber Support scheme (anyone completing a course here is automatically fully insured for 6 days' underwater activity). Female divers also take note that the tanks here are all squat steel tanks, making them a much more comfortable shape on your back, & significantly easier to cart down the beach to the boat. Nitrox diving was introduced in 2008. Mnemba sites are visited every couple of days; Hunga is a frequent destination; Kichafi, Mbwangawa & Haji all feature on the east coast; Tumbatu is a weekly excursion; & Big Wall at Mnemba (advanced divers only) is favoured over Leven Bank for safety & quality of marine life. EADC also has bases within Essque Zalu, Royal Zanzibar, Z Hotel & Doubletree by Hilton; for hotel guests confined water assessments take place in the pool at Z or Royal

Zanzibar. US$70/110/190/400 (plus US$30 to Mnemba Atoll) for 1/2/4/10 dives; Discover Scuba US$95; Open Water US$480; Advanced US$380; Nitrox US$300.

Rising Sun Diving Centre m 0777 440883–5/88; e bookings@risingsun-zanzibar. com; www.risingsun-zanzibar.com. Operating out of the all-inclusive Royal Zanzibar Hotel, this is the north coast sibling of Rising Sun Dive Centre (see page 289) at Breezes on the Michamvi Peninsula. It offers diving & watersports to hotel guests, but only scuba courses & trips to non-residents. It is a fully accredited PADI 5* Gold Palm Resort with National Geographic status & like its sister operation has state-of-the-art technology, quality equipment & experienced staff. Safety is taken seriously with instructors being covered by DAN insurance & guests are actively encouraged to join the scheme. PADI courses are taught on site whilst existing divers are taken out to less-visited local reef sites. Mnemba dives are offered on request but the focus here is on max underwater time & min transfer time. US$85/170/464/695 for 1/2/6/10 dives; Open Water US$672; digital photography US$386: daily equipment rental (regulator, BCD, wetsuit, mask & fins) US$39; underwater digital camera rental (inc CD of images) US$46.

Spanish Dancer Dive Centre (see advertisement on the final page of the 2nd colour insert) ☎024 2240091; m 0777 417717/430005; e contact@spanishdancerdivers.com; www. spanishdancerdivers.com. Taking its name from both an attractive marine creature (a nudibranch – a kind of sea slug) & its owner's nationality, Spanish Dancer is based in an open rondavel on South Beach & is run by David & Shee, with 3 other expat dive instructors & a dive master. The team regularly dives 20 sites, including Mnemba (35mins by speedboat), Leven Bank (divers must have a min of 20 logged dives), & for 5 months (Oct–Dec; Apr–Jul) takes advanced divers to waters just south of Pemba. Equipment & integrated BCD/12l steel tanks seem in good condition, & are pre-loaded for divers onto their 2 boats, which are both capable of carrying 15 divers on a 2-tank trip. Oxygen & first-aid kits are standard on all boats. Only the instructors carry surface marker buoys, so you may want to consider taking your own. The dive centre is PADI accredited & teaches in German, French, Spanish, Hebrew & English, with confined water sessions in the lagoon off the beach. There is a live-aboard diving option available with the owner's daughter, Sabine, on catamaran *Julia*. US$132/226/320/475 (plus US$47 for Mnemba) for 2/4/6/10 dives; Discover Scuba US$117; Open Water US$585; Dive Master US$1,169.

🤿 **Zanzibar Watersports** ☎ 024 2233309; m 0773 165862; e info@zanzibarwatersports.com; www.zanzibarwatersports.com. With PADI 5* Gold Palm Instructor Development Centre status, offering all PADI qualifications to instructor level, Zanzibar Watersports has 2 Nungwi outlets: 1 at Ras Nungwi Beach Hotel for guests only (the original one), & 1 within the central Paradise Beach Bungalows complex, which is open to everyone. The Ras Nungwi centre offers the same high quality as the hotel; equipment, service, safety & staff all seem top-notch here. For guests coming to learn to dive, it's worth emailing in advance; there's a home-study option which allows all the Open Water course reading & paperwork to be done before you arrive. Confined-water sessions for beginners are held in either the pool or the adjacent lagoon in front of the hotel. A strict refresher policy means that all divers who have not donned scuba gear for 6 months must do a refresher course on arrival. 4 permanent instructors, a dive master & 8 local boat captains & snorkel crew keep everything shipshape on board the 4 large dhows. 2 of these are capable of taking 10 divers on a 2-tank dive trip, whilst the other 2 sailing dhows are used for sunset cruises

& snorkelling trips. Dive sites are predominantly on the west side of the island; though trips to Mnemba are also run regularly. The 12 sites they most frequently visit are painted on the centre's wall; they vary according to visibility & weather conditions. Trips to Leven Bank & Mnemba's Big Wall are strictly for advanced divers & above. Dive departure times vary & may require a short minivan transfer if the water in the lagoon is too shallow for their boat. At the Paradise Centre, divers may benefit from the pool or swish surroundings, but they do enjoy reduced rates. From here, daily snorkelling & diving trips head to Mnemba, whilst divers also have a choice of 21 other local sites. 2 canopy-covered boats are on hand to accommodate max 20 people & 4 expat PADI instructors; a local dive master & 4 boat crew are always on hand. Safety is taken seriously with life-rings, lifejackets & first-aid equipment on all boats, plus a thorough safety briefing including a lesson on using the onboard radio. There are also 1- & 2-man kayaks, waterskiing & wakeboarding equipment available & sunset dhow cruises for the more sedentary visitor. US$55/100/295/460 (plus US$65 for Mnemba) for 1/2/6/10 dives excluding equipment; Refresher US$30; Open Water US$550; Advanced US$440; US$15 equipment hire (mask, fins, BCD, regulator, wetsuit); kayaks US$10pp/hr; waterskiing US$70/15mins; windsurfing US$30/hr. At the Paradise branch group deals available for 4+ persons.

Sailing Aside from local sunset dhow trips, there are few opportunities to sail on board more modern vessels on this stretch of coast. For live-aboard 'learn-to-sail' options and simple cruising, *Julia* (see below), is the only real option.

⚠ **Dive 'n' Sail Zanzibar** m 0774 441234; e info@dive-n-sail.com, yachtjulia@hotmail.com; www.dive-n-sail.com. Dive 'n' Sail operates a lovely 50ft Admiral catamaran, *Julia*, specialising in live-aboard dive trips & fishing excursions to Pemba & Mafia. Available for charter with its own professional skipper, chef, deckhand & optional dive instructor, the boat is fully equipped for diving & deep-sea fishing. On board are 4 en-suite dbl cabins, a large galley & saloon area complete with stereo & DVD player, an outside deck & sunbathing trampoline. Complete with a Bauer 'Mariner' dive compressor for refilling tanks, it has 8 full sets of dive equipment, including 16 aluminium cylinders,

BCDs, regulators, depth gauges, weight-belts & weights. With some notice, PADI Advanced Open Water & speciality courses can be taught on board. Dinner usually comprises the daily catch, so fishing is a frequent activity. Day or overnight trips to the reefs around Mnemba are possible, although the boat is more likely to be used by serious divers for week-long ventures to Pemba. US$1,320/day private boat charter (1–5 persons) for min 4 days, excluding dives; dives US$42/dive for first 10 dives, then US$36; US$108pp Mnemba Island snorkelling day trip (min 4 persons); US$66 dive supplement; US$480 half-day fishing.

Fishing Nungwi's proximity to some of Africa's best deep-sea fishing grounds – Leven Bank and the deep Pemba Channel – offers serious anglers outstanding fishing opportunities. (For details on the fishing seasons see *Chapter 3, Natural environment*, page 51 In addition to the weather-beaten local dhows which plough the coastal waters, three operators currently offer game fishing in fully equipped, custom-built boats.

⤙ Fishing Zanzibar e gerry@fishingZanzibar. com, info@fishingZanzibar.com; www. fishingZanzibar.com. Operated by Gerry Hallam, Fishing Zanzibar have 4 sport-fishing boats based in Nungwi: *Unreel, Surreel, Cobia & Sansuli*, as well as a 50ft sailing yacht, *Walkabout*. The sport-fishing boats are kitted out with a stand-up fishing chair, outriggers, downriggers, Shimano fishing gear (line classes 25–80lb) & a full selection of lures, & take small charter groups (max 4 anglers) to Leven Bank & the Pemba Channel. Anglers are taken in search of black, blue & striped marlin, sailfish, yellowfin tuna, spearfish, dorado, trevally, king & queen mackerel, barracuda, & wahoo (travelling at 85km/h, these are amongst the fastest fish in the sea). Night fishing for broadbills is an option, as are live-aboard trips. As members of the International Game Fish Association, a catch-&-release approach to billfish & sharks is encouraged, except when fish are injured or in the event of a possible record catch. US$500–1,000 1/2 day; US$1,000–2,000 full day, including lunch; live-aboard US$1,300–2,500/day for 4 persons; rates vary by boat.

⤙ Game Fish Tours m 0753 451919; e gamefish@zanlink.com; www. gamefishlodge.2itb.com. Based out of Game Fish Lodge, this South African operation runs half-day, night fishing & 2-day Pemba tours for reef & bottom fishing. They have 2 boats: *El Shaddai* & *Karambisi*. *El Shaddai* is a 14ft fibreglass Super Dolphin ski boat kitted out with a fish-finder & Penn & Scarborough tackle. *Karambisi* is a Magnum 25ft game-fishing vessel offering plenty of deck space & a harness chair for fighting fish. Focusing on the serious game-fishing market, Karamibisi has Shimano Tiagra 30WA, 50WA & 80WA rods & reels spooled with IGFA yellow 15kg, 24kg & 36kg fishing line, 8" Scarborough reels spooled

with Berkley Whiplash Pro 37.8kg Dacron line & a selection of lures, feathers & rapalas. Karambisi also has a toilet & sleeping facilities so is used for the multi-day Pemba trips. US$220pp/6hr charter (max 2 persons) on *El Shaddai*; US$165pp/6hrs (max 3–4 persons) on *Karambisi*; 2-day Pemba US$550pp on *Karambisi*.

⤙ Zanzibar Big Game Fishing ☎024 2233767/2512; e info@rasnungwi.com; www. rasnungwi.com. Arguably the best game-fishing operation on Zanzibar, & certainly the longest established, Zanzibar Big Game Fishing (previously known as Ras Nungwi Fishing), is a division of Zanzibar Watersports (see opposite). They are extremely well kitted out for both professional fishermen & have-a-go holidaymakers, with 3 sport-fishing boats, professional tackle & international safety equipment. *Haraka*, a 2006 model Gulfcraft Sport Fishing 35 is used to access distant fishing grounds, *Timimi*, a custom-built Windy 24 with a fighting chair for big-game fishing, & *Suli Suli*, a 24ft T-top fibreglass boat with open decks for fly fishing, are all available for guest use. On board modern, purpose-built fittings, experienced skippers & a raft of state-of-the-art technology are utilised. A full set of tackle is provided along with Shimano, Fenwick, Harnell or KC rods & Shimano or Penn international reels, spooled with 80lb, 50lb & 30lb mono line, although clients can bring their own if preferred. Tag-&-release fishing is encouraged for all big fish unless it is the fisherman's 1st-ever catch, his biggest to date, or if it is likely to be an east African or All Africa record. 1/2-day (5hr) outings depart at either 06.30 or 13.30; whole days depart 06.30. Rates include charter of boat, skipper, bait, tackle equipment & lunch. US$400/550 half/full day on *Suli Suli*; US$550/750 half/full day on *Timimi*; US$650/950 half/full day on *Haraka*.

Kiteboarding In recent years, kiteboarding has grown in popularity and Nungwi is no exception. Steady winds (approx 15–20 knots) for most of the year, level beaches, warm clear water and protected, shallow lagoons make it a great place for both beginners and more experienced kiters. The quiet, long, sandy beach on the eastern side of Nungwi cape allows for easy launching and landing, although, like all of Zanzibar's east coast, the tidal change is significant and this affects the exposed beach area. The fringe reef here creates a calm and sheltered lagoon, which is ideal for kiting, and from May to September affords great opportunities for wave-riding and surfing. There is no seaweed farming here, and consequently no danger from concealed underwater canes. It's worth checking if centres are certified by the International Kiteboarding Organisation (IKO) if you are interested in quality assurance and training courses.

🐟 Kiteboarding Zanzibar

e kiteboardingzanzibar@gmail.com. Kiteboarding Zanzibar is IKO-certified, using up-to-date Cabrinha, NPX & Dakine equipment, with qualified, experienced staff on hand for safety & lessons. Their Nungwi base is in a small but neat, thatched chalet alongside Parasailing Zanzibar, whilst a kite-mobile is used to transfer kit & kiters to selected beaches in Nungwi & Matemwe (season dependent – Nungwi Jun–end Sep; Matemwe end Dec–Mar), & perform on-the-spot maintenance & repairs. Under the management of Seif Hassan, there are usually 2–4 instructors based here, approx 15 kites, & with proof of certification you can hire equipment here, as well as sign up for lessons.

Motorised watersports The last few years have seen a dramatic change in the range of aquatic activities offered on the north coast. Once strictly a swimming, snorkelling, diving and fishing place, Nungwi now has several companies offering increasingly thrilling, motorised watersports. From stunt wakeboarding to sedate

JET-SKIS: THINK BEFORE YOU HIRE

Jet-skiing is one of the fastest growing watersports; but its arrival on the north coast is understandably controversial. For some it is a thrilling addition to the aquatic activity selection, while for others it is a cause for very real concern. If you do choose to take to the waves, make it an informed decision.

Firstly, remember that you would be unable to hire a motorbike or a speedboat without proper training and a licence; a jet-ski is an equally powerful machine yet neither of these is required. Very careful consideration of your own abilities and experience is necessary before you hire. The waters around Nungwi are full of activity: local dhows and ngalawas sailing, women fishing, carefree holidaymakers swimming and snorkelling, and dive operators doing scuba training. The risk of collision is potentially quite high if you find yourself out of control, and the results horrendous to contemplate.

In addition to the safety issues, there are also areas of shallow reef and diverse resident marine life here, so the environmental impact must be considered. Underwater sound pollution is one of the probable reasons for the decline in north shore dolphin sighting, there have already been cases of damage to the reefs at low tide, and local concerns about the impact on fish breeding habits are understandable.

If you are still keen to hire, the operators listed on pages 234–9 are reliable: the machinery is good quality and well maintained. However, there is a danger in this part of the world that the visible success of a company will encourage less reputable individuals to begin hiring out secondhand, poorly maintained jet-skis. This is likely to result in more sound and fuel pollution and a rise in accidents, so do avoid any casual approaches, however good a deal they appear to be.

parasailing, and jet-ski safaris to fast-paced banana boats, the coastal waters are significantly busier and the range of activities vastly increased.

🪝 Zanzibar Parasailing 📞0779 073078; e hello@zanzibarparasailing.com; www. zanzibarparasailing.com. Parasailing flights are a very recent arrival in Nungwi, & already a popular one. This Turkish-run company uses specially adapted boats, & participants are harnessed to a parasail & then winched into the air from a platform at the rear of the accelerating boat. It's unquestionably thrilling & offers spectacular island panoramas. Solo or tandem 'flights' are possible, as is an optional dip in the sea on your descent. The flight itself is 10mins long, though several people may be on your boat, resulting in a trip lasting up to an hour. In spite of the company's name, parasailing is only one of the thrill-seeking water activities available. Escorted Tumbatu jet-ski safaris (identical in nature to those offered by Zanzibar Watersports, page 236), stereo or mono waterskiing with lessons are available too, & wake-boarding, knee-boarding & an 8-person banana

boat or ringos are also on offer. On a practical note, jet-ski drivers must be over 16, though no experience is necessary; parasailing is open to anyone over 8. Parasailing US$80/120 solo/tandem; jet-ski safari US$200/220 1/2 riders/bike; jet-ski rental US$50/15mins; waterskiing US$45/10mins; wake-boarding US$45/10mins; banana boat US$15pp/15mins; ringos US$30pp/10mins.
Zanzibar Watersports (see full listing under *Diving* section, page 236) Escorted jet-ski safaris (1hr 15mins) head from the Paradise Beach base in Nungwi to Tumbatu, where riders can have a quick swim before pushing on to Kendwa and back around the coast to the watersports centre. Drivers must be over 16 & no experience is necessary; passengers can be as young as 8. 2011 Yamaha 110 HP 4-Stroke jet-skis can also be hired for individual use. Jet-ski safari US$180/200 1/2 riders/bike; jet-ski rental US$50/15mins.

Spa and well-being
Temporary henna tattoos have long been de rigueur in Nungwi. Painted onto your skin by friendly local ladies on the beach, they seem to be a rite of passage for backpackers. As elsewhere on Zanzibar, the beach and bars are full of people with vaguely Arabic- or Celtic-style rings round their biceps. Many clearly believe they look cool; the reality seems highly variable though. Be warned that the henna can badly mark bed linen, which naturally annoys the hotel owners – many will charge for stains. For all-out African beach chic, hair-braiding services are also available by the same ladies, along with basic beach massages. For a less public massage experience, try one of the following.

Baraka White House Spa & Boutique (*Body treatments US$20/hr; manicures US$10*) In a small, immaculate room adjoining Baraka's Restaurant on West Beach, 2 very friendly therapists, Harriet & Tina, offer excellent treatments on kanga-covered massage tables. From deep muscle rubs to Indian head massage, foot treatments to facials, their super little business offers them all. They are both beauty-trained, with Harriet previously having worked in Bluebay's commended East Coast Spa, so the standard is above that available on the beach; that said, this is not in any way a 'spa'.
Malaika Spa (*Body treatments US$30/hr; manicures US$10*) Alongside & linked with Safina Bungalows, this small, neat massage room is home to friendly Conchesta. Trained in Dar, she offers scrubs, facials, beauty treatments & spice

oil massages, both aromatherapy & Ayurvedic. The room is fan cooled, & she tries hard to ensure guests relax & enjoy their treatment.
Peponi Spa (*Body treatments US$50–120/40–80mins; manicures US$40/1hr; waxing & eyebrow tinting/threading US$10–35*) e peponi-spa@rasnungwi.com Set in the tropical gardens of Ras Nungwi Beach Hotel, Peponi Spa offers both guests & non-residents 'an array of rejuvenating, pampering & holistic treatments'. It is the area's best spa by far. Run by internationally qualified therapists & using natural oils & ingredients, treatments are carried out in calm, minimalist rooms decorated with stylish monochrome photographs, billowing linen curtains & freshly picked red hibiscus flowers. With the soothing music & intoxicating aromas of a professional spa

operation, this is a wonderfully relaxing place to spend a few hours, & who could resist the hour-long Peponi Zanzibari Glow (sea salt to exfoliate; aromatic oils to nourish) to bring out their holiday tan?

The Zalu Zanzibar Spa *(Facials US$120/90mins; body treatments US$80–280/60mins–3½hrs; manicures US$55/1hr)* ✆ 0778 683 960; e ezz. retreat@essquehotels.com. Within the Essque Zalu Hotel, this small spa pavilion fans out into sweet-smelling treatment rooms, a Vichy shower room, a sauna/steam & gym area. Using healingEARTH products that blend the organic oils of indigenous African plants, the small team of therapists offer a range of beauty treatments, massages, body polishes & finishing touches from waxing to manicures. There are loungers amid the encircling gardens for pleasant pre- & post-treatment chilling, though the space is limited & it's not a place for all-day relaxing.

Zanzi Yoga m 0776 310 227; e info@ yogazanzibar.com; www.yogazanzibar.com. Founded by South African Marisa van Vuuren, Yoga Zanzibar, based at Flame Tree Cottages, offers individual yoga sessions & longer retreats year-round. Trained in India, Marisa is a registered teacher with the worldwide Yoga Alliance, & teaches relaxation, pranayama (breathing techniques), sun salutations, asanas (postures) & reiki. The teaching comes from Hatha Yoga based on the Ashtanga Primary Series sequence, & classes are suitable for all levels with small groups ensuring a personal approach & flexibility. Yoga Retreats include morning & sunset yoga classes *(*08.00 & 17.15; duration 1hr 15mins)* in the cotton-covered garden pavilion or the sea-facing rooftop, followed by breathing & meditation, & short discussions on yogic techniques. This a lovely option for those seeking some body & mind well-being. Life coaching, fire poi workshops & mandala painting are also available.

Turtle sanctuaries
There are two neighbouring operations which allow close-up turtle viewing in Nungwi's tidal pools. Clear signposts will take you to either, but please read the descriptions of both carefully before planning a visit, as their backgrounds and motives are quite different.

Baraka's Turtle Aquarium Owned by Mr Baraka of Baraka Beach Bungalows on West Beach, this aquarium is signposted at a bend in the road on the way to the East Beach area. It opened in direct competition with the long-established sanctuary scheme at the neighbouring Mnarani Natural Aquarium. Although it has a lovely tidal pool with a couple of large parrotfish, pretty Picasso fish, red snapper & 15 resident green turtles, all of whom appear to be healthy & well fed (for US$4.50 they practically leap out of the pool to take seaweed from your hand), this is fundamentally a business & not a conservation project. To compound this, on our most recent visit we were saddened to be told by a very friendly, if ill-informed, manager that not only could we swim with the turtles (US$6), but that if we held onto the flippers 'like a motorbike' we could ride them too. Clearly, this is a practice to be discouraged in every way & your support is probably better directed at the original rehabilitation & research scheme next door (see listing below).

Mnarani Natural Aquarium ☉ 09.00–18.00 daily. Hawksbill turtles have traditionally been hunted around Zanzibar for their attractive

shells, & green turtles for their meat. In 1993, with encouragement & assistance from various conservation bodies & some dedicated marine biologists, the local community opened the Mnarani Natural Aquarium. In the shadow of the lighthouse, at the northernmost tip of Zanzibar Island, the aquarium was created around a large, natural, tidal pool in the coral rock behind the beach. Originally set up to rehabilitate & study turtles that had been caught in fishing nets, the aquarium project expanded to ensure that local baby turtles were also protected. Turtles used to nest frequently on Nungwi Beach, although sadly, in some part due to hotel lighting, this is now a rare occurrence. If a nest is found, village volunteers now mark & monitor new nests, whilst local fishermen rescuing turtles caught in their nest receive a small fee. The resulting hatchlings are carried to small plastic basins & small concrete tanks at the aquarium where they remain for 10 months. By this time, they have grown to 25cm & their chances of survival at sea are dramatically increased. All bar 1 of these turtles are then released into the sea, along with the largest turtle from the aquarium pool. The 1 remaining baby turtle is then added to the pool, ensuring a static population of 17 turtles. Currently, this equates to 4 hawksbills (Swahili: *ng'amba*), identified by the jagged edge on their shell, sharper beak & sardine diet, & 13 seaweed-loving green turtles (Swahili: *kasakasa*). The aquarium manager, Mr Mataka Kasa, keeps a logbook detailing all eggs, hatchlings & releases. On 5 Jun 2005, the sanctuary released its first tagged turtle as part of a worldwide monitoring programme, & now all large turtles are released with an 'address tag' to track their movements. In spite of the aquarium being little more than a glorified rock pool, it's fascinating to see the turtles at close quarters. Further, the money raised secures the project's future & goes towards local community schemes, in a bid to demonstrate the tangible value of turtle conservation to the local population. With luck, this will lessen the trade in souvenir shell products & ensure the species' survival. When timing your visit, the water is clearest about 2hrs before high tide (Swahili: *maji kujaa*). US$5; 50% discount for children.

Village life

Dhow-building & harbour activity As well as being a tourist destination, Nungwi is also the centre of Zanzibar's traditional dhow-building industry. A number of hardwood trees, particularly good for boats, grow in this area (or at least did grow here, until they were chopped down to be made into boats). Generations of skilled craftsmen have worked on the beach outside the village, turning planks of wood into strong ocean-going vessels, using only the simplest of tools.

It is a fascinating place to see dhows in various stages of construction, but do show respect for the builders, who are generally indifferent towards visitors, and keep out of the way. Most do not like having their photos taken (ask before you use your camera, or join the village tour listed below for easier opportunities), although a few have realised that being photogenic has a value, and will reasonably ask for payment.

Fishing continues to employ many local men, and it's magical to watch the fishing boats bobbing in the sparkling waves of the morning, and then set out to sea in the late afternoon. There can be as many as 40 going out at once, their distinctive lateen sails silhouetted against the evening sky – it's probably been unchanged for centuries. Early in the morning, around 06.00, they return with their catch to the beach fish market. The spectacle is worth the early start, but if you don't make it, there's a smaller re-run at around 15.00 each day.

Like the east coast, Nungwi's other key marine industry centres on its seaweed. Local women tend this recently introduced crop on the flat area between the beach and the low-tide mark. The seaweed is harvested, dried in the sun and sent to Zanzibar Town for export. (For more details, see box, *Sustainable seaweed farming*, page 290.)

Cultural village tour (*US$15pp*) The base for the Nungwi Cultural Village Tours is adjacent to Mnarani Aquarium, and indeed run by the same volunteers. From the clearly marked bungalow, the two-hour walks take in the aquarium, fish market (best visited early morning when the day's catches are landed), mosques, dhow-builders, basket-weavers and even touch on the uses of surrounding medicinal trees. A pleasant, guided trip, it offers visitors a different view of the community here, and gives photographers a great opportunity to capture the dhow-builders (always ask permission first). The money generated from these tours goes back into the community and is donated to a range of beneficiaries, from the kindergarten to the dhow-builders.

Lighthouse The lighthouse at Ras Nungwi is still in operation, although it is not open to visitors. As it is a designated 'strategic point', photographing it is officially not allowed; the marines on guard may point this out. There have been a few muggings in this area, so be aware when walking on the cut-through pathways here, especially if carrying expensive cameras, and be sensible about walking here in anything other than broad daylight.

KENDWA

On the west coast, about 4km south of Nungwi, is the tiny village and beautiful beach of Kendwa. What a relief after the noise and crowded development of Nungwi! It's a serene place (most of the time), with some well-spaced, simple places to stay, a clutch of beach bars, a dive school, and a glorious, wide, sandy beach, which doesn't suffer the vast tidal changes of the east coast.

Until the arrival of La Gemma Dell'Est in late 2005, Kendwa catered almost exclusively to backpackers and those in search of simple, low-budget escapism. Since then, yet more large resorts have been, and continue to be, built on the coast between Les Toits de Palme and Nungwi, yet the main stretch of sand at Kendwa remains a peaceful place to chill out and has a feeling of space not found in neighbouring Nungwi. Development is coming to this part of the coast, but it is slower and the plots not so visibly cramped. Things do liven up in the evenings, with bonfires, barbecues and full-moon beach parties, but apart from these it's a haven of peace. Let's hope it can stay this way.

GETTING THERE AND AWAY From Nungwi you can simply **walk** along the beach at low tide. If you plan on doing this it's imperative that you are aware of tide times before setting off: with steep coral cliff bordering the beach, there is nowhere to escape the incoming tide. It is also worth noting that there have been a few incidents of robbery on the 1.5km stretch of beach between Baobab Beach Bungalows and Diamonds La Gemma Dell'Est, so single travellers are not advised to take this route.

A good option is to travel by **boat** or **canoe** from Nungwi. Several places in Kendwa run a free transfer service, or it's easy to find a local boatman who will take you for a few dollars, but do check their reliability with others first.

If you're **driving**, turn off the main road about 4km south of Nungwi, and follow the very rough, undulating track for about another 2km. A high-clearance vehicle is essential. The public **bus** (Route 14) and **dala dalas** (No 116) from Zanzibar Town to Nungwi will drop you off at the same junction on the tar road, leaving you to walk the final 20 minutes to the sea.

WHERE TO STAY All of Kendwa's accommodation choices are on the coast; there are no village-stay options here. For convenience, they are all listed running from south to north (see map, *Nungwi & Kendwa*, page 220), in the order they would be approached by visitors arriving from Zanzibar Town.

Unless stated otherwise, hotels listed below offer air conditioning and en suite bathrooms as standard,

Kilindi (15 rooms) \024 223 1954; e reservations@kilindi.com; www. elewanacollection.com. Exclusive & upmarket without being pretentious, the complex offers pavilions spread out over 20ha & overlooking a sweep of white beach. Reminiscent of Greek Orthodox churches, the domed, 2-tier pavilions are dotted among the dense, indigenous shrubbery &

each is accessed through heavy wooden Zanzibari doors. Rooms are divided into 2 halves, split by a small flight of steps. On 1 side is the spacious circular bedroom, with a mosquito net-draped dbl bed in the centre & a wardrobe & dressing table around the edge. All are equipped with a safe & a minibar fridge. Outside are his-&-hers plunge pools, 1 raised above the other. On the other side of the stairs is the open-sided bathroom, where the sea is visible from the open window. Below this is a tranquil seating area, strewn with cushions & sunloungers. It's strikingly simple with lovely Moorish detailing in the beaten metal lanterns, coloured glass & little indulgences: Port decanters to tasty petit fours. With a personal butler to bring you whatever you may desire, including your meals, you may never wish to leave your pavilion. However, if you can be tempted away, head for the attractive restaurant & bar for a spiced mixed fruit juice or a deliciously chilled South African wine. This distinctly colonial chic area oozes a casual, funky vibe. The waterfall behind the bar catches the eye, while the umbrella-shaded deck is perfect for b/fast in the sunshine. Dinner on the other hand is served by candlelight next to the infinity pool, & is accompanied by a great selection of world music. The adjoining lounge is adorned with smart black & white photographs, & Wi-Fi enables modern communication. The spa offers massages & body wraps in a laid-back atmosphere. Kilindi is also ecologically sensible, with rainwater collected & stored under each pavilion to keep it cool, whilst also providing water for the pools, showers & toilets. With its extensive grounds & stunning accommodation, this is a place for getting away from the stresses of modern life. Most definitely one of Zanzibar's top spots! 🏖

🏠 **Kendwa Beach Villa** (7 rooms) No contact details. Neighbouring Mocco Villa on a tiny plot, this place seems to be in a perpetual state of semi-completion & is very basic. Accessed up concrete stairs from the beach, the spartan rooms are off a dark central corridor & boast little: orange lino floors, simple beds & an adequate toilet & cold-water shower. Some rooms have a fan, though only some work, & all have dim electrical lighting. There is a thatched beach restaurant, which is a popular hangout for Italian package holidaymakers, & it's best to ask for Mohammed if you're looking for a room. **$$**

🏠 **Mocco Villa** (16 rooms) No contact details. Rebuilt in 2010 following a fire, this small, single-unit villa is in fact a collection of independent rooms. Sitting on the very edge of the coral cliff at the start of a new parade of budget development, Mocco's 4 original rooms are neat & clean with showers & 4-poster beds, although the plastic floor sheeting lets the place down a little. The rooms are all named after island towns, with 'Kidoti' enjoying the best sea view & commanding a consequential

supplement. At the back, a newer block offers very simple rooms, including a family room. There is an affiliate restaurant on the beach from where cocktails can be enjoyed to MTV tunes & traditional seafood specials are served at comfortable coir sofas. Ask for Juma at the restaurant if you're interested in staying here. **$$**

🏠 **Eden Viaggi Kendwa Beach Resort** (90 rooms) www.edenviaggi.it. Originally, the petite sibling of Amaan Bungalows in Nungwi, this place has now been extended & taken over by Italian all-inclusive holidaymakers. Tripling in size in recent years, its rooms run from the sandy beach, up the coral-rock cliff through sloping, tropical gardens to reception & up the bumpy track behind the village. There are 4 categories, from the older rooms in small apricot, castellated buildings to a large 2-storey thatched block of holiday apts & the newly built, spacious deluxes. Those closest to the water command a worthwhile premium. All rooms are simply furnished, have mini fridges, reasonable en-suite facilities, & can accommodate 2–4 people. There is a pool, beach volleyball, soccer, tennis, boules & an extensive all-day entertainment programme. The large beach restaurant & bar (Ngarawa) serves food & drink all day under a huge makuti shade. Alternatively, the Tutti Frutti Bistro dishes up crêpes & *gelato* to residents only, & there is the à la carte Essence, where tagines & Arab *shwarmas* are popular with local expats as well as visitors. Although Kendwa Beach is beautiful, the small section immediately north of here is where the village fisherfolk pull ashore & park their dugouts & nets, & can get a little messy; though arguably this is far preferable to the nightly 'theatre' performed on the beach by Eden's Italian staff. **$$$**

🏠 **La Rosa Dei Venti** In spite of opening only in 2003, La Rosa Dei Venti began to feel decidedly tired & unkempt only a few years later. In mid 2008, it was sold to a new owner & closed for redevelopment. Coastal land is rarely left unused for long in these parts, & by early 2012, construction of an extensive collection of low-lying bungalows was well under way. There may well be a new resort here by the time you visit.

🏠 **Kendwa Rocks** (35 rooms) 📱 0777 415473/5; e booking@kendwarocks.com; www.kendwarocks.com. The 1st property to open on this stretch of beach, Kendwa Rocks celebrated its 15th birthday in 2010. It's part-owned & run by Ally Kilupy, a Zanzibari Rastafarian who grew up welcoming tourists at his mother's guesthouse in Stone Town before spending some time in Germany & south London, & completing a trans-African motorbike trip. On his return to Zanzibar, Ally put his tourism skills to use & now runs a successful operation here. There's a wide range of accommodation, getting booked up roughly in order of luxury. The coral-stone bungalows are all named after African countries with suitably themed interiors. All have large Zanzibari beds & a veranda; each has mains electricity & mosquito nets. Most of these rooms can be used for dbl or trpl occupancy. The beach bungalows are spread out in a semicircle on a lovely stretch of sand. They are constructed from coconut panels & makuti, & all boast lots of lights, simple cane furniture & an inviting batik hammock on their private verandas; only a few steps from the sea, their location is excellent. Above the bungalows & beach area, towards the road, are 8 new rooms in the 2-storey North & South wings. They have nice sea views from the shared balcony. There's a terrace of simple, motel-style rooms; small, with a shared ablution block, & usually used by guests arriving without a reservation. There is also a 19-bed mixed dorm for use by groups of off-duty VSO workers & those waiting for space elsewhere. Here, there are 2 rows of sgl, net-covered beds & a bank of lockers with a functional, if not pretty, shower & toilet block immediately behind; check at the time of booking as there has been talk of creating a new dorm. On the beach, the Mermaid Bar is the epitome of backpacker drinking dens: a hip DJ messes on decks in the corner, smiling staff stand behind a well-stocked bar festooned with laminated lists of cocktails, while sun-kissed travellers recline writing diaries & drinking. In addition, a boat-shaped beach bar has opened on the foreshore, serving Italian coffees, juices & spirits, & is surrounded by chunky timber furniture (the remnants of a cargo ship) & a bonfire area. The place is totally chilled, so don't expect anything to happen fast, just sit back & enjoy the sea views. On Sat nights (22.30 onwards) the bar hosts an infamous beach party (US$7pp), a messy affair that's often still in full swing at sunrise. Revellers come from all over the island to experience the cocktails, bonfires, dance beats, acrobatic shows, &, somewhat bizarrely, the Michael Jackson impressionist. Things can get a bit rowdy, & the frequency, scale & noise from this event, & other Kendwa copycat events, are starting to change the atmosphere here a little. Complaints from beach-lovers seeking a tranquil retreat are on the rise but if it's your thing, the monthly Full Moon Party may be worth checking out. **$$–$$$**

🏠 **Sunset Bungalows** (80 rooms) m 0777 413818/414647; e sunsetbungalows@hotamil.com, sunsetbungalows@gmail.com; www.sunsetkendwa. com. An increasingly faded, upturned surfboard on the beach marks Sunset Bungalows' location. The board is in fact the sign for a sizeable beachside structure, once a backpackers' drinking den known as the 'Bikini Bar', but now clearly aiming at a more affluent crowd – though Happy Hour has stuck (15.30–18.30; 2 cocktails for US$7). Outside, on wide wooden decking, diners indulge in Zanzibari curries with chapattis (US$5–8), stone-baked pizza (US$4–5) & surf 'n' turf grills (US$8–10). On the beach in front is a shaded hammock area & a bonfire pit surrounded by wooden benches, making it a popular after-dinner drinks spot, while floodlit beach volleyball keeps the energetic entertained, & the relaxed laze in the local massage tent. Set back from the sea, on the beach behind the restaurant & bar, 2 widely separated rows of bungalows have been built. Of either timber or stone, these are extremely pleasant with bold fabrics, mains electricity, an electronic safe & AC in some. A terrace in front of each looks out onto sand & feathery casuarinas. Higher up, on the coral cliff above the beach, the standard rooms (no AC) are in thatched cottages dotted around a pretty garden, overflowing with hibiscus & bougainvillea. Huge 'apt' buildings at the rear offer spacious rooms with high ceilings, coconut-wood furniture, built-in cushioned baraza benches & garden-view terraces. 2 large apricot-coloured buildings, Chaza & Lulu. each have spacious rooms with sweeping views over baby palms. The quaint beach retreat vibe of Sunset may have faded with development, but it remains a reliably good choice on this stretch of beach & is remarkably convenient for divers using Scuba Do (see *What to see and do*, page 247). Be warned, though – the DJ at the Fri night beach party could well be spinning his discs until gone 04.00. **$$–$$$**

🏠 **White Sands Beach Hotel** (32 rooms) PO Box 732, Kendwa; m 0777 411326; e ajvtours@zanlink. com. There has been fairly constant, low-level renovation & rebuilding at White Sands, though our last visit revealed the possibility of it all being absorbed & redeveloped by a new neighbouring property. This may or may not materialise. At the time of writing, the reception & all of the accommodation is perched on a coral cliff above the beach & is surrounded by neat gardens filled with aloes, papaya & bougainvillea. The cosy standard rooms are clean & functional. The bright-red floor, fabric-screened wardrobe, wall-mounted fan, cheerful paintings & concrete baraza with cushions & table are all perfectly adequate. A little larger & with a beach-view terrace are the mid-class rooms; significantly larger in size, the king-size rooms have a large dbl bed, with plenty of room for another & a bigger terrace. The floors in these rooms are covered with dyed makuti mats, whilst the walls are decorated with African murals: the artwork of local talent, Moses. The mock rock art & swaying Maasai dancers may be a little crude for some but the rooms are certainly bright & individual. All have en-suite bathrooms, but the standard-class rooms do not yet have hot water. The newest rooms are tucked behind the old in cottages with flat roofs & a tin shade over the veranda. They have large square bedrooms with huge Zanzibari beds, blue kanga curtains to offset the brilliant white walls & hot-water en suites. None of the later rooms has a sea view which may be a negative at the price, though it's barely a stagger to the beach. There are no safes in the rooms, but a deposit box is available at reception. If you're accessing White Sands from the beach, look out for the old oil barrel suspended under a small makuti shade & the lodge's red & white sun & sail logo. The drum is the restaurant's outside advertisement: 'Lobster tomorrow? Ask today! Kitchen open all day.' Whether you go for the lobster or the alternative burgers, curries & pizzas (US$4–8), the large circular bar & split-level restaurant is a fun hangout. Built on the beach, it has swings to rival bar stools & a sunken central lounge filled with cushion-covered coir-rope sofas facing the satellite TV. A surrounding raised platform of tables for 2 creates a feeling of enclosure, & a couple of king-size beds are laid out for those lazy afternoons, & punters can even treat themselves to a relaxing massage here. Standard & mid-class **$$**; new room **$$$**

⌂ **Les Toits de Palme** (10 rooms) m 0777 418548/0777 851474; e depalme@live.com. Under joint French–Zanzibari ownership, Les Toits de Palme has retained its simplicity & size whilst all around has been magnified. Its simple rooms are in bungalows raised above the beach on coral rock. Decorated in white & marine blue, each has a free-

standing fan, hot-water shower & dbl/twin beds. They are a little tired, but clean & with a lovely view of the beach. In addition, there are also new bandas down on the sand, each of which has varnished palm sides, a tiled floor, mossie nets & dbl or twin beds. They offer fabulous views & there is 1 concrete cottage in a similar vein. There's generator electricity from 18.00–midnight, when the atmospheric light of storm lanterns takes over. On the beach, a round shaded deck houses the simple restaurant, whose badly misspelt menu offers fresh salads (US$4), pizza & pasta (both US$5–7) as well as appealing Swahili specialities such as Chuku Chuku stew (*US$5*). Being a little distanced from the beach party bars further south gives a pleasant retreat feel, but at the time of writing there is currently a land dispute court case regarding this place, which could spell imminent change. **$–$$**

⌂ **Uzuri Zanzibar** On the site of Kendwa Breezes Beach Lodge, Czech developers were on site & negotiating to level & redevelop this plot in 2012. Plans for a 100-room, luxury villa resort with a well-known Middle Eastern hotel management company were touted, & we await news of them coming to fruition … or not.

⌂ **Diamonds La Gemma Dell'Est** (96 rooms) \024 2240013; e fo.gemma@diamonds-reosrts. com; www.diamonds-resorts.com. La Gemma Dell'Est is a large hotel, managed by the Swiss-based Italian firm PlanHotel SA, & is still one of the more stylish of Zanzibar's large resorts. Sensitive architecture & stunning landscaping create a feeling of tremendous space, while minimal tidal changes allow for swimming in the sea all day. The hotel's rooms have been cleverly built along the natural contours of the landscape, making them appear lower-density & fairly unobtrusive, while also allowing each a sea-view veranda. Approach corridors may be dark, but inside the rooms are comfortable, each having a king-size bed or twin beds with mosquito net, satellite TV, minibar, electronic safe & an en-suite marble bathroom; everything you'd expect from a good, modern hotel. Thoughtfully planted screens offer privacy on each terrace & the lawns & swathes of established exotic vegetation make a beautiful foreground to the setting sun over the Indian Ocean. The beach here is wide & beautiful, with nice loungers & makuti umbrellas dotted around the raked sand. The enormous, floodlit pool is also set right on the beach, with a children's area, jacuzzi, waterfall & swim-up cocktail bar. There is hotel security on the beach to ensure no hassle for sunbathers yet Kendwa's clutch of beach bungalows & their associated bars & restaurants are an easy 10min walk south. La Gemma has several bars & restaurants, from the sleek Pavilion serving tasty Mediterranean buffets to the Coral Cove al fresco pizzeria by the pool, & the intimate, à la carte seafood restaurant, Sea Breeze, at the end of the jetty. With the exception of the last, all food & drink is on a totally flexible, all-inclusive basis, & the Italian influence ensures that the food is invariably very good. By day, there's a PADI diving centre (see *What to see and do*, opposite), outdoor gym, countless watersports, beach volleyball, sailing & even snorkelling over the artificial reef – created when the jetty was built – to keep everyone occupied, then the selection of optional evening entertainment kicks off with everything from quizzes to musical Swahili beach BBQs. Children are well catered for, & the staff's attitude is extremely positive towards families, making La Gemma 1 of Zanzibar's best choices for those with kids. 👑

🏠 **Diamonds Star of the East** (11 villas) 📞024 2240089; e info.sote@diamonds-resorts. com; http://staroftheeast.diamonds-resorts.com. A hotel within a hotel, Star of the East is the swish new sibling of La Gemma, & sits within its grounds, though masked from view & guests by a high wall & grandiose tower entrance. A member of Small Luxury Hotels of the World, the 1- & 2-bedroomed villas are seriously stylish: amazing contemporary bedrooms are flooded with natural light. There are high-end fixtures & fittings, waterfalls & fountains, walk-in wardrobes, indoor & outdoor showers, a glazed courtyard, a beautiful keyhole pool in the spacious garden, cushioned daybeds, & a lounge with all the latest mod cons. If you need anything, personal butlers carry pagers 24/7 & have 6mins to be at your beck & call! The fine dining Ocean Blue restaurant & Tiara bar are in a thatched building at the centre of the complex, around which the pool snakes seductively. It's stylised & very sophisticated, but it all comes with an exceptional price tag, & however luxurious, it's hard to justify when the resort is not directly on the beach & is surrounded by an all-inclusive resort & a neighbouring construction site. There are far more private places at this end of the market, not that this appears to be affecting occupancy levels. Access to all the facilities at La Gemma is included. 👑

🍴 WHERE TO EAT

Virtually all the hotels on Kendwa Beach have an affiliated beach bar and restaurant offering cold drinks, casual dining and uninterrupted sea views. The menus and quality are close to identical, relying heavily on the day's catch for fresh seafood, with a number of Swahili curry and fresh pizza options. They are all open to anyone who cares to wander by and, as with many places on Zanzibar, this includes a number of friendly (and hungry) neighbourhood cats.

SHOPPING

With the increase in accommodation and visitors, Kendwa now has two small, local-style 'supermarkets': **Ndiro Supermarket** on the very edge of the cliff at the southern end of the beach and **Mwakamini Supermarket** on the village side of Kendwa Rocks. Both sell basic supplies of tinned food, crisps, sweets and water, but little else. For **curios**, the ever-increasing span of Maasai-manned stalls on the beach bordering La Gemma offers colourful paintings, beaded jewellery and occasionally carvings. Quality varies considerably so shop around and don't be blinded by the sun into making second-rate purchases.

WHAT TO SEE AND DO

Sunbathing, beach volleyball, diving and snorkelling are the main activities in Kendwa – it's a terribly laid-back beach hangout. The vast majority of the hotels and guesthouses will hire out basic snorkelling gear, organise day trips by boat to Tumbatu Island, and offer sunset dhow cruises; some will rent out kayaks, too.

Watersports

For fun below the waterline, Kendwa's now has two primary dive operators:

Scuba Do Diving (UK) +44 (0)1326 250773; m 0777 417157/0748 415179; e do-scuba@scuba-do-zanzibar.com; www.scubado.demon.co.uk, www.scuba-do-zanzibar.com. Until recently, Scuba Do was Kendwa's only dive operation. Owned & operated by a British couple, Christian & Tammy, it is a highly professional & well-equipped dive centre, based on the beach next to Sunset Bungalows' restaurant (& at La Gemma for resort guests). As well as a thoroughly nice guy, Christian is a PADI Master Instructor & the only Emergency First Response Instructor Trainer in Tanzania; Tammy is a PADI Master Scuba Diver Trainer & exceptional at teaching even the youngest children to snorkel & dive. She is also one of the hyperbaric chamber operators. There are up to 10 permanent dive leaders based here (season dependent), taking a max of 6 divers each to 1 of their repertoire of 20+ reef sites, chosen according to conditions & diver experience. Diving is done from 6 high-powered RIBs (rigid inflatable boats), allowing fast access to dive sites (Mnemba is reached in 30mins, as opposed to nearly 2hrs by dhow), & GPS navigation pinpoints precise dive entry points. There's plenty of good, new equipment – 'Buddy Explorer' BCDs, Sherwood regulators, masks & fins, & Reef wetsuits – & they have a code of stringent safety procedures. We were impressed that all divers are issued with surface marker buoys, whilst marine radios maintain contact between boats & base. Their on-site Bauer air compressor is regularly tested, & there's an emergency oxygen re-breather & a full medical kit. As part of this adherence to safety, Scuba Do will not

INTERNATIONAL COASTAL CLEAN-UP DAY

On the third Saturday of September every year since 2005, the team at Scuba Do Diving has galvanised Kendwa into a successful beach tidy. As part of International Coastal Clean-up Day, co-ordinated by conservation foundations Project AWARE and Ocean Conservancy, the aim is to collect and prevent debris littering seaside locations and aquatic environments, thus protecting their beauty and health. In Kendwa, the initiative has been greeted enthusiastically by villagers, residents, hotel staff and even thoughtful tourists, and their efforts to make a difference are clear: Kendwa does have one of the island's cleanest beaches. Ideally, the village will ultimately take ownership of this event, and to effect this Scuba Do have provided wheelbarrows to help with ongoing collection.

At the first beach clean-up, 82 people (75% from the local community) collected 108 bags (730kg) of rubbish, but only two years later, in 2007, this had grown to 106 volunteers and a massive 1,002kg in 168 bags. Sadly, the composition of the rubbish is changing too, and while village waste declines, tourist waste increases. Whilst this increase in litter, a manmade mix of drinks bottles, food wrappers, discarded building materials and plastic bags, is disturbing, this community's involvement to better the environment is positive.

Tammy and Christian at Scuba Do are totally committed to their community and work hard throughout the year to educate local schoolchildren and elders, as well as many hotels, about the effects of rubbish on the environment. In an impressively shrewd move, their latest initiative is to photograph the collected rubbish and send the images to companies whose branding is clearly visible. The aim being to request their assistance in promoting social awareness of litter related problems.

Do help their efforts by disposing of rubbish responsibly and if you're on holiday in the area in mid September, don a pair of rubber gloves and join in the clean-up campaign: snorkellers can fill crates in the shallows whilst landlubbers comb the sand. Be sure to guess the total waste weight too, and you may even win a prize at the end of the day.

take any divers underwater without proof of their qualification & insist on a US$50 PADI refresher dive with anyone who hasn't been underwater for 6 months or boasts fewer than 100 logged dives. When out of the water, the team are also involved in extensive community work, most notably their commitment to training Zanzibaris & Tanzanians to become qualified dive masters & instructors, & the annual beach & underwater clean-up project (see box, *International Coastal Clean-up Day*, page 247). Snorkelling trips US$45-85 Tumbatu/Mnemba; US$120/230/330/420 for 2/4/6/8 dives; scuba equipment hire US$15/day; digital camera hire (inc CD) US$50.

Zanzibar Watersports 024 2233039; m 0773 235030; e info@zanzibarwatersports.com; www. zanzibarwatersports.com. The 3rd island base for this established watersports company is at Kendwa Rocks. In a purpose-built, thatched bungalow, efficient staff can arrange PADI courses & an array of watersports, both motorised & not, using good-quality equipment. Full company details can be seen in their main Nungwi listing (see page 236). US$65/115/310/460 (plus US$30 for Mnemba) for 1/2/6/10 dives (inc equipment); refresher US$30; Open Water US$499; Advanced US$310; equipment hire (mask, fins, snorkel) US$15; kayaks US$10pp/hr; waterskiing US$50/15mins.

MKOKOTONI

On the west coast of the island, about 21km south of Nungwi, Mkokotoni is a lively fishing village. Although there's no accommodation here that we could find, it's worth a short detour to soak up some rural atmosphere and vibrant village life. The bustling market, where Tumbatuans and local Zanzibaris buy and sell all manner of fresh seafood, is crowded, noisy and full of energy. Around this, an abundance of tumbledown stalls display piles of coconuts, fruits, vegetables and spices whilst in the harbour behind age-old techniques are used to repair and build the next generation of dhows.

In 1984, a major hoard of Chinese coins was discovered on the beach north of the village, indicating that this was once a prosperous trading port between the East, Arabia and Zanzibar, long before the arrival of the Europeans. Colonial rule brought the few grand administration buildings glimpsed along the central avenue of sweet almond trees, but today village life is still centred on simple trade with neighbours.

GETTING THERE AND AWAY Few tourists visit Mkokotoni, and those who do are usually part of a **tour** *en route* to Tumbatu Island. The village can be accessed on a fast tar road from both Mahonda to the south and Kivunge to the east.

By public **bus**, Route 1 runs hourly from approximately 05.30 to 20.00 from Darajani Terminal in Zanzibar Town to Mkokotoni; as do frequent **dala dalas** (No 101) from Creek Road.

REGIONAL EXCURSIONS

About 12km south of Nungwi, on the main road to/from Zanzibar Town, are the ruins at Fukuchani and Mvuleni. These are the remains of large houses dating from the 16th century. They're worth a short stop if you're **driving** this way, and a possible excursion from Nungwi if lying on the beach gets too much.

FUKUCHANI RUINS Fukuchani Ruins are on the edge of the village of the same name. Beside a large school on the western side of the road, there's a small signpost under a baobab tree which will point you in the right direction, along a track that bisects the local football pitch. The ruins are known locally as the 'Portuguese House', but although some Portuguese settlers may have built houses on Zanzibar during this period, this structure is considered by archaeologists to be of Swahili and not foreign origin. The ruins are well maintained and the surrounding land has been mostly cleared of vegetation.

Built in the 16th century, Fukuchani is a fortified dwelling that may have belonged to a wealthy merchant or farmer. It is constructed of coral bricks, with arched doorways and rectangular niches in the walls of the main room, and surrounded by a stone wall in which small holes have been inserted. It has been suggested that these are gun slits for the purposes of defence, but a more recent theory suggests they may have been to hold projecting beams which supported a raised walkway, so that anyone inside the enclosure could see over the wall. The ruins are in good condition, compared with many others on Zanzibar of a similar age, and quite impressive. Buildings of a similar style have been found at other sites along the East African coast, though – alongside the ruins at Mvuleni – Fukuchani represents the finest domestic stone house architecture of this period.

Behind the ruin, a path leads to a small beach. Across the channel you can see Tumbatu Island, with the lighthouse at its northern tip clearly visible. At the southern end of the island are the remains of a large town, dating from around the 12th century. (For more details, see box, *Tumbatu Island*, below.)

MVULENI RUINS Mvuleni Ruins lie just to the south of Fukuchani, on the other side of the road (east), where you'll see a small signpost. Next to a few huts and a small shop, a path leads through banana and palm plantations to reach the site. Like Fukuchani, this structure was probably once a fortified house that would have belonged to a powerful member of the community. It, too, was thought to be the work of Portuguese invaders until recent research suggested that it is more likely to be Swahili in origin. The house was once larger than the one at Fukuchani, with thicker walls, but the ruins are in poor condition, and are partly overgrown, obscuring some of the architectural features. Substantial sections of the walls remain standing, though, complete with carved door arches, conveying something of the impressive building that this once was. One of the most interesting features of this house is the large natural cavern just northeast of the house, outside the main wall. Crystal-clear, salt water flows through the cave, collecting in a pool visible beyond an entrance fringed by vegetation: this was probably a source of water when the house was occupied.

TUMBATU ISLAND

Tumbatu is one of the largest of Zanzibar's offshore islands, measuring about 8km long by 2–3km across. The people of the island, the Watumbatu, speak their own dialect of Swahili. They have a reputation for pride and aloofness, and are reputed not to welcome visitors to their island. The Watumbatu men are traditionally known as the best sailors on Zanzibar, or even on the whole east African coast.

On the southern end of Tumbatu Island are a group of Shirazi ruins, thought to date from the 12th century. An Arab geographer writing in the 13th century recorded that the Muslim people of Zanzibar Island were attacked (by whom is not clear) and retreated to Tumbatu Island where they were welcomed by the local inhabitants, who were also Muslim, and it is assumed that these people were responsible for the Shirazi ruins.

The ruins were probably abandoned in the early 16th century, but the Watumbatu still claim to be descended from Shirazi immigrants.

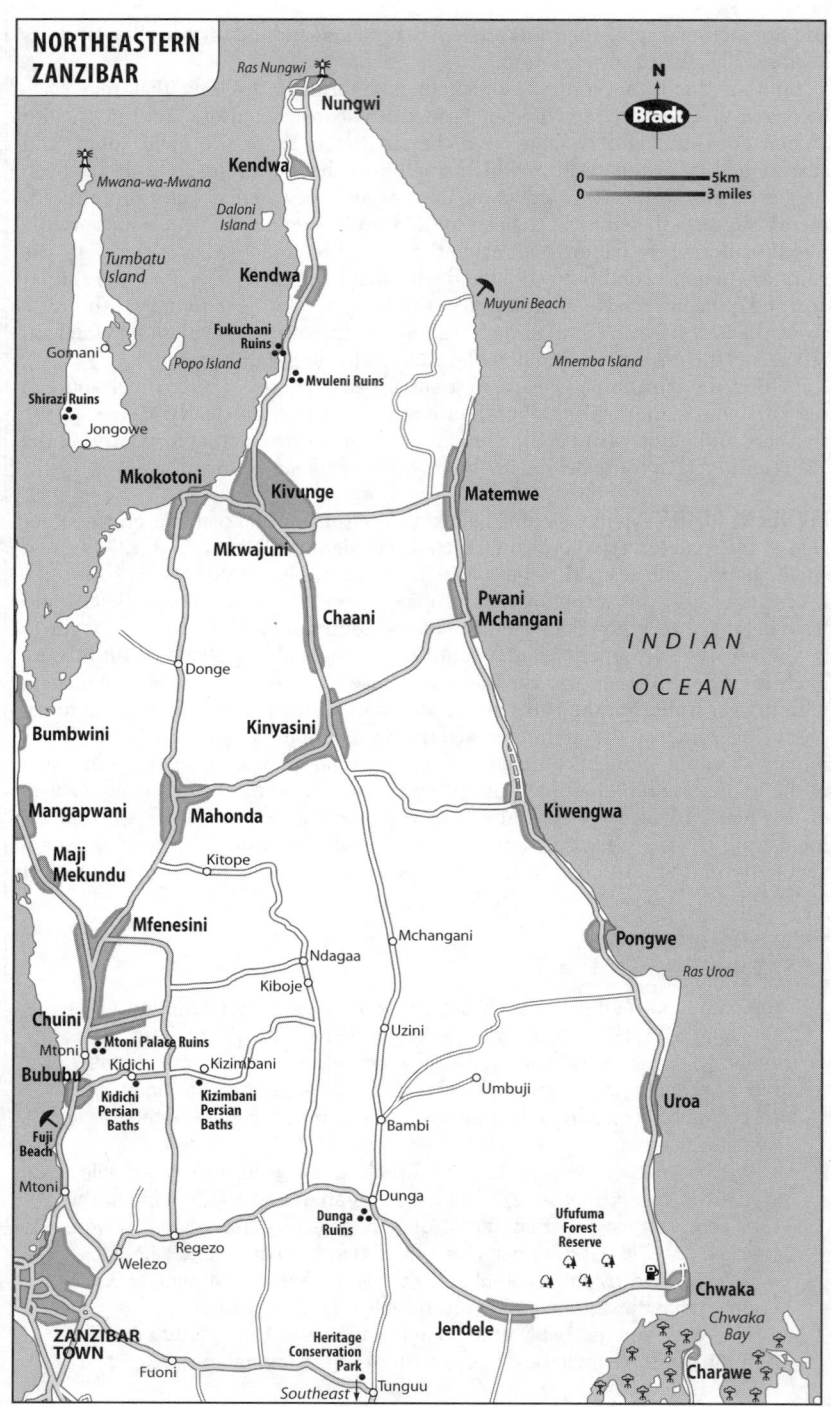

NORTHEASTERN ZANZIBAR

Ras Nungwi
Nungwi
Kendwa
Mwana-wa-Mwana
Daloni Island
Kendwa
Tumbatu Island
Muyuni Beach
Fukuchani Ruins
Gomani
Popo Island
Mvuleni Ruins
Mnemba Island
Shirazi Ruins
Jongowe
Mkokotoni
Kivunge
Matemwe
Mkwajuni
Pwani Mchangani
Chaani
INDIAN
OCEAN
Donge
Kinyasini
Bumbwini
Mahonda
Kiwengwa
Mangapwani
Kitope
Maji Mekundu
Mfenesini
Ndagaa
Mchangani
Pongwe
Kiboje
Ras Uroa
Chuini
Uzini
Mtoni Palace Ruins
Mtoni
Kidichi
Kizimbani
Bububu
Kidichi Persian Baths
Kizimbani Persian Baths
Umbuji
Fuji Beach
Bambi
Uroa
Mtoni
Dunga
Regezo
Dunga Ruins
Ufufuma Forest Reserve
Welezo
Chwaka
ZANZIBAR TOWN
Heritage Conservation Park
Jendele
Chwaka Bay
Fuoni
Tunguu
Charawe
Southeast

N
Bradt
0   5km
0   3 miles

250

9

Northeastern Zanzibar

The east coast of Zanzibar boasts an almost continuous expanse of picture-perfect beach; it's arguably the island's greatest attraction for visitors. Stretching from Nungwi on the northernmost tip of the island to the mangrove swamps of Chwaka Bay, the superb, powder white-sand beaches of the northeastern coastline are breathtaking in length and beauty. Less than 1km offshore, waves break along the fringe reef which runs the length of the island, and the warm, turquoise waters of the Indian Ocean attract divers, swimmers and fishermen. Bordering the sand, an almost unbroken strip of picturesque coconut palms provides shade for traditional fishing villages and sunbathing honeymooners, and completes many people's vision of paradise.

The beaches along Zanzibar's east coast slope very little. Consequently, when the tide is out, the water retreats a long way, making swimming from the beach difficult. It does, however, allow for fascinating exploration along the top of the exposed reef. Washed-up seaweed can also be a surprise here for uninformed visitors, see box, page 272.

Compared with those found in Nungwi to the north, the accommodation choices in the northeast tend to have more space, both in their private grounds and between properties. However, most are still within easy walking distance along the seashore, and make useful refreshment stops on long beach walks. The central stretch of the coast around Kiwengwa is the busiest, with its cluster of large, Italian, package-holiday resorts, but there has been less tourism development to the north or south of this area, and it's still possible to find some lovely, individual places that seem to be virtually on their own.

Access from Zanzibar Town to the east coast is easy, on both private and public transport. The extension of the tar road has improved the journey and shortened transfer times, though close to the sea there is currently little more than a narrow, bumpy track connecting the villages from Pongwe to Matemwe, necessitating very slow progress and either a 4x4 vehicle or the hastening of the end for your vehicle's suspension.

MATEMWE

A long, linear village, Matemwe is the most northerly of the east coast settlements. Although less than 20km south of Nungwi, it marks the end of the coastal road heading north. It's a quintessential Swahili fishing village: little houses set among masses of elegant coconut palms with dhows and ngalawa (dugout canoes) bobbing in the water. The sand is so white and smooth here that the wind blows it into mounds that look like snowdrifts. In spite of some recent expansion, this remains a quieter section of coast, with some great accommodation options and the added bonus of swift access to Mnemba's reefs for divers.

Matemwe is very much a working beach, especially close to the village centre, and this is part of its attraction for visitors looking for just a bit more than sea and sunshine. The main employment here is fishing, and the dhows and ngalawa go out most evenings, delivering their catch onto the beach in the morning. There's also some seaweed farming here: look out for the makeshift racks of purple fronds drying in the sun. The local people are relatively friendly and don't seem to mind tourists watching the scene, but this isn't a spot to be intrusive with in-your-face photography.

Sadly, like many villages on the island, Matemwe has a litter problem. In spite of Matemwe Lodge arranging regular rubbish collections, plastic bags and general household garbage can be seen caught in bushes and strewn on the ground. With continued assistance from local hotels, this will hopefully improve.

GETTING THERE AND AWAY If you are **driving**, there is a direct road to Matemwe from Mkwajuni, on the island's central north–south road. Alternatively, turn east after Kinyasini to Pwani Mchangani, and head north along the new tar road.

If you're staying at one of Matemwe's smarter accommodation options, **transfers** to/from Zanzibar Town can be arranged by them. Alternatively, a private **taxi** or **minibus** can be organised by a Zanzibar Town tour company or hotel (see *Chapter 6, Tour companies*, pages 134–7).

By public transport, there's a frequent daily **dala dala** service (No 118) and public **bus** (Route 16) from Zanzibar Town to Matemwe village, which then continues up the coast to within about 2km of Matemwe Lodge.

WHERE TO STAY Unless stated otherwise, hotels listed below offer air conditioning and en-suite bathrooms as standard.

Travelling from north to south along the beach, the various options for accommodation are:

Kasha Boutique Hotel (11 rooms)
m 0776 676611/22; e info@kasha-zanzibar.com; www.kasha-zanzibar.com. Accessed down a very bumpy track, Kasha is the northernmost hotel in Matemwe, located on the top of a coral cliff. Despite being on a sizeable plot, the villas are crammed into 2 close rows set just back from the beach. Inside each is a substantial open-plan living room & bedroom. In the centre of the room is a plasma TV which has no channels but can be used to watch one of the limited DVDs available from reception. There's a powerful shower, twin sinks & an Arabian-style bath but no door except on the toilet, so be prepared to get familiar with your travelling companion. From the bedroom, glass doors lead out to the patio, where there's a plunge pool & a cushioned baraza for lazy afternoons. The view depends on which row the villa is in – from the front row it's across the natural vegetation to the sea, but from the back row it's the villa directly in front. This also means that 2nd-row villas are lacking in privacy: the room access path runs immediately in front of the terraces & plunge pools. All rooms are equipped with safes, & European plugs, but adaptors are available. Towards the beach, there's an infinity pool with views across to Mnemba, a small poolbar & a simple spa. A coastal path & some wooden stairs lead down to the sea, which at high tide covers the bottom few steps, swallowing the beach. Various signboards along this route have formal health & safety disclaimers on them – & there are additional ones in the rooms – making swimming off-putting for some, & certainly less carefree for most. Away from the beach, the high-ceilinged makuti-thatched main area contains the Nargili Bar, where guests can try the cocktail of the day (US$9, or US$6 during happy hour 18.30–19.30), the Sama Restaurant, where à la carte b/fasts & pretty basic European-style dinners are served, a TV room & a small curio shop. Although well-finished & relaxed, with plenty of comforts, Kasha is a fairly pricey place, which doesn't quite live up to expectation, but this doesn't discourage the young honeymooners who rave about it. FB. 👑

⌂ **Zi Villa** (4 rooms) ✆ (South Africa) +27 (82) 8233347/+27 (11) 7983600; e allan@starlight. co.za; www.zivilla.co.za. North of Matemwe village, in a bay called Fisherman's Cove, Zi Villa is a private villa owned & let by a South African couple. This large, well-equipped house is an excellent base for groups who are comfortable being relatively remote & self-sufficient. Stylish, spacious interiors, packed with interesting *objets d'art*, all mod cons & a superb view out to Mnemba Island are all guaranteed. The eloquent Zanzibari manager, Seif, & the housekeeping team, including a nightwatchman & resident chef, do their utmost to accommodate requests. There are 4 bedrooms, 3 dbls & a twin, 3 of which have direct access to a large wraparound deck & an en-suite bathroom. The upstairs master bedroom, or Sultan's Suite, has an enormous bed, large TV with video player, private sundeck, indoor jacuzzi & its own bathroom. There is 24hr mains electricity & hot water. The bright, light & airy lounge has comfortable sofas, a satellite TV & DVD player, a library of English books, & access to the pool deck through large French doors. Here, there's a deep pool, with great sea views, & a sunbathing area of hammocks & loungers. The fully stocked Fifo Bar, complete with pool table, music centre & dartboard, also accesses the deck & beach, & completes the package. FB. 🍴

⌂ **Matemwe Retreat** (4 rooms) m 0777 475788/0774 414834; e reservations@ asilialodges.com, matemweretreat@asiliaafrica. com; www.asiliaafrica.com. Bordering Matemwe Lodge is its exceptional younger sibling, Matemwe Retreat. Comprising just 4 imposing, castellated villas, the Retreat is one of Zanzibar's most impressive & exclusive places to stay. Each villa has been thoughtfully & creatively designed & has strikingly unusual interiors, panoramic ocean views, a private roof terrace & highly original, locally produced furnishings. The heavy timber entrance allows access to the enormous private deck, where dbl hammocks gently sway, sofas invite siestas & a dhow-shaped peninsula table anticipates dinner *à deux*. The interior is decorated in neutral coffee & cream colours, with a mix of Swahili style & minimalist tendencies, & thoughtful touches like luxurious linens & modern conveniences are indicative of the attention to detail & price tag. There is a king-size bed, plenty of storage, a private bar & good use

of reclaimed dhow-wood throughout. The large bathroom boasts a circular shower (complete with star-like LED ceiling), separate toilet & a bath beside the sea-facing picture window for truly indulgent soaking. At the top of the internal spiral staircase, a door leads to the idyllic private roof terrace. A 2-tier area, half is devoted to sun worshippers & the other to a super-sized corner sofa under pole shading. With an easterly outlook, the terrace catches the first rays of dawn, making for wonderful photographs & all-day sunbathing. There is also an infinity plunge pool, complete with alcove waterfall, which offers stupendous views. Service is top-notch with a friendly villa butler taking care of your every need. Menus are discussed daily & almost anything seasonally available is prepared on request. Food & drinks can be served anywhere: the beach, roof terrace or veranda. Retreat guests can use the small beach that the villas share, & are also free to walk the neat sandy paths to Matemwe Lodge (5mins) & have free use of all of their communal facilities. It's important for sociable guests to realise, however, that there are no public areas at Matemwe Retreat itself – no central lounge, bar or restaurant. This is really a place to get away from it all & indulge in exclusive solitude. FB. 🍴

⌂ **Matemwe Lodge** (12 rooms) m 0777 414834; e matemwe@asiliaafrica.com; www. asiliaafrica.com; ⏱ Jun–Mar. Just past the northern edge of Matemwe village, occupying a windswept spot beside a sweeping sandy beach, Matemwe Lodge is a very good, smart yet informal place. Popular with well-travelled, unpretentious couples, it's relaxed & quiet & is not really the place for families seeking action-packed adventures. Perched on the edge of a low coral cliff, lapped by the waves, each of the thatched cottages has a superb view across the water to Mnemba Island. All rooms have been upgraded into impressively stylish, individual suites, some split-level, with private, curved verandas. Coconut-wood dbl beds are covered in bright appliqué throws; polished concrete floors are strewn with cheerful woven mats; & wooden lattice shutters conceal built-in wardrobe space. The newer suites have decadent baths, as well as a sunken, cushioned baraza that looks out through wide shutters to the sea. On the terrace, a dbl hammock & director's chairs make the

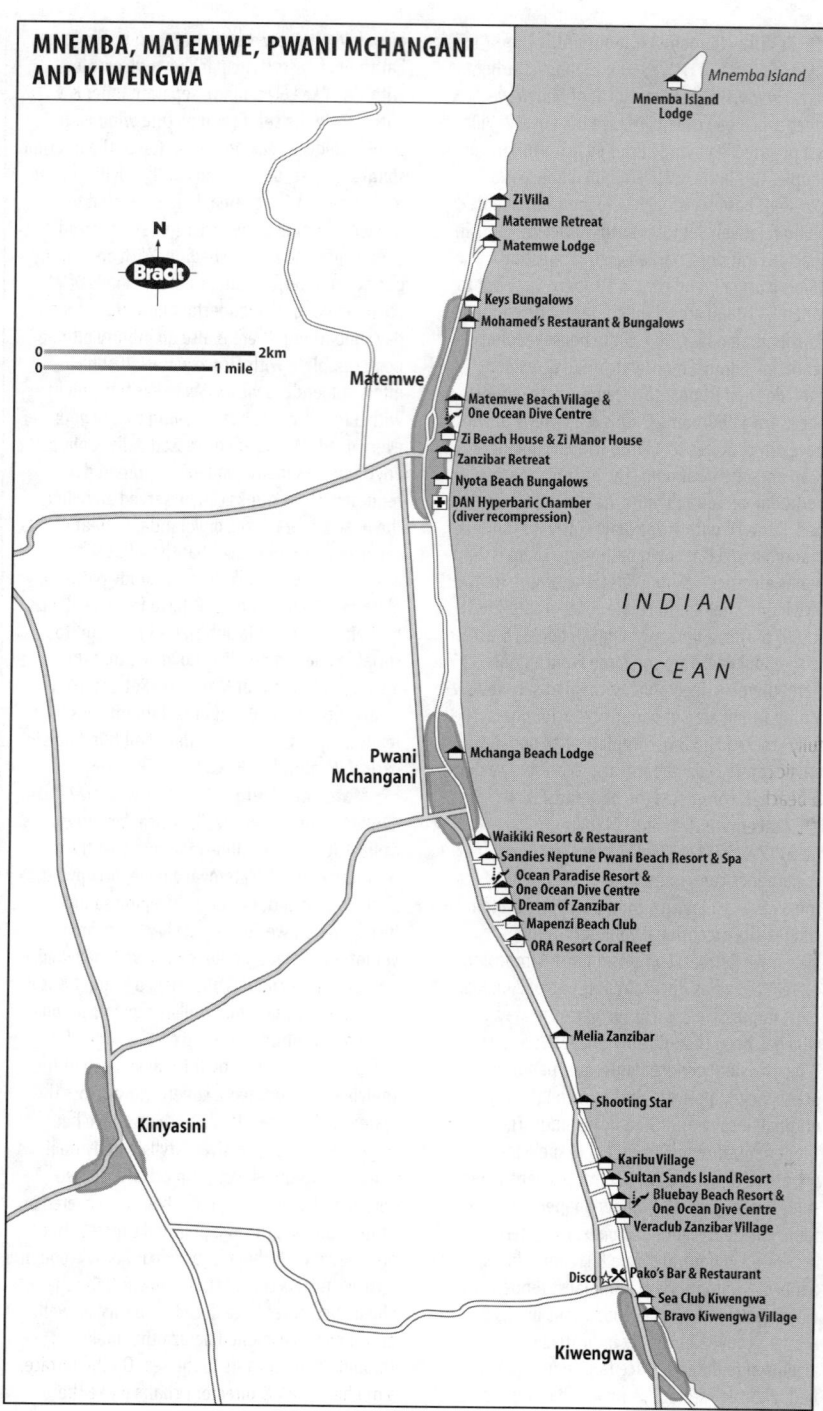

MNEMBA, MATEMWE, PWANI MCHANGANI AND KIWENGWA

Mnemba Island

Mnemba Island Lodge

Zi Villa
Matemwe Retreat
Matemwe Lodge

Keys Bungalows
Mohamed's Restaurant & Bungalows

Matemwe

Matemwe Beach Village &
One Ocean Dive Centre
Zi Beach House & Zi Manor House
Zanzibar Retreat
Nyota Beach Bungalows
DAN Hyperbaric Chamber
(diver recompression)

INDIAN

OCEAN

Pwani
Mchangani

Mchanga Beach Lodge

Waikiki Resort & Restaurant
Sandies Neptune Pwani Beach Resort & Spa
Ocean Paradise Resort &
One Ocean Dive Centre
Dream of Zanzibar
Mapenzi Beach Club
ORA Resort Coral Reef

Melia Zanzibar

Shooting Star

Kinyasini

Karibu Village
Sultan Sands Island Resort
Bluebay Beach Resort &
One Ocean Dive Centre
Veraclub Zanzibar Village

Disco   Pako's Bar & Restaurant
Sea Club Kiwengwa
Bravo Kiwengwa Village

Kiwengwa

N

Bradt

0   2km
0   1 mile

perfect seaside retreat. In the older rooms is a small lounge area with a veranda boasting a dbl sofa & a dbl hammock. Constant mains electricity, a solar-powered hot-water system, retractable mosquito nets, free-standing fan (on request), large Zanzibari safe box & a relaxing daybed are standard in all suites. Matemwe also recently added a self-contained beach house with 3 bedrooms, sleeping a max of 6, located just a few mins along with beach. It is well suited to families or groups & comes with a private pool, & its own chef and butler. Below & behind the cottages, a stone path meanders through lush tropical gardens to the swimming pools, the main dining area & onwards to the beach. The beach ends where Matemwe Lodge begins, resulting in virtually no passing foot traffic & very little hassle. Some locals have set up curio stalls, but few approach guests & it's relatively low-key compared with other stretches of this coast. There is an infinity pool with a clear view across to Mnemba Island, & another pool below it, connected by a gently tumbling waterfall, offering protection when the coastal wind blows. The adjacent bar is a beautifully polished old dhow flanked by an enormous sperm whale skeleton. Tasty buffets & plated dinners are served by friendly, uniformed staff in an open-sided dining room overlooking the beach. All guests stay on a FB basis &, space permitting, visitors will be welcomed for dinner with 24hrs' notice. 2 day rooms (US$50), complete with shower area, have been added so that those leaving late in the afternoon can enjoy their final hours on the beach or sunbathing by the pool. 2 dhows are based at the lodge for snorkelling & sailing excursions, free escorted reef walks can be arranged at low tide (local villagers, who already work as the lodge's boatmen, are being trained to guide these), & a large wooden chess set (complete with prawns as pawns) is set up *en route* to the beach. Fishing & diving trips can also be arranged. For the more sedentary, there's in-room massage, a library & a stack of board games. There is complimentary internet access with the facility to download digital pictures from cameras & burn them to CD or DVD: this is especially useful for post-safari guests arriving with full memory cards.

With close proximity to the local community & a desire to contribute to development, the company & guests have given time & money to supply the local villagers with fresh water, build a primary school, provide 2 deep-sea mashua dhows for fishing, assist with much-needed rubbish collections & teach English. Matemwe is one of very few lodges on the island with a staff member dedicated to community relations & development. If this appeals but something more exclusive is required, neighbouring Matemwe Retreat (see listing above) is the lodge's private villa alternative. FB. **$$$$$**– 🏆

🏠 **Che Che Vule** (4 rooms) m 0778 919525; e info@chechevule.com, reservations@ moivarosouth.com; www.chechevule.com. Originally a private villa, Che Che Vule underwent significant renovation & expansion 4 years ago & is now a luxury villa, catering to families, small groups & even intimate wedding parties. Managed by a delightfully welcoming Italian lady, Carola, & backed by the experienced team at Moivaro, it is a cool, comfortable Swahili-style beach house, with personal, understated service. There are 4 spacious bedrooms, 2 with en suites & balconies. High makuti ceilings, concrete floors & brilliant white interiors keep the place cool, with touches of colourful kanga fabric, chunky timber furniture & lanterns offering style & comfort. There is a large dining table, which seats 8, a spacious lounge & a veranda framed by delicate cotton curtains. An honesty bar operates (bottled water free of charge), otherwise a butler will try hard to meet your needs. Locally recruited staff are on duty 24hrs to provide all necessary catering, housekeeping & security services, & though day trips around the island can be arranged, the sail-cloth shaded pool, local beach walks (bring your own reef shoes), tropical garden hammocks & leisurely BBQ lunches (veggies well catered for) are tough to leave. This is a place to laze in the sun & chill out with family and friends … take your lead from long-term resident 'Speedy' the tortoise. No credit cards. Zanzibar Town transfer US$80/up to 8 people. **$$$$$**–🏆

🏠 **Green and Blue** (14 rooms) m 0772 390086; e welcome@greenandblue-zanzibar. com; www.greenandblue-zanzibar.com. Standing at the opposite end of a curved beach from Matemwe Lodge, Green and Blue is a terrific new lodge that opened for business in late 2011. On a pleasantly large & strikingly landscaped plot, the 2-person bungalows are all identical bar their view, whilst the Ocean Front Villa, which is larger, sleeps up to 4. Colourful interiors are meticulously designed & laid out: ochre washed walls, a net-draped bed with indigo sheets, plus an upstairs lounge that can double as another bedroom. On each bungalow's veranda, shaded by banana trees & palms, are a stylish plunge pool & an outdoor shell-encrusted shower. Lovely as these rooms are, the beachfront public areas are the real draw. In a large 2-storey makuti structure, the lounge, bar & restaurant, are cantilevered over the beach, offering fabulous sea views & equally appealing breezes. The excellence continues in the restaurant, where 2 celebrated Austrian chefs (both hailing from Michelin-starred establishments) aim to make this one of the finest restaurants on the island – given their determination so far, we have great faith. Adjacent to this area, 2 large & inviting pools run down to the beach & are linked by a cascade of water, which guests can walk underneath. Tulia Spa, in the centre of the gardens, offers various therapies in the open air as well as candlelit treatments for romancing couples, who also get private use of an additional, more sedate pool. It's the attention to detail that really makes this place stand out, from the handmade welcome packs, to the planting on the roofs so that the rooms blend in to the surroundings. Its German–Austrian owners & managers have plenty of hospitality experience & are off to a flying start. FB; BB & HB also available. **$$$$$–** 🥢

🏠 **Keys Bungalows** (6 rooms) m 0777 411797/0714 665654; e allykeys786@yahoo. com; www.allykeys.com. Behind a collapsing mkeke palm gate, Keys is a friendly beach bar with some surprisingly nice little rooms in gardens of casuarinas, palms & papayas. This is a good option for beach-focused backpackers seeking a chilled hangout for their ocean activities. Accommodation is in individual coral-rock cottages or within a larger whitewashed building & each room is small but clean & pleasant. Behind heavy Zanzibari doors, there are nicely carved dbl beds, cheerful kanga curtains, cupboards made from cleverly adapted ngalawa boats (complete with integrated safe), & wet-room-style bathrooms. Fans, mosquito nets, cold water & a small veranda with cane & hide chairs

are all standard; 2 rooms now boast hot water, too. The circular bar above the beach is the centre of activity here with gentle reggae music & a sociable crowd. The wine may be lukewarm & from a box, but the spirits are all imported & the mood's happy. From the comfort of a hammock, bar stool or beachfront baraza, it's possible to arrange snorkelling & boat trips with the local crew (half-day Mnemba snorkelling US$30pp), but anything more will require a trip to one of the larger resorts. Meals are possible with some notice, & include some imaginative ingredients from mustard mayo to chorizo, or simple snacks are available all day from the Snake Menu (sic). For now, Keys seems to be a good option in this price bracket, but 2011 saw the start of an incongruous, 4-storey semi-built structure literally on the boundary so this may change. **$$**

🏠 **Mohamed's Restaurant & Bungalows** (5 rooms) m 0777 431881/0715 431881. Follow the clear sign from the main road & you'll find these small, basic cottages: they're hidden behind a high wall in the heart of Matemwe village. Owned & managed by Mohamed, this little complex offers 3 twin & 2 trpl rooms, each with mosquito nets, fans & tiled, immaculate bathrooms with cold-water showers & flush toilets. The rooms here are basic but fairly clean, & although the beds don't always have linen, this can usually be arranged. Simple meals can be organized with a day's notice. The beachfront location & price continue to make this a great backpacker option. **$$**

🏠 **Mitende Easy Africa Club** (16 rooms) m 0772 990021; e mitende.easyafrica@gmail. com, info@mitende.com; www.mitende.com. Run by an Italian father & son duo, Mario & Andrea, since 2010, & undergoing gentle upgrading. The 2 large villas by the entrance here are bright & spacious, if uninspiring & soulless. They are predominantly used by families & groups, with 1 villa featuring an open-plan, self-catering kitchen & lounge area. Electricity, hot water, mosquito nets & deckchairs on the terrace all come as standard. In addition to the villas, there are 10 rooms in traditional bungalows, 1 of which has an interconnecting door for family use. Set back from the beach behind a garden, these are clean, with a high Zanzibari dbl bed, a daybed & a mosquito net. The mekeke & makuti ceilings are high & unusually constructed, which combined with the gauze windows allows the cooling sea breeze to circulate.

Facilities & activities are quite limited, but there is a beachfront restaurant, drooping volleyball net, Swahili massage, local fishing excursions on request, & Wi-Fi in the works. The raised swimming pool is at the heart of the complex, surrounded by shaded loungers, & there's a dive centre, Scuba Libre (*www.scubalibrezanzibar.com*), behind the restaurant. For self-drivers, there is the advantage of secure parking behind the metal gate. Villas **$$**; bungalows **$$$**

⌂ **Azanzi Beach Hotel** (35 rooms) m 0775 044171; e cara@azanzihotels.com, res@anthology. co.za; www.azanzibeachhotel.com. Don't be misled by the extremely bumpy & unattractive approach road, for behind the high Azanzi gates, a confident team awaits. Snaking through the centre of the hotel are water features & a sinuous swimming pool, somewhat surprisingly shaded under the main makuti thatch. The room décor has strong ethnic influences, with heavy theatrical curtains & pretty good facilities. All have minibar & tea/coffee facilities as standard, with villas offering additional outdoor showers, deluxe villas offering a small outdoor jacuzzi, & luxury suites boasting the most internal space & a small private garden or terrace. At the beachfront side of the property, there are deep-cushioned chairs in the lantern-strewn lounge & a restaurant on the breezy mezzanine level. Aquatic activities are well-catered for with an efficient One Ocean dive centre (see *What to see and do*, page 260) & an Afrikite kite-surfing base on site, as well as a small catamaran for cruising & some fun glass-bottomed kayaks (capacity 2 adults &1 child). Zanzibari massage & yoga instruction are available, or there's a TV lounge & basic games rooms. Families are welcome, as are honeymooners, & couples in search of a beach wedding. FB. **$$$$$–** ♨

⌂ **Matemwe Beach Village** (22 rooms) ✆024 2238374; m 0777 417250; e matemwebeachvillage@zitec.org; www. matemwebeach.net; ⏰ Jun–Mar. Operating a 'no shoes, no news' policy, Matemwe Beach Village is a place to relax on the beach, read a book & indulge in the occasional dive or massage (US$15/hr). This is a simple, unassuming beach resort popular with European family groups & young honeymooners. The compact Kijiji rooms (1 with AC) are next to one another in a series of rows, a mere hop, skip & a jump from the beach. The interiors are simple but stylish with blues & lilacs giving a cool, nautical

air, & thoughtful touches from hats to towels provided. With a mixture of king-size, sgl- & twin-bed combinations, all have mains electricity, fans, mosquito nets, candles & handy torches. Outside, a selection of chairs sit on a small terrace & the sound of the sea & the massage banda beckon. Forming a cul-de-sac of dbl-storey rondavels with steep pitched thatch are the Shamba suites. Cross the threshold & enter the highly stylised interior of designer Ivan Sutila. Matching hats, kangas & beach bags greet every guest at the door. The spacious central lounge area has built-in seating, & the bedroom is airy with a large dbl bed & pastel lilac linen. The en-suite shower is a stand-alone circular feature, whilst the very separate toilet is dressed to look like a throne with swathes of blue & purple circus-style fabrics streaming up towards the roof. On the galleried upper level, these suites have large mattresses covered in cushions, & a suspended dbl bed. Fun as these rooms are, their real disadvantage is that they are set at the back of the complex, & even from the upper level, their views are limited. The one-off Asali Suite is most frequently used by honeymooning couples keen to take advantage of its private plunge pool & dedicated chef. The resort's raised lounge area, overlooking the beach, encourages lazy afternoons & evenings. The area is thatched but the walls are made of billowing cream canvas to create a cool, intimate den. The adjoining restaurant offers a daily, à la carte menu at individual tables. An attractive pool area complete with pole-shaded bar & sloped loungers makes cooling low-tide dips possible, but be aware that there is little shade here. The One Ocean PADI 5* IDC dive centre is housed behind the pool (see *What to see and do*, page 260); upstairs in the makuti thatch a DVD & TV lounge offer sports fans & sunburnt guests a shady retreat. All HB. **$$$$–** ♨

⌂ **Sele's Bungalows** (7 rooms) m 0776 931690/0777 413449; e info@selesbungalows. com; www.selesbungalows.com. A British–Zanzibari joint venture, Sele's is a hip budget hangout with a buzzing atmosphere, friendly staff & relaxed vibe. The funky, fruit-bedecked bar is currently a real draw for non-residents & guests. Food is served on the upper deck, & it's a good option for fresh seafood with a local twist: staples like spicy octopus, grilled kingfish or giant prawns in coconut curry are popular. The simple rooms are a mix of sizes – some at the back of the property are decidedly bijou though perfectly nice – & have varying facilities. All have hot-water en suites, Zanzibari beds & a free-standing fan. There is a safe available in the manager's office, & its use is recommended for any valuables. No credit cards. **$$–$$$**

⌂ **Villa Kiva** (11 rooms) m 0772 224222; e villakiva@villakiva.it; www.villakiva.it. Villa Kiva is a smart, Italian-run villa, with some rooms in the villa & others in rondavals. It boasts a comfortable central lounge, a bar, 2 restaurant areas & a small L-shaped pool. Even the tiny gift shop has beautifully displayed products, showing an eye for detail & high level of care. Bleached furniture, pale cushions, billowing voile curtains & a wide timber deck all give a cool, uncluttered look, & aid the relaxed vibe. The place exudes a home-from-home feel & is a place to escape not to party. On the villa's 1st floor, the spacious master suite has a wrought-iron 4-poster bed, AC & fan & a small chill-out area. Decorated in white with Tanzanian trims, it's a lovely cool spot & has a spectacular balcony sea view. This room's only potential negative is drifting noise from the restaurant below. Other villa rooms can be cleverly interconnected for groups or families up to 6. The rondavals have sea or garden views & each has its own small terrace & 2 rooms high in the makuti roof with peephole windows . An infant cot & even a portable hob can be provided in the larger rooms on request.All rates HB; *F*B US$20 pp supplement. **$$$$– ⬤**

⌂ **Zi Beach House & Zi Manor House** (4 rooms each) (South Africa) +27 (82) 8233347/+27 (11) 7983600; e allan@starlight. co.za; www.zivilla.co.za. In neighbouring houses in the centre of Matemwe village, Zi Beach House & Zi Manor are within the 'Zi' property portfolio, which includes Zi Villa to the north. Let mainly to groups of friends & families from South Africa, these thatched houses can be rented for self-catering escapes or with a resident chef for those wanting a little more pampering. The house interiors are very similar in style: varnished coconut floors, family dining areas, a central bar, games facilities (pool table in Zi Manor; darts in Zi Beach), comfortable sofas for watching DVDs & neutral colour schemes sprinkled with African *objets d'art*. There are 4, neatly decorated en-suite bedrooms in each house, all with fans, AC, French doors & outdoor access to the garden or an upper balcony. The beach is

immediately in front, making high-tide swimming a popular pursuit, but this is a significant seaweed farming area, so do beware not to trip over or damage the underwater plantations. There is a swimming pool at each villa as well as a shared RIB (rigid inflatable boat) for fishing trips & a quad bike for beach excursions; dive centres can be found at nearby resorts. Zi Beach: self-catering US$128/day for 2–8 guests; Villa inc chef, FB US$320/461/691 2/4/8 guests. Zi Manor: self-catering US$128/day for 2–8 guests; Villa inc chef US$360/518/778 2/4/8 guests; 35% supplement in Aug & Dec. **$$$$– ⬤**

⌂ **Zanzibar Retreat** (10 rooms) m 0776 108379; e info@zanzibarretreat.com; www. zanzibarretreat.com. Behind a wall of cascading bougainvillea, immediately next door to Zi Manor, this pleasantly peaceful hotel is popular with Nordic expats from the Tanzanian mainland & even when fully booked is exceptionally quiet by day. With 8 rooms accessed from its broad, wraparound veranda & 2 1st-floor, interconnecting rooms (1 with balcony), it is a personal place to stay & better suited to older couples seeking solitude than energetic youngsters. The main building has decorative Moorish arches, a shady veranda & a small central courtyard from which the stairs ascend to 2 rooms. The upstairs private balcony has a wonderful view, & it is possible to see all along the coast from Mnemba Island to Kiwengwa. The bright, standard rooms are on the ground floor have polished dark timber floors, well-made louvred wardrobes, large Zanzibari beds & a dbl shower. High ceilings, fans & AC ensure they are always cool, whilst Wi-Fi adds a touch of modern convenience. Outside is a well-tended garden & an attractive view through the beachfront mangroves to the sea & bobbing ngalawa boats, which can be enjoyed from the restaurant or at the nice circular bar. Talk to the fisherman-cum-gardener to arrange a reef or village walk. The hammock-filled raised beach & large pool are assets at low tide but for those keen to hit the ocean, activities, including diving, can be arranged at One Ocean in Matemwe Beach Village (10min walk; see page 260). **$$$$**

⌂ **Sunshine Hotel** (16 rooms) m 0774 388662/ 0773 236578; e office@sunshinezanzibar.com; www.sunshinezanzibar.com; ⊙ Jun–Apr. On a sweeping curve of white sand, the vibrant Sunshine Hotel welcomed its1st guests in Jun 2010. Although occupying a relatively small plot of land, the immaculate gardens, stylish architectural touches & calm efficiency lend this hotel a cool intimacy & prevent it from feeling claustrophobic. Run by the helpful & friendly Doris, originally from Austria, Sunshine offers light rooms set in 2-storey chalets among banana tree-filled gardens. They share a similarly sunny colour scheme inside but vary slightly in location & facilities. The Sunshine Suites have 2 sea-view rooms on the top floor & 2 garden-view rooms on the bottom; set back from the beach are the 2 Garden Retreats; whilst 2 luxury rooms are found right on the sea shore, these are more secluded & therefore popular with honeymooners & those in search of a little privacy. All have dbl or twin beds draped with mosquito nets, a small cushioned seating area, a safe & 3 electric fans – 1 ceiling, 1 bed & 1 free-standing. The luxury rooms also have private plunge pools & beach bandas, & either a garden or terrace, depending on which floor they are on. The furniture in these rooms is recycled from a disused Stone Town pier, while the ceiling shape channels the wind, negating the need for AC & contributing to the hotel's eco-friendly policy. Back on the beach, the main area houses the restaurant, which serves up daily specials of fresh seafood & Zanzibari curries as well as an eclectic cocktail list. Upstairs is a chilled lounge with a couple of computers & a small library; the internet connection comes and goes. A small waterfall cascades into an infinity pool shaded by dhow sails, & the sunloungers are popular hangouts. While providing plenty of opportunities to relax, Sunshine has a lively buzz & should appeal to sociable young couples as much as urban escapists. HB. **$$$$**

⌂ **Nyota Beach Bungalows** (10 rooms) m 0777 484303/439059; e info@ nyotabeachbungalows.com; www. nyotabeachbungalows.com; ⏲ Jul–May. Opened in Dec 2004 by Italian Patrizia & Edi from Pemba, Nyota's simple rooms showed great care had been taken in decorating the stone-&-thatch cottages with bright fabrics, nice furniture & natural ornaments, & originally received high praise from guests. Recently though, gripes with the bathroom plumbing, the lack of backup generator (no fan/hot water if no electricity) & some mediocre food have somewhat dampened its initial appeal. That said, it is set on a very lovely stretch of sand, close to the mosque in the centre of Matemwe village (be warned – call to prayer starts early). There are 2 beachfront cottages, a selection of dbl & twin rooms in neat 2-storey structures & a family room for 3 people. Each room has a fan, mosquito net & mains electricity. There's a small dbl-storey lounge & bar area overlooking the ocean, which is used by both residents & guests; alternatively, the cushioned benches outside each room make a comfortable spot to chill, overlooking the banana & papaya trees in the garden. Diving & snorkelling trips can be arranged through one of the larger resorts nearby, & email access is available. **$$$**

⌂ **Panga Chumvi** (4 rooms) m 0772 177204/0777 862899; e pangachumvi@gmail. com; www.pangachumvi.com. This small locally owned place offers surprisingly good accommodation, currently with a Briitish expat manager, a stone's throw from a pretty quiet stretch of beach. The layout is somewhat unusual, with a couple of private (unfenced) houses lying at the centre, but the selection of room types – a villa, bungalows & a refurbished beach house – & tranquillity make it worth a look. Mchanga Mdogo Villa has 2 dbl & 2 twin rooms, all with a pleasant veranda & some interconnecting if required. The terraced bungalow rooms have been built with an eye on traditional Swahili cooling techniques, & maintain the same attention to detail with coconut-wood furniture, quality linen & some outdoor space. The beachfront Baharini bungalow & banda offer sea-facing rooms. There is a small on-site restaurant & bar, complete with pizza oven, offering the usual Swahili fare, but otherwise it's quite a private place to be. Community support is strong, with the owners heavily involved in Matemwe life & some interesting projects: supporting a village taxi service, fishing boat & chicken-farming project. Equally impressive is their commitment to environmental awareness at this little resort – an aspiration which sadly not all others on the island share. **$$$**

WHAT TO SEE AND DO Apart from lazing on the beach, or going for long walks along it, there are the usual diving and snorkelling possibilities which can be arranged through One Ocean's two local centres:

One Ocean – Matemwe Beach Village
e oneoceanmatemwe@zanlink.com. This is one
of the nicest centres around, & the whale-tail
reception desk is bound to bring a smile to even
the most nervous of water babies. It's a 5* PADI
dive school offering a range of certification courses,
Mnemba dive trips & snorkelling excursions. The
staff are happy to accept referral certificates from
guests who've completed dive-course classroom
work before arriving in Zanzibar, or to teach in
English or French from scratch in the pool & at
sea. Using RIB *Natie* or a purpose-built dhow,
MV *Jessica*, dive trips depart from Muyuni Beach
(a 35min dala dala ride) at 08.00 each morning.
Only twice a month do high tides allow for dhow
departures from the resort's own beach. 12 divers,
grouped by ability, are accompanied by 2 guides,
& it is not necessary to stay at the resort to use
the dive centre. US$120/325/500 for 2/6/10 dives;
equipment rental US$15/day; PADI Open Water
US$500; snorkelling trips US$45.

One Ocean – Azanzi m 0779 111888
e oneoceanazanzi@zanlink.com; www.

zanzibaroneocean.com. This may be the newer
centre, but its resident pair of instructors are
experienced in both the company & Zanzibar's
underwater scene. PADI courses from complete
beginner to Dive Master are taught in English,
German, French & Dutch, with confined water
exercises taking place in the shaded swimming
pool. Novice divers can also opt to dive with an
instructor without committing to a full course
through the PADI Discover Scuba scheme.
Equipment is all brand new, with multiple brands
of masks & fins available, long & short wetsuits,
Scubapro BCDs & regulators, & a variety of tank
sizes, including 8 litres for children. MV *Caroline*,
a purpose-built dhow, is based here permanently
allowing for daily morning dives to Mnemba, &
guided snorkelling excursions head out on an RIB
named *Alice*. Extras abound with Zanzibari spiced
tea & snacks on offer aboard the boat, & dry bags
& sea sickness tablets free to all. Open to guests
& non-guests 7 days a week. US$120/325/500 for
2/6/10 dives; equipment rental US$15/day; PADI
Open Water US$500; snorkelling trips US$45.

MNEMBA ISLAND

Lying approximately 2.5km off the northeast coast of Zanzibar, Mnemba Island
is a picture-perfect coral atoll. Previously uninhabited, it is now privately leased
by &Beyond (formerly Conservation Corporation Africa, or CC Africa) and has
become one of Africa's ultimate beach retreats.

At its centre is a tropical forest, home to nothing more dangerous than cute suni
antelope, a population of cooing red-eyed doves, butterflies, an ancient well and
some Ader's duiker (Africa's most endangered forest duiker with fewer than 300
remaining in the wild). The island's circular perimeter is 1.5km of soft, brilliant
white coral sand: perfect for romantic evening strolls, migrating wading birds,
scuttling ghost crabs and nesting turtles. In the turquoise sea around, some of east
Africa's best coral reefs hide in a relatively unspoilt aquatic wonderland. There are
virtually no insects on the island, making it a very low-risk malarial area.

Officially titled Mnemba Island Marine Conservation Area (MIMCA), the
island is part of a coral formation supporting a staggering variety of marine life,
which was once threatened by overfishing and a general disregard for the fragility
of the environment. Sustained lobbying by &Beyond and the government resulted,
however, in the area being declared a Marine Conservation Area in November 2002
and its future has now been secured.

A US$3 levy is charged on all watersports, notably snorkelling and diving, within
the protected zone. This revenue is paid into a community conservation fund, the
primary purpose of which is to show local fishermen and their communities the very
real economic value in protecting rather than exploiting these exceptional reefs. In
addition to the money generated from MIMCA park levies, the lodge and Africa
Foundation (&Beyond's social development partner) have invested US$180,000
in community projects on Zanzibar close to Mnemba: building eight classrooms,

a windmill and ablution blocks, refurbishing the doctor's house, supporting the orphanage and assisting villagers with access to clean water.

GETTING THERE AND AWAY Mnemba Island guests are **chauffeur-driven** from the airport or Stone Town to Muyuni Beach, north of Matemwe, from where it's a 15–20-minute **ski-boat** ride to the island. It is not possible to visit the island unless you have a booking.

WHERE TO STAY Unless stated otherwise, hotels listed below offer air conditioning and en-suite bathrooms as standard.

Mnemba Island Lodge (10 bandas) (South Africa) +27 11 8094300; e inboundsales@andbeyond.com; www. andbeyond.com; ⊕ Jun–Mar. The crème de la crème of &Beyond's impressive portfolio, Mnemba Island Lodge is the height of rustic exclusivity: a place where the term 'barefoot luxury' is reality. Overlooking the beach from the forest's edge, its secluded, split-level bandas are constructed entirely of local timber & hand-woven palm fronds, beautifully finished in a herringbone pattern. These are large & open-plan & are the favoured retreats of both the rich & the famous, together with a few harmless hermit crabs. Furnished simply but tastefully, each banda has a huge bed & solid wooden furniture, softened with natural, ivory-coloured fabrics & plenty of forest-view windows. As a place to escape the trappings of the modern world, in-room facilities stretch only to electricity, a simple fan, a padlocked wooden box for valuables, a couple of cotton bathrobes & a torch. A palm-covered corridor leads to a stylish timber-&-glass bathroom. Built-in barazas on the thatched beach-facing veranda are perfect for afternoon siestas & lazy b/fasts, whilst in front, private beach *salas* (shaded, open-sided beach huts) feature traditional Zanzibari loungers for leisurely hours on the beachfront. The uncluttered indulgent luxury, peaceful isolation & stunning situation make this a blissfully romantic haven. Mnemba's cuisine is predictably excellent, with plenty of fresh seafood, fruit & vegetables, & the flexibility to cater for individual needs exceedingly well. Guests can choose what, when & where to eat, from leisurely b/fasts in bed to candlelit, lobster dinners on the beach. An engaging 'butler' is assigned to each room, & from arrival will subtly go about tailoring each guest's stay. In line with its environmentally aware beginnings, the lodge strives to be eco-friendly. Water is desalinated, the beaches are rid of any manmade debris, & organic waste is recycled & the rest shipped off the island. Solar power is used wherever possible, including to heat the water, & guests are encouraged to do their bit by the eco guide left in each room. The lodge is also involved in marine- & turtle-conservation projects: watch out for the beach signs heralding new hatchlings. Children under 12 are accepted at the lodge, though only 2 are allowed on the island at any time. 1 extra bed can be put in with parents, or there are 2 bandas close to each other for convenience. Mnemba is unquestionably expensive, but its flexibility & service levels are second to none, & its idyllic location & proximity to outstanding marine experiences are very hard to match. Visa & MasterCard accepted. Price includes FB & activities. ☺

WHAT TO SEE AND DO An American couple, Eli and Robin, run a professional **dive centre** on the island and for qualified PADI divers, up to two dives per day are included in the lodge rates. PADI courses are naturally available and one-on-one tuition may be expensive but the quality instruction and warm, shallow waters make for excellent training. Once divers are qualified, a number of superb dive sites are within 15 minutes of the lodge, from tranquil coral gardens dancing with colourful reef fish and gentle turtles to steep drop-offs: the haunt of huge, deep-water game fish. Over a delicious hot chocolate on the boat back to shore, sightings of dolphin pods are not uncommon, and even humpbacks can be spotted in season.

For the non-diver, there's snorkelling, double kayaks, windsurfing, power kiting, sailing, and fly- or deep-sea fishing. Hot stone, aromatherapy, deep tissue massage and reiki are all available, too.

PWANI MCHANGANI

'Pwani' means beach in Swahili and this is certainly the focus of village life. This area is particularly noted for its seaweed collection, and the dramatic low tides see women and children take to the shallow water to harvest their marine quarry, which is then usually dried on the beach. The men, like most on Zanzibar's coast, concentrate on fishing, and the village boasts one of the island's main seafood markets.

Mass-market tourism is less developed than on the coastline around Kiwengwa (9km south), and Pwani Mchangani retains a more traditional air as a result. It's a sizeable village in the seaside coconut belt, where children and poultry run riot, colourful washing is strung between thatched houses, and conservative attitudes dominate.

GETTING THERE AND AWAY To travel from Zanzibar Town to Pwani Mchangani on public transport, take **dala dala** No 117 towards Kiwengwa or the 118 towards Matemwe, or local **bus** Routes 15 or 16. Those with a **hire car** approaching from the north or west coast should take the right turn about 1km north of Kinyasini at Kikobweni, straight into the village. The simple coastal track north and south has now been joined by a smart new tar road, making travel along the coast infinitely faster and more comfortable.

WHERE TO STAY Unless stated otherwise, hotels listed below offer air conditioning and en-suite bathrooms as standard.

Mchanga Beach Lodge (10 rooms) m 0773 952399/569821; e tradewithzanzibar@zantel.com; www.mchangabeachlodge.com. Mchanga Beach Lodge is run by a wonderfully dedicated German–American couple, Thomas & Gloria Zimmermann. Simple, stylish construction, high-quality interiors & a happy, efficient staff are testament to their concerted efforts & good natures. The location itself is stunning: on a deep, powder-sand beach between Pwani Mchangani & Matemwe, where the sea is crushed coral & urchin free, making for perfect swimming & paddling. There are steeply thatched, whitewashed rooms: 6 sea-view lodge rooms, 2 garden twins & 2 garden suites, the last ideal for families with a dbl baraza seating area which neatly converts into an additional sleeping spot for adults or older children. These rooms also have additional outdoor terracing for private relaxation. All of the rooms have an intricately carved Zanzibari 4-poster bed covered in white soft cotton, fine wool blankets & turquoise & indigo batik throws, as well as a semicircular cushion-covered baraza alcove & a small sand-covered terrace for morning

tea. Touches like light switches within mosquito nets, beach baskets brimming with towels, & jugs of water by the door to wash the sand from your feet show great attention to detail. Equally, a thoughtful mix of hand-crafted wooden shutters, electric ceiling fans, AC & traditional high-beamed ceilings all ensure rooms remain cool whatever the time of day. Outside, through flower-filled gardens, towards the oceanfront palm grove, there is a lovely swimming pool, relaxed bar & an open-sided makuti restaurant. Food is a seasonal mix of Swahili specials with traditional cooking methods & tropical produce. There are beach bandas & cheerfully covered coir loungers for sunbathing & snoozing, a simple massage room, boules & board games, & even the 'Macycle' bike rental service. Diving can also be arranged with nearby PADI centres. This is currently one of Zanzibar's best beach havens: delightfully simple, small & personal. No children under 12. All rates FB; airport transfer US$58 each way.

Waridi Beach Resort & Spa (62 rooms) www.waridibeachresort.com. Waridi is a package holiday resort favoured by young Italians. An assortment of room categories cater for couples & families, with satellite TV & all the usual mod cons as standard. There are 2 restaurants serving largely pasta-based dishes, a beach bar & a cushioned shisha lounge. A small fitness room, table tennis, pool, bike rental, & a 4-room spa with jacuzzi, sauna & steam room, are all on site, with entertainment staff coercing guests to participate in a range of activities from sports tournaments to cabarets. In addition, a large number of Maasai beach boys (most with adopted Italian names) congregate around the beach entrance to this property, playing football with the guests, & taking the opportunity to recommend their neighbouring souvenir stalls & 'guiding' services. **$$$$**

🏠 **Villa Dida Resort** (9 rooms) m 0773 130793; www.villadida.com. A relatively new, small-scale resort, Villa Dida is under Tanzanian–Italian ownership, & is largely used by Italians on bush 'n' beach package trips organised by the owner's tour company. Described as a 'big Swahili villa', Dida focuses firmly on the sea view. Rooms are simple with ochre, rust & white colour schemes, polished concrete floors, coconut wood furniture & mkeke mats. There is deliberately no AC, though double fans are fitted in all bedrooms for comfort. Equally, fish & vegetables for the restaurant are sourced from the local community as much as possible to keep food miles low. An inviting pool in the palms, large jacuzzi & plenty of makuti beach umbrellas make lazing in the sun appealing, & activities from local massage to jeep rental can also be arranged. Rates include flights from Italy. **$$$$$**

🏠 **Next Paradise Boutique Hotel** (16 rooms) m 0765 925832; e info@zanzibar.it; www.zanzibar.it. Next Paradise is a lovely, quiet property under Marina & Stuart's Italian–Slovenian ownership. Set in an immaculate coconut grove, the resort's hub is a trio of interlinked, circular makuti structures: a large international restaurant, a small bar complete with life-sized carved Maasai & an eclectic music selection (Pink Panther to Queen during our visit), & a reception area. From here, Arusha stone paths meander to rooms housed in an assortment of multi-storey villas around the complex. All rooms & suites are different, but the interior of each is clearly the product of a high degree of thought, care & investment. Bathrooms clad in metallic mini

mosaics, vibrant chiffon curtains, impressive appliqué wall hangings, & luxurious bed linen all feature, along with AC, safes, fans & Wi-Fi. Families are well catered for with large, interconnecting rooms & wide verandas to ensure everyone has plenty of space. There is a small swimming pool, but other activities are limited with no equipment for snorkelling or on-site dive centre. A good option for couples hoping to relax in tropical surroundings. Min 3-night stay; 7 nights high season. HB. **$$$$$–**🛏

🏠 **Garden Palms** (11 rooms) m 0777 77 1000; e gardenpalms@gmail.com; www.gardenpalms.pl. Immediately next door to Next Paradise, this Polish-run resort offers immaculate rooms, with refreshingly few large resorts on the doorstep. Built in a U-shaped formation around a good-size central pool, & overlooking the beach, are the 2 neat rows of accommodation, an open-sided seafood restaurant & a dive centre. The rooms – available in a terrace or as detached bungalows – are all extremely spacious, with bright interiors, tiled floors, coconut-wood furniture & sea view terraces. Perhaps lacking a little in soft furnishings & character, they remain pleasant, cool retreats after a day in the sun. Equally, the surrounding landscaping needs time to grow & soften the rather stark sand, yet this place has great promise as a quiet, efficient retreat. **$$$$**

🏠 **Waikiki Resort & Restaurant** (15 rooms) m 0773 286881/0777 877329; e waikikibooking@hotmail.com; www.waikikiafrica.com. This delightful hotel is refreshingly small & personal, run enthusiastically by husband & wife team, Flavio & Sarah, an Italian–English couple. Life here focuses on the buzzing central restaurant, where guests quaff wine & enjoy homemade leisurely lunches, & the funky beached dhow bar *Cassiopeia* – home to British mixologist James & a chilled cocktail-drinking crew. Across the resort, the multi-lingual staff check everyone's OK & a vibrant atmosphere prevails. In addition, every Fri from 22.00 Flavio DJs on the beach to a large party crowd (up to 400 revellers). All bungalows are individually decorated with striking tropical murals. Of the rooms, 'Safari' rooms are particularly spacious, & room 6 in this category has the best beachfront location. There is some basic activity equipment, free Wi-Fi, & a small massage zone. For more organised sport, diving is available through One Ocean at Matemwe Beach Village (free transfer, 10mins; see page 260), & kite-surfing courses & equipment through on-site operators Kite Zanzibar (see *What to see and do*, page 266). Links to the new neighbouring stables (horses & camels) may mean simple beach riding may be possible sometime soon. In spite of doubling in size, Waikiki remains welcoming, making it somewhere fun & offbeat on this stretch of coast. From a security perspective, this resort is one of the few covered by CCTV. Rooms **$$$**; bungalows **$$$$**

🏠 **Sandies Neptune Pwani Beach** (154 rooms) 📞 024 2240396; **m** 077 4567893/4 **e** info.neptune@sandies-resorts.com; www. neptunepwani.sandies-resorts.com. With 4 established resorts in Mombasa this is the Neptune Group's 1st departure from the Kenyan coast, though it is now managed by PlanHotel (Zanzibar resort stalwarts). Neptune Pwani is a sizeable hotel extending from the beach up along the coral cliff behind. Striking dbl-storey accommodation blocks with steep makuti thatch & external timber staircases are laid out in imposing rows on the lush lawns. There is little that is soft, gentle or environmentally in keeping, rather the scale, colour & harsh geometry are quite arresting. Inside, things improve: spacious bedrooms are decorated with locally crafted furniture & there is crisp linen & wide balconies. Satellite TV, tea-/coffee-making facilities, mini fridge & electronic safe are all standard. There is an extensive network of swimming pools (the largest on the island) with a child-friendly paddling section, popular swim-up bar & disco music throughout the day. A selection of non-motorised watersports is also available, & divers can make arrangements with Scuba Do (see page 247) or any of the local centres. For relaxation, the autonomous Mvua African Rain Spa above reception is suitably sweet smelling & is staffed by delightful Indonesian & Thai therapists. Offering flower-filled baths, scrubs & professional massage & beauty therapies, this is a good place for guests & non-residents alike to break from the sun for a few hours. **$$$$$**

🏠 **Ocean Paradise Resort** (98 rooms, 8 suites) **m** 0777 439990–3; **e** info@ oceanparadisezanzibar.com; www. oceanparadisezanzibar.com. Ocean Paradise is a big hit with UK honeymooners enticed to the resort by the free bottle of bubbly, fruit basket

& private lobster dinner for newlyweds. The imposing reception is a huge semicircular area, with a high, vaulted makuti roof. From here, sweeping stairs curve round what is intended to be an impressive waterfall, into manicured gardens, the beautiful central pool area, & beach-level accommodation. There are superior rooms & junior suites, all in neat, pale yellow rondavels. The circular bedrooms are stylishly understated in neutral tones & all have mains electricity, satellite TV, electronic safe & a minibar. There is even a nice laminated card of useful Swahili phrases. Each room has an outside seated terrace area accessed through French doors. The junior suite rooms are exactly the same in design as the superior, but with 2 separate rooms they are twice the size. Half of these have a king-size bed & sitting room, whilst the others have 1 king-size & a twin room, which can be used by families. Transfers around the complex by golf cart can be arranged for guests with limited mobility. If splashing in the seaside pool or reclining on the beach isn't stimulating enough, there's a daily schedule of hosted activities typically including coconut weaving, Swahili lessons & beach soccer. Alternatively, there's a One Ocean Dive Centre for scuba & snorkelling (see *What to see and do*, page 260), canoeing, windsurfing, fishing, volleyball, table tennis, billiards & a small fitness centre. Beach bikes can also be rented (US$7.50). For families, there's a children's pool & 'animators' to engage children in Butlin's-style activities; cots are available & English-speaking babysitting services are provided at a standard US$5/hr. Every night musicians perform, treating guests to traditional Swahili ngoma drumming or Maasai acrobatics. Evening meals at the Jahazi Restaurant overlook the performers & are usually themed. Non-residents with a booking are also welcome to eat here. When the cabaret entertainment is over, the Jungle Disco (Fri & Sat) & terraced Bahari Bar can get lively. **$$$$$**

🏠 **Dream of Zanzibar** (157 rooms) **e** info. dreamofzanzibar@planhotel.com. This all-inclusive PlanHotel property is an architectural interpretation of the grand old Arab–African palaces: makuti thatched buildings with shaded arcades, open terraces & palm-filled vistas. The detached reception area is a striking introduction with a large open-sided lounge area filled with primary coloured cylindrical lanterns suspended from the thatch. From here, accommodation heads downhill towards the beach. Bedrooms are very spacious & pleasant, with dark teak furniture, orange & white fabrics & a raft of mod cons including satellite TV, DVD-CD player & minibar. For sea views opt for the Junior Suites, or one of the 3 Royal Suites for a private plunge pool. There are 3 restaurants in the grounds, the international, buffet-style Cape to Venice Brasserie, the Andiamo Pizza Co & the seafood à la carte Blue Vanilla, as well as a couple of cocktail & juice bars. With 2 pools, a well-equipped gym, a professional spa, games room & diving through Scuba Do (La Gemma, Kendwa, see page 247), activities galore are available, although this is not a resort for coercive group activities. **$$$$$**

Mapenzi Beach Club (87 rooms) m 0774 414268/ 0774 414493; e info.mapenzi@sandies-resorts.com; www.planhotel.com. Owned & managed by Swiss–Italian hoteliers, PlanHotel, Mapenzi is a comfortable resort on a nice stretch of coast. In spite of its size, it is a relatively serene place, catering to a large number of Italian package holidaymakers (25 rooms used exclusively by operator Eden Viaggi), especially between Aug & Easter. Increasingly though, British & South African families are staying here, enticed by the positive attitude towards children (easy availability of cots, highchairs & babysitting). The reception area is shaded by impressive makuti thatch supported by a tremendous network of poles, & plays ethereal music to arriving guests. From here, wide corridors lead to a mezzanine-level daybed & evening shisha corner, a curio shop & stylish boutique, a business centre offering internet & the massage zone. Raised above the beach, the long swimming pool, with children's area & jacuzzi, is surrounded with loungers, & affords views across the entire complex.

The cottages closest to the sea fetch the premium rate but all rooms offer 24hr mains electricity, mosquito nets, electronic safe, fridge, & a veranda. In true European-resort style, 'animators' encourage active participation in games & activities but at least there is a Swahili influence evident in their offerings, & their manner is not as intolerably coercive as at the all-inclusive Italian resorts. Tingatinga painting, village excursions & ngoma drumming lessons are just as likely to feature alongside archery & boules here. There's a daily fitness programme of aqua aerobics & jogging, & catamarans, bicycles, windsurfers & snorkelling equipment can be hired. Football & volleyball matches benefit from properly marked pitches, &, diving is organised through Scuba Do & sister-property La Gemma (see page 247). By night, entertainment ranges from live bands to acrobatic shows & quizzes. Mapenzi is all inclusive & meal times & cuisine are set, though a seafood à la carte menu is also available. Meals are served in the spacious restaurant or new pizzeria, though Thu night sees the weekly Swahili BBQ by the pool. There are 2 bars, including 1 in the central area which opens at 22.00 for cabaret, karaoke & late-night revelling. Drinks are included in the room rates but long drinks are free only from 18.00 to midnight; it's a cash bar thereafter. Late checkout rates are reasonable at US$50/4hrs, & well worth considering for those with afternoon flights. **$$$$$–♛**

ORA Resort Coral Reef (45 rooms) m 0777 415549; e coralreef@zanzinet.com; www.zanzibar-coralreef.com; ⌚ Jul–Apr. Coral Reef was opened by 3 Italians & virtually every guest here is a fellow compatriot. It is allegedly now managed by Italian hospitality group, ORA Resorts, though their presence, or that of any other management, was notably absent during our last visit –wilfully unhelpful staff lent it an uneasy air. The sparse reception area is naturally raised above the beach & decorated with simple murals showing acrobatic Maasai. From here a long central path leads to the swimming pool, complete with its own elegant palm island & sadly a roped monkey at the shower. Signs from the main path indicate the direction of various rooms, some of which are a fair stretch from the beach. The bungalow architecture is Arabic in style: white walls with arched windows & flat roofs. There are standard rooms on the hillside, each either dbl or twin, plus superior & seafront rooms on the beach. Each has mains electricity, mosquito nets, & hot-water shower. The standard & some superior rooms have fans only, whilst 7 of the latter enjoy AC. There is an electronic safe, left-luggage facility & Wi-Fi access (US$24/ week) available at reception. Buffets are served for every meal in a restaurant beside the sea. In the past, it was dark & smoky with the feel of a school dining hall, though outside is a very pleasant deck with large navy parasols & a lovely view along the beach through the extensive Tingatinga painting gallery. Once open-sided, this area is now behind a high wall, following a high-tide incident. $$$$-$$$$$

🏠 **Melia Zanzibar** (117 rooms) m 0777 444477; e reservations.melia.zanzibar@melia.com; www.meliahotels.com. In May 2011, Spanish hotel group Melia, took over this Kempinski resort. Much has remained of the original property, but some interiors have suffered under the new management & the once clean lines & contemporary style have been diluted. Set in 12ha of immaculate gardens, the spacious guest rooms & suites are housed in contemporary coral-rock buildings, each with its own private terrace or balcony. Angular in design with Moorish influences evident in the carved timber balconies, patterned shutters & cool courtyards, the architecture is some of the most modern on the island; it's strikingly different from any other large resort here. In addition to the standard rooms, there is a vast presidential villa & 6 smaller villas, each with a private pool. All rooms have Zanzibari beds & heavy floral cushions & curtains, & the quality & number of in-room facilities reflect the resort's association with a serious European hotel group. Each offers satellite TV with movie channels, tea-/coffee-making facilities, a minibar, an electronic safe, his & hers bathrobes, 24hr room service & even a shoe-shine facility. Bathrooms have a contemporary free-standing bath &, in safari style, an outdoor shower in a pebbled Zen courtyard. There are 2 restaurants: a themed buffet at Spice Market where seating spills out onto the garden patio, & a daily set menu at Aqua, overlooking the sea. Drinks & snacks are available poolside, or there's tapas on the jetty, a book-filled Library Bar & a cushioned shisha lounge on the coral cliff. For exercise & total relaxation, the Anantara Spa Zanzibar is one of the island's best well-being facilities. It is a contemporary area with private treatment rooms & professional Thai therapists, a large outdoor pool with sundeck & pool bar, a 23m lap pool & a fully equipped fitness centre. If being outside is preferable, there's basketball, tennis, a stunning swimming pool & a number of watersports on offer, & even sunrise yoga in the amphitheatre. There is no dive centre here but diving can be easily arranged. The resort is on the edge of the coral cliff so there's no real beach to speak of immediately in front of it. If it's lying on the beach you're after, then it's a golf buggy trip 1km south to Gabi Beach – the resort's satellite beach bar on Kiwengwa Beach. 🛏

WHAT TO SEE AND DO Any lodge or resort can arrange one or more of the ubiquitous Zanzibar Island tours (see *Chapter 5*, pages 133–4). For diving, contact the One Ocean Dive Centre at the Ocean Paradise Resort and for kiting, the Kite Zanizbar base at Waikiki is your best bet (see below).

🏄 **Kite Zanzibar** m 0773 114976; e info@kitezanzibar.com; www.kitezanzibar.com. Based at Waikiki (see *Where to stay*, page 263) this IKO-registered kite centre offers instructor-led courses as well as hiring out North branded equipment to experienced kiters. Beginners can join small groups (max 4 pupils/instructor), intermediates can top up their skills, & professionals can practise freestyle & wakestyle acrobatics. Beginner lesson on sand (3hrs) US$160; Intermediate lesson (6hrs) US$295; Advanced lesson (9hrs) US$432.

🤿 **One Ocean – Ocean Paradise** 📞 024 2238374; m 0777 453892; e oneocean@zanlink.om; www.zanzibaroneocean.com. The most recent of the One Ocean dive centres, this is a professional, PADI-accredited operation offering reliable equipment, custom-built dive-boats, knowledgeable staff & the usual array of certification courses. Most dive trips are dbl dives (perhaps because of the resort's distance from the better reefs), including a light lunch in between. Non-guests can also dive from here. US$174/489/750 for 2/6/10 dives; Open Water US$726; Dive Master US$994; snorkelling trips US$70; underwater camera hire US$32.

KIWENGWA

A small, traditional coastal village with a stunning beach, Kiwengwa is also the heart of Zanzibar's package-holiday industry. A glut of exclusively Italian, all-inclusive resorts cluster along the beach immediately around the village, with several other large hotels spaced along the coast to the north. That said, with continuous in-house entertainment and exhaustive facilities, the guests at all of these resorts are rarely seen outside of their chosen hotel's perimeter walls, so the area around is generally quite quiet. The contrast between the dusty Zanzibari fishing villages and the lush, European hotel grounds is stark, and sadly the bigger developments and their visitors have often displayed a depressing lack of environmental and social consideration towards the local area and population. However, there are some who have made real efforts over many years, notably Bluebay and Shooting Star, and are good options on what is a truly beautiful beach.

GETTING THERE AND AWAY The easiest way to reach Kiwengwa from Zanzibar Town is along the good tar road, via Mahonda and Kinyasini. The small coastal road, both north and south, is narrow, sandy and badly maintained, so **4x4** vehicles are advisable if you choose to travel it. In 2006, an excellent tar road was opened which runs north to Matemwe, parallel to the old road and just slightly inland of it.

You can come by **taxi**, **rented car** or **motorbike**, or arrange a minibus through a **tour company**. By public transport from Zanzibar Town, **dala dalas** (No 117) run between 06.00 and 19.00, whilst the public **bus** on Route 15 passes through the village five-times daily. The 'official' stop for both is in the village; though for a small fee the driver may well drop off at individual hotels. The major resorts and upmarket hotels all arrange **transfers** from the airport and Stone Town.

WHERE TO STAY Unless stated otherwise, hotels listed below offer air conditioning and en-suite bathrooms as standard. Looking from north to south:

Shooting Star (16 rooms) m 0777 414166; e star@zanzibar.org; www.zanzibar.org/star. Standing on a coral cliff above the stunning Kiwengwa Beach, Shooting Star is a firm favourite with young, well-travelled Europeans. Built & run by the charismatic Eliamani 'Elly' Mlang'a, a charming & engaging Tanzanian, & his family, this small hotel is a delightfully social place, despite the high number of honeymooners who visit. The 3 garden rooms border the lodge's central area & have a dbl/twin bed, mosquito net & en-suite bathroom. They are small & simply furnished but light, bright & perfectly adequate. The sea-view cottages are a step up with lovely decorations & each offering mosquito nets, a large shower & a private terrace. All have comfortable Zanzibari beds, colourful Tingatinga pictures & dyed makuti mats. In line with the lodge's child-friendly attitude, 4 of these cottages have been designed with families in mind & include a dbl bedroom & separate twin-bedded upper room. Named after the island's trade winds – the Kusi from the south & the Kaskazi from the north – 2 separate villas offer luxurious accommodation & some real privacy.

Each suite is entered through a pair of intricately carved Zanzibari doors flanked by large potted palms. Inside, both temperature & style are cool: high-quality finishes, antique furniture, AC & whirring ceiling fans. In the entrance hall, curved baraza benches are covered in a mass of cushions, Swahili-style interior-design books are piled on the coffee table & a dressed Zanzibari daybed awaits tired travellers. With an adjoining shower, dressing room & kitchenette (complete with well-stocked fridge), this area is easily converted into an extra bedroom for families. Continuing up the curved staircase at the rear, the spacious master bedroom boasts a super-king-size Zanzibari 4-poster bed, twin baraza benches & a large lockable chest for valuables. Windows have shutters to keep out the midday sun, but when opened they afford views along the coast in both directions. Up a further flight of stairs, the roof terrace is the perfect place for privacy. Enjoy a sunrise coffee, stretch out on the cushioned baraza or indulge in a moonlit bubble bath for 2, all overlooking the island vegetation & ocean beyond. There is also a private garden on the ground floor with a small plunge pool surrounded by soft sand, coir loungers & a little bar. Tasty snacks & fruit are available & meals can be served here or at the main restaurant. For all guests a stunning horseshoe infinity pool & sundeck in front of the main lodge area afford superb views over the ocean, barrier reef & beach below, as well as the opportunity for a cooling dip when the tide's out. Alongside, a circular 'beach' area has been created. A simple shower is secreted under a nearby palm for rinsing off before heading to the bar. Dining is split among 3 adjoining areas: 2 beneath makuti thatch & 1 under date palms, but all surrounded by tropical vegetation. Meals here are simple & filling, but it's the lively bar & relaxed lounge area that is the true heart of Shooting Star. Elly's invariably on hand to offer friendly advice & help with planning, whilst card & board games are available for those content with a bottle of wine & a quiet seat. There is also a Star Bar under suitably star-shaped makuti thatch on the beach. With the waves literally crashing underneath at high tide, this is a terrifically friendly evening hangout – especially before the famed lobster beach BBQ (an extra US$45pp). Diving & snorkelling trips can be organised, , & fishing trips with the locals on outboard boats will give a totally different take on life on the ocean wave. For relaxation, a seaside spa room is available for massages &, appropriately, seaweed wraps. There's a phone for guest use &, with satellite connection, fast internet access. All rates FB; B&B & HB rates available; transfer from Zanzibar Town US$60. **$$$$$–**⚱

🏠 **Karibu Village** (168 rooms) m 0777 417328; e direzione.karibu@zanzinet.com; www. ventaglio.com. One of several similar all-inclusive, all-Italian resorts on this coast, this is exclusively sold to Italians as a package holiday. All of its rooms are classed as standard with little variation bar the number of beds they contain: dbls, twins, trpls & families all catered for. Group activities are encouraged here & there's canoeing, windsurfing, archery, aqua gym, volleyball, snorkelling & even yoga at sunset. As one would expect at an Italian property, there's a very relaxed attitude towards children; cots & highchairs are readily available & during school holidays there are separate kids' clubs. **$$$$**

🏠 **Sultan Sands Island Resort** (76 rooms) PO Box 3276, Kiwengwa; ☎024 2240240/1/2/4;

e mail@sultansandszanzibar.com; www. bluebayzanzibar.com. The newer sister property to the neighbouring Bluebay (see below), Sultan Sands is a large hillside resort where rooms are in thatched rondavels dotted among planted terraces above the beach. The split-level interiors house a dbl bed, sofa-bed lounge & modern facilities including satellite TV & minibar. All the rooms are single storey with very few having a sea view, but the gardens are well tended with snaking coral-stone paths to the beach. In the main building, arches, courtyards, fountains & colourful scattered flowers set the cool, calm tone in the reception. There is a pool, the Casablanca Lounge & the Mwambao all-day restaurant. While once a place to relax with a book, the hotel has recently jumped on the animation programme bandwagon & offers a wide range of activities from Oscar movie evenings to coconut-throwing competitions & w/end discos. If this still isn't enough to keep you occupied, energetic guests can venture next door to Bluebay where further facilities abound. Christmas, New Year & Easter supplements apply. Airport transfer US$40 pp each way. **$$$$$–**⚱

🏠 **Bluebay Beach Resort** (112 rooms) ☎024 2240240/1/2/4; e mail@bluebayzanzibar. com; www.bluebayzanzibar.com. Set on a lush, gently sloping site, rooms are in thatched, 2-storey villas. All of the spacious rooms in the original complex have 2 large, dark wood 4-poster beds or 1 king-size, a dressing area & private balcony or terrace; the garden & deluxe rooms also have a lounge area. Minibars, satellite TV, electronic safes, tea-/coffee-making facilities & mosquito nets are also standard. Deluxe rooms enjoy a bath & a private outside shower. Honeymooners are welcomed with arches of fresh flowers adorning their doors, & families are equally well catered for with interconnecting rooms, a children's pool, playground, the possibility of babysitting & an on-site nurse at Sultan Sands. There are 2 rooms kitted out with a shower shelf & ramp for visitors with limited mobility. There are oodles of activities from canoeing to catamaran sailing & waterskiing, a One Ocean centre on site for diving & snorkelling trips, a large freshwater swimming pool with jacuzzi & a floodlit tennis court. The professional Oasis spa offers Vichy treatments, massage tables with a sea view, a steam room, open-air whirlpool with loungers & an adjoining fitness centre. There is

Wi-Fi in the communal areas for US$8/hr. The Makuti Restaurant, Bahari Grill & Pool Bar cover everything from extensive dinners to coffees & cocktails, with the majority of guests staying here on an HB basis. Bluebay is proud of being a 'Green Globe 21' organisation: a sustainable tourism certification. . It recycles all room & laundry waste, purifies water to keep its gardens green, incinerates all garden & kitchen rubbish, soundproofs generators, uses energy-efficient fittings, & collects rainwater from its specially designed roofs. In addition, the gardens are planted only with indigenous species. Christmas, New Year & Easter supplements apply. Airport transfer US$40 pp each way. **$$$$$**–🛥

🏠 **Veraclub Zanzibar Village** (63 rooms) m 0777 466233/414988, 0741 320987; e veraclubznz@zitec.org; www.veratour.it/villaggi/zanzibar/ zanzibar.html. Most of Veraclub's all-inclusive guests come on charter flights from Italy. Whilst simply lying on the shaded loungers, beside the sea or the lovely pool, clearly holds great appeal for most, the energetic Italian & Zanzibari 'animators' are keen to encourage participation in a variety of games, competitions & shows. Countless activities are encouraged, but you can escape the archery tournament by heading for a massage at the beauty centre, Ibiscus, or down the new Pontile jetty. Accommodation is in traditionally built bungalows with makuti thatch roofs & the en-suite rooms, some suitable for families, are clean, comfortable & recently renovated. Each has a safe & a private, polished-wood terrace with cane furniture, but no TVs. **$$$**

🏠 **Sea Club Kiwengwa** (200 rooms) m 0777 414351; e sckiwengwa.recep@renthotel.org. Like its neighbouring resorts, Spanish & Italian package holidaymakers throng Sea Club's lush gardens & stretch of beach. Each of its rooms is decorated in pastel colours, with light rattan furniture. Suitable for up to 3 adults or a family of 4, they have a minibar, safety-deposit box (for which there's an extra change) & a private balcony or veranda. As with most all-inclusive resorts, there are buffets for every meal, with the welcome addition of the African Hakuna Matata Restaurant & an à la carte seafood establishment, Matunda. The ever-present resident entertainers run an extensive programme of daytime events & evening shows, with a dedicated children's club for those aged 4–12. The hotel also boasts floodlit tennis courts & a basketball court, along with the usual assortment of beach & watersports at the Blue Diving centre. **$$$**

🏠 **Bravo Kiwengwa Village** (200 rooms) e bckiwengwa.recep@altamarea.it; www.bravoclub.it. Another big resort full of Mediterranean tourists & here even the resort signs & piped music are in Italian. With the bungalows & dbl-storey blocks, the grounds feel quite built-up in spite of the profusion of tropical greenery. Some rooms come with a sea view, whilst others are able to accommodate up to 4 people. All rooms have fridge, safe & individual terrace. The usual array of excursions & activities is available, including the hyped inter-guest football & volleyball tournaments. 1 of the resort's real assets is its lengthy pier, which allows easy access to the sea, even when the tide's out. If taking part in the nightly cabaret isn't enough, there's a disco, too. **$$$**

🏠 **Baby Bush Lodge** (12 rooms) m 07773 332847; e babybushlodge.zanzibar@gmail.com; www.bbzanzibar.com. The approach to Baby Bush Lodge is not for the faint hearted: a steep, rocky descent from the tar road (4x4 recommended, if not essential), before a left turn along a sandy track through the village. Visible from quite a distance, it's raised high on the cliff & spread across 3 towering structures, a mix of fairly crude coral rock, pole & makuti construction. The central multi-level, open-sided chill-out lounge/bar/restaurant actually affords quite a pleasant view across the ramshackle tin rooftops below to the sea, & the wide sofas encourage guests to relax & listen to retro tunes – this is the best part of the lodge. Below the bar, there are some fairly basic, & not very appealing backpacker rooms (sgl & bunk beds available; only some with mossie nets) with shared functional bathroom facilities & low rates. Larger, more expensive rooms are available above the central area & up the steep, irregular stairs. These have pretty uninspiring interiors with mkeke mats, netted windows, a dbl bed, & a small shower. Overall, it's hard to escape the slightly grubby feel of the place. **$$–$$$**

WHAT TO SEE AND DO The major resorts and hotels can organise the normal tourist trips and watersports, as can tour operators in Zanzibar Town (see *Chapter 6*,

Tour companies, pages 134–7). For diving, there are One Ocean dive centres at the Bluebay Beach Resort and Ocean Paradise (see below).

↙ One Ocean Bluebay & Ocean Paradise

m 0777 414332/453892 (Ocean Paradise guests); e oneocean@zanlink.com; www. zanzibaroneocean.com; ⊕ (office) 08.00–17.00 Thu–Tue. Well-equipped & managed, these PADI 5* dive centres offer the usual array of courses & dive opportunities, including pool-based training & refresher courses taught in Italian & English. *Manta,* a custom-built dive boat, is shared by One Ocean Bluebay & Ocean Paradise, & concentrates its attentions on sites around Mnemba Island. Helpful staff are always willing to answer questions & give underwater advice. PADI courses can be taught in English, Swahili, Italian & Spanish. All One Ocean dive centres are open to both hotel guests & non-guests. US$135/375/565 for 2/6/10 dives; equipment rental US$15/day; PADI Open Water US$620; snorkelling trips US$60; underwater camera hire US$32.

PONGWE

Northwest of the Ras Uroa headland, a series of idyllic, palm-fringed, sandy coves make up Pongwe. Except for a tiny fishing village and a handful of small, individual accommodation options, there is very little else here: and that's its magic. Blissful beach relaxation, away from everything.

GETTING THERE AND AWAY Pongwe Beach and Nature Safari Lodge can arrange **minibus** transfers from Stone Town, or these can be organised by local tour companies (see *Chapter 6*, pages 134–7). By public transport, **bus** Route 6 and **dala dala** No 209 (only three per day) from Stone Town travel to Pongwe, with dala dala 214 to Uroa often continuing to Pongwe village: ask the individual drivers.

Self-drivers will be pleased to find that the bumpy mix of sand and coral rag which once made up the coastal road is now paralleled with a smooth, fast tar road up to Kiwengwa and beyond. A **4x4** can still negotiate the original route, but patience and a good suspension are necessary for any degree of comfort.

WHERE TO STAY Unless stated otherwise, hotels listed below offer air conditioning and en-suite bathrooms as standard.

⌂ Pongwe Beach Hotel (16 rooms) m 0784

336181/0773 169096; e info@pongwe.com; www. pongwe.com. Standing within its own quiet cove, under a shady oasis of coconut palms, this is a simple little lodge in a lovely location. In spite of its uninspiring name, it is a well-managed, good-value haven for relaxing on a beautiful beach. There are airy, whitewashed bungalows, furnished with traditional Zanzibari beds & mosquito nets. 3 rooms are located in the pretty garden, while the remaining have beachfront views. Dbl & trpl rooms are available, with some rooms capable of taking 4 beds at a squeeze. There are plenty of inviting hammocks & loungers, a small library, a kite for seaside entertainment, free kayak hire & an array of other individual & group beach games. The reef is only 15mins offshore & the resort has its own dhow for sailing, snorkelling trips (US$15, no time limit), & game or line fishing that can all be arranged at the 'Captain Ali Boti' beach shack. On the rock to the north of the beach, beside the border with Nature Safari Lodge is a lovely infinity pool. Large enough to swim lengths & with an imported beach area & decked surround, this area is a popular, if slightly exposed, spot when the tide's out. Yellow-clad pool attendants are on hand to supply drinks & fresh fruit at 16.00. Pongwe is especially proud of its food with tasty lunches from US$5 & varied set menus for dinner, including succulent spiced meats from the professional tandoori oven. With a little notice, children are warmly welcomed & there are great children's discounts. HB. **$$$$$**

⌂ Seasons Lodge Zanzibar (see advertisement on the final page of the 2nd colour insert) (11 rooms)

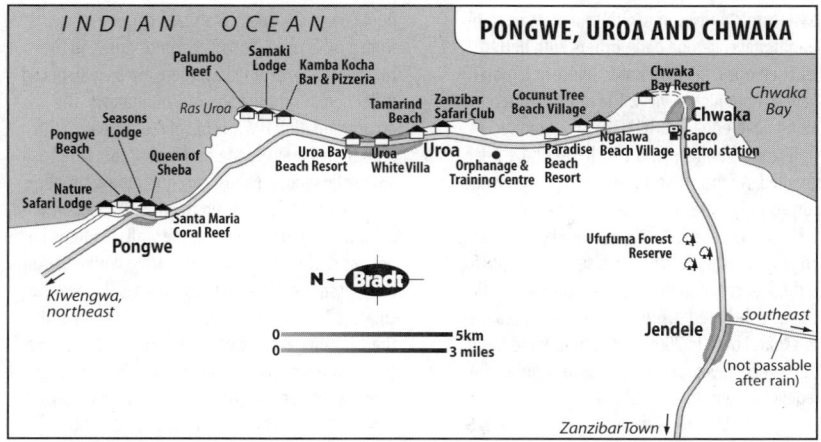

PONGWE, UROA AND CHWAKA

Palumbo Reef
Samaki Lodge
Kamba Kocha Bar & Pizzeria
Chwaka Bay Resort
Chwaka Bay

Seasons Lodge
Ras Uroa
Tamarind Beach
Zanzibar Safari Club
Cocunut Tree Beach Village
Chwaka

Pongwe Beach
Queen of Sheba
Uroa Bay Beach Resort
Uroa White Villa
Uroa
Orphanage & Training Centre
Paradise Beach Resort
Ngalawa Beach Village
Gapco petrol station

Nature Safari Lodge
Santa Maria Coral Reef
Pongwe

N Bradt

Ufufuma Forest Reserve

Kiwengwa, northeast

0 — 5km
0 — 3 miles

Jendele
southeast
(not passable after rain)

Zanzibar Town ↓

m 0776 107225; e info@seasonszanzibar.com, seasonslodge@gmail.com; www.seasonszanzibar. com. With dreams of starting up a boutique beach hotel, Irish–Ugandan owner Michael scouted out this peaceful spot in 2008. He soon started building using natural materials & local craftsmen, some of whom he trained on the job, & the resulting Seasons Lodge opened in early 2012. The bright & fresh cottages & top-floor rooms (1 dbl, 1 twin & 2 trpls) are bathed in sunlight from the numerous windows & all have fans & folding louvred doors to allow the sea breezes to enter, so no AC is necessary. Being just metres from the sea, there are 180° ocean views from all balconies & terraces. In the en-suite bathrooms sit a cast-iron claw-footed bathtub & 2 sinks, with solar heated water on tap. The cottages are a little more private than the rooms, & each has its own garden. The striking chokaa limestone design of the buildings gives a pretty mottled effect. The owners have made a conscious & commendable effort to limit their carbon footprint by growing their own herbs & spices & by composting their waste, using it to fertilise the garden (which they credit for the luscious & abundant indigenous plants). As well as the home-grown vegetables, chickens, goats, ducks & turkeys are kept here by locally employed staff. There are even plans to install solar electricity throughout. After a hard day's sunbathing lie back in an easy chair & sip on a Scottish malt whisky in the ingeniously named Bar Es Salaam which has a large wall-mounted TV, popular with homesick sports fans. The Temple Bar, a throwback to the owner's Irish roots, offers similar fare down on the sand. While the romantic cottages, privacy & sweeping

vistas would suggest that honeymooners are the main target market, the owner has included a small splash pool on the side of the main pool for his young daughter, & visiting children are welcome to use it, too. If sea splashing & beach lounging isn't enough, the lodge also has mountain bikes & kayaks for guest use. $$$$$

🏠 **Queen of Sheba** (10 rooms) e info@ santamaria-zanzibar.com; www.queenofsheba-zanzibar.com. Adapted from a private house, Queen of Sheba has the same owners as Santa Maria Coral Park (see below), & is well signposted off the main road. Friendly staff greet visitors in the airy central area, & the low-key, happy vibe is immediately apparent. There are few frills here but for the more budget-orientated traveller this is a good option on this stretch of coast. In the original villa there are 2 dbl rooms with a shared bathroom; the sgl, dbl & trpl rooms in the newer houses are clean & extremely large, with Spartan décor & bougainvillea-clad terraces. The upper rooms offer good sea views, & soon all will offer hot-water en suites. There's a pleasant stretch of beach below the restaurant & it's blissfully quiet thanks to little development in the immediate vicinity. For a little aquatic action, fishing & snorkelling can be arranged on the owner's boat (US$2,030pp), otherwise just lie back & chill. $$–$$$

🏠 **Nature Safari Lodge** (10 rooms) m 0777 223816; e mosses.znz@yahoo.com. This is a very rough & ready place, better suited to the self-sufficient. Surrounded by dense vegetation, on an attractive beach, are mud huts, with crude, painted-brick exteriors. All rooms have only

271

basic furnishings, some with thin mattresses on traditional coir-rope beds, others with better wooden ones. All are painted white or lemon & have a fabulous sea view. The rooms are accessed along neat, edged paths & there's a 'nature trail' from the site, along which trees have been labelled. A fenced central enclosure, somewhat surprisingly called a 'zoo', is home to a few small tortoises, rabbits & a tethered monkey. Adjacent is an empty restaurant/bar area serving simple food & drink at crude shell-encrusted concrete tables. The British-based owners had allegedly planned to expand back in 2009, but current word has it that Czech developers may now be scoping out redevelopment here. If it happens, it will likely change the take-it-as-it-comes vibe & cost. **$$**

🏠 **Santa Maria Coral Reef** (10 rooms) m 0777 432655; e info@santamaria-zanzibar. com; www.santamaria-zanzibar.com. Opened by an entrepreneurial local named Suleiman, this is a delightful hideaway. With no other developments currently along the beach here, & very low-density population, this really is a place to get away from it all & relax. Set in a coconut grove, in the middle of a sweeping bay, there are a well-spaced collection of simple bandas & bungalows. The accommodation is a mix of sgl & dbl storey, with high thatch & suspended ceilings. Rooms are basic with solid wooden beds, coconut-rope & timber shelves, colourful mats on the floor & block-printed buxom mermaids adorning the walls. 6 rooms have hot water & there is 24hr electricity, with a backup generator. Arguably, the best room is the new & smarter 'Mount Zion', though it is set back within the coconuts, & the coral rock & timber building at the front does boast superb views along the bay. Lunch & dinner options are usually freshly cooked fish or chicken with rice & cost around US$6. Dhow snorkelling trips can be arranged to the reef beyond the bay, or there's a simple thatched lounge/library area for enjoying a cooling drink & a good book. The capable manager, Juma, will happily help organise anything; he's friendly & helpful & speaks English & Italian with ease. **$$**

UROA

The small village of Uroa is on the coast about halfway between Kiwengwa and Chwaka. Neat bundles of wood are piled 'jenga-style' by the roadside, quirky pedestrian crossings have been painted on the road, and village life appears active and ordered. It's a traditional, slow-paced place, centred on fishing and seaweed collection. There have been a few low-key accommodation options here for many years, but 2008 saw the start of larger developments at either end of the village. So far these resorts have not set the trend for a flood of all-inclusive properties in the area, but with coastal land at such a premium, this may not be the case for long.

GETTING THERE AND AWAY Approaching from the south on the 9km of blissfully tarred road from Chwaka, you'll pass cultivated, plantation-style fields of casuarina pines; from Kiwengwa, 11.5km to the north, there is now a fast tar road too, with the old coast track the preserve of **4x4** drivers alone. In early 2008, work began to widen the road here into a serious two-lane tar highway.

Dala dala No 214 plies the route from Stone Town to Uroa six times a day, between 06.00 and 18.00, whilst the public **bus** on Route 13 adds another five

---

BEACHED SEAWEED

From December to mid February, some of the beaches on the east coast have large patches of brown seaweed washed ashore from the ocean by the wind. This can be quite a shock if you expect pristine, picture-postcard tropical beach conditions. The seaweed normally stays on the beaches until the start of the rainy season, when it is carried back out to sea. After March, and up until November, the beaches are mostly clear.

services from 08.00 to 16.00. If you prefer, private **minibuses** and **taxis** can also be arranged by most reliable Zanzibar Town tour operators (see *Chapter 6, Tour companies*, pages 134–7).

WHERE TO STAY Unless stated otherwise, hotels listed below offer air conditioning and en-suite bathrooms as standard. Going from north to south, the accommodation options here are:

ORA Palumbo Reef (102 rooms) m 0732 940178. Now managed by ORA resorts, the majority of guests here are on Italian package holidays, hence the pasta stations in the restaurant & Italian-speaking 'animators' encouraging guest participation in the day's activities. Accommodation is in 4-storey blocks, & all rooms have basic mod cons with Zanzibari beds. There's a pleasant swimming pool snaking down to the beach, a popular pool bar, thatched restaurant area & an adjacent TV lounge. The usual island excursions can be arranged, or there's an on-site spa. **$$$$**

Samaki Lodge (35 rooms) m 0772 633063/0774 467669; e samaki@samakilodge. com; www.samakilodge.com. Owned by the same Mr Palumbo as its immediate neighbour, Samaki differs in both architecture & vibe, & is not under ORA management. Its design is marked out by striking shell-encrusted coral walls (doing little for any environmental awareness credentials) & a fish skeleton logo ('samaki' means fish) which adorns lights, room numbering & all signage. Overlooking the pool, but set back from the beach, the L-shaped main building houses most of the accommodation & the public areas. There's a buffet restaurant & a piano tucked away for musical guests, with no organised activities, making this a much quieter establishment than Palumbo Reef, albeit still predominantly Italian. Additional rooms are located beside the beach, in a separate building. Access from these to the main area is less than salubrious, on a rough path bordered with barbed wire, but they do afford a little more intimacy & a sea view. **$$–$$$$**

Uroa Bay Beach Resort (61 rooms) m 0778 672809/0779 881505; e info@uroabay. com, uroa.bay@gmail.com; www.uroabay.com. Italian-owned but international in approach & clientele, this resort is spread over a large, lawned plot with a series of makuti-thatched accommodation blocks stretching back from the beach. Smart, well-spaced dbl, trpl & family rooms are available, the last wheelchair accessible with walk-in showers & level floors. Seafront & sea view, the latter being a little further back from the sea, are otherwise identical: tiled, spacious rooms with 1 king & 1 sgl bed, cream & burgundy interiors, & wide terraces. TV, fridge & electric safes are standard throughout. The communal area houses the internet room, a simple boutique, Jua buffet restaurant, Rafiki bar &, behind the tropical mural, a massage room. Nearby, but apart from the accommodation, is the small Disco Mwezi for evening entertainment. There's also a floodlit tennis court, beach volleyball area, 5-a-side football pitch, & a large swimming pool. FB. **$$$$–$$$$$**

Coconut Tree Village (64 rooms) m 0773 201867/0772 270162; e info@coconuttreevillage. com, reservation@coconuttreevillage.com; www. coconuttreevillage.com. Pulling up at Coconut Tree, you could be forgiven for thinking you were arriving at a low-budget, crumbling safari park. Life-size animal sculptures litter the entrance & landscaping: grimacing gorillas point at the gate, some sun-bleached giraffe greet you inside, whilst zebra & kudu hide in the vegetation around room terraces. Opened in Feb 2011, it is undoubtedly a curious place. The terraces of standard & superior rooms are identical except in furniture choice. Newer rooms are in multi-storey buildings dotted around the complex. The central area has rows of sofas, angled to the TV & its fuzzy African soap opera, & a restaurant. There's also a small gym & a pool. The beach here is not great, but plans are afoot to build an affiliate restaurant beside Obama Beach in Kiwengwa & provide guests with a shuttle bus to the sandy stretches further north. Currently this resort is very quiet, so negotiating rates should be possible. **$$$**

Uroa White Villa (5 rooms) m 0778 879577; e uroawhitevilla@gmail.com; www. uroawhitevilla.com. In the centre of the low-density village, with clear signposting, this place sits on a fairly compact, walled plot, where white buildings stand on 3 sides of a quadrangle, & a row of beachfront fir trees makes up the 4th. Its rooms are divided between the main villa & 2 thatched bungalows. The main villa, with its blockwork walls, tin roof & red-painted floor, has all the character of a government administration building. The 1 family room inside is clean & cool, with 3 Zanzibari dbl beds in 2 adjoining rooms, & a shared en suite. There are 4 quiet & functional bungalow rooms, spartan in appearance with little more than a bed, small coconut-wood table, & a 'fitted' wardrobe constructed from rough timber planks. Outside there's a terrace with chairs. Also in the villa is a central lounge, with a selection of Italian & German books, & a separate open-sided restaurant. The food here is all freshly cooked & the seafood-dominated menu is subject to availability. Snacks, such as chapattis, will usually cost US$1–5, with à la carte dinners ranging up to US$12. Snorkelling equipment can be hired (US$15) & fishing trips with the locals are always possible; there's a beach nearby. The villagers here are relaxed around visitors, & not (yet) overwhelmed by their numbers, so wandering into the community is also a possibility. **$$–$$$**

⌂ **Tamarind Beach Hotel** (16 rooms) m 0777 413709/411191; e tamarind@zanzinet. com; www.tamarind.nu. Along a particularly stunning stretch of coconut-lined beach, & with joint Norwegian–Zanzibari ownership, the very helpful Said Ali, & Scandinavian Trond manage peaceful Tamarind. The semi-detached cottages built from coral-stone blocks & cement are each entered through traditional Zanzibari doors. All rooms have a dbl bed (although extra beds are easily obtained for twin or trpl occupancy), mains electricity, 2 ceiling fans & mosquito net, plus an en-suite 'wet-room'-style bathroom. Interiors are simple & in parts could do with some upgrading. There is a safety-deposit box at reception for valuables, a small TV room & a large central pool with integrated childrens pool. The restaurant (lunch & dinner US$15pp) offers indoor dining at individual tables & fresh produce, with an emphasis on seafood, whilst the adjoining bar produces fabulous freshly squeezed juices & lots of cocktails. Children are generally welcome at the hotel, a cot is available & babysitting can be arranged with the staff, but, beyond playing in the pool, sea & sand, activities are limited. **$$$**

⌂ **Zanzibar Safari Club** (50 rooms) m 0777 844481; e reservations@zanzibarsafariclub. com; www.zanzibarsafariclub.com. The mock cannons resting on red-brick plinths scream of the idiosyncrasies hidden behind Safari Club's imposing gates. South of Uroa village, this is a slightly kitsch medley of Arabian & Indian styles, marketed primarily to groups from Europe & South Africa. Run by efficient, if brusque, staff, the resort has all the trappings of a large hotel (business centre, modern in-room amenities, tennis court) but the feel of a hospitality training school, which ties in with its links to the wildlife lodges of the Tanzanian mainland. In the heart of the resort, the central pool is lovely, & surrounded by tidy rows of sunloungers, & there's an idyllic, peaceful, palm-fringed beach for those who want to dip in the sea. The standard rooms & suites are a riot of colours & designs, both inside & out. A stream of different designers came & went during the development of this resort, which explains the eclectic design. The Disney-like orange cottages with green-tiled roofs sit in orderly rows around the organised complex. At the entrance to each, a Zanzibari bench, covered in cushions, sits on a small terrace, & an arched door, leads to a décor of distressed Van Gogh: every piece of wooden furniture has been painted in bold colours & limed to create an aged, beach-hut quality. Yet the rooms have all the essential hotel mod cons, including a fridge, satellite TV & electronic safe. The Zanzibari beds are covered in mosquito nets trimmed with patterned fabrics, & each room has its own boiler. Reasonably sized but mediocre buffets are served in the circular, poolside Mwangaza Restaurant, or alternatively the quiet Ocean View Restaurant serves Swahili cuisine beside the beach. At the end of the jetty, the Zinc Discotheque allows guests to boogie above the waves. Impressive sound & light systems, a good Kenyan DJ & a free pool table for non-dancers make this an entertaining, if noisy, after-dinner hangout. Even when no-one turns up, the music plays on until 02.00 every night. This hotel is very secure with a multi-gate security entry, good locks on room doors, safety-deposit boxes at reception & security guards on patrol. No children under 12 years are allowed. No credit cards accepted. **$$$$$**

⌂ **Paradise Beach Resort** (63 rooms) m 0775 088729/0777 699000; e bookings@ hotelzanzibar.com. Between Uroa & Chwaka rises the truly massive makuti roof of Paradise Beach Resort's reception. The place has undergone several management & name changes; most recently, in late 2011, new Dutch owners arrived with renovation plans. Beyond the vast open reception, there are 56 rooms in the main resort area & a further 7 at the satellite Beach House, 15mins' walk north along the beach (close to Tamarind Beach Hotel). Each of the rooms has a fridge, electronic safe, hot water & capacity for dbl or trpl occupancy. The Premium room has a lounge area & a TV & CD player, whilst the Luxury rooms are identical but lack the audio-visual equipment. The 1st-floor suites are simpler but thoughtfully decorated & still very spacious. In a small coconut grove, there is a central sundeck & a popular pool. There's a large buffet & à la carte restaurant, complete with open kitchen, & a sundown area on stilts over the sea, which may yet become an alternative dining venue. Kayaks are available for guest use though the beach here is not Zanzibar's finest, with landed seaweed strewn across little sand. At low tide, the outline of sunk concrete slabs are also visible (a failed bid by previous owners to bank up the sand in front of the hotel), while the current owners have plans to build a 200m rock wall out to the reef line in an attempt to trap sand & increase their beach size. The visual & environmental impact of this new plan is not to be underestimated. Plans to create a dive centre, conference centre & spa are also afoot. **$$$$**

✗ WHERE TO EAT

✗ Kamba Kocha Bar & Pizzeria
⏱ 10.30–24.30. 'In this bar you'll never drink alone' claims the signage, & popular it is. Italian-owned & Masaai run, this timber-clad bar & restaurant is a busy seaside hangout for guests of the neighbouring resorts. Inside, the bar is decorated with graffiti: declarations of love & alcoholic words of wisdom adorn every inch of the interior. Outside on the sand, pub benches & mosaic-topped tables sit under makuti umbrellas & the clay oven serves up pizza for US$5–9 alongside a host of daily cocktails. **$$**

CHWAKA

Halfway down the east coast, directly due east of Zanzibar Town, Chwaka is a large fishing village overlooking a wide bay fringed with mangrove swamps. In the early 19th century, Chwaka was a major slave port, exporting human cargo across the Indian Ocean to Arabia. In more recent times, its sea breezes and lack of mosquitoes made it a popular holiday destination for British colonial administrators and affluent Zanzibari dignitaries: their grand, crumbling villas remain along the shoreline north of the village. Today, apart from some coastal researchers, there is not much in the way of facilities or activity, besides the large, lively seafood market, where for the best atmosphere, arrive in the mornings when the fishing boats dock, laden with the day's catch.

Chwaka Bay itself supports the largest swathe of mangrove forest on Zanzibar and forms a significant part of the Jozani-Chwaka Bay National Park, Zanzibar's only national park. The government is currently working with international charities, like CARE International, and conservation bodies, to develop and manage the forest as a conservation area and income-generating ecotourism project. Some tours to explore the mangroves are possible, and do make an interesting diversion. There is little accommodation in Chwaka and few visitors, but it's possible to take a boat across Chwaka Bay to head further down the east coast, which may attract the adventurous.

GETTING THERE AND AWAY Chwaka can be reached by public **bus** (Routes 6 and 13), **dala dala** (Nos 206 and 214) or by **hired car** or **bike**. Tourist **minibuses** do not usually come here, although you could privately hire one through a tour company (see *Chapter 6, Tour companies*, pages 134–7). However you choose to travel, if you approach from the west, the smooth, tarmac road through the island's lush interior is a pleasure.

If you are heading to or from the southeast coast, and don't want to go back to Zanzibar Town in between, you can hitch a ride on an octopus-fishing **boat** (high tide only) across Chwaka Bay to Michamvi on the peninsula north of Bwejuu. Local people regularly travel this way, but only the occasional intrepid tourist is seen

MANGROVE FOREST DEPLETION

Mangroves are salt-tolerant, resilient, evergreen trees, anchored by stilt-like roots in the intertidal zone (eg: *Rhizophora mucronata*) or simply growing in sandy muddy bottoms (eg: *Avicennia marina*), or even perched on fossil coral pockets with minimum soil. They are found in sheltered bays and river estuaries, where the waves have only low energy levels, and are vital components of the tropical marine environment. They ensure shoreline stability by protecting soft sediment from erosion, providing nutrients for sea organisms, and offering sanctuary to migratory birds, juvenile fish, shellfish and crustaceans.

Mangroves are nevertheless one of the most threatened habitats in the world. Environmental stress from changing tides and pollution takes its toll, but increasingly it's human interference that is the primary cause of irreparable damage. On Zanzibar, this is certainly the case: many people rely on the forests for fuel (firewood and charcoal), lime burning, boat repair and dugout manufacture, as well as material for house construction. Mangrove wood is dense and, because of its tannin content, it is termite-resistant, making it preferable for house construction. Income is also generated from trading in cut wood, poles and charcoal. The absence of alternative income-generating activities means heavy dependence on mangroves.

Ominously, as the rural population continues to grow, so does the demand for this fragile resource. It is therefore critical to fully understand and address the needs of the villagers in order to have any chance of developing successful conservation initiatives.

Chwaka Bay is fringed by Unguja's largest area of mangrove forest, approximately 3,000ha and accounting for 5% of the island's total forest cover. Here, fairly dense stands of diverse mangrove species, zoned by their tolerance to the conditions of the area (eg: volume of water and salt levels), are drained by a number of lovely creeks.

Over the last 60 years, assorted management plans have been drawn up with the communities bordering the forests, in a bid to control overexploitation in the area. From issuing permits to control harvesting, imposing mangrove taxes and limiting creek access, each has successively failed to halt rapid deforestation. Ever-changing forestry policy, lack of serious patrolling, a decline in the authority of village elders to command community support, insufficient alternative income sources for villagers, and minimal resources are all cited as reasons for the failure.

Conservation and development organisations continue to attempt to halt deforestation in the area, improve villager understanding of the forests' importance and lobby local and national government for support; but, without doubt, these valuable natural resources will be irretrievably ruined unless human activities are carefully controlled.

here. Boats from Michamvi come across to Chwaka's fish market most mornings, returning around noon. There are no set schedules, so you will need to ask around on the beach. A ride should cost little more than a few dollars.

WHERE TO STAY

⌂ Chwaka Bay Resort (30 rooms) m 0774 040400; www.phoneandgo.it. North of Chwaka village on the coast road, past some near-derelict grand colonial villas, Chwaka Bay Resort has been turned into yet another all-inclusive Italian resort. Its former Swedish owners handed over their property to Euro internet operator 'Phone & Go' in 2006 & the complex is now filled with social groups of 30-somethings from Rome & Milan. Little has changed in the accommodation, though it has been recently renovated, & the original rondavels, known as bungalows, remain light & spacious thanks to their 3 large windows, & come with AC and en-suite bathrooms. The simple, dark wood furniture all matches & beds can be made up as dbls or twins. Arguably, these rooms have more character than their newer siblings. The newer villas (each with 4 independent rooms), are referred to as 'deluxe' & these have lockable drawers as safes, mosquito nets & constant hot water controlled by an in-room boiler. Each room has a terracotta-tiled terrace or balcony with chairs, a coffee table & a view to the beach. The ground-floor rooms in these buildings are a mix of dbls, twins & trpls, whilst upstairs all the rooms have a dbl bed. Rooms in both categories are raised up away from the sand.

The beach here isn't as good as many on the east coast, but daily boat trips to the other side of the peninsula are arranged to 'Paradise Beach' with its satellite bar, grill & loungers. Alternatively the kidney-shaped swimming pool is pleasant enough for a cooling dip, & there's a sunken pool bar for cocktails & juices. Coir-rope loungers & striped metal deckchairs sit on the surrounding tiles, some shaded by umbrellas, & all enjoying views of palms along the coast. Like a giant board game, the resort's concrete paths are seemingly colour-coded: green leads between the bungalows whilst blue takes you around the pool & gardens. The former décor disaster in the restaurant & lounge has thankfully been rectified & now buffet meals & drinks are enjoyed under makuti thatch with a more muted colour scheme. **$$$–$$$$**

UFUFUMA FOREST HABITAT

The Ufufuma Forest conservation project was set up by the people of nearby Jendele village. It aims to protect the forest habitat and to educate the villagers in sustainable use. The 102 local volunteers, led by the dedicated and charismatic Mr Mustafa Makame, hope to make it a place for both locals and foreigners to visit, and to preserve the traditional worship of *shetani*, or spirits, which is performed here (see box, *The Shetani of Zanzibar*, pages 40–1). The forest area is at present only 1km², but the villagers are leaving the surrounding 4km² area uncultivated to allow the forest habitat to expand in size. Tiny paths, marked with periodic, mid-blue arrows, wind through thick vegetation, whilst underfoot a tangle of roots clings to coral rag. A visit here is not a great wildlife experience, nor is it meant to be, although you might be fortunate enough to see skittish red colobus (as we did; apparently early morning is best), island birdlife, snakes and lizards. Honey is also collected from the forest, so look out for the canopy-height hives. A few villagers act as guides, but they are not wildlife specialists and don't know a lot of the bird names. They are trying to learn, however, and are very enthusiastic about Ufufuma's cultural importance – which is the primary reason for a visit here.

There are many underground caves hidden in the dense forest undergrowth: three are shetani caves being used by the local traditional healer (aka 'witch-doctor'), which tourists may also visit. It is a source of great joy and comfort to the local Zanzibari people who come to these caves to speak with the spirits. When local people are sick or troubled they come to these sites with the local traditional healer and perform rituals and recitations to cure themselves. The cave entrances are adorned with tattered strips of red and white fabric and surrounded by piles of

UFUFUMA'S USEFUL TREES

As in most African societies, many of the trees and plants found in Ufufuma Forest play an important role in the daily lives of the local population. Be it for medicinal or practical use, religious or cultural significance, the flora is fascinatingly versatile when viewed through the eyes of a resident guide. The trees below are a sample of what's to be seen and learnt. They are listed by their Swahili name, as the guides will not know them by anything else.

MCHOFU Across the island, the branches of this tree are commonly used as an all-purpose timber for firewood and furniture. Here, only its fruits are used as a cure for coughs, colds and flu.

MDAA (*Euclea natalensis*) Ufufuma's answer to Colgate: this is the local toothpaste. The villagers chew on a piece of the tree's root to ensure a bright, white set of teeth and healthy gums. In 1991, research into this custom by the South African Medical Research Council at the University of Stellenbosch showed that oral bacterial growth was indeed suppressed by this chewing, giving the practice some scientific validity. Sadly, it also concluded that the daily exercise is too limited to have a truly beneficial effect: this is probably backed up by the smiles around you.

MKOMWE (*Caesalpinia bonducella*) Mkomwe's Latin name derives from the Arab word *bonduc*, meaning 'hazelnut'. It's easy to see why when presented with the neat spherical seed kernels (Swahili: *komwe*) from within its fruit. These are the traditional pieces used in games of *bao*, but the dual-purpose seeds of this tree can also be boiled with water to produce a drink for sufferers of stomach ache.

MKUYU The roots of this wild fig are boiled with water to form a drink. Given to pregnant women, the concoction is believed to have an abortive quality.

MLALANGAO Hunting for birds is a patient but ingenious process. Local men must first study the avian movements in the forest, watching flight paths and routines. To catch the birds, they cut the trunk of the mlalangao tree with a *panga* (long blade machete), collect the sap (Swahili: *utomvu*), and boil it to form a type of latex. Back in the forest, the chewing-gum-textured latex is smeared onto the branches where birds have been observed resting. Then the men wait … for when the birds do land, they simply stick to the latex from where they are easily collected and taken home to make soup.

MUWAVIKALI This sweet-smelling tree is boiled with water and the resulting liquid is drunk to combat symptoms of malaria.

MKAAGA Seek out the young leaves on this little bush. They'll provide you with the freshest tea.

sweet offerings, often rotting, from sugar cane to Coca-Cola. Inside, the caves are dank and spooky, with the smell of smoke from recent fires and resident colonies of bats. It's a fascinating insight into a rarely seen aspect of Zanzibari culture.

Mr Mustafa and his small team believe wholeheartedly that in protecting the forest there is potential for the local communities to benefit financially from conservation tourism; they are simply unsure how to achieve their goal. Gaining support from all of the villagers is difficult – many want the timber for firewood and rocks for building, and perceive little monetary gain from conservation. But Mr Mustafa is determined, and, whilst searching for a solution, he travels to Ufufuma from Zanzibar Town every Sunday on his moped, keen to inspire and educate the villagers about protecting the forest. He even chairs the local NGO.

Six villages in the vicinity already benefit from the income of the forest. All of the money goes directly to the community leaders, who assess their village's primary needs, be it cattle medicine, wells or school materials, and channel the money as appropriate. If more people visit the forest, accepting that it's not a slick tourism enterprise, the village coffers will slowly increase, and in turn the communities will begin to see the benefits of preserving rather than plundering their surroundings. We wish the Ufufuma Forest conservation project every success.

ARRANGING YOUR VISIT To visit Ufufuma Forest, it is best to make contact in advance, to ensure that an English-speaking guide is available at the time of your visit (Mr Mustafa Makame; m *0747 491069*; e *himauje@yahoo.com*). The price of a visit is variable as a single tariff system has yet to be adopted. However, for a guided forest walk lasting a few hours, a visit to the caves, and usually a gift of fresh fruit or coconut refreshment, expect to pay US$5 per person per guide, and then volunteer to make a larger donation to the community fund. If you want to see a full shetani ceremony, consisting of about seven hours of singing, dancing and assorted rituals, this costs US$50 (for one or two people), and will have to be booked in advance and take place at a time convenient to the local 'doctor'. As the forest floor can be damp and rugged, be sure to take sturdy shoes, and, in the hot season, plenty of water to drink.

GETTING THERE AND AWAY To reach Ufufuma from Zanzibar Town, take the road west towards Chwaka: the forest is on the left, about 5km before Chwaka. There is currently a small, slightly rusted sign but no specific parking place, and only concealed paths lead into the forest. If you have contacted the Ufufuma volunteers in advance, then a welcoming party will likely be waiting for you. However, if your visit isn't scheduled, stop at Jendele village and ask in the market area for an official forest guide.

To reach the forest on **public transport**, talk to the dala dala drivers heading towards Chwaka (Nos 206 or 214), and ask to be dropped in Jendele village; be aware this is a sprawling village with little tourism connection so it may not be an easy task.

DUNGA RUINS

Equidistant from Chwaka and Zanzibar Town, in the lush centre of the island, lie Dunga Ruins. Close to the modern village of Dunga, these are the remains of the palace built for King Mohammed, the Mwinyi Mkuu (great chief) of Zanzibar. Constructed between 1846 and 1856, the palace may have been built on the site of an earlier house. Prior to this, the residence of the Mwinyi Mkuu had been at Kizimkazi or Unguja Ukuu (see pages 321 and 334 respectively).

Local legend tells that when Dunga Palace was built, slaves were buried alive in the foundations, while others were killed and their blood mixed with the mortar. It was believed that this would bring strength and good fortune to the house. There may be some truth in this story as, in the 1920s, a nearby well was found to be half full of human bones. Today, in the centre of an overgrown garden, only the main walls of the palace remain, but it is still an imposing ruin and retains something of its original grandeur.

A few old passages, pillars and staircases can also be seen. The windows are empty and their decorative frames are now in the House of Wonders in Zanzibar Town (see *Chapter 6*, page 185), along with the Mwinyi Mkuu's sacred drums and horns. The latter were part of the royal regalia and both were kept at Dunga during King Mohammed's rule. The drums, carved from mango wood and inscribed with Arabic, were said to beat spontaneously to warn the king of impending trouble. The horns were kept in a secret hiding place, known only to the Mwinyi Mkuu. When he was near death, their location would be revealed to the heir apparent. Mohammed died in 1865 and was succeeded by his son Ahmed, but he died of smallpox in 1873, leaving no male heir. His two sisters had married into prominent families of Arab landowners, but the ruling dynasty came to an end.

A Swahili royal line is believed to have existed on Zanzibar prior to the first Shirazi immigrants arriving from Persia in the 10th century AD. Leading figures among the Shirazis are thought to have married into the family of the then Swahili ruler, as the Mwinyi Mkuu later claimed to be descended from a Shirazi prince. During the following centuries, while the island was controlled by the Portuguese, and later by the Arabs and British, a Mwinyi Mkuu continued to be regarded as the traditional leader by the people of Zanzibar.

GETTING THERE AND AWAY About 14km from Stone Town on the road to the east coast, or 30 minutes' drive inland from Chwaka, the ruins sit in the centre of the island on the southern side of the road. It is also possible to reach Dunga from the south, along the dirt track from Tunguu, on the main road to the island's southeast; a **4x4** is necessary for this route. By **dala dala** from Zanzibar Town, it's possible to reach the ruins on the Chwaka services, Nos 206 and 214, or by public **bus**, Routes 4 and 6.

Southeastern Zanzibar

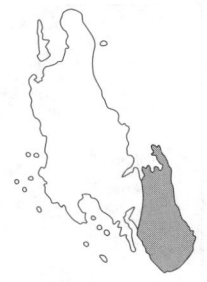

From the finger of the Michamvi Peninsula to the coastal curve at Makunduchi, the southeast of Zanzibar offers, in many ways, a continuation of the powder-white sandy beaches and traditional fishing villages found from Matemwe to Chwaka Bay. Certainly the environment here, with its large tidal range and fringe reef parallel to the beach, is almost exactly the same.

A decade or so ago, the area around the villages of Paje, Bwejuu and Jambiani used to be the busiest part of the east coast, especially for backpackers, as there was a good choice of cheap places to stay. However, things have changed in recent years and the variety of accommodation has increased considerably, whilst the arrival of tourism to the peninsula's furthest reach at Michamvi Kae has opened up a whole new area. A scattering of mid-range and upmarket options have appeared, with more imagination and thought going into their design and ethos, and the success of a few large family resorts has widened the area's appeal.

The fast tar roads may mean that the bulk of budget travellers are currently opting for livelier environs in northern Zanzibar, around the burgeoning Nungwi and Kendwa areas, but pockets of growth around new beach bars, 'flashpacker' retreats and kitesurfing centres are returning here too. There remain a large number of rather uninspiring guesthouses along the southeastern coast, many almost indistinguishable from the next, but among them some gems are worth seeking out.

The end result is that southeast Zanzibar now offers some of the island's quieter beach spots available to a genuine mix of budgets. The palm-fringed beaches here invariably seem wilder and more ramshackle than their counterparts on the northeast coast, and probably still offer fewer makuti-shaded cocktail bars than those of Nungwi and Kendwa. With the exception of a couple of larger all-inclusive properties, the southeast of the island is still generally an area for a lower-key, lower-impact beach retreat.

MICHAMVI PENINSULA

Along the length of the Michamvi Peninsula's 10km east coast, the sand is the fine, powder-white stuff of 'paradise' advertising, and the sea is a suitably sparkling cobalt blue. Few local people live here, concentrating instead in Bwejuu to the south or the village of Michamvi Kae, beside Chwaka Bay. Almost all of the accommodation in this area is currently high quality, and each place is individual in its style and customers. However, the number of hotels has more than doubled since 2005, and more are being built. For the immediate future, come for the pristine, palm-fringed beaches, good diving opportunities and a sense of space, and hope that development stalls.

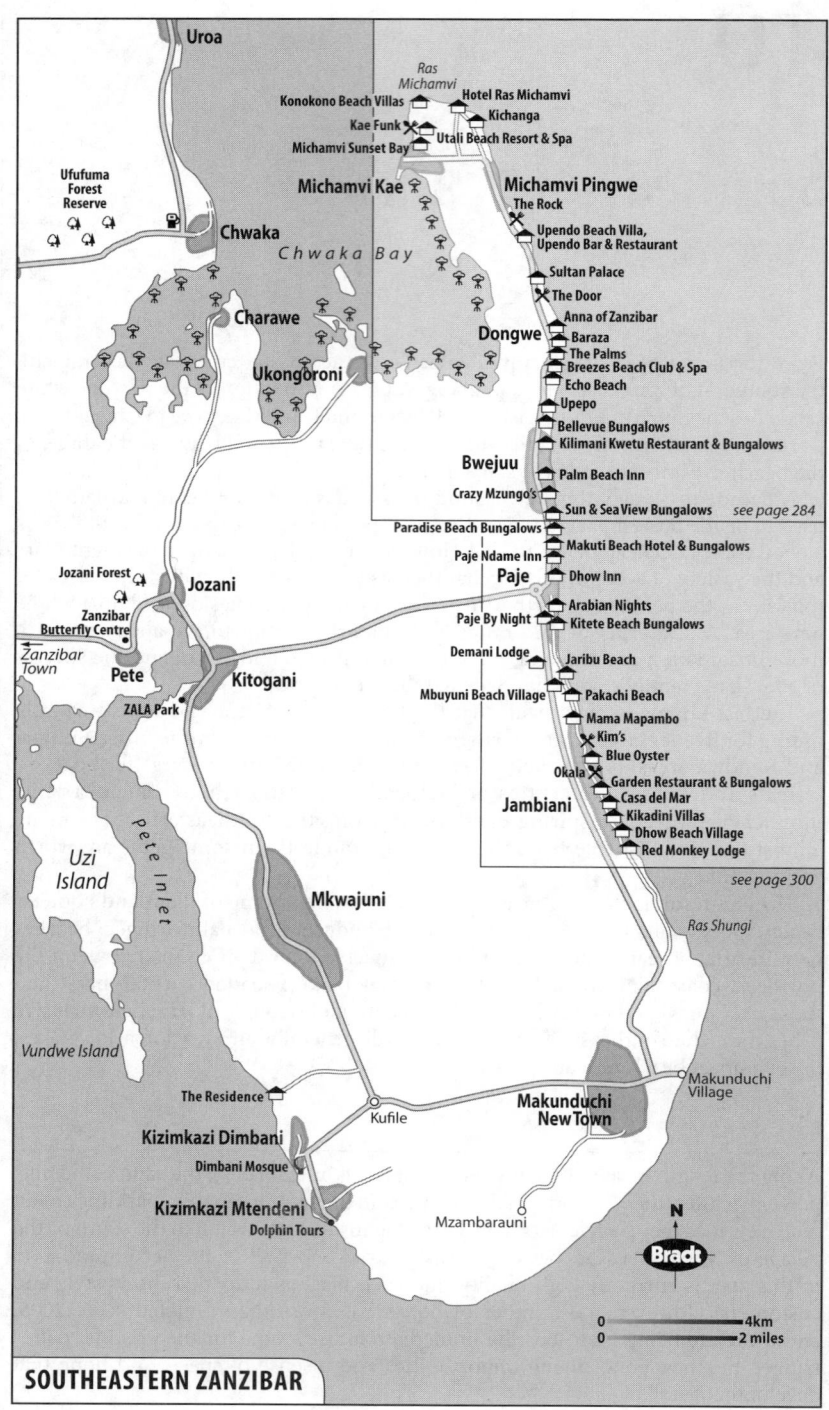

Uroa

Ras Michamvi

Konokono Beach Villas
Hotel Ras Michamvi
Kichanga
Kae Funk
Michamvi Sunset Bay
Utali Beach Resort & Spa

Ufufuma Forest Reserve

Chwaka

Chwaka Bay

Michamvi Kae

Michamvi Pingwe
The Rock
Upendo Beach Villa, Upendo Bar & Restaurant

Charawe

Sultan Palace
The Door
Anna of Zanzibar
Baraza
The Palms
Breezes Beach Club & Spa
Echo Beach
Upepo
Bellevue Bungalows
Kilimani Kwetu Restaurant & Bungalows
Palm Beach Inn

Dongwe

Ukongoroni

Bwejuu

Crazy Mzungo's

Sun & Sea View Bungalows   *see page 284*

Paradise Beach Bungalows

Makuti Beach Hotel & Bungalows

Paje Ndame Inn

Paje

Dhow Inn

Jozani Forest

Jozani

Arabian Nights
Kitete Beach Bungalows

Paje By Night

Zanzibar Butterfly Centre

Zanzibar Town

Pete

Kitogani

Demani Lodge
Jaribu Beach

ZALA Park

Mbuyuni Beach Village
Pakachi Beach
Mama Mapambo
Kim's
Blue Oyster
Okala
Garden Restaurant & Bungalows
Casa del Mar
Kikadini Villas
Dhow Beach Village
Red Monkey Lodge

Jambiani

Uzi Island

Mkwajuni

Pete Inlet

see page 300

Ras Shungi

Vundwe Island

The Residence
Makunduchi Village

Kufile

Makunduchi New Town

Kizimkazi Dimbani

Dimbani Mosque

Kizimkazi Mtendeni

Dolphin Tours

Mzambarauni

N

Bradt

0 ——— 4km
0 ——— 2 miles

SOUTHEASTERN ZANZIBAR

GETTING THERE AND AWAY All of the accommodation on this stretch of coast will arrange **transfers**, though most international guests will set this up in advance with their tour operator. For those with a **hired car**, north of Bwejuu there is a single fast tar road, so getting lost is virtually impossible; a bumpy coastal track also heads north, although the arrival of the tar highway has rendered it into more of a footpath, and it is almost impassable at points. There is little in the way of public transport on the peninsula, but **dala dala** No 324 from Zanzibar Town will sometimes continue from Bwejuu towards Michamvi Kae village. If your luggage is not too bulky it's probably easier to **cycle** or arrange a local transfer.

WHERE TO STAY This peninsula is the location for some of the island's most luxurious hotels. These are described in this section from north to south.

Unless stated otherwise, hotels listed below offer air conditioning and en-suite bathrooms as standard.

Michamvi Sunset Bay (20 rooms) m 0778 662872/0777 878136; e matt@michamvi.com, brad@michamvi.com; www.michamvi.com. The only east coast resort facing west across water, Michamvi Sunset Bay underwent a complete renovation in 2011, & also turned away from large, energetic groups. At the northern end of Michamvi Kae village, overlooking the mirror-like Chwaka Bay, it's now a relaxed, family-friendly resort with a casual vibe. There's a small restaurant & a breezy bar overlooking the pretty beach. The bedrooms are in 2-storey villas set out in an arc around the mosaic pool. Entering from the back, the rooms are light & spacious with contemporary furnishings, retractable mosquito nets & original Zanzibari art (any piece can be bought with 100% of sale price going to the artist). The new bathrooms have a double shower, with 4 rooms enjoying a bath, too. Every room has either a private balcony or ground-floor terrace, complete with seating. Sunset mangrove safaris (US$50, up to 4 people) are available & several watersports are possible from the quiet beach, whilst divers are collected by the off-site Peponi Diving centre (see *What to see and do*, page 304). Personalised village tours are arranged directly with the community. The team here are very adaptable & children are warmly welcomed by the hands-on management, with under-12s staying free of charge. Equally, there is an impressive commitment to the local community. Several sensible, well-resourced – financially & practically – projects are in place. On a large scale, manager Brad, a trained horticulturalist, is piloting a vegetable-growing scheme with the ultimate aim of having the villagers cultivate &

sell their produce to not only Sunset Bay, but other peninsula hotels too. An English teacher is funded to teach adults in the village, with plans to create a local hotel school. There is also an ambitious scheme to run a freshwater pipeline from Paje to serve the Michamvi Kae community. Even small ideas reap great rewards, however: from staff swimming lessons to job exchange programmes & profit-sharing, this place firmly lives up to its 'Making a Difference' philosophy. It's also a lovely remote spot on an increasingly crowded island. **$$$$-$$$$$**

Utalii Beach Resort & Spa (127 rooms) \024 5500098; m 0786 927300; www. utaliiresort.com. For the last 4 years, this fairly sizeable development has been under construction immediately next door to Michamvi Sunset Beach. Finally opening its doors in early 2012, the circular, 2-storey buildings house rooms with clean (if a little spartan) interiors, tiled floors, French doors to some terrace space, shower rooms & an array of add-ons from mini fridges to safes. There are 2 pools, a small selection of watersports & the Maisha Spa offering Thai, African & European treatments. Inside the main makuti thatched area, the multi-coloured underlighting & dark furniture of the Pavilion Bar try a little too hard, but perhaps put some guests in the mood to check out the Crab Nightclub (© 22.00 onwards daily). For more sedate evenings, à la carte or set menu dining is available in the open-sided restaurant, whilst daytime snacks & lunches are served from the Michamvi Beach Cove Restaurant on the beach. **$$$$**

Sagando Hostel m 0773 193236; e sagandohostel@gmail.com. In the village of

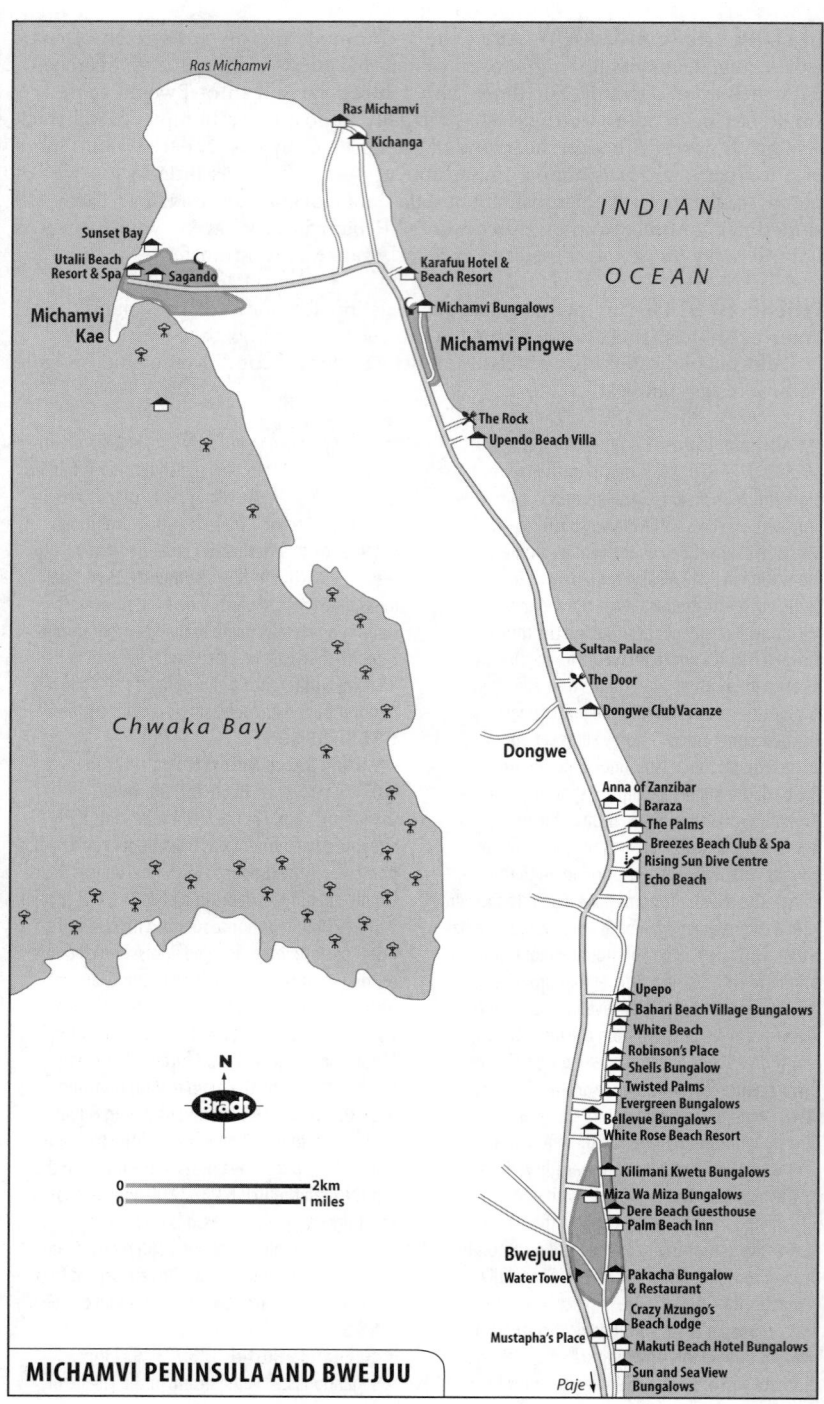

INDIAN

OCEAN

Ras Michamvi

Ras Michamvi
Kichanga

Sunset Bay
Utalii Beach
Resort & Spa
Sagando
Karafuu Hotel &
Beach Resort
Michamvi Bungalows

Michamvi
Kae
Michamvi Pingwe

The Rock
Upendo Beach Villa

Chwaka Bay

Sultan Palace
The Door
Dongwe Club Vacanze

Dongwe

Anna of Zanzibar
Baraza
The Palms
Breezes Beach Club & Spa
Rising Sun Dive Centre
Echo Beach

Upepo
Bahari Beach Village Bungalows
White Beach
Robinson's Place
Shells Bungalow
Twisted Palms
Evergreen Bungalows
Bellevue Bungalows
White Rose Beach Resort

N

Bradt

Kilimani Kwetu Bungalows

Miza Wa Miza Bungalows
Dere Beach Guesthouse
Palm Beach Inn

0   2km
0   1 miles

Bwejuu
Water Tower
Pakacha Bungalow
& Restaurant

Crazy Mzungo's
Beach Lodge
Mustapha's Place
Makuti Beach Hotel Bungalows

Paje
Sun and Sea View
Bungalows

MICHAMVI PENINSULA AND BWEJUU

Michamvi Kae, away from the beach, Sagando is a trio of very simple backpackers' bungalows. The basic rooms are all en suite, & of a standard expected at the bottom end of the budget scale. **$**

⌂ **Konokono Beach Villas** (24 rooms) m 0777 2265431; e reservations@konokonozanzibar.com; www.konokonozanzibar.com. Konokono opened its doors in 2010 & promptly closed them again the following year. Currently under extensive refurbishment, including the addition of a further 13 villas, the lodge is due to reopen in May 2013 with a new, & much needed, beachside restaurant & a spa. The large, contemporary villas all have their own secluded gardens with plunge pools, & are well spaced over this extensive plot. There are plans to redesign the colourful gardens & raised pool, the latter being distinctly uninspiring given the space, setting & overall quality of the resort. With more focus on the environment & better beach & pool facilities, standards & guest praise are likely to remain high here. **$$–$$$**

⌂ **Hotel Ras Michamvi** (15 rooms) ✆024 2231081; e info@rasmichamvi.com; www.rasmichamvi.com. Opened by Mr Suleiman of Jambo Guesthouse in Stone Town (see *Where to stay*, page 158), this little resort sits high up on the coral cliffs at the very tip of the peninsula. It's in a very quiet corner of the island, so unless you have your own transport or enjoy extremely long walks it's really quite remote; this is also its charm for the escapist. Bordered by peach & pink hibiscus bushes, the paths around the complex are all on slightly raised boardwalks with makuti thatch & neatly planted macramé hanging baskets. Rooms are surprisingly nice with tiled floors, quality Zanzibari beds & large blue bathrooms. There are some rooms classed as 'disabled-friendly' with ramp entrances & walk-in showers, though the beds remain fairly high to be practical to those who are truly wheelchair-bound. There is an impressive semicircular restaurant offering reef panoramas & glimpses into the open kitchen. Outside this, steep steps lead down the cliff to a small private cove, where the sand is at its deepest & best in Jun/Jul. **$$$**

⌂ **Kichanga** (23 rooms) m 0773 175124/193775; e info@athomehotels.com; www.athomehotels.com. Kichanga is an attractive cliff-top lodge above a lovely sandy cove at the northernmost tip of the Michamvi Peninsula. Its cottages are of stone-&-thatch or rustic timber construction & are

in staggered rows to give a mix of beach-facing & garden outlooks. Interiors are a little sparse, especially in the family rooms, & slightly tired but they do all benefit from large wooden terraces. Mosquito nets, fans & safes are standard throughout. In the main building there's an internet point, local tailor (US$15/top), a lounge bar & an Italian-influenced buffet restaurant (tomato & mozzarella chapatti, pasta stations, etc).

There are organised snorkelling trips, canoe rental & kite-boarding; even beach towels are provided. The cove geography means that very few non-residents come even close to the beach, & children are pretty safe from wandering too far. The sand here migrates, & is at its best from Aug–Dec; the beach gets progressively rockier as the Kaskazi wind blows. There is a pool popular with young families, a massage banda for local treatments (US$25/hr) & a pool bar for midday drinks & snacks. **$$$–$$$$$**

⌂ **Karafuu Hotel & Beach Resort** (89 rooms) m 0777 413647/8; e khbr@karafuuzanzibar.com; www.karafuuzanzibar.com. Karafuu is as friendly & stylish as you would expect from an Italian-owned resort. Beautifully carved chaise-longues sit on polished granite floors in reception, antique clocks adorn the walls, cosmopolitan young couples sip margaritas around the swim-up pool bar, & all around an air of cool confidence & sophistication pervades. Its rooms are all terrific, smart & newly painted. They're divided into 3 categories, based solely on proximity to the beach, with only the junior suite having a sea view. The rooms all have big beds with neat wrought-iron seats at the end of each, a daybed & minibar. Outside, a wide terrace with tasteful wooden furniture looks out onto gardens filled with beautiful white lilies & coconut palms. Children are warmly welcomed & well catered for with a children's playground & a sectioned-off baby area within the main pool. There's also a large diving & watersports base beside the pool, the Karafuu Dive Centre (see *What to see and do*, page 289). **$$$$–**🏆

⌂ **Michamvi Bungalows** (2 rooms) m 0777 490027; e ilyasnasib@yahoo.com. At the northern end of Michamvi Pingwe village, overlooking the palms, beach & emerald waters below, these rock bungalows are pretty basic with dbl beds, a cold-water en-suite shower & small private terrace. The manager, Mr Ilyas, is very accommodating & the small octagonal restaurant, decorated with shell mobiles & psychedelic flowers, serves fresh fish to order. There can be a reasonable number of villagers touting for trade on the beach but otherwise this is really a simple place to get away from it all. **$$**

🏠 **Upendo Beach Villa** (3 rooms) m 0777 244492; e info@upendozanzibar.com; www. upendovilla.com Adjacent to Upendo Bar (see *Where to eat and drink*, page 289), this mint-green, makuti thatched villa is a dream retreat for hip, travelling friends. Much like the affiliated lounge bar, attention to detail is evident in all aspects of this chic hideaway. Overlooking the beach, lagoon, & the Rock Restaurant, this is a super spot for escapists. It's close to the village, but far from the large resorts & crowded budget haunts elsewhere on the island. Very much aimed at cool urbanites seeking a sexy retreat, it's an open-plan villa with cool, brilliant white interiors, high makuti ceiling (exc the bedrooms), & a sea-facing wraparound deck complete with inviting swinging beds & a plunge pool (there's also a swimming pool by the bar). There are 3 spacious dbl bedrooms – Kamma, Raaga & Ishtaa – all with simple built-in furnishings, stylish bathrooms, & splashes of colour from circular mkeke mats & vibrant artwork. A private chef is on hand to prepare food to order, or give you a lesson in spicy Swahili cookery, & there's a family-style timber table beside the open kitchen for social meals. An iPod docking station, raft of design & fashionista magazines, & guest library hint at the low level of guest activity expected here – but with a beautiful breezy deck, beach frontage & good food & drink, it's easy to see why just chilling is de rigeur. FB. **$$$$–$$$$$**

🏠 **Sultan Palace** (22 rooms) ☎ 024 2240173; m 0777 423792; e Sultanpalacezanzibar@ zanlink.com; www.sultanpalacezanzibar.com. It was a sad day when Sultan Palace closed in 2006, but happily, it reopened in Aug 2011, brighter & even lovelier than before. Set high on a coral cliff, overlooking a deserted pristine beach, this elegant place has lost none of its olde-worlde charm. The rooms are divided into Flower Rooms, & Ocean, Garden & Imperial suites, with Ocean & Garden being identical apart from the view (though there is a better view of the sea from the Garden suites here than from many sea-view rooms at other nearby hotels). The Flower Rooms are the simplest, & are located at the back of the

plot, away from the sea. Inside the extremely spacious Garden Suites are beautifully ornate pieces of carved Zanzibari furniture, a bed draped in a lace-trimmed mosquito net, & some tasteful locally sourced antiques. Each suite is a different colour & co-ordinated so that the shell pattern on the bedspread matches the cushions, the room information folder & even the hairdryer. There's also AC, a walk-in wardrobe, an electronic safe, an umbrella & a large bathroom. The Imperial Suites are larger still, with 2 dbl beds, vast bathrooms & his-&-hers showers in sculpted Arabian baths. Out the front is a sundeck with sunloungers overlooking the ocean below. Each room is named after a flowering plant, & its name is ornately painted on a ceramic tile on the door post & in reception, where a row of keys hangs below the gold flower paintings. The arabesque main area is laid out in a circle, with striking stained-glass windows, fading old Africa maps & fascinating black-&-white photos of Zanzibar of days gone by. Up 1 floor, the restaurant has a breezy interior & a great view over the sea at b/fast time. Dinner here is a 3-course affair, & the local chefs have been expertly trained by Italian cooks, allowing them to create some of the most delicious food on the island. Down on the beach is another restaurant, open for snacks & drinks. The gracious & attentive manager Paola will welcome you with open arms, & is on hand to deal with any requests, day or night. If you like, she'll even join you for a delightfully civilised cup of homemade lemongrass tea & slice of homemade cake in the poolside pavilion in the afternoon. The infinity pool is a recent addition, & has a stunning location on the edge of the cliff with the deserted beach below. This is a really excellent hotel, & also great value. FB. 👑

🏠 **Dongwe Club Vacanze** (76 rooms) ☎ 024 2240251/2; e book@dongweclub.co.tz; www. dongweclub.co.tz. The name Club Vacanze gives away this resort's origins & market: it's an all-action, family-friendly, unquestionably Mediterranean holiday spot, with a predominantly Italian clientele. There are spacious rooms, 4 of which are suites, an all-inclusive restaurant offering international food & Swahili theme nights, & a long jetty for over-water dining & promenades. **$$$$$–**👑

🏠 **Anna of Zanzibar** (5 villas) m 0773 999387; e info@annaofzanzibar.com; www.

annaofzanzibar.com. Staying here feels like being welcomed into a friend's home & the spacious villas are cosy & full of charm. Split into 3 rooms – a living room, bedroom & bathroom – all are filled with homely touches like deep armchairs, dressing tables, framed black-&-white photos & an abundance of cushions. The 2 resident dogs complete the home-from-home vibe. On a practical note, all the bedrooms are fitted with minibars & a safe; for proximity to the sea, book rooms 4 & 5. The villas surround the pool, which sits behind a lovely section of powdery sand, where b/fasts & special dinners are served. On occasion, tasty 3-course meals are also eaten at the formal table in the dining room. The lounge is a popular place to kick back; there's a large satellite TV & DVD collection, plus a good range of novels left by previous guests. Free, reliable Wi-Fi is available all over the property, & laptops are available to take to rooms. For more indulgent entertainment, there's an outside bathtub & 2 massage treatment rooms (US$40/hr), or the hotel also has a telescope for stargazing. Commendably, the owners here are spearheading a campaign to provide benches for local schoolchildren who would otherwise sit on the floor, & are matching every dollar donated – so please do contribute if you stay. FB. Min stay 7 nights over Christmas & New Year. Airport transfer US$57/vehicle each way. 🛏

🏠 **Baraza** (30 rooms) e info@baraza-zanzibar. com; www.baraza-zanzibar.com. Baraza is the youngest sibling of Palms & Breezes, & offering an all-inclusive option at a similar level it aims to be a more child-friendly luxury hotel. With strong Omani influences in its architecture, ornate gardens, & plunge pools, its target is clearly affluent families who are not interested in the island's activity-focused mega-resorts. White-washed, flat-roof villas are divided into categories based on their proximity to the sea & bedroom numbers. All have a spacious lounge, mod cons & décor of golden fabrics & glittering cushions. The imposing Presidential Villa also offers 2 massive rooms & a lap pool. Each villa has a numbered umbrella on the beach, complete with a pair of sunloungers for the sole use of the room's occupants, though the pool appears to be the focus of afternoon chilling. Diners have a choice of the Sultan's Restaurant, which serves Indian food, or the more traditional Livingstone Restaurant which

is Swahili in influence. The food at either of these is excellent, with top-notch chefs spinning tasty twists on popular dishes. Afterwards, sip liqueurs or browse in the atmospheric library, which is open till late. The lavish spa feels more like an Arabian palace theatre set filled as it is with swathes of fabric & antique-style artefacts from the Middle East & India. Scented treatment rooms & a further courtyard pool offer respite from the outside heat, while the more energetic enjoy a fully equipped fitness centre, yoga room & tennis courts. Shoppers may be tempted by the Aladdin's Cave curio shop, which sells a range of art, swimwear, crockery & even furniture, all in a similar Arabian style to the hotel's own. Despite the opulence, families are welcome at Baraza & the kids' club is filled with colourful toys, games, a small paddling pool & even miniature beds for afternoon napping. Given the success of its sister hotels & the affiliation with the respected Rising Sun Dive Centre (which also has a small base here; see page 289) it's no surprise that Baraza is proving to be a slick, quality operation. FB. 🛏

🏠 **The Palms** (6 rooms) m 0774 440882; e info@palms-zanzibar.com; www.palms-zanzibar.com. Immediately adjacent to Breezes & owned by the same family, The Palms is significantly more exclusive & expensive. With just 6 large, luxurious villas, it attracts young, affluent honeymooners lured by image & intimacy. This is certainly a small, stylish option, but though the resort area is private, it's important to remember that it sits immediately next door to a family-friendly, 74-room resort, & everyone shares the same beach: romantic dinners for 2 on the sand may be subject to intrusion. Palms set out to achieve 'understated elegance', & this has broadly been achieved. The colonnaded Plantation House is the main resort building, housing its bar/lounge, dining room & mezzanine library. Here, antique cabinets, carved dark wood sofas & natural palm mats rest on highly polished floors, while heavy old-fashioned fans spin in the high makuti thatch. The billowing organza curtains & afternoon tea on the deck complete the colonial feel. At the ocean end of the building, tarnished mirrors & candles fill a dining room set with sparkling crystal glasses & simple flower arrangements. Individually named after exotic spices, the villas sport shaggy thatch roofs & a large curved front terrace. Through French doors, there is a lounge area with picture windows revealing the bedroom beyond. Decorated in brown, cream & apricot, with Arabian brass lanterns & wooden furniture, the huge rooms are classically elegant but feature all mod cons: minibar, safe, satellite TV & DVD player. There's a bathroom with a bath & even a private outdoor plunge pool. The villas share a small, split-level, tiled swimming pool, & each is also allocated a private banda overlooking the beach, where intimate dinners can also be served (tide dependent). Makuti shades draped with panels of indigo fabric make these a good place to escape the heat of the day & survey the beach beyond. For most activities, head to neighbouring Breezes (see below), though Palms does have a tiny spa, The Sanctuary. FB; minimum age 16. 🛏

🏠 **Breezes Beach Club & Spa** (74 rooms) m 0774 440883–5; e info@breezes-zanzibar. com; www.breezes-zanzibar.com. A perennial favourite with honeymooners & families, Breezes is a large, efficient, family-run beach resort. Amid extensive gardens are rooms in whitewashed villas, virtually identical in size & interior, decorated in muted neutral colours, & with all the amenities of a good hotel. The rooms are comfortably furnished with large beds, & all have safe, fridge & sofa bed, but deliberately no TVs. The suite & deluxe categories are closer to the sea, & are upstairs & downstairs respectively. The suite also features a walk-in dressing room, slightly larger bathroom & wraparound balcony with sunloungers. The recently added 2-floor villa sleeps 6 people in 4

deluxe rooms, similar to the other rooms apart from the TV & DVD player. There is a large pool at the centre of the resort, surrounded by verdant lawn & a great stretch of beach. Tall palms & makuti umbrellas offer shade at both, & wooden loungers are comfortable for reading & relaxing.

The Rising Sun Dive Centre is based between the beach & pool (see *What to see and do*, opposite) & watersports can also be arranged here. Filled with the aroma of cinnamon & cloves, the Frangipani Spa is a great retreat: modern treatment rooms, a calm candlelit relaxation room, private jacuzzi, steam room, hair salon, & a team of Thai & Balinese professional masseuses ensure you leave purified & pampered. For indulgent couples, there's also a private spa for 2. The yoga studio (with genuine yogi), fitness centre & floodlit tennis court complete the spiritual & physical well-being offered. There's a baffling number of restaurants: the Salama Dining Room for b/fast & evening table d'hôte, Breakers on the beach for lunchtime sustenance, & the intimate Sultan's Table offering Indian cuisine in a wood-panelled tower filled with red velvet cushions & brass lanterns. For private dining *à deux*, The Tides comes complete with its own chandelier & staff. For a cocktail & bar snack, the shady Pool Bar is a fun spot, with soft sand on the floor, coir-rope sofas & smiling staff in funky indigo-blue batik shirts. By night, the sophisticated & atmospheric Baraza Bar is a cool drinking den; shrouded in silk, it offers whisky, liqueurs & cigars. **$$$$–$$$$$**

✖ WHERE TO EAT AND DRINK

✖ **Kae Funk** m 0777 439059/222346/001692/ 0779 351382; e kaefunk@hotmail.com; ⏰ 11.00 until last customer leaves, daily. Owned by Eddy of Nyota Bungalows in Matemwe (see *Where to stay*, page 259), this feet-in-the-sand, reggae beach bar is funky indeed. Tucked away along a sandy road at the northern end of Michamvi Kae, the bar itself is quite impressively constructed from multiple boats, driftwood, rusted bicycles, & all manner of flotsam & jetsum. Ask Simba behind the bar for a cold drink or hit the massive array of liqueurs & spirits lining the multi-tier bar backdrop, then head to the upper deck, recline on cushioned swings in the shady garden, or grab an ngalawa table & order some coconut spice curry (lunch & dinner, 1 day's notice required). Music is played all day, & fireside beach parties are a regular occurrence, with Facebook

being a significant publicity tool for this little bar. Chilled, entertaining & open 24/7, this Rasta hangout is an understandably popular hangout for social backpackers & open-minded travellers. **$–$$**

✖ **The Rock Restaurant** m 0777 835515; e info@therockrestaurantzanzibar.com; ⏰ lunch daily. Probably the most remarkable location of any Zanzibar restaurant, The Rock is perched on top of a marooned, seriously undercut coral-rock outcrop, just off the shore of the Michamvi Peninsula. Accessed by wandering across the sand at low tide, or by boat or breaststroke at high tide, the local team in this dilapidated building, with its cheery yellow window frames (no glass) & sealife murals, serve up a simple 'catch of the day' menu. It's very basic, quirky & often empty, but the views are terrific, the staff friendly & the experience unique. Calling in advance to arrange food is probably a good idea, especially if you're coming any distance. $$$

✗ **Upendo Bar & Restaurant** m 0777 244492; e info@upendozanzibar.com; www.upendolounge.com; ⊕ 10.00 until last customer leaves, daily. On a gorgeous sweep of beach directly opposite The Rock, Upendo is the perfect place to while away an afternoon. Opened by a flamboyant British lady, Trish Dhanak's cool confidence & clear vision are paying off already. This is a chilled-out beach bar, where gentle female bar staff mix tantalising cocktails & exotic mocktails: try the US$6 Upendo signature drink (Sky vodka shaken with guava juice & honey, then topped with sparkling wine) or the Apple Virgin Mojito. London lounge music is piped into the shady, cushion covered beach barazas, & tasty treats are cooked to order. Delights range from salt & pepper squid (US$5) to loaded beef tacos (US$9) to the 'So Loaded' seafood fiesta sharing platter (US$100), comprising 1kg rock lobster, slipper

lobster, crab, prawns, octopus, calamari & catch of the day. If you're too comfortable (or full) to move, there are even service bells provided. Sun brunches could well become an island institution here, though it's worth a trip any time. Understated beach chic: a perfect place to just lose time. Rooms are also available in the affiliated villa next door (see *Where to stay*, page 286). $$$

✗ **The Door** m 0777 414962; ⊕ lunch & dinner daily. Accessed from the beach, you'll find The Door on top of the coral cliff above the Rafiki shop; from the tar road, it's signed down a bumpy track. This is a good place for fresh seafood, though book in advance for dinner. It's a sizeable shady restaurant with friendly staff & a great outlook over the waving palm fronds to the Blue Lagoon (the only place where swimming is possible in this area of coast at low tide). After some fried squid with lemon rice (US$6.50) or a divine 2-person whole grilled lobster (US$40), leave your things behind the bar & take a cooling dip or snorkel. $$$–$$$$$

WHAT TO SEE AND DO With many of the hotels on this stretch offering a gamut of activities in idyllic grounds, few visitors need step outside their own resort in search of entertainment. Divers, however, may need to head to a neighbouring property to find a dive centre. Excluding the one at the Italian-speaking, all-inclusive Club Vacanze, the **dive schools** on the peninsula are as follows:

↝ **Karafuu Dive Centre** m 0777 413647/8; www.karafuuzanzibar.com. Formerly Kaskazi Sports Centre, the Karafuu Hotel has now taken over the management of this dive & watersports centre which sits within its grounds (see *Where to stay*, page 285). It has all the latest branded equipment, as well as welcoming divers who bring their own (10% discount if you do), & offers everything from PADI to windsurf courses, kitesurfing, canoeing & mountain biking. Dive accessories, from dive computers to underwater Seadoo scooters, can also be hired. Diving US$50/85 sgl/dbl; US$165/230/345 for 4/6/12 dives; Open Water US$390.

↝ **Rising Sun Dive Centre** m 0777 4408835/88; e bookings@risingsun-zanzibar.com; www.risingsun-zanzibar.com. This smart, efficient company is based on the edge of the beach at Breezes Beach Club (see *Where to stay*, opposite), but is independently owned & operated. The scuba kit here is regularly updated & remains in excellent condition. All Rising Sun instructors & clients are also covered by DAN (Divers Alert Network) insurance,

but for those travelling throughout the continent they recommend taking out insurance online with DAN Europe (*www.daneurope.org*). The dive school is geared to take both beginners & experienced divers looking for PADI speciality courses. Using GPS & echosounder technology, several brand-new sites have been discovered, & the team are always keen to show experienced divers underwater treasures rarely visited by other companies. Rising Sun is also the only PADI National Geographic Dive Centre in east Africa & regularly works with Sea Sense, a Dar-based charity supporting dugongs & turtles. The centre also offers windsurfing, kitesurfing & sailing (wind dependent) on top of the snorkelling safaris (US$15/25 child/adult) & fishing trips that include skippered boat rental & speedboat trips to the mangrove forests. Payment in cash or travellers' cheques only. US$80/160/450/700 for 1/2/6/10 dives; Open Water US$520; Digital Photography US$240; daily equipment rental (regulator, BCD, wet suit, mask & fins) US$35; underwater digital camera rental (inc CD of images) US$45.

BWEJUU

Bwejuu is about 4km north of Paje. Sitting just back from the beach, the village itself is a dense network of dusty alleys and cramped houses, interspersed with towering palm trees. Bwejuu, like many of Zanzibar's east coast villages, has experienced alarming population growth in recent years, which, combined with the increase in tourism on the coast, is putting great pressure on the resources here. Given that around 80% of the children frequently fail even the basic school exam, the village's problems sadly look set to increase.

SUSTAINABLE SEAWEED FARMING

Seaweed has been harvested by coastal dwellers for centuries. This practice led to the export of red seaweed from Zanzibar to Europe in the 1950s, and continued until the wild stocks became exhausted. However, in the late 1980s, following initial scientific experiments by the University of Dar es Salaam, several development organisations and private companies began working with Zanzibar's north and east coastal communities to develop and promote the commercial cultivation of seaweed. This later expanded to the rest of the island, neighbouring Pemba Island and more recently on the mainland coast.

Providing initial funding, seedlings and technical skills, the aim is to encourage sustainable resource management, an essential prerequisite for long-term economic growth and employment, particularly for women. It is estimated that 15,000–20,000 people (90% of whom are women) are currently engaged in seaweed farming, providing a much-needed household income for many coastal workers. The revenue from this trade is also a great foreign-exchange earner for Zanzibar's economy.

Seaweed is used commercially as a source of carrageenan, a natural gelling agent produced from it by alkaline extraction. Used in the manufacture of toothpaste, cosmetics, medicine and also as a thickening agent in many food products, particularly some which are milk-based, this is a valuable, natural product.

With real market demand, several species of seaweed are now farmed, though the most common are the reliable, profitable strains of *Kappaphyicus alvarezii* (*cottonii*), *Eucheuma denticulatum (spinosum)* and *Kappaphycus striatum*. By hammering wooden stakes into the sandy intertidal zone, and stretching lines of coir rope or nylon monoline a foot above the seabed, cultivation lines are prepared and small seaweed stems are attached. Each plot can have up to 50 rows of strings 30cm apart, each line carrying ten to 15 cuttings. The seaweed grows at a rate of 7% per day, increasing to tenfold its original weight in a fortnight. This rapid growth allows farmers to harvest their crop every six weeks; a total of 697kg of dry seaweed is harvested annually per farmer, earning them an average US$50–100 per month, although some earn more with increased effort.

The seaweed is then dried in the sun for a few days, bagged, and sold to seaweed brokers who transport it to Zanzibar Town and onwards to Europe and the USA. Replanting of seedlings can be done immediately, using fragments from the old crop, ensuring sustained farming and income. According to statistics from the Department of Marine Resources Zanzibar, the current production and export volume is 12,500 tonnes per annum.

In 2006, a group of female seaweed farmers in the northern Zanzibar village of Kidoti were trained under the Zanizbar Seaweed Cluster Initiative (ZaSCI)

The local people do some fishing and the women make coir rope from coconut husks (see page 53), but seaweed farming is the major industry and Bwejuu retains a very traditional atmosphere.

North of the village, towards Michamvi, it is still a quiet area, excellent for escapism, where there are plenty of places to enjoy just the sound of the waves and the wind rustling in the trees. Like the rest of the east coast, the tide goes out for miles, and as long as you're not hankering after a cool dip, there's a great feeling of space. There are still a few huts and houses dotted among the palms, but generally speaking the local population thin out and, in their place, you'll find a wide choice

(*www.secitz.com*) to further increase their income by making finished products out of seaweed. Known as Tusife Moyo ('we should not lose heart'), they are members of the Zanzibar Seaweed Cluster Initiative who are promoting innovative methods of farming seaweed, such as deep-water floating lines, promoting working together with neighbouring villages and the invention and production of value-added products. Working under the Pan-African Competitiveness Forum (PACF – Innovative Clusters Programme), the Kidoti women (aided by the Small & Medium Enterprises Competitiveness Facility and the Tanzania Commission for Science and Technology), acquired the necessary machinery to manufacture seaweed soap (they also make soaps infused with aromatic spices). Other groups under the ZaSCI that make seaweed products are located in Paje (Furahia Wanawake Group) and Bweleo (Bado Tupo Bweleo & Jitegemee Group). The first 600 bars of seaweed soap were produced in March 2008, packaged neatly in specially created seaweed boxes and distributed for sale. Spurred on by their success, members of the Zanzibar Seaweed Cluster Initiative have already embarked on diverse products from seaweed powder, foods such as biscuits, salads and cake, to body creams and scrubs for spas, and shampoo. The women's commitment and determination are deeply impressive, and have inspired similar projects elsewhere on the island. In Paje, the smart new Seaweed Center (*www.seaweedcenter.com*) works in conjunction with ZaSCI to help improve and maintain working conditions for the village's 450 seaweed farmers, who earn an average of US$1 per day, training them to make organic seaweed soap, providing marketing and sales channels, and ultimately increasing their earnings. It is very much hoped profitability here will allow for expansion of this and similar projects.

The personal income generated from seaweed farming and its products has helped significantly to improve many villagers' standard of living. In many parts of Africa, farming has been traditionally regarded as women's work, and this remains the case with seaweed farming on Zanzibar. Consequently, much of the money earned stays in the hands of these rural women, who would not normally have their own source of income. The advent of seaweed and the more recent development of seaweed product manufacture have resulted in many having a degree of freedom and empowerment previously impossible. Money is often used for school fees, house improvements, kitchenware or even luxuries like radios and cassette players. The villagers of Paje have collectively built two day-care centres for their children with their profits. Thus, sustained trade in these fast-growing marine algae and related products may just be a viable way out of poverty for many Zanzibari families.

Southeastern Zanzibar   BWEJUU

10

of places to stay from all-inclusive resorts to upmarket boutique hotels and simple bungalows. The beach to the north is beautiful, and the water deep turquoise, making this an ideal place to relax for anything from a day to a week.

Since the arrival of the tar road up the centre of the peninsula, a great deal of the tourist traffic has withdrawn from the winding village paths, making things a lot more pleasant for both the residents and drivers, neither of whom appreciated the resulting dust or track corrugations. However, there have been reliable reports of an increase in threatening snatch-and-grab crime on the isolated tracks from beach accommodation to the bus stops on the main road. Single travellers, especially women, are naturally advised to be careful and ideally to avoid unknown, remote routes. These are undoubtedly disturbing occurrences, but for now at least the assailants seem more interested in stealing bags than causing physical harm.

GETTING THERE AND AWAY From the roundabout at Paje, connecting the island's main east–west artery to the southeast's new tar road, **self-drivers** should turn north on the well-signposted road towards Michamvi. This fast, smooth road now runs all the way to the outskirts of Michamvi Kae. Most of the beach hotels have clear signs marking the relevant turning off the tar road, and we have marked those present in mid 2012 on the area map. Tracks spring up as quickly as new hotels though, so do be aware that more of these less official routes will appear by the time you travel. If you are keen to head into the centre of the village, follow signs to Palm Beach Inn. This will take you along the old coastal road: a narrow, bumpy, dusty track that wanders between village huts and palm trees. It's not for the faint-hearted as children and chickens regularly dart across the road, and navigation through Bwejuu village's tracks is tricky and often without room for a three-point turn. If you're **on foot** or **bicycle**, hit the beach and enjoy the sea breeze as you travel.

Dala dala No 324 leaves Zanzibar Town for Paje three times a day, and often travels onwards to Bwejuu: check with the individual drivers as some will turn south at Paje for Jambiani.

From Bwejuu and the beaches north, adventurous travellers heading to the north of the island can opt to hitch a lift with the octopus fishermen across the bay from Michamvi Kae to Chwaka. This is a fun way to avoid backtracking round the hinterland, but agree costs clearly in advance and don't chance it if you can't swim.

If you come to the Bwejuu–Paje–Jambiani area by **tourist minibus**, many drivers will be keen to take you to the hotels and lodges where they expect to be paid a good commission, often regardless of your own requests. (Read our comments in the box in *Chapter 6, Guides and the 'papaasi'*, page 142.) If you take a minibus from Zanzibar Town, then we strongly advise that you agree precisely where you want to go before departing, and preferably have a reservation in advance.

WHERE TO STAY Bwejuu has something to cater to almost every taste and budget. The accommodation options below have been divided between those in the immediate vicinity of the village, and those strung out along the coast to the north of the main settlement. The pick of the bunch, offering great value for money in their class, is Bellevue Bungalows for its laid-back vibe, food and cheery bungalows; Robinson's Place for its character and eco-credentials; Makuti Beach Hotel for peace and escapism; Crazy Mzungos Flashpackers for stylish chilling budget-style; and Echo Beach for raising the bar on all fronts in Bwejuu.

Unless stated otherwise, hotels listed offer air conditioning and en-suite bathrooms. They are listed as you will see them travelling south to north.

Bwejuu village

⌂ **Sun and Sea View Bungalows** (11 rooms)
m 0718 102633; **e** info@sunandseaviewbungalows.
com; www.sunandseaviewbungalows.com.
Covering a large, flower-edged plot beside the
beach, this is a quiet corner. At the end of the
entrance path, a rough-hewn, pink coral-stone
building houses the reception & restaurant area.
It's a relaxed place with cheerful African music
playing at the bar & neat tables set with red, shell-
covered tablecloths. The large rondavels contain 2
independent en-suite rooms. Simple & clean, they
have red-&-white tiled floors, 2 fans (1 standing
& 1 ceiling), nets & mains electricity. Unusually for
many budget rooms, there's plenty of natural light,
& a bath as well as a shower. The hospitable owner is
often around the property & his thoughts about the
island, its people & politics are enlightening; with
time he can also arrange village tours covering the
school, clinic & local occupations. There is no pool,
but otherwise this is a reasonable choice, & kayak
hire is included in the price. **$$$**

⌂ **Makuti Beach Hotel & Bungalows**
(11 bungalows) **m** 0774 372947; www.makuti-
beach-hotel.com. Just metres from the beach on
a beautiful patch of sand speckled with shrubs,
these simple bungalows are shaded by makuti
thatch, which channels the sea breezes & negates
the need for AC (apart from in the 2 suites).
Pristine dbls & trpls are compact but contain all
you need, with 4-poster beds, yellow floors, bright
white walls & matching mosquito nets. Sea green
bathrooms with hot-water showers gleam, whilst
outside is a small deck with a sofa & a fabulous sea
view where hammocks & makuti shaded loungers
are on hand for beachside chilling. Relaxation is
definitely in order, as management refuse groups,
ensuring peace & quiet to this idyllic corner. The
simple bar & restaurant is little more than a few
kanga-covered chairs & tables dotted around in
the sand under a makuti roof, whilst upstairs the
lounge is strewn with animal appliqué cushions, a
few books & a world map. Come here to escape the
stresses of modern life. **$$$**

⌂ **Mustapha's Place** (10 rooms) ☏ 024
2240069; **e** mustaphas@africamail.com; www.
fatflatfish.co.uk/mustaphas. Set back from the
beach, across the sandy road, Mustapha's Place
is a long-established, totally chilled, slightly
eccentric hangout. Its original name, Mustapha's
Nest, bore reference to both its Rastafarian owner,

Mustapha, & the site's overwhelming population
of bright yellow weaver birds, which have sadly
not been seen for a number of years hence the
name change. Set around a neat, sandy circle
(complete with bonfire, swings & miscellaneous
pieces of coir rope & wood furniture) are 6 uniquely
decorated bandas, 2 of which share a bathroom.
An additional room is set further back beside the
beehive (honey available on request), while 3
newer 2-storey rooms are spread among the trees.
Inside, the white adobe walls are decorated with
brightly painted patterns or pictures, & colourful
kangas are used to cover the solid beds & as
curtains. The floors & surfaces of the bathroom
are newly tiled in sparkling white & jet black,
with plants sprouting from soil-filled bottles &
deliberately placed holes in the floor – a crude,
back-to-nature feel that will not suit everyone. The
bar & restaurant area is as laid-back as the reggae
tunes it plays, & is repeatedly praised for its food.
Camping **$**; rooms **$$**

⌂ **Crazy Mzungos Flashpackers & Beach
Lounge** (5 rooms) **m** 0779 912498; **e** jack_
mohd@yahoo.com. Under joint South African–
New Zealand ownership, Crazy Mzungos started
life as a trendy beach lounge. Soon a chic beach
house was added, & hey presto, some of the most
stylish, chilled-out budget beach accommodation
in the area appeared. It's easy to spot from the
road with its eye-catching orange sign depicting
a cartoon deranged monkey, or from the beach
by the Jack Daniels' VW Beetle wedged into the
sand. The Beach Lounge is still the main attraction
(see *Where to eat and drink*, page 298), but next
door is a well-finished villa. It's a lovely spot for
families & groups, but couples taking the rooms
individually may find their style cramped by fellow
guests. Sequinned curtains, comfy chairs & beds,
traditional ceilings, satellite TV, AC & fans, with an
upstairs terrace, & beach bed & swing downstairs
combine to make the villas feel like a summer
beach house. Each room has its own bathroom,
where power shower fans will be happy to see the
giant shower heads for a full-on steam session.
The rooms share 2 modern kitchens of which the
downstairs one is slightly better equipped, & can
be used by either guests or a private chef. **$$**

⌂ **Pakacha Bungalow & Restaurant** (8
rooms) **m** 0751 084811; **e** pakachabungalow@
hotmail.com. A small village restaurant run
by friendly Bwejuu resident, Ali Chamnda, the

accommodation here comprises 6 recently refurbished rooms, each with twin dbl beds & a cold-water shower, & 2 further rooms added in 2012. These have the same facilities as the other rooms but more colour with blue & turquoise linen & lime green curtains. Some rooms have AC whilst others have only a large ceiling fan, & 1 has a well-equipped kitchenette. There is a very basic 'relaxing area' upstairs with some less than stylish armchairs & a few concrete planters, but there is a pleasant sea view through the trees. The 'honeymoon suite' comes with a TV & DVD player. The adjacent Makuti restaurant serves big b/fasts of fruit & Spanish omelette, & Swahili dinners (octopus in coconut cream US$7; whole crab US$10; grilled fish US$6). Rates reduce by half in low season. **$$**

🏠 **Palm Beach Inn** (21 rooms) ☎024 2240221; m 0777 410070/419191/0773 414666; e palmbeach@zanlink.com/info@palmbeachinn.com; www.palmbeachinn.com. In the heart of Bwejuu, sandwiched between the dusty village track & the beach, Palm Beach Inn sits behind a high, secure gate. Opened in 1990 by Niala Jadawi, a local girl & influential former MP, this is a real hotchpotch of a place. The management makes an admirable effort to employ Bwejuu residents, particularly single mothers, & female staff have been taught to design & make woven bags to sell for extra income. Accommodation is in detached cottages & in a central building, & all rooms (from sgl to trpl) have 24hr mains electricity, universal adaptors, orange mosquito nets & a fridge. Kamilo's suite, with its sea view & tiny lounge area, is viewed as the best room, but this depends upon your taste & is not for minimalists, who may prefer the simplicity of the Abdi Karume room.

There is a split-level, circular dining room & easy chairs in a lounge area where games & cards are available. Although there are windows facing the sea, the restaurant is enclosed on all sides to give shelter from the evening wind. Most guests stay here on a B&B basis, but other basic meals are available: the staple fish, vegetable & rice dishes of the island cost around US$10. There is a large menu but, as is often the case, it's invariably only the 'specials' menu that shows what's available that day. Order food as early as possible & accept that service is slow. There's a well-stocked bar of beer & spirits, as well as traditional dancers & stage entertainment.

An inviting pool nestles among beds of cacti, frangipani & large-leafed climbers, & the grounds are also home to 3 very old tortoises, a sizeable pigeon coop, & a few painted tables & chairs. Although it's located beside the ocean, there is a fence between the lodge area & the beach. The beach immediately outside the property is strewn with sharp coral rock, & litter from the village, & staff also warn against taking valuables onto the sand due to the risk of theft. Also think twice about a night-time stroll on the beach, as high-speed motorbikes bypass the bumpy village lanes by taking to the sand. **$$$**

🏠 **Dere Beach Guesthouse** PO Box 278, Bwejuu; ☎024 240197/231017 m 0777 864818/471840. Once a reasonable backpacker haunt, this place has now completely degenerated. In the centre of the village, the beach immediately in front of the guesthouse is covered in litter, while inside is dark & unwelcoming & the whole place has a generally unkempt look & unpleasant air. The en-suite rooms are grubby & basic with saggy mattresses, torn mosquito nets & ripped lino flooring. It is hard to do anything other than recommend not staying here. **$$**

🏠 **Miza Wa Miza Bungalows** (14 rooms) Opened by Rastafarian artist Ibrahim & his Austrian wife, Miza Wa Miza was once an offbeat place brimming with character. Sadly, it was looking a bit tired on our last visit, where we saw no sign of life apart from some forlorn-looking dogs & an inquisitive cat. The rooms have all been left to deteriorate & the dusty restaurant had obviously not been used in a while. We await news to see if it will reopen to its former glory. **$$**

North of Bwejuu village
🏠 **Kilimani Kwetu Restaurant & Bungalows** (4 rooms) ☎024 2240235; m 0777 465243 (Wadi), 0777 214133 (Clemens); e info@kilimani.de; www.kilimani.de. Opened in 1994 as a partnership between 5 Germans & the villagers of Bwejuu, Kilimani Kwetu is rooted in community development. Built by local people from local materials, on a gentle hill to the north of the village overlooking the sea, this is a relaxed spot, with a positive impact on those who live in the area. Wadi & a delightfully friendly local team manage Kilimani Kwetu & are happy to help any visitors. Rooms are in 2 white, thatched bungalows which were renovated in 2010. Surrounded by palms &

sweet almond trees, the rooms are basic if a little uninspiring, with painted concrete walls. They have simple furniture, 2 deckchairs, mosquito nets with inside fan, & en-suite bathrooms with a cold-water shower. Electricity is available & there's a traditional well on site. The neat restaurant serves fresh fish & vegetarian dishes on the daily set menu, & b/fast boasts homemade tropical fruit jams & locally produced honey; culinary-inspired guests can even learn some Swahili recipes from the chef if they wish. Take any one of several zigzag paths, 50m to the sea, & there's a private beach area for guests, with makuti umbrellas, deckchairs & the Kilamani Beach Café, serving wine & beer. Development projects centred on Kilimani Kwetu have successfully financed the construction of an adult education centre & library in the past, & it remains a place for visitors keen to immerse themselves in local life. **$$$**

🏠 **White Rose Beach Resort** (30 rooms) m 0776 659662; e gm.whiterose@oraresort.eu; www.oraresort.eu. White Rose Beach Resort reopened in 2006 after a complete refurbishment, & by the time it was taken over by Ora Resorts in 2008, the place had magnified in size & the room interiors had been considerably modernised with fridges & electric safes. Despite the resort-like promise here, the rooms are disappointing & distinctly tatty. Rising from the beach up the hill behind, there are garden rooms set on the slope above the coconut line, superior bungalows with slightly better views, & sea-view rooms which actually look out over the pool. The white-stone garden bungalows are all the same basic design with wide verandas, spacious bedrooms & en-suite bathrooms, whilst the pool-side rooms are in 2-storey buildings with small individual balconies or terraces. The pool is worthy of note, with an interesting 3-level design, including a splash pool. It's a peaceful place with pleasant landscaping, several sun umbrellas & coir-rope chairs. The beachside Romantic Restaurant is pre-order only, while the pool bar, shop & massage room provide guest diversions & there's a secure parking area for self-drivers. **$$$$**

🏠 **Bellevue Bungalows** (9 rooms) m 0777 209576; e bellevuezanzibar@gmail.com; www.bellevuezanzibar.com. On the top of a high rise of coral rock, this is a thoroughly relaxed, gentle place offering one of the best budget deals on the island. In recent years Bellevue has flourished & since the

arrival of a young Dutch couple, Melanie & Dim, in Dec 2007, it has taken on a new energy. Building on the good work in recent years to establish pretty gardens, they have transformed the restaurant, lounge & rooms with vibrant co-ordinated colours & original solutions for storage & lighting. The recently added house which accommodates the honeymoon suite & 2 downstairs rooms has been done up in the homely, relaxed vibe of the rest of the property – moulded bathrooms, colourful bedspreads & jangly shell curtains. The whole building can be used as a family house, which shouldn't break the bank as children up to 4 stay free. The clean, spacious dbl rooms with fans are in 3 thatched bungalows & have good bathrooms with solar-heated water, matching linen, fluffy towels, fishing-basket shelves & even bedside reading lights. Each room has a sunrise terrace, with clever kanga woven coir dividers to create privacy & the raised level allows for a cooling breeze & a great outlook (the nearby residential villa is hidden by clever planting). Chef Chulla makes terrific tapas as well as a variety of fresh European & Swahili cuisine (US$5–7). Scrumptious b/fasts of spice-infused juices, fresh bread, pancakes, locally produced honey & homemade jams are a great start to the day, too. With a 50m walk down to the beach & free transfers to Dim's kitesurfing school (see *What to see and do*, page 305) in Paje, the focus is on traditional seaside activities & the chance to chill under the storm lanterns with a cold beer in the evening. The team here are all justifiably proud of their achievements, & at this price their continued success is virtually guaranteed. **$$$**

🏠 **Evergreen Bungalows** (14 rooms) 024 2240273; e zanzievergreen@yahoo.com; www.evergreen-bungalows.com. The rooms are in 2-storey beach bungalows: those upstairs are in the apex of the makuti thatch & are accessed by steep steps at the front of the chalets. The older of these rooms are extremely simple, with no real windows downstairs, though the open-weave palm mesh does allow some light & air to penetrate. Plans are afoot to make some changes, but for now, the upstairs rooms are much better & lighter with high ceilings, solid walls & balconies, simple wooden furniture, mosquito nets & a cold-water en-suite bathroom concealed behind a batik curtain. The central bar & restaurant is spacious, & snacks & meals are available throughout the day (chapatti

US$2; fried calamari with tartar sauce US$6). Evergreen is affiliated with African Blue Divers (see the Echo Beach Hotel listing, opposite). **$$$**

🏠 **Twisted Palms** (10 rooms) m 0776 130275; e twistedpalms@zanzibarone.com; http://twistedpalms.zanzibarone.com. In Jul 2008, run-down & dreary Twisted Palms was bought by new Italian owners, who have since worked wonders. Now vibrant & colourful, with original artwork adorning the walls, the whole place has been significantly upgraded to become a welcoming & friendly beachside retreat. Rooms are divided between the beach & the small hill behind the property, but all contain 3 beds with delightfully eccentric purple sheets & blue mosquito nets to go with the rainbow of colours on the outside walls. Simple furnishings, cooling fans, en-suite bathrooms with European flush toilets & hot-water showers painted with tropical fish are standard. 2 of the beachside rooms are quads, & 1 has a bunk bed, useful for those travelling with little ones. Well-tended gardens filled with shells & shaded by palms host a swinging beach sofa, great for afternoons with a good book from the book exchange. The explosion of colour continues in the restaurant, which is the only one in Bwejuu to sit on stilts above the sea. It is open from 11.00–21.30 every day with the menu changing depending on what the daily catch is. Non-guests are welcome to sample the food, & the seafood platter (US$15) comes highly recommended. **$$–$$$**

🏠 **Shells Bungalow** (10 rooms) PO Box 4666; m 0787 400772/400772. There are 6 bungalows here named after Tanzanian places – Serengeti to Kilimanjaro – as well as 4 rooms in the neighbouring villa available from Sep–Jan. Although the bungalows are a little rough on the outside, each is in fact colourful, large & clean, with a big dbl bed, some basic furniture & an adequate bathroom with flush toilet & cold-water shower. Tingatinga pictures show thoughtful decorating attempts, & there's 24hr electricity, plus a backup generator. There's a good stretch of beach here, where sunloungers under shady palms & no hassle make for a relaxed atmosphere. There's an extensive African & Indian menu but it's probably best to order in the morning if you want to eat dinner. **$$**

🏠 **Robinson's Place** (6 rooms) m 0777 413479; e ann@robinsonsplace.net; www.robinsonsplace.net; ⊕ Jun–Mar. This is a delightfully offbeat family home set in lovely mature gardens, beside a superb beach. To Ann & Ahmed, the fascinating European–Zanzibari couple who own & run the place, being here is about a particular lifestyle choice rather than business, hence you can expect a very friendly welcome, a gentle & relaxed pace, but none of the trappings of a commercial lodge. Robinson's does its best to be fairly self-sufficient – keeping chickens across the road & growing tropical fruit. Simple meals are served either under the trees or on rugs & cushions on the floor in the main lounge area. There is no electricity, so wind & solar power are used to light the restaurant, portable solar lamps & petrol lamps are found in the rooms & all cooking is done in clay pots on open fires. In an effort to conserve wood, the only hot meal of the day is dinner (US$10). For lunch, guests often wander along the beach to Breezes (see *Where to stay*, page 288) where for a fee they can also enjoy a dip in their pool. Robinson's rooms cater for a max 12 people so advance booking is invariably necessary. All rooms are very different in style & are divided amongst 2 small houses & a Robinson Crusoe-esque, 2-storey treehouse. The master bedroom in the main house is huge with a dbl & three-quarter bed, bright fabrics, & beer bottles filled with flowers. Attached, but not interconnected, the main house 'guest bedroom' is small but pretty with a three-quarter bed, a daybed & vibrant orange linen. The proximity & contained feel of these 2 rooms make the house perfect for a family with older children. House Bondeni, literally meaning 'house in the corner', is a lovely, airy, L-shaped room with white walls, cheerful kangas on both the European & Zanzibari dbl beds, & woven palm mats on the floor. For a little more privacy, across the road the secluded Marakesh Lodge has treetop views from the open sides in the upstairs dbl room, while shady hammocks make the most of the cooling breezes. Downstairs the bathroom adjoins a further room containing a sgl bed covered with striking purple linen. The *pièce de résistance* is Robinson's House, a rough-hewn, wattle-&-daub, 2-storey affair under a large tree on the edge of the beach. Upstairs is a basic but fun 'honeymoon suite' from where, under a lovely mangrove & makuti roof, the dbl bed looks out through the shell mobiles & trees to the ocean beyond. Downstairs is a small, clean sgl room with its own sea view. All rooms, except the master & Marakesh Lodge, share immaculate bathroom facilities. There are 2 cold-water showers & 2 toilets, each separated by stylish cream curtains, & a large open-ended central area with mirrors & sinks. These are cleaner & more pleasant than many of the en-suite facilities offered by Zanzibar's more mid-range properties; certainly the best 'shared facilities' that we've seen in Africa! Several dogs roam the property as effective security guards. Min 2 night stay, cash only. **$$**

🏠 **White Beach Hotel** (6 rooms) m 0776 789181; e info@whitebeachhotelzanzibar.com; www.whitebeachhotelzanzibar.com. In 2009, the site of the former Hammond's Guesthouse was bought by the current Czech owners, who have ambitious plans for the property's improvement. The old rooms have been demolished, & replaced instead with bungalows built in a row either side of the main building. The cool interiors are a little featureless but are furnished with Zanzibari beds, frilly mosquito nets, sturdy coconut wood cupboards, fans & bathrooms with hot-water showers. Out in front, travel-weary guests can recover on the shaded deck filled with potted plants, or can head down to the sweeping beach which is dotted with comfortable sunloungers. Overlooking the sand, the restaurant serves up a daily menu of mainly pizza (US$7.50). From the loud music playing at 09.00 to the snoozing revellers on the beach-facing sofas, it would appear that the bar is the main hub of activity & it shows movies & sports on a giant screen. Manager Radic's future vision includes a swimming pool & 24 additional rooms, though quite where all of this is going to fit on the small plot remains to be seen. For the moment though, free airport pickups & long-stay discounts make White Beach a pretty good deal. **$$$**

🏠 **Bahari Beach Village Bungalows** (4 rooms) m 0773 687219/0772 623084; e baharibungalows@gmail.com. This extremely simple local hotel may seem more like a home for abandoned dogs, but there are in fact basic but clean rooms to be found among the trees. Mismatched sheets on rickety beds with mosquito nets but no AC or fan may put off those in search of creature comforts, but the shower rooms are clean & it's peaceful, with plenty of dappled shade corners. **$$**

🏠 **Upepo** (2 rooms) m 0784 619579; e shareefznz71@hotmail.com; www. zanzibarhotelbeach.com. Under Canadian–Zanzibari ownership, Upepo offers clean en-suite rooms, which are spacious with huge comfortable beds, fans & traditional ceilings. 1 room faces the beach & 1 is set a little back with a view of the lush garden, where carved wooden zebras peer through the foliage. With just 2 rooms there'll only ever be 4 guests or fewer here, so you may think you'll have the place largely to yourself; don't be fooled though as the animated beach restaurant & bar attracts large numbers with its relaxed vibe & iced sangria (see *Where to eat and drink*, page 298). **$$$**

🏠 **Echo Beach Hotel** (12 rooms) m 0773 593260/593286; e echobeachhotel@hotmail. com; www.echobeachhotel.com. In 2007, British expats Sue & Andrew Page swapped life at their quaint Loire Valley B&B to create Echo Beach. Opened in the same year, this small, friendly lodge has high aspirations & is receiving some admirable reviews. 4 small detached cottages & 3 dbl-storey houses with 2 rooms in each are arranged in an arc behind the inviting kidney-shaped swimming pool, & there are 2 cottages at the rear of the property offering more privacy & a daybed in the loft. Almost every room has a sea view from its private terrace, & each is attractively screened with billowing fabric panels in a rainbow of colours, giving this lodge an original take on the Zanzibari norm. Room interiors vary slightly, though all are similar in style: a 4-poster dbl bed swathed in a mosquito net, feature wallpaper, African bedside lamps, carved wardrobes, highly polished floors, good AC, ceiling fans & open bathrooms with huge walk-in showers. The large open-sided lounge/dining room is under high makuti thatch with gleaming aqua tiles on the floor; the food is consistently very good (Andrew is a chef) & the pre-dinner bar chatter makes it a cheerful hangout. It looks out towards the sea through a coconut grove, & the lovely stretch of beach is a stone's throw away. Echo Beach is more about relaxing than action, but hydrophiles can head for the on-site watersports centre, African Blue Divers, to arrange dive trips (US$80 per dive) & courses. Children can stay at the discretion of the management, so advise at time of booking, & there are tentative plans to build a new garden cottage & extend one of the current ones to create 2 new family rooms. All rates are HB, including a 3-course à la carte dinner. 🍽

✗ WHERE TO EAT AND DRINK Nearly all of the hotels cater for guests and non-residents alike (see individual listings), with **Echo Beach** (see page 297) and **Bellevue Bungalows** (see page 295) deserving a special mention for their tasty offerings. In addition, there are a few small shops and local-style eating-houses in the village itself, and increasingly a few European-style beach café-bars, all of which also offer accommodation.

✗ Crazy Mzungo's Beach Lounge m 0779 912498; e jack_mohd@yahoo.com. Relaxed Crazy Mzungo's is popular with both party-goers & locals. The former are attracted by the Crazy Cocktail specials including Crazy Juice (US$15), 750ml of mixed alcoholic drinks. Meant for sharing, these pitchers are accompanied by the warning: 'contents may destroy your mind'. Zanzibari patrons tend to come more for the international football broadcast on a tiny TV screen, while the drinking tourists also flock back on Sun mornings to refresh & revitalise with the famous Crazy Brunch, served from 11.30–15.00. All day b/fasts & fresh organic food are a real draw, as is the Wed BBQ night. After all that gorging, replete diners can head for the beach bed, or wear it all off with a spot of volleyball. Internet access costs US$7/hr. $$$

✗ Upepo m 0784 619579; e shareefznz71@ hotmail.com; www.zanzibarhotelbeach.com. You can't fail to hear the Cuban beats emanating from this chilled restaurant-cum-bar, which with only 6 tables offers a personal touch on local & international cuisine, influenced by the joint Tanzanian–Canadian ownership. Rum is quite clearly a best-seller, as bottles of it line the shelves behind the bar. Thirsty beach-goers can cool off with a fruity sangria, but there's also a range of seasonal fish dishes, curries, bowls of pasta & pancakes for the hungry, though if you're after lobster they'll need prior notice to request it from the fishermen. There's a good vibe here, & you may well find that you linger longer than intended. $$$

WHAT TO SEE AND DO Most visitors to this area are kept occupied by resort activities and sun-worshipping. If you're staying somewhere small or simply fancy a change, you can explore the offshore reef with **snorkelling** gear hired from Palm Beach Inn (see page 294), in the village (around US$5 per day for mask, snorkel and flippers), or, with better kit, from Rising Sun Dive Centre at Breezes (see page 235). At low tide, the long **intertidal walk** to the ocean is a rewarding excursion in itself, but be sure to top up the suncream and drink lots of water on the way. You can also hire bikes (US$10) or scooters (US$40) from local villagers, with a little help from your hotel, and ride a few kilometres north up the beach to the 'lagoon' at Dongwe, in front of The Door Restaurant, where the break in the reef means it's possible to swim and snorkel off the beach even at low tide (if hiring a scooter, see *Chapter 5, Hired vehicles*, page 127, and *Driving licences*, page 132).

PAJE

Paje is a small fishing village, straggled along the coast; it's centred on the point where the main road from Zanzibar Town joins the new tar coast road, which heads north to Bwejuu and south to Makunduchi. Its location at this junction makes it the easiest place on the coast to reach by public transport and contributed to its early success as the backpackers' choice location. With the rise in Nungwi's dominance over the livelier side of the budget scene, the percentage of travellers heading to Paje has reduced (even if real numbers probably continue to rise). By and large, the area surrounding the village remains a quiet spot for an idyllic beach break. Genuine interaction with the local community is virtually non-existent here, with only the beach traders mixing with the tourists.

GETTING THERE AND AWAY To reach Paje, the main tar road from Zanzibar Town leads through Tunguu, Jozani and Kitogani before reaching the coast. From Paje, a relatively new tar road then leads north to Bwejuu and Michamvi, whilst another heads south to Jambiani and Makunduchi, in the far southeast corner of the island.

Paje can be reached by **public transport** (dala dala No 324 or bus Route 9), **tourist minibus** or self-drive **rental car**, **motorbike** or **bicycle**. If you want to go north beyond Bwejuu or south past Jambiani, there's no regular public transport, so you'll need to have your own wheels, be willing to hitch on a local ngalawa, or enjoy a really long, hot walk.

WHERE TO STAY There are several places to stay in Paje, most of them closely clustered at the southern edge of the village. All the accommodation here is small scale, individual and relatively cheap; most places are owner-run. Not all hotels are on the beach though, so choose carefully if it's a sea view you're after.

Beside the main group of guesthouses is a private house, locally known as 'Paje Palace'. Ignore the aesthetic damage that this pink-and-mint monstrosity may do to your architectural sensibilities, and be grateful that it has brought floodlighting to its immediate surroundings, including the beach, as it is generally felt to have increased security here in the evenings.

Unless stated otherwise, hotels listed below offer air conditioning and en-suite bathrooms as standard. Hotels are listed from north to south.

⌂ **Paradise Beach Bungalows** (12 rooms) ☎024 2231387; m 0777 414129; e paradisebb@ zanlink.com, saori@cats-net.com; http:// paradisebeachbungalows.web.fc2.com/. Opened 20 years ago by a diminutive Japanese lady, Saori Miura, who abandoned the corporate rat race to travel in east Africa, Paradise is a cheap beach retreat offering basic facilities & great sushi. There are clean & tidy rooms, of which 3 are larger, dbl-storey options. The original rooms are in semi-detached cottages with 2, three-quarter-size traditional Zanzibari beds with flowery sheets & mosquito nets. Some of these have interconnecting doors for groups of friends or families. The bathrooms are basic concrete rooms with mostly hot-water showers, but 1 dbl & the dormitory are cold-water only. The new chalets are a better bet with a simple but spacious, ground-floor bedroom with a dbl & a three-quarter-length bed, neat coconut-wood shelves & a Zanzibari chest for storing valuables. Outside, stairs lead from the veranda to a private roof terrace with a picnic table, chairs, washing line & view into the surrounding palms & frangipani trees. There is now electricity here with low-level lights helping significantly at night, & storm lanterns still used for atmosphere; power cuts are frequent though so a good torch is essential. The central restaurant houses tables covered in pink batik tablecloths &

glasses of fresh flowers, & a small multi-lingual library. The evenings see guests come here to read, play cards, chat & eat, all sheltered from the sea breeze by retractable wooden shutters. The home-cooked food is all good quality, especially the Japanese options of fresh sashimi & tempura, but supplies are limited so order dinner well in advance & check Saori is around if you're coming for the sushi. B/fasts are simple affairs of fruit, fresh bread & a selection of local preserves. Next to the restaurant, a 2-storey, hexagonal lounge area offers cushioned seating, good sea views & some shade during the heat of the afternoon. In spite of its very basic amenities, Paradise's quiet location, Japanese food & inexpensive rates do mean that it can get very busy, so advance booking is advisable. It is also worth being aware that there are a number of docile-looking dogs dozing around the gardens – from experience, their bite is stronger than their bark. **$$**

⌂ **Paje Ndame Village** (31 rooms) m 0777 886611; e info@ndamezanzibar.com; www. ndamezanzibar.com. Since German manager Hans Ehrentraut took over in 2011, Paje Ndame has been catering mainly to German families & is consequently at its busiest during the European school holidays in Jul & Dec. Rooms in 2-storey villas or neat bungalows are all bright & clean with shiny pink flooring, baby-blue tiled bathrooms,

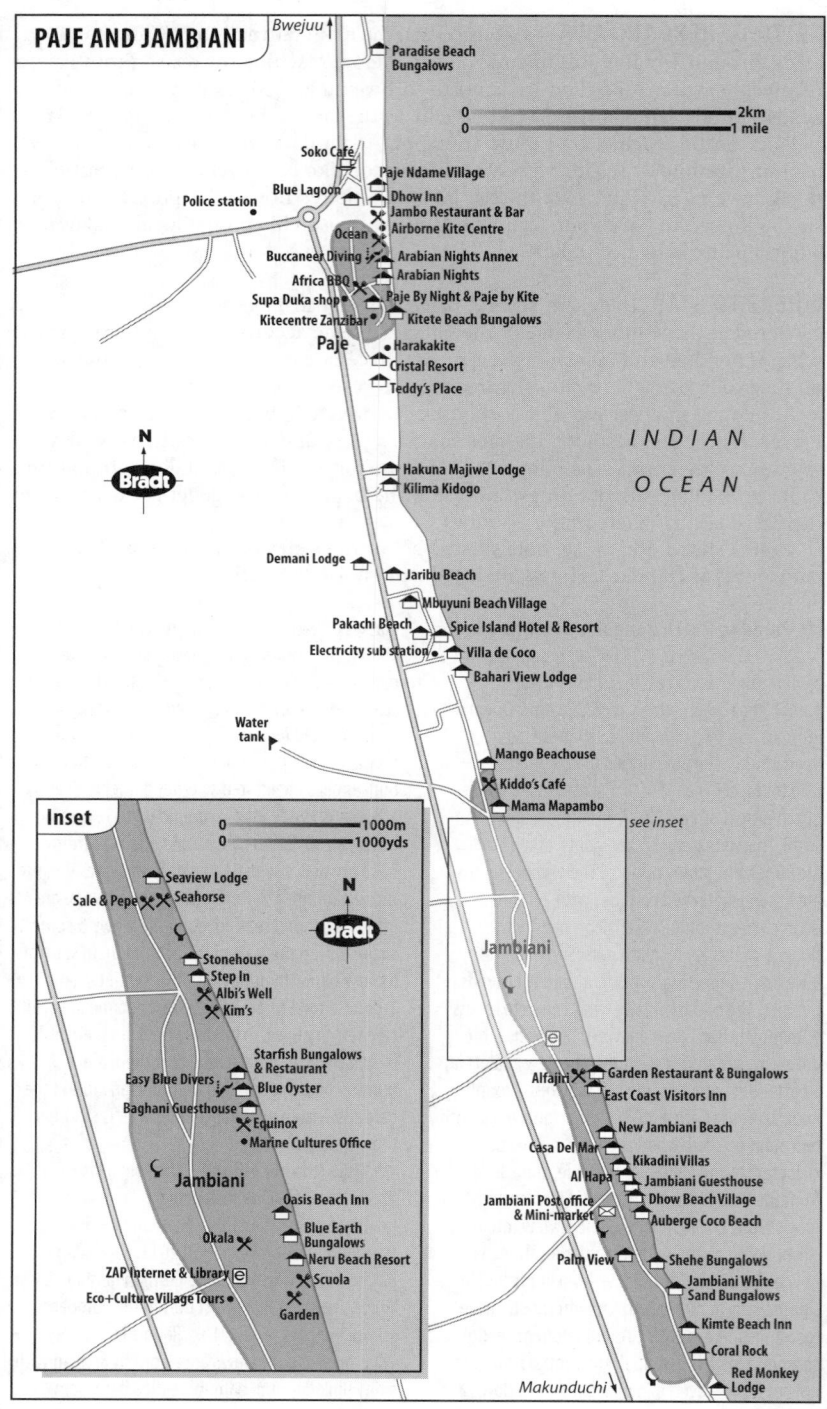

PAJE AND JAMBIANI

Bwejuu ↑

Paradise Beach Bungalows

0 ———————————————— 2km
0 ———————————————— 1 mile

Soko Café
Paje Ndame Village
Blue Lagoon
Police station
Dhow Inn
Jambo Restaurant & Bar
Airborne Kite Centre
Ocean
Buccaneer Diving
Arabian Nights Annex
Arabian Nights
Africa BBQ
Supa Duka shop
Paje By Night & Paje by Kite
Kitecentre Zanzibar
Kitete Beach Bungalows
Paje
Harakakite
Cristal Resort
Teddy's Place

INDIAN

OCEAN

N
Bradt

Hakuna Majiwe Lodge
Kilima Kidogo

Demani Lodge
Jaribu Beach
Mbuyuni Beach Village
Pakachi Beach
Spice Island Hotel & Resort
Electricity sub station
Villa de Coco
Bahari View Lodge

Water
tank

Mango Beachouse
Kiddo's Café
Mama Mapambo

see inset

Inset

0 ———————————————— 1000m
0 ———————————————— 1000yds

N
Bradt

Seaview Lodge
Sale & Pepe
Seahorse

Stonehouse
Step In
Albi's Well
Kim's

Starfish Bungalows
& Restaurant
Easy Blue Divers
Blue Oyster
Baghani Guesthouse
Equinox
Marine Cultures Office

Jambiani

Oasis Beach Inn
Okala
Blue Earth
Bungalows
ZAP Internet & Library
Neru Beach Resort
Eco+Culture Village Tours
Scuola
Garden

Jambiani

Alfajiri
Garden Restaurant & Bungalows
East Coast Visitors Inn
New Jambiani Beach
Casa Del Mar
Kikadini Villas
Al Hapa
Jambiani Guesthouse
Jambiani Post office
& Mini-market
Dhow Beach Village
Auberge Coco Beach
Palm View
Shehe Bungalows
Jambiani White
Sand Bungalows
Kimte Beach Inn
Coral Rock
Red Monkey
Lodge

Makunduchi ↓

& either a shared semicircular balcony with a good sea view or a garden terrace. All rooms have mains electricity, fans, mosquito nets & bedside lights. The resort sits along a lovely long stretch of soft beach on which guests laze, enjoy an African massage & watch the world go by. There's a pleasant seafront restaurant & bar, a curio shop with a reasonable selection of colourful local paintings, a new circular beach bar for sundowners & a popular beach volleyball court. Activities are relatively limited but the youthful crowd seems happy playing cards, snorkelling from a local ngalawa, or renting bicycles & embarking on cultural tours of Paje village (US$10pp). Child & student reductions available. **$$$**

⌂ **Blue Lagoon** (8 rooms) m 0774 368468; e abel@savanna-ocean.com; www.savanna-ocean.com. Set a row back from the beach opposite the Dhow Inn, Blue Lagoon consists of a ring of rooms around a central circular courtyard, which is also the location of a smattering of recycled-dhow tables that make up the restaurant. Attempts have been made to spruce up the unimaginative rooms with local art work, but they are still large AC-cooled boxes with simple coir-rope, wood & animal-hide furniture. Up on the 2nd storey, the bar is raised above the courtyard, & you'll need to be early to save a seat on its kanga-covered sofas when the plasma TV is on. Out in the front of the building, a well-used snooker table is wedged into the sand, & at reception a limited but useful shop sells essentials such as suncream. Blue Lagoon's accommodation is mostly used as a base by students who are happy to live on a diet of pancakes (US$3) & burgers (US$8) & don't seem to mind the lack of beach access. **$$**

⌂ **Dhow Inn** (6 rooms) m 0777 525828; e info@dhowinn.com; www.dhowinn.com. Neighbouring Paje Ndame to the south, Dhow Inn's 3 Dutch owners are on site & keen to warmly welcome guests & live up to their 'come as a guest, leave as family' motto. The modern rooms form a circle around a small ochre-washed courtyard & are vibrantly finished with sunny wall shades & tangerine sheets. Hot water, fans, mosquito nets & even free Wi-Fi are standard. Set 40m back from the water's edge, the rooms don't have a sea view but the atmospheric bar-restaurant does. There is a flexible dining programme with Full Moon pool parties & regular poolside BBQs for those who simply don't want to leave the water's edge. It's also worth noting that if you can't get a room, non-guests are welcome to use the pool as long as they buy something – perfect for cooling dips when the tide is out & temperatures are searing. If you fancy a further jaunt then ask at reception for help renting bikes & cars. Dhow Inn is a chilled & sunny choice, so we hope that the 28 additional rooms currently under construction (completion early 2013) don't change its relaxed character. **$$$$**

⌂ **Arabian Nights Annex Hotel** (18 rooms) m 0777 844443/0775 045194; e arabiannightsannex@hotmail.com; www.zanzibararabiannights.com. Being newer, Arabian Nights Annex seems superior to its nearby sister property Arabian Nights (see below). It's well finished, with fresh coats of burnt orange paint & matching red & gold furnishings. This warm colour scheme continues to the rooms, where gold curtains & lampshades plus generously proportioned carved coconut-wood beds are cosy & inviting & even the mosquito nets are gold trimmed. Sparkling white bathrooms with tropical-fish shower curtains diverge from the theme a little, while modern paraphernalia such as electric safes & flat-screen satellite TVs make life easier. The rooms are located in various 1- & 2-storey rondavels set around tidy gardens, where there's also a palm-shaded pool looking out over the waves. The only real drawback is the rather unnecessary fence between the hotel & the beach, covered in signs announcing that the area is 'private'. By contrast, the garden terraced Cinnamon Restaurant is open to passers-by wishing for a flavour of its Swahili cuisine. **$$$$**

⌂ **Arabian Nights** (12 rooms) ☎ 024 2240190/1; m 0654 080808; e anights@zanzibararabiannights.com, anights-arabian@hotmail.com; www.Zanzibararabiannights.com. Tucked down a narrow alley to the beach beside Kitete Beach Bungalows, Arabian Nights is one of Paje's more mid-range, sedate options. Its rooms are in yellow coral-rock cottages with thatched roofs. Some surround the large, private pool & others face directly onto the beach. In keeping with the hotel's evocative name, soft golds & decorative spices influence the room décor. Very spacious bedrooms have walk-in wardrobes & floral tiled en suites. 2 sea-facing suites have a private plunge pool. The upstairs Swahili & European-mix restaurant is open to all, & there is an efficient on-site dive school, Buccaneer (see *What to see and do*, page 304). Free Wi-Fi. **$$$$**

Kitete Beach Bungalows (21 rooms)
024 2240226; m 0778 160666; e kitetebeach@
hotmail.com; www.kitetebeach.com. Kitete has
moved on from being just an old villa offering
basic rooms. Guests are still welcome at the
original house opposite Paje By Night, known as
Kitete Cottage, with its bright entrance & simple
rooms, but walk a little further along the beach &
you'll reach Kitete's new, blush-pink villas & the
restaurant. Here, immaculate rooms are modern &
offer much better facilities. Sunny yellow interiors,
mains electricity, a fan, mosquito nets & a small
outside terrace/balcony feature in all. The rooms
are fresh & clean, with crisp linen, modern clip-on
bedside lights & an informative guest information
sheet. There is also a lovely family villa with 3
cheerfully decorated bedrooms, 2 bathrooms &
a central dining area. The Kitete View Restaurant
occupies the prime spot next to the beach, &
offers stunning views along the sand from its 1st-
floor location, but unfortunately lacks buzz. The
decent chef serves up traditional Swahili dishes
(US$5.50–12) alongside specials such as lobster
thermidor (*US$30*). Down on the sand, a gift shop
also rents out bicycles for local jaunts. **$$$**

Paje By Night (21 rooms) m 0777 460710;
e info@pajebynight.net; www.pajebynight.
net. Opened in 1984, when it was the only hotel
with electricity on the peninsula, this is an
unpretentious joint where jovial Italian manager
Marco warmly welcomes 'the young & the not
so young any more'. The row of hammocks at the
entrance hints at the pervading mood before you
even get inside, for this is a slightly hippy, take-
it-as-it-comes place. Come here for the relaxed
vibe & social atmosphere rather than for chic
style, modern facilities or endless activities. Set
50m back from the beach, & without a sea view,
the hub of PBN is the bar. Chunky black sofas are
dotted all around, as are wooden tables & faux-fur
chairs, & colourful lanterns furnish the adjoining
makuti TV lounge, which screens international
news & sport virtually all day. An open-sided
makuti structure is used as a simple massage
area, whilst the neighbouring rondavel with its
spider's-web rope pattern is a quiet reading spot.
The food quality is good with a definite Italian
slant: fresh pasta & pizza are always available &
occasionally Marco himself will knock up some
great homemade ravioli. Seafood & Swahili BBQs
are a weekly occurrence whilst the social cocktail

bar is open 24hrs. Around the garden area are
spacious standard rooms with a dbl/twin bed, &
king-size rooms. The latter refer to the larger size
of the room not the bed, for only 9 of the rooms
have a king-size bed while the other 2 are trpls.
There is mains electricity available throughout
the complex, & every room has hot water, tiled
floors with colourful mats, cheerful batik pictures
& a fan. Room 1 is a newly decorated family
bungalow with 2 bedrooms, a shared bathroom
& a spacious entrance hall. Each of the bedrooms
has 2 sgl & 1 dbl bed with mosquito nets, vibrant
curtains, a small desk, wardrobe & ceiling fan,
& AC if you're willing to pay US$10 extra for the
remote. Designed & proudly built by Marco, the
2-storey 'jungle bungalows' are very rustic. Within
the downstairs coral-stone walls are twin beds
& a small, hot-water bathroom; fumble upstairs
in the dark & there's an additional dbl bed in the
makuti roof space. Although a baby's cot was once
borrowed from the village for a visiting child, the
basic facilities & party spirit here are not really
conducive to holidaying with infants. Primary
guest activities seem to be sleeping & sunbathing
on the beach, then chilling over cocktails & fresh
juices before building up to serious parties. On a
practical note, there's free internet access, a safety-
deposit box in the office & in the king-sized rooms,
& night-time security. Visa, MasterCard & Amex
subject to 5% surcharge. **$$$**

Cristal Resort (24 rooms) m 0777 875515;
e info@cristalresort.net; www.cristalresort.net. In
Jun 2012, the Cristal Resort absorbed the adjacent
hotel, the Kinazi Upepo, to create a sizeable
beachfront plot just south of Paje village. This
French–American-owned place has received mixed
reviews, perhaps because its marketing imagery
sets expectations too high. That said, it's clear that
a great deal of thought is going into producing
neat accommodation & a pleasant environment,
& aspirations to improve are evident. There are
3 room types: 5 rather uninspiring 'deluxe' cubes
with thatched roofs & glass windows, 6 deluxe
bungalows & 13 'Ecologic' cabins, whose greying
timber sides are falling victim to salt erosion.
The last have more character by far & are dotted
around the beach, though they miss out on the AC
& bath. The safari-tent layout of the eco-cabins,
with the bathroom concealed behind the coral-
rock headboard, is particularly nice. There's a good-
size swimming pool & an impressive dhow cocktail

bar, while down on the beach a lively canteen-style restaurant serves salads, seafood & sushi by day & cocktails by night. Tucked behind the rooms is an on-site dive centre, Peponi (see *What to see and do*, page 304). Online booking discount. **$$$**

⌂ **Teddy's Place** (9 rooms) m 0774 137413; e karibu@teddys-place.com; www.teddys-place.com. The former Kizingitini Disco now markets itself as a locally owned hostel, which sums up the level of accommodation here. While acceptable, the thatched bandas are very basic, with sand-covered floors & window-free walls offering no ventilation or natural light. The bandas range from sgl to cramped dorms. Inside, furnishing consists of little more than a bed, an ill-fitting mosquito net & a standing fan, & all rooms share a hot-water shower room.

Although basic food is available it appears drinking is the main focus, with a large upturned dhow used as a bar. It's worth noting that Teddy's has no direct beach access, & is not visible (or signposted) from the sand. To reach the sea, guests must walk down a winding path, climb a ladder over a wall, & pass by the raised lounge, locally known as 'Amsterdam', which gives a clue as to what goes on here. **$-$$**

⌂ **Hakuna Majiwe Lodge** (20 rooms) m 0777 454505; e hakunamajiwe@gmail.com; www.hakunamajiwe.net. About 2km south of central Paje, & now accessed from the main tar road to Jambiani, is Italian-owned Hakuna Majiwe. Meaning 'a place without stones', a reference to the wide beach & expansive intertidal flats here, it certainly has a lovely position & the benefit of relative isolation. The large, en-suite beach bungalows are very nice indeed, with varnished floorboards, fluffy towels, fans & impressive 4-poster beds. Wide individual decks have inviting swinging beds & a cushioned bench, whilst makuti-shaded loungers are tucked amid the low beach vegetation to provide

some privacy. There is a huge (slightly lacking in atmosphere) open-sided makuti restaurant & a baraza lounge with a dartboard; a swimming pool set back from the beach; & 2 on-site tailors running up made-to-measure beachwear from kanga fabric (*www.magoeastafrica.com*). Sadly, we have heard of staff being mistreated here, so in spite of the location & facilities we must refrain from a wholehearted recommendation until we've been able to learn the truth behind these allegations. **$$$$–$$$$$**

⌂ **Kilima Kidogo** (9 rooms) ☎ (South Africa) +27 (84) 225 5500; m 0777 201088; e kilimakidogo@live.com, kilimakidogo@gmail.com; www.kilimakidogo.co.za. Hakuna Majiwe's southern neighbour, Kilima Kidogo is essentially a fully staffed villa, though rooms can be booked individually. Owned by South African twins, Dina & Joey, it's very much their home from home & retains that comfortable feel throughout. With en-suite bedrooms in the main villa & a small gateside cottage in the bougainvillea-filled garden, it represents very good value for groups looking for quality accommodation & beachfront privacy. Under high makuti thatch, the central villa area has a pool table & satellite TV, a beautifully set table beside the open kitchen & a small lounge full of games, jigsaws & books; bedrooms are tastefully furnished with rustic beds, quality linen & colourful scatter cushions. There is AC, fans & an electronic safe as well as open wardrobes & shuttered windows. There is a licensed bar & small restaurant under makuti on the beach, & a flat roof overlooking the sea for sunrise sea views. Hadji is the friendly on-site tour guide who books island tours & hires out jeeps & bikes. For the less energetic, the beachfront spa offers various soothing therapies. Unfortunately, the curio shop here sells shells from the beach; please do not buy them as it will only encourage this practice further. **$$$**

✕ **WHERE TO EAT AND DRINK**   All of the hotels above welcome non-guests to eat and drink, with most serving a mix of Swahili flavours and international-style dishes. On top of this, a smattering of local and European-style cafés and restaurants have appeared in recent years, all serving suitably filling and tasty treats.

🍽 **Soko Café**   Just past the roundabout in Paje, this bright pink building is well signposted & impossible to miss. A cross between a café & a market, it sells traditional food, refreshing

smoothies & juices, homemade local ice cream, & fresh bread & sweets. Try an iced cinnamon latte to cool off in the midday heat. **$$**

🍴 **Jambo Restaurant and Bar** Fri night is party night at Jambo's, where beverages including beer & wine are served from 08.00. There's a limited menu of spaghetti & burgers, but most come for intoxicating cocktails sipped on shady sunloungers. Simple & cheap b/fasts of spiced tea & fruit are also popular. $$$

✕ **Ocean Restaurant** The smart Ocean Restaurant opened in late 2011 at the far north of Paje village, next door to Buccaneer Diving. It's accessed over an unnecessary bridge from the beach, which at high tide is partially underwater.

The menu is a classic selection of Italian-style food, including pasta, steak, seafood & grilled chicken dishes washed down with a glass of wine or a cold beer. $$$

✕ **African BBQ** m 0712 567988. Just around the corner from Paje by Night, Rastafarian-run African BBQ is not much more than 2 tables covered by makuti thatch & decorated with pictures of Bob Marley. Unsurprisingly, everything on the menu is barbecued, from fresh seafood & home-grown garden vegetables to chicken & spiced beef skewers, all served with salad & chips or rice. $$$

WHAT TO SEE AND DO The primary activities in Paje are sunbathing on the beautiful beach and swimming in the sea. If staring out at the waves breaking along the fringe reef pricks your curiosity, there are two dive schools in the vicinity for underwater adventures and more recently a number of European-run kitesurfing schools have popped up for above-the-waves action. Be aware that kitesurfing is seasonal though, with the best times being December to February, or even better, from June to August. For those tired of the salt and sand, Dhow Inn's pool (see *Where to stay*, page 301) is open to non-residents as long as they purchase something from the bar.

Diving

🤿 **Buccaneer Diving** ☎ 024 2240190/91; m 0728 630369; e info@buccaneerdiving. com; www.buccaneerdiving.com. Based within Arabian Nights (see *Where to stay*, page 301), Buccaneer Diving is an efficient 5* PADI dive school. It has large classrooms, a swimming pool for course work, & a resident team of 3 experienced instructors & a dive master, who between them speak 6 languages. Their reception bears the hallmarks of a reputable, safety-conscious operation with clear certification from DAN & PADI on display, a dive-briefing board & some enticing underwater photography. Sgl/dbl dive US$50/90; sailboat snorkelling US$11; Mnemba Island snorkelling trip US$90.

🤿 **Peponi Diving** m 0773 523781; e info@ peponidiving.com; www.peponidiving.com. Part of Cristal Resort & based within their grounds (see *Where to stay*, page 302), Peponi is a PADI centre offering courses from Discover Scuba to Dive Master, as well as speciality modules. Beginners can do their confined water in the hotel pool, & there is a designated classroom for the theory elements. Managed by experienced dive instructor Philippe, the small team & guests here have access to new (under 2 years) Aqualung Seaquest equipment, full & shorty wetsuits & 12l aluminium tanks. The centre's shaded local boat, *Bahati*, can take 10 divers, & carries oxygen, first aid, & a spare engine for safety. PADI Open Water US$450 over 5 days.

Kitesurfing

🏄 **Airborne Kite Centre** m 0715 548464; e info@airbornekitecentre.com; www. airbornekitecentre.com. Airborne's knowledgeable staff consist of 2 instructors, 2 interns, 2 helpers, & the owner who can tell you all you need to know about their IKO-accredited courses & private lessons. For something a little different, day trips kitesurfing at Mnemba Island, reef-kiting lessons & full-moon trips are available, as well as a variety of local tours & excursions. Kite-rental costs US$65/1/2-day, US$115/full day.

🏄 **Harakakite** m 0777 244416/85; e info@ zanzibarkiteschool.com; www.zanzibarkiteschool. com; ⊕ Dec–Mar & mid May–Oct. Meaning 'fast kite' in Swahili, Harakakite has been offering IKO-accredited courses for 4 years. All levels are catered for, & children are accepted from the age of 3 (strength, comprehension & concentration allowing!) as long as they are accompanied by an adult, & from 9 on their own. The number of instructors here depends on the season, but there's 1 permanent instructor & founder, Mathias. A 4hr beginner's discovery course costs US$100, while a 10hr complete course costs US$200, with a max 4 per group. After all that surfing, guests can head to the small café which offers a selection of drinks & snacks. Equipment rental is available to tour operators only.

⚓ Kite Centre Zanzibar

e kitecentrezanzibar@gmail.com; www. kitecentrezanzibar.com; ⏱ mid Dec–mid Mar & mid Jun–mid Oct. Owned & operated by Dim of Bellevue Bungalows in Bwejuu (see *Where to stay*, page 295), this IKO-accredited activity outfit was one of original kiting operations on the island – and certainly the only dedicated centre on this stretch of coast. The trend has taken off though and plenty others have followed Dim's lead now. It continues to offer high-quality, branded kit, lessons & courses, experienced instructors & a thoroughly exhilarating seaside diversion. The courses are open to all abilities (you do need to be able to swim though), but if you are a novice to the sport, take along a T-shirt, plenty of sunscreen & a sense of humour. Beginner course (3x3hrs) US$370; board & kite rental US$60/½-day, US$100/day, 370/week. The centre also offers sea safaris to learn about local fishing techniques & seaweed farming, with all profits going to the village.

⚓ Paje By Kite

e info@pajebykite.net; www. pajebykite.net. As the name might suggest, this IKO centre is on the same plot & affiliated with the quirky Paje By Night hotel (see *Where to stay*, page 302). It opened in Dec 2011, & offers kiteboarding lessons from beginner to advanced level, taught by 3 instructors, as well as wakeboarding, speedboating, tubing & other water & motor combinations. Equipment rental is a steal at just US$20 for the full gear, while courses cost US$40/hr for a group of up to 4, or US$65/hr for private lessons.

An informative diversion is the new **Seaweed Center** (m *0777 871377*; e *info@seaweedcenter.com; www.seaweedcenter.com*). Given the visibility of seaweed farming, it's well worth checking out these lovely new 'headquarters' to better understand its very real importance to the community. Information boards are clear and guided tours are available. A few bars of organic seaweed and spice soap also make perfect, lightweight souvenirs.

There is also an old **mausoleum** nearby: a low rectangular edifice with a castellated wall, inset with antique plates and dishes. This design is thought to have originated in Persia, and may indicate that this part of the island was settled by Shirazi immigrants prior to the western side of the island, near present-day Zanzibar Town. Ask one of the local villagers to escort you for a small fee.

JAMBIANI

Straddling the provinces of Kibigija and Kikadini, Jambiani village is a sprawling, linear coastal village. Beginning a few kilometres south of Paje, it spreads for about 6km down the coast towards Ras Shungi. With around 8,000 permanent residents, of whom half are children, Jambiani still has a relatively low population density, even though it's experienced a 25% increase in the last four years. It benefits from having nursery, primary and secondary schools and a medical centre. All warmly welcome visitors to donate money to improve facilities; indeed the nursery was built entirely by money raised by the local village NGO, not by the government. There are several basic food stores, a local craft shop (selling delicious natural honey), a friendly post office and a bakery.

The village's name comes from the Arabic word *jambiya*: a dagger with a markedly curved blade. Local legend holds that early settlers found such a knife here; proof that others had been in the area before them. It emits an active community spirit; on a village tour with the local Eco+Culture team (see *What to see and do*, page 318), Jambiani is probably the best place on the island to gain genuine insights into Zanzibari village life and enjoy rewarding community interaction.

The beach is wide, and is the hub of daily life: work, rest and play. For visitors it's a place to catch some sun and explore the fascinating tidal flats, for children it's a place to cool down, run and play football; for local men it's a launch for their picturesque ngalawas, and for the large number of seaweed-farming women it's a valuable natural asset.

Alas, for tourists, Jambiani has lost some of its energy in recent years and is increasingly run-down. It now offers a disappointing lack of variety in its choice of places to stay: depressingly deserted hotels and a lack of characterful

JAMBIANI MARINE AND BEACH CONSERVATION (JAMABECO)

The Jambiani Marine and Beach Conservation (JAMABECO) organisation was founded in Jambiani village in 2001, receiving official recognition in February 2005. It aims to eradicate beach pollution and destruction in the area by providing villagers of all ages with environmental education. It hopes ultimately to improve villagers' incomes by promoting sustainable, long-term use of the local marine resources.

Jambiani village life revolves around the sea – fishing, seaweed farming, coir-rope manufacture and beach tourism – so the quality of the sealife and coastal environment has the ability to impact directly upon the vast majority of villagers. Well-managed resource use and protection is important in maintaining and developing all of these industries and incomes.

The 34 JAMABECO committee members operate a year-round education programme to advocate environmental conservation; plant trees along the beaches; and regularly patrol and clean the beaches and village, removing the broken glass, bottles, batteries, iron materials and huge number of plastic bags that litter many of Zanzibar's coastal villages. Since 2003, they have also organised annual clean-up days to mark International Environment Day on 25 June. In addition, they follow Scuba Do Kendwa's excellent example (see page 247) and participate in September's annual International Coastal Clean-up Day.

With support and sustained education, we must hope that their efforts pay off in Jambiani, and that the message spreads to other coastal settlements. Without question, there is already significantly less litter here than in most of Zanzibar's other villages.

Partnered with JAMABECO, Swiss-run **Marine Cultures** (*www.marinecultures. org*) works in a similar way, encouraging villagers to find sustainable ways to cultivate and harvest marine products. This non-profit organisation enables farmers to contact their buyers directly, allowing them to cut out the middleman and reap greater financial reward from their produce. The Marine Cultures office in Jambiani is located next to the Equinox Restaurant and welcomes visitors who wish to find out more about their ongoing projects. They are currently investigating sponges, with the hopes of starting up sponge harvesting in the village. There's currently a test farm, and if this is successful they hope to teach locals to cultivate and sell sponges (in a similar way they do seaweed), providing them with much-needed employment.

More information is available from Abdu M Vuai or Makame Simai (e *jamabeco@yahoo.co.uk*). To visit in Jambiani, ask for directions to the JAMABECO office or head to Okala Restaurant, where owner Mohammad (*okala@marinecultures.org*) is an enthusiastic member of both organisations.

accommodation options combine to give the place an empty feel, sending many visitors north to Paje where there's more going on.

There is clear evidence of coastal erosion too, with most hotels protected from the waves by aesthetically challenged concrete walls and rock breakwaters, creating a two-tier beach – above and below the defences. That said, the beach is kept clean thanks to two dedicated community organisations (see box, *Jambiani Marine and Beach Conservation*, opposite) who arrange litter collections and local environmental education, and the sand here is simply never as busy as the northern beaches of Nungwi and Kendwa.

GETTING THERE AND AWAY The paved road has made travel to and from Jambiani a pleasure compared with the past. The road runs inland of the village with a number of well-signposted turns to various coastal lodges. The old uneven, meandering 'highway' through the village remains, though it is no longer possible to travel all the way to Paje along the coast, thanks to various boundary walls along the way.

You can reach Jambiani by **private vehicle** or **tourist minibus**. In addition, **dala dala** No 309 runs from Zanzibar Town about five times a day, and the public **bus** (Route 9) to Paje sometimes continues as far as Jambiani: it's important to check each individual bus's destination though. It's also worth noting that most public transport heads only as far south as Auberge Coco Beach. To get to the more southerly resorts, you will have to either make a special plan with the driver, walk, or wait for one of the few daily dala dalas that continue on to Makunduchi.

At the southern end of Jambiani village, the dirt road heads inland past the Red Monkey Lodge to meet with the main road for the final 10km to Makunduchi. Zanzest Beach Bungalows is the only hotel along this stretch of road, and public transport is extremely limited. If you want to keep heading south to Makunduchi, you may be lucky and find a lift on one of the occasional vehicles on the main road, otherwise, if you decide to walk, it takes a very hot three to four hours.

 WHERE TO STAY With a long stretch of small guesthouses and no resorts, nothing on this stretch of coast qualifies as upmarket. Kikadini once tried to raise the bar here, but unfortunately its early promise has significantly waned. There's little with real stand-out character, but of the mid-range options, Blue Oyster and Casa del Mar are very pleasant and far ahead of the pack, with newcomer Mama Mapambo following close behind. The Red Monkey Lodge at the far south of town is probably the best of the budget-choice places to stay, if you don't mind the more relatively remote location. One of the better hotels in the area was the Sau Inn, but unfortunately a fire in late 2011 razed it to the ground. In recent years, as hotels have emptied and tourists have headed north, a number of hotel owners have turned their properties into villas aimed at long-term rental, which may be an option worth considering for larger groups. The places below are listed from north to south, though development seems to be constant, so expect a few more names by the time you arrive. Unless stated otherwise, hotels listed below offer en-suite bathrooms as standard.

🏠 **Demani Lodge** (11 rooms) m 0772 263115/0777 460079; e demanilodge@gmail. com; www.demanilodge.com. Catering for those on a tight budget who still want a decent standard, Swedish-managed Demani is truly a backpackers' place, filled with chill-out music, good vibes

& offbeat characters. The simple but well-constructed thatched bandas have fans, mosquito nets & sturdy beds made from varnished tree trunks. All rooms share neat bathrooms, where the walls are covered in colourful murals by local artist 'Chris Da Vinci'. While some rooms have concrete floors, many visitors prefer the desert-island feel of the sand-covered floors, even though scratchy grains in the bed are inevitable. The dormitories have 6–9 beds under a high A-frame ceiling, making them seem less cramped than they could be, & the largest one's a bargain at US$12/bed. Even cheaper are the camping spots, but you'll need your own gear. Hearts & stars hang from the makuti-ceilinged bar, where the lower level has swings, benches & a fire pit, & the upper chill-out zone is strung with rainbow-coloured hammocks & scattered with floor cushions. This upper area is a good spot to catch a cooling evening breeze, but you'll need to be quick to save the cocktails-at-sunset sea-facing sofa. Tasty meals made from locally sourced ingredients are all served here for rock bottom prices – check out the blackboard marked 'cheap shit', filling comfort food for those on even the tightest of budgets. Demani helpfully offers Wi-Fi for US$0.30/day. It also rents bikes for US$4/day, useful for reaching the beach which is found across the road & down a private sandy path. **$$**

🏠 **Jaribu Beach Hotel** (9 rooms) m 0776 739572; e jaribubeachhotel@hotmail.com; www.jaribubeachhotel.com. Meaning 'try' in Swahili, the Jaribu Beach Hotel may in fact need to try much harder. Its rooms opened in late 2011 & have remained pretty much unoccupied ever since; it's not hard to see why. With a solid coconut wood bed, traditional-style ceiling & freshly painted walls, they start off well but falter with cheap chairs & a complete lack of decoration. The wet-room bathrooms are damp & tatty & there's no fan. The ominous red bars on the windows are reminiscent of a prison, & the exaggerated explanation by the staff as to why no sea swimming should be attempted (due to rocks & sea urchins) may make you wonder: why bother staying at all? But it's a peaceful spot raised up on the rocks allowing for cool winds & sea views. The terrace restaurant is basic & heavily seafood focused, but a good meal can be had for US$6pp. Staff were enthusiastic about possible improvements during our last visit, such as adding a pool to the rocky garden, but change is unlikely to come quickly. **$–$$**

🏠 **Mbuyuni Beach Village** (24 rooms) ☏ 024 2240149; m 0777 843622; e mbuyunibeachvillage@yahoo.co.uk, uhurul3@hotmail.com; www.mbuyuni.com. Mbuyuni is 200m north of Pakachi & currently reached on the bumpy coastal track. Plans have been in place for a while to build a road directly from the north–south tar highway, but this more than likely still won't be completed by the time you travel. Accessed from the beach road, you will first pass the restaurant, about 50m south of the accommodation, sitting atop the coral cliff. Decorated with paintings of golden hued sunsets, the à la carte cuisine is both Swahili & international, with a range of spaghetti & fish dishes for US$8, & there's a lengthy cocktail menu (try a Zanzibar Pirate: local gin & Cointreau with lime, orange & passionfruit juice). The 'village' itself has 2 rows of thatched bungalows running perpendicular to the sea, with established flower beds & wide sandy paths. The rooms are simple with tiled floors, sky blue walls & matching sheets, but an enormous red bathroom spoils the quaint feel a little. All offer a fan, mosquito net & shower; some of the rooms also come equipped with a mini fridge. The seemingly constant construction work that surrounds the site makes the place feel half finished, but you can easily distract yourself in the cooling pool. **$$**

🏠 **Pakachi Beach Hotel** (8 rooms) m 0777 423331; e pakachi@hotmail.com; www.pakachi.net. Appropriately, *pakachi* means 'border', for this pleasant little hotel is situated on the coral rock roughly halfway between the centres of Paje & Jambiani. The European management who recently took over have injected the place with character & created a friendly, rustic haven. 3 new, 2-storey, A-frame beach bandas amid flower-filled gardens, each with 2 rooms, channel the breeze nicely & offer a lovely view from upstairs. Inside, the rooms are simple & spotlessly clean, with kanga curtains, large ceiling fans & en-suite bathrooms. There is also a 2-bedroom family house available. On the other side of the bumpy road, the bar/restaurant sits overlooking the sea. The chef, Gaudi, rustles up both local & international dishes, with recommendations coming in for his pizzas. The coastline is very rocky at this point, so it's not always ideal for shore swimming, but the intertidal zone makes for fascinating beachcombing at low tide. A much-needed pool & a simple Island Spice spa have recently been added for guest enjoyment. **$$**

🏠 **Spice Island Hotel and Resort** (34 rooms) m 0777 512512/0775 020113; e reservation@spice-island-hotel-resort.com, office@spice-island-hotel-resort.com; www.zanzibar-holidays.com. A breath of fresh air among what seems like a row of identikit guesthouses, the Spice Island Hotel is an organised & professional operation managed by the energetic Tina, with excellent facilities & helpful staff but without the feeling of some of the larger, more generic resorts elsewhere on the island. The 17 terracotta bungalows, each containing 2 rooms, are all sea facing but not all have sea views, which may cause some confusion when booking. There's both AC & a fan, although the trpl-layered construction of makuti-steel-makuti keeps the temperatures cool & so these are not always necessary. Each room has Zanzibari beds scattered with fresh flowers & a particularly ornate piece of furniture for added interest. All have clean en-suite bathrooms, & some even have 2 separate toilets. Within the pleasant garden, filled with over 5,000 plants & complete with a fountain, the 30m kidney-shaped swimming pool & mini baby pool is the main focus of all the fun. Here, guests sunbathe & read while their children amuse themselves with pool games, stopping only for lunch in the vast restaurant where European & Zanzibari fusion food is served. Stressed parents might prefer to interrupt their poolside lounging with a massage in the Lemon Spa. For further respite, the plush leather sofas in the huge makuti lounge are a particular draw, & the sequinned cushions & saxophone music add to the relaxed feel. Spice Island's beachfront is 100m long, allowing plenty of space for the Water Sport Center Zanzibar (*www.watersportcenterzanzibar. com*). Here water babies can participate in all manner of activities, from banana boats to fishing, & parasailing to aqua aerobics (US$60 for 6, 30-min sessions). Particularly unusual is supping, a form of stand-up paddle boarding, which costs US$90 for a 3hr introductory session. In the middle of the beach, the 100m-long jetty has a bar at the end, where an international wine list is a fitting accompaniment to sunset. If entertainment is still required, then there's always the TV, library, & the volleyball court, or the hotel rents out cars & bikes. **$$$$**

🏠 **Villa de Coco** (11 rooms) m 0776 110691; e villadecoco@gmail.com; www.villadecoco.net. Beside the electrical substation, about 400m off the tar road south of Paje, Villa de Coco is an Italian-run lodge, currently catering to fellow citizens on all-inclusive package holidays with the Italian operator, Phone & Go. That said, if there's space outside high season, the friendly owners, Marco & Manuela, will happily accept ad hoc visitors. The majority of the rooms are in 3 rows of coconut-wood bungalows;

inside they are small but neat with attractive coconut floorboards, kanga-hung walls, clean beds, fans, open wardrobes & a small terrace. There are also 2 separate rooms, set back across the dusty car park in a new 2-storey villa, which also houses the massage room. There is a makuti-thatched restaurant serving pasta, & the chill-out lounge by the beach is a great place to relax & play snooker. **$$$**

🏠 **Bahari View Lodge** (13 rooms) m 0776 716020; e africanview@yahoo.com, bahariviewlodge@yahoo.com; http://bahari-view-lodge.de. The former Mount Zion Long Beach Bungalows changed hands in 2009 & is now Bahari View Lodge. Apart from the addition of a small pool, not much has changed, & 'Mount Zion' remains ornately carved into the door frames. This is the most northerly of Jambiani's resorts, situated along the village road just before you reach the brick wall that now stops traffic continuing to Paje along the coast. The coral-rock bungalows sit amid overgrown gardens & offer moderately clean, sparsely furnished accommodation with ceiling fans & Heath Robinson-style mosquito nets. There are also 2 pagoda-like makuti structures on the beach, which contain banda rooms & a small shared WC/shower. These are very basic with coir-rope beds & little else, but are only used when the other rooms are full. The varnished palm-frond door offers limited security, so guests are advised to secure any valuables elsewhere. The buzzing circular beach bar is adorned with Rasta Revolution posters & seems to be the preferred hangout for a good number of local Rastafarians. Bahari View is an adequate establishment in a reasonably attractive situation, but the rather gloomy bungalows & rickety bandas remain overpriced. Banda **$$**; bungalow **$$$**

🏠 **Mango Beachhouse** (3 rooms) m 0773 498949; www.mango-beachhouse.com. At Kiddo's Café (see *Where to eat*, page 316) & with the same management, this quirky guesthouse has 3 very different, self-catering rooms spread across 2 buildings, each made distinct by the owner's eye for unique decorative items & styles: 1 room has batik elephant sheets, 1 has a large orange bathroom, & 1 is adorned with shells hanging from the ceiling. All are brightened up with fresh flowers & bold paintings & share a kitchen with a hob, a kettle & a zebra print fridge. Out the front, comfortable sunloungers are spread out on the sand. For every week booked guests are offered a free night, an offer well worth taking up as this is a place to linger. **$$$**

🏠 **Mama Mapambo** (5 rooms) m 0772 671073/0774 134767; e mamamapambo@gmail.com; www.mamamapambo.altervista.org. New in 2011, cheery Mama Mapambo adds a splash of much-needed colour & character to the guesthouses along this stretch of beach. A wonderfully vibrant sign will direct you to this Italian-owned place, & don't let the lack of spoken English put you off as the rooms are delightful & high quality, each painted a different shade. 3 rooms have a sea view & all have 4-poster beds draped in colour-trimmed nets as well as gauzed windows for mosquito defence. Walk-in wardrobes are a bonus, as is AC, & bathrooms are modern. Up a spiral staircase, 2 Jungle Rooms have wooden A-frame ceilings & zebra-striped beds, & the modern bathrooms feature a shower in a circular pod in the middle of the room – a striking & original design. To round it all off, the exterior of the whole lodge is painted a sunny yellow to match the owners' warm dispositions. A choice of bright & breezy seating areas both upstairs & down offers plenty of cushions & overlooks the sand. Unsurprisingly, the food is most definitely Italian with large bowls of spaghetti & cheesy pizzas being the staples. The owners have put their hearts & souls into this project, & it shows. **$$$**

🏠 **Seaview Lodge** m 0777 282877/0719 427232; www.seaviewlodgezanzibar.com. Next to Bahari View, there is nothing fancy here but the local owners are trying hard to offer clean, simple accommodation, if a little overpriced. Decorated with painted sealife outside, the bungalows have low twin beds (although 1 room has a large dbl), en-suite showers & a small fan as standard. Murals have been attempted on the walls, but these look unfinished, or were perhaps painted in the dark! There are a few loungers in front of each room, & even a beach shower for rinsing off salt water (but bear in mind the water immediately in front of the lodge is predominantly used for seaweed farming so you'll have to wade out quite far for a dip in the sea). The beach restaurant is supposedly open 24hrs, with market availability determining the menu, & it's a casual spot to watch the local beach activity. Check out the simple Tamarind Spa, where you can treat yourself to a body scrub with local spices, as well as waxing, facials & hair braiding.

Seaview Lodge is also the base for Indian Ocean Magic Tours (Indoma) (024 2234797; m 0777 415465; e info@indomatours.com; www.indomatours.com). **$$$**

✗ **Stonehouse** (7 rooms) m 0777 874771; e karibu@stonehouse-zanzibar.com; www.stonehouse-zanzibar.com. This former family house was converted to a guesthouse 5 years ago, & still retains much of its homely feel, though not in a good way. The disappointing rooms contain nothing more than a bed covered in a bubblegum pink bedspread, & the mint green bathrooms are all outside. The former occupants of the house have left the place messy & littered with junk (a long-forgotten Christmas tree stands in the lounge), & piles of abandoned dirty clothes & peeling lino fixed with duct tape do little to impress. Guests are welcome to use the well-equipped kitchen, but if you don't fancy cooking, the owners can rustle up simple meals with a bit of notice. Stonehouse doesn't seem to know if it has apts or a beach house, & is ridiculously overpriced for what you get. **$$$**

🏠 **Blue Oyster Hotel** (13 rooms) 024 2240163; m 0783 045796; e blueoysterhotel@gmx.de; www.zanzibar.de. In lovely gardens of oleander & hibiscus, Blue Oyster remains one of the friendliest, most cared for & best-value hotels in its range. The main 2-storey building has ground-floor rooms around a rear palm courtyard & a wonderfully breezy 1st-floor restaurant, from where the wide veranda overlooks the ocean. Further accommodation is available in a trio of smaller 2-storey buildings, all of which come with en-suite facilities & balconies. There is a lovely raised stretch of sand in front of the hotel, which has been laid with loungers, shaded by makuti parasols & softened with tropical planting – a perfect sunbathing spot, especially if you also opt for one of Zena's coconut-oil massages (US$20). With exceedingly friendly staff, clean rooms, good beds, running water & electricity, & an attractive location, this is a fine deal for the price. In the restaurant, snacks & sandwiches cost around US$5, delicious salads US$6, or pizzas & good evening meals like coconut-infused octopus with rice around US$10. Kemi Tours & Travel are based at Blue Oyster (m 0782 214127; kemitours@gmail.com; www.kemitours-zanzibar.com); contact for advice on day trips, safaris & watersports, or simply to hire reef shoes for US$1 per day to avoid those pesky sea urchins. **$$$**

⌂ Baghani Guesthouse (8 rooms)
m 0777204634; **e** husseink@yahoo.com. Just a short hop south from the Blue Oyster, a statue of 2 leaping dolphins forms the arched entranceway to Baghani from the beach. In a small sandy garden you'll find a deserted bar made out of tree trunks, & various tables with vases of bougainvillea. Behind this, spread over 2 storeys, the spartan rooms contain nothing more than chunky coconut-wood beds, a desk & a chair. The owner, the brother of Starfish's owner, (see page 316) confidently proclaims all windows have a sea view, but a bar view might be a more appropriate description. The 2 bathrooms are shared so that 2 rooms use 1, & 6 use the other. Upstairs an open-sided lounge offers a cooling spot, but most head for the bar. **$$$**

⌂ Oasis Beach Inn (7 rooms) **m** 0779 351346/0778 162009; **e** phabo2@yahoo.com. This rather run-down resort lies about 750m south of the Blue Oyster, just along the beach. The rooms are literally 20m from the sand, but the luxury ends there; inside, ripped plastic sheeting on the floor, grime-encrusted fans & a rusty shower show a total lack of care. Mismatched furniture fills the dark rooms, while limescale & mould cover the bathrooms, which are not helped by a lack of doors on the toilets. In early 2008, a bar & new restaurant were constructed, & all attention seems to have been focused here. Some rooms are scheduled for extension, though we have little faith that the standard or service will improve to match. **$$**

⌂ Blue Earth Bungalows (8 rooms) PO Box 4226, Zanzibar; ☏024 2240351; **m** 0777 846597; **e** info@blueearthbungalows.com; www. blueearthbungalows.com. Approaching Blue Earth from the beach, you could be forgiven for thinking the desolate, overgrown walled plot was yet another slice of abandoned half-built wasteland. But look closer & you'll see a discrete row of thatched bungalows hidden along the far wall, each containing 2 rooms. Within, the aroma of freshly laundered linen wafts from the Zanzibari beds which sit on a cool blue-tiled floor. Furnishing is simple, with just a wardrobe, fan & a lamp, but strangely no table to put it on. Flowery green curtains complete the look. 2 rooms have TVs & AC, but other than that, the rest are indistinguishable. Bathrooms are again basic but have hot-water showers & are spotlessly clean. In front of the

rooms stands the Dimbuni Restaurant, which is little more than a couple of tables under a makuti roof. Here a menu of seafood, curries & sandwiches is on offer, though the probability of anything on the menu actually being available seems low. There's a lot of unused space here, & for such basic accommodation, the price should be lower. **$$$**

⌂ Nuru Beach Resort (9 rooms) PO Box 20, Jambiani, Zanzibar; **m** 0754 280249; **e** krytontz@ yahoo.com; www.nurubeach-resort.com. Next to the primary health-care unit, about 50m south of the Oasis Beach, Nuru is a new hotel, having been the dire Rising Sun Hotel in a former incarnation. The clean rooms contain a bed, a chair, a desk & shelves fashioned from branches & coir rope, & there is a fan, but that's it. Despite the lack of decoration, it's clean & tidy, & the blue bathrooms gleam. The Polish flag flies proudly at the beachside entrance, reflecting the nationality of the owners & most of the clientele; non-Polish guests may find checking in a struggle, as not much English is spoken here, & to make matters worse, there's no obvious reception. There are leafy gardens which have been brightened up with concrete moulded flamingos – perhaps not to everyone's taste. **$$$**

⌂ Garden Restaurant & Bungalows (6 rooms) The damage Sau Inn's fire caused spurred Garden Restaurant's British owners to get renovating & improving, & they're doing a great job. New fixtures & fittings have updated the spacious rooms while keeping them simple; new nets, screens & ceilings have been added to reduce mosquito numbers, & everything has been thoroughly cleaned & repainted to include bold animal artwork. Manager Jenny has redesigned the garden, which she hopes will grow to a lush & green space. Meanwhile, a brand-new kitchen & bar should smarten up the restaurant (see *Where to eat*, page 316), which is popular for its curries & crêpes. The whole place has a lot of potential, & with Jenny's enthusiasm & dedication, there are hopes that this could be a high-quality operation in the near future. **$$$**

⌂ East Coast Visitors Inn (40 rooms) ☏024 2240150; **m** 0777 045479/417312; **e** visitorsinn@ zitec.org, visitorsinn@hotmail.com; www. zanzibarvisitorsinn.com. Situated about 150m south of the charred remains of the Sau Inn along the village main street, past the health centre & the school, this is quite large for a budget place.

10

Reception is tucked under the 'Karibuni' arch & is a popular spot for locals to watch TV, while the rooms are in white bungalows above the beach. Some rooms have been given a fresh coat of paint & have larger beds & a desk, while the older rooms are a little run-down with saggy ceilings & worn carpets. All offer AC, mini fridges, satellite TV & tiled floors, & some have a dining table too. Alternatively, meals are available in the cheerfully fruit-painted Visitor's Palate Restaurant for around US$5, where there's also a snack bar & a pool table. There is a nice stretch of beach here & shade to be had under the casuarina trees. Children under 7 stay free. **$$$**

🏠 **New Jambiani Beach Hotel**
(6 rooms) m 0779 351317/0716 415466; e jambianibeachhotel@yahoo.com; www. jambiani-beach-hotel.com. Owned & run by a German woman, Marlies Lehmann, Jambiani Beach Hotel first opened in 1987 as a joint venture with her Zanzibari husband. Following their separation & contentious land division, the place fell into disrepair & closed. However, in early 2008, Marlies began a rebuilding programme, hence the addition of 'New' to the hotel name. The resulting bungalows are solid, bright white & shiny with sturdy beds, a small lounge area, spotless bathrooms, free-standing fans & a terrace. The planting in the flourishing gardens has finally grown to shield the rooms from the beach, although why they are set so far back from the water's edge is unclear. There is a beach restaurant, popular with local lads, & here a variety of meats & seafood are served in various guises, with snacks available between meals. There's a tiny on-site dive centre, Xplore Ocean Divers (m *0773 456666;* e *xodivers@hotmail.com; US$90 for dbl dives*), where all manner of watery activities can be arranged but note they are not PADI accredited. **$$**

🏠 **Casa Del Mar** (14 rooms) m 0777 455446; e info@casa-delmar-zanzibar.com; www.casa-delmar-zanzibar.com; ⊕ Jun–Mar. This is among the more aesthetically pleasing beach lodges in this part of Zanzibar, consisting of rooms in 2 thatched dbl-storey houses, & a 2-room bungalow made almost entirely of organic material. It's owned & managed by a young, gentle Palestinian couple, with impressive enthusiasm, skill & environmental awareness. All of the unique lodge furniture & *objets d'art* were made on site & every palm uprooted during its construction has been

successfully replanted. Community relations are very strong, with the vast majority of the staff (14 out of 17) being Jambiani residents & the school & clinic receiving regular support. These credentials aside, the accommodation & friendly vibe are good reasons to stay, too. The ground-floor rooms are dbls with a mosquito net, fan & terrace overlooking the gardens, while the 1st-floor suites are dbl storey with a downstairs lounge (or children's room) & balcony, & a galleried bedroom high in the makuti thatch. The circular restaurant is in a shady spot with colourful cushions, tropical planting & good food; there's a detailed noticeboard of local activities & island excursions, & the lodge has its own boat for snorkelling trips (US$15pp/day). **$$$–$$$$**

🏠 **Kikadini Villas** (8 rooms) m 0777 707888; e reservations@kikadini.com; www.kikadini.com. On a large beachfront plot in the centre of the village, the unique villas that make up Kikadini are stylishly designed, owned & managed by a Norwegian couple, Sylvia & Torgeir Barner. Kikadini clearly aims to be a boutique hotel: striking architecture, high-quality furniture & finish, & definite individuality. Sadly, it doesn't quite pull it off & service has suffered with an absent manager & high staff turnover in the last few years. Each of the beach-facing villas is architecturally & decoratively different, from 3-bedroomed Villa Palm with its Moorish feel, pretty patio & inner courtyard, to the seclusion of villas Maroc & Pwani. There are also 2 sgl rooms in the reception building. The interiors feature eclectic *objets d'art* & huge Zanzibari oil paintings alongside soft linens & comfortable furniture, yet their size makes them feel spartan. All have AC, electricity, fans, small fridges & plenty of space, with Wi-Fi, bottled mineral water & beach towels provided as standard. Shady roof terraces above each villa have a bathtub, although as this is shared with all guests in the villa, it is only really of practical use if you have rented out the whole building. For an extra US$5 guests can dine in their villa, although again the same rule applies, & exotic-sounding menus in fact taste disappointingly bland. A new pool surrounded by bougainvillea has unfortunately cut off the beach views from the main villa & from Villa Palm, making the property seem smaller & sadly missing a beautiful sandy beach space. Other public spaces include an Arabic-style shisha lounge, which fits in with the slightly Moroccan feel (US$15 a pipe). In a bid to maintain a calm haven for guests, children under 12 cannot stay unless a villa is exclusively booked. Although still the only property of its kind, sadly, what was once one of the best & most original accommodation options on the island has lost some of its shine, gaining instead an uneasy atmosphere & uncertain future. $$$$$

🏠 **Al Hapa Hotel** (3 rooms) m 0773 048894; e alhapa.bungalows@africamail.com; www.alhapazanzibar.n.nu. In association with the local villagers, this Swedish–Zanzibar-owned hotel opened in 2011. Offering a cosy & intimate stay, right on the beach, there are plans to slowly extend, add a pool & improve the facilities in the beachfront garden. Inside, bright yellow walls & huge flowery floor tiles clash with tangerine sheets, but rooms are clean & fresh & are equipped with fans, mosquito nets & hot-water showers. It's fairly simple but added touches such as scattered shells on the simple coir & driftwood shelves lend a dash of beach homeliness, & those staying in the twin room are treated to 2 squishy dbl beds. Reserve your hammock, classically tied up between curving palm trees, & lie back with one of the many well-read books. The simple restaurant & circular beach bar is the spot for seafood dishes such as sizzling calamari fritters (US$7) & evening postcard writing next to an almost shrine-like wall of Bob Marley memorabilia. $$$

🏠 **Jambiani Guesthouse** (5 rooms) m 0773 147812; e anne@zanzibar-guesthouse.com, martin@zanzibar-guesthouse.com; www.zanzibar-guesthouse.com. Jambiani Guesthouse is in the coconut line immediately above the beach at the southern end of the village. It's a small, thatched building, clearly signposted off the main village road, best booked by a group of friends or a family. A simple villa, it has 5 clean dbl rooms (1 en suite), 2 shared bathrooms, a small kitchen-lounge & a veranda overlooking the sandy beach & ocean. The local caretaker, Rama, lives on site & can help with local tours, snorkelling equipment (free) &, if necessary, catering. The weekly rates are not really discounted, but you can check availability online. $$

🏠 **Dhow Beach Village** (8 rooms) m 0777 417763; e dhowbeachvillage@yahoo.com, info@dhowbeachvillage.com; www.dhowbeachvillage.com. Set in the coconut line above the beach, Dhow Beach Village is a good option in this price range. Set in 2 neat rows, the rooms are small but stylishly simple, with solid wooden furniture, retractable mosquito nets, a small ceiling fan & a little outside terrace. The tiled bathrooms have constant hot water for post-beach (or party!) showers. The quite attractive pizza restaurant at the centre of the complex is lined with red hessian, & offers both Swahili & European favourites, & there's an octagonal bar, Day n Nite, on the beach. Serving cocktails 'when they feel like it', the bar is also the focus for the all-night Sat Happy Happy Beach Party when camp fires & the tunes of DJ Kweli attract locals & budget travellers. Pricing of rooms is dependent on size, not location, with Room 3 on the beach being arguably the best but not the most expensive. Room-rate discounts of up to 50% are available in low season. $$

🏠 **Auberge Coco Beach** (5 rooms) m 0732 940154; e cocobeach@zanlink.com. This long-standing small lodge offers simple dbl rooms which become more & more run-down as the years pass. Fading bedding, clunky fans, mildew-covered bathrooms & a small terrace lead onto a shady garden of coconut palms & sweet almond trees. It's a quiet spot & in the past, several travellers recommended the hedge-enclosed restaurant here, which is decked out in vinyl records, shipping memorabilia, & turtle-shells. However, what was once a list of exciting seafood is now a sparse menu of overpriced fish, beef & chicken dishes – remember to order at lunchtime for dinner. Visa is accepted with 5% surcharge. $$$

🏠 **Shehe Bungalows** (20 rooms) m 0777 843622; e shehebungalows@hotmail.com; www.shehebungalows.co.uk. Along the beach, about 1km south of the centre of Jambiani, Shehe was one of the first backpacker refuges in the village & has been operating for over a decade. Popular on the budget-travel trail for many years, it had been heading downhill but efforts have been made to spruce it up & it has regained some of its former glory. The accommodation is divided between a short terrace of beachfront rooms & a larger complex of small bungalows. The former have been tidied up with pretty paintings on the outside & a fresh coat of paint inside, clean Zanzibari beds & cold-water bathrooms with crimson floral tiles. In the fuschia pink (bring your shades!) main complex, further south along the beach past a couple of private houses, there are a good number of bungalows, of varying ages &

comfort. The newest of the rooms are set around a sandy courtyard towards the back, which has been fenced off from the beach. Given the geographical separation of Shehe's accommodation, you may have to ask around a little to find someone who can help you view rooms or check in. There is around a US$5 discount on rates Mar–Jun. **$$**

🏠 **Jambiani White Sand Bungalows** (8 rooms) m 0775 044382/0777 450565; e whitesandbungalows@yahoo.com. With a lovely location right on the soft sandy beach, the White Sand Bungalows live up to their name. Identical yet unremarkable bungalows, each is painted with tropical fish & decorated with seashells pushed into the cement. Accessed via a small corridor, all have fans. The owners claim that no AC is necessary due to the sea breezes, but these are barely detectable once you're inside, & even less so once inside the mosquito net. Bathrooms are long & thin with patterned floor tiles & a rusty mirror & taps, but there is hot water. Lunch & dinner need to be requested in advance, & contain such delights as 'cow'. Considerable discounts are available in low season. **$$**

🏠 **Kimte Beach Inn** (8 rooms) m 0773 055992; e kimte@lycos.com; www. kimtebeachinn.com. Straddling the road, about 500m beyond Shehe, at the quieter end of the village, this Rasta-managed lodge offers a warm welcome & its ever-popular bar boasts a good location on a great stretch of beach. The rooms are all within a sgl-storey house, with orange windows & a tin roof, on the right of the road as you head south of the village centre. Inside it's cool but otherwise rather basic, & corridor walls are adorned with vast murals & the spartan rooms & 7-bed dormitory (US$20pp) house little more than ceiling fans & beds. 4 rooms share a bathroom, & the dorm has its own for occupants to share. Being in an out-of-village location with a seaweed filled beach, limited in-room facilities & little sign of general upkeep, the rooms are probably a touch overpriced. **$$**

🏠 **Coral Rock Hotel** (14 rooms; 2 villas) m 0776 031955; e coraltrees@yahoo.co.uk. Towards the southern end of Jambiani, Coral Rock recently merged with its neighbour, the former Gomani Guesthouse, to create a chilled-out hotel with excellent ocean views. A South African–Zanzibari partnership, the hotel lives up to its name, with the bungalows, pool & restaurant all perched along the rocks above the beach.

Smartened up following the merger, the standard rooms are divided among 7 thatched bungalows. Rooms have sunken beds, local paintings for decoration, mosquito nets & AC. Quirky carvings & beautiful furniture have been added for extra interest. There is a small red concrete terrace in front of each with a few deckchairs. There are also 2 houses behind the bar, which can be taken exclusively by families, though they are mainly used by locals. The glass-fronted Rocky Bar at the end of the complex offers terrific views of the craggy, notch-cut headlands to the south, & the extensive seaweed farming in front of the hotel. It's a funky hangout for sundowners with a nice vibe & free Wi-Fi. Chilling out is definitely the order of the day here, with an original triangular infinity pool & sun terraces that look out over the sand, though unfortunately this is often covered with seaweed. With a private location, much improved rooms & a cool bar, Coral Rock is establishing itself as one of the better Jambiani options at this price. **$$$$**

🏠 **Red Monkey Lodge** (12 rooms) m 0777 713366; e info@redmonkeylodge.com; www. redmonkeylodge.com. About 2km from the centre of Jambiani, on an increasingly bumpy track, Red Monkey is set on the low coral cliffs & named after the Kirk's red colobus monkeys that live in the adjacent forest & pass through the grounds most days. A recent management change has increased standards & quality, but as expected, prices have risen to match. Still, rooms are delightful, there's a nice view of the beach (which is reached by a short flight of steps), & the German–Zanzibari staff are very friendly. The incredibly spacious rooms, complete with large ceiling fans, mosquito nets & high-pressure showers (some also have mini fridges), are extremely clean & represent one of the better budget deals in this part of Zanzibar. There are a few raised flower beds & palms, & up in the restaurant on the coral cliff, a skilful chef prepares fresh fish & other good meals for about US$15. **$$$**

🏠 **Zanzest Beach Bungalows** (12 rooms) m 0777 430992; e info@zanzest.co.tz; www. zanzest.co.tz. Way down the beach from Jambiani village, high up on the coral rock, stands Zanzest, which is run by the former manager of Kimte. Basic palm-thatched bandas have been brought a level above the norm by shell & coconut decorations, patterned lamps & psychedelic zebra print sheets. Zanzest caters for the budget end of the market with 2 dorms sleeping 8 & 5, & just 2 rooms with private cold-water bathrooms. Simple catch-of-the-day meals & pizza are available in the open-sided bar, which is laid out with benches & kanga-covered tables. It's simple, but a little different from standard Jambiani accommodation, though not helped by its location. **$$**

✕ WHERE TO EAT

Virtually all of the places to stay listed above have affiliated restaurants, most of which serve a fairly standard range of seafood and island curries. **Casa del Mar** and the **Blue Oyster** are both recommended for food, as is the lower-budget **Starfish Bungalows**, but as with most places along this stretch of beach, you'll probably have to order in advance as ingredients are bought fresh. Good-quality meals at all of these, naturally with a seafood emphasis, cost US$5–10, and drinks, snacks and lunches are also readily available. If your taste buds get the better of your wallet, you can often pay by credit card.

Unusually for a Zanzibari village, there are also some really very good local-style restaurants which, with a bit of notice, will prepare an excellent medley of island dishes for you to sample (talk to them in the morning if you want to eat that afternoon or evening). Kim's and Okala, listed below, warrant special mention – don't be discouraged by the ramshackle exteriors and sand floors; the food is very tasty.

If you just want supplies, there are a number of small local shops. The **Jambiani Post Office & Mini Market** on the main village road, near the Auberge Coco Beach, doesn't quite warrant its prominent signposting throughout the village, but it does supplement the usual local fare with a selection of tinned foods and a few imported goodies (sweets and crisps), and it also sells stamps.

✕ **Albi's Well** m 0786 231988; ⏱ 11.30–17.00 daily. Part of the adjoining Jambiani Tourism Training Institute (JTTI), Albi's Well is staffed by students who wish to gain experience in the tourism industry. Tasty fusion food such as wraps & pizzas are on the light-bites menu, as are rich coffee & tempting cakes. Colourful cocktails are shaken & stirred at the pretty pink bar, & there's a green-walled deck overlooking the sea. Dinner is served on Fri nights only & must be pre-booked, & the varied menu takes on a different theme each week – Japanese & Italian are some of the more popular choices. Many of the students here also study tour guiding – ask one of them to practise their skills on you if you fancy a local excursion. All proceeds go to the JTTI, all tips go directly to the students, & with some of them having gone on to run lodges & hotels in Jambiani, or even set up their own business, this is a cause worthy of your support. **$$$**

✕ **Equinox Restaurant** m 0772 608241; ⏱ lunch & dinner, daily. Owned by a local Rastafarian, known as Captain Cook, Equinox is tucked behind a woven makuti fence. Chances are that Captain Cook will find you before you find him, but if not follow the signs from Blue Oyster & you'll locate it with ease. Originally opened in 2006, Equinox suffered a major setback following a fire, but with great determination on the part of its young, entrepreneurial owner, it was rebuilt in 2008 & has flourished ever since. It's very basic, casual place, doubtless influenced by Cook's own friendly, informal manner. With a flag-flying rondavel bar & outdoor seating, it's primarily a place to chill out & chat in the village. There is some simple cooking equipment & if you're keen to eat (fish in masala US$7; grilled octopus US$6.50), Captain Cook will proudly read you the glowing multi-national reviews in his little red guest book. There are plans to add a couple of rooms here at some point in the future. **$$$**

✕ **Kim's Restaurant** ⏱ lunch & dinner, daily. Owned by a charming local entrepreneur, Kim, this simple, shaded restaurant is the realisation of a childhood dream. This place serves authentic Zanzibari cuisine for lunch & dinner (best ordered in advance), all freshly prepared by Kim & his mother. The spicy fish samosas (US$3.50), fish soup (US$2.50) & coconut-crusted fish with mango chutney (US$9) are particularly tasty. The small palm-clad shack & sand on the floor that make up the restaurant only add to the local flavour, & this is one of a few reliably good village dining options in Jambiani. Kim's is well signposted from the Blue Oyster Hotel. **$$$**

✘ **Seahorse Restaurant** ⊕ lunch & dinner, daily. Just to the north of the Blue Oyster Hotel, this fab little place offers fresh home-cooked Zanzibari cuisine in its breezy beachside restaurant. Spiced curries & grilled lobster go for around US$7, with light snacks about US$4, served up by friendly staff by candlelight (if you come after sunset). The simple makuti roof is spruced up by simple shell mobiles, & the menu is full of witty comments that make for amusing reading. $$$

✘ **Step In Restaurant & Bar** ☎0652 718964; e jack.b@gmx.net; ⊕ lunch & dinner, daily. From the outside, Step In is an attractive prospect, & although the inside is an expanse of concrete, there's an extensive menu of octopus, coconut crusted fish (US$6) & a range of tempting desserts & snacks (if they're available). For dehydrated patrons, there's an array of funky cocktails. $$$

✘ **Alfajiri** m 0779 347669; e matteopatrizia@ hotmail.com; ⊕ lunch & dinner, daily. The previous Pingo Restaurant burnt down in the Sau Inn fire, but was soon replaced by the modern & lively Alfajiri. Impossible to miss from the beach, a large sandwich board declares its presence & it serves European-style food such as sandwiches & burgers, as well as the ubiquitous seafood. Equally, just pop in for a refreshing cold beer or a spiced tea. $$

✘ **Garden Restaurant** m 0776 586193; ⊕ 11.30–late. Follow the yellow sign from the ruins of the Sau Inn or access this place from the beach; either way it's very clearly marked. With lovely sea views from its newly renovated beachfront plot (see *Where to stay*, page 311), Garden Restaurant is breezy & popular, & boasts friendly staff & a mixture of both Zanzibari & European menu options, including curries & crêpes. A shiny new bar was added in 2012. $$

✘ **Kiddo's Café** m 0773 498949; e pl-stern@ web.de; ⊕ 10.00–18.00 daily. Tucked off the main road through the village between Mama Mapambo & Bahari View Lodge, or accessed from the beach, this is an understated, calm café where gourmet fruit-juice concoctions are mixed by the dreadlocked, cool dude after whom the bar takes its name. It's a place to retreat, order a cafetière of fresh coffee or something exotic (Kiddo's Mix of pineapple, passionfruit & mango juices with coconut milk & ginger is divine), grab a paperback from the recycled dhow bookshelf (an eclectic mix from Nick Hornby to Louis de Bernières is available), kick back & relax in the treehouse-like

upper bar or under the sailcloth shade in the sand garden below. Kiddo's is particularly convenient for those staying at the affiliated Mango Beachhouse next door (see *Where to stay*, page 309). $$

✘ **Okala Restaurant** m 0777 430519; e okala_6@hotmail.com; ⊕ lunch & dinner, daily. In a small, unremarkable makuti building, just up from the beach (between Nuru Beach Resort & Oasis Beach Inn), Okala's food far exceeds any expectations arising from its architecture. Run by a small co-operative of Jambiani families, the Zanzibari food here is really excellent by any standards, making the restaurant well worth a visit. The woven makuti walls, sand floor & crude shell mobiles may discourage some from entering, but we highly recommend that you do. With some notice, the team here can prepare a fabulous meze of Swahili curries, grilled seafood & tasty vegetable accompaniments. Filling up on fresh coconut rice, wilted spinach with lime & rich tomato fish curry is a real Zanzibari treat. Individual dishes, such as grilled octopus or fish, are US$5–6, with special items, like the amazing (and enormous) coconut-crusted jumbo prawns costing US$10. If you like what you taste, the Okala team also offer short courses in Zanzibari cooking. The team here are closely involved with JAMABECO & Marine Cultures (see box, *Jambiani Marine and Beach Conservation*, page 306) & several community projects, so ask them if you're interested in what's happening, or arrange to end your Eco+Culture village tour (see page 318) with a deliciously satisfying lunch here. $$

✘ **Palm View Restaurant** ⊕ lunch & dinner, daily. Well signposted from the beach, Palm View can be hard to spot despite the distinctive bright red & orange sign. In a small makuti-covered courtyard, a book-like menu of pizza, pasta, seafood & sandwiches, which also includes anomalies such as goulash for US$8, can be devoured along with an extensive list of milkshakes & juices. Despite the extensive menu, as with anywhere in Jambiani, it's worth ordering a few hours ahead to ensure availability. $$

✘ **Sale E Pepe** ⊕ lunch & dinner, daily. This rather sparse restaurant does itself no favours with a dull black & white colour scheme inspired by its name but it's saved by its long list of exotic curries. It's located in the village, but is easy to find from the beach – look for the large sandwich board with a range of delicious dishes written in chalk. The owner here also owns a house in Jambiani that he rents out to long-term visitors – ask at the bar for further information. $$

✕ Starfish Bungalows and Restaurant
(2 rooms) m 0777 419558/0771 682884;
e mbarakaameir@yahoo.com, bookings@
starfishzanzibar.com; ⏲ lunch & dinner, daily.
Primarily a seafood restaurant, the rooms here
appear to be an afterthought. It has received
consistently good reviews from diners who come
for the fresh seafood, grilled & fried in a range of
sauces. The friendly owner is the brother of nearby

Baghani Guesthouse managers, & offers his own
very ordinary, ensuite rooms. Come for the food, &
stay if you're desperate. $$
▱ Scuola Restaurant ⏲ lunch & dinner,
daily. This very simple café is little more than a
small hut on the beach. A huge sign welcomes
you to the 2 tables where you can tuck into pasta
& soup, though curiously no drinks are on offer at
all. $

OTHER PRACTICALITIES

Bureaux de change If you need money, there's a bureau de change at the East
Coast Visitors Inn (see *Where to stay*, page 311). Alternatively, Auberge Coco Beach
(see *Where to stay*, page 313) and Casa del Mar (page 312) might be able to give you
cash back from a bank card (though you'll need to have a meal at the restaurant first).

Internet The best bets for internet access are the hotels (mid range and above)
– but even these are likely to be painfully slow and unreliable. **Casa del Mar** (see
Where to stay, page 312) provides internet access for US$3 per half-hour, as does
Blue Oyster (page 310) and **Kikadini Villas** (page 312), and though Wi-Fi is
increasingly widespread, the budget hotels will charge and connection speeds will
be highly variable.

WHAT TO SEE AND DO As with most of Zanzibar's coastal villages, the main focus
of the tourist agenda is swimming and sunbathing. **Diving** and **snorkelling** can
be arranged through local dive centres and **kitesurfing** is currently experiencing a
popularity surge.

COIR-ROPE PRODUCTION

The fruit of the evocative coconut palm does not look as many imagine: it
has a smooth, leathery, green skin. The brown nuts sold in supermarkets
worldwide are simply the central element of the fruit. Between the well-
known shiny shell and green exterior is a coarse fibrous husk known as coir; it
is from this that rope is made.

The patient process begins when the husk is separated from the nut. The
fibres are then buried in the sandy intertidal zone and covered with a cairn
of coral rock. Over the coming six to ten months, microorganisms in the
surrounding sand cause the husk tissues to begin biodegrading, in a process
known as retting, loosening the fibre strands. The remains are then uncovered,
beaten and sun-dried. When dry and clean, the long fibres are simply rubbed
together to form strands which can be twined to the required thickness of rope.

According to the Royal Botanical Gardens at Kew, the total of world coir-
fibre production is about 250,000 tonnes, with over 50% of the coir fibre
produced annually consumed in its countries of origin. This bears out on
Zanzibar where the relatively waterproof nature of the coir and its resistance
to saltwater damage make it an invaluable material for boat rigging, fishing
nets and seaweed-farming lines. As a tourist, you are likely to benefit from its
more recent application in the manufacture of sunloungers, hammocks and
the beds used by budget hotels.

If you want a change from the beach and water, though, Jambiani has some options. The **Eco+Culture village tour** is excellent and is probably the island's best insight into genuine rural life. Do be aware, however, that of late a few villagers have apparently been operating copycat walks. It is well worth taking the time to seek out Kassim or the Eco+Culture office (see below), not only for their knowledge and friendliness, but also to be sure that your money is going to be directed back into vital village projects that range from the kindergarten to the planned handicraft shop for the women's co-operative.

About two hours' walk outside Jambiani is a large underground cavern called **Kumbi**, which contains a natural spring. According to local legend, it was lived in at one time but today it is a traditional shrine and local people go there to pray and make offerings. You'll need a local guide to show you the way and it's an interesting trip; even if the cave doesn't leave you in awe, the walk is pleasant. Around the village, you can also see several **old tombs** decorated with plates and dishes, similar to the mausoleum at Paje.

For self-guided exploration, bicycles can be rented from a number of hotels – try Casa del Mar, which charges US$10 per day.

Eco+Culture Jambiani Cultural Tours

📞 024 2233731; m 0777 410873; e info@ecoculture-zanzibar.org, hajihafidh@yahoo.co.uk, kassimmande@hotmail.com; www.ecoculture-zanzibar.org. Meet in the small, signposted makuti hut under a grove of coconuts in the centre of the village (opposite the school), or be collected on foot from your hotel for these well-run, enlightening community-focused walks. Organised & guided by resident Kassim Mande (m *0777 469118*) & his colleagues, a percentage of your fee goes directly towards community development initiatives, a direct result of the organisation's original NGO status. Depending on your enthusiasm & heat tolerance, the tours last anything from a few hours to the best part of a day & take in many aspects of everyday life. Spend time helping the women make coconut paste, reciting the alphabet in unison at the efficient kindergarten & meeting the *mganga* (traditional healer). Kassim's presence, reputation within the community & ability to translate allow for genuine interaction with the Jambiani residents & a thoroughly engaging time. The trip can also be arranged in advance from Eco+Culture's Stone Town office on Hurumzi Street (see *Chapter 5, Tour companies*, page 134).

Jambiani Wellness Centre e habszanzibar@yahoo.ca; www.handsacrossborderssociety.org;

🕘 09.00–14.00 Mon & Tue, Thu & Fri. Opened in 2003 by a joint Canadian–Zanzibari NGO, Hands Across Borders, the Jambiani Wellness Centre primarily offers chiropractic treatment, homeopathic remedies & other therapies free of charge to the local community. The exact treatment on offer depends on the skills of the volunteers at the time but tourists are welcome to visit for massage, acupuncture, breema or homeopathic treatments & even Chinese medicine. A donation of at least US$15 is asked *in lieu* of a fee. The charitable work of the group now extends well beyond the clinic boundaries, with current community projects including the Jambiani Tourism Training Institute (JTTI), a vocational school which educates adults about tourism & starting up a business & also provides on-the-job training at the Albi's Well Restaurant (see *Where to eat*, page 315).

Kumbi Cavern About 2hrs walk outside Jambiani is a large underground cavern called Kumbi, which contains a natural spring. According to local legend, it was lived in at one time but today it is a traditional shrine and local people go there to pray and make offerings. You'll need a local guide to show you the way and it's an interesting trip; even if the cave doesn't leave you in awe, the walk is pleasant. Around the village, you can also see several old tombs decorated with plates and dishes, similar to the mausoleum at Paje.

MAKUNDUCHI

The ill-defined settlement of Makunduchi lies at the southeastern end of Zanzibar Island, and is divided into two distinct parts. On the coast is the small fishing village of 'old' Makunduchi, with some local huts and houses, a few holiday cottages, and a small beach from where you can sometimes spot dolphins. Then, about 2km inland is 'Makunduchi New Town', complete with one main road, some dusty side streets, a bank, post and telephone office, police station, small shop and a few incongruous blocks of austere flats, built as part of a 1970s East German aid scheme.

With the exception of July's Mwaka Kogwa Festival (see box, *The Mwaka Kogwa Festival at Makunduchi*, below), Makunduchi hardly receives any visitors. It is significantly quieter than Bwejuu or Jambiani – not that they are particularly noisy – and its community focuses on seaweed farming and fishing, not tourism.

GETTING THERE AND AWAY From Zanzibar Town, Makunduchi can be reached by public **bus** (Route 10), **dala dala** (No 310), or by **rented car**, **scooter** or **bike**. There are no tourist minibuses working regularly on this route, although you could

---

THE MWAKA KOGWA FESTIVAL AT MAKUNDUCHI

If you happen to be visiting Zanzibar during the last week of July, try to reach Makunduchi. Every year there's a large festival here called the Mwaka Kogwa, when local people come from all over the island for a great get-together of singing, dancing, drumming, making new friends and meeting old ones. It's no problem for tourists to see the festival, and when it's taking place several of the tour companies run day trips to the village (see *Chapter 5*, pages 134–7).

The festival is also called Mwaka Nairuz and it originates from Persia, marking the start of the New Year in the Shirazi calendar (for more details on the Shirazis in Zanzibar, see *Chapter 1*, *History*, page 5) and involves several rituals, including a mock fight where men from different parts of the village beat each other with banana stems. It is believed that this fight gives each combatant a chance to vent his feelings, and in this way the disagreements and arguments of the past year are exorcised so that the New Year can be started peacefully. (Although this is a mock fight, it can still get pretty serious. Fortunately the men are only fighting with banana stems – they used to do it with real clubs and cudgels.)

While the men are beating each other, the women have a far more genteel way of celebrating: dressed in their finest clothes, they parade around the village singing about love, families and village life.

The next stage of the festival is the ritual burning of a traditional hut, which has been built especially for the purpose. A local healer goes inside before the fire is lit and runs out again when the hut is burning strongly. It is thought that the burning of the hut symbolises the passing of the old year and also ensures that, during the coming year, should any house in the village catch fire its inhabitants will escape unharmed.

After the fighting and the hut-burning, a large feast is held with all the villagers bringing food and eating together. People from other parts of Zanzibar are welcomed, as a local tradition holds that any villager without a guest must be unhappy.

After the eating, the music starts – traditional ngomas and taarab (see *Music and dance*, page 40), but these days may include some more modern amplified sounds as well. The locals dance into the night, and die-hard party animals move on to the beach to continue singing and dancing until dawn.

always hire one for exclusive use through a tour company. You can also reach Makunduchi from Jambiani (see *Getting there and away*, page 307).

🏠 **WHERE TO STAY** Accommodation in Makunduchi consists of just one solitary hotel, La Madrugada. However, despite the isolation, visions of remote shorelines should be banished – the hotel beachfront is full of locals going about their business – and so a stay here is not the tranquil seclusion you may be envisaging.

🏠 **La Madrugada Beach Resort** (37 rooms) m 0714 045634; e abdul1234@hotmail.com. The only large resort in the southeast, La Madrugada Beach Resort is an enormous high-gated complex, which was purchased by an Afghan businessman in 2011. Plans are afoot for a large-scale renovation into a full-on resort with a new name & image. For the moment though, the 2-storey buildings surround 2 pools (1 freshwater & 1 saltwater), each emblazoned with the hotel name in mosaic, which will likely remain regardless of any future name change. There are 3 rooms per building with the upper level accommodating the large suites, & standard dbl rooms, complete with small terraces downstairs & balconies upstairs. Inside, blue sheets adorn Zanzibari beds & the rooms are large & clean, with beautiful hand-painted birds of paradise on the wall in the bathroom. Conversely, there are several hideously painted restaurant & bar areas, along with a discotheque with a stage for live music or enthusiastic dancers. Outside, what would be a pleasant beach is spoilt by a local dirt road running between it & the hotel. But at least the new owners are conscious of the impact that this hotel has on the village & they have several worthy ideas for community development projects: notably building new classrooms for the local school & teaching English to locals. Let's hope the managers make good on their resort & development plans, because at the moment it's hard to see why anyone would come all this way for the existing charms of La Madrugada. **$$$$$**

11

Southwestern Zanzibar

For most of Zanzibar's overseas visitors, the island's southwest corner holds little more than day-trip opportunities to see dolphins from Kizimkazi and troops of red colobus monkeys in Jozani Forest. Yet some of the best marine, animal and historical conservation projects on the island lie on the coast between Chukwani (10km south of Stone Town) and the ruins at Unguju Ukuu, and on the coral reefs of Chumbe Island and the Menai Bay Conservation Area. Few people stay in this area, in part because accommodation options are limited, with most opting instead for the endless beaches of the east coast or the buzz of Zanzibar Stone Town. Away from the main tourist attractions, the villagers in these parts rarely encounter many visitors, and their welcome is one of genuine friendliness. It's a refreshing contrast to the more crowded and visitor-centric feeling taking over significant parts of the island's north and east coasts.

KIZIMKAZI

The village of Kizimkazi lies at the southwestern tip of the island, about 12km west of Makunduchi. In a beautiful bay, it is one of the island's oldest settlements and the former home of the Mwinyi Mkuu (the traditional ruler of Zanzibar). It is steeped in history, though there is little evidence of this today.

Kizimkazi has a sizeable population, a school, a dispensary, a reasonable selection of places to stay, and a burgeoning tourist industry based on dolphin-watching. Bottlenose and humpback dolphins are regularly seen off the coast here and Kizimkazi has become the major launch point for boats taking visitors out on viewing trips.

Technically, Kizimkazi consists of two villages: Kizimkazi Mkunguni and Kizimkazi Dimbani. Most boats go out to see the dolphins from the larger of the two, Kizimkazi Mkunguni, and this is generally just called Kizimkazi. As the number of tourists has grown over the last few years, so too has the number of 'guides', touts and hustlers taking to the streets – sadly some of them can be quite aggressive, rude and generally unpleasant. If you're driving, watch out for the squad that wait for custom on the roadside by the entrance to the village.

Kizimkazi Dimbani is 2km north along the coast from 'main' Kizimkazi (3km by road); it is smaller, much quieter and arguably prettier, and a few boats do depart from here as well. There are far fewer touts, probably because it's mainly groups who come here, and just three places to stay. Dimbani is also the site of east Africa's oldest mosque.

GETTING THERE AND AWAY Most people come to Kizimkazi by tourist minibus or as part of a **day tour**; the alternative is to come by **hired car**, **scooter** or **bike**.

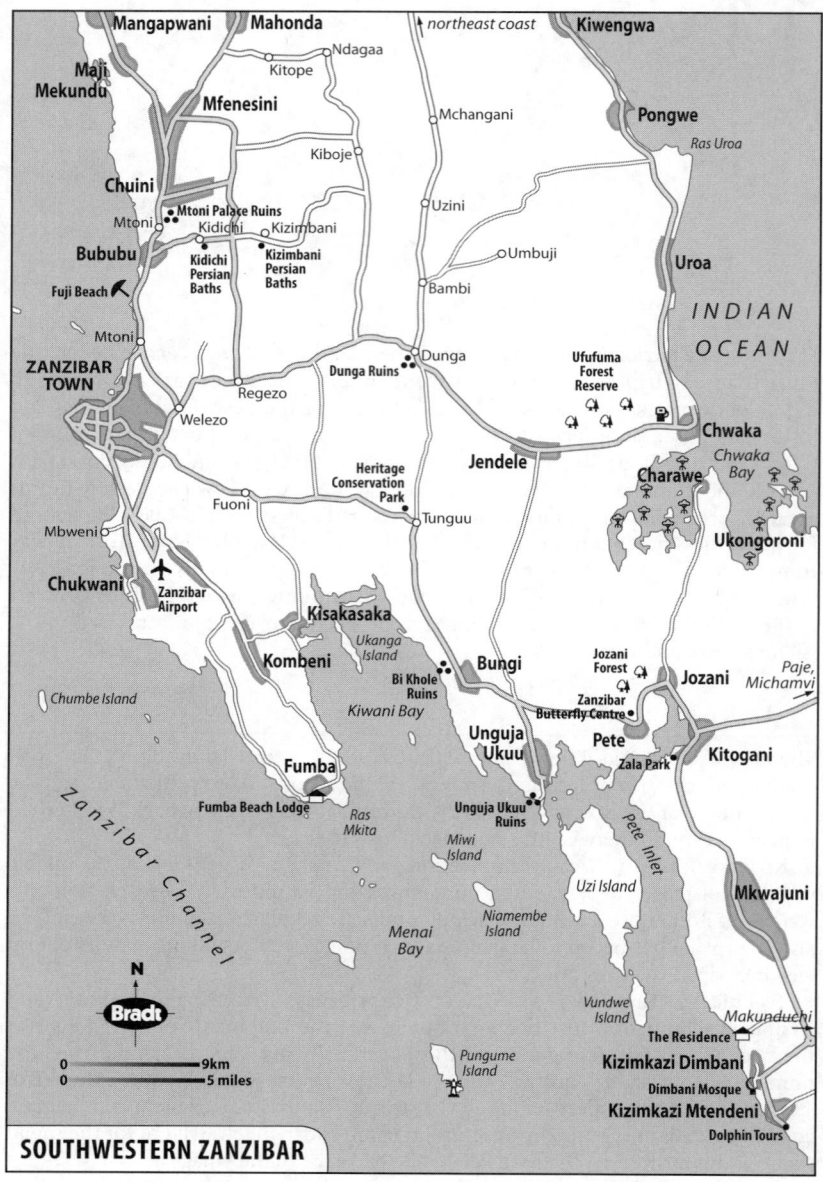

To reach Kizimkazi Dimbani, turn off the main road between Zanzibar Town and Makunduchi at Kufile junction and follow this road to a fork, heavily adorned with miscellaneous accommodation and tour signs. Here, right goes to Kizimkazi Dimbani and the ancient Shirazi mosque; left goes to the main part of Kizimkazi (Kizimkazi Mkunguni).

It is also possible to get here independently from Zanzibar Town on one of the five daily **dala dalas** (No 326), by public **bus** or tourist **minibus**. Some buses

(Route 10) running between Zanzibar Town and Makunduchi stop in Kizimkazi Mkunguni, but if this cannot be arranged, get off the bus at Kufile junction and walk along the tar road, predominantly downhill, to Kizimkazi Dimbani (3km) or Kizimkazi Mkunguni (6km).

WHERE TO STAY
Unless stated otherwise, hotels listed below offer air conditioning and en-suite bathrooms as standard.

Kizimkazi Dimbani

L'Oasis Beach Hotel (36 rooms) 027 2507089; m 0757 557802; e info@loasistanzania.com; www.loasiszanzibar.com. Resort-style L'Oasis is family focused, with standard & family rooms each sleeping 4, & space for an extra bed in the family rooms. It's a nice enough place with rooms built in a row either along the beachfront or behind the irregular-shaped pool. Colourful murals decorate the outside walls of each, whilst inside traditional Zanzibari beds have been painted white. At one end of the beach the restaurant/lounge/bar is cantilevered over the sand, while a blue wall divides the property from the surrounding grasslands. Wi-Fi is available & there's a curio shop in the thatched reception area. **$$$$**

Karamba (20 rooms) m 0773 166406; e karamba@zanlink.com; www.karambaresort.com. This attractive clifftop lodge started life as a large restaurant, aimed almost exclusively at dolphin-viewing tour groups. It has since been transformed into smart bungalows & is one of this coast's most appealing places to stay. In spite of the linear layout, rooms all have individual interiors & are thoughtfully decorated in nautical blues & whites with a splash of sunshine yellow in the luxury rooms. Some boast outdoor circular baths, whilst others have blissful open-air showers hewn in coral rock. Check out the villa's whitewashed walls filled with coloured glass bottles cemented into the brickwork. Here, a spacious upstairs terrace allows for sleeping under the stars. There's a sea view from every veranda though the harbour vista from the cushioned lounge/restaurant is arguably the finest of them all. Here, fresh sushi (US$20 sharing platter) & tapas dishes (US$3–6 each) are served at tables or the dhow bar. Once the tour groups head home in the afternoon & real peace & quiet returns here, cocktails overlooking the sunset dhow activity makes for a quintessentially Zanzibari experience. There's a lovely pool overlooking the beach & yoga,

reiki & Ayurvedic therapies are also available. Standard **$$$**; lux **$$$$**

Kizi Dolphin Lodge (6 rooms) 0777 422843/410253; e kizilodge@yahoo.com. Looking like a block of flats, Kizi's opened in Jul 2011. Reception is up 1 floor & it's best to just go up, as calls & knocks are likely to be ignored. You'll enter a small room with a b/fast table, & more often than not the staff will be glued to endless low-budget horror movies. A small balcony with a few tables & sofas looks out over a construction site; the rooms – spread over 3 floors – are a little better with shiny tiled floors, wooden desks & chairs, & Zanzibari beds. 3 have AC, the rest fans. There's no beach access here & Wi-Fi costs US$5 per day. The lodge appears to have delusions of grandeur & is very overpriced for such basic accommodation. **$$$**

Kizimkazi Mkunguni

Unguja Lodge (12 rooms) m 0774 477477/857234; e info@ungujalodge.com; www.ungujalodge.com. The accommodation & service here is up with the best on the island. Run by a friendly, unpretentious Dutch couple, Ralph & Elies, it's a small, quiet place. The rooms (8 with sea views) are enormous & unusual, & are dotted around the dense gardens between a few large baobabs. Under vast, steep *makuti* roofs, the interior walls conceal a cushioned lounge, shower room, mezzanine seating area & a fully enclosed bedroom. The 3 'baobab villas' have AC & a plunge pool, whilst 6 'sea-view villas' & the 2, 3-bed family villas have direct views over the coral cliff to the ocean below. The furniture is island-produced from coconut wood, & the artwork contemporary. The main restaurant & bar area is a similar mix of modern & traditional – curved white walls, low-hanging *makuti* thatch & terraces of square tables with directors' chairs. Punched brass lanterns cast a patterned glow at night, wall-mounted basketry adds colour, & 3 large fans enhance the sea breeze. Buffet meals are served 3 times a day, with social, pre-dinner drinks at the bar from around 18.30. By day, there is a lovely pool surrounded by bougainvillea, hibiscus & fan palms to one side & wide *makuti* umbrellas & timber loungers to the other. Alternatively, there is the beach. Diving instructor Nick runs the purpose-built PADI dive centre for guests only, & snorkelling & shore diving are possible, with good sightings of lionfish & even sea horses being reported on the closest reef (70m away), though most people choose to boat dive (Menai Bay 2-dive trip US$120pp). Dive courses & other water-based activities – dhow cruises to sea kayaking & surfing – are all organised. There is also a village tour, escorted by 1 of the local staff, costing US$5, all of which is donated to vital village projects. All rates HB; children 2–18yrs have a 50–75% reduction. **$$$$–⚸**

🛖 **Swahili Beach Resort** (19 rooms) m 0777 844442; e info@swahilibeachresort.com; www.swahilibeachresort.com. At the far side of Kizimkazi Mkunguni village is Swahili Beach Resort. Inside, guests are welcomed into a large reception area, from where views extend to the swimming pool & sea beyond. Spacious rooms are all in sgl-storey, lemon-painted coral bungalows except the 4 'cabanas'. Each is named in Kiswahili after a marine creature & there is a fan, AC, mini fridge, TV & broad terrace as standard. The bedroom interiors are perfectly fine, if a little dated in décor, & the bathrooms spotless. There is a central, mosaic tiled pool, with a small children's pool, & the on-site PADI Paje Dive Centre (e paje@pajedivecentre.com), which, like the resort, shares the same owners as Arabian Nights in Paje (see *Where to stay*, page 301). Local tours by dhow & speedboat are possible, kayaks can be hired & the usual island excursions are offered. All rates FB; HB available. **$$$$**

🛖 **Dolphin Bay Resort** (30 villas) m 0684 868385; m 0772 930333; e reservation@dolphinbay-resort.com; www.dolphinbay-resort.com. The furthest south of Kizimkazi's options, the Dolphin Bay is located on a huge beachside plot down a sandy & bumpy track. The resort is simply vast, feeling more like a small town than a relaxed beach lodge. Within the walls, 2-storey villas each contain 3 bedrooms, plus 2 spacious shared lounges, 1 on the ground floor, 1 on the 1st, both with TV, plus a veranda & a balcony. Decorated in white, rooms are modern & well equipped with mosquito nets & a safe, & there's a shower & bath in the en suite. Downstairs is a kitchenette with a fridge & a kettle, but this is not meant for self-catering, & instead guests head to the restaurant for all meals. While these villas are best suited to families (cots available) or groups, it is possible to rent the rooms individually, just be prepared to get up close & personal with other room occupants. Most of the villas have their own decent-sized swimming pool, while the rest share the enormous main pool, looking out over the sea. The Barracuda Restaurant has pretty sea views too, as it's raised up on the coral rock. Diners have a choice of 3 European-inspired courses, & b/fast is à la carte. The circular main area is built around a large algae-filled fish pond, which functions mostly as a mosquito breeding ground. Here a games room & a small curio shop sit alongside the restaurant, & pre-dinner Rock Shandies are sipped on the jetty. Despite the space, at the time of research there was not a single guest staying here. **$$$$**

🛖 **Promised Land Lodge** (8 rooms) m 0779 909168/39; e promisedland.znz@hotmail.com; www.promisedlandlodge-zanzibar.com. French–Zanzibari owned & run, Promised Land has been open on & off since 2002. Currently it's open again, offering brick-built rooms in 1 building as well as newer, detatched thatched bandas. Rooms are simple, with nothing more than a bed, fan & some shelves, but they are jazzed up by a colourful kanga ceiling & matching curtains, & jet black bathrooms. The bandas have more character than the rooms & have open-air bathrooms, but are quite dark. There are relaxation opportunities aplenty, with an outdoor bed inside a thatched 'tent' & a fire pit surrounded by swing benches; Bob Marley tunes play on repeat in the beach bar & shady seafood-focused restaurant. The lodge suffers slightly from the lack of a pool, but one's supposedly in the pipeline. **$$**

North of Kizimkazi

🛖 **The Residence** (66 rooms) ☏ 024 5555000; e info-zanzibar@theresidence.com; www.theresidence.com. Just 3km north of Kizmikazi Dimbani stands as one of the most talked about hotels on the island, a place where movie stars & supermodels wouldn't seem out of place. Set on a delightfully calm stretch of powdery beach, with gently lapping waves washing up intricate pink & lilac shells, the Residence offers plush villas, each with its own generously sized swimming pool & a personal butler. They are divided into 6 categories, with varying views, sizes & number of bedrooms, but all extremely well appointed with satellite TV, CD & DVD player, broadband internet access (US$3/hr), minibar, safe, bathrobes, slippers ... the list goes on. Indoor & outdoor showers plus a bathtub are found in the contemporary curvaceous, glass bathroom. Each guest is provided with a bicycle to explore the complex, but you can also give reception a call for a lift in a golf buggy. It's worth bearing in mind that the oceanfront villas have little privacy from passing beach-goers (& each other), & the patio doors leading onto the pools are clear glass, so close curtains for modesty. The main complex is spread over a number of buildings, including 2 restaurants: the Dining Room, with Arabic & African influence, & the Pavilion, with Middle Eastern & Mediterranean dishes. These are complemented by 2 bars, the modern Dining Room Bar & the more traditional Library Bar. The adjacent swimming pool is raised up above the deck, & with glass sides observers are able to clearly see under the water – an unusual & intriguing design. The spa complex has yoga classes as well as therapies, & is the first hotel spa to offer ohashiatsu, an energy-based massage therapy. For further beautifying, there's a 'hair spa' & hairdressing pavilion. To burn off the rich food, hit the gym, head for the tennis courts or out on a nature walk or take part in the watersports. The Residence is not a small & intimate lodge, but nor does it pretend to be. As with its Mauritian & Tunisian counterparts, this is a vast complex, with bowing staff pandering to every whim. On arrival, there's even someone to unpack for you, plus a tempting selection of welcome chocolates. With all this, plus scheduled evening entertainment, there's plenty to keep you amused, & for anything else your butler will be on hand to assist at any time. Despite all the luxury, it's hard not to feel that it's all a bit sterile – you could be anywhere in the world. ♛

✕ WHERE TO EAT In the main part of Kizimkazi, near where the boats are launched, is the **Jichane Restaurant**, mostly serving lunches for the tour groups from Zanzibar Town.

In Kizimkazi Dimbani, there are two places – both geared mainly to feeding large groups. **Karamba** is mentioned above (see page 323), and serves fresh sushi, pasta and traditional Swahili seafood dishes from around US$6. **Cabs Restaurant** (m *0777 415554*), on the opposite side of the harbour mouth, has meals like chicken and chips or grilled seafood for around US$5.

WHAT TO SEE AND DO The main reason people visit Kizimkazi is to see the dolphins, but if you're keen on history you might also want to stop off at the ancient Shirazi mosque in Kizimkazi Dimbani.

Kizimkazi Mosque Hidden behind its new plain walls and protective corrugated-iron roof, the mosque at Kizimkazi Dimbani is believed to be the oldest Islamic building on the east African coast. The floriate Kufic inscription to the left of the *mihrab* (the interior niche indicating the direction of Mecca) dates the original mosque construction to AD1107 and identifies it as the work of Persian settlers, working under the orders of Sheikh Said bin Abi Amran Mfaume al Hassan bin Muhammad. The silver pillars on either side of the niche are decorated with pounded mullet shells from the island of Mafia, and the two decorative clocks, which show Swahili time (six hours' different from European time), were presented by local dignitaries. However, though the fine-quality coral detailing and columns date from this time, most of the building actually dates from an 18th-century reconstruction, attested to by a further inscription, to the right of the *mihrab*. The more recent additions of electrical sockets and flex have not been installed with a comparable degree of style or decoration.

The shallow coastal waters around Kizimkazi have been favoured by dolphins for many years (quite possibly for millennia) because the area offers a reliable food supply and is a good place to nurse calves or simply to rest and socialise. Two species of dolphin are resident all year round: the Indo-Pacific bottlenose dolphin (*Tursiops aduncus*) and the Indo-Pacific humpback dolphin (*Sousa chinensis*). The bottlenose dolphin is more sociable, and more readily observed, whereas the humpback dolphin is a shyer creature.

Studies conducted have revealed that there are about 150 bottlenose and 60 humpback dolphins inhabiting the area. A catalogue of all the individual dolphins has been compiled based on the shape, nicks and marks of their dorsal fins and most of the animals have been given names. (Look closely if you see the dolphins and you'll notice that they all look different.)

Tourists first started coming to see dolphins at Kizimkazi in the early 1990s. The continued presence of these popular creatures has attracted growing numbers of visitors, such that tourism has now created new job opportunities for the local villagers. Contrary to the practices of other fishing communities in the Indian Ocean, the fishermen of Kizimkazi are very protective of the dolphins and no longer hunt them, seeing instead the economic rewards from conservation.

In 1997, villagers from Kizimkazi also helped to arrest dynamite fishermen from Dar es Salaam, knowing their methods destroyed the coral reefs and important habitats for the dolphins. Today, other fishing methods, such as drift nets, pose the greatest threat to the dolphins as they are liable to get tangled up in the nets and drown.

Over the years there have been a number of studies carried out at Kizimkazi, to monitor the interaction between dolphins and tourists. It's widely believed that the overall effect is detrimental. However, on a positive note, in 2005, all the stakeholders involved in dolphin tourism formed an association, the Kizimkazi Dolphin Tourism Operators Association (KIDOTOA), and they are working towards getting a management plan in place. Training courses have also been initiated where boat operators are taught how to conduct their tourism activities in a responsible, sustainable way. Further, a system of certifying those who have taken the course is also being considered.

On the whole, the creation of KIDOTOA is very promising for the conservation and management of both the dolphins and the tourism. It is still early days and many boats continue to compete for the best views of the dolphins but it is now up to everyone to make sure that this new strategy is put in practice. As a tourist you should secure a copy of the existing dolphin tourism guidelines (see box, *Dolphin-watching guidelines*, page 328) and ask the boat operators to follow them strictly. This should minimise the impact on the dolphins and ensure that they remain in the area for many years to come.

This section is based on information from the Marine Mammal Education & Research group at the Institute of Marine Sciences, Zanzibar, and Dr Per Berggren, Department of Zoology, Stockholm University, Sweden.

Outside the mosque are some old tombs, a few decorated with pillars and one covered by a small makuti roof. The pieces of cloth tied to the edge of the tombs are prayer flags. The raised aqueduct which carried water from the well to the basin where hands and feet were washed is no longer used: running water is piped straight into a more recently built ablution area at the back of the mosque.

Archaeological evidence suggests that when the mosque was built Kizimkazi was a large walled city. Tradition holds that it was founded and ruled by a king, Kizi, and that the architect of the mosque itself was called Kazi. Legend has it that when the city was once attacked by invaders, Kizi prayed for divine intervention and the enemies were driven away by a swarm of bees. Later the enemies returned, but this time Kizi evaded them by disappearing into a cave on the shore. The cave entrance closed behind him and the enemies were thwarted once again.

Today, very little of the old city remains, but non-Muslims, both men and women, are welcome to visit the mosque and its surrounding tombs. It's normally locked, and you'll probably have to find the caretaker with the key (he lives nearby, but is usually under the trees near the beach a few hundred metres further down the road). Show respect by removing your shoes and covering bare arms and legs (this part of the island is very traditional so, out of politeness, your arms and legs should be covered anyway – see *Clothing*, page 100). On leaving you'll be shown the collection box and be able to make a donation.

Dolphin tours

Most visitors come on all-inclusive 'dolphin tours' which include road transport, the boat, snorkelling gear and lunch. If you don't take an all-in tour, or want to spend the night at Kizimkazi, you can make your own way here, then hire a boat on the spot or arrange to join a group.

Generally, dolphin-viewing trips last for about two to three hours – usually enough time to locate the dolphins – although some captains trim the time down to about 90 minutes. Sometimes tourists become bored if they don't get quick and easy sightings, and decide to go back even sooner.

Dolphin tours are often promoted in a misleading light. It is important to realise that sightings cannot be guaranteed, and swimming with the dolphins is a rare occurrence. This is not a Florida-style dolphinarium; these are wild animals and their whereabouts cannot be predicted. It is they who choose to interact with people, not the other way around.

Observing dolphins in their natural environment, as with any other animals, requires time and patience. Shouting and excessive movement will not encourage them to approach your boat. Be satisfied with passive observation – do not force the boat driver to chase the dolphins, cross their path, or approach too close, especially when they are resting. If you decide to swim, slip quietly into the water and avoid splashing. Never jump in. Stay close to the boat and let the dolphins come to you instead of you trying to catch up with them. You could try attempting to excite their curiosity by diving frequently and swimming below the surface, maintaining your arms alongside your body to imitate their own streamlined shape.

In reality, unless you charter your own boat and go out early in the morning, so as not to be disturbed, you're unlikely to be able to put any of these theories into practice. On some days it's not unusual to see 20 or more boats, carrying at least ten people each, all chasing the dolphins and desperate for a sighting. When the dolphins are seen, big groups of people jumping in do little to entice them any closer. One visitor commented: 'it's billed as "swimming with dolphins" but it's actually "jumping into the water a long way from the dolphins"'; another called it a 'shambolic turkey-hunt'.

It's little wonder that the dolphins are beginning to head for somewhere more peaceful. In recent years, the number of sightings has definitely gone down. They used to be almost guaranteed, but it's not unusual now for groups to return without having seen a single dolphin. Sadly, as the disturbances from too many boats and people increasingly outweigh the benefits of food and shelter, this trend is likely to continue, with fewer and fewer dolphins appearing in Kizimkazi's waters in the future.

When to visit The best time of year to see the dolphins is between October and February. From June to September, the southerly winds can make the seas rough, while during the rainy season (March to May) conditions in the boat can be unpleasant. Regardless, out at sea you're likely to get wet anyway. You should also protect yourself against the sun.

Organised tours Most people who visit Kizimkazi come on a fully organised tour. These are easily arranged before you arrive, in Zanzibar Town, or by one of the hotels elsewhere on Zanzibar. Costs for these tours vary between US$35 and US$100 per person from Zanzibar Town, including transport to/from Kizimkazi, the boat, all snorkelling gear and lunch.

These prices vary considerably depending on the season, the quality of the vehicle, the standard of driver and guide, the number of passengers, and whether you want a private tour or are happy to share with others. Obviously they also depend upon where you are coming from: if you're taking a day trip from Zanzibar Town, then it's going to be cheaper than driving here from Nungwi.

Private boat charter Excursions can be arranged with local fishermen through any of the guesthouses and restaurants in Kizimkazi Mkunguni and Kizimkazi Dimbani. (The latter is more group orientated; it might be harder finding spare seats here unless you can muster a group together.) Traditional wooden fishing boats are most commonly used, although several fishermen have upgraded to modern fibreglass boats. Chartering a boat costs about US$40 and if you're in a small group, you can of course share these costs, although you'll probably find that for groups of five or six the price for a boat may go up to about US$50. You can also hire snorkels, masks and flippers (around US$5–10pp) from the souvenir stalls beside Jichane Restaurant. This is essential if you want to get in the water and observe the dolphins below the surface – which is highly recommended. As competition between the boatmen is stiff, some include free snorkel gear in the price of the boat, so it's always worth asking.

Cabs Restaurant in Kizimkazi Dimbani (see *Where to eat*, page 325), has a fleet of boats for dolphin-viewing. It caters mainly for large groups from the all-inclusive east coast resorts, but it's reckoned by local operators to be one of the safest and best-organised outfits based here, so it may be a good bet if you don't arrive with a trip pre-booked.

JOZANI-CHWAKA BAY NATIONAL PARK AND AROUND

Roughly halfway between Zanzibar Town and the broad beaches of the southeast coast is a lush area of protected forest reserve, the Jozani-Chwaka Bay National Park, and small, rural villages lining the road. It's a gentle part of the island, with little development and some of Zanzibar's best opportunities for viewing land animals. The communities here are increasingly involved in a number of conservation projects and even though the forest is an ever-popular, sometimes busy, destination for visitors, the neat boardwalks, diversity of dense vegetation and terrestrial mammals make for a great escape from the sunloungers and souvenir stalls of the rest of the island. For smaller-scale insect and reptile encounters, the new Butterfly Centre and Zala Park (see page 333) are worthy add-ons to a trip in the area.

JOZANI-CHWAKA BAY NATIONAL PARK (⏱ *07.30–17.00 daily; admission US$8*)

This national park incorporates the largest area of mature indigenous forest remaining on Zanzibar, although today it is only a tiny remnant of the forest that once covered much of the island. It stands on the isthmus of low-lying land which links the northern and southern parts of the island, to the south of Chwaka Bay. The area is prone to flooding in the rainy season, giving rise to its unique 'swamp-forest' environment, and the large moisture-loving trees, stands of palm and fern, and high water table and humid air give the forest a cool, 'tropical' feel.

Historically, local people have cut trees and harvested other forest products for many centuries, but commercial use started in the 1930s when the forest was bought by an Arab landowner and a sawmill was built here. In the late 1940s, the forest came under the control of the colonial government and some replanting took place. Jozani has been protected since 1952 and, as the forest areas in other parts of the island have been cleared, much of the island's wildlife has congregated here. The forest was declared a nature reserve in the 1960s, but despite this the trees and animals were inadequately protected. Local people cut wood for building and fuel, and some animals were hunted for food or because they could damage crops in nearby fields.

Nevertheless, Jozani Forest retained much of its original natural character and now forms the core of the island's first national park, Jozani-Chwaka Bay National Park.

Developed from a partnership between the Zanzibar government's Commission for Natural Resources and the charity CARE International, with funding from various sources including the government of Austria, the Ford Foundation and the Global Environment Facility, the park now has clear targets to protect natural resources and improve conditions for local people and wildlife in the area.

When to visit Keen naturalists who want to watch wildlife undisturbed, or those who just like a bit of peace and quiet, should try to visit the reserve either very early in the morning or in the early afternoon, as most groups come at about 09.00–10.00 on their way to the coast, or 15.00–16.00 on their way back. The monkeys and birds seem subdued in the midday heat, so from about 14.00–15.00 seems to be the best time for watching their behaviour.

Getting there and away The entrance to Jozani Forest is on the main road between Zanzibar Town and the southern part of the east coast, north of the village of Pete. You can visit at most times of the year, but in the rainy season the water table rises considerably and the forest paths can be under more than 1m of water. The reserve is clearly signposted, and the entrance fee includes the services of a guide and the mangrove boardwalk (see below).

Many **tour companies** include Jozani on their east coast tours or dolphin tours, but you can easily get here by frequent public **bus** (Routes 9, 10 or 13), **dala dala** (Nos 309, 310, 324 or 326), **hired bike** or **car**. Alternatively, take a tourist **minibus** heading for the east coast, and alight here. This road is well used by tourist minibuses and other traffic throughout the day, so after your visit to the forest you could flag down a vehicle and continue to the coast or return to Zanzibar Town, though it's best to be waiting roadside by 17.00, when the frequency of buses decreases.

Getting around the forest A network of **nature trails** has been established. The main one takes about an hour to follow at a leisurely pace, with numbered points of interest which relate to a well-written information sheet which you can buy for a nominal cost at the reception desk. There are also several shorter loops. Some other information leaflets and species lists are also available, and there are a few very good display boards and other exhibits.

As you walk around the nature trails, it's possible to see lots of birds and probably a few colobus and Sykes' monkeys, but these animals are shy, and will leap through the trees as soon as they hear people approaching. On the south side of the main road live two groups of monkeys who are more used to humans and with a guide you can come and watch these at close quarters. This is ideal animal viewing – the monkeys are aware of your presence but not disturbed. They are not tame, and don't come close, but just get on with their usual feeding, playing, grooming or resting. As the colobus monkeys look so cute, some visitors have been tempted to try to stroke them or give sweets to them. This is bad for the monkeys, but can be bad for tourists too – several people have been given a nasty nip or scratch. (See box, *Rules for responsible monkey-watching*, opposite, for the rules to follow.) Look but don't touch.

South of the forest, a long thin creek juts in from the sea, and is lined with mangrove trees. A fascinating **boardwalk** has been constructed, the only one of its type in east Africa, so you can easily and harmlessly go deep into the mangrove to experience this unique ecosystem. This is also a community project, and revenue from visitors coming to the boardwalk helps fund local development projects.

Jozani's flora Several distinct habitats exist within Jozani's borders – evergreen bushland to the west; dense groundwater forest of laurel wood (*Callophyllum inophyllum*), screw palm (*Pandanus rabaiensis*) and untidy oil palms (*Elaeis guineensis*) in its heart; thickets of flowering *Macphersonia gracilis*, cloves (*Eugenia*), and cabbage trees (*Cussonia zimmermannii*) to the north; and mangrove forest forming the eastern border along Chwaka Bay, dominated by the common red mangrove (*Rhizophora mucronata*), yellow mangrove (*Ceriops tagal*) and grey mangrove (*Avicennia marina*).

Other trees in the reserve include moisture-loving palms (five species, of which three are true palms), figs (two species) and red mahogany, plus some introduced species such as Sydney blue gum. Red mahogany (*Khaya nyasica*) was formerly regarded as an introduced exotic, but the weight of evidence is that it is native or anciently naturalised; this tree is found on other Indian Ocean islands and, like the mangrove, its seeds can float and survive in seawater. Although the size of the trees in Jozani is impressive, few trees become truly huge as the soil is too shallow to allow deep roots to penetrate, and they get blown over by strong monsoon winds. With several diverse habitat types, each brings its associated and equally varied wildlife to the reserve.

Jozani's mammals Several rare and endemic animal species occur in Jozani, making it a major attraction for wildlife fans. Even if you've got only a passing interest, a visit can be fascinating. The main reason most visitors come here is to see some of the resident red colobus monkeys (see box, *Kirk's red colobus*, page 332); their local name is *kima punga* meaning 'poison monkey' and they are unique to the Zanzibar archipelago. Many wildlife fans rate the red colobus of Jozani as one of the best monkey-viewing experiences in Africa. Nowhere else can you get so close to a monkey in the wild that is not aggressive or likely to bite, and is also attractive, endearing and very rare.

Brochures produced in the mid 1990s said there were 1,500 individual colobus monkeys in Zanzibar, but this was an estimate, and more accurate surveys in 1997

KIRK'S RED COLOBUS

Kirk's red colobus (*Procolobus kirkii*) are named after Sir John Kirk, the 19th-century British consul general in Zanzibar, who first identified these attractive island primates. They are endemic to the archipelago and one of Africa's rarest monkeys. Easily identified by their reddish coat, pale underside, small dark faces framed with tufts of long white hairs, and distinctive pink lips and nose, the monkeys are a wildlife highlight for many visitors to Zanzibar.

Kirk's red colobus live in gregarious troops of five to 50 individuals, headed by a dominant male and comprising his harem of loyal females and several young (single births occur year-round). They spend most of the day hanging out in the forest canopy, sunbathing, grooming and occasionally breaking away in small numbers to forage for tasty leaves, flowers and fruit. Their arboreal hideouts can make them hard to spot, but a roadside band at the entrance to Jozani-Chwaka Bay National Park allow for close observation and photography.

Timber felling, population expansion and a rise in agriculture have resulted in the rapid destruction of the tropical evergreen forests in which the Kirk's red colobus live, thus dramatically reducing population numbers. Researchers estimate that around 2,700 of these monkeys currently exist, a fact verified by their classification as 'endangered' on the IUCN Red List (2004) and their inclusion in Appendix II of CITES.

Human behaviour has undoubtedly caused the decline in Kirk's red colobus population numbers, yet now tourism may help to save them. With national park status now protecting their habitat in Jozani Forest, and visitor numbers increasing, the local communities are beginning to benefit from the tangible economic rewards that come from preserving these striking monkeys. If this continues, the future survival of the species should be secured.

put the figure at around 2,700. The red colobus population of Jozani is growing, which is partly a result of conservation efforts. However, recent research shows that this is most likely caused by monkeys fleeing ongoing destruction of the small patches of forest elsewhere on the island into the safety of the Jozani area, rather than their numbers increasing as the result of breeding. Researchers think that Zanzibar's total population of red colobus is probably stable, but emphasise that habitat destruction is still a major threat.

Other residents of Jozani include a population of blue or Sykes' monkey (*Cercopithecus mitis albgularis*), which you are also quite likely to see. The forest is also home to Ader's duiker (*Cephalophus adersi*), a species of small antelope found only on Zanzibar and some parts of the Kenyan coast, and suni (*Nesotragus moschatu moschatus*), another antelope which is even smaller than the duiker, but both of these are extremely shy and unlikely to be seen. The Ader's duiker is virtually extinct in Kenya now and is one of the two rarest antelopes in the world. Its only chance of survival is on Unguja. Its population is between 400 and 1,000 and efforts have been under way over recent years to ensure its survival, including protecting Jozani, working with local communities to establish sanctuaries and the proposed translocation of some individuals to Chumbe Island.

There are even reports of leopards (*Pathera pardus adersi*) in Jozani. If present they would be a local subspecies, smaller than the mainland version, although the veracity of these claims is very questionable. (For more details of wildlife in Jozani and Zanzibar, see *Wildlife*, pages 52–63.)

Jozani's birds Jozani has a fairly good bird population, with over 40 species recorded, although many of the forest birds are shy and therefore hard to spot. Species occurring here include Kenya crested guineafowl (*Guttera pucherani*), emerald-spotted wood dove (*Turtur chalcospilos*), little greenbul (*Andropadus virens*), sombre greenbul (*Andropadus importunus*), cardinal woodpecker (*Dendropicos fuscescens*), red-capped robin-chat (*Cossypha natalensis*), dark-backed weaver (*Ploceus bicolour*), golden weaver (*Ploceus xanthops*), olive sunbird (*Nectarinia olivacea*) and crowned hornbill (*Tockus alboterminatus*). An interesting endemic is the Fischer's turaco (*Turaco fischeri*), which is slightly larger than those on the mainland, with blue-purple on the wings instead of green. In the mangroves you'll see various kingfishers, including the localised mangrove kingfisher (*Halcyon senegaloides*), sunbirds and coucals.

If you're especially keen on birds, it is well worth engaging the services of a bird guide. Jozani has two bird specialists on the staff: Ali Addurahim is an ecologist and chief bird guide; Ali Khamis Mohammed was trained by the other Ali, and also knows his stuff. They have a bird checklist and a copy of the big fat *Zimmerman Birds of Kenya and Northern Tanzania* book, which includes most species that occur on Zanzibar.

AROUND JOZANI-CHWAKA BAY NATIONAL PARK

Zanzibar Butterfly Centre (e *mail@zanzibarbutterflies.com*; *www.zanzibarbutterflies.com*; ⊕ *09.00–17.00 daily; admission US$5pp*) The Zanzibar Butterfly Centre (ZBC) in Pete aims to show visitors the forest's fluttering friends close up whilst also generating income for local villagers and preserving the forest.

Villagers around Jozani-Chwaka Bay National Park are being encouraged to protect the surrounding vegetation in an unusual initiative which has them trained to sustainably farm native butterflies. Participants (currently 26 farmers) are taught to identify butterfly species, gently capture female butterflies, net small areas for breeding, harvest eggs, plant appropriate caterpillar fodder and ultimately collect the resulting pupae for breeding the next generation and sale back to the centre. The pupae are then sold on to overseas zoos and live exhibits or displayed for visitors in the large, netted tropical garden. Here, 200–300 colourful butterflies can be seen in the enclosure, making for a fascinating diversion and one of Africa's largest butterfly exhibits. There are good guides and clear informative signs to explain the project and butterfly lifecycle, and experienced photographers can also get some wonderful shots.

The income generated from visitors to ZBC is channelled back into further funding local conservation and poverty-alleviation projects, whilst the message is made clear to the communities that protecting the natural habitat of these insects provides much-needed income. The centre is a fun, worthwhile 30-minute stop, and its location just outside Jozani Reserve, makes it a convenient addition to a forest trip.

Zanzibar Land Animals Park (m *0777 850816*; e *mohdayoub2@hotmail.com*; ⊕ *10.00–17.00 daily; admission US$8 adults, children free*) The Zanzibar Land Animals Park (ZALA for short) is in the village of Muungoni, just south of Kitogani, where the main road from Zanzibar Town divides into roads towards Paje and Makunduchi.

At first glance it's just a zoo, with various pens and compounds to hold the animals (mostly reptiles). However, this community-based project, run by the tireless and enthusiastic Mohammed Ayoub, has a more important purpose. It's primarily an education centre where groups of Zanzibari schoolchildren come to learn about their island's natural heritage.

For tourists this is one of the few places on Zanzibar where you can observe snakes and lizards at close quarters; the chameleons are particularly endearing. Also look out for the geometric tortoises which are not native, but were brought to the park by customs officials who confiscated them at the airport from a smuggler of exotic pets. There are a few other species on display, most notably the small group of tree hyrax who spend time in their pen and time in the nearby forest. These part-time zoo animals come back mostly at feeding time, then seem quite content to rest or play in their pen before returning to the trees at nightfall.

Zala Park is only about 3km down the road from Jozani Forest Reserve, and can be combined with a visit there. If you have an overwhelming interest in wildlife, conservation or education, it is sometimes possible to stay in the small one-roomed guesthouse, though this is often used by visiting volunteers. Mohammed offers a nature trail in the nearby forest and mangrove stands, and can organise guided walks if you are interested in seeing more of this area; ideally, this should be arranged in advance.

Zanzibar Heritage Conservation Park (*small entry fee*) This rather grand-sounding place is actually a fairly low-key project run by some local people. Located to the north of the main road from Zanzibar Town to the east coast, west of the village of Tunguu, the park has some game birds on display (which are not that interesting), and a vast garden (which is more interesting) full of spices, herbs, fruit trees and medicinal plants. Everything is labelled, and sometimes a guide is available to show you round and explain the uses of the different plants. Consider visiting on the way to Jozani Forest.

UNGUJA UKUU AND BI KHOLE RUINS

For keen fans of history and archaeology, there are two places of interest in the southwest of the island. Both are just off the main road between Zanzibar Town and Jozani-Chwaka Bay National Park, Paje and Kizimkazi, so make convenient stop-offs *en route* there or to the southwest coasts.

There is now also an excellent full-day dhow trip in the Menai Bay Conservation Area which launches from Unguja Ukuu and is run by ethical local operator Eco+Culture (see *What to see and do*, page 338).

WHERE TO STAY

Menai Bay Beach Bungalows (10 rooms)
m 0777 411753; www.menaibaybungalows.
com. Set beneath the palms along an impossibly
beautiful crescent beach at Unguja Ukuu, these

bungalows closed in 2008, but a new hotel is
under construction in their place, so do check if
you're planning on being in the area.

WHAT TO SEE AND DO

Unguja Ukuu This is the site of the oldest known settlement on Zanzibar, dating from the end of the 8th century AD. It was believed to have been founded by early Shirazi immigrants from Persia, but recent archaeological evidence from here and other sites on the east coast of Africa suggests that it was Swahili in origin. Research at Unguja Ukuu is still taking place and more evidence may yet come to light.

Unguja is the local name for Zanzibar Island today, and Ukuu means 'great'. It is believed that the settlement may have been quite large, but was probably abandoned in the 10th century when the local Muslim population came under attack. An Arab geographer, writing in the 13th century, recorded that the people of 'Lenguja' had taken refuge from their enemies on the island of Tumbatu, off the northwest shore of Zanzibar Island (see box, *Tumbatu Island*, page 249).

Despite this site's fascinating history, today there is very little remaining that would be of any interest to anyone except the keenest archaeologist – just some shallow earth pits and the remnants of a few crumbling walls.

Getting there and away To reach this site, you need to pass through the modern village of Unguja Ukuu, reached by turning south off the main road between Zanzibar Town and the southern part of the east coast, at a junction about halfway between the villages of Tunguu and Pete. South of the village, a small track branches off the dirt road that leads to Uzi Island (reached by tidal causeway); follow this to reach the remains of old Unguja Ukuu. If you don't have a **car, dala dala** No 308 takes passengers to Unguja Ukuu from Zanzibar Town as does the public **bus** on Route 8.

Bi Khole Ruins Situated about 20km to the southeast of Zanzibar Town, the Bi Khole Ruins are the remains of a large house dating from the 19th century. Khole was a daughter of Sultan Said ('Bi' is a title meaning 'lady') who came to Zanzibar in the 1840s, after Said moved his court and capital from Oman. With her sister, Salme, she helped their brother, Barghash, escape after his plans to seize the throne from Majid were discovered (see the *History* and *Economy* sections, pages 3 and 30).

Khole had this house built for her to use as a private residence away from the town; she is recorded as being a keen hunter and a lover of beautiful things. The house had a Persian bathhouse where she could relax after travelling or hunting, and was surrounded by a garden decorated with flowering trees and fountains. The house was used until the 1920s but is now ruined, with only the main walls standing, and these are often overgrown.

The main front door has collapsed into a pile of rubble but this is still the way into the ruin. Directly in front of the door is a wide pillar, designed so that any visitor coming to the door would not be able to see into the inner courtyard, in case Khole or other ladies of the court were unveiled. In this room are alcoves and niches with arabesque arches, although the windows are rectangular. With some imagination, it's possible to see what an impressive house this once was.

Getting there and away The Bi Khole Ruins lie a few kilometres to the west of the main road from Zanzibar Town to the southern part of the east coast, about 6km south of the village of Tunguu. The road passes down a splendid boulevard of gnarled old mango trees, supposed to have been planted for Khole (though they may date from before this period): about halfway along is the track to the ruins. If you're travelling on public transport, take any of the **buses** (Routes 9, 10 or 13) or **dala dalas** (Nos 309, 310, 324 or 326) heading to the southeast and ask the driver to tell you when to alight.

FUMBA AND MENAI BAY

At the far end of the island's southwestern peninsula, on an increasingly rutted coral road 15km from Zanzibar Town, is the peaceful village of Fumba. It's a quiet, scenic place and very few tourists ever come here, which gives it a good deal of its charm. There is only one upmarket lodge offering accommodation, but day trips to the marine conservation area of Menai Bay are run by two reputable operators (Safari Blue and Eco+Culture – see *What to see and do*, page 338), so even if you can't stay it's still possible to get a taste of this area. From the beach south of the village, local fishermen take their *ngalawa* outriggers and dhows to the islands and fishing grounds beyond, and here too is the departure point for

INTEGRATED SEAWEED AND SHELLFISH FARMING

Tremendous effort is being made by the government, research institutions and NGOs to increase the returns from seaweed production (see box, *Sustainable seaweed farming*, pages 290–1). At the beginning of 2006, a pilot scheme began to integrate seaweed and shellfish farming. Funded and supported by the Institute of Marine Sciences in Zanzibar, Woods Hole Oceanographic Institute in Massachusetts and the McKnight Foundation, the scheme aims to maximise workers' time by engaging them in the farming of both seaweed and shellfish, particularly oysters. Some 200 women from Fumba, Bweleo, Nyamanzi and Unguja Ukuu are now involved in the project and it's hoped that the benefits of a dual income will considerably improve their independence and standard of living.

To initiate this work, the Institute of Marine Science worked with the Western Indian Ocean Marine Sciences Association (WIOMSA), the Coastal Resource Center (CRC) at the University of Rhode Island and USAID on a programme called Sustainable Coastal Communities and Ecosystems (SUCCESS). All of these operators aim to promote the inclusion of shellfish on tourist hotel menus so as to increase its overall consumption. It is hoped that this raised demand for shellfish will drive market prices up, and ultimately improve the incomes of the shellfish collectors and farmers.

The SUCCESS programme has successfully developed a floating line system for seaweed farming and adapted it to shellfish and mabe pearl farming. (A mabe pearl is a hemispherical pearl which has grown against the inside of an oyster's shell, rather than in its tissues.) The pearl farming, which started in 2006, had the first crop of 28 mabe pearls in November 2007. The mabe pearls were subsequently sold, with 19 of these being bought by a US company for US$2,000. The company donated three resulting necklaces back for the project's first Zanzibar pearl auction in February 2008. These pieces, together with the remaining raw mabe pearls earned the group of seven (three men and four women) a further US$1,000 at auction, and clearly shows the tremendous success for the aptly named project. There are currently an estimated 400 oysters implanted for mabe pearls at different stages of development and this is set to be a potentially significant marine crop.

The group have also been trained on other aspects of entrepreneurship including pearl and shell polishing, making ornaments, packaging and marketing, as well as running co-operatives. Three of these people, all women, have become so successful that they are earning approximately US$170 per month out of the part-time activity. This is significant: a low-ranking government officer will earn US$70 per month, and 50% of the island population is still on the US$1 per day poverty line. The group, together with the seaweed soap manufacturers of Kidoti (see page 291), have been successfully selling their merchandise to tourists and residents and we very much hope that the opportunity and their entrepreneurial skills can be passed on to other coastal communities within the archipelago.

one of the boat trips. It's truly stunning in the surrounding waters but if you also want to get a deeper insight into the community, ask around for a local villager called Issa Kibwana, who conducts small tours of the nearby fruit and spice plantations, or arrange a meeting with him through Sama Tours (see *Chapter 5, Tour companies*, page 135).

GETTING THERE AND AWAY To get here, take the road from Zanzibar Town towards the airport, then fork left (east) down a main road just after a petrol station. This will lead you northeast, before turning east and heading south, along the airport runway's eastern boundary fence. Leaving the airport behind you, you'll continue southeast along a bumpy, but picturesque, tree-lined road.

After around 5km there is a right turn from the main road, signposted to the Menai Bay Conservation Area. You can continue straight on or turn right to get to Fumba, as these roads join up at the rocky, southern end of the peninsula. Alternatively, if you don't have your own transport, take one of the four daily local **buses** (Route 7) from Zanzibar Town.

WHERE TO STAY

⌂ **Fumba Beach Lodge** (26 rooms)
m 0777 860504/878025; e reservations@ fumbabeachlodge.co.tz, info@fumbabeachlodge. co.tz; www.fumbabeachlodge.com. Built on 16ha of private land, including 3 separate sandy coves, Fumba Beach Lodge is just 30mins from the airport, & is currently the only upmarket lodge in the WWF's Menai Bay Conservation Area. It remains one of the island's best places to stay. Designed & built by Edwin van Zwam, a Dutchman with a solid African background, Fumba was created in line with contemporary safari camps, & the result is a fabulously original place, with clean lines & bold colour. Its interiors were a little less slick on our most recent visit, but not much more than a refreshing coat of paint is needed. There are well-spaced, deluxe rooms with canopied dbl beds, mains electricity, en-suite showers, fans & a sea view; 3 can become family rooms using inter-connecting doors. There are also special suites with huge dbl beds, sunshine-yellow details, beautifully carved wooden wardrobes with safes & tremendous views. There's a stylish outside shower & a dbl bath with a view. Large, shuttered terrace doors open onto a private deck & the beach beyond,

or there's a delightful rooftop terrace with views out to Kwale Island. 2 of these suites are built on the edge of a low coral cliff, around a baobab tree, into which an additional large outdoor bath has been set. Beside the large, infinity pool is a comfortable cushioned lounge & a restaurant specialising in seafood, though candlelit meals are often enjoyed on the beach. Nearby, the outside bar, Dhow FumBar, is a stunning spot for sundowners or pre-dinner aperitifs. The tropical Baobab spa has been expanded, though still incorprates its original open-air treehouse. With high makuti for shade, & curved internal walls for privacy, it's a pleasant enough afternoon experience. This is an African spa with local therapists – don't come expecting sophisticated Thai masseuses, though neither will you be charged premium prices. Yoga classes can also be arranged. For more active excursions, there's a well-equipped on-site dive centre & some wonderful day trips around Menai's idyllic islands. The lodge has got involved in local community projects including school & water initiatives, & is a member of the Fumba Peninsula Environmental Conservation Organisation.
$$$$$–♛

WHAT TO SEE AND DO The Menai Bay Conservation Area has a number of picturesque, uninhabited islands and sandbanks to explore as well as some fascinating marine life. It's well worth taking one of the full-day **sailing** and **snorkelling** excursions here, either through Fumba Beach Lodge, if you're a guest, or with Safari Blue departing from the Fumba Peninsula or Eco+Culture departing from Unguja Ukuu.

11

Some shade is available on these boats and beaches, but remember to apply sunscreen and preferably wear a T-shirt for protection when snorkelling. Towels and waterproof shoes are also recommended as you'll most likely have to wade out to the boat across coral rock.

Eco+Culture ☎024 2233731; m 0777 410873; e ecoculturetours@gmail.com; www.ecoculture-zanzibar.org. This socially & environmentally aware tour operator (see page 134) runs a fabulous full-day Menai Bay excursion: the Unguja Ukuu Boat Trip. On a traditional dhow, small groups are taken past rich mangrove forests to the pristine beaches of Miwi, Nianembe or Kwale islands & accessible sandbanks. Snorkelling kit is provided & the shallow reefs around the bay & islands provide excellent opportunities to spot brightly coloured fish & corals. After a good amount of time in the water, a delicious BBQ lunch is prepared on the beach, which invariably features a selection of freshly caught fish, Swahili side dishes & tropical fruits. On all trips, there is an English-speaking guide alongside the 2 crew & local chef, all of whom are happy to answer questions & talk about the surroundings & traditions of the area. Life jackets, a small first-aid kit & outboard motor are also kept on board for emergencies. Eco+Culture have a firm policy of limiting numbers on their trips with the express aim of protecting the environment & making the trip more enjoyable for their guests. Max 8 people per dhow & only 12 guests (in 2 boats) are ever taken out at the same time. This is a real pleasure & one of the main differentiators of this trip over its competitor. Trip leaves Stone Town at 08.00, returning at 17.00; US$70pp for 4 peeople, US$55pp for groups of 8.

Safari Blue m 0777 423162; e adventure@zanlink.com; www.safariblue.net; ⊕ (tours) Sat–Thu. Trips are made on traditional sailing dhows, 8–10m in length, which have been kitted out with Yamaha outboard engines, life jackets, sunshades, boarding ladders, first-aid kits, fire blankets & waterproof bags for cameras & valuables. Public liability & marine insurance complete the adherence to safety.

The trip pauses at a few of the bay's islands & sandbanks for exploration, a tasty lunch & relaxation, in between guided snorkelling forays & hopeful spotting for humpback & bottlenose dolphins. The 1st stop of the day is usually Kwale sandbank for gentle snorkelling. If conditions allow, a 2nd snorkelling session takes place at West Kwale. Sailing on further, BBQ seafood lunches await on Kwale Island, where tamarind trees offer shade (vegetarian/non-fish options must be ordered in advance). It's worth noting that there's also a toilet block on the island. There's a visit to a mangrove lagoon, where swimming is possible during high tide, a walk across the island, & a chance to try your hand at sailing a ngalawa, before the dhow's lanteen sail is hoisted & the boat heads back to Fumba. Fumba Beach is remote with no formal changing facilities, so it's best to wear swimwear under your clothes & bring beach shoes & a towel.

The experience has been recommended by many travellers in the past, although there have been an increasing number of complaints about the sheer volume of people & the number of boats being taken out. In some ways, Safari Blue has started to become a victim of its own success, though for now it remains one of the best island excursions. Trip leaves from close to Fumba Beach at 09.30, returning about 17.00; US$60 adult, US$30 child aged 6–14 years, children under 6 years free; transfers from Stone Town to Fumba cost an additional US$60/vehicle.

CHUKWANI

The small village of Chukwani, to the south of Zanzibar Town, is about 5km beyond Ras Mbweni. Southwest of the village, on the coast, is the Chukwani Palace. It was built by Sultan Barghash in 1872 and used mainly as a place to recuperate after illness, as the air here was supposed to be particularly healthy. The palace was built as a smaller version of the House of Wonders (see page 185), without the tower. During the reign of Sultan Ali bin Hamoud (sultan from 1902–1911) the palace was used by government officers.

Today, most of the palace has been demolished, leaving only the bathhouse. The new buildings around the ruins are used by the army, so visitors are not allowed to enter but you can get a good view from the air if you fly out of Zanzibar, as the palace lies only a few kilometres southwest of the airport.

CHUMBE ISLAND

Chumbe lies about 10km south of Zanzibar Town, and is one of the largest of the offshore islands in this area. The coral reef surrounding Chumbe Island is in very good condition because until recently the island was inside a military area and public access was not allowed. Consequently, it has not been damaged by high volumes of tourists, transfer boats or the destructive fishing techniques employed by local fishermen. The reef on the western side of Chumbe Island was officially gazetted a Marine National Park (the first in Tanzania) in 1994, and the island has

COCONUT CRABS

Common on Chumbe Island, yet endangered elsewhere in the south Pacific and Indian Ocean, the rare and remarkable 'coconut crab' (*Birgus latro*) is the world's largest land invertebrate.

A member of the Coenobitidae family, it is one of only a few hermit crabs that is wholly adapted to spending most of its life away from the sea. In some areas coconut crabs are known to move several kilometres inland; however, they do begin life in the sea, with the female depositing hatched eggs in the water as planktonic larvae (*zoea*). Over a matter of a few weeks, the larvae develop claws to become *megalopa*, and sink to the seabed as tiny crabs, in search of a protective shell. They retain these shells when they reach land, discarding them only when their carapace is fully hardened. Unlike other hermit crabs, these creatures develop a dual-purpose shell over their abdomen, similar in appearance to a lobster. This guards against water loss and saves on 'house-hunting'. And without the need to fit inside abandoned shells, the coconut crab is free to grow indefinitely, accounting for its serious size (adults have been recorded with a 1m leg span).

Nocturnal by nature, the crabs scavenge and feed on decaying vegetation, fruit, small animals and, naturally, coconuts. Although adept at climbing palms to reach the coconuts, these crabs do not actually have any special adaptations for scaling tree trunks. The crab will use its powerful claws to heave itself up to the coconut, snip it off the palm using its sharp pincers, descend the tree backwards (facing up), gather its prize and feast. With its razor-sharp claws, the crab attacks the coconut, ripping away the husk, cracking its shiny nut and devouring the flesh inside.

The coconut crab is listed on the IUCN endangered species list, with no record of the number in existence. Habitat destruction, human hunting and introduced predators continue to threaten their global survival. Happily, Chumbe Island reports a healthy population and is working to gain international support for the protection of this amazing species. Guided by one of the island's staff, you are likely to be able to watch them forage by night (especially in the salubrious surroundings of the camp's compost heap) – but keep still and quiet; the crabs have poor eyesight and so detect predators and threats by vibrations.

Southwestern Zanzibar CHUMBE ISLAND

11

since been declared a forest reserve. Together, the island and reef are known as Chumbe Island Nature Reserve or Chumbe Island Coral Park (CHICOP).

CHICOP's own information states: 'Chumbe Island is a rare example of a still pristine coral island ecosystem in an otherwise heavily over-fished and overexploited area. It includes a reef sanctuary and a forest and bird sanctuary of exceptional biodiversity'. This has been verified by various global conservation and scientific bodies, including IUCN, WWF and UNESCO. A specialist from the Australian Institute of Marine Sciences called Chumbe 'one of the most spectacular coral gardens to be found anywhere in the world'.

Over 400 species of fish have been identified in the marine park and other marine wildlife frequently seen includes turtles, dolphins, and seasonally even the great humpback whale. On the island, 60 species of bird have been recorded, including breeding pairs of the rare roseate tern (*Sterna dougallii*). The island is also home to various lizards and a population of rare giant coconut crabs (see box, *Coconut crabs*, page 339). Six Ader's duiker (*Cephalophus adersi*), an endangered small antelope whose range is restricted to a handful of coastal forests in and around Zanzibar, were reintroduced to Chumbe Island in 1999 and 2000, and the small population is reproducing and appears to be thriving in the dry and rough coral-rag forest on the island.

Buildings of historical and cultural interest on Chumbe include a **lighthouse** built by the British in 1904 and still clearly visible from ships approaching Zanzibar from Dar es Salaam. The lighthouse is still functioning but is now also used as an observation tower with a spectacular view of the island and the marine park. There is also an old **mosque** built in an Indian style unique to Tanzania which is still frequently used by the local Muslim staff. A cottage originally built for the lighthouse keepers has been converted into a **visitor information centre**, including an education room for local schoolchildren who are brought here by the Chumbe management and other conservation organisations to learn about local environmental issues.

Tourism is being developed on Chumbe in a very sensitive manner. Former fishermen have been employed as park rangers on the island. They have been trained by CHICOP and now take visitors on **guided walks** along trails in the dense forest and along the intertidal flat around the island at low tide. The most popular excursion on the island is the **guided snorkelling tour** to the protected reef, where the tourists learn more about the delicate coral reef ecosystem. Profits from tourists visiting the island are channelled back into local education and conservation projects.

Chumbe Island's unique situation has been recognised by an almost unparalleled string of awards for its responsible approach to tourism, and its ecologically sensitive approach to the environment. Meanwhile Chumbe seems effortlessly to combine a tourist attraction with a centre for ongoing education projects for the local people. It is an exceptional place.

GETTING THERE AND AWAY For tourists, **day trips** to the island are available when the island isn't full – these cost US$95 including all transfers, snorkelling equipment, guides and lunch – but visitors are encouraged to spend at least one night here and two or three would be perfect.

⌂ WHERE TO STAY

⌂ **Chumbe Island Lodge** (7 rooms) ☎ 024 231040; m 0777 413582; e chumbe@zitec. org; www.chumbeisland.com; ⊕ mid Jun–mid

Apr. Run as part of the Chumbe Island Coral Park (CHICOP), this superb, trailblazing lodge is an example of truly eco-friendly accommodation.

Its bungalows are simple but clean, comfortable, ingeniously designed & genuinely ecologically sensitive. Each 2-storey, dbl bungalow is made from predominantly local materials using traditional construction techniques, & employing cutting-edge eco-architectural systems. Downstairs there's an open-fronted lounge terrace, complete with sea-view hammock & animal mosaics. Upstairs, the bedroom comprises a comfortable mattress on the floor, mosquito net, & a stunning view of the ocean or stars,through the triangular front wall. The bungalows are completely self-sufficient with solar panels to provide electricity, funnel-shaped roofs to catch, filter & store rainwater (there is no good groundwater on the island), & 'compost toilets' to avoid septic tanks & the pollutants they often produce. Used water from the showers goes onto flower beds where specially chosen plants absorb nutrients before the water drains into the ground. This accommodation is unique in Zanzibar, & very unusual in the whole of Africa. The central area is a huge, star-shaped makuti structure – perfect for catching the sea breeze in the heat of the day. Simple, fresh meals are served on the terrace (at the sounding of a large gong), & there's a lovely upper deck of hammocks & chairs where the reference library & education centre can also be found. Activities are all escorted & focus on learning about the surrounding environment & ecology. They include snorkelling (scuba diving is prohibited) on the nearby reefs, forest walks & walks across the intertidal zone, with its plethora of rock pools. The coconut crab is a nocturnal creature & seldom seen in daylight, but if you ask the staff to take you into the woodland at dusk or after dark, you are virtually guaranteed to see several! The lodge is a private company with not-for-profit aims, & ploughs its proceeds back into great community education & conservation initiatives, making it not only a stunning holiday spot, but a worthy cause. FB includes soft drinks, guides, transfers & all activities; reduced rates Oct–Nov & Mar–mid Apr. ☗

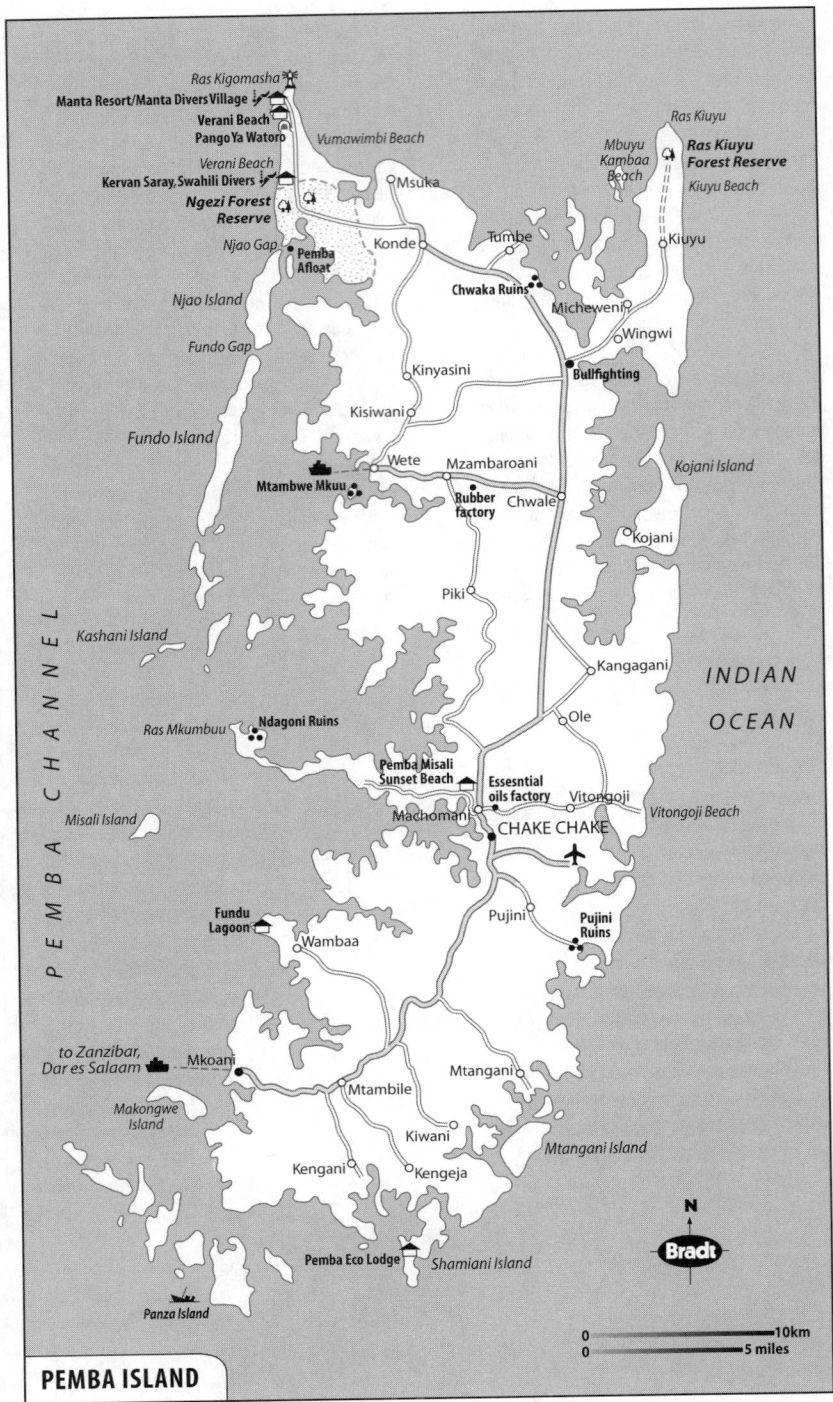

Manta Resort/Manta Divers Village
Verani Beach
Pango Ya Watoro
Ras Kigomasha
Vumawimbi Beach
Verani Beach
Kervan Saray, Swahili Divers
Ngezi Forest Reserve
Njao Gap
Pemba Afloat
Njao Island
Fundo Gap
Fundo Island
Msuka
Konde
Tumbe
Chwaka Ruins
Micheweni
Wingwi
Bullfighting
Kinyasini
Kisiwani
Wete
Mzambaroani
Mtambwe Mkuu
Rubber factory
Chwale
Kojani Island
Kojani
Piki
Kashani Island
Kangagani
INDIAN OCEAN
Ras Mkumbuu
Ndagoni Ruins
Ole
Pemba Misali Sunset Beach
Essential oils factory
Machomani
Vitongoji
Vitongoji Beach
CHAKE CHAKE
Misali Island
PEMBA CHANNEL
Fundu Lagoon
Wambaa
Pujini
Pujini Ruins
to Zanzibar, Dar es Salaam
Mkoani
Makongwe Island
Mtambile
Mtangani
Kiwani
Mtangani Island
Kengani
Kengeja
Ras Kiuyu
Mbuyu Kambaa Beach
Ras Kiuyu Forest Reserve
Kiuyu Beach
Kiuyu
N
Bradt
Pemba Eco Lodge
Shamiani Island
Panza Island
0   10km
0   5 miles
PEMBA ISLAND

12

Pemba

Pemba Island lies about 80km to the northeast of Zanzibar Island (Unguja), and about the same distance from the Tanzanian mainland, directly east of the port of Tanga. Smaller than Zanzibar Island, at just 67km long, it covers an area of 985km² and has a more undulating landscape, even though its highest point is only about 95m above sea level. But one of the first things that most strikes the visitor is how green it is. More densely vegetated than Zanzibar (with both natural forest and plantation), Pemba has always been seen as a more fertile place. The early Arab sailors called it El Huthera, meaning 'The Green'. Today, as always, far more cloves are grown here than on Zanzibar Island.

With 362,168 inhabitants at the last census, in 2002, Pemba is – like Zanzibar Island – one of the most densely populated areas of Tanzania, although this is no urban jungle. Most of the population live in traditional square houses, with a wooden frame and mud walls, the thatched roofs occasionally upgraded to corrugated iron. The largest town on Pemba is Chake Chake, the island's capital and administrative centre, about halfway down the western side of the island. The island's other main towns are Wete, in the northern part of the island, and Mkoani, in the south, which is the main port.

As in Zanzibar as a whole, the people are predominantly Muslim. Right across the island, women wear the veil, most in bright colours but some in sombre black, while schoolgirls look immaculate in the uniform dark skirts and cream veils. Typically it's a subsistence economy, with cloves the only real revenue earner, and few jobs available, so the nascent tourist industry brings much-needed employment. Despite the current lack of job prospects, Pembans remain optimistic and hope that the 2015 elections will bring new opportunities and further increases in the government-set clove prices, thereby improving the quality of life on the island. Pembans are naturally hospitable, but while English is spoken in the larger hotels, and by most of those who regularly come into contact with tourists, few villagers speak anything other than Swahili, so it's advisable to learn at least a few words of the language.

The low number of tourists to the island can make the independent traveller stand out, and visitors to Chake Chake, Mkoani or Wete will find they are likely to be the only foreigner in town, and a cause of much interest to the locals. Inland villages are visited even less; those passing through will be greeted with a mixture of broad grins and suspicious stares, while excited children squeal '*Mzungu!*' (white person). There is some concern as to the effect that increased tourism will have on Pemba. As infrastructure, roads and telecoms gradually improve, it is inevitable that confidence to invest in the island will eventually increase, prices will rise and the island will change. Hopefully, this transition will be carefully and positively managed.

HIGHLIGHTS

For today's visitor, Pemba's greatest attractions include long, empty beaches, some excellent diving and snorkelling, particularly around Misali Island, and the unspoilt forest reserve at Ngezi. There are several small historical sites which, although not 'must sees', certainly repay a visit if you use just a little imagination. Perhaps more important, though, with under 10,000 visitors per year, and little in the way of tourist facilities, Pemba is still a place where travel for its own sake (by car, bus, bike or on foot) remains a prime reason for visiting.

NATURAL HISTORY AND ENVIRONMENT

Verdant and very fertile, Pemba was once densely forested, although all that remains now is Ngezi Forest, on the northwestern tip of the island. Nevertheless, numerous spice and fruit trees dominate the rest of the landscape. **Cloves** represent the biggest cash crop, with Pemba responsible for the vast majority of cloves exported from Zanzibar, and sales monopolised by the government (see box, *Cloves*, page 54). For several months each year, cloves are left to dry in the sun on mats by the side of the road.

Consumption of almost all other **fruit and spices**, however, is restricted to domestic use. Mango, banana, avocado, coconut, citrus fruits, pineapple and papaya grow almost side by side with less familiar fruits such as breadfruit, custardfruit,

WITCHCRAFT ON PEMBA

For the people of east Africa, the island of Pemba is particularly known as a centre for traditional medicine and witchcraft. The British writer Evelyn Waugh, in his classic travel book *Remote People* (1931), described Pemba as a centre of 'black art' learning, and went on to record how:

> novices would come from as far as the great lakes [of central Africa] to graduate there. Even from Haiti, it is said, witchdoctors will come to probe the deepest mysteries of voodoo. Nowadays everything is kept hidden from the Europeans, and even those who have spent most of their lives in the country have only now and then discovered hints of the wide, infinitely ramified cult which still flourishes below the surface.

Sixty years later, little had changed. A 1995 travel story in a British newspaper reported that the village of Vitongoji, in the centre of the island, was 'the capital of Pemban sorcery ... a place of dark secrets. Some years ago a witchdoctor was arrested for eating children in the course of his duties.' This report may have been tongue-in-cheek, but it's an inescapable fact that local people seeking cures for spiritual or physical afflictions still come to the local doctors of Pemba from Zanzibar Island, mainland Tanzania, Kenya, and even as far as Uganda and Congo.

As a visitor to Pemba from the West, you shouldn't expect to be taken to see any cures or ceremonies. This type of thing is strictly for the locals. Even the most innocent of questions about witchcraft from tourists will be met with nothing more than embarrassed smiles or polite denials. (For more details on traditional religion and witchcraft, see pages 40–1.)

plantain, tamarind, bungo and jackfruit (a huge and hard sponge-looking thing that yields an improbably sweet flesh). Spices such as ginger, vanilla, cinnamon and pepper also grow in abundance.

Of the three **primates** that inhabit the island, the most visible is the Pemba vervet monkey (*tumbili au kima*; *Cercopithecus aethiops nesiotes*), while the small-eared galago or bushbaby (*komba*; *Otolemur garnettii garnettii*) is more likely to be heard than seen, its human-sounding cry disturbing many an otherwise peaceful night. A small population of Kirk's red colobus is also present in Ngezi Forest.

Relatively easy to spot is the **Pemba flying fox** (*popo wa Pemba*; *Pteropus voeltzkowi*), a large fruit bat which is the only fully endemic mammal on Pemba, and is classified as a globally endangered species. Its name comes from its orange fur and dog-like snout and ears. This animal seeks out the high canopies of undisturbed forest with a ready supply of fruit and tree blossoms. Pemba flying foxes roost throughout Pemba, particularly along the west coast and on islands off it, but are readily seen at Ngezi Forest where the forest rangers monitor their whereabouts, and at Kidike. They feed on soft fruits and weigh up to 1.5kg. Local people consider their flesh a delicacy; it tastes like oily chicken.

The **Zanzibar tree hyrax** (*pelele*; *Dendrohyrax validus neumannii*) is present not only at Ngezi but also on Njao and Fundo islands, whereas the rare and threatened **Pemba blue duiker** (*paa wa Pemba*; *Cephalophus monticola pembae*) and **marsh mongoose** (*chonjwe*; *Atilax paludinosus rubescens*) are found only in Ngezi Forest.

Bird species on the island include three endemics: the russet or Pemba scops owl, which is fairly common in the clove plantations and at Ngezi, the Pemba white-eye and the Pemba violet-breasted sunbird. A number of sub-endemic species include the Pemba green pigeon, the African paradise flycatcher and the Pemba African goshawk. Without doubt, the best place to see birds on Pemba is in the Ngezi Forest. (For more details, see pages 371–2.)

GETTING THERE AND AWAY

TO/FROM THE MAINLAND

By air Daily services between Dar es Salaam and Pemba are run by ZanAir and Coastal Aviation (for contact details, see page 124), although all flights go via Zanzibar, and some may involve a change of plane. The duration of the flight is just over an hour. At the time of research, **ZanAir** operates two daily flights between Dar es Salaam and Pemba: 09.00 from Dar via Zanzibar, arriving Pemba at 10.15, and a direct service, departing Dar at 13.45 and arriving in Pemba at 14.30. This route is US$300 return, including tax.

Coastal Aviation operates two daily flights from Dar to Pemba, which travel via Zanzibar then onwards to Tanga on the Tanzanian mainland. Flights depart Dar at 10.45 and 14.00, arriving in Zanzibar at 11.15 and 14.30 before arriving in Pemba at 11.45 and 15.05, with the later flight waiting for earlier connections from Selous and Ruaha. The one-way fare from Dar is US$130 and from Zanzibar US$95. The onward 20-minute flight to Tanga leaves Pemba at 15.15, and costs US$95. For return journeys, the flights leave Pemba at noon and 16.35, arriving in Zanzibar at 12.30 and 17.05, and landing back in Dar at 13.20 and 17.35. Fares are the same as for the outbound trip. **Tropical Air** also flies from Zanzibar to Pemba daily, leaving Zanzibar at 08.00 for the half-hour flight. Return flights depart Pemba at 10.05. Flights cost US$90 one-way. These can be used to connect with flights to/from Tanga and Dar.

If you're coming from any other part of Tanzania or Kenya and want a direct flight, your only option is to **charter a plane**. In Dar, Nairobi or Mombasa, a travel agent will be able to help you. Spare seats on charter flights are sometimes sold to individuals. Once again, the best thing to do is contact a travel agent, who will probably phone the airport or one of the local charter companies to see if anything is going your way.

On leaving Pemba, don't forget that there is a US$6 **departure tax** (made up of US$5 'safety' tax, and a further US$1 airport tax), and be prepared to hand this over in cash. This tax is usually included for Coastal Aviation flights, but it's best to check before travelling. The modern terminal has few facilities – just a small shop selling drinks and snacks and a couple of toilets.

By sea The most reliable scheduled ships from the mainland to Pemba are the *Kilimanjaro* and *Sea Bus I & II*, run by **Azam Marine**, and *Sea Express I, II* and *III*, run by **Fast Ferries**, which between them sail daily between Dar and Zanzibar Island, continuing on to Pemba (Mkoani). The fare between Dar and Pemba is US$45–60. Ferry timetables on all routes, especially the slow ferries, can change with little or no notice, and boats do not run during high winds or Islamic holidays. During Ramadan services will be limited. The *Seagull* and the *Sepideh*, once the most reliable of the ships, now run an extremely limited and unreliable service at irregular times, so it's best not to depend on these. Similarly, you can in theory reach Pemba by dhow from Tanga or from Mombasa, in Kenya, although police at the port are unwilling to let tourists board, with good reason – the safety record on these boats is pretty dire (see page 127), and it's worth remembering, too, that services are irregular and far from idyllic. Most dhows from Tanga or Mombasa go to Wete, but a few go to Mkoani.

Immigration formalities Whichever type of boat you use to reach Pemba from the mainland (Kenya or Tanzania), you need to show your passport to the immigration officials at the port. This is a very relaxed and low-key affair. So low key in fact that sometimes the office is empty, and you have to go to the police station in town to present your credentials, or get redirected to wherever the immigration staff might be.

TO/FROM ZANZIBAR ISLAND

By air Scheduled flights run by **ZanAir** and **Coastal Aviation** between Pemba and Dar es Salaam (see above) touch down on Zanzibar Island in both directions. The one-way fare for non-residents ranges from US$95–115, plus the departure tax of US$5.

Your other option for reaching Pemba from Zanzibar Island is to fly with one of the local **air-charter** companies based in Zanzibar Town. If you can get a group together and charter a whole plane, it can sometimes be cheaper per person than buying a ticket on a regular flight. Alternatively, these companies will often sell spare seats on charter flights to Pemba. In high season there are flights at least every other day, so it's worth contacting the companies direct, or getting a travel agency to do it for you, to see if there's anything going. (For contact details, see *Chapter 5, Scheduled flights*, page 124.)

To book scheduled or charter flights to the mainland from Pemba, contact ZanAir's agent opposite Barclays Bank in Chake Chake, or Pemba Aviation & Airport Services (the Coastal agent) on the other side of the road. Alternatively you can phone the airport control tower (✆ *024 2452238*) and enquire yourself. This is a fairly standard procedure – the charter companies often tell the tower if they're looking for passengers to fill spare seats.

By sea Nearly all passenger ships, and some cargo ships, coming into Pemba arrive at the town of Mkoani (at the southern end of Pemba Island), while it's mostly cargo ships and dhows that go to/from Wete (at the northern end of Pemba Island). Very few ships or dhows, other than local fishing boats, go to/from Chake Chake. (In fact the old harbour of Chake Chake is silted up and only canoes can get here; the town's port is now at Wesha, about 10km west along the coast.) Schedules given below were correct at the time of research, but are notoriously unreliable and subject to change.

For more details on buying tickets to Pemba on one of the ships listed below, see *Chapter 5, Passenger ships and ferries*, pages 125–6. To buy tickets on Pemba, contact the relevant local agent in Chake Chake, Mkoani or Wete (see pages 355, 362 and 365).

MV *Kilimanjaro* & *Seabus I, II* & *III* Run by Azam Marine, these boats share the Dar–Zanzibar–Pemba route. Departures from Dar are at 07.00 on Mon, Thu & Sat, & after a 30min stopover in Zanzibar the ferries leave at 09.30 to Pemba. Returning, ferries depart Pemba at 12.30 & Zanzibar at 16.00. These can all be booked online at www.azammarine.com. One-way fare non-residents Dar–Pemba US$75.

Noora In theory, there is a weekly Sun service on the *Nora* between Tanga & Wete, leaving Wete at 08.00. The return journey on Tue leaves Tanga at 08.00 but timings are erratic & this service is none too reliable; for the current state of play, & for details of any other boats on this route, contact one of the tour operators in Chake Chake (see page 355).

Sea Express I & II These speedboats owned by Fast Ferries Ltd commenced operations between Dar, Zanzibar & Mkoani on Pemba in 2005. At the time of writing, 1 of 2 Fast Ferries was departing Zanzibar every day at 07.00, 09.45 or 10.00 depending on the day for the 3hr crossing to Pemba; for the return Pemba to Zanzibar boats were departing at 11.00 or 13.30. Journeys from Dar to Zanzibar depart 07.00 & 09.00, arriving 2–3hrs later. One-way fare non-residents Zanzibar–Pemba US$45; Dar–Pemba US$65.

Serengeti The most reliable of the slow boats is the passenger ship *Serengeti*, operated by JAK Enterprises. The 6–8hr crossing between Zanzibar Town & Mkoani runs 3 times a week (currently Tue, Thu & Sun), departing at 22.00, returning the following day. One-way US$20.

Most of Pemba's **dhow** traffic goes to/from Tanga on the mainland, and only occasionally do dhows go between Zanzibar Town and Pemba. Of those that do, most land at Mkoani. Although it is illegal in Tanzania for tourists to travel by dhow, and not especially safe, some intrepid travellers still report finding captains willing to take them on board. If you're determined to consider this, see *Chapter 5*, page 127.

TOURIST INFORMATION

Tour operators are the most reliable source of tourist information, although they will of course expect any bookings to be done through them. The Zanzibar Tourist Corporation (ZTC) has an office in Chake Chake, where staff may be able to assist, but their main purpose is to regulate the tour operators on the island rather than provide visitor guidance.

GETTING AROUND

Pemba's road system was given a boost in 2005 with the completion of the tarred road across the island from Mkoani to Konde, paid for by the World Bank. North of Konde, and elsewhere, however, most of the roads are pretty poor, with access to some of the outlying villages requiring 4x4 vehicles, particularly in the rainy season.

From Chake Chake to Wete, a bumpy alternative to the main road is the 'old' – and, more direct – road via Mzambaroani, which goes through some beautiful scenery. This has recently been tarred in places, but the road conditions are not great and time-wise, the new road is considerably quicker, despite the apparent diversion.

Options for getting around on Pemba are limited, although public transport allows independent travellers to see at least some parts of the island. To get further afield independently you'll have to hire a bike, motorbike, car or boat. It is also possible to arrange a car with driver, or an organised excursion, through hotels and guesthouses, a local tour company, or direct with the drivers.

For many travellers, the easiest way to set up an excursion or a tour of the island is to contact a driver, either direct (see below) or through your hotel or guesthouse. Alternatively, there are a number of companies in Chake Chake and Wete that can organise this for you (see pages 355 and 365).

TAXIS AND CAR HIRE It is rare for tourists to hire cars in Pemba, and it's not the easiest thing to organise, but with some effort it can be done through the tour companies in Chake Chake. Organising this in advance with erratic communications is challenging, and do bear in mind that conditions in Pemba for the self-driver are not great: few signposts, overconfident local drivers, sandy or rocky roads, and livestock in the street and remote hotel locations. For those heading north, the drive from Wete to the Ngezi Peninsula is particularly tough, and not at all easy to navigate.

Alternatively, it's pretty straightforward to rent a car with a driver for around US$60 a day, including petrol, depending on the distance you want to travel. Most of the hotels can organise this for you, as can tour companies. Try contacting one of the following individuals (giving plenty of notice), both of whom offer tours to various places of interest around the island. They are reliable, interesting guides, and both speak excellent English.

🚗 **Said Mohammed** m 0777 430201. Based in Chake Chake & known to everyone as Saidi. Offers city tours, spice tours, transport to the north & east (inc 4x4 by arrangement), & visits to all Pemba's places of interest.

🚗 **Suleiman Seif** m 0777 431793. The driver for Fundu Lagoon also offers a range of tours. He is a mine of information & is particularly knowledgeable about the island's spice & fruit trees.

In Chake Chake, vehicles and drivers wait for business outside Barclays Bank, near the clock tower; in Mkoani and Wete they can be found near the market. Rates vary according to the vehicle: pickups, saloon cars, minibuses, Land Rovers and small Suzuki 'jeeps' are often available. Rates are also negotiable and should be discussed fully (and agreed) in advance. To give you an idea, a trip from Chake Chake to Wete or Mkoani costs about US$40 return. If you're planning a tour, a newish vehicle covering a round trip from Chake to Wete, Ngezi Forest and the Manta Resort and back would cost about US$150 per vehicle. All rates include petrol. Whatever you hire, part payment in advance is usually required, and the first stop is likely to be the petrol station.

Although in theory it's possible to self drive, in practice this is less easy to set up. Some of the tour companies, such as Coral Tours or Msewe Travel in Chake Chake, may be able to help, with costs starting at US$60 per day. Do check the insurance details, and see pages 127–8 for further information.

MOTORBIKE AND BICYCLE HIRE Bikes can be hired from any of the tour operators in Wete or Chake Chake, while elsewhere it's perfectly possible to hire both motorbikes and pedal bikes on more of an ad hoc basis. The system seems to involve simply finding somebody who is not using their bike and doesn't mind making some extra shillings lending it out to tourists. Rates start at about US$10 per day for a bicycle, and US$30 for a motorbike. Alternatively, you can sometimes arrange to hire a bike or motorbike through your hotel. Tell the staff what you want to do, and they may well know someone who can help you out – prices will be the same as mentioned above. Sharook Guesthouse in Wete rents out bikes for around US$10 a day. For details, see page 365.

Be warned that motorbikes or scooters – locally known as *piki piki* – can be extremely dangerous, both on pot-holed side roads and on the main north–south road, where erratic driving, sharp bends and numerous chickens or goats are just some of the hazards. If you're determined to go this route, remember that you probably won't be insured. Check that your vehicle is in reasonable condition, particularly the tyres and the rims, and don't even consider it if you've no previous motorbike experience.

BUS, MINIBUS AND DALA DALA Pemba's main form of transport is dala dala (see pages 130–1). Pemba used to be served by quaint old buses (actually converted trucks with wooden benches and canopies on the back), but these days they've been replaced by more modern dala dalas (converted pick-ups) or the occasional minibus. Routes and numbers are listed below. On the main routes, of which the number 606 seems to have the most frequent service, there are several buses each day (at least one an hour after 06.00 until midnight), but on the minor routes buses might operate only a few times – or just once – per day, and that'll be in the morning. Services to/from Mkoani are tied in closely with ship arrival and departure times. In fact, it seems that Pemba Island's entire public transport system revolves around ship timetables. The fare on the longer routes (eg: Chake Chake to Mkoani) is about US$1.50. For shorter trips it's half that. The most useful routes for visitors are as follows, though it's worth noting that dala dalas will stop to collect or drop off passengers at any point along their route.

Route

601	Wete to Konde
602	Chake Chake to Konde
603	Chake Chake to Mkoani
606	Chake Chake to Wete
305	Chake Chake to Wesha (Chake's port)
316	Chake Chake to Vitongoji (5km east of Chake Chake)
319	Chake Chake to Pujini
330	Chake Chake to Wambaa
10	Wete to Wingwi/Micheweni

Other buses connect Chake Chake and, to a lesser extent, Wete with outlying villages. There will be a station manager at the bus depot in each town so check with him for details.

BOAT HIRE Aside from booking through one of the hotels, there's no organised means of getting from Pemba across to the individual islands, although it's worth asking any of the tour operators in case they can help. Alternatively, some of the local fishermen are prepared to carry passengers for a fee, which is fine for short distances, but do remember that the longer crossings – especially to Misali Island – could take a considerable period of time, and be pretty uncomfortable, especially in rough seas.

ACCOMMODATION

Pemba has a very small number of places to stay compared with Zanzibar Island but there is increasing variety, from rock-bottom hotels and a smattering of guesthouses through to more exclusive spots on the coast: one mid-range hotel, an eco lodge, and a highly exclusive tourist hideaway. While rumours of further options have been mooted for some time, Pemba Eco Lodge (see *Where to stay*, page 364) is the only new accommodation to have appeared in recent years. A dip in visitor numbers to Pemba, especially independent travellers, has had a negative impact on the accommodation options, as lack of income and investment has forced many to close. While nobody wants Pemba to turn into the cramped sprawl seen along some of Zanzibar's beaches, with so few facilities and lack of a reliable public transport network it is difficult for the independent traveller to visit, so most come on pre-paid trips to the larger lodges, and bypass the smaller, simpler hotels completely.

As on Zanzibar Island, all accommodation on Pemba must officially be paid for with hard currency: US dollars in cash being preferred, and, unless otherwise stated, anything else (eg: pounds sterling, euros) may not be accepted. If you have only Tanzanian shillings, these are usually accepted at the current rate of exchange. Breakfast is normally included in the room price; other meals are payable in Tanzanian shillings. As on Zanzibar Island, during quiet times many of the lodges and guesthouses on Pemba lower their rates, and even if reductions aren't advertised, it's worth asking. At the cheaper places, rates are often negotiable at any time of year.

FOOD AND DRINK

All the hotels on Pemba serve food, although at the cheaper places it has to be ordered, even by residents – sometimes quite a long time in advance. The island's main towns have simple restaurants where you can get local dishes, featuring varying combinations of chicken, fish and chips, or Indian-influenced dishes such as pilau and biryani.

Roadside stalls proliferate during market hours, most selling variations on meat kebabs (*mishkaki*) and omelettes. For a cheap meal, try *chipsi mai yai* – an omelette filled with chips, sometimes served with shredded cabbage, for around US$1. On the drinks front, it's easy enough to get branded fizzy drinks such as Coke and Fanta, and look out for the local pineapple drink, brand-named Zed, a strong alcoholic tipple with a dangerously low price. If you fancy a snack (or a simple souvenir), seek out the tamarind sweetmeat sold in small, hand-woven palm-leaf baskets. Called *haluwa*, it's made from oil and sugar, costs just a few shillings, and is so sweet that one packet will happily serve a whole group. Open it with caution, though – *haluwa* is very sticky. The best on the island is said to come from Wete.

For lunches or picnics, you can buy fruit at the markets and roadside stalls in Chake Chake, Mkoani, Wete or Konde. You can also buy bread – either from the occasional stall, or from men on bikes with baskets of fresh loaves on the back. Shops in the towns sell a reasonable range of food in tins and packets, imported from the mainland or elsewhere in the Indian Ocean, but in the smaller villages this kind of stuff is more difficult to find.

OTHER PRACTICALITIES

BANKS AND BUREAUX DE CHANGE Banking is limited to Chake Chake, which has branches of the People's Bank of Zanzibar and Barclays Bank; the latter even has an ATM (⊕ *08.30–16.00 Mon–Fri, 09.00–13.00 Sat*). The banks will change money, but expect a wait of 30 minutes or so, and be advised that US dollars are best. Financially, you may do slightly better at a bureau de change. A couple can be found in Chake Chake but they may not have shillings available and the rates still won't be favourable. There's one in the ZTC building, and there are various less reliable local exchanges dotted among the shops. An alternative is to ask at a local shop or seek advice from staff at your hotel who may be able to direct you to a local trader who could change cash dollars, though naturally rates may well be higher than at the banks. If you're travelling to Pemba from Dar es Salaam or Zanzibar, you'd be well advised to change money at one of the bureaux de change at the airport or in town before travelling to Pemba. Travellers' cheques are unlikely to be accepted anywhere.

COMMUNICATIONS Although there are communications centres in each of the main towns, the introduction of yellow public phone booths has made these somewhat redundant for the visitor. Phones take TTCL phonecards, which cost US$10 and are available from the Tanzanian Telecommunications office and numerous other outlets – just look for the TTCL sign outside. International calls cost US$1.50 a minute. For a fee, Coral Tours also have a landline that tourists can use (see *Travel and tour companies*, page 355). For more general information on telephone services into and out of Zanzibar, see pages 116–17.

There are post offices in Chake, Wete and Mkoani and Konde (⊕ *usually 08.00– 13.00 & 14.00–16.30 Mon–Thu, 08.00–noon & 14.00–17.00 Fri, 09.00–noon Sat*), but public email services are confined to the internet bureaux in Chake Chake (see page 358).

ELECTRICITY Since joining the mainland Tanzania grid in 2011, the electricity situation on Pemba has improved and power cuts have become far less frequent than they used to be. However, the power is still only on for eight to 14 hours a day, after which it switches to a less-consistent battery store. Backup generators are still necessary, though this is a drastic improvement on recent years.

HOSPITALS AND PHARMACIES The island's main hospital in Mkoani is a modern place, built with overseas aid. Although it is staffed by dedicated Chinese, Cuban and Tanzanian doctors, the hospital suffers from shortages of drugs and other essential supplies. There's also a smaller hospital in Chake Chake, which has Western doctors and the island's only obstetrics unit, while X-ray facilities are based at the hospital in Wete, near the ferry port.

There are several pharmacies, including near the hospital in Chake Chake (close to the museum), where reportedly most things are available – if you know what you're looking for, that is.

ACTIVITIES

DIVING Recreational diving off Pemba is for the most part confined to the Pemba Channel on the more sheltered west of the island. Misali Island in particular provides a wonderful array of corals and fish life. Unlike the reefs around Zanzibar Island, many of the reefs off Pemba fall away into steep walls, offering opportunities for some exciting drift dives and the chance to see creatures such as the spotted eagle ray, with its 3m wingspan. Despite Pemba's undoubted reputation for the big pelagics, such as barracuda, trevally, giant groupers and the endangered Napoleon wrasse, sightings of shark are extremely rare on the west of the island, and even to the south. If it's sharks that you're after, you need to deep dive on the east of the island, where the steep walls and fast currents attract hammerheads.

Most of the operators use either speedboats or motorised dhows to get to the dive sites. While the former are undoubtedly faster, there's a lot to be said for the leisurely pace of a dhow, giving the opportunity to take in the beauty of the islands or to watch large teams of fishermen working with their nets from narrow wooden boats. On the way to the dive sites, particularly in the morning and further north, you may be joined by schools of common or spinner dolphins, just tagging along for the ride, and occasionally humpback whale sightings have been reported.

Diving on Pemba, as on Zanzibar Island, is good all year round, with visibility ranging from 10m to 30m or even more. Between December and March, the water is warm – around 30°C, but even quite early in the season the water temperature is a reasonable 25°C or so, and most operators have good wetsuits if you didn't bring anything suitable. (For more details, see box, *Zanzibar diving and fishing seasons*, page 113.) Visibility, current and thus the choice of dive sites are strongly affected by the state of the tide: not just the level, but also whether it is spring or neap. Be guided by your dive instructor on this – it's important: there are a number of dives that should not be attempted by beginners, especially in the southeast of the island. On almost all boats, entry is a backward roll into the water.

Dive sites Although much of the reef around Pemba was adversely affected by the El Niño of 1998 (see page 387) and the situation hasn't been improved by dynamite fishing (which sadly continues, despite being illegal), pristine, virgin reef can still be found, and groups do tend to be small, so divers, especially at advanced levels, are spoilt for choice. Dive sites on Pemba tend to have been given different names by the individual dive outfits, so the following is an overview of what to expect.

Particularly popular is the protected area to the west of **Misali Island** (see pages 362–4), with its calm waters and spectacular coral gardens, where most (but not all) of the dives are suitable for novice or relatively inexperienced divers. Improbably giant clams hug the reef, as do numerous smaller creatures, such as exquisitely coloured nudibranchs: keep an eye out especially for the 30cm Spanish dancer, only visible at night. At one dive site to the northwest of the island, currents can be strong, making it more suited to advanced divers with considerable experience. The rewards can be great, however, with eagle rays and some big pelagics. Dives around the southwestern tip of Pemba are for the most part in the vicinity of **Panza Island**, and are also normally recommended for advanced divers, as the currents can be strong. Sites here are relatively spread out, with 'blue dives' offering good opportunities to see pelagics. There's also the wreck of a 1950s freighter in 12m of water.

North of Misali, some excellent sites around **Ovinje Gap**, **Fundo Gap** and **Njao Gap** with their steep walls are usually better explored by more advanced divers with plenty of experience, able to cope with strong and sometimes unpredictable currents. Diving through the 'gaps' between the islands can be seriously exciting, earning plenty of comparison with fairground rides and express trains. Even the more leisurely drift dives may not be suitable for a just-certified novice, so be clear of your limitations and do be sure to tell your dive leader if you have any doubts. **Manta Point**, just off Fundo Gap, is a great circular dive, affording regular ray sightings, as its name would suggest, although the number of mantas has significantly dwindled with overfishing. Also present are huge mushroom and cabbage corals; even if you don't get to see the manta rays, there are plenty of ocean-going fish in the vicinity, and all sorts of nudibranchs. Out of the currents, gentler dives offer plenty to see, while sheltered lagoons to the east of the islands are good locations to learn to dive and hone your skills. North of Njao Gap, however, the quality of the reef is poor, and dive operators rarely visit the area.

Dive companies There are currently four dive operators in Pemba, each linked to one of the island's resorts and with its own style. Be sure to check out what is available and choose the right operator for you. Equipment is available to hire from all companies, with standards generally pretty high. All offer PADI-certified courses, including the popular Discover Scuba and Open Water; night dives can usually be organised with advance notice. For those interested in underwater photography, cameras can be rented from Fundu Lagoon (US$30/1 dive; US$50 including image CD) or from Swahili Divers, who run photography courses.

On a practical note, some of the operators do not carry water on their boats, so check this before you leave and take your own if necessary, particularly in hot weather. For other practical advice, see pages 110–13.

For comparison purposes, prices below have been given for a single- or two-tank dive, and the PADI Open Water course. Inevitably, though, options vary considerably, and many other courses are offered, so do check these out.

360 Dive Pemba m 0776 718852; www. themantaresort.com. On the northwestern tip of the island, this efficient 5* PADI dive school is run by Manta Resort (see *Where to stay*, page 370) & has good access to most of Pemba's west coast dive sites. As many guests here come with their own equipment, the regulators, BCDs, marine conservation fees, boat trips & wetsuits are charged separately, with packages offering better value. Dive US$52/104 sgl/dbl; Open Water US$540.

Dive 710 \ 024 2232926; m 0774 438668; e info@fundulagoon.com; www.fundulagoon. com. Dive 710, the professional yet friendly dive centre at Fundu Lagoon (see *Where to stay*, page 362), is a PADI 5* Gold Palm operation used exclusively by the resort's guests. Its location, just 20mins or so by speedboat from the dive sites of Misali Island, makes it possible to leave at a civilised hour for the morning dive & be back in time for lunch. A more leisurely day allows for 2 dives, with a picnic lunch on the island. Dive at Misali US$75/150 sgl/dbl (further afield additional US$15 per dive, min 4); Open Water US$650.

Pemba Misali Divers m 0775 044713/7; e info@pembamisalidivers.com; www. pembamisalidivers.com. Pemba Misali Sunset Beach's dive centre (see *Where to stay*, page 357)

is found in Wesha, a small village west along the coast from Chake Chake. Diving can be arranged to sites all around the island, including Misali Island (US$130/170 sgl/dbl dive) & although the centre is not PADI affiliated, equipment is the latest in Scuba Pro gear. Considerable discounts are available for divers wishing to stay at the hotel. Dive US$ 80/120 sgl/dbl.

Swahili Divers m 0773 176737/8; e resort@ kayakpemba.com; www.swahilidivers.com. The longest-established dive operator on Pemba is a relaxed & friendly outfit run by Raf Jah, who has lived & dived in Pemba for over a decade. In 2007, the company, which was the 1st on the island to attain PADI 5* status, moved from Chake Chake to its new base at Kervan Saray Beach (see *Where to stay*, page 370) in the northwest, near Ngezi Forest. From here, Raf or his crew take divers all over the central & northern dive sites of the island in fast RIBs, with the nearest dive sites just a 4min journey. There are 2-tank dives every morning (departing 09.00; returning 13.30), with afternoon dives at 14.30, each taking a max 5 divers. Snorkelling is also on offer, as are sunset cruises. Dive US$ 60/140/160 sgl/dbl/tpl; equipment US$30pp/day; Open Water US$550, or US$650 for individual tuition.

Live-aboards There used to be a number of live-aboards operating around Pemba, with many originating in Kenya. Recently these have all but ceased to operate, with only one new arrival on the scene. **Pemba Island Sailing** (\ *0768 123464; e sailing@ ecoTZ.com; www.sailing.ecoTZ.com*) launched in October 2011, and operates a fully crewed, live-aboard catamaran called *Kaskazi*. Accommodating up to eight or, more comfortably, six guests, the boat sails from September to November and March to May, when the weather and sea are calmest. Charters are available from as few as three days, with bespoke itineraries usually including snorkelling, diving (request in advance to ensure a qualified dive master is present) and swimming, with wakeboarding and waterskiing from the motorized dinghy or mangrove kayaking also available. Guests are collected from Pemba Airport before being transferred to the port at Wesha, near Chake-Chake, where dinghy transfers take seafarers to board *Kaskazi*. The boat moves daily, mainly among quiet lagoons surrounding the island, with the multi-national crew working hard to ensure a relaxed and enjoyable trip.

SNORKELLING While there is no shortage of places to swim and snorkel off Pemba, most are viable only at high water. One of the best places for snorkelling lies in front of the visitor centre on Misali Island, where – in just a few feet of water, and regardless of the tide – countless fish and other underwater life can be seen in almost perfect visibility. As you drift through the water, keep an eye out for unicornfish, sea goldies, cleaner wrasse, deep red and blue parrotfish, and the startling Moorish idol. Giant clams grip the reef, and sea cucumbers edge along the sandy bottom; you may even spot a grouper. Other possibilities include areas around the sandbanks that dry out at low tide along the west coast. Snorkelling trips can be organised through all the hotels and lodges; expect to pay US$20–40, depending on the distance to the site.

FISHING The waters of the Pemba Channel are well known for their abundance of fish, including blue marlin, sailfish, barracuda, trevally, mahi mahi, rainbow runner and kingfish. Fishing is offered by **Kervan Saray Lodge** (see *Where to stay*, page 370) from a 7m Yamaha vessel, kitted out with electronics and echo sounder, and sometimes ranging as far as 8km offshore. This is suitable for two serious fishermen, or three if they know each other, and needs to be booked in advance. Trolling, fly fishing, spinning gear and vertical jigging rods are all available for rent. (US$250pp/ day, plus fuel and lures; equipment hire US$50pp/day).

Fundu Lagoon (see *Where to stay*, page 362) also offer four- to five-hour trips for their own guests on boats captained by Rusty Rauscher, the only International Game Fish Association-accredited captain in Tanzania. Costs range from US$300 per half day on the *Karambizi* (max 2) to US$500 per half day on the *Vumba* (max 4). This is a scenic trip and includes drink and all food. Fundu's chef can cook up any fish caught for dinner. Long fishing trips, lasting up to a week can be arranged in advance, but most are for the day only.

Pemba Misali Sunset Beach (see *Where to stay*, page 357) offers big-game fishing in the Pemba Channel on their catamaran, Glacier Bay 2670, with a two-person queen-sized berth, electric toilet and shower. These are booked through Hooked on Fishing (*www.fishzanzibar.com*) who charge US$1,200 for a full day including all fishing gear, tackle and bait, mask and snorkel, lunch and refreshments.

For something more low key, **Manta Resort** (see *Where to stay*, page 371) offers fishing trips for US$50 an hour and locally guided handline trips for US$40. Alternatively, you could try asking around in the harbours at Wete, Wesha or Mkoani; there are few fishermen nowadays who are prepared to take visitors on board. The boats are small, however, and safety records are none too great, so you'd do better to stick to one of the established operators.

KAYAKING All the larger tourist lodges and hotels have kayaks, with short guided trips offered by **Fundu Lagoon** for their guests. The **Manta Resort** includes kayaking trips, while at **Swahili Divers** (see *Dive companies*, page 353), marine anthropologist Cisca Jah runs kayak tours under the name Kasa Kayaking. A half-day guided mangrove tour with snacks and support boat costs US$70.

CHAKE CHAKE

Chake Chake is the largest town on Pemba, just over halfway down the western side of the island. The island's capital and administrative centre, it forms the hub of the bus and dala dala network. Although Chake Chake has been settled for as long as Zanzibar Town, it has never achieved the same degree of importance, and thus has little in the way of grand palaces or the winding narrow streets of the old Stone Town, although part of the Omani Fort, near the hospital, is open to the public as a very informative museum.

When the first edition of this guide was researched in the early 1990s, Chake Chake – and Pemba itself – was a sleepy backwater. Today, it's a bustling community with more than a hint of modernity: there are a couple of phone shops, and many of the tin-roofed houses have sprouted satellite dishes. In other ways, though, it's still very quiet and traditional, with ox-carts trundling up the high street (although there are even more scooters). The market, around the bus station, is lively, and the old port, down the hill from the town centre, is also worth a walk. Down the back streets, particularly on the road opposite the market, are countless shops selling everything from foodstuffs and car parts to plastic mops and all types of clothing. In tiny booths, tailors will knock you up a suit or skirt on an ancient treadle sewing machine. The whole place is more peaceful than Zanzibar Town, with a laid-back atmosphere, and tourists get no hassle at all, just friendly hellos or shy waves from children, so it's great just to stroll around.

TRAVEL AND TOUR COMPANIES The tourist who arrives in Chake Chake in the hope of organising something on the fly could well be disappointed, since the town is less geared to visitors than in the past.

Azam Marine Next to the market, this is the main agent for the *Kilimanjaro & Seabus I, II & III* (see *Getting there and away*, page 347).
Coastal Travels Ltd ☏ 024 2452162; m 0777 420702; m (Airport) 0777 418343; ☉ 07.30–17.00. This helpful bureau, almost next to Barclays, is set up to handle bookings of Coastal Aviation flights between Pemba & Zanzibar, Tanga & Dar.
Coral Tours ☏ 024 2452045; m 0777 437397; e coralnasa@yahoo.com; ☉ 08.00–16.00 daily. Enthusiastic & incredibly helpful Pemban manager Nassor has been running Coral Tours since 2000 & has built up extensive local knowledge of everything from the dala dala routes to up-to-date road conditions. He's happy to give out tourist information & book all manner of accommodation, tours & tickets, plus car, motorbike & bicycle hire. A whole day trip to the north of the island including Kidike, Ngezi Forest & Vumawimbi Beach, plus lunch & an English-speaking guide costs US$55pp,

but is cheaper if you can get a group together. He also books ferry & flight tickets. The shop can be found on the ground floor of the ZTC building opposite the adult training centre.
Imara Tours and Travel ☏ 0242 452648; m 0777 842084; e info@imaratours.com; www. imaratours.com; ☉ 08.00–15.30 Mon–Fri, 08.00–14.00 Sat, 09.00–13.00 Sun). Located on Chachani St, next door to the People's Bank of Zanzibar, Imara offers a range of tours & water-based activities on Pemba as well as ferry & flight bookings, car hire & bike hire (US$20 per day).
Msewe Travel (see advertisement on page 372) m 0777 229468/0754 015148; e admin@ msewetravel.com, msewetours@gmail.com; www.msewetravel.com. Managed by the very friendly & enthusiastic Kassim, Msewe is down a tiny side street just across the road from Barclays Bank. The office provides lots of information on excursions, flights, ferries, diving, bullfighting &

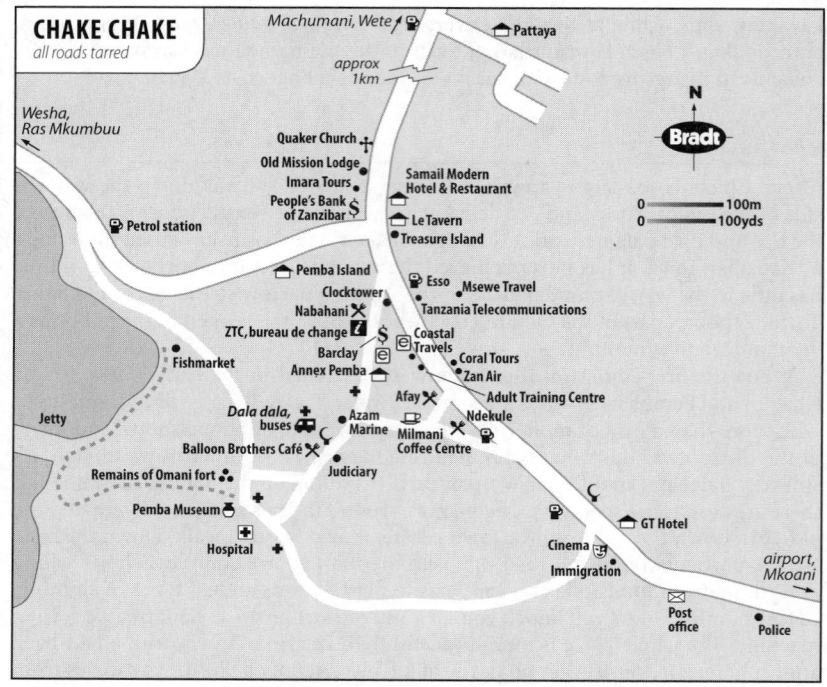

transfers can be found, as well as safari options on the mainland, which are arranged through their Arusha office. They have a further base in Pemba Airport. Full-day tours of Pemba cost around US$90 for 2 people.

ZanAir 024 2454990; m 0775 044101. The booking office for ZanAir flights is just down the hill from Barclays Bank, diagonally across from Coastal Travels.

WHERE TO STAY Chake Chake's renowned Old Mission Lodge, for years the home of Swahili Divers and a first-rate hangout for laid-back scuba enthusiasts, closed its doors when owners Raf and Cisca Jah moved their operation north to Kervan Saray Beach (see *Where to stay*, page 370). This left something of an accommodation vacuum for a while, though fortunately there are now a few decent and central alternatives, of which the Samail is probably your best bet.

Annex Pemba Hotel (15 rooms) 024 2452216; m 0777 428303/90041; e pembaislandhotel@yahoo.com. The sister hotel to Pemba Island (see next), this is another strict Muslim establishment with no alcohol allowed & a marriage certificate compulsory for couples. Rooms are spread over 3 floors leading off a central communal area with a sofa & a TV, which also doubles as reception. Shiny yellow & orange tiled floors & white walls enclose simple fan-cooled rooms with mosquito nets & shaky old TVs. The bathroom, which is so small that the toilet is

underneath the shower head. Guests are welcome to use the rooftop restaurant at the Pemba Hotel. **$$$**

Pemba Island Hotel (16 rooms) 024 2452215; e pembaislandhotel@yahoo.com. This clean hotel is a welcoming & pleasant place to stay in the centre of town. Painted white with bright pink decorative tiles, it's easy to spot just down the hill from the People's Bank of Zanzibar. En-suite rooms have dbl beds (even the 'singles') with AC/fans, mosi nets, TV & fridge; splashes of colour come from pink curtains, red plastic chairs

& green bathrooms. In keeping with the hotel's strict Muslim ethos, no alcohol is permitted on the premises, & a marriage certificate is required for a couple to share a room. Rooftop restaurant. **$$$**

🏠 Hotel Le Tavern (8 rooms) ☎024 2452660. On the main street, opposite the People's Bank of Zanzibar, Le Tavern is above a small row of shops – look for the blue & white striped awning. If you're asking for directions here, forget French; it's pronounced 'lay' Tavern. Clean, en-suite rooms with sgl beds have nets, fans & crackling TVs (local channels only), but are in desperate need of a fresh coat of paint. Meals to order around US$5. **$$**

🏠 Samail Modern Hotel & Restaurant (16 rooms) m 0776 627619/0718 010960; e samailmodernhotel@yahoo.com. The new kid on the accommodation block, Samail opened in

Apr 2012 in a freshly painted 3-storey building next door to Le Tavern. The bright restaurant serves a selection of spiced chicken & fish dishes with rice or biriyani (US$3.50) on glass-topped tables. Cakes, bread & fresh fruit juices make for quick snacks & there's even an ice-cream machine. Upstairs, spacious rooms are cooled by both AC & fans, & all have TVs; bathrooms are fine & functional. **$$**

🏠 GT Hotel (8 rooms) m 0777 418532. An ugly concrete monstrosity which is perpetually under construction yet shows no signs of improvement, & rarely has guests. Owner Omar speaks no English, & the place is clearly aimed at locals & cash-strapped backpackers; you'd have to be pretty desperate to stay here. **$**

One by one, the small collection of clean and basic guesthouses just north of town have closed down, leaving just one, plus a new resort further along the coast in Wesha:

🏠 Pemba Misali Sunset Beach (20 villas) ☎024 2233882; m 0775 044713/7; e info@ pembamisalibeach.com; www.pembamisalibeach. com. North of Chake Chake, near the village of Wesha, Pemba Misali Sunset Beach's row of pea green villas occupies a pretty waterfront spot, with sea views for all. Inside, is a neutral interior, wooden king or twin beds & shiny white bathroom. AC, ceiling fans & mosquito nets are standard, as are shuttered, handcrafted louvre doors. There's plenty of privacy & space, & outside a small terrace faces the sunset. Cantilevered over the sea, the restaurant offers romantic sunset views while serving up a mix of Indian, Arabic, Swahili & European meals along with the

fisherman's daily catch. Diving is arranged through the on-site Pemba Misali Divers (see page 353) and all sorts of local trips can be organised. Camping facilities are also available. **$$$$**

🏠 Pattaya Guesthouse (6 rooms) m 0773 172445. This simple local guesthouse is fine if you want a feel of Pemban suburban living. Rooms, 1 of which is en suite, have nets & ceiling fans, & are named after local football teams. To get here, head north out of town, then take the first major right turn you come to – look out for the big white wall with railings on the top. Pattaya Lodge is signposted on your left, about 20m from the junction. Simple suppers of chicken & rice cost US$4 & must be ordered in advance. **$**

✕ **WHERE TO EAT AND DRINK** All the hotels and guesthouses listed above will serve meals to non-residents, although normally food has to be ordered several hours in advance. Elsewhere, most of the town's street restaurants open from approximately 07.00 until 15.00, when the market closes.

There's no shortage of **street stalls** around the market or on the main road near Le Tavern selling simple hot food during these hours, with *chipsi mai yai* at US$1, beans and rice for around US$1.30, or chicken and rice at US$3. In the same area around the road junction, more small stalls open up in the evening, selling food such as fried fish and chapattis.

✕ **Pemba Island Hotel** ⏱ 07.00–10.00 & 19.00–22.00. A large TV dominates this hotel's pleasant rooftop restaurant, which boasts views across the town to the trees beyond. For evening

meals, you'll need to order ahead. Food available includes vegetable dishes (rice US$2) & chicken curry at US$6. Soft drinks only. **$$–$$$**

✕ Bismillah This is one of the better small places around the market, & is good for a no-frills lunch. $$

✕ Ndekule Restaurant Set among the shops in the town centre, this is a good, local-style place, clean & tidy with wipe-clean plastic tables. There's usually only a few choices, such as chicken & chips or fish & rice (or vice versa) for about US$0.50. If you stroll in at lunchtime you should find something ready, while for those in a hurry there's a small take-away stand outside. $$

✕ Samail Modern Hotel & Restaurant Samail's modern ground-floor restaurant cunningly displays its cakes & ice cream in the window to tempt in passers-by. For something more substantial, hot meals such as spiced chicken & fish dishes are served with rice or biriyani (US$3.50). No alcohol. $$

✕ Afay Restaurant Popular with local people, central Afay is often open till around 22.00, with the terrace closing at 19.00, depending on trade & whether there's any food left. It serves good tea & offers pleasant service. $

✕ Balloon Brothers Café Close to the market, there's quite a choice of snacks here – samosas, cake, popcorn & *chiahoro* (like Bombay mix), as well as more substantial dishes such as *mishkaki*, or *chipsi kasava*, which are so good they inspire long queues during the lunch hour. To one side of the stand, a small seating area is available for diners. $

⊡ Milmani Coffee Centre Down a narrow side street between Afay & Ndekule, Milmani serves freshly brewed spiced coffees for just TSh100. $

✕ Nabahani Restaurant m 0777 460414. A friendly local choice next to Barclays Bank, Nabahani serves chicken & dumplings, curry & rice, soup, biriyani & omelettes for around US$2. It even does take-away. $

SHOPPING Chake Chake's **market** is in the centre of town, around the bus station. In the narrow streets leading away from the market, small shops sell an almost infinite variety of goods. If you're craving *mzungu* food, look no further than the **Why Not shop** at the northern end of town, opposite the Old Mission Lodge, where the likes of chocolate, cereal, biscuits, cheese triangles and even Pringles may be in stock, as well as good fruit juice for US$1.

OTHER PRACTICALITIES

Post and internet The post office is on the way into town from Mkoani, on the left-hand side. For internet users, **Chake Chake's Adult Training Centre** (⊕ *07.30–22.00; TSh1,000/hr*), opposite Coral Tours, has five computers and is the most reliable internet café in town. Alternatively, **Tawasul Internet** is found opposite the NMB bank and there are a couple of computers at **Naeem Telecommunication** next to Chake Chake Library, both costing TSh1,000 per hour.

WHAT TO SEE AND DO Chake Chake itself has a dusty charm that repays a walk through its small market, and around its narrow streets and alleys crowded with shops selling a wide range of goods. Definitely worth a visit is the informative **Pemba Museum** (⊕ *08.30–16.30 Mon–Fri, 09.00–16.00 Sat/Sun; admission US$3*). Located in part of the town's 18th-century Arab Fort, it retains the original wooden door, but other features were lost during restoration, and the cannons at the entrance came from Wete. Diverting exhibits are clearly laid out on five broad themes, covering every aspect of Pemba's history, economy and culture. Of particular interest are the display on the ruins of Pemba, and the room on the island's maritime history and boatbuilding, complete with a model of a *mtepe* – a boat made of coconut rope, with sticks for nails and a sail of palm leaves, that was in use until the 1930s; the original is in the House of Wonders in Zanzibar Town (see page 185). In addition to exhibitions on politics, fishing and farming, and a jailhouse (the fort was at one time Pemba's prison), there is also a considerable amount of space devoted to Swahili society. Several rooms are set out like the interior of a Swahili house, complete with relevant furniture and implements for cooking, while related displays focus on individual aspects of Swahili culture, from initiation and burial rituals to the use of herbal plants and traditional musical instruments. In the final archives room, researchers will delight in papers that have been painstakingly boxed and labelled.

AROUND CHAKE CHAKE While most places in Pemba are within easy reach of Chake Chake, there are a few places of interest that are particularly well placed for those staying in the town. Of these, the easiest to get to is the flying fox centre at Kidike (see below). It is also possible to visit the **essential oils factory** (admission US$2), where a guide can tell you about the production process. To get there, head north out of Chake Chake to the village of Machomani, then turn right towards Vitongoji; it's a ten- to 15-minute drive from the town centre, or you could take the No 316 dala dala. Oils are extracted from a variety of plants – cloves, of course, but others include citronella and eucalyptus. Interestingly, spent cloves are used to power the burners. You could combine this with a trip to Vitongoji Beach, another 10km or so to the east.

There are also a couple of archaeological sites relatively close to the town that give a glimpse into Pemba's past and provide a great reason for a day out in the country. The route to Pujini Ruins, for example, passes through scenic fields and farmland and a few small villages, while a visit to Ras Mkumbuu usually involves a beautiful boat ride down the bay, and a walk through a grove of massive palms.

Kidike (⊕ *09.00–18.00 daily; admission US$5*) Home to more than half of Pemba's flying foxes, Kidike is a shared initiative between villagers and the government. Located about 7km north of Chake Chake, it is clearly signposted from the main road. Several tour operators run trips here, and individual drivers charge around US$25 from Chake Chake, including entrance. Alternatively, you can take a dala dala from Chake Chake, and then walk the 45 minutes or so along the 3.5km track to the reserve.

Pujini Ruins The Pujini Ruins, the remains of a fortified palace built around the 15th century by Swahili people, lie about 10km to the southeast of Chake Chake, near the village of Pujini. Locally the place is called Mkame Ndume, meaning 'milker of men', derived from the name of a reputedly despotic king who ordered the palace walls be built by local inhabitants who were forced to carry large stones while shuffling on their buttocks.

Today, the ruins of the palace cover an area of about 1.5ha, and the remains of the defensive ramparts and surrounding ditches can still be seen, although much of the area is overgrown. The ditch was once connected to the sea by a 1km-long channel. Inside the walls, a team of archaeologists working here since the mid 1990s have found remnants of three large buildings, and an underground shrine with plaster bas-reliefs on the walls, and several other features. It is also possible to see some wide stairways that presumably allowed access to the defensive ramparts, the remains of a walkway that joined the town to the shore, and the site of the well. Legend tells of a wall that was built across the well so that the ruler's two wives, who lived in separate parts of the palace, would never meet if they came to get water at the same time.

The ramparts are the most interesting feature of the Pujini Ruins, in that they can be seen and appreciated by any visitor, and also because there is nothing else like them at any other Swahili site along the east African coast. They were built when the

Swahili civilisation was at its zenith (see *History*, pages 5–6), and when the presence of Portuguese ships in the area posed a very real threat. It seems, however, that the walls may not have been strong enough to withstand the invaders: some Portuguese records dating from the 1520s mention the sacking of a fortified 'treasury' on the east coast of Pemba.

Archaeological evidence suggests that, although the palace may have fallen on hard times after this invasion, it remained occupied (or was possibly re-occupied) and was only finally abandoned in the 19th century. Remains of other buildings, including a mosque, have been found in the area around the palace, suggesting that it did not stand alone, and that a town or larger settlement also existed here – possibly for many centuries.

Getting there You can **walk** the 8km or so from Chake Chake to the Pujini Ruins and back in a day, or take **bus** Route 319 as far as Pujini village, but it is easier to travel by **hired bike** or **car**. To get there, leave Chake Chake on the road south, and turn left onto a dirt road just after the tar road turns off to the airport. Follow the dirt road to a fork near a small dispensary, where you go left. At the next junction, go right to reach a flat grassy area which is usually wet. The ruins are amongst the trees and bushes on the far side of the grassy area. (If you get lost, ask for directions to Mkame Ndume.)

Ras Mkumbuu Ruins

The headland of Ras Mkumbuu is at the end of a long peninsula about 14km to the west of Chake Chake. The relatively well-preserved ruins are at the tip of the peninsula and also seem to be called Ndagoni (although Mkumbuu and Ndagoni may have been different places). This is the site of a Swahili settlement, thought to have been one of the largest towns on the coast (and in east Africa) during the 11th century. It is also considered to be the site of the earlier port of Qanbalu, where Omani sailors traded in slaves and timber.

Today, the remains of a large 13th-century mosque can still be seen, although they are becoming very overgrown, and there are also several 14th-century pillar tombs, graves with a tall 'chimney' at one end, used to mark the burial place of prominent Muslims. Pillar tombs are found in other parts of east Africa and are held to be one of the most distinctive forms of monument built by the Swahili people. The tombs here are in poor condition, although an inscription on one states that they were restored in 1916.

Getting there The easiest and most enjoyable way to reach the ruins is by **hired boat**, or on an **organised tour** – which may also visit Misali Island (see page 362) on the same day. Near the ruins is a small fishing village, and to reach the mosque and tombs you walk through maize fields and a plantation of tall palms with smooth white trunks. A road from Chake Chake leads westwards along the peninsula towards Ras Mkumbuu, but it becomes impassable and turns into a track for the final 5km, which is negotiable only on foot or by bike.

SOUTH OF CHAKE CHAKE

The main road from Chake Chake south to Mkoani follows a winding route through hilly terrain clothed by an abundance of fruit trees, interspersed by villages at every turn. Bananas grow freely, with jackfruit, passion fruit, breadfruit, mango and papaya all very much in evidence. In season, cloves lie drying on mats by the side of the road, their scent pervading the air. Look out in particular for the trees to the east of the road that are home to the Pemba flying fox.

MKOANI Mkoani is the smallest of Pemba's three main towns, but the passenger-boat services linking it to Zanzibar Town and the mainland make the port the busiest and most important on the island. Any time a boat is docking or leaving there's a buzz in the air, and perhaps the opportunity to watch boats being loaded with cloves for Zanzibar, but for the rest of the time Mkoani is very quiet and sleepy. Although a few businesses are located near the port, and the market is just along the coast, the main town of Mkoani is up the hill towards Chake Chake. A footpath leads up some steps from opposite the port towards the town, cutting out the bends. The deserted port area is unlit at night and it's not advisable to walk there unaccompanied.

Where to stay
For some visitors, Mkoani remains the main gateway to Pemba, and a couple of local guesthouses cater for this, but the closure of some in recent years reflects the increasing reliance by visitors on air travel.

Zanzibar Ocean Panorama (4 rooms)
024 2456166; m 0773 545418; e info@
zanzibaroceanpanorama.com; www.
zanzibaroceanpanorama.com. Hot on the heels
of the Jondeni, & just down the road, Zanzibar
Ocean Panorama opened in 2012. The name was
obviously inspired by the excellent sea view from
the guesthouse's advantageous location high up
on a hill. Don't let the slightly ramshackle exterior
of the bungalows put you off; inside, the rooms are
better than expected, with stone floors, Zanzibari
beds, a desk & chair, fan & AC, a fridge, & clean
en-suite showers. Outside, each has a tidy terrace
with a hammock facing the sea. B/fast is served in
the shaded restaurant (other meals with advanced
notice; dinner US$15). **$$**

Jondeni Guesthouse (8 rooms) 024
2456042; e jondeniguesthouse@hotmail.com.
Once by far the best place to stay in Mkoani, the
guesthouse is to the north of town, a dusty 10–
15min walk uphill from the port, & looks out over
Mkoani Bay. The bungalow is set in lush gardens,
complete with hammock, & the friendly staff make
staying here a pleasure. Clean, simple rooms – some
en suite – have Zanzibari beds, AC, fans & mosquito
nets. A bed in the 6-bed dormitory is available for
US$15pp. Bathrooms are fine if a little dark. Drinks
& meals such as grilled octopus with mashed potato
(around US$7) are available, taken on a dhow table
on the shady terrace overlooking the sea – a perfect
place for whiling away a hot afternoon. There's also
a TV, or if you're feeling more active, snorkelling,
sailing, fishing & island tours. **$–$$**

Where to eat
Apart from the hotels above, both of which serve food, places to eat in Mkoani are very limited. There's a small restaurant close to the hospital, at the

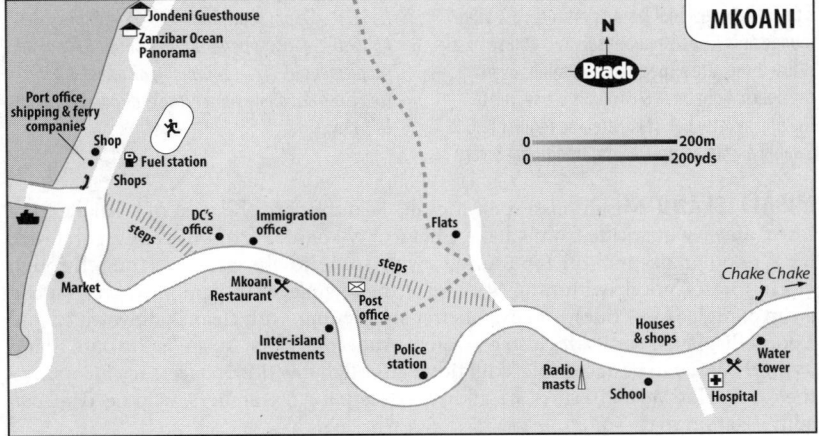

eastern end of town, but that's pretty well it. A couple of stalls sell fruit, sweets and biscuits for the passing boat-passenger trade.

Travel agents and tour companies Almost next to the quay, Mkoani's port office is open from 08.00 to 15.30 daily. Tickets can be bought here for the ferries that run between Pemba and Zanzibar Island (see page 347).

Other practicalities Aside from the hospital, towards the eastern end of town, Mkoani has very little to offer the visitor. A couple of communications centres lie on the road near the port, and in the centre of Mkoani is the post office and a small shop selling groceries, towards the north of town.

WAMBAA The small village of Wambaa is to the north of Mkoani. Nearby is the long and idyllic Wambaa Beach, facing southwest overlooking Mkoani Bay and out towards the Pemba Channel. At its northern end lies Pemba's most exclusive hotel, Fundu Lagoon.

⌂ Where to stay

⌂ **Fundu Lagoon** (18 rooms) Reservations ☏ 024 2232926; hotel m 0774 438668; e info@ fundulagoon.com; www.fundulagoon.com; ⊙ mid Jun–mid Apr. It's not difficult to see why honeymooners & retired couples flock to this secluded lodge, 15mins by boat from Mkoani. Combining the flexibility of a hotel with the individuality of a smaller lodge, it's a relaxed hideaway on the beach with attentive service & a lively atmosphere. Linked to the central area by sandy walkways, tented rooms nestle among the trees to form the core of each carefully designed, thatched bungalow. Inside is wicker & wood furniture of wicker & small en-suite bathrooms showcase the hotel's own range of handmade aromatherapy toiletries. Each bungalow has its own veranda, facing out to sea, whilst suites offer a private plunge pool & superior suites a 2-storey lounge area. The restaurant serves 3-course meals – fish dishes are a speciality – & tables overlook the beach; light bites & cocktails are served in the breezy jetty bar. There are also regular BBQ & Swahili nights, complete with traditional & very enthusiastic singing & dancing. When it comes to activities, snorkelling, kayaking & fishing are on offer, & there's a fully equipped dive centre (see *Diving*, page 353). Rather less strenuous are the sunset dhow cruises, boat trips to Misali Island & poolside loungers with panoramic ocean views. There's also a popular treatment room with a wide range of massages & beauty treatments (US$15– 120), & a games room with satellite TV. Excursions to the village of Wambaa can be arranged, as can hair braiding, & in the evenings a local lady is on hand to give free henna tattoos. It's quite isolated here but that's part of the appeal. It's also fairly relaxed, & bare feet are actively encouraged. It's worth noting that researchers for this book & holidaymakers have consistently disagreed over the quality of the finishing & food. *Hillside US$370–435pp; beachfront US$405–480pp; suite US$580–545pp; superior suite US$660–750pp; sgl supplement US$135–240/night; all rates FB & inc canoe use & a dhow sunset cruise; airport transfer US$45pp.*

MISALI ISLAND Misali (also spelt Mesali) Island lies to the west of Chake Chake town, an easy boat ride from Chake Chake or Mkoani. Surrounded by a coral reef, it's a popular destination for tourists, with some idyllic beaches, trails through virgin forests, good swimming (it's one of the few places in Pemba where you can swim at high or low tide), and even better snorkelling, with clear shallow water, and a good display of corals. It's also a favourite spot for divers. Misali is the only island around Pemba to be accessible in all tides, although low tide is necessary for visiting the caves. No overnight stays are allowed, except for researchers, who need special authorisation to do so.

The island is covered in forest, with a mix of evergreen and deciduous species, and most notably many large baobabs. Vervet monkeys cavort among the branches, peering down at visitors. Birds to be spotted here include red-eyed dove, mangrove kingfisher, paradise flycatcher, Pemba white-eye and Pemba sunbird. Fischer's turaco has also been recorded. An increasing number of green sea turtles are successfully nesting on the beach on the western side of the island, with hawksbill turtles also present.

Locally, Misali has 'holy island' status. When the Prophet Hadhara found himself without a prayer mat, it is said that he made use instead of the teardrop-shaped island which faces Mecca; the word *msala* means 'prayer mat'. The strong Islamic environmental stewardship ethic is being used to support management and environmental education, and the island was a 'sacred gift for a living planet' from the Islamic faith as part of a millennium celebration organised by WWF in 2000.

The notorious pirate Captain Kidd is reputed to have had a hideout on the island in the 17th century, and even to have buried treasure here. Today, the island and the surrounding reef are incorporated in the government-owned Misali Island Marine Conservation Area, under the auspices of the Misali Island Management Committee. Formed as a partnership between the Zanzibar government, the local fishermen's association and the Pemba Ecological Conservation Authority (PECA), with support from CARE International, the committee is dominated by fishermen, while the rangers, who can also offer guided island tours, are employed by PECA. It's not entirely satisfactory, with considerable concerns locally about infringements of the no-take zone to the west of the island, and armed soldiers have recently been introduced to support the rangers. In its previous incarnation as MICA (Misali Island Conservation Association), PECA's authority covered a smaller area. With the change to MICA, a larger area is still covered by the same number of rangers, whose workload has now escalated while their motivation has decreased.

Almost two-thirds of the revenue from visitors goes towards managing the island, with the rest earmarked for community development. Conservation measures involve the input of local fishermen, who can continue working here in a managed environment. As just one example of how the scheme is working, local fishermen are prevented from camping on the beach itself (they camp among the trees), so as not to disturb turtles nesting. Additionally, the nests are monitored and protected, along with the rest of the island, by the rangers.

Just 1.4km long, and covering a total area of 90ha, the island consists of 15,000-year-old uplifted coral, with a surrounding coral reef to a maximum depth of 64m. Mangroves fringe much of the island, making a fascinating place for snorkelling during spring high tides. A series of walking trails has been established through the forest, where there are three caves that are considered sacred. In time of need, local people would come to one of the caves with a witchdoctor to pray for help, making payment in the form of a chicken, a goat or even a cow. It takes about 2½ hours to walk round the island (at low tide only), taking in an intertidal trail to the west of the island. At the landing point for visitors, there is a shaded information centre, with benches for picnics, rudimentary toilets and displays on what to see with a good map showing the various trails. On the beach in front, a few sunbeds and umbrellas have been set out, but banish all thoughts of commercialism – it remains a tranquil spot visited by just a few people at any one time.

Getting there Misali Island can be reached by **hired boat** from Chake Chake or Mkoani (see the *Boat hire* and *Travel and tour companies* sections on pages 349 and 355 respectively). There are also **organised excursions** run by various local tour operators, as well as by individual hotels for their guests. In addition, a few of the dive centres based in the northern part of Zanzibar Island run trips here. Occasionally, the island is also visited by groups from passing cruise ships and live-aboards.

Some unlicensed **fishing boats** run to the island, but few have life jackets or backup engines. One that does is the *Victoria*, owned by Captain Hamoud, who can be found at Chake Chake's port area of Wesha. Pemba Misali Divers (see *Diving*, page 353) can also arrange boats to the island.

SHAMIANI ISLAND Surrounded by magroves, Shamiani Island, also called Kiweni Island, is a remote and beautiful spot east of Mkoani, just 100m or so off the far southeastern tip of Pemba Island. Shamiani was originally settled by Persian immigrants in the 17th century, who built the island's first mosque, the ruins of which can still be visited. Shamiani's population of around 150 families rely on fishing and farming for their livelihood and live in just one small village with a school, a doctor and a mosque. Until recently there were no visitors, as the island was accessible only to the very determined. Now, the development of a new, eco-friendly lodge brings a smattering of tourists, providing income and employment to the island, as well as endless fascination to the local children, still not used to the unfamiliar ways of the *mzungu*. The tourist industry on the island is still in the fledgling stages, and there's no electricity, cars or bikes on the island, just boats.

Getting there Travel to Shamiani involves taking some form of transport from Chake Chake to the village of Kengeja, reached by branching off the main Mkoani to Chake Chake road at Mtambile. Then from either Mpene or Kiwimbini harbours, both located on small inlets south of Kengeja, locals wade across but visitors sail across to Dongoni, Shamiani's access point. Guests heading to Pemba Eco Lodge will have the entire transfer from Chake Chake organised by the lodge.

🏠 Where to stay

🏠 **Pemba Eco Lodge** (see advertisement on the 1st page of the 2nd colour insert) (5 bungalows) ✆ 0732 495077/88; e info@pembalodge.com; www.pembalodge.com; ☉ May–Mar. Pemba Eco Lodge, with an emphasis on the 'eco', is the vision of enthusiastic Pemban Nassor Ali, owner of the popular Mnarani Beach Cottages (see *Where to stay*, page 228) on Zanzibar. Focused on those seeking both privacy & R&R, it is designed to create minimum environmental impact. Inspiration has been taken from Chumbe Island's excellent example of how an eco lodge might work, & some of the staff have trained there, as well as at Mnarani. The 4 dbl & 1 family timber-frame bungalows are constructed from natural materials, with makuti thatch, woven palm walls & locally crafted coconut wood & recycled dhow furniture. Features include not just solar-powered lighting (which can make the room seem a little dark), hot water, & composting toilets, but also a building design that harnesses the breeze from the Pemba Channel, obviating the need for energy-guzzling AC. No plastic bottles are used & rainwater is collected in a 10,000 litre reservoir. Access to the lodge is an adventure in itself: arrive by traditional (though motorised) boat through the mangroves, passing sailing villagers & children heading for school, schoolbooks held above their heads as they wade across at low tide. Boats dock at Dongoni in a low or neap tide & it's a hot & hard 20min walk over unforgiving coral rock to the lodge, with luggage carried by porter or ox-cart. For all other tides the boats can land right on the beach. There are plans to build a resthouse at Mpene, where guests can wait for the tide to come in & avoid this walk. Dinner is 'catch of the day' cooked over a gas flame. Filtered drinking water is free in the bar, there's an honesty bar & all non-alcoholic drinks are included in the rates. There's no pool, but the beach is simply stunning, with white sand & turquoise sea; it's also blissfully deserted. When the tide's in, kayaking trips can be undertaken in the mangroves. There's also a 30ft catamaran with 2 cabins, based between here & Mnarani in Nungwi. For something more cultural, try a Pemban cooking class or a trip to the local village. The lodge is heavily involved with the conservation of green turtles – they pay compensation to the fishermen for any caught up in fishing nets that are brought in. These turtles are put in a tidal lake to breed & groups are released every 6 months, an event that guests are welcome to get involved in. There is very slow dial-up internet here but do not rely on it; instead come for ecological sensibility & peace & quiet on a deserted beach. *US$220pp FB inc soft drinks, kayaking & snorkelling.*

WETE

The second-largest town on Pemba, Wete is at the head of a large inlet on the west coast, in the northern part of the island. Spread out down a long central street, it's quieter than Chake Chake, with more ox-carts and fewer mopeds. For most travellers Wete is a good base for exploring northern Pemba: from here Tumbe, the Chwaka Ruins, Konde and Ngezi Forest can all be easily reached. The people are exceptionally friendly and willing to assist, although as most just pass through on their way to the northern resorts, you'll more than likely be the only foreigner in town.

Wete has a large harbour, mainly used by cargo ships and dhows. It can sometimes be busy here, with vessels from Tanga offloading cement or timber, and loading up with cloves, coconuts or other Pemban commodities. Local ferries also sail across the inlet to Mtambwe Island, where you can get to the ruins of Mtambwe Mkuu, and to Fundo Island.

GETTING THERE AND AWAY North of Chake Chake, the dense vegetation of the south gives way to open pasture and scrubland. The main road bypasses Wete entirely as it hugs the eastern side of the island, but it is still the quickest route between the two towns. The turn-off to Wete is about 20km from Chake Chake at the village of Chwale. From here it's a reasonable, intermittently tarred road to Mzambaroani, past the rubber plantation where what look like old flannels are hung out on racks to dry in the sun, before winding the last few kilometres to Wete.

GETTING AROUND If you want to reach the places of interest around Wete independently, Royal Tours can help with **car hire** and the Sharook brothers can hire out **bikes** for US$30 per day.

TRAVEL AND TOUR COMPANIES Various shacks and shops along the main street advertise that they sell ferry tickets, but the only tour operator is **Royal Tours & Travel (m** 0778 143426/0777 429244; **e** royaltours@live.com). Up in the north of town, this helpful office handles everything from tour guiding services, flights, hotels, Pemba tours, diving and snorkelling and it sells tickets for the fast ferries. Good English is spoken, as long as the manager is in.

For additional services, the **Sharook Guesthouse** (see *Where to stay*, below) offers a good range of tours: a boat ride to Mtambwe Mkuu Ruins costs US$5 per person; a minibus to Ngezi Forest costs US$35. Highly recommended all-day trips to Fundo Island cost US$30 for the whole motorboat (seating up to ten) or US$27 for a dhow; or you can go to Misali Island for US$50.

WHERE TO STAY

Sharook Guesthouse (5 rooms) 024 2454386; **e** sharookguest@yahoo.com. Owned & run by the Sharook brothers, this guesthouse is in the lower part of town, on a quiet side street near the market & bus station. It's a small, family-run place with a peaceful & friendly atmosphere.

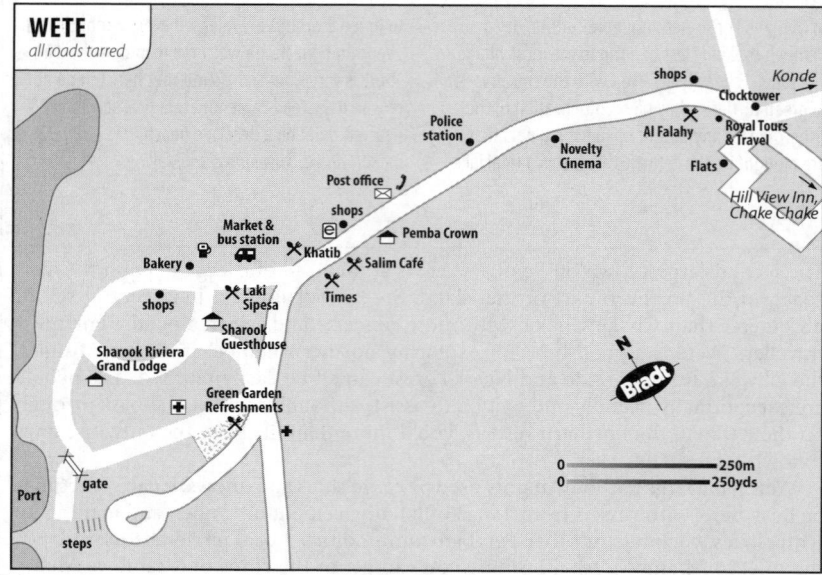

With its own generator, it offers constant running water & functioning TV. Dinner (US$10), with local dishes, must be ordered well in advance, & is served in front of the TV in the dining room. Bike hire (US$10/day) can be arranged, as can a range of tours around the island. **$**

🏠 **Sharook Riviera Grand Lodge** (8 rooms) Located in a sleepy, residential area overlooking the harbour, this rather impressive-sounding annex to Sharook Guesthouse is not nearly as magnificent as the name suggests. The building itself is newly constructed, & inside sgl & dbl rooms plus a dorm are filled with Zanzibari beds covered in colourful bedspreads, & have a fan, AC & an en-suite bathroom with hot water. The communal space is made up of the b/fast room & a lounge with a computer & TV. Meals can be ordered in advance & are freshly prepared; juices, water & soft drinks are served but no alcohol. There are plans for a rooftop restaurant. **$**

🏠 **Pemba Crown Hotel** (12 rooms)
📞 024 2454191; m 0777 4936667; e sales@ pembacrown.com; www.pembacrown.com. Pemba Crown is a 3-storey hotel above a row of shops on the main street, right in the centre of Wete. Since it opened in 2007, it has become Wete's best accommodation option. The rooms are comfortable, & the staff smiley & helpful. Spotless bedrooms come with AC, fans & TVs, while

colour is added by pretty linen. Soaps are even provided– a rarity in Wete's basic guesthouses. All rooms have a large balcony overlooking a busy street, & it's interesting to see people going about their everyday business. B/fast is the only meal served. **$$**

🏠 **Hillview Inn** (10 rooms) m 0777 863310/428365; e omarjumakhatib@yahoo. co.uk. When approaching Wete from Chake Chake, you'll spot the large signpost to Hillview just before reaching the town itself. In a rather unsavoury residential area, the basic rooms contain little more than a bed, fan, mosquito net & crinkled lino flooring. 5 rooms have a bathroom, while the others share, although strangely the rooms all cost the same (TSh20,000). Decoration comes in the form of mismatched curtains & rather scary paintings of dogs. 1 room has a balcony with a disappointing view of a hill, hence the hotel's name. The whole place could do with a good scrub & a fresh coat of paint, but the linen is freshly laundered & the manager a jovial, helpful sort. They are incredibly proud of their modem, & charge guests US$6.50 for a week's painfully slow internet. The room price includes a 'continental' b/fast but other meals must be ordered in advance for around US$6. **$**

✗ WHERE TO EAT All the hotels and guesthouses serve food with advance notice, and Wete also has a choice of local eating-houses, most open until the last buses have left at 16.00. Several are located to the west of town, close to the port and bus station. **Green Garden Refreshments**, a pleasant open-air café, sells omelette and chips or beans and rice for around US$1, with more expensive meals, based on beef and chicken, also available. It's open all day, but not always at weekends. Opposite the market and bus station, **Laki Sipesa** (which means '100,000 has no value') serves pilau rice and meat, plus bread, chapattis and tea, while next door is the **Khatib Restaurant**, which dishes up omelettes and bread and has a fridge full of cold sodas outside it. There's also a good bakery next to the market.

Further up the main street, away from the port, is the **Salim Café**. A large place with loud television, it's popular with locals, who recommend the biryani and pilau at US$1 each. Unusually, it's open all day from 07.00–22.00. Next to Salim, the best choice in town is the **Times Restaurant**, worth going to for the air conditioning alone, but it also serves up good pizza, curries, grilled meats (US$4), fishcakes (US$1.50) and sandwiches (US$2), all served on neatly laid tables and accompanied by English-language newspapers. Up towards the clock tower in the north of town, the **Al Falahy Hotel**, which is not a hotel despite the name, serves tasty snacks and fried bread. Nearby, a number of small local cafés vie with street stalls selling the usual range of fare, including – we've heard – very good octopus and chapattis, with sugar-cane juice to drink at TSh150.

OTHER PRACTICALITIES The **post office** (⊕ *08.00–13.00 & 14.00–16.00 Mon–Thu, 08.00–noon & 14.00–17.00 Fri*) is on the right of the main street about halfway towards the port. Wete's only **internet café** is found in the small row of shops opposite the Pemba Crown Hotel, where there's also a bureau de change, although shortages of Tanzanian shillings are common and the rates aren't great.

BULLFIGHTING ON PEMBA

Somewhat surprisingly, the island of Pemba is a place where you might see Iberian-style bullfighting. The origins of this sport are uncertain although it is thought to have been introduced by the Portuguese during the 16th century. Bullfights take place close to Wingwi, in the northeast of the island, during holiday times, mostly between August and November after the harvest and before the short rains, but also between December and February after the short rains. Local matadors put on a brave display, posing in front of the bull, goading him into a charge and then standing aside at the last moment, much to the appreciation of watching villagers. At the end of the fight, the bull is not killed but praised by the fighter, and sometimes decorated with flowers and leaves, then paraded around the village.

If you happen to be in Pemba when a bullfight is planned, it's worth going to see, but, although sometimes it can be a lively and fascinating spectacle, a few visitors have reported that in reality some bullfights can be fairly uneventful, and seem to involve a group of local wide boys annoying an apathetic cow by beating her with sticks, while the local girls shriek loudly.

Exactly when a bullfight is about to take place is hard to find out. Ask at your hotel or a reliable tour company, such as Msewe Travel in Chake Chake (see page 355) for more details.

12

WHAT TO SEE AND DO

Mtambwe Mkuu The ruins of Mtambwe Mkuu are on the small island of Mtambwe, which is joined to the mainland at low tide, directly south of Wete. For over 1,000 years, it was one of the most prosperous ports of east Africa. The 'Mtambwe hoard', a collection of coins found near the beach in 1984, included gold coins dating from 11th-century Egypt, and one of very few examples of pre-colonial minted silver currency anywhere in east Africa. Despite its rich past, there's little to see at Mtambwe Mkuu these days, although a trip there from Wete is a very pleasant way to spend the day.

Getting there and away From Wete harbour you go by small **dhow** or **canoe** to Mtambwe village, then **walk** south, west and north around a creek and through mangrove swamps to reach the ruins. Apparently, when the water is high, you can get cut off at the ruins, or be forced to wade back to Mtambwe village through the mangroves, so careful checking of the tides is recommended. Sharook Guesthouse or Royal Tours (see page 365) in Wete can arrange tours or give you advice.

NORTH OF WETE Although there are more direct routes from Wete to the north of the island, it is quicker to head east to Chwale, then take the main tarred road north. This also has the advantage of passing close to many of Pemba's places of interest, so makes for an interesting journey in its own right.

From Chwale, the landscape is mainly farmland, dotted with coconut palms as it heads up the east coast. Just before the turn-off to Micheweni, in an area generally known as Wingwi, is a rather unprepossessing stretch of green which, come the end of the year and at times of government celebration, plays host to the island's bullfights (see box, *Bullfighting on Pemba*, page 367).

Kiuyu Peninsula To the east of the main north–south road, a narrow isthmus separates the rest of Pemba from the Kiuyu Peninsula. A rough road, north of the 'bullring', leads to the village of Micheweni (about 5km), which has a school, a hospital and a few shops, but no place to stay. (Confusingly, Micheweni is also sometimes called Wingwi, the name not only of the area but also of another village a few kilometres to the south.) The road deteriorates from here passing through the village of Kiuyu, and becoming a deep-red dirt track, reminiscent of mainland Africa, before it reaches **Ras Kiuyu Forest Reserve**, almost at the tip of the peninsula. It's a remote and somewhat inaccessible place, smaller than the forest at Ngezi (see pages 371–2) and with a less impressive range of vegetation and wildlife. Nevertheless, it has been highly recommended as a day trip from Wete or even Chake Chake, as much for the interesting journey through the fields and villages as for the forest itself. The unspoilt Kiuyu Beach, to the east of the forest, is an added attraction.

Getting there and away By **public transport**, you can catch an early dala dala from Wete to Micheweni. From here, it's a 5km walk to the village of Kiuyu and another 5km into the forest itself. About 3km beyond Kiuyu village, a narrow track branches right (east) to Kiuyu Beach. Nearby, another track branches left to a small beach on the west of the peninsula called Mbuyu Kambaa. The only alternative is to hire a driver with a **4x4**, since the road beyond Micheweni is unsuitable for other vehicles.

Chwaka ruins Continuing north from the bullring, near the coast, are the ruins of the town of Chwaka. Dating from as early as the 9th century, the town was active as a port in the 15th century, probably linked to a network of villages trading with the east African coast and beyond. The ruins are sometimes referred to as Harouni, a reflection of the town's association with a local king called Harouni, who was the son of Mkama Ndume, builder of Pujini (see pages 359–60).

The most easily recognised buildings are two small mosques, standing well apart. The larger and better-preserved Friday mosque is also the site of the king's tomb. Local legend has it that the two mosques were built because the king's two wives were constantly at loggerheads, and that the town was eventually destroyed by the second wife's family.

There are also remains of houses and tombs. Nearby stood another group of tombs and an 18th-century fort built by the Mazrui group of Omanis, and on the other side of the road are some more remains called Old Tumbe. As with most of Pemba's ruins, don't go expecting a major archaeological find, but it's an interesting place and offers free rein to the imagination.

Getting there and away Chwaka is signposted to the east of the main road between Wete and Tumbe, just north of where it crosses a swampy area on an embankment with metal crash barriers on either side. The ten-minute **walk** takes you through cassava fields and past lofty palms, with a splendid view over the bay towards Micheweni as you approach the ruins themselves.

Tumbe The village of Tumbe, not far from the Chwaka Ruins, has the largest fish market on Pemba. Particularly busy in the mornings, it attracts people from all over the island to buy fish, which they carry away in plaited baskets strapped to the back of bicycles. It's an interesting place for visitors to watch the boats come in with fish of all sizes.

Tumbe lies off the main tar road about 5km east of Konde, and can be reached by **bus** or **bike** from Wete, or with a **hired car**. A **dala dala** stops at the junction, from where it's a pleasant walk through the long, narrow village to the coast; by car, it's about a ten-minute drive from the main road.

Konde Near the end of the tarred road, the small town of Konde is also the end of the road for the dala dala network, and the last place to stock up for a picnic before venturing further north to Ngezi Forest and Vumawimbi Beach. Men on bicycles weave up and down the dusty main street, with palm-leaf baskets strapped to the back laden with produce. During market hours, until 14.00, fruit stalls line the road, and there's a bakery selling fresh bread. There's also a restaurant where dishes such as pilau and *chipsi maiyai* can be bought for around US$1.50. Konde is well known for making excellent breads.

NGEZI PENINSULA

The Ngezi Peninsula is the northernmost point on Pemba, jutting out from the northwestern corner of the island. Beyond Konde, a significant area is taken up by **Ngezi Forest**, the last remains of a huge tract of indigenous forest which used to cover much of Pemba.

Curving round the eastern side of the peninsula is **Vumawimbi Beach**, one of the most beautiful on Pemba, with miles of dazzling white sand flanked by pristine forest. Here and there fishermen sit and mend their nets, watching over their ngalawas as they wait for the tide, and occasionally an ox-cart rolls along the sand. Rumours have abounded for years about the construction of a hotel, but for now the beach remains remote and unspoilt. You can walk to the beach across the fields from Ngezi Forest or the Manta Resort, or go with a driver.

The west of the peninsula is flanked by the long expanse of **Verani Beach** with, at its northern end, a place called **Pango Ya Watoro** ('the cave of the fugitives'). At low tide, sandbanks dry out offshore, and boat trips from the nearby Manta Resort take visitors out with a picnic to swim and snorkel. It's possible to walk along the beach to the **lighthouse** near Ras Kigomasha, but only at low tide, so do check carefully before setting out; there's an alternative route through the fields if the water is up. Built by the British in the 1800s, the lighthouse offers some outstanding views out to sea and across the lush green landscape of northern Pemba. It costs US$4 per person to climb the 95 narrow steps to the top – just ask at the house nearby for the lighthouse keeper.

GETTING THERE AND AWAY You can get from Wete as far as Konde by **dala dala**, but from there you'll have to **walk** the 5km along the road, bordered by farmland, to the Ngezi Forest entrance gate. If you make an early start this walk is a nice part of the day out. Alternatively, and especially if you want to go on to one of the beaches, you'll need to hire a **car** from Wete or Chake, for which you can expect to pay US$50–70 for the day, or travel as part of an **organised tour** (see pages 365 and 355 respectively). Beyond the entrance gate to Ngezi Forest the road is rough, and to get to the beach is sandy too, so unless it's dry a high-clearance **4x4** is recommended.

WHERE TO STAY It's possible to visit the forest and beaches around Ngezi for the day, and stay overnight in Wete or Chake Chake. Alternatively, there's one basic guesthouse and a couple of more upmarket places to stay nearby.

The Manta Resort (17 rooms) m 0776 718852; e stacey@themantaresort.com; www. themantaresort.com; ◔ Jun–Apr. Overlooking the northern end of Verani Beach, in a truly stunning location, the Manta Resort is a smart beach resort catering to divers through its own PADI dive centre, 360 Dive Pemba (see *Diving*, page 353), & landlubbers alike. The seafront villas are built on, with panoramic views across the Pemba Channel. With AC, a big dbl bed, small lounge area & en-suite bathroom, these are the resort's premium rooms. The superior garden rooms set behind the villas are less open, with views across the gardens but optional interconnecting doors make them good for families. They are cool inside, with AC & rustic 4-poster beds. Standard garden rooms are more basic, with standing fans only. A central area serves as dining room, bar, lounge & lobby, with a big terrace looking out to sea & steps leading down to the beach & a 2-tiered beach bar, though be careful of sea urchins. For entertainment & relaxation, there is a pool, a cocktail bar & a small selection of books. There's deliberately no TV or phones, though the lack of any music takes a little away from the atmosphere, especially in the eerily

quiet bar. Aside from watersports, guests benefit from a wide range of birdlife & some interesting walks to the lighthouse, Vumawimbi Beach & Ngezi Forest (5km). Other options include kayaking (free), boat trips & small-scale fishing (US$50/hr), plus hand-line fishing with a local fisherman (US$40), as well as village tours & massages in the Kipepeo Spa, where 1 massage per day is included in the FB rates. Internet is available, & there's Wi-Fi & a computer in the lounge. No children under 7. FB; airport transfer US$40 pp, under 12 free. ⚓

Kervan Saray Beach (22 rooms) m 0773 176737/8; e resort@kayakpemba.com; www. kervansaraybeach.com. Owned & managed by Turkish adventurer Raf Jah & his Dutch anthropologist wife, Cisca, Kervan Saray Beach is a simple & unpretentious affair. Located close to the small village of Makangale, its thatched cottages are just above a sand & rock beach that is excellent for swimming at high tide. Bungalows contain cool & spacious rooms, with a dbl bed raised up on a plinth, complete with orange-trim mosquito net, an en-suite bathroom & a solar-heated outdoor shower. There is generator power 18.00–06.00 for light, but laptops & cameras can be charged in the office at other times. The rooms are really lovely, with fresh flowers, slatted windows & oodles of colour, but be sure to ask for a newer one, as older, un-refurbished rooms have cold water only & though pleasant, are a tad worn out. The lodge boasts a PADI 5* Resort Dive Centre with a team who are experienced in the surrounding reefs & sometimes challenging waters (see Swahili Divers, page 353). Snorkellers, sunbathers & cruisers are more than welcome to hop on board, too. Birdwatching tours can be arranged to see Pemba's 4 endemic species. Trips are free for guests who pre-book as birders, but park fees are extra (see below). Kayaking (US$70pp for a half-day), fishing, local hikes & trips to the Ngezi Forest are also on offer. Aside from making sure everyone has a good time, the lodge is trying hard to maintain a low carbon footprint & to work with the local community. **$$$$**

🏠 **Verani Beach Hotel** (5 rooms)
m 0777 414408/2; e info@veranibeach.com; www.veranibeach.com. The friendly smiles & owner's warm welcome give a good 1st impression but alas the rooms spectacularly fail to live up to the initial promise. The 5 rooms are spacious enough with traditional ceilings, a table & 2 colourful beds draped in mosquito nets, but there's no electricity (paraffin & pressure lamps provide lighting), & cracked floors & ceilings are open to the elements & some pretty huge spiders. The bathroom is very compact, & bathers must sit on the toilet in order to shower. If you can't stomach the room, you can try camping (US$15pp inc b/fast) with tents provided at extra cost. 6 hours' notice is needed for all meals (US$7–10) except b/fast, as fresh ingredients are bought to order. The lodge offers fishing trips, using traditional boats & also owns a small sailing boat & a motorboat for snorkelling & Misali Island trips. Creek safaris are also offered – sail along the coast to explore the mangroves & indulge in a spot of snorkelling (US$25pp). There are plans to add more rooms & move the restaurant to the rocks overlooking the sea, so let's hope the standards improve at the same time. The hotel can arrange transfers. **$$**

NGEZI FOREST RESERVE (⊕ *07.30–15.30 daily; admission short tour US$5pp, longer tour or birdwatching US$10; transit fee US$2; night walks by prior arrangement*) This reserve is virtually all that remains of a vast area of indigenous forest that used to cover much of the island. One of the highlights of Pemba, especially if you have an interest in wildlife, is that it offers the opportunity to discover Pemba as it once was. It's advisable not to arrive too early because mosquitoes remain active in the morning.

A 2km **nature trail** takes in sections of moist forest, and several large ponds. A **guided walk** with the rangers takes about an hour, and is a must if you want to have a brief insight into the forest's different habitats and to spot some of the animals and birds that live among the trees. Tips are negotiable, but it's reasonable to give around US$5 for a small group. Birdwatching trips can be organised, too, as can walks in the late evening, or at night, when you have a much better chance of seeing the Pemba flying fox and the russet scops owl. To set up a trip of this ilk, contact the rangers' office in advance, during opening hours.

History Historically, the forest was used by local people, as it provided timber, fuelwood, edible plants, medicinal plants, and material for baskets and ropes, but at the same time areas of forest were being cleared for small-scale agriculture, and since the early 19th century for large plantations – especially for cloves. Although the first forest inventory was carried out in the 1920s, it wasn't until 30 years later that the reserve was established. Even then, a commercial sawmill owned by one Vi Arnjosh continued to extract timber until the mid 1960s, when the government officially took control. The rude hut in which he lived and the rusting remnants of his sawmill can be seen on the nature trail.

Through the 1970s and 1980s Ngezi was virtually ignored by the government, while encroachment and overuse by local people endangered the forest and its wildlife. Then, in 1995, funds were received from the Forest and Park Service of

12

Finland, and a management plan was drawn up to preserve the remaining forest by strengthening conservation efforts and improving management. In this way, people from the ten villages within the reserve could still utilise the forest, but at a sustainable rate, and wildlife could also benefit. It is hoped that the forest can be developed to attract tourists as a way of raising revenue – which would in turn ensure its future protection.

Ecology The reserve covers just 1,476ha but the variety of soil types has resulted in a wide range of vegetation. Dominant are 943ha of tropical moist forest, which once covered most of the island. Found mainly in the central and eastern parts of the reserve (the part most easily reached by visitors) it has some trees reaching over 40m in height – most notably the *Odyendea zimmermanii*, known locally as *mbanko*. Also to be found is the endemic Pemba palm (*mpapindi*; *Dypsis pembanus*), an ornamental tree whose red seeds are attractive to birds.

Other vegetation types include swamp forest, coastal thicket, heathland, pockets of mangroves and palms, and raffia stands. The mix is unique in east Africa, with several species more usually found in lowland mountain regions, as well as those more often found in coastal areas, plus eastern Indian and Malagasy species, and even a southeast Asian wild banana. There are also several introduced tree species.

The forest is home to several animal species, most notably the Pemba flying fox. Other animals found in Ngezi include the Pemba vervet monkey, the greater bushbaby, Zanzibar tree hyrax (*pelele*; *Dendrohyrax validus neumannii*), blue duiker (*paa wa pemba*) and marsh mongoose (*chonjwe*; *Atilax paludinosus*). A band of wild European pigs, descended from domestic animals introduced by the Portuguese centuries ago, also lives in the forest. As most people on Pemba are Muslim and abstain from pork, these animals are not hunted.

For birdwatchers, Ngezi Forest is undoubtedly the best place on Pemba, with all the endemics and sub-endemics present here. Visitors could also see palm-nut vultures, crowned hornbills, red-billed hornbills and kingfishers, as well as turacos and starlings. (For more details, see *Chapter 3, Natural environment*, page 51.)

13

Mafia Archipelago

While Zanzibar is entrenched as probably the most popular ocean resort in East Africa, the small archipelago around Mafia Island, 160km to its south, remains virtually unknown. Poor communications with the mainland and a rather unfortunate name have not served Mafia well, but a growing trickle of visitors over recent years, currently around 4,000 annually, have been unanimous in singing the island's praises. A few interesting Swahili ruins notwithstanding, Mafia lacks for an equivalent to Zanzibar's atmospheric Stone Town, so that it cannot be recommended as an alternative destination for those whose primary interest in Tanzania's islands is cultural or historical.

By contrast, the combination of a clutch of small, high-quality lodges, offshore diving and snorkelling that ranks with the very best in the Indian Ocean, and a conspicuous absence of hassle and crime, make it the ideal destination for those seeking an exclusive but low-key Indian Ocean retreat. Paradoxically, perhaps, Mafia also has considerable potential for budget travellers seeking a truly off-the-beaten-track and adventurous experience, and once boats connecting Mafia to the mainland become more reliable, their numbers are sure to increase.

The Mafia Archipelago, which lies approximately 20km east of the Rufiji River Delta in central Tanzania, probably became isolated from the mainland some 20,000 years ago. The archipelago consists of about 15 sandstone and coral-rag islands and numerous smaller atolls and sandbars, none of which reaches an elevation above 80m, and all but two of which are little more than 1km² in extent. The central island, known today as Mafia (though it seems that this name applied to the archipelago rather than any specific island prior to the 20th century), is by far the largest, approximately 50km long by 15km across. The second-largest island is Juani, about 8km long and up to 4km wide, which lies to the southeast of the main island and was the centre of local political activity in medieval times. Sandwiched between these two larger islands, the tiny Chole Island superseded Juani as the local centre of trade in the Omani era.

The archipelago's estimated population of nearly 41,000 lives in rustic fishing communities and farming villages dotted all over Mafia and the smaller islands, although many of the islands are theoretically uninhabited. The largest town and port on Mafia Island is Kilindoni in the southeast, the site of the airstrip, and the main landing point for dhows from the mainland. A couple of hotels can be found along the beach from Kilindoni, as well as a few local guesthouses in the town itself, but the centre of upmarket tourist development is Chole Bay on the southeastern side of the island. Here a number of tourist lodges, ranging in standard, line the coast around Utende, roughly 10km from Kilindoni by road. Further accommodation options are found on Chole Island within the bay, and, more recently, up in the north of the island near Ras Mbisi and Bweni.

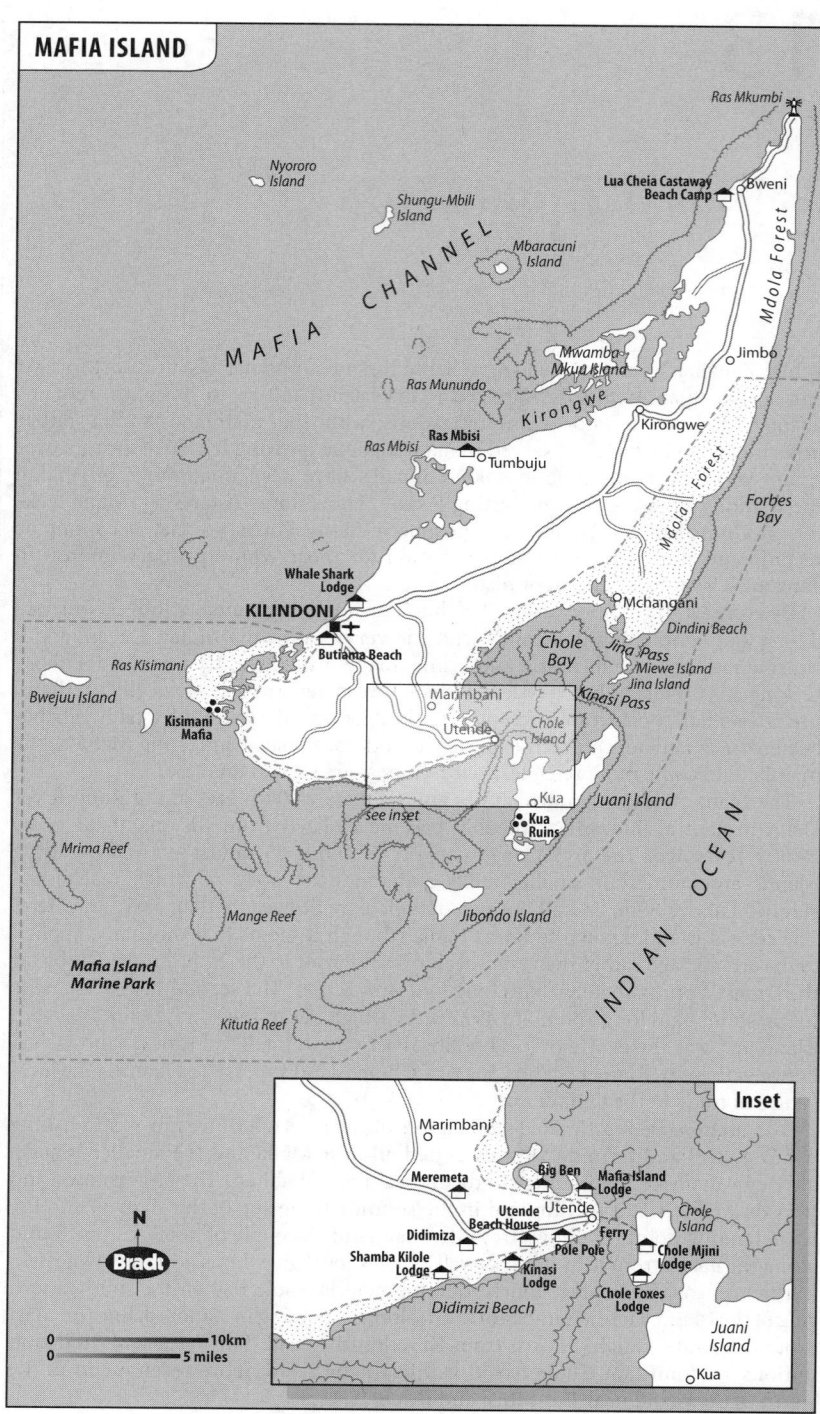

MAFIA ISLAND

Ras Mkumbi

Nyororo Island

Shungu-Mbili Island

Lua Cheia Castaway Beach Camp
Bweni

Mbaracuni Island

M A F I A   C H A N N E L

Mwamba-Mkua Island

Jimbo

Ras Munundo

Kirongwe

Kirongwe

Mdola Forest

Ras Mbisi
Ras Mbisi
Tumbuju

Forbes Bay

Mdola Forest

Whale Shark Lodge

KILINDONI

Mchangani

Dindini Beach

Butiama Beach

Chole Bay

Jina Pass
Miewe Island
Jina Island
Kinasi Pass

Ras Kisimani

Marimbani

Bwejuu Island

Utende

Chole Island

Kisimani Mafia

Kua

See inset

Kua Ruins

Juani Island

Mrima Reef

I N D I A N   O C E A N

Mange Reef

Jibondo Island

Mafia Island Marine Park

Kitutia Reef

N

Bradt

| 0 | 10km |
| 0 | 5 miles |

Inset

Marimbani

Meremeta

Big Ben
Mafia Island Lodge

Utende Beach House
Utende

Didimiza

Pole Pole
Ferry

Chole Island

Shamba Kilole Lodge

Kinasi Lodge

Chole Mjini Lodge

Chole Foxes Lodge

Didimizi Beach

Juani Island

Kua

VEGETATION Natural vegetation on Mafia ranges from tidal mangrove thickets (eight species of mangrove grow here), marshland, heath and scrubby coastal moorlands to palm-wooded grassland and lowland rainforest, although the evergreen forest was cleared for coconut plantations in the 1980s. Baobabs are prominent along with the native *Albizia*. A patch of coastal high forest, the Chunguruma Forest, is a dense tree canopy interlaced with lianas and having an abundant floor covering of ferns.

WILDLIFE

Mammals A large, reed-lined lake in central Mafia, probably a relic lagoon dating from when the island was joined to the mainland, harbours about 20 hippo that were washed out to sea during flooding in the Rufiji River system. Unpopular with locals, they eat from the rice farms at night and can cause considerable damage, but are hard to see. Other island fauna includes a colony of flying foxes (the lesser Cormoran fruit bat), while bush pigs are found in Mdola Forest and Juani Island. The pigs eat the cassava from farms on Juani, so are a menace to farmers, who try to trap the pigs where possible.

Mdola Forest stretches along the east coast of Mafia Island for about 30km, from Bweni to Chole Bay, and has a high level of diversity, as well as a number of endemic species, such as the blue duiker, a subspecies endemic to Pemba and Mafia. Other fauna includes at least one bushbaby species, the genet, and the black-and-rufous elephant shrew. Monkeys (Sykes' and vervet) and squirrels were introduced for the pot by the Portuguese.

Reptiles and insects The leaf-litter toad has been recorded in Mdola Forest, and may be endemic to Mafia; the writhing gecko is found both in Mdola Forest and on the Tanzanian mainland. The monitor lizard is known locally as *kenge*. Butterflies (there are five endemics) are best seen in the wet season, particularly around Ras Mbizi and mangroves, which flower during the rains.

Birds More than 120 species of bird have been recorded on Mafia, including five different types of sunbird. The island is of particular interest for its concentrations of resident and migrant shorebirds, which have breeding grounds in northern Europe but come to Mafia from October to March for the nearby mangrove estuaries, where they feed on the mudflats. Waders include ringed plover, crab plover, grey plover, Mongolian plover, great sandplover, curlew, whimbrel and turnstone, and the island is also a nesting area for fish eagles and open-billed storks.

MARINE LIFE Of far greater ecological importance than Mafia's terrestrial habitats is the immensely rich marine environment, which provides some of the finest snorkelling and diving sites in the Indian Ocean. It may be surprising that the biodiversity of the Rufiji–Mafia complex has global significance, and of 21 sites in east Africa has been described as having 'one of the world's most interesting and diverse ecosystems'. The coral-reef habitats around Mafia have a diversity of species rivalled only by rainforests, with at least 380 species of fish and 48 of coral. The beds of seagrass (12 species of which are found here, the only flowering plants to have colonised the sea) and the deep open waters support some of the planet's most endangered marine life.

Four species of turtle live in Mafia's waters, and two of these use Mafia as a nesting ground. The hawksbill (*Cretmochelys imbricata*) lays eggs between

December and January; the green turtle (*Chelonia mydas*), between April and June. The east African coast is one of the last strongholds for the critically endangered dugong (*Dugong dugon*), and during the 1960s and 1970s these gentle sea cows were regularly caught in the shark nets of Mafia's fishermen. Despite two separate sightings in 1999, there are fears that the dugong may now be extinct here.

The lowland coastal forest of the eastern seaboard has been 'recognised as a critical site for biodiversity', and the intertidal flats are important for octopus, while in the open sea marine mammals like the humpback whale give birth and nurse their young. Sadly the demand for shark-fin soup in the Far East is one contributor to diminished populations of shark along the coastline. The large pelagics such as marlin, billfish and tuna also inhabit the deeper sea.

Oceanographers often talk of the Rufiji River Delta–Mafia–Kilwa area being one extended ecosystem. It's particularly exciting that a coelacanth was caught here in 2003. Archaeologists have found fossils of this very rare, bony fish which dates back to the era of the dinosaurs, and today's specimens are almost identical.

From October to April, whalesharks are seen in the area. Chole Mjini on Chole Island is the headquarters for the newly formed Mafia Island Whaleshark Conservation Project and during the season offers regular dhow excursions for guests to visit these gentle giants, which are spotted mainly on the western side of the island near Kilindoni.

CLIMATE

The Mafia Archipelago experiences a tropical climate tempered by ocean breezes. Rainfall averaging 2,000mm a year occurs mainly between April and May, although November can also be wet. February and March are hot and humid, while a strong southerly wind, the *kusi*, blows during July. The best holiday period is from June until mid October, when the islands enjoy blue skies with temperatures kept pleasant by light coastal breezes. The water temperature varies from 24°C to 31°C while the air temperature rarely exceeds 33°C or drops below 20°C.

HISTORY

Little is known about the early history of the Mafia Archipelago, but presumably it has been settled for millennia, and it may well have participated in the ancient coastal trade with Arabia. The eminent archaeologist Neville Chittick regarded Mafia as a strong candidate for the 'low and wooded' island of Menouthesias, described in the 1st-century *Periplus of the Erythrian Sea* as being two days' sail or 300 *stadia* (roughly 50km) from the river port of Rhapta (which, according to this theory, was situated in the Rufiji Delta). Although the anonymous writer of the *Periplus* also mentions the sewn boats and hollowed-out tree canoes that are still used widely on Mafia today (as they are elsewhere on the coast), several other aspects of the description count against Mafia. Two days rather exaggerates the sailing distance from the island to the Rufiji Delta; furthermore, either the *Periplus* was mistaken in its assertion that there are 'no wild beasts except crocodiles' on Menouthesias, or the crocs have subsequently vanished and the island's few hippos are a later arrival.

The earliest known settlement on the archipelago, Kisimani Mafia, was situated at Ras Kisimani in the far southwest of the main island. Archaeological evidence suggests that this town, which covered about 1ha, was founded in the 11th century, possibly by a favoured son of the Sultan of Kilwa. Several coins minted at Kilwa have been unearthed at the site, as have coins from China, Mongolia, India and Arabia, all minted prior to 1340. A second important town, Kua, was probably founded in the 13th century, again as a dependency of Kilwa, and it must surely have usurped Kisimani as the islands' political and economic hub soon after that. In its prime, Kua was probably the second-largest city along what is now the southern coast of Tanzania, boasting seven mosques as well as a double-storey palace and numerous stone homesteads spread over an area of more than 12ha.

Following the Portuguese occupation of the coast, Kua was chosen as the site of a Portuguese trade agency in 1515, when a fortified blockhouse was built at the town. The name Mafia (more accurately Morfiyeh) was well established by this time, and the islands are marked as such on the earliest Portuguese naval charts. Several explanations have been put forward for the origin of this name (see box below). Because the archipelago lies 20km offshore, Mafia attracted a large influx of refugees from the mainland during the cannibalistic Zimba raids that dealt the final deathblow to so many coastal settlements during the late 16th century.

Control of Mafia changed hands frequently in the 17th century as Portugal's fortunes declined. An Omani naval raid in 1670 effectively terminated the Portuguese presence on the Mafia islands, and by 1598 the entire east African coast north of modern-day Mozambique was under Omani control. Little is known about events on the islands over the next two centuries. In about 1829, however, the archipelago was attacked by the cannibalistic Sakalafa of Madagascar, who succeeded in wreaking havoc at Kua, one of the few coastal towns left untouched by their Zomba forebears 250 years earlier. Kisimani, though also attacked by the Malagasy, stumbled on into the 1870s, when a devastating cyclone dealt it a final death blow, but Kua was abandoned to go to ruin.

One reason why Kua was not resettled after 1820 is that a new seat of the Sultanate of Zanzibar had been founded on the north end of Chole Island barely ten years earlier. Known as Chole Mjini (Chole Town), this settlement was also attacked by the Sakalafa, but it was soon rebuilt to emerge as the most important town on the islands. Chole became the established home of a number of wealthy Omani traders and slave owners, while the main island of Mafia, known at the time as Chole Shamba (Chole Farm), was occupied by newly established coconut plantations and the slaves who worked on them. Although Chole was not as directly involved in the slave trade as Pangani, Bagamoyo or Kilwa Kivinje, it was an important stopover for slave ships heading between Kilwa and Zanzibar, and the ruined mansions that survive today indicate that it was a very wealthy settlement indeed.

Mafia was part of the Zanzibar Sultanate throughout the Omani era, and it should have remained a part of Zanzibar in the colonial era, according to a treaty that placed it under British protectorateship along with Zanzibar and Pemba

WHAT'S IN A NAME?

There are a number of suggestions for the source of the archipelago's name, but it isn't derived from the Sicilian crime syndicate. It may have origins in the Arabic word *morfiyeh* meaning 'group', describing the archipelago of Mafia, or be named after the Ma'afir, an Arab tribe from Merku (Mocha) in present-day Yemen. An unlikely suggestion is that the name derives from the Arabic *mafi* meaning 'waste' or 'rubbish', or perhaps from sthe Swahili *mahali pa afya* meaning 'a healthy place to live'. The authors would be grateful for any further suggestions!

13

islands. However, in the complex Anglo–German treaty of 1890, Mafia was ceded to Germany in exchange for a part of what is now Malawi, and it has been administered as part of mainland Tanzania ever since. In 1892, Germany sent a local administrator to Chole, who constructed the two-storey Customs House that can still be seen on the beach today.

In 1913, Germany relocated its administration from Chole to the deeper harbour at Kilindoni on the main island. Two years later, Mafia was the first part of German East Africa to be captured by British forces. The island was subsequently used as the base for a series of aerial assaults on the German cruiser *Königsberg* which, having evaded capture in the Rufiji Delta, was finally sunk on 11 August 1915. A six-cent German Tanganyika Territory stamp overprinted 'Mafia' by the British and listed at £9,000 in the Stanley Gibbons catalogue makes philatelists one of the few groups of people aware of the existence of the islands.

ECONOMY

Coconuts were the main source of income for the islands until the 1970s, when the price of coconut products dropped, and the fishing industry grew in importance. Cultivated since the 19th century, coconuts remain a secure income source and, although the trees are still climbed by hand, some 30 tonnes are exported to Dar daily in dhows. Coconut products have a number of local uses: leaves are used for roofing, coconut coir makes doormats and ropes, and even the ribs are used to make fishing traps and brooms. The wood can also be used to make furniture.

Other produce grown on Mafia is used for subsistence farming, particularly the primary crop, cassava. Rice, sweet potato, maize, pumpkin, okra, banana, pineapple, passionfruit, lime, mango and tomato are also seen growing on the islands, some of which are exported to Dar. Cashew nuts are either sold locally or exported, and the cashew fruit is used to make local beer. At subsistence level, mushrooms, raffia fibre, medicinal plants and game (monkey, bush pig and duiker) play an important role. Mangrove trees provide many raw materials; their wood is used for building poles, and boatbuilding and repair. Dead mangrove branches are used for firewood; leaves, bark and fruit are all used for medicines and colour dyes. Firewood is collected to burn coral rag for lime, and also for charcoal, which is sold to locals, hotels, and at Kilindoni, as well as exported.

The sea is vital to the livelihood of many of Mafia's inhabitants. Seaweed farming exists on a small-scale basis, used for export and for processing food additives. It is grown on lines attached to wooden stakes across the seabed of shallow lagoons, and is dried on palm leaves. Traditionally the intertidal area has been the women's domain, where they fish for octopus at spring tide. In the 1990s, however, men too began collecting octopus on the intertidal flats, as fish catches were declining yet prices increasing. Now 60% of octopus is caught by men, often through free-diving. Sea cucumbers are harvested for export to Zanzibar or Dar, then out to the Far East. Fish is also exported. Chole and Jibonde were well known for their boatbuilding in the past, but this now is in decline. You can still see people working in the shipyards, but more of the work is now repairing smaller dhows rather than building large cargo-carrying boats.

RELIGION AND CULTURE

The majority of the islanders are Muslim, but there are also many Christians, and both are sometimes mixed with local beliefs which are older in origin. While traditionally reserved, the islanders are tolerant of visitors provided they dress discreetly and behave in a manner becoming to local customs. Mafia women wear the colourful patterned kanga of the Swahili coast (see box, *Kangas and kikois*, page 102), and on weekends and religious holidays men exchange Western dress for the long, white *kanzu*. Older folk who remember the British era can speak some English, as can staff working at the tourist lodges, but it can help to know a little Swahili when talking to other islanders.

Mafia is a conservative society, and the passing visitor is unlikely to be asked for handouts. Children who beg from tourists are quickly reprimanded by their elders. Please make sure that you, and your travelling companions, keep it this way. (For further information, see page 117.)

GETTING THERE AND AWAY

BY AIR The most efficient way of getting to Mafia is by light aircraft (Cessna Caravan or AIRVAN) with **Tropical Air** who operate a 10.00 service from Dar es Salaam to Mafia, or with **Coastal Travel**, who run two scheduled flights from Dar es Salaam every day, costing US$120 for a single flight: the first leaves at 10.30, arriving in Mafia at 11.00, and the second at 15.00, arriving at 15.30. These flights both wait for the Selous plane to arrive before departing. If enough people are flying, **Safari Airlink** operates two daily flights to Mafia from Dar, leaving at 08.15 and 16.40, landing at 08.50 and 17.15 respectively. The return flights leave Mafia at 09.20 and 17.40, arriving in Dar at 09.55 and 18.15, costing US$200 each way. If one of these flights is not running, you can sometimes persuade Coastal to fly by paying for a minimum of two passengers. Coastal also fly from Kilwa to Mafia daily (departing 11.50; arriving 12.20) for US$190 one-way and Zanzibar to Mafia twice daily, usually via Dar (09.30–11.00 and 14.00–15.30), costing US$150 single.

You can also **charter planes** to Mafia from a range of companies in Dar es Salaam and Zanzibar, with the cost of a small aircraft from Coastal or Tropical costing around US$900.

The flight path to Mafia is within sight of the Rufiji River Delta, at 40km^2 the largest delta in east Africa with the region's greatest concentration of mangroves. The views are impressive; the dhows look tiny as they go about their fishing unfeasibly far from shore. Be warned though that with plans currently stalled on the new 1.9km runway, arrival on Mafia's uneven gravel airstrip is usually a bumpy.

Note that an airport departure tax of US$5 per person, which includes a US$1 'safety fee', is payable in cash on leaving Mafia, although flights with Coastal normally include this in the ticket price.

Airline operators

✈ **Coastal Aviation** 107 Upanga Rd, Dar es Salaam or Dar Airport; ☎ 022 2117959 (HQ)/022 2842700/1 (Dar Airport)/024 2233112; m 0785 500009 (Zanzibar Airport); e safari@coastal.cc; www.coastal.cc

✈ **Safari Airlink** Dar es Salaam ☎ 022 5504384/0044, (0)1452 862288 (Gloucester, UK);

m 0777 723274 (Dar); e flights@safariaviation. info; www.flysal.info

✈ **Tropical Air** Zanzibar; ☎ 024 2232511 (HQ); m 0773 511679 (Zanzibar Airport)/0773 618367 (Dar Airport); e info@tropicalair.co.tz; www. tropicalair.co.tz

Mafia Airport Mafia's small airport (⊕ *around 08.00–18.30, unless there's an early-morning flight*) is situated on the edge of the main town of Kilindoni, a 15km drive from Utende, where most of the tourist lodges are located. It's Mafia's centre of communication for visitors, and even if visitors arrive on Mafia by boat they tend to be directed the 1km from the harbour to the airport.

Currently, the airport has a simple waiting room with huge leather sofas and basic toilets, while outside a reasonable curio shop sells kangas, kikois and imported wooden carvings for those last-minute souvenirs. Plans for a new terminal and decent runway have been 'ongoing' for many years now. There's no longer a currency exchange at the airport, but there is a branch of the National Microfinance Bank in Kilindoni, albeit the ATM only accepts cards from account holders. Lodges will take credit cards, but it's still wise to bring an amount of cash with you.

MAFIA ISLAND MARINE PARK

Over the past 2,000 years, turtle-shell, mangrove poles and seashells have been part of east Africa's trade to Arabia. By the 1960s, however, it had become clear that natural resources were not coping with human progress. In Tanzania, dried and salted fish, exported to the mainland, contributes more to the national protein consumption than meat and poultry combined. Dynamite fishing became very popular on Tanzania's coast, despite the destruction that it causes to fish populations and to coral. Small-mesh, beach-seine nets were catching all sizes of fish, again damaging populations. In some areas the only source of building materials has been coral, used as bricks and in the production of lime: this was the second-largest industry on Mafia at one time. Mangrove wood is very hard, insect-resistant, and makes excellent building material, so vast areas were cleared to provide timber, fuelwood, farmland and salt pans for salt production.

In the 1970s, four islands were declared marine reserves to slow the damage, but in the absence of facilities to police the park, fishermen ignored the rules and continued as usual. By 1995, it was clear that conservation had become an urgent priority, so the following year a partnership of investors, communities and the government set up the Board of Trustees of Marine Parks and Reserves of Tanzania, and on 6 September 1996, an area of Mafia extending across 822km² was gazetted as Tanzania's first marine park, to protect the ecosystems as well as the future livelihood of coastal people. The park embraces most of the southern and eastern shore of Mafia, including Chole Bay and associated reefs, a number of isolated atolls to the south of the main island, and the reefs enclosing Juani, Jibondo and Bwejuu islands.

The marine park now owns seven boats and has one full-time park warden plus many rangers. The park authorities are aiming to co-operate and collaborate with local residents, using community-based projects to dispel conflict between groups. If the islands are to be protected, the success of the marine park is imperative. Mangroves trap river sediments that would be otherwise washed out to sea and, along with coral reefs, protect the shoreline from the erosion of rising sea levels. The natural forest shields the island's crops from storm damage from the ocean, and a healthy ecosystem helps in the recovery from natural disasters such as cyclones, hurricanes and floods. Significantly, wetlands have also been shown to provide clean water, perhaps the most significant issue in terms of sustainable development of the islands.

For further details, contact the warden in charge, Mr George Msumi, Mafia Island Marine Park (☏ 023 2402690; e mimpMafia@raha.com).

Visitors holding a hotel reservation will be met at the airport for their transfer. If you don't have a reservation, most of the lodges have representatives who speak English, and can radio the lodges to organise accommodation subject to availability. They can also help individual travellers to find a Land Rover taxi, costing a fixed price of Tsh 40,000 (US$25.50) to Utende one-way; note that you'll cross the border into the marine park *en route*, so have the fee (US$20pp/day) for the requisite number of days ready in US dollars cash, and remember to keep your receipt as proof of payment when you leave the island. Taking a tuc tuc will be cheaper but it takes longer.

BY BOAT The options for budget travellers who wish to visit Mafia are limited to boats that connect Kilindoni to the mainland. Many of these dhows are uncomfortable and crowded and the trip can take anything from ten to 24 hours. The safety record is none too inspiring; sailing dhows have a reputation for hitting reefs, as these are very dangerous waters that require an experienced captain. Equally, if it's too windy, none will sail. If you want to take a boat, make sure you check that they're properly licensed to carry passengers or vehicles, and at the very least have marine radios and life jackets on board.

For the incorrigible, a tide table is incorporated in the free booklet, the *Dar Guide*, available from bars and hotels in Dar es Salaam. This is invaluable when trying to organise a boat trip to Mafia, as the boats have to arrive at high tide, and often leave on a high tide, too. In Kilindoni though, a jetty is under (slow) construction, which would mean that boats no longer have to restrict their arrival to high tide. This should lead to a much more regular service in the future.

The closest mainland port to Mafia is Kisiju, 30km from Dar, and 45km southeast of Mkuranga on the Kilwa road. From the Kariakoo bus depot in Dar, you take a bus to Kisiju and then a dhow to Mafia. Make sure you arrive in Kisiju before 14.30, when the last dhow leaves for Mafia. Another possibility from Dar es Salaam is via Kimbiji, easily reached by catching the motor ferry from the city centre to Kigomboni (boats leave every ten minutes or so and take five minutes) then a dala dala direct to Kimbiji (about one hour). There are also dhows connecting Mafia to Kilwa Kivinje. Finally, a rather sporadic service runs from Niamisati in the Rufiji Delta once a day, leaving around midday and arriving in Kilindoni six hours later, before departing for the return journey at around 19.30. To reach Niamisati it's a three to four hour drive from Dar, or two hours' taxi ride from Mbalala.

GETTING AROUND

The island infrastructure is basic. Hardly any villages are connected to mains water or electricity and at the time of writing there are no tarmac roads. Throughout the island the best you'll find is a bouncy sandy track. Vehicles are few, mainly Land Rover pick-ups and 4x4s belonging to the hotels and other organisations. Most local people use bicycles and motorbikes to get around, although the former are quite hard work on the sandy roads. **Bicycles** can be rented by arrangement with the New Lizu Hotel in Kilindoni (see *Where to stay*, page 386), or from any of the lodges.

A not very reliable **minibus** runs every three hours or so between Kilindoni and Utende charging around US$1 one-way. It seats a minimum of 12 and has no fixed timetable – it departs when it's full. **Dala dalas** shuttle between Kilindoni and Utende, and these pick people up along the way. They're not the most comfortable means of getting around, but are a good way of meeting local people and really getting to understand life on Mafia. Alternatively, the even bumpier option of a **motorbike taxi** can be picked up in Kilindoni. **Hitchhiking** is an accepted means of getting about, but it usually entails a long wait. Islanders also use *jahazis*, widely referred to in English as dhows, to commute between Kilindoni and outlying villages on Mafia, and for inter-island travel.

Free maps of Mafia can be obtained from Mafia Island Marine Park office.

🏠 WHERE TO STAY

Mafia isn't really the place for easy backpacking, but budget travellers who do come here may stop in Kilindoni itself. Meanwhile, the majority of Mafia's tourists head straight through town and over to one of the more upmarket small lodges in Utende or on Chole Island, although recently added properties in Bweni and Ras Mbisi are encouraging tourists to venture a little further.

Unless stated otherwise, hotels listed below offer en-suite bathrooms as standard.

UTENDE The number of accommodation options around Utende is steadily increasing, with five new lodges having sprung up since the last edition of this book. There's now a fair amount of choice, even for those on a tighter budget, although the more upmarket places remain the most popular.

🏠 **Pole Pole** (7 bungalows) e book@polepole. com; www.polepole.com; ⊕ Jun–Mar. Pole Pole, meaning 'slowly, slowly' in Swahili, is a superb destination for relaxation. This Italian-managed lodge is designed to be fairly luxurious whilst still a little rustic; smart without being pretentious. Set in a garden of coconut palms, & connected by pathways of the softest sand, Pole Pole has a small beach, perhaps 100m wide, with mangroves on either side. The large bungalows, built almost entirely from organic materials, have modern bathrooms, including a flush toilet with an eco-friendly sewerage system – waste water is collected into a phytopurification bamboo pool where it is filtered for use on the garden. The bedroom has a polished wooden floor, some stylishly simple furniture, a ceiling fan, & 24hr electricity plus a back-up generator; dbl or twin beds are surrounded by a walk-in mosquito net. Large double-doors lead onto a very wide, shaded veranda overlooking the sea below, complete with some relaxing daybeds & chairs. In keeping with its chill-out vibe, Pole Pole operates a strict mobile-phone policy with guests requested to keep phones on silent mode & only make calls from within their rooms. Italian-influenced 4-course dinners are served in the restaurant; Swahili dinners are offered once a week or on request. Service is attentive & helpful, & there are also 2 good local masseuses. Pole Pole has a lovely sail-shaded swimming pool, or snorkelling,

diving, game fishing & island excursions are offered. 1 dhow trip – usually including some snorkelling & perhaps a BBQ picnic lunch – is normally offered every day on a complimentary basis. Between Oct & Mar the lodge operates trips to see (& on occasion swim with) the migratory whalesharks. If you're looking for somewhere small, comfortable & fairly remote with great diving & snorkelling, & involving very low-key excursions, then Pole Pole offers very good value indeed. *FB; minimum age 10.* 🛏
🏠 **Kinasi Lodge** (14 bungalows) m 0777 418256, operations; m 0741 242977; e stay@ mafiaisland.com; www.kinasilodge.com; ⊕ Jun–end Mar. A 5min walk along the beach from Pole Pole brings you to the more formal Kinasi Lodge. This Indian Ocean hideaway is named for the indigo pass through the outer reef that leads into Chole Bay. Kinasi has large, landscaped lawns studded with coconut palms, which slope steeply down to a small sandy beach & the ocean. There's a swimming-pool area, complete with poolside bar & grill, & dotted around are solid, self-contained bungalows with makuti roofs & stone verandas furnished with armchairs & addictive hammocks. Inside, Zanzibar-style queen-sized beds are enveloped in vast mosquito nets. Throughout the hotel great attention has been paid to soft furnishings. The lodge's multi-level, open-sided bar & lounge area contains a top-notch reference library, book-swap service & comfortable long couches & armchairs

plus a TV & free Wi-Fi. The adjacent dining area serves an eclectic fusion menu & themed dinners ranging from a seafood fondue to poolside Swahili nights. A separate grill & pizza kitchen has also been installed for more casual dining, & meals can be either in a group or individually. There's a well-stocked walk-in wine cellar & cocktail bar for pre-dinner wine tastings & canapés. Kinasi has its own fully equipped watersports & PADI dive centre beside the beach, & the resident instructor can arrange dives in & around Chole Bay, as well as snorkelling trips, windsurfing, kayaking & game fishing. An 'activity manager' in the lodge organises the various excursions (at additional cost), which include the usual range of dhow trips, village visits, & 4x4 excursions across the island, plus the unique option of borrowing mountain bikes to explore local villages. The lodge has also constructed a 2hr nature trail for birdwatching along the coastal flats & through patches of coastal scrub. To complement these activities, the Isis Spa has 3 treatment rooms, including the romantic Pharaoh bath, & 2 charming, professional Thai therapists. **$$$$$**

🏠 **Mafia Island Lodge** (34 rooms) m 0786 303049; e info@mafialodge.com; www. mafialodge.com; ⊕ Jun–Apr. This very simple lodge, built by the government in 1971, is situated on 1 of the island's few open, palm-lined beaches, directly opposite the ruins of Chole Mjini on Chole Island. The lodge consists of reasonable, box-like rooms, with standard & superior rooms available for couples, friends & families. The rooms have recently undergone a much-needed refurbishment but have retained their terracotta-tiled floors & sea-facing French windows. There's 24hr hot water, & despite the uninspiring interiors & a rather featureless garden, it's a reliable, functional place offering access to Mafia's superb diving without breaking the bank. The bar/restaurant is a large & fairly pleasant spot, with an airy terrace & a seafood menu. Myriad games are available & there is a small shop selling a few essentials. There's also an internet access point (US$10/hr), a pool table & equipment for beach volleyball. Diving is arranged through the PADI affiliated Sea Point Dive Centre, whose instructors speak English, French & Italian. Mafia's only real tour company, Mafia Island Tours, is based here & is an obvious choice for booking excursions: a short hop to Chole Island for a village tour (US$10pp); & a half-day trip to the Kua Ruins & Channel (US$25pp); picnic/snorkelling trip to Marimbani or Kitutia

(*US$55pp*) & a full-day excursion to Ras Mkumbi or Bwejuu Island (US$60pp). Diving US$48; equipment US$20/day. **$$$$**

🏠 **Shamba Kilole Lodge** (6 rooms) m 0786 110671; e info@shambakilolelodge.com; www. shambakilolelodge.com; ⊕ mid Jun–mid Apr. Quiet & peaceful, Shamba Kilole's 3 chalets & 3 suites each have a different theme & colour scheme. They're all agreeably decorated with ochre exteriors, traditional ceilings, reclaimed dhow furniture & mosquito nets. Each has a couch that doubles as a 3rd bed, as well a fan, 24hr electricity & a semi-open bathroom. A cosy 2-storey lounge is filled with wooden & coir-rope chairs, shelves stuffed with books, & cats who steal the comfiest spots. There is beach access, but it's more of a 'bush beach', with the sea itself not visible due to the band of mangroves between it & the lodge. Swimming is difficult, but for those who do fancy a splash, walking for just a few mins brings you to a small bay where water access is easier. Diving is the main focus here, & there's a classroom & pool for novice/refresher dives. Alongside it, emerald lawns are perfect for candlelit Italian dinners or wine tastings from the well-stocked cellar. The lodge tries its best to be eco-friendly, with all wood taken from authorised cultivators, rainwater collection & no sceptic tank. It's a delightful place to stay, popular with honeymooners. **$$$$**.

🏠 **Big Blu** (3 rooms) m 0784 918069; e infodiving@bigblumafia.org; www.bigblumafia. com. What started off as a dive centre in 2005 now has 2 dbl & 1 trpl room, & although the diving emphasis remains, guests do not have to be divers to stay. Palm-woven bungalows house pretty bedrooms, decorated with pastel kikois & blue mosquito nets, plus there's a hot-water shower. Meals, including a 3-course b/fast, are offered in a chilled-out restaurant right on the beach. As well as dive trips (US$70 dbl dive, US$100 intro dive), the dive centre has 3 instructors & 2 dive masters teaching a range of courses. Big Blu also offers seasonal whaleshark-watching trips, snorkelling, fishing, dhow sandbank trips & windsurfing. Considerable discounts are available for room & dive combinations. **$$–$$$**

🏠 **Meremeta** (6 rooms) m 0787 345460; e meremetalodge@hotmail.com; www. meremetalodge.com. Quirky Meremeta receives consistently favourable reviews for its friendly atmosphere & relaxed vibe. Chintz dominates, & everything here is decorated: fish & whalesharks are painted on the pink walls & giant shells & driftwood adorn the gardens, but it all adds to the charm. Rooms are a vision in pink, filled with carvings,ornaments & a fan. Outside a small veranda covered in cushions is filled with ornamental trees, silk flowers & swathes of fabric draped from the ceiling. 1 room is actually a tent with solid walls around it & makuti thatch above it, to give a 'camping' feel. Outside, chickens roam among the pineapple & passionfruit trees, & the active can rent quad bike (US$75/hr), motorbikes & mountain bikes. **$$**

⌂ **Didimiza** (4 rooms) m 0784 303554/0685 266727; e alawia75@yahoo.com. Simple Didimiza offers 3 dbl & 1 family room, all connected by flower-lined sandy paths. Solid wooden beds & towel-filled shelves furnish the rooms, while smiling whalesharks offer light relief on the walls & yellow bathrooms are tidy

& clean. 3 meals a day are served around 1 communal table, which along with the lounger-filled garden is the only relaxation space, as there is no beach access. **$$**

⌂ **Utende Beach House** (5 rooms) m 0755 828825/0713 784547; e bluehousemafia@yahoo.com; www.bluehousemafia.com. High up on a steep hill, with only a glimpse of sea through the trees, is backpacker-focused Utende Beach House. The rooms are identical & all named after nearby islands. There's just about enough floor space for a bed, but not enough to walk around it, although there is a fan & bright blue mosquito net. Basic bathrooms have no hot water but they're clean & functional. Meals are served in the makuti thatched dining area; it's compact with just 2 tables & a bar. The pretty beach is reached down a precariously steep sandy path. **$$**

CHOLE ISLAND The two lodges on Chole are polar opposites – one an originally designed, ecologically friendly retreat, and the other a bottom of the scale backpacker hangout. Regardless of your accommodation choice, all visitors to the island must pay a US$10 per person village levy on arrival (including those staying at Chole Mjini).

⌂ **Chole Mjini Lodge** (6 treehouses, 1 chalet) m 0748 520799; e 2chole@gmail.com; www.cholemijini.com; ⊕ Jun–Mar. This fabulous lodge, situated on the northern side of Chole Island, boasts large, treehouse bedrooms perched high in the baobabs, amongst the crumbling 19th-century ruins of Chole Mjini. This place is emphatically not catering for people seeking Sheraton-style luxury or a conventional beach retreat – there is no electricity for starters (lighting is by paraffin lamps at night, so bring a good torch!) & the waterfront in front of the lodge is overgrown with mangroves. Nevertheless, this must rank as one of the most original & aesthetically pleasing lodges on the east African coast. It's also an atmospheric base for exploring Chole Island & the surrounding waters. Lunch is usually served at group tables in a family atmosphere, with fresh seafood & vegetable dishes in a mixture of African & European styles, usually with tasty sauces. B/fast & dinner are served at individual tables dotted around the garden, jetty or ruins. 6 of the bedrooms stand high on stilted platforms; 3 are in or beside their own huge baobab tree. Each is made almost entirely of wood, thatch & local materials by the local people of Chole – & the sheer quality of the carpentry says much for

the islanders' reputation for building fine dhows. All rooms are slightly different, but climb the stairs & inside you'll generally find a large dbl bed surrounded by a walk-in mosquito net, an open wardrobe & dressing area, & a large, padlocked wooden box for your valuables. Most also have an upper floor, with relaxing daybeds or hammocks. Each of these treehouse rooms has private ablutions – but all are separate & down on the ground. The sit-down toilet is a long-drop, using ash to keep it dry & composting; they rank as one of the cleanest long-drops in Africa. Hidden from view behind a circular bamboo enclosure, the ingenious, open-air showers are good & hot. Another popular contraption is the pulley system used to deliver morning coffees to guests; children will love playing with it! Chole Mjini has just 1 more conventional chalet, which is on the ground level, next to the lodge's main lounge/dining area. Its walls are open to the breeze, & it has a huge bed, a conventional flush toilet (the only one on the island) & a large sunken bath. It's not quite as romantic as the treehouses, but might be just the place if stairs to the toilet don't appeal. Finally, a recent addition to the lodge's range of accommodation is a converted 40ft wooden dhow with 6 berths, allowing guests to spend a night or 2 on the water or fly-camping on a secluded beach. In keeping with the eco-friendly ethos, a community fee is included in the rates. There's no dive centre here, but scuba activities can be arranged through Big Blu or Sea Point at Mafia Island Lodge just across the water (see page 382), & it's possible kite-surfing trips will be possible between Chole & Utende in the future. There is no pool here, or any beach to lie on, but there are organised walks, snorkel trips & excursions to nearby sandbars (usually 1–2 complimentary trips organised every day). Visitors need to accept the lodge for what it is & then a really enjoyable stay is almost guaranteed. Rate includes FB & US$10 village levy & daily activity; Mafia Airport transfers US$40/vehicle. 🛏

🏠 Chole Foxes Lodge (3 rooms) 📞023 2010209; m 0787 877393/0654 512639; e cholefoxeslodge@rocketmail.com; www.cholefoxeslodge.webs.com. Named after Chole's population of flying foxes, the 2nd lodge to open on the island pales in comparison with the 1st. Tiny, messy & extremely basic rooms have very few facilities & little maintenance. The palm-weave bathrooms appear to have been added as an afterthought, with cold concrete floors, long-drop toilets & no running water. Down a sandy path, a couple of wooden tables overlook the sea, & a few coir-rope loungers are dotted about the garden. Apathetic staff are exceedingly unhelpful, bordering on rude, & at US$45pp, the rooms are so overpriced it's laughable. **$$$**

BWENI Up until 2010, there was nowhere to stay in Bweni, and its beautiful beach could be visited only on a day trip. The opening of a high-end beach lodge here has brought more visitors and the added bonus of a wind-generated electricity supply to villages in this remote corner of the island, although the lodge itself uses solar power.

🏠 Lua Cheia Castaway Beach Camp
(6 rooms) m 0777 424588; e stay@mafiaisland. com; www.luacheiabeach.com; ⏰ Jun–end Mar. In the far north of Mafia, at Angel's Beach near Bweni, stands Lua Cheia. On a 2km stretch of white sand scattered with shells, its appeal is in its isolation – guests can truly escape modern life & there's a max of 12 guests so it's never crowded. The owners (those of Kinasi Lodge, see *Where to stay*, page 383) have tried to leave the area as natural as possible; there's no electricity, & solar power is used for the water, lights & fans, which are assisted by sea breezes. Tented rooms lie under thatched bandas & all have verandas overlooking the beach from where there are lovely views of the surrounding bays. The style is simple but comfortable, with dhow timber & leather furniture. Nightly driftwood fires are used for cooking & there's a limited but good bar selection. Apart from appreciating the remote, desert island feel, you can explore by dhow or kayak, try out windsurfing, snorkelling or visit the nearby lighthouse. Swimming off the beach is always possible, even in low tide. There's currently no dive centre, though there are plans to set one up. For those who prefer to remain above the water, catch & release game-fishing trips are offered in partnership with Fishing Tanzania (*www.fishing-tanzania.com*), who have 3 twin-enjoined boats & provide all gear. Rates don't include the bumpy 55km transfer from Mafia airport (US$120/vehicle, 1-way). **$$$$**

RAS MBISI The soft white sand and deserted beach is a great location for the Ras Mbisi Lodge, which has opened this area up to those who wish to linger longer than just a day.

🏠 Ras Mbisi Lodge (9 rooms) m 0754 663739/0753 284397; e contact@mafiaislandtz. com; www.mafiaislandtz.com; ⏰ Jun–Mar. From the airport, after a drive of 45mins down a very bumpy, sandy track, guests reach this relaxed & chilled-out lodge, found just metres from 8km of deserted beach. The room décor makes use of clean lines & soft creams & browns, while in the bathroom solar-heated water is pretty effective, & locally made coconut oil soaps are provided. There's an emphasis on the eco-friendly here, with local coconut wood from sustainable sources used for construction, power generated from a biomass gasifier which is fuelled by waste, locally crafted furniture, freshly caught seafood & juicy fruit & vegetables grown in the on-site garden. The full English b/fast is a throwback to when manager Michelle lived in the UK. Hungry guests can even treat themselves to elevenses & afternoon tea, complete with cake & biscuits. For evening indulgence, a good wine list features quality South African wines. Various activities & excursions can be booked, including trips to Chole, Chungaruma Forest, fishing, kayaking & snorkelling, although

it's worth noting that it's a bit of a trek across the island to Chole Bay in order to go diving. If you don't fancy leaving the lodge's peace & quiet, there's a refreshing pool for afternoon dips. Ras Mbisi is involved in local community projects & is raising money for children's desks at nearby Chungaruma school. FB, with tea & coffee & use of kayaks & vehicles included. Road transfer from Mafia Airport US$30/vehicle. **$$$$**

KILINDONI The guesthouses in town are all pretty basic, with little to draw travellers to them. For a far better bet, head to the more upmarket Butiama Beach.

⌂ **Butiama Beach** (10 rooms) e maura@ coraldivers.co.za; www.butiamabeach.com. On the edge of the Mafia Island Marine Park & just a 10min walk south along the beach from Kilindoni, or a bumpy 10min drive over sand, the spacious, well-designed rooms are colour co-ordinated & creatively decorated. 2 conjoined rooms are good for families, who will appreciate the relaxed, laid-back vibe of the place, plus kids love the stuffed whaleshark hanging up in the bar. Sandy pathways & planted flowerbeds lead from the rooms to the circular bar with snooker table & the newly constructed swimming pool. It's worth noting that snorkellers & divers must head to the other side of the island around Chole Bay, a 30min drive, where they can visit Big Blu (see page 382), also owned by Butiama. Fishing enthusiasts are encouraged, with the lodge being the only one on Mafia to offer deep-sea fishing from their 2 boats, & guests can also borrow kayaks & snorkelling gear. **$$$$**

⌂ **Whale Shark Lodge** (6 bandas, camping) ☎ 023 2010201; m 0755 696067; e carpho2003@ yahoo.co.uk; www.whalesharklodge.com. Outside central Kilindoni, a 15min walk from the airport, this camp (formerly Mafia Pwani Camp) is one of the only basic lodges that offers a relaxing atmosphere. It's also an excellent area for spotting the rufous elephant shrew, as well as vervet monkeys. The camp is in a beautiful, peaceful area overlooking the sea, & has considerable potential. Its individual tangerine hued bandas (3 en suite & 3 with shared bathroom) are sizeable & clean, with nets on windows & sturdy coconut-wood beds made up with colourful batik sheets, fans & 24hr electricity. Sandwiched between the garden & the beach below, the covered lounge & bar is encircled by comfy wooden chairs. Here, filling

seafood dishes (US$7–8) are offered as well as a selection of sandwiches, & a wine list. Despite the good standard of building, facilities are very basic: bathrooms have seen better days & there's no hot water, but the lodge tries hard to make the best of what they have. If you follow the steep pathway down to the beach, you'll come to the campsite (US$7). Whale Shark has its own boat which is used for snorkelling trips, & they rent out motorbikes on request. **$$**

⌂ **Classic Visitor's House** (12 rooms) m 0719 045307/0688 145763. This very basic guesthouse has recently installed Western-style toilets, but that's about the only redeeming feature. The owner speaks English, so the manager (who doesn't) will call him if needed. The cramped rooms are filthy & poor-quality bathrooms are shared. There are 3 newer en-suite twin rooms with similarly basic interiors, although an ancient TV has been added. There is no restaurant here. **$**

⌂ **Ibizza Inn** (5 rooms) No contact details. Found around the back of the main street, this is the most comfortable of the central Kilindoni guesthouses, & by far the cleanest. The sofas might be straight out of the 1970s, but the rooms are bright & cheery, with TV, large bathrooms & AC in some. The entrance hall doubles as a cosy lounge & TV room, & feels homely & welcoming. That said, Ibizza is most definitely aimed at locals. **$**

⌂ **New Lizu Hotel** (5 rooms) Bookings c/o Post office, Mafia; ☎ 023 2010180. Used by local traders, New Lizu is a 1min walk from the market, & 10mins from the dhow landing jetty. With 24hr electricity, mosquito nets & fans, it is fairly clean but extremely basic. All but 1 room (a sgl) share washing facilities, with water very limited. Toilets are flushed with a bucket; hot water can be boiled on request. The hotel also offers a laundry service, a stationery shop, a phone & an internet café (US$1/30 mins). A simple bar/restaurant sells sodas & rice & seafood meals, but no alcohol. **$**

CAMPING There is a campsite at **Whale Shark Lodge** (see opposite) and if you have your own tent, **Meremeta** in Utende (see page 384) offers camping for US$10 per person including breakfast. Otherwise, check with the marine park authorities before camping independently, as it's not legal to camp in Tanzania unless you're in a specified area. Don't take any chances.

DIVING *with Jean de Villiers*

Many people visit Mafia purely for its diving, which is often considered the best anywhere in east Africa. It's easy to dive two sites outside the bay on a single outing; the trip out and back can also be great for fishing, sunbathing, sailing and dolphin-spotting. The marine park off Chole Bay is home to 48 species of coral, including giant table corals, delicate sea fans, whip corals and huge stands of blue- and pink-tipped staghorn coral.

As well as the spectacular variety of reef fish there are turtles and large predatory fish such as grouper, Napoleon wrasse and barracuda. Stingray, manta rays (rare) and several species of shark are encountered in Kinasi Pass. November to January is best for the more common black-tip and white-tip reef sharks. The corals of Chole Bay, in the heart of the marine park, have recovered dramatically from damage caused by El Niño (of 1997–98) and the destructive fishing practices used before the establishment of the park, and the number of fish is now increasing again. The number of manta rays has sadly decreased significantly in recent years.

Almost all Mafia's best diving is in depths of less than 26m. Between June and September you can dive only within the lagoon-like Chole Bay, albeit in almost any weather. For the more challenging dives outside the bay, you have to wait until the calmer conditions in mid-September to November. Outside the bay the average size of the fish is bigger, and you've a good chance of seeing a 2–3m grouper; these are friendly and let you come quite close. Inside the bay, visibility from June to September tends to be 10–15m, whereas in October to February it can be 25m, and high tide gives better visibility than low tide. Mafia is good for beginner divers, as it's very safe inside the bay. However, diving outside the bay on an outgoing tide can be extremely dangerous, with strong currents that can sweep you out to sea: in this position, if you miss your rendezvous with a boat, the next stop is Mogadishu. Make sure you check the tides before you set out.

When diving in the open ocean, divers are advised always to carry two means of signalling: one audible (a whistle or air horn) and one visible (an inflatable surface marker, a flare, strobe light or mirror). In addition, always wear a full wetsuit as protection against exposure, and drink water before commencing a dive. Don't take any risks or push the safety boundary while diving here; it's a long way to the nearest decompression chamber in Zanzibar. Note that you can't buy diving insurance in Tanzania – you must have this before you travel; it can be arranged online.

All of the lodges on Mafia offer diving excursions as well as full PADI courses. Chole Mjini, Pole Pole, Kinasi, Butiama Beach and Mafia Island lodges (see *Where to stay*, pages 382–7) all offer specialist diving courses with every conceivable type of dive site – reefs and bommies, channels, walls, caves, drift, ocean and night dives. All these are accessible in a day, while diving safaris catering for 12 people can be arranged to destinations further afield such as Ras Mkumbi, Forbes Bay southeast of Mafia, and the spectacular reef complex around the Songo Songo Islands, which lie about 80km south of Mafia and about 50km north of Kilwa, and so an overnight trip is needed.

DIVING AND SNORKELLING SITES IN MAFIA MARINE PARK There are at least half a dozen more scuba-diving sites in the park and numerous snorkelling sites. Wherever possible, names given are those used by local fishermen.

The first three sites are relatively close together and can be reached on a stronger drift dive starting near the Pinnacle in Kinasi Pass. These sites sometimes suffer from being in the mouth of a bay in that the visibility can be poor for a few days after stormy periods at sea and when tidal currents are very strong at full moon or new moon.

Kinasi Pass: South Wall *Dive depth: max 27m. Recommended for experienced divers or beginners under professional supervision.* Justifiably Mafia's most famous dive site, this has it all: wall with caverns, big critters and spectacular corals. At times huge volumes of water flow through the pass, creating an exhilarating drift dive, or dive at slack water to enjoy the 30m wall and its resident potato cod and giant grouper. Schools of snappers and sweetlips are often here, as are their predators: barracuda, giant trevally, jacks, cobia, wahoo and kingfish. Rays and morays are common, with whalesharks, eagle rays and stingrays seasonal visitors (late Dec–Mar is best). Finish the dive in a splendid coral garden, and maybe catch up with a Napoleon wrasse or a feeding turtle.

Utumbi (or Kinasi Wall) *Dive depth: 5–25m. Recommended for all certified divers. Outstanding snorkelling site nearby, mainly at low tide.* If you don't tackle the pass right off then this is the must-do dive in Mafia. About 300m before the pass, inside the bay, is a truly gorgeous reef: the ease of access and safe, sheltered location and the obliging currents all add up to a world-class dive. The corals rapidly change from soft corals (gorgonians and whip corals at the pass end), to more and more hard corals, until finally you find yourself in shallow gardens of tabular and staghorn acropora and gold-hued fire coral. The fish fauna is mostly typical reef inhabitants, with a huge variety of multi-coloured wrasses, parrotfish, damsels, surgeons, triggerfish and anthiases. Big wahoo and barracuda cruise off reef, and 2- to 3ft greasy cod and malabar grouper are abundant.

Kinasi Pass: Pinnacle *Dive depth: max 29m. Recommended for experienced divers or beginners under professional supervision.* In the entrance of the bay, 50m north of Kinasi Wall, this pinnacle rises sharply to within 8m of the surface, usually surrounded by a school or two of sweetlips or trevally and their attendant predators. When the visibility is good, this is the most likely place within the bay to meet a bull shark (or zambezi). We also occasionally come across a 3m guitar fish (shark that is half ray, with a flat, triangular head) and a huge, mottled green-black giant grouper accompanied by a bevy of attendant yellow-and-black-striped pilotfish. It's an excellent site at slack water.

Dindini or Shangani Wall *Dive depth: max 24m. Recommended for experienced divers only.* Dindini is only accessible seasonally: it's directly in front of surf-pounded cliffs. There are a lot of fish: big fish, small fish, sharks, rays and also turtles. In periods of good visibility, usually November–March, this is one of the better places in Mafia to see sharks, along with Mkadini (usually reef sharks).

It's also good for large groupers and, very occasionally, big-game fish like tuna, sailfish and marlin. The wall has many caverns and U-shaped tunnels, and some deep, unexplored caves where there is the occasional appearance of a big shark or other large creature. The dive ends on the top of the wall, with really spectacular powder blue, purple and pink alcyonaria soft corals teeming with fish, especially red-toothed triggerfish, and a variety of surgeons.

Mlila or Jina Wall *Dive depth: max 24m. Recommended for experienced divers or beginners under professional supervision.* Seasickness can be a problem due to sea surges. Just over a kilometre away, the wall has formed a slight fold close to the cliffs. It starts out quite mediocre but rapidly changes as you get where fishing boats seldom penetrate. In the pocket there are more grouper than you'll probably ever see. There are also lots of other fish around and this is likely to be your best chance of seeing big Napoleons or getting close to a feeding turtle. At the base of the wall is a lot of coral, with many holes to investigate; look out for lobster and small stingrays, snappers, moray eels as well as giant and ribbon-tailed rays.

Milimani – 'mountain tops' in Swahili *Dive depth: max 20m. Recommended for all skill levels; often used for courses and Discover Scuba experiences.* The most often-requested repeat dive in the park. This is a long reef inside the bay, characterised by spectacular coral turrets rising above corals to form mini mountains and alleys. A gentle entrance in just 6m of water over pure white sand makes this the easiest dive in the park, and the diversity of the coral is phenomenal: the topology of the reef is stunning and it just goes on and on. As you explore the twisting, turning reef interspersed with mounds of coral teeming with fish you may become so absorbed that you suddenly find you're in 20m with a towering reef above. A small gap in the reef is an excellent place to view planktivores, usually swarms of counter-shaded fusiliers and schools of unicorns but occasionally (in the right season) a cruising stingray, accompanied by a flotilla of remoras and pilotfish. There are also a lot of layfish, nudibranchs and moray eels. You can end the dive by climbing over the reef crest to look for turtles or to join the millions of kasmira and blackspot snappers in the very shallow water among the magnificent fire corals.

Miewe Shoulder – the 'Washing Machine' *Dive depth: max 25m. In slack water possible for all levels, in deep water just outside the bay during spring tides, 2hrs before high tide, this is almost white-water diving & only for experienced and advanced divers who can control their buoyancy instinctively and know how to surf currents without fear of injury.* Outside the bay, this is a sloping fringing reef north of the pass, with a fabulous diversity of fish, corals and topology. The reef is teeming with fish but you can't stop because the relentless current drags you over the top. The trick is to then drop down into one of the many deeper pools that lie just behind the jagged reef crest for a 'rinse and spin' cycle and watch the fish rush in and out. When you have been thoroughly wrung out you leave this lunar landscape of craters and spires and head south, across the current as much as possible, and will soon drift along the drop-off through Kinasi Pass for a very satisfying and relaxed end to an awesome experience.

Mkadini *Dive depth: max 25m. Recommended for all skill levels.* Outside the bay, off Miewe Island, there is a short vertical step in shallow water (12–14m max). This flattens out into a deeper shallow-sloping reef. There are many alcyonaria

13

soft corals and diverse hard corals, lots of turtles (green and hawksbill), diverse groupers (back-saddled, lyretail, greasy cod, potato cod), schools of batfish and a good chance to see white-tip reef sharks and dolphins.

Juani Reef *Dive depth: max 30m. Recommended for experienced divers or beginners under professional supervision.* Outside the bay, a sloping fringing reef south of the pass extends for 12km. This is a good place to see turtles (green and hawksbill), guitar fish and white-tips, as well as stunning alcyonaria soft corals.

Mange Reef *Dive depth: max 24m. Recommended for all skill levels.* South–southeast of Chole Island (12 nautical miles), this is another beautiful coral-encrusted sandbar, once feared by local fishermen because of the many sharks. There is a good variety of reef fish and this is easily combined with Kitutia (see below) for an excellent day trip with a sandbank picnic.

Chole Wall *Dive depth: max 16m. Recommended for all certified divers; good training site.* Reef inside the bay; gentle slope. About 1km in length with lots of coral and reef fishes. A grand skin-diving site when the weather is calm.

Musambiji *Dive depth: max 16m. Recommended for Open Water or equivalent; good training site.* This is a submerged island inside the bay, with diverse walls and sloping fringing coral reefs. Unfortunately a combination of coral damage and poor visibility mean that it is rarely dived these days.

Kitutia *Dive depth: max 20m. Recommended for all skill levels.* Once a fantastic dive site, Kitutia was badly degraded by El Niño some years ago, although it's recovering rapidly and regaining much of its former glory. It is a spectacular sandbar encrusted with corals, ideal for a day of mellow dives, snorkelling and swimming. Combined with a picnic and a fabulous sail home, it's the perfect day out.

AROUND MAFIA ISLAND

Although Mafia is predominantly visited for its waters, many choose to explore the islands, and see some of Mafia beyond the marine park. It's easiest to arrange this through one of the lodges. For a good English-speaking guide, ask for either Moussa from Big Blu (see *Where to stay*, page 382) or Halfani at Sea Point (see *Where to stay*, page 382), who was sponsored through school by Pole Pole, where he also once worked. Having extensively researched these islands he is now also a knowledgeable snorkel guide. To go it alone, you could either hire a bike, or negotiate a price with the 4x4 drivers parked in Kilindoni to take you on an excursion.

KILINDONI All arrivals on Mafia pass through Kilindoni, the main town as well as the island's airport and sea port, but few visitors venture into Kilindoni for any length of time. New by east African standards, the town was established by the Germans in 1913 on discovering that Chole Island lacked a deep-water anchorage. While it has none of the Arab architecture of Stone Town on Zanzibar, its coral and lime-mortar shop-houses with quaint signs and rusting corrugated-iron roofs exude an ambience of old Indian Ocean days.

At first, Kilindoni appears to have all the accoutrements of a small town: a district hospital, school (complete with science laboratories), police station, bank, petrol station, post office, airport, mosque and churches. Then suddenly the sandy road opens into a square full of clothes for sale, music and activity, as well as a cluster of tuc tucs awaiting business.

Peaceful rather than bustling, the **market** is the centre of local life. Tomatoes, chillies, potatoes, onions, limes, coconuts, dried prawns, bananas, cassava and whatever the trader can get his hands on are arranged in little piles. A large amount of food here is from Dar, grown elsewhere on the Tanzanian mainland. Spices are from Zanzibar, naturally, all wrapped up in little plastic packets. Baobab seeds for kids to chew are sold in piles and the fish stalls are pungently gathered together a little further off. Other stalls sell pottery, kangas and secondhand clothes, and if you're brave enough to buy a homemade snorkelling/diving mask, ingeniously made of pieces of metal stapled to thick black rubber, it'll set you back US$2.50. In stark contrast to the ramshackle surroundings, there's a video rental store and a surprising number of mobile-phone shops, with some unexpectedly up-to-date models available; it seems everyone in town owns one.

A number of small **local shops** are of interest to the visitor, and most are found on the square or just off it down one of the five road branches. Here various stalls, shacks and shops sell a surprising variety of goods for such a small place. A couple of local tailors tout for business while a tiny shack sells various snacks and sundries. On the square itself the **KMB MIN mini-market** sells cold Cokes and Fantas for US$0.50, as well as items such as chocolate, toilet paper and toothpaste, although note that suncream is a rare commodity – the locals don't use it so it's next to impossible to find. If you're desperate, lighter skinned lodge staff might be able to lend you some, but far better to come well prepared. The **Kisoma Store** next to New Lizu sells basic stationery and offers internet access from four computers.

There are more stores on the road descending to the dhow landing. The **Market General Supply Store** and the **Peace and Love** sell soft drinks, and off the main square, Utende Road has a rather vulgar monument presented by the fish factory. On the left is a grey weather-beaten **mosque** and further along the Roman Catholic **church**, one of at least six churches.

The **landing** in Kilindoni usually has 15–20 *jahazis* moored on the beach. Whether unloading fish or mending their nets, the fishermen object strongly to being photographed, as do the people frying cassava chips and cooking octopus on small stoves under the trees.

✖ **Where to eat** The popular **Hakuna Matata** bar sells basic meals such as chicken and chips for rock bottom local prices. To find it, take the left-hand fork at the collection of dala dalas when arriving in Kilindoni from the airport. It's on the left just as the road starts to turn – look out for a map of Mafia painted on the wall. Alternatively, it's a well-known establishment, so just ask. It is near a cluster of two or three other local restaurants offering similar fare. A basic African establishment, the tiny **Royal Pub Mafia**, with a woven palm door, may be rather surprised by visitors, but sells local beers: Kilimanjaro, Tusker, Serengeti, Bin Bingwa for US$1, and Konyagi (a local firewater with rather descriptive flames on the bottle) for US$2.50. This local bar also sells food: chips are US$0.50, egg and chips US$1, and a beef kebab US$1.50. Another basic, open-sided restaurant is found opposite New Lizu – look for the plastic chairs and tables behind a large gate. Chips, omelettes and rice dishes are on offer.

Other practicalities The **National Microfinance Bank** (⊕ *08.30–15.00 Mon–Fri, 08.30–12.30 Sat*), is located on airport road but note that its ATM can only be used by account holders. The **post office** (⊕ *08.00–13.00 & 14.00–16.30 Mon–Fri, closed Sat*) is just past the bank, but be aware that your letter may take months to leave Mafia. A better option may be to ask your lodge to post your letters in Dar es Salaam.

NORTH OF KILINDONI One of the few places that travellers visit on Mafia is the lighthouse at Ras Mkumbi, via the charming village of Bweni. This is approximately 47km north of Kilindoni, and the drive there, over bouncy sand roads that follow or run parallel to the west coast of Mafia, takes about two hours direct, or all day if you want to include swimming and a picnic. Note, though, that while there are some stunning white-sand beaches along this coast, with excellent swimming opportunities, the sea on this side of the island is largely devoid of the underwater attractions around Chole Bay to the east. The excursion is best organised through one of the lodges; you'll find an English-speaking guide is invaluable. Alternatively, a full-day excursion to Ras Mkumbi with Mafia Island Tours costs US$65 per person. Bring everything you are likely to need from your hotel, not forgetting clothes to cover knees and shoulders, suncream, and insect repellent in case you return after dark.

Driving across Mafia is a good way of seeing the island, and finding out about everyday life. As you drive through the villages, you'll see crops of mangoes, pineapples, bananas, cassava and cashew nuts, as well as sweet potatoes, which grow after the rainy season. About 8km from Kilindoni is a picturesque swamp covered in mauve lotus. Small tilapia and catfish dart among the reeds. Further on, the old agricultural village of **Kirongwe**, with a tradition of making clay pots, counts a score of houses, a handful of shops and a market selling the usual dried octopus, bananas and coconuts. Beyond here the countryside is intensively cultivated with beans, pigeon pea and cassava, and – rather less attractive – numerous indications of slash-and-burn agriculture. Sykes' and vervet monkeys raiding the crops flee at the sound of any vehicle.

The north of Mafia is markedly different from the wetter southern part of the island, which is dominated by vast coconut plantations. After **Jimbo**, where you may see local blacksmiths working by the side of the road, the landscape suddenly becomes more undulating open grassland with outcrops of mia'a or palm, and baobabs similar to those on the mainland coastal plain. Birdlife is plentiful with bee-eaters and lilac-breasted rollers flashing amongst the trees and large flocks of guineafowl scuttling off the road. While only about 30m above sea level, it is noticeably cooler here than on the coast.

Bweni village, built behind 2km of beach, was an obvious spot for tourism development, and realised its potential in 2010 with the opening of Lua Cheia Beach Camp (see *Where to stay*, page 385). The village's traditional Swahili-style houses of coral and lime plaster are dotted among slender coconut palms. You need to stop to collect the lighthouse key from a keeper in the village, and will be soon surrounded by excited and curious children, delighted at the chance to shout *Mzungu!* at the unexpected visitor. Their behaviour is polite, however, and their fascination mixed with a fear of the unknown, although this is sure to change as the new lodge becomes more popular. Bweni women are experts at weaving striped prayer mats from the palms on the plateau, and you only need to show interest for items to be shyly produced. The larger mats are 2.5m by 1.5m, and cost around US$4; smaller oval mats go for US$3.

The **lighthouse** at **Ras Mkumbi** is a 3km drive on a good stretch of road from Bweni. Built on coral rag on the northern tip of Mafia, it is worth climbing the 15m up to the top of the red-and-white structure for a spectacular view of the Mafia Channel lying between the archipelago and the mainland. The stretch of deep-blue water is reputed to offer some of the best big-game fishing in east Africa. This working lighthouse also has concrete outbuildings, now owned by Pole Pole (see page 382), who organise trips to the area. One of the buildings has basic rooms with beds and mosquito nets, but no running water. At present it is used for overnight fishing trips but is being developed into a small guesthouse.

The grassy area in front of the lighthouse leads towards a rocky beach which offers half an hour or so of exploration at low tide. Black kites swoop low over the cliffs, while further out fishermen search for octopus in their race against the tide. It's possible to rent a bike from the village, or to go on a forest walk to see birds and monkeys. Snorkelling, fishing and diving trips can also be organised in this area.

KISIMANI MAFIA Kisimani (Kiswahili for 'the place of the well') lies on Ras Kisimani, at the south end of the island 30 minutes' drive from Kilindoni, or a two-hour boat trip. The town was an important centre during the Shirazi domination of Kilwa between the 12th and 14th centuries (see page 376). The hands of the sultan's chief mason were cut off after he built the palace, so that he could never repeat the task. The story goes on to claim that this was why a few months later Kisimani was inundated by the sea. There is little left of the submerged medieval settlement, but you can see the well for which it is named on the beach. Wandering about, you might find a few coins and pottery shards.

The shady coconut palms are a nice spot for a picnic, and there's a lovely beach with good birding and snorkelling, but bring everything you want to eat or drink.

UTENDE The majority of Mafia's tourist lodges lie along the beach below this small village, at the end of the 15km road west from Kilindoni. Many of Utende's inhabitants are Makonde people from the mainland, who keep their fishing boats in Chole Bay. One or two shop-houses sell strings of dried octopus and fish. Like everywhere else on Mafia, the village is quite safe to explore, being only ten minutes' walk from any of the hotels. The beach in front of Utende (close to Mafia Island Lodge) is where local dhows leave for Chole Island.

Schools here are developing with aid from the lodges. A new primary school was built on the site of the old school, offering Standards 1–6, and nursery education for 31 pupils. Since 2000, this has been financed by Pole Pole who sponsor some of the pupils. The government was then helped to build another school building for seven to 14 year olds. Visitors are welcome to visit the projects of the non-profit community development organisation Karibuni Onlus (*www.misaada.it*), which aims to improve education and health care in Utende village and all over Mafia. They have sponsored students and contributed towards the building and upkeep of a school and a well in Utende, but they also provide volunteer doctors, distribute mosquito nets all over the island and are renovating a school in nearby Kiegeani. Mafia Island Tours offers a trip to see the well and the school, plus learn about Karibuni Onlus's work for just US$5 per person, all of which goes directly to the organisation.

Utende also has a couple of small shops, and you'll notice a number of buildings made with cement blocks and corrugated iron. Although not picturesque, cement blocks are relatively cheap and an easy material for building, while corrugated-iron roofs last longer than a palm-leaf roof, which has to be replaced every three years or so.

OTHER EXCURSIONS Most other villages on Mafia are inaccessible by road and, like the offshore islands, may be visited only by boat. Given advance warning, the lodges can usually arrange trips to visit them.

13

However, the most popular excursions are probably those to isolated sandbars. You'll sail to these from your lodge, and then the boat crew will set up some shade on the beach, and cook lunch over a barbecue. Meanwhile, you can relax, sunbathe, swim and snorkel with nothing around you except miles and miles of deep-blue ocean. Trips like these are included by some of the lodges, for which others will charge you extra, depending on the destination (US$40–60 per person per trip is typical).

Destinations for excursions include Chole, Juani and Jibondo islands, described in the following pages, and several smaller spots including:

Mchangani Village The end of an interesting excursion winding for nearly 3km up a creek on the north side of Chole Bay. Sykes' monkeys can be seen in the mangrove forests and fish eagles are commonly observed. The village lies on the east bank of the creek, and takes about an hour to reach. Depart only on a high tide. If you would rather walk, it takes 90 minutes over sand and rock.

Dindini Beach Likewise accessible only at high tide. It faces the ocean from Mafia Island just north of Chole Bay, and from December to February can see big waves. Behind the beach is a large, sea-fed rock pool, which contains a variety of marine life. There are also low sand dunes and interesting vegetation on the coral rag.

Didimizi Beach This is the lovely beach seen from Chole Bay, around 4km from the main tourist lodges, or a 45-minute walk. You could arrange for a vehicle going to Kilindoni to drop you at the turn-off and walk back, not forgetting to take refreshments and a hat. Alternatively, a short trip by dhow brings you straight to the beach dotted with little pyramids of sand caused by the white ghost crabs that scuttle around – they'll be all you share the sandbar with.

Bwejuu Island Off Ras Kisimani to the west of Mafia, Bwejuu has its own small village and makes a good day trip. Located between the Rufiji River Delta and Mafia's main island, it offers good snorkelling at Mange Reef, as well as diving and fishing. You can also camp on Bwejuu Island for a few nights. Further afield, the Rufiji River is close enough for trips which can go all the way to the Selous Game Reserve.

Ras Mbisi Only 90 minutes by road from Kilindoni, it has an ideal beach for picnics, swimming and snorkelling, and is now the location of the new upmarket Ras Mbisi Lodge (see *Where to stay*, page 385).

Mbaracuni Island Lying 12km northwest of Mafia, this island can be visited by arrangement. Uninhabited, quiet and said to be very beautiful, it is used by fishing dhows. This is a good place to see black kites and occasionally two or three fish eagles.

Miewe Another small, uninhabited island used by fishermen to clean and dry fish, it can be visited for picnics, as can the sandbank of **Marimbani**. If you're interested in sailing a little further, and for a good chance of seeing dolphins, you can take a day excursion to the island of **Kitutia**. After a couple of hours under sail, you'll be rewarded by some stunning snorkelling on a reef which surrounds a pure-white sandbank. This is all covered by the sea at high tide, so the trip needs to be timed carefully.

Chole is the lush, tropical island lying to the west of Kinasi Pass. With the adjacent islands of Juani and Jibondo, it forms a barrier between Mafia and the open ocean. The shallow reef in front is rich in soft corals, sea anemones and sponges, and, sloping to 15m, it is a good spot to practise drift diving. The bay itself is ideal for sailing, windsurfing and kite surfing. The town of Chole Mjini was the main urban centre on the archipelago for much of the 19th century, the home of wealthy merchants whose plantations lay on the main island of Mafia (see *History*, page 376). Ruins dating from this era include a reasonably preserved **German Customs House** on the waterfront, and several more **ruined mansions** dating to the Omani era. A path behind the new market leading to the village brings you to a **prison**, whose broken cells are invaded by tangled tree roots. Farther along and also in ruins is a **Hindu temple**.

Hanging upside down in a nearby baobab is a colony of **fruit bats** of the same family as the Comoros Islands' lesser flying fox (*Pteropus seychellenis comorensis*), found in the Comoros, the Seychelles and Mafia, but nowhere on mainland Africa. Each evening the bats fly across Chole Bay to feed on the cashew nut and mango trees of Mafia, as well as marula fruit, figs and mangrove flowers. Like the Comoros bats they dip over the surface of the water – an action which scientists believe may be an attempt to rid themselves of parasites. A more enchanting local explanation claims 'they are washing before evening prayers'. Bats are nocturnal, so it's imperative for the continuation of the Chole colony that visitors allow them to sleep in the day, ensuring that neither they nor their guide throw stones at them, or shake their tree, just to wake them up and take photos of the bats in flight. Remember that it is a bat sanctuary.

Chole's human population was estimated at 5,000 during the early years of German rule, but today it is no more than 1,000. The islanders cultivate smallholdings of cassava, beans, mangoes, paw-paw, citrus (including very sweet oranges) and passion fruit. Encouraged by the lodges, these smallholdings have flourished and produce is now exported to Mafia, with the oranges also making their way to the mainland. Most of the menfolk fish, while many of the women are engaged in catching octopus beyond the mangroves at low tide. Winding past traditional houses, the path brings you to a beach where fishermen can be seen mending nets, or making sails and coconut-coir ropes. Chole was once a centre of boatbuilding, and boats are still repaired and occasionally built on the island. The boatyard is indicated on the circular walk available from Chole Mjini, about half an hour from the lodge.

The Norwegian Women's Front and Chole Mjini Lodge have been instrumental in much of Chole's development. They have funded the building of a hospital and a free clinic for the under fives, a kindergarten, a market, and the Society for Women's Development (which runs savings and loan schemes). They have also helped to set up a school, so that children no longer have to walk across to Juani Island at low tide, and a learning centre to help educate adults.

For places to stay, see page 384. Note that Chole Mjini Lodge does not cater to passing custom or serve meals to non-residents.

GETTING THERE AND AWAY The lodges at Utende (see page 382) operate **boat trips** to Chole, or you can visit it independently from Mafia, or on a '**bat and village tour**' with Mafia Island Tours (US$10). A dhow dubbed the '**Chole taxi**' leaves the beach in front of Mafia Island Lodge every 30 minutes or so throughout the day – last sailing at 16.00 – a crossing of ten to 15 minutes depending on the wind and tide, for a cost of US$0.60 one-way for visitors. It is also possible to charter a local boat across for a fee of about US$10.

On arrival you will need to hand over a village levy of US$10 per person – which goes straight to the village – payable at the Red Herring Café where the boat docks. You can also charge camera batteries here because there's no other electricity on the island. If you plan to stay more than a few hours on the island it is advisable to bring a picnic and refreshments from your hotel, and note that you'll have to wade a short distance from the boat. Make sure that you're wearing shoes, as there are stingrays in this area.

There is no motorised transport on Chole Island, and the locals all use **bikes**.

JUANI ISLAND

The boat trip from Mafia to Juani, site of the ruined city of Kua, takes about ten minutes longer than the one to Chole, but the island can be approached only at high tide. The landing, in a small bay sheltered by dense mangroves, is covered in thousands of opened oyster-shells, so remember to wear good shoes, as you'll have to wade to shore. Seafood is the staple diet on Juani, but, unlike Chole, Juani has no well water, and locals practise rain-dependent cultivation.

Beneath three big baobabs near the landing, your shoes crunch on the rocky paths of a buried civilisation. Bits of blue-and-white Shirazi pottery suggest trade links with China are embedded in the dirt. In the past, people from the mainland came to Juani to bathe in a seawater cave reputed to have curative properties for rheumatism. It is a long, difficult walk across to the ocean side, where there are also said to be three turtle-nesting beaches. The Kua Channel slices a tiny chunk off Juani as it opens into Chole Bay. It makes a superb picnic excursion with birdwatching and swimming. A friendly grouper lives in one of the rock pools at the southern end.

The ruined city of **Kua** (see *History*, page 377), spread across 6ha on the west coast of Juani, was the Shirazi capital of Mafia. It was one of the few east African ports to be continuously inhabited from medieval times into the early 19th century, when it was sacked by raiders from Madagascar. A trail hacked out of the undergrowth leads up to a large building shedding masonry: the former palace, still revered locally as a 'spirit place' where offerings such as bits of glass are left. The ruins here have been defeated by the powerful strangler figs that dominate a number of the walls, and the tomb of the sultan himself has been destroyed by a tree growing in its centre. The path passes other ruined edifices, including two 14th-century mosques and a series of tombs.

The buildings are made from coral rock and lime cement, which does not survive well in this sea air. Looking at cracks in the walls you wonder how long they will remain standing, with the occasional monkey as the only inhabitant. If you see the caretaker, he expects and deserves a small gratuity; ask him to show you the foundations of the house referred to in the box *Kua's revenge*, opposite.

You depart on a beautiful sail home between the islands, watched by the scores of ibis on the mangroves. There is a guide and map of the ruins, as well as the report on its archaeology, in the library at Kinasi Lodge (see *Where to stay*, page 383).

JIBONDO ISLAND

Jibondo is a long, low-lying island another 20-minute sail from Juani. This traditional village community is rather different from the rest of Mafia, and the atmosphere is somehow more charged than in other villages. Coming ashore, a big **jahazi dhow** is one of the first things you see. Built 15 years ago, it has never been

The political relationship between Kisimani and Kua is unclear, but an intriguing if unverifiable oral tradition recounted by T M Revington in an essay in *Tanganyika Notes & Records* suggests that it was not always amicable:

The people of Ras Kisimani constructed a ship, and when it was finished and still on the stocks, they made a feast to which they invited the people of Kua. From amongst the guests they took by force several children, laid them on the sand, and launched the ship over their bodies. When the Kua people heard what had been done at Ras Kisimani, they were infuriated and thought out a scheme of revenge. Seven or eight years later, when they thought that the incident had been forgotten, an invitation was sent to the inhabitants of Ras Kisimani to attend a wedding at Kua. When the guests arrived in the evening they were ushered to a room that had been especially prepared beneath a house; the hosts one by one left their guests on the excuse of inquiring into the food, until only an old man remained to entertain them. This he did so well that the doors were bricked up without the guests perceiving it. The bodies are there to this day. So, too, is the sealed-off basement in which the bodies lie, according to the site's caretaker, who claims that it is situated below the ruins in front of his hut.

launched and is subsequently something of a museum piece, but the old men sitting under the quinine tree nearby have already learned its value to tourism, wanting to charge US$1 for a photo.

Behind the boat is a rather plain white **mosque**, built in 1979. Some of its furniture was taken from the queen's palace in the ruins at Kua, and it's worth wandering around the back to see the carved wooden door from Kua (by contrast, the window frames were made of wood from India). This is all set off by the pungent smell from the row of long-drop loos that literally drop into the sea. Jibondo does not have a fresh water supply, so the islanders depend on frequent deliveries from Mafia's main island.

Jibondo people are well known as shipbuilders and, as on Chole, use only traditional tools. Even the nails are handmade and the holes are plugged with local kapok and shark fat. Local women play a prominent role in trading as well as fishing. They also sail boats, which is unusual in African society, and are more affable and confident than women elsewhere. Jibondo people also collect and dry seaweed to export.

Another unusual aspect of Jibondo is that cultivation is carried out at one end of the island while the people live in an urban community at the other. The village, which consists of traditional Swahili-style houses with makuti roofs, is laid out in a grid pattern. As on Chole and Juani, there is no transport other than boats which shelter on the western side of the narrow neck of the island.

The island has one school, easily identified by the football field in front. If the tide is good for fishing, the children – encouraged by their parents – go straight out on the water, ignoring lessons. In a year, only one child is likely to leave the island and go to secondary school on Mafia. There are, however, three *madrasas* on the island, where there is a strong Muslim faith. There are no other social services, and only a basic shop. On the other side of the island is **Flamingo Beach**, which makes an interesting two-hour trek. The village trail and sailing dhow with Mafia Island Tours costs US$30.

TANZANIA

NATIONAL PARKS & GAME RESERVES

1 Burigi GR
2 Biharamulo GR
3 Rubondo Island NP
4 Grumeti GR
5 Ikorongo GR
6 Serengeti NP
7 Maswa GR
8 Ngorongoro CA
9 Lake Manyara NP
10 Arusha NP
11 Mt Kilimanjaro NP
12 Gombe NP
13 Moyowosi GR
14 Kigosi GR
15 Mahale NP
16 Ugalla River GR
17 Tarangire NP
18 Mkomazi GR
19 Katavi NP
20 Uwanda GR
21 Kisigo GR
22 Rungwa GR
23 Ruaha NP
24 Udzungwa NP
25 Mikumi NP
26 Sadani GR
27 Selous GR

KEY

Capital city ■
Other city ●
Town ○
Surfaced road
Unsurfaced road
Railway
National park
International boundary

0   200km
0   100 miles

14

Southern Tanzania Safaris

with Philip Briggs

In recent years, there has been increasing interest in southern Tanzania's Ruaha National Park and Selous Game Reserve. For decades these areas have been overshadowed by their more famous northern counterparts (Lake Manyara, Ngorongoro Crater and the Serengeti), but today the secret is out, and southern Tanzania is a favourite amongst safari aficionados as well as first-time visitors who are put off by the crowds which so often mar the northern parks.

Zanzibar is barely 200km from the Selous, the largest of all Tanzania's (and indeed Africa's) game reserves, making it easily accessible by air. Ruaha is further – about 400km from Zanzibar, and having been extended to cover an area of 22,200km² in 2008, is now Tanzania's largest national park.

Gradually a 'southern circuit' has developed, with many individuals and small groups flying to Selous (and sometimes also Ruaha) before finishing their trip with time on the islands. Daily flights make this a very straightforward option. If you want to combine the parks of southern Tanzania with a trip to the islands as part of your travels, then this chapter aims to help you plan your trip, and enjoy it to the full.

OVERVIEW OF YOUR TRIP

It's often difficult for first-time visitors to decide which reserves to visit – so an overview here might help.

If you're planning on a beach-and-safari trip then first be mindful that safari time will usually cost much more than beach time; it's often double the nightly cost. For example, an uncomplicated safari lodge will easily cost US$350 per person per night, whilst you'll have to try hard to find a mid-range beach lodge at more than US$180 each per night. The reason for this is partly that most safari lodges include a full day of activities and all your meals, whereas a beach lodge often provides only a room and breakfast; and partly because the logistics at most safari lodges are that much more expensive.

With this in mind, consider how long you want to spend on each part of your trip. A 50/50 split (a week on safari and a week by the beach) is typical for a two-week trip, but this depends on your priorities and budget.

If you decide on five nights or less on safari, then our advice is that you should probably stick to Selous – and spend all your time there. If you decide on eight nights or more on safari, then you should consider combining time in Selous with time in Ruaha – as then the extra cost of flying between the parks is worth it for the change in scenery and environment. If you decide on six or seven nights on safari, then it's less clear if Ruaha is worth the extra travelling or not; you need to consider your own personal requirements.

Extending over 47,500km², the Selous (pronounced 'Seloo') is Africa's single largest game reserve, three times larger than the Serengeti, more than twice the size of South Africa's Kruger National Park, and roughly 50% bigger than either Belgium or Swaziland. It is, furthermore, the core sanctuary within the greater Selous-Niassa ecosystem, which extends over 155,000km² of practically uninhabited wilderness in southern Tanzania and northern Mozambique – the largest chunk of comparably untrammelled bush left in Africa.

The claim that the Selous lies at the core of the greatest surviving African wilderness is supported by the prodigiously large mammal populations protected within the reserve and the greater ecosystem. The elephant herd of 65,000–70,000 represents more than half of the Tanzanian population, and 5–10% of the African total. The buffalo, estimated at 120,000–150,000, and the reserve's 40,000 hippo and 4,000 lion are probably the largest such populations on the continent. The Selous also harbours an estimated 100,000 wildebeest, 35,000 zebra, 25,000 impala and significant herds of greater kudu, hartebeest and eland. It is also one of the most important sanctuaries in Africa for the endangered black rhinoceros, African wild dog, and sable and puku antelope.

BACKGROUND INFORMATION That the Selous ranks as one of east Africa's most alluring and satisfying safari destinations is not in dispute. However, given that much of the publicity surrounding the Selous bangs on about its vast area, prospective visitors should be aware that the extent of the reserve is in practice something of a red herring. The Selous is divided into two disproportionate parts by the Rufiji, Tanzania's largest river, which together with the great Ruaha, a major tributary, runs through the reserve from west to east. About 90% of the Selous lies to the south of the river and has been divided into a number of privately leased hunting concessions, all of which are off-limits to casual tourism. A proportion of the northern sector has also been set aside for hunting concessions. The remainder – no more than 5% of the reserve's total area – forms what, to all intents and purposes, is the Selous Photographic Reserve. The lodges (and most activities for visitors) are actually concentrated within an area of about 1,000km² immediately north of the Rufiji.

Fortunately, this photographic part of the Selous is wonderfully atmospheric, a dense tract of wild miombo woodland abutting the meandering Rufiji River, and an associated labyrinth of five pretty lakes connected to each other and the river by numerous narrow streams. Arriving by light aircraft, as most visitors do, it is exhilarating to sweep above the palm-fringed channels teeming with hippo and waterfowl, the swampy islets where immense herds of elephant and giraffe graze alongside each other, and exposed sandbanks where antelope drink and all manner of shorebirds scurry about.

No less exciting are the boat excursions along the Rufiji, which generally culminate with a brilliant red sun setting behind the tall borassus palms and baobabs that line the wide sandy watercourse. Gulp-inducing dentist's-eye views of the Selous's trademark gigantic crocs can pretty much be guaranteed from the boat, as can conferences of grunting, harrumphing hippo – and you'd be unlucky not to be entertained by herds of elephant, buffalo or giraffe shuffling down to drink.

The most memorable aspect of the boat trips, however, is the profuse birdlife. Characteristic waterbirds along this stretch of the Rufiji include yellow-billed stork, white-crowned and spur-winged plovers, various small waders, pied and malachite kingfishers, and African skimmer. Pairs of fish eagle and palmnut vulture perch high on the borassus palms, seasonal breeding colonies of carmine and white-throated bee-eater swirl around the mud cliffs that hem in some stretches of the river, and pairs of trumpeter hornbill and purple-crested turaco flap between the riparian trees. Worth looking out for among a catalogue of egrets and herons is the Malagasy squacco heron, a regular winter visitor, while the elusive Pel's fishing owl often emerges at dusk to hawk above the water.

Game drives along the network of rough roads to the north of the Rufiji are reliably rewarding, especially towards the end of the dry season, when large mammals concentrate around the five lakes. More frequently seen ungulates include impala, common waterbuck, bushbuck, white-bearded wildebeest, eland, greater kudu, buffalo and common zebra.

The northern sector of the park has been dubbed 'Giraffic Park', with some justification, as herds exceeding 50 individuals come down to drink in the heat of the afternoon. Giraffes seem exceedingly common here, which is odd as they are entirely absent south of the Rufiji. The river also forms a natural barrier between the ranges of the distinctive white-bearded and Niassa races of wildebeest. The endangered African wild dog is commonly observed, as is the spotted hyena, while leopards are common but elusive, and cheetahs exceedingly rare.

Much in evidence are Selous's lions, with two or three different prides' territories converging on each of the five large lakes. The lions typically have darker coats and less hirsute manes than their counterparts elsewhere in east Africa. During the dry season, the lions of Selous evidently rely on an unusual opportunistic diurnal hunting strategy, rarely straying far from the lakes, where they rest up in the shade to wait for whatever ungulate happens to venture within pouncing distance on its way to drink.

The Selous receives few visitors when compared with Tanzania's more famous northern parks – about 1% of tourist arrivals to Tanzania. Particularly if you are based at one of the western lodges – Beho Beho, Sand Rivers and Amara – it is still possible to undertake a game drive in the Selous without coming across another vehicle.

Whereas the national parks of northern Tanzania are dominated by large impersonal hotels that evidently aim to shut out the bush the moment you enter them, the Selous boasts a select handful of low-key, eco-friendly, thatch-and-canvas lodges whose combined bed capacity amounts to little more than 300 visitors. Furthermore, because the Selous is a game reserve and not subject to the regulations that govern Tanzania's national parks, visitors are offered a more primal and integrated bush experience than the usual repetitive regime of one game drive after another. In addition to boat trips, all lodges offer guided game walks for those aged 12 and over (16 at Lake Manze and Impala), which come with a real likelihood of encountering elephant or buffalo – even lion – on foot. Better still are the overnight fly-camping excursions offered by some of the camps, which entail sleeping beneath a glorified mosquito net in the middle of the bush.

Note that the roads within the Selous become impassable after heavy rain. Hence camps here close towards the end of the wet season, in April, and reopen in July.

Entrance fees An entrance fee of US$75 per person per day is charged (US$50 for park fees and a US$25 conservation charge). This is payable in hard currency. On most organised trips this will be included in the overall price, but it's worth checking this when booking. All lodge rates below include park fees. There has been talk of these fees increasing in the near future so do check before you travel.

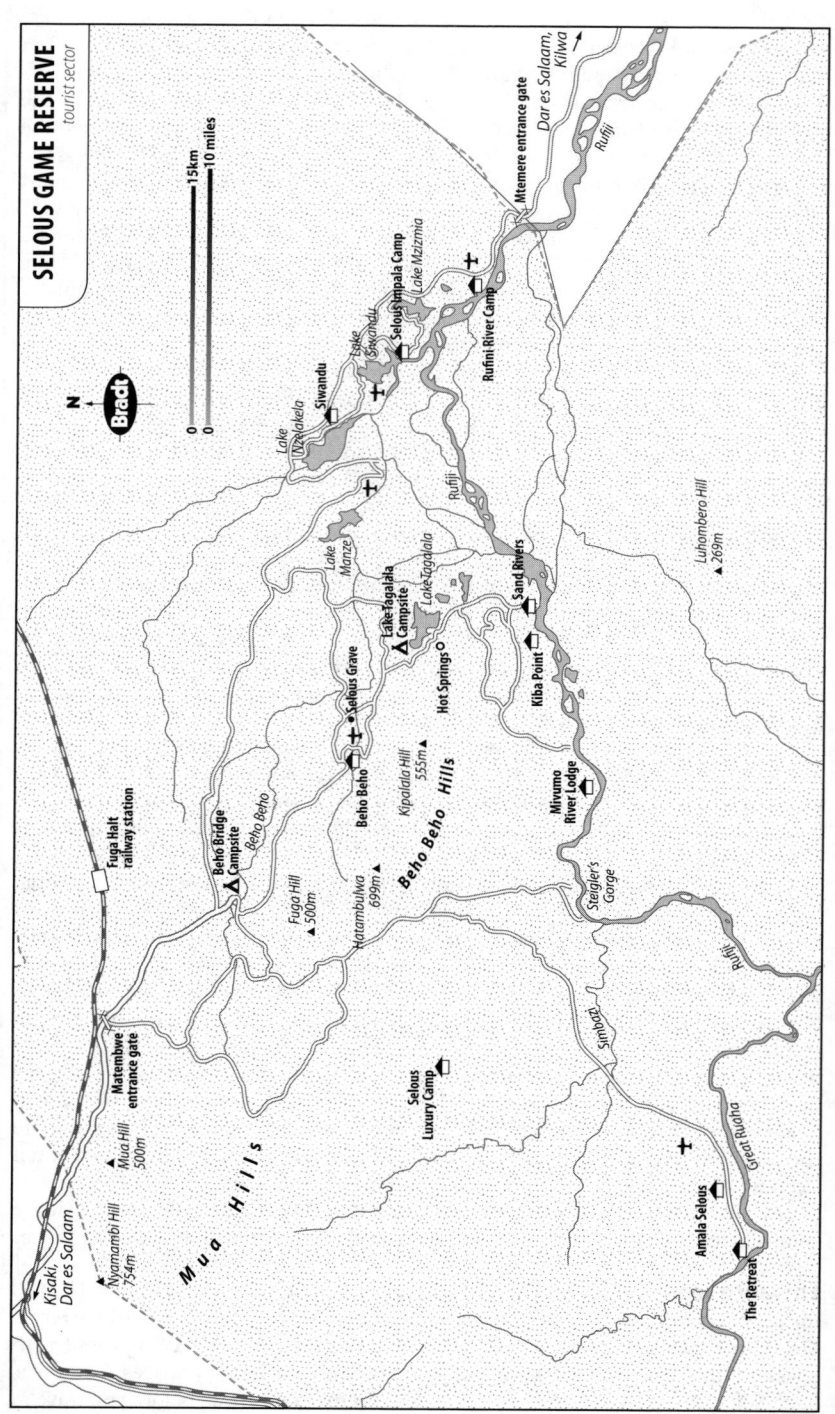

SELOUS GAME RESERVE
tourist sector

N

0   15km
0   10 miles

Bradt

Kisaki;
Dar es Salaam

Nyamambi Hill
754m ▲

Mua Hill
500m ▲

Matembwe
entrance gate

Fuga Halt
railway station

Beho Bridge
Campsite

Fuga Hill
500m ▲

Beho Beho

Matambulwa
699m ▲

M u a   H i l l s

Selous Luxury Camp

Selous Grave

Beho Beho

Kipalala Hill
555m ▲

B e h o   B e h o   H i l l s

Lake Tagalala
Campsite

Hot Springs

Lake Tagalala

Sand Rivers

Kiba Point

Lake
Manze

Lake
Nzelakela

Lake
Siwandu

Siwandu

Lake
Siwandu

Selous Impala Camp

Lake Mzizimia

Mtemere entrance gate

Dar es Salaam,
Kilwa

Rufiji

Rufiji River Camp

Rufiji

Mivumo River Lodge

Steigler's Gorge

Simbazi

Luhombero Hill
269m ▲

Amala Selous

The Retreat

Great Ruaha

Rufiji

Further information Two useful booklets are *Selous Game Reserve: A Guide to the Northern Sector* by Rolf D Baldus and the glossier *Selous: Africa's Largest & Wildest Game Reserve* by Rolf D Baldus and L Siege. Most lodges stock both and they are similar textually. For details on the man behind the park's name, read *The Life of Frederick Courtney Selous* by J G Millais, published by Gallery Publications and available in Zanzibar.

GETTING THERE AND AWAY Many tour operators, both overseas and in Tanzania, offer a variety of trips to the Selous. These usually include flights to/from the reserve, accommodation and activities. Most use frequent daily **flights** between Dar es Salaam and Selous operated by **Coastal Airlines**, **Safari AirLink** and **ZanAir**. These generally connect very easily to/from Zanzibar. The early-morning Coastal flight continues to Ruaha daily. Once inside the parks, these flights will all stop at any of the camp airstrips by prior arrangement, although it is not possible to fly between camps in the Selous – for this, a road transfer must be arranged in advance.

If you are travelling in mainland Tanzania it's perfectly possible to reach the Selous by **road**, although that's generally more costly than flying. For full details of these options, Bradt's *Tanzania* guide by Philip Briggs is highly recommended (see *Appendix 2*).

WHERE TO STAY Over the last few years, accommodation options in Selous have increased significantly, although the sheer size of the park still ensures privacy in the majority of areas. All of the camps listed below are within the park boundaries and levels of service and experience are almost invariably high. A growing number of camps are found along the sandy road leading to the Mtemere Gate, while Sable Mountain Lodge is located 1km outside the Matambwe Gate. For further details of these see Bradt's *Tanzania* guide by Philip Briggs.

⌂ **Amara Selous** (12 suites) ☎ TZ +255 784 747 265; e sales@highlifemarketing.com; www. amara-tanzania.com. In 2010, Amara Selous opened in the far west of the park overlooking the Great Ruaha River. Marketed as a 'boutique camp', its designer's influence is apparent throughout, with stylish leather furniture & black glass chandeliers in the cosy lounge, plus interesting *objets d'art* scattered throughout the property. The tiered main area looks out over the river & the tempting pool. The half-tented, half stone-built suites offer plenty of light & space, AC (although with gauze windows its efficiency is somewhat dubious), & a private deck & plunge pool overlooking the river. The en-suite bathroom is decked out in high-quality fittings & tiles, & has both an indoor & outdoor hot shower. Activities focus on game drives plus romantic sundowners & bush dinners under the stars. While tired parents relax with an in-suite massage, children will be educated & entertained on the popular 'Amaradillos' programme, a series of informative games & activities designed to teach children

about the local flora & fauna. All participants are given a colourful workbook that keen children will love to fill in & keep. The service at Amara is slick & the camp well run, & although there's a fair amount of game around, it's a little sparser than the more easterly lodges. But for a relaxing & indulgent safari it's a great choice that would especially appeal to honeymooners. *US$1125/775 sgl/dbl FB inc drinks & all activities & park fees.*

⌂ **Beho Beho** (9 units) ☎ 022 2600352–4/(UK) +44 (0)1932 260618; e reservations@behobeho. com; www.behobeho.com. Beho Beho's site was used for a safari camp as early as 1972, one of the first such sites in the Selous. It still has an unusual location for this park, high on a hill in an area dotted with baobabs. In 2004, it was virtually rebuilt & completely refurbished, & is now widely regarded as the best lodge in the Selous. Accommodation is in very large & attractively decorated en-suite bandas built of local stone on the footslopes of the Beho Beho Hills, on the west side of northern Selous. All have large bathrooms with great outdoor showers. The bedrooms have canopied king-size beds, ceiling

14

fans & 24hr electricity. All are slightly different, & each has a separate area that is part lounge, part veranda. This lies under a high thatched roof, with almost a whole wall open at the front. The elegant dining area serves very high-quality food, with everyone usually sitting around the same table. Afterwards there are vast sofas to relax in around the bar area, & a full-size slate-bedded billiards table. Slightly down the slope, the swimming pool & its sundeck command a spectacular view. In 2012, the brand-new Bailey's Banda was completed, a private house named after the camp's owner. With 2 bedrooms & a lounge & dining room with its own chef, it's a welcome escape for those in need of privacy. Beho Beho is the only lodge within Selous set away from the river, but a permanent pool in the valley below supports a resident pod of hippos & attracts plenty of game & birdlife. Although very comfortable, what has really gained such a top reputation for the camp is the quality & enthusiasm of its guiding team. Being in a relatively remote area of the park, you'll find few other visitors in the vicinity. The camp's activities include 4x4 game drives, boat trips on Lake Tagalala, & particularly good walking safaris. (It's not unknown for morning activities to last for 5 or 6hrs if you are enthusiastic & energetic.) Nearby sites of interest include some World War I trenches (complete with scattered artefacts), the grave of Frederick Courtney Selous & a group of hot springs set in a patch of riparian woodland. Beho Beho also offers a super-luxurious treehouse in the branches of an ancient leadwood tree. With a dbl bed that can be taken outside to sleep under the stars, this is a romantic option. It is expensive, but the camp is certainly the best in Selous & arguably one of the best camps in Tanzania. The camp actively prefers guests to book through an operator rather than directly, & you will almost certainly get a better rate by doing so. *US$995pp sharing or single, FB inc drinks & all activities; Treehouse extra US$350pp & Bailey's Banda extra US$1000 on top of normal room rates.*

🏠 **Lake Manze Tented Camp** (12 tents) 📞022 245 2005/6; e reservations@adventurecamps. co.tz; www.adventurecamps.co.tz. Lake Manze Camp is part of the highly regarded Adventure Camps circuit, joining sister-property Impala Camp in the Selous, plus Kwihala Camp & Mdonya Old River Camp in Ruaha National Park. Distinct from many of the other camps in the park, Lake Manze is about being in the wilderness & enjoying

bush simplicity: atmospheric paraffin lanterns replace electricity, bathrooms are open air & there is fireside dining under the stars. Dotted under borassus palm trees, the tents are spacious & surrounded with gauze windows to allow for long views & a cooling breeze, furnishings are simple but high-quality wrought-iron & canvas furniture, & there is an en-suite bathroom complete with hot shower & flush toilet. Perhaps the greatest asset of the tents is their shady stone veranda, from where their slightly raised position affords good views across the lake, floodplain & passing wildlife. Activities are varied with 4x4 safari drives, boat safaris & morning walks all available, & with a high standard of guiding, Lake Manze is an excellent choice for a good value safari in the Selous. *US$405/680 sgl/dbl, FB for drive-in clients (no activities); US$885–955/820–890 inc FB & activities; inc park fees.*

⛰ **Lake Tagalala & Beho Beho Bridge campsites** These little-used official campsites have no facilities worth talking about, but they both boast a great setting & bush feel. Camping must be arranged in advance or at the Matambwe or Mtemere Gates. *Camping US$20pp exc park fees.*

🏠 **Mivumo River Lodge** (12 rooms) 📞+255 22 2118113/4; e darreservations@serena.co.tz; www.serenahotels.com. Now run by the Serena hotel group, Mivumo is set along the river in the Stiegler's Gorge area, with its suites – all with AC & en-suite bathroom with both a free-standing tub & an outdoor shower – designed for both privacy & luxury. Nearby, the Presidential suite is a vast complex of rooms connected by artificial rivers & waterfalls which flow through the lounge, bathroom & 2 bedrooms. Guests can laze in their own plunge pool, or take in the latest news on satellite TV in the lounge with a drink from the minibar. The river view is shared by a 3-tier central lounge, library & dining area, as well as an extensive pool. Visitors should be aware that though plenty of crocs, hippos & birds can be seen on a riverboat trip, the land-dwelling game in this area is fairly dispersed, & therefore full-day game drives are offered to reach better frequented areas. *US$845/1225 sgl/dbl FB & activities, inc local drinks, activities & laundry, park fees; children over 7 welcome.*

🏠 **Rufiji River Camp** (14 rooms) 📞(UK) 01452 862288, 📞022 2862357; m 0784 237422/0713 237422; e fox@safaricamps.info;

www.tanzaniasafaris.info. One of the 1st lodges to be established in the Selous, the ever popular & reasonably priced Rufiji River Camp is situated at the eastern extremity of the photographic northern area of the reserve, overlooking an atmospheric stretch of the Rufiji River alive with hippos & crocs & regularly visited by elephants. Owned by Foxes Safari Camps, who also own Ruaha River Lodge, the camp was extensively renovated in 2012. The number of tents decreased & their size & privacy increased, while fixtures & fittings were upgraded. The interiors are pleasant but simply furnished, with dbl/twin beds & an en-suite bathroom with a flush toilet & solar-heated shower. The camp is frequently visited by monkeys & numerous birds, & occasionally by more exciting large mammals. Rufiji River Camp has traditionally offered an excellent range of boat & foot activities, as well as half-day game drives encompassing the 3 nearby lakes, full-day excursions further afield & overnight fly-camping. The guides are generally experienced Tanzanians, most of whom have been guiding here for many years; many have worked as game scouts before joining the lodge. For guests who don't want to venture far, there's a swimming pool for in-camp relaxation. *US$415–490/730–820 sgl/dbl, FB, inc activities & park fees.*

🛖 **Sand Rivers Selous** (8 rooms plus private camp) `022 2865156; e info@nomad-tanzania.com; www.nomad-tanzania.com. Set above a wide, sandy bend in the Rufiji River, Sand Rivers Selous has been regarded as the top camp in the Selous for many years, & still puts up very stiff competition to Beho Beho. Sand Rivers' pedigree is top-notch: it's run by Nomad Tanzania & is the sister-camp of Chada Katavi, in Katavi National Park, & Greystoke Mahale, in Mahale National Park – both of which are top camps & names to conjure with in the safari world. Like Beho Beho, Sand Rivers is situated in an isolated area of the Selous, the wild southwest of the photographic section of the reserve, which is visited by vehicles from the other lodges infrequently. It is a very comfortable lodge with a large, open-fronted, thatched boma dotted with large sofas sporting sumptuous cushions, but it stands on a wide curve of the Rufiji River & being able to watch the life of the river adds greatly to the special feel of the place. For those who need to be closer still to the water, there is a stylish curved swimming pool under a large baobab tree. Meals are high quality & eaten either

together around a large table, or separately if guests prefer. The lodge's stone-&-thatch cottages are large & elegant with large dbl/twin beds, walk-in mosquito nets, an en-suite bathroom with flush toilet & a private balcony. There are 5 standard rooms, 2 suites (with small plunge pool & separate lounge area) & the Rhino House – a private 'honeymoon cottage' offering private dining & game drives. All the rooms are open fronted, & raised up to look out over the river. For something more private, Sand Rivers has a satellite camp a few kilometres from the main camp. With just 4 cottages, it can be booked only by groups or families of up to 8 people for their exclusive use. The style is similar to that of Sand Rivers, with the addition of a plunge pool at each of the cottages, plus a private chef & guide. Sand Rivers' activities focus on 4x4 game drives (the plains around nearby Lake Tagalala are one obvious goal), boat trips along the river & up through the impressive Stiegler's Gorge, & walking safaris. The standard of guiding is exceptionally high & the camp is very proud of its Tanzanian guides, some of whom have been there for many years. Sand Rivers also runs very popular fly-camping trips, whereby a couple of guests sleep out on a dry riverbed with their guide – usually having had a meal under the stars, complete with table-linen, crystal glasses & some fine food. Usually these are run for 1 or 2 nights as part of a longer stay at the lodge. *Standard room from US$700pp, FB inc most drinks.*

🛖 **Selous Impala Camp** (8 units) `022 245 2005/6; e reservations@adventurecamps.co.tz; www.adventurecamps.co.tz. This unpretentiously tasteful camp boasts a magnificent location on a wooded stretch of the Rufiji. It's relatively small, with just 8 Meru-style tents, built on wooden platforms with a private balcony. These are very comfortably furnished, in a bright & warm style. There is a family option here, with 2 full-size tents sharing 1 platform allowing parents to have their own space but remain within easy access of their children. The camp also uses Maasai guards to escort guests to their rooms at night. Impala has one of the most scenic locations in the park & its thatched lounge & communal deck look out over the river to mountains, although your gaze is usually drawn back to the Rufiji River by the elephants & other wildlife which visit it. Activities are fairly flexible, including game drives

& boat trips, & the camp has a lovely swimming pool – allowing you to look out over the river & to the hills while you're in the pool. Fly-camping trips are a wonderful way to get closer to nature, & are surprisingly comfortable, with long-drop toilets, bucket showers & sinks, & a chef to prepare all meals. Impala has high standards of service, a great team & excellent prices, & though it isn't as luxurious as Siwandu & Sand Rivers, it's stylish enough & tremendously good value. This has made it justifiably popular & you need to book a fair bit in advance to stay here. In combination with its sister-camps in Selous (Lake Manze Camp) & Ruaha (Kwihala Camp & the rather more spartan Mdonya Old River Camp), safaris are varied & particularly excellent value. *US$450–610/770– 1,090 sgl/dbl for drive-in clients (no activities); US$510–685/740–1,090 sgl/dbl inc activities; all rates FB; inc park fees.*

🏠 **Selous Luxury Camp** (12 tents) 📞 +255 22 2118113/4; e darreservations@serena.co.tz; www.serenahotels.com. Formerly known as Selous Wildlife Camp, the 2nd of the Serena hotel group's offerings lies on the Simbazi River, a tributary of the Rufiji. Each of the individual tents, sheltered under grass thatch, is identical, with soft carpeted floors, comfy sofas & sparkling chandeliers & has its own bathroom. Interiors are rather dramatically decorated with high-quality dark wood furnishings, & dressing gowns & slippers are provided. Central to the lodge is a natural waterhole, overlooked by the dining area & lounge. There's also a viewing deck & an infinity swimming pool. Guest can take part in nature walks, river cruises & game drives, which often last a full day in order to reach the well-dispersed game. *US$710/960 sgl/dbl FB & activities, inc local drinks, activities & laundry, park fees; children over 7 welcome.*

🏠 **Siwandu** (13 rooms) 📞 022 2128485; e reservations@selous.com; www.selous.com. The former Selous Safari Camp, this plush lodge is set back slightly from the shores of Lake Siwandu. Approaching across the water, all you see of the camp over the treetops are the tall apexes of the main bandas, which have been built on stilts. The camp has recently been divided into a main camp with 9 rooms, known as 'Siwandu', & a smaller section with just 4 rooms called 'Siwandu Private Camp'. Both provide accommodation in raised, spacious en-suite tents, which are set far apart from each other & have fans, open-air showers & a private

deck. The main camp's lounge & dining area is a fabulous stilted treehouse lit at night by dozens of gas lamps. The main camp has a separate swimming pool. The private camp's tents are in essence identical to the main camp, though they are more luxuriously appointed & as a group have their own dining area on decking near the pool. Private camp is booked on an exclusive-use basis only. Game drives, boat trips, guided walks & fly-camping are all offered here – although the camp is geared more for driving & boating than it is for walking. A recently purchased pontoon boat, apparently the only one in east Africa, allows for relaxing lake trips with chilled drinks & tasty snacks provided. In short, Siwandu Camp is a very high-quality, professional operation that pays great attention to detail – especially where comfort & food are concerned. *US$963–1,286/642–857 sgl/ dbl main camp & private camp; inc 2 activities daily; all rates FB & inc park fees; exc drinks.*

🏠 **The Retreat** (12 rooms) 📞 +255 783 213 951; e welcome@retreat-africa.com; www.retreat-africa.com. In a remote section of the park, is the strikingly stylish Selous Retreat. Architecturally impressive, its ochre walls, Omani arches, stunning pool deck & impressive array of African *objets d'art* are testament to its Swiss owners' attention to detail & high standards. Reminiscent of a fort, the imposing main building is entered through a 200-year-old carved wooden door from Rajasthan. Accommodation is divided between the main clay 'fort', hillside tents & riverfront suites (complete with waterside plunge pools & viewing decks), including a honeymoon hideaway boasting a private chef, guide, butler & pool. 2 tents at Hippo Point share a pool bar & dining area. The tents, raised on teak decks, are spacious & well furnished & all have inviting outdoor baths to complement the en-suite facilities. In the public areas, there are lovely shaded lounge areas & the lodge also has a well-equipped, professionally run outdoor spa on the riverbank. With an array of traditional massage & holistic treatments available, including crystal & sound therapy, this is a great place to relax. Massages can even be included as 1 of your 2 activities per day. Food is served in the main restaurant overlooking the infinity pool & river or, for romantics, atop one of the 2 towers for panoramic views. Cocktails & sundowners' spots are equally varied, with bars both riverside & raised on the hillside. If you can drag yourself away from the obvious comfort of the lodge, activities include game drives, river cruises (when the river is high enough), guided walking & line fishing. Open 4x4 vehicles & aluminium boats are used for these, with Tanzanian guides (who have received mixed reports) escorting all trips. Fly-camping needs to be pre-booked & costs an additional US$325pp. As there is more emphasis on sitting back & relaxing than game viewing, the Retreat appeals to honeymooners & those looking to get away from it all. *From US$770pp, FB & 2 activities/day.*

RUAHA NATIONAL PARK

With the addition of the Usangu Game Reserve in 2008, Ruaha doubled in size to become Tanzania's largest national park. It extends over 20,200km². of wooded hills and open plains to the west of Iringa, and it lies at the core of a greater ecosystem that is 2½ times larger, embracing six other protected areas including the contiguous Rungwa and Kizigo game reserves. Ruaha is widely regarded by Tanzania's safari cognoscenti to be the country's best-kept game-viewing secret, and it has unquestionably retained a compelling wilderness character that is increasingly savoury when compared with the package safaris and 100-room game lodges common in the parks of northern Tanzania. Let's hope it stays this way.

BACKGROUND INFORMATION The dominant geographical feature of the park is the Great Ruaha River, which follows the southeast boundary for 160km, and is known to the local Hehe people as the Lyambangori (Ruaha being a corruption of the Hehe word *luhava*, which simply means 'river'). Only the small part of the park around the river is developed for tourism, with just six small lodges currently operating. Its limited 400km road circuit sees relatively few visitors and has a reassuringly untrammelled mood.

Ruaha has a hot and rather dry climate, with an average annual rainfall of around 500mm falling almost exclusively between October and May, and peaking in February and March. Daytime temperatures in excess of 40°C are regularly recorded, particularly over October and November before the rains break, but a very low humidity level makes this less noticeable than might be expected, and it cools down reliably at night. The best game viewing is generally from May to November, but the bush is greener and prettier from January to June, and birding peaks during the European winter months of December to April. The vegetation of Ruaha is transitional to southern miombo and eastern savanna biomes, and a wide variety of habitats are protected within the park, including riparian forest along the watercourses, swamps, grassland and acacia woodland. The dominant vegetation type is brachystegia woodland, and several areas of the park support an impressive number of large baobab trees.

The floral variety of Ruaha is mirrored by the variety of wildlife likely to be seen over the course of a few days on safari. The most common ungulates, not unusually, are the widespread impala, waterbuck, bushbuck, buffalo, zebra and giraffe, all of which are likely to be encountered several times on any given game drive. The park lies at the most southerly extent of the range of several east African ungulate species, including lesser kudu and Grant's gazelle. Yet it also harbours a number of antelope that are rare or absent in northern Tanzania, most visibly the splendid greater kudu – some of the most handsomely horned males you'll come across anywhere in Africa – but also the more elusive roan and sable antelope. The elephant population is the largest of any Tanzanian national park, despite heavy losses due to poaching in the 1980s, with some 12,000 elephants migrating through the greater Ruaha ecosystem. The most impressive pair of tusks weighed in the 20th century – combined weight 201kg – were from an individual shot in Ruaha in the 1970s, but the poaching of the recent past means you're unlikely to see anything comparable these days.

14

Ruaha is an excellent park for predators. Lions are not only numerous and very habituated to vehicles, but the prides tend to be unusually large, often numbering more than 20 individuals. The park also boasts a justified reputation for good leopard sightings, and, while it's not as reliable as the Seronera Valley in the Serengeti, leopard are usually seen every few days and they are less skittish than in many game reserves. Cheetah, resident on the open plains, are quite often encountered in the Lundu area – known locally as the mini Serengeti – northeast of the Mwagusi River. More than 100 African wild dogs are thought to be resident in the greater Ruaha ecosystem. Wild dogs are known to have very wide ranges, and their movements are often difficult to predict, but one pack of about 40 individuals regularly moves into the Mwagusi area, generally hanging around for a few days before wandering elsewhere for a couple of weeks. Visiting in July gives a higher chance of seeing a wild dog, as they are normally denning, and are thus easier to locate than at other times of year. However, in recent years their behaviour has been more varied, and so this seasonal activity is not as reliable as it once was. Black-backed jackal and spotted hyena are both very common and easily seen, and the rarer striped hyena, though seldom observed, is found here at the southern limit of its range.

With 587 species recorded, Ruaha also offers some excellent birding, once again with an interesting mix of southern and northern species. Of particular note are substantial and visible populations of black-collared lovebird and ashy starlings, Tanzanian endemics associated with the Maasai Steppes, found here at the southern extreme of their distribution. By contrast, this is perhaps the only savanna reserve in east Africa where the crested barbet – a colourful yellow-and-black bird whose loud sustained trilling is a characteristic sound of the southern African bush – replaces the red-and-yellow barbet. Ruaha is also the type locality for the recently described Tanzanian red-billed hornbill (*Tockus ruahae*), a Tanzanian endemic that is very common within its restricted range. Raptors are well represented, with bateleur and fish eagle probably the most visible large birds of prey, and the localised Eleanora's falcon quite common in December and January. The watercourses support the usual waterbirds.

Ruaha is best visited between July and November, when animals concentrate around the river. Internal roads may be impassable during the rainy season (December to May), when many of the camps are closed.

National park fees There is a conservation fee of US$30 per person per night (US$10 for children aged 6–16) which must be paid by Visa, MasterCard or Tanapa smartcard – cash is not accepted. On most organised tours this will be included, but it's worth checking this when booking.

Further information The *Ruaha* booklet, published in 2000 by the African Publishing Group, is normally available at the lodges, and contains useful maps, animal descriptions and checklists, and details of where to look for localised species.

GETTING THERE AND AWAY The most straightforward way to reach Ruaha from Zanzibar is by Coastal Aviation's daily scheduled **flights** via Dar es Salaam, which also serve the Selous Game Reserve. Typically these cost about US$330 per person one-way between Selous and Ruaha, or US$380 per person one-way between Dar and Ruaha.

As with the Selous, if you are travelling in mainland Tanzania you can reach Ruaha by air from Dar es Salaam, without going to Zanzibar. It's also possible to get there by **road**, although this is usually at least a two-day trip; for more details see Bradt's *Tanzania* guide by Philip Briggs.

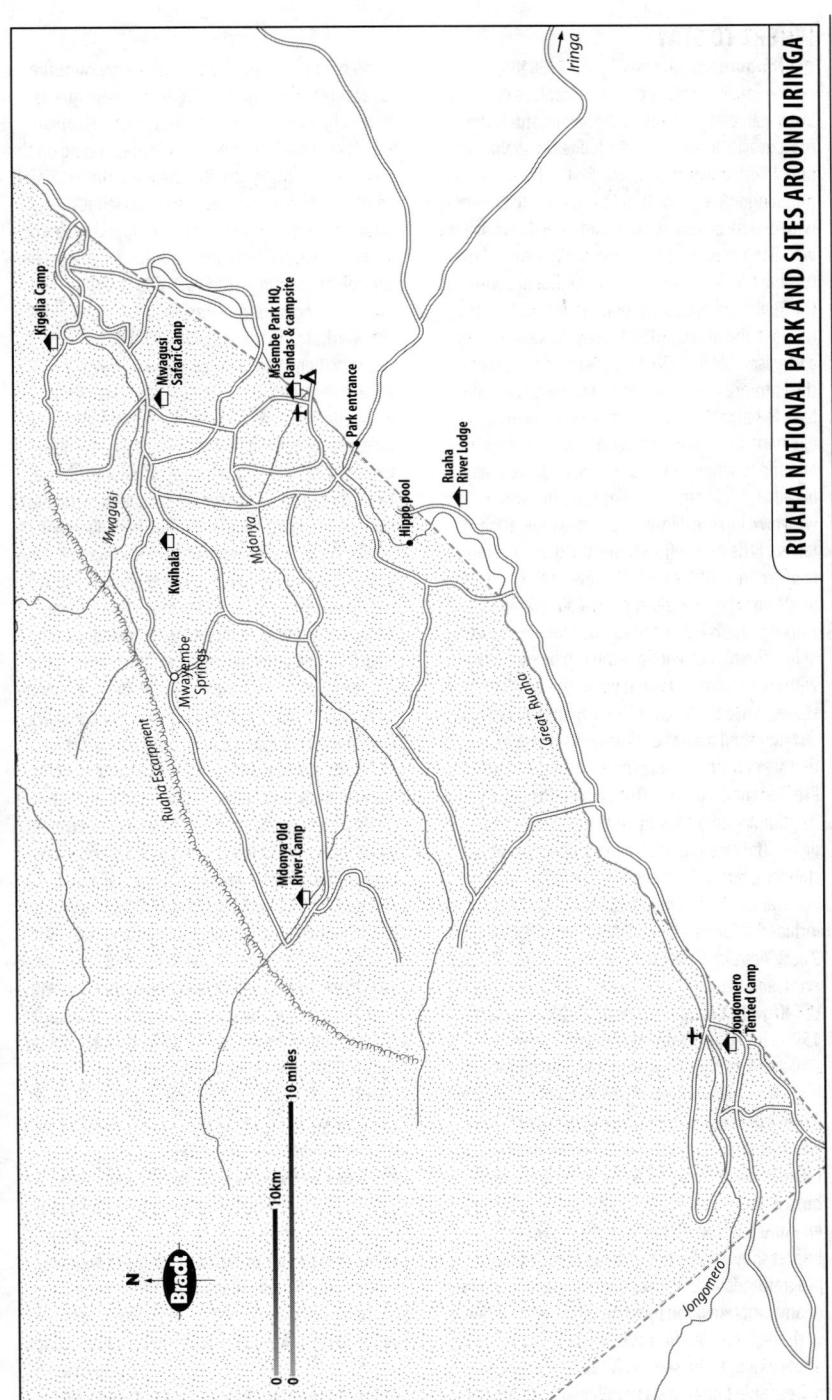

RUAHA NATIONAL PARK AND SITES AROUND IRINGA

⌂ WHERE TO STAY

⌂ Jongomero (8 tents) ☎ 022 2128485; e reservations@selous.com; www.selous.com. Sister-camp of Siwandu in the Selous, this is the most overtly luxurious of the lodges in Ruaha, & the only 1 with a swimming pool. Stylish & excellently run, Jongomero consists of spacious tented rooms with private balconies carved into the dense riverine woodland bordering the eponymous seasonal river. It's about 500m upstream of its confluence with the Ruaha, where a semi-permanent pool hosts a resident pod of around 50 hippos. Jongomero has a very isolated feel, situated 60km southwest of the entrance gate, & the little-used road running back towards the entrance gate often yields good elephant & buffalo sightings. The area to the south of camp functions much as a private game reserve because so few other vehicles head this way, but with lower game densities & dense vegetation, it takes a little more effort to see the game here than in other areas of the park. However, this is more than made up for by the top-notch guiding & fascinating walking safaris led by the camp's manager & head guide. The birdlife within camp can be excellent, with Livingstone's turaco topping the gaudiness stakes, while the localised Bohm's spinetail can be distinguished from the other swifts & swallows that soar above the camp by its distinctive bat-like fluttering. For something a bit different, try fly-camping to complement the existing game drives. The catering is to an exceptionally high standard, but, unlike several other lodges in this price range elsewhere in Tanzania, drinks are not included. *US$821–1,143/547–762 sgl/dbl, FB & inc 2 activities/day & park fees; walking safaris US$35pp extra park fee.*

⌂ Kigelia Camp (6 tents) ☎ +255 769 204 159; e info@afrikaafrikasafaris.com; www.afrikaafrikasafaris.com. Rustic yet elegant Kigelia is a semi-permanent camp found tucked away in a grove of sausage trees (*Kigelia africana*), from where it takes its name. Secluded & spacious tents blend in surprisingly well with the surrounding bush & are airy with plenty of light. Inside, the en-suite bathrooms' hot water is provided in bucket showers. Each tent has a mobile phone, programmed with the manager's number, in case of any problems. The open-sided lounge is filled with solid wooden furniture, made from reclaimed dhow wood, & the shelves & tables scattered with coffee table books. It's a popular spot for afternoon

tea & biscuits. In the evening, a roaring campfire is set up overlooking the riverbed, where guests gather for pre-dinner stargazing. Tasty 3-course meals are usually served outside, depending on the weather. The main activities here are the extremely comfortable game drives with knowledgeable & informative guides in vehicles equipped with soft, sofa-like seating, hot-water bottles & blankets for the colder mornings. *US$708–845/1,140–1,360 sgl/dbl FB inc laundry & park fees.*

⌂ Kwihala (6 tents) ☎ 022 2452005/6; e reservations@adventurecamps.co.tz; www.adventurecamps.co.tz. With the same tent designer as Kigelia & with a similar layout yet completely different style, Kwihala was opened by Adventure Camps in 2006 to join sister-camp Mdonya. Canvas tents are spacious & tastefully decorated, with glass beads & the camp's signature blue baobab design adding a touch of interest. En-suite bathrooms are simple & stylish, with a hot bucket shower which has been cleverly disguised to look like a regular shower. The lounge & dining room are adjoined & set back from the tents, while a short walk away is the campfire, where safari-goers gather in the evening to discuss the day's sightings. Dining locations vary, but a popular choice is a tasty bush dinner served under the stars by lantern light. The camp cleverly mixes style, luxury & comfort while managing to retain a feeling of wilderness. As well as the usual game drives, safari walks & night drives are offered here, although these are not always available & cost extra (US$35pp per walk & US$70pp per night drive). Kwihala's popularity has increased steadily over recent years, mainly due to its great value, good management & excellent standard of guiding. With plenty of game in the surrounding area – leopards are regularly sighted here – it's a justifiably popular choice. Following on from its success here, Kwihala has plans to open a luxury camp nearby in the next couple of years. *US$490–530/810–860 sgl/dbl inc activities & park fees; all rates FB.*

⌂ Mdonya Old River Camp (12 tents) ☎ 022 2452005/6; e reservations@adventurecamps.co.tz; www.adventurecamps.co.tz. Like its sister-camp, Selous Impala Camp, Mdonya Old River Camp was set up with help from Coastal Aviation. It stands on the wooded banks of the 'old' Mdonya River, which has not flowed in earnest since a newer path was carved by the river a couple of decades back. Comfortable rather than luxurious, the en-suite

Meru-style tents all have a private veranda, while the culinary emphasis is on tasty home-style cooking eaten beneath the stars. Mdonya Old River makes no apologies for being a fairly simple camp; it's aiming for a fairly elemental experience of Africa, & not for the comforts & fripperies that so many camps seem to have been striving for in recent years. There's no electricity, although the open-air bathroom does have a hot-water shower & a flushing toilet. A few sofas dot the lounge area, while the bar is really just a tree with bottles stored in the nooks & crannies. Isolated though it may be, the camp offers good access to the superb Mwagusi Sand River game-viewing circuit. The old riverbed is an important wildlife passage, & plenty of animals pass through camp daily, most profusely impala, warthog & giraffe, but also the occasional lion or elephant, while the helpful staff will gladly show you nocturnal visitors such as honey badger, genet & bushpig. The birding is also superb, with the likes of purple-crested turaco, bearded woodpecker, crested barbet, black-necked weaver, orange-breasted bush-shrike & green-winged pytilia among the colourful & conspicuous residents. *US$335/540 sgl/dbl for drive-in clients (exc activities); US$405–435/680–740 inc activities & park fees; all rates FB.*

🏠 **Msembe Camp** (11 rooms) PO Box 369, Iringa, Tanzania; no telephone; e kudumse@hotmail.com. This national park camp near the HQ lies close to the river & some extensive open plains teeming with game. The accommodation isn't up to much – prefabricated en-suite dbl & family bandas that look like they must get seriously hot in the middle of the day – but it's the cheapest on offer within the park. There's a shower with hot water & the newer bandas have more space & indoor bathrooms. Bedding, firewood & water are provided, & drinks & very basic provisions can be bought at the nearby staff bar, but it's best to bring all food with you. *US$20pp for old bandas, US$50pp for new bandas, room only.*

🏠 **Mwagusi Safari Camp** (13 tents) ✆(UK) +44 (0)1822 615721; m 07525 170940; e oeas. co@btinternet.com; www.mwagusicamp.com. This small & exclusive tented camp, situated on the north bank of the seasonal Mwagusi River, is one of the most alluring lodges anywhere in east Africa, immensely comfortable, yet with a real bush atmosphere. Set up by Chris Fox in 1987, the accommodation is strung along the riparian woodland fringing the river & consists of spacious walk-in tents, enclosed in a wood, thatch & reed

shelter, each of which has a vast shower & toilet area, & a private balcony with inviting armchairs & hammocks. Because the lodge is owner-managed, the service is top-notch, & includes some great touches – most memorably, starlit bush dinners around a campfire in a clearing above the camp or in the riverbed. Game viewing is superb, with elephant & greater kudu regularly putting in an appearance, & plenty of birds hopping around the trees. Although wild dog habits have become more changeable in recent years, leopard are regularly sighted in the area, several lion prides are resident, & the closest game-viewing circuits are situated far enough from the larger Ruaha River Lodge & park headquarters to let you feel you have the whole park to yourself. Game walks with an armed ranger are also offered, with a good chance of encountering elephants & other large animals on foot, & it is best to book these in advance. For early risers, Mwagusi also runs free early-morning bird walks around the camp, a lovely way to start the day. *US$660/1,190 sgl/dbl inc all activities, meals & park fees; drinks are extra; US$41/ group plus US$10pp for ranger-guided walks.*

🏕 **Ruaha River Campsite & Mdonya Campsites 1 & 2** PO Box 369, Iringa, Tanzania; no telephone; e kudumse@hotmail.com. With no facilities other than a patch of ground to pitch your tent, these camping spots offer the cheapest accommodation inside the park. *Camping US$30pp exc park fees.*

🏠 **Ruaha River Lodge** (26 rooms) ✆(UK) 01452 862288, ✆022 2862357; m 0784 237422/0713 237422; e fox@safaricamps.info; www.tanzaniasafaris.info. This scenic & comfortable camp is the oldest in Ruaha, situated on a rocky hillside above a set of rapids on the Ruaha River some 15km from the entrance gate. Game viewing is excellent from the camp, with rock hyrax scuttling around everywhere, hippo resident in the river, elephant passing through regularly, & many other animals coming down to drink. Accommodation, in fixed tents or unpretentious stone cottages, is simple but each has a dbl & a sgl bed & a comfortable lounge area. Ruaha River Lodge is actually divided into 2 camps, with 12 rooms along the river & 14 rooms further up the hill. 1 dining area is raised up with great views over the river; the other is down nearer the water, giving a closer view of the animals that drink there. Fly-camping & walking safaris can be arranged. *US$380–450/660–740 sgl/dbl inc most activities, meals & park fees; drinks & walking safaris are extra.*

14

Bradt Travel Guides

Africa

Africa Overland	£16.99
Algeria	£15.99
Angola	£18.99
Botswana	£16.99
Burkina Faso	£17.99
Cameroon	£15.99
Cape Verde	£15.99
Congo	£16.99
Eritrea	£15.99
Ethiopia	£17.99
Ethiopia Highlights	£15.99
Ghana	£15.99
Kenya Highlights	£15.99
Madagascar	£16.99
Madagascar Highlights	£15.99
Malawi	£15.99
Mali	£14.99
Mauritius, Rodrigues & Réunion	£16.99
Mozambique	£15.99
Namibia	£15.99
Nigeria	£17.99
North Africa: Roman Coast	£15.99
Rwanda	£16.99
São Tomé & Príncipe	£14.99
Seychelles	£16.99
Sierra Leone	£16.99
Somaliland	£15.99
South Africa Highlights	£15.99
Sudan	£16.99
Swaziland	£15.99
Tanzania Safari Guide	£17.99
Tanzania, Northern	£14.99
Uganda	£16.99
Zambia	£18.99
Zanzibar	£15.99
Zimbabwe	£15.99

The Americas and the Caribbean

Alaska	£15.99
Amazon Highlights	£15.99
Argentina	£16.99
Bahia	£14.99
Cayman Islands	£14.99
Chile Highlights	£15.99
Colombia	£17.99
Dominica	£15.99
Grenada, Carriacou & Petite Martinique	£15.99
Guyana	£15.99
Haiti	£16.99
Nova Scotia	£15.99
Panama	£14.99
Paraguay	£15.99
Peru Highlights	£15.99
Turks & Caicos Islands	£14.99
Uruguay	£15.99
USA by Rail	£15.99
Venezuela	£16.99
Yukon	£14.99

British Isles

Britain from the Rails	£14.99
Bus-Pass Britain	£15.99
Eccentric Britain	£16.99
Eccentric Cambridge	£9.99
Eccentric London	£14.99
Eccentric Oxford	£9.99
Sacred Britain	£16.99
Slow: Cornwall	£14.99
Slow: Cotswolds	£14.99
Slow: Devon & Exmoor	£14.99
Slow: Dorset	£14.99
Slow: New Forest	£9.99
Slow: Norfolk & Suffolk	£14.99
Slow: North Yorkshire	£14.99
Slow: Northumberland	£14.99
Slow: Sussex & South Downs National Park	£14.99

Europe

Abruzzo	£16.99
Albania	£16.99
Armenia	£15.99
Azores	£14.99
Belarus	£15.99
Bosnia & Herzegovina	£15.99
Bratislava	£9.99
Budapest	£9.99
Croatia	£15.99
Cross-Channel France: Nord-Pas de Calais	£13.99
Cyprus see North Cyprus	
Estonia	£14.99
Faroe Islands	£16.99
Flanders	£15.99
Georgia	£15.99
Greece: The Peloponnese	£14.99
Hungary	£15.99
Iceland	£15.99
Istria	£13.99
Kosovo	£15.99
Lapland	£15.99
Liguria	£15.99
Lille	£9.99
Lithuania	£14.99
Luxembourg	£14.99
Macedonia	£16.99
Malta & Gozo	£14.99
Montenegro	£14.99
North Cyprus	£13.99
Serbia	£15.99
Slovakia	£14.99
Slovenia	£13.99
Svalbard: Spitsbergen, Jan Mayen, Franz Jozef Land	£17.99
Switzerland Without a Car	£15.99
Transylvania	£15.99
Ukraine	£16.99

Middle East, Asia and Australasia

Bangladesh	£17.99
Borneo	£17.99
Eastern Turkey	£16.99
Iran	£15.99
Israel	£15.99
Jordan	£16.99
Kazakhstan	£16.99
Kyrgyzstan	£16.99
Lake Baikal	£15.99
Lebanon	£15.99
Maldives	£15.99
Mongolia	£16.99
North Korea	£14.99
Oman	£15.99
Palestine	£15.99
Shangri-La: A Travel Guide to the Himalayan Dream	£14.99
Sri Lanka	£15.99
Syria	£15.99
Taiwan	£16.99
Tajikistan	£15.99
Tibet	£17.99
Yemen	£14.99

Wildlife

Antarctica: A Guide to the Wildlife	£15.99
Arctic: A Guide to Coastal Wildlife	£16.99
Australian Wildlife	£14.99
East African Wildlife	£19.99
Galápagos Wildlife	£16.99
Madagascar Wildlife	£16.99
Pantanal Wildlife	£16.99
Southern African Wildlife	£19.99
Sri Lankan Wildlife	£15.99

Pictorials and other guides

100 Alien Invaders	£16.99
100 Animals to See Before They Die	£16.99
100 Bizarre Animals	£16.99
Eccentric Australia	£12.99
Northern Lights	£6.99
Swimming with Dolphins, Tracking Gorillas	£15.99
The Northwest Passage	£14.99
Tips on Tipping	£6.99
Total Solar Eclipse 2012 & 2013	£6.99
Wildlife & Conservation Volunteering: The Complete Guide	£13.99

Travel literature

A Glimpse of Eternal Snows	£11.99
A Tourist in the Arab Spring	£9.99
Connemara Mollie	£9.99
Fakirs, Feluccas and Femmes Fatales	£9.99
Madagascar: The Eighth Continent	£11.99
The Marsh Lions	£9.99
The Two-Year Mountain	£9.99
The Urban Circus	£9.99
Up the Creek	£9.99

Appendix 1

LANGUAGE *with thanks to Said el-Gheithy*

PRONUNCIATION Pronunciation of Swahili is generally straightforward: every syllable is sounded and there are no 'silent endings'. In longer words the stress is on the penultimate syllable. The most confusing feature for learners is that many words have a prefix and suffix which change according to subject and tense. However, when speaking, beginners can ignore these additions, and still be understood.

Of course, the best way to learn is to listen to the people around you. For more detailed information, use a phrasebook (see *Appendix 2*, page 420), or visit the Institute of Kiswahili and Foreign Languages (see page 180).

USEFUL SWAHILI WORDS AND PHRASES The following basics are necessarily very simplified, and may not be grammatically correct, but by using them you will be understood in most situations. Many Zanzibaris will be delighted to hear a visitor using a few Swahili words – even if they are mispronounced or put in the wrong order!

Introductions and greetings Introductions and salutations are very important in Swahili culture, particularly when speaking to adults or people older than yourself, even if the age difference is slight. (Children are not usually greeted by adults outside their family.)

The most common forms of address are the traditional Muslim greetings (in Arabic), regardless of the religion of the people being greeted, each with its own response:

Salama aleikum	Peace be with you
Aleikum salam	And peace be with you (response)

You can also use the following greetings when addressing older people:

Sblakheri	Good morning
Msalkheri	Good afternoon/evening
Shkamoo	(a general greeting which can be used at any time of day)
Marahaba	(response to '*shkamoo*')
Habari zako or *hujambo?*	How are you?
Al humdul allah	Everything is well (response: literally 'Thanks be to Allah')

For people of the same age, and especially for friends, you can use *Habari*, which means 'Hello' (also meaning 'How are you?', literally 'what news?'). The reply might be *Al humdul allah*, or the more casual *Nzuri* ('good'), *Nzuri sana* ('very good') or *Safi* ('fine'). In areas

413

where Swahili is not spoken as a first language the reply is often *Mzuri*, with an 'M', rather than 'Nzuri'. *Habari* can also be used for 'Excuse me' (when attracting somebody's attention), but it is still considered impolite to simply say '*Habari*' ('hello') to someone older than you.

Mambo is an even more casual way of greeting friends, meaning 'how's it going?' The response is *Poa* (something along the lines of 'neat', 'cool' or 'dandy').

Although *Jambo* also means 'Hello', Zanzibaris never use this word speaking to each other, and it tends only to be used by Zanzibaris talking to tourists. (In the same way, the oft-quoted '*Hakuna matata*' – 'no problem' – is mock-Swahili-for-tourists imported from Kenya, and not used by Zanzibaris. If you want to express this idea, a more correct alternative would be '*Hamna neno*' or '*Haidhuru*'.)

Children in Zanzibar greet adults with *Chechei*, usually followed by the title of the adult. The response is the same.

Even when speaking in English a Swahili acquaintance will ask 'How are you?', 'How are things today?', 'How is your husband/wife/friend?' You should do the same. Launching straight into any subject without the opening questions is rude. Traditional Zanzibaris expect women to be less forward than men, although in areas used to tourists this does not apply.

Hodi means 'Hello, anyone at home, can I come in?' used when knocking on somebody's door. *Karibu* is the response, meaning 'welcome' (literally 'come near').

You may hear the word *mzungu* ('white person') directed to you, particularly by children, but it is not disrespectful.

The basics

Goodbye	*Kwaheri*
Welcome	*Karibu*
Please	*Tafadali*
Thank you (very much)	*Asante* (*sana*)
yes	*ndiyo*
no	*hapana*

Conversation starters and enders

What is your name?	*Jina lako nani?*
My name is Susie	*Jina langu Susie*
Where are you from?	*Unatoka wapi?*
I am from …	*Mimi ninatoka …*
	(the *mimi* is often dropped)
Where do you live?	*Unakaa wapi?*
Where are you staying? (ie: locally)	*Umefikia wapi?*
I am sorry, I don't understand	*Samahani sifahamu*
I don't speak Swahili	*Sijui Kiswahili*
I speak a very little Swahili	*Nazungumza Kiswahili kidogo tu*

Other useful words and phrases

OK (agreement)	*sawa*	there is	*ipois*
sorry (condolences)	*pole* (not used for apologies)	there…?	*iko …?*
		there isn't…	*hakuna …*
where?	*wapi?*	how much?	*bei gani?*
what	*nini*		(literally 'what price?')
here	*hapa*	how many shillings?	*shillingi ngapi?*
there	*hapo*		

I want to go to Bububu		*Nataka kwenda Bububu*	
Where is the bus for Makunduchi?		*Liko wapi basi la Makunduchi?*	
Where is the ruin?		*Liko wapi gofu?*	
I am ill		*Mimi mgonjwa*	
Where is the hospital?		*Iko wapi hospitali?*	
Where is the doctor?		*Yuko wapi daktari?*	
I am lost		*Nimepotea*	

left	*kushoto*	tomorrow	*kesho*
right	*kulia*	yesterday	*jana*
straight on	*moja kwa moja*	bank	*benki*
near	*karibu*	shop	*duka*
far	*mbali*	market	*soko*
today	*leo*	café, eating-house	*hoteli ya chakula*

Food and drink

beef	*nyama ya ngombe*	water	*maji*
chicken	*kuku*	tea	*chai*
eggs	*yai*	coffee	*kahawa*
fish	*samaki*	milk	*maziwa*
potato	*viazi*	sugar	*sukari*
rice	*mchele*		

The word *soda* means any fizzy drink in a bottle. In the smarter hotels in Zanzibar Town, if you want soda water try asking for a club soda.

Numbers

1	*moja*	21	*ishirini na moja*
2	*mbili*	30	*thelathini*
3	*tatu*	40	*arobaini*
4	*nne*	50	*hamsini*
5	*tano*	60	*sitini*
6	*sita*	70	*sabini*
7	*saba*	80	*themanini*
8	*nane*	90	*tisini*
9	*tisa*	100	*mia*
10	*kumi*	101	*mia na moja*
11	*kumi na moja*	102	*mia na mbili*
12	*kumi na mbili*	200	*mia mbili*
20	*ishirini*	300	*mia tatu*

Time Swahili time starts at 00.00, the hour of sunrise, which is at 06.00 in Western time.

What time is it?	*Saa ngapi?*	08.00	*saa mbili*
07.00	*saa moja* (literally	noon	*saa sita*
	one o'clock)	13.00	*saa saba*

When finding out about bus or boat departures, check if the time you've been told is Swahili time or Western time. This can be complicated further by some buses leaving outlying villages very early in the morning.

Appendix 2

BOOKS
History and background

General histories of Africa The following books are general histories of Africa or the east African region, which include sections on Zanzibar. Some are old and now long out of print, but make interesting reading if you can find them – try a specialist historical bookshop. Pakenham's classic history of Africa from the 1870s onwards is particularly compulsive, and often reprinted in paperback. Taylor's book about the European settlers who 'stayed on' in east Africa after the countries gained independence, looks at the colonial past in the present context, and neatly combines history with contemporary travel writing.

Coupland, R *The Exploitation of East Africa 1856–1890: The Slave Trade and the Scramble* Faber, London, 1939

Davidson, B *The Story of Africa* Littlehampton Book Services Ltd, London, 1984

Freeman-Grenville, G S P *The East African Coast: Select Documents* Oxford University Press, 2nd edn, 1975

A History of East Africa Oxford University Press, London, 1963

Pakenham, T *The Scramble for Africa* Weidenfeld & Nicolson, London, 1991

Prestage, E *Portuguese Pioneers* A & C Black, London, 1933

Taylor S *Livingstone's Tribe* HarperCollins, London, 1999

Early histories of Zanzibar The next six books cover Zanzibar specifically, but they are old guidebooks and histories from British colonial days. Most are out of print, though a local Zanzibar publisher, Gallery Publications, has reprinted some of the titles.

Brode, H *Tippu Tip: His Career in Zanzibar and Central Africa* Gallery Publications, Zanzibar, 2002. This is a reprint of the original 1903 study of the career of Tippu Tip, Zanzibar's most famous (or infamous) trader. A fascinating and highly readable account of life on Zanzibar and the east African mainland over a century ago.

Gray, J *History of Zanzibar from the Middle Ages to 1856* Oxford University Press, London, 1962

Ingrams, W H *Zanzibar: Its History and People* Witherby, London, 1931

Lyne, R N *Zanzibar in Contemporary Times* Darf, London, 1905. Reprinted 1987

Ommanney, F D *Isle of Cloves* Longman, London, 1957

Pearce, Major F B *Zanzibar: The Island Metropolis of Eastern Africa* Fisher Unwin, London, 1920

General histories of Zanzibar and the Indian Ocean

Hall, R *Empires of the Monsoon* HarperCollins, London, 1999. A fascinating history of the lands around the Indian Ocean, including good sections on Zanzibar.

Hamilton, G, *In the Wake of da Gama* Abacus, London, 1951

Hamilton, G, *Princes of Zinj* Hutchinson, London, 1957. Comprehensive and accessible historical accounts, with an emphasis on readability, sometimes at the expense of accuracy.

Modern histories of Zanzibar

Nurse, D and Spear, T *The Swahili: Reconstructing the History and Language of an African Society* The Ethnohistory Series, University of Pennsylvania Press, Philadelphia, 1985. This is an excellent, short, readable book which argues convincingly that the Swahili culture is more of an African (and less an Arab) phenomenon than previously thought. Highly recommended.

Horton, M C 'The Swahili Corridor'. This article was published in *Scientific American* 255(9) 86–93 (1987). Horton has been one of the most influential archaeologists to work on the east African coast, and has done excavations and surveys on Pemba and Unguja (Zanzibar Island). This is an excellent short piece that touches on some of the Mediterranean connections with east Africa.

Mapuri, O *The 1964 Revolution* (published 1996). This short, locally published book is a concise history of Zanzibari politics, covering the period from 1964 up to the 1995 elections.

These three books are modern, post-revolution, textbook-style histories:

Martin, E B *Zanzibar: Tradition and Revolution* Hamish Hamilton, London, 1978

Sheriff, A *Slaves, Spices and Ivory in Zanzibar* James Currey, London, 1987

Sheriff, A, and Ferguson E D *Zanzibar under Colonial Rule* James Currey, London, 1991

Zanzibar and Oman Four modern and very detailed books, with specific reference to the Oman–Zanzibar link:

Al-Maamiry, A H *Oman and East Africa* Lancers Books, New Delhi, 1979

Al-Maamiry, A H *Omani Sultans in Zanzibar* Lancers Books, New Delhi, 1988

Bennett, N R *A History of the Arab State of Zanzibar* Methuen, London, 1978

Bhacker, M R *Trade and Empire in Muscat and Zanzibar* Routledge, London, 1992

Railways and ships

Hill, M H *The Permanent Way* East African Literature Bureau, Nairobi, 1949 and Miller, C *The Lunatic Express* Macmillan, Ballantine Books, Random House, 1971. These two books are histories of the east African railways, both with good sections on Zanzibar.

Patience K *Zanzibar and the Bububu Railway* (published by the author, 1995). A fascinating little booklet about the only railway on Zanzibar, which existed at the beginning of the 20th century.

Patience K *Zanzibar and the Loss of HMS Pegasus* (published by the author, 1995) and Patience K, *Zanzibar and the Shortest War in History* (published by the author, 1994). Two excellent booklets written and published by Zanzibar historian Kevin Patience. Well researched, they describe in full events which might otherwise be confined to the footnotes of history. The gunship *Pegasus* was sunk during World War I and this book also contains background information on British naval ships in east Africa, while *Shortest War* describes the 1896 bombardment of the sultan's palace, with several fascinating archive photos.

Patience K *Königsberg: A German East African Raider* (published by the author, 1997). The *Königsberg* was the German gunboat which sunk the British *Pegasus,* fully described in an earlier book by the same author. This painstakingly researched book covers historical events before and after the *Pegasus* incident, including the *Königsberg's* final sinking by another British ship in the Rufiji Delta, southwest of Zanzibar. The chapter describing the present-day position of the *Königsberg's* relics scattered all over east Africa is particularly interesting.

Architecture and history

Mwalim, M A *Doors of Zanzibar* Gallery Publications, Zanzibar, 2002. Using hundreds of photographs by Uwe Rau, this fascinating book catalogues the unique doors which have become an icon of Zanzibar Stone Town, and covers the various Indian, Arabic and Swahili influences.

Pitcher, G and Jafferji, J *Zanzibar Style* Gallery Publications, Zanzibar, 2001. This celebration of Zanzibari architecture is listed under *Large-format photo books* below.

Siravo, F, and Bianca, S *A Plan for the Historic Stone Town* Gallery Publications in association with the Aga Khan Trust for Culture, Zanzibar, 1997. A large and detailed discussion document, full of fascinating photos, plans and drawings, which analyses the current situation then proposes a major and systematic plan for the repair, preservation and conservation of the many old buildings in Stone Town. This is a vital reference for anyone interested in the history and architecture of Zanzibar.

Sheriff, A *Zanzibar Stone Town: An Architectural Exploration* Gallery Publications, Zanzibar, 1998. With skilful photographs by Javed Jafferji and illuminating text by a leading Zanzibar historian, this handy little pocket-sized book is an ideal guide and companion for your strolls around the narrow streets of Stone Town. Highly recommended.

Sheriff, A *The History and Conservation of Zanzibar Stone Town* James Currey, Ohio, 1995. This book is part of Currey's Eastern African Studies series, and although quite academic in tone, it has a lot of useful information for anyone keen on the history of Zanzibari architecture.

Princess Salme

Ruete, E (born Salme binte Said Al-Busaidi), *Memoirs of an Arabian Princess from Zanzibar* Gallery Publications, Zanzibar, 1998. This book is a translation of *Memoiren einer Arabischen Prinzessin,* which was first published in 1888. It was also reprinted by Markus Wiener Publishing (New York, 1989), but the latest translation is now easily available in Zanzibar bookshops. It is a very readable first-hand account by a unique figure in the history of Zanzibar, providing a good overview of the period and several fascinating personal insights. Highly recommended.

Ruete, E (born Salme binte Said Al-Busaidi), *An Arabian Princess Between Two Worlds: Memoirs, Letters, Sequels to the Memoirs,* ed E Van Donzel, E J Brill Publishing, Leiden, Netherlands, 1993. Volume 3 in a series on Arab History and Culture. This is a very detailed and comprehensive account of Salme's life in Zanzibar, Germany and Syria. Includes a biography of her son, Said-Rudolph Ruete. Expensive and hard to obtain.

Travel and exploration

Batchelor, J and J *In Stanley's Footsteps* Blandford Press, London, 1990, and Wilson, C, and Irwin, A, *In Quest of Livingstone* House of Lochar, Scotland, 1999. Two books in which British couples follow the routes of the great explorers in Africa. Livingstone started many of his travels in Zanzibar. The Batchelors mount a full expedition, while Colum Wilson and Aisling Irwin trace Livingstone's final journey through Tanzania and Zambia at a more grass-roots level.

Burton, Richard Francis *Zanzibar: City, Island and Coast* London, 1872. Many early European explorers in Africa mentioned Zanzibar in their journals, but Burton, perhaps the most 'colourful' of them all, is the only one to write a specific book on Zanzibar. Although published first over a century ago, reprints are sometimes available.

Hugon, A *The Exploration of Africa* New Horizons, Thames & Hudson, London, 1999. This is a fascinating and beautifully illustrated little book, with good coverage on the journeys of Livingstone, Stanley and others in east Africa.

Moorehead, A *The White Nile* Hamish Hamilton, London, 1960. A classic book on the history of European exploration in the east African region. Often reprinted. Readable and recommended.

Mountfield, D *A History of African Exploration* Domus Books/Hamlyn, London, 1976 and Richards, C, and Place, J *East African Explorers* Oxford University Press, London, 1960. Two books on exploration in Africa, although both out of print and hard to find, including some mentions of Zanzibar where many journeys began and ended.

Royal Geographical Society (ed John Keay), *History of World Exploration* Paul Hamlyn, Reed International, London, 1991. Includes sections on the exploration of east Africa.

Teal, J *Livingstone* Putnam, New York, 1973. A fine biography of the great explorer.

Waugh, E *Remote People* Duckworth, 1931, republished 1985 by Penguin Books, UK, as part of their 20th Century Classics series. Waugh travelled to many parts of Africa, including Zanzibar, as a newspaper correspondent, and his dry observations are as engaging today as they were when first written.

Large-format photo books

Jafferji, J, and Rees Jones B *Images of Zanzibar* HSP Publications, London, 1996. Much of east Africa has been covered by publishers of lavishly illustrated 'coffee-table' books, but until recently Zanzibar seems to have escaped their notice. Local photographer Javed Jafferji has made up for this with a portfolio of his finest work, showing rich colours and an eye for detail perfectly capturing the spirit of the islands.

Jafferji, J, Jafferji, Z and Waterman, P *A Taste of Zanzibar: Chakula Kizuri* Gallery Publications, Zanzibar, 2001. Not hungry? You will be if you read this bountiful cookbook which celebrates (and helps you create) Zanzibar's delicious cuisine, enhanced with 250 mouthwatering colour photos.

Pitcher, G and Jafferji, J *Zanzibar Style* Gallery Publications, Zanzibar, 2001. This sumptuous and stimulating book combines evocative photos by Javed Jafferji and text by Gemma Pitcher to explore the themes that have inspired Zanzibar's unique architecture and interior design – from Europe, Oman and India, as well as of course the natural forms of Africa – and also covers related aspects such as crafts, textiles and furniture. Listed by *The Times* as one of the 'Top 20 travel books for Christmas' 2001.

Sheriff, A *Historical Zanzibar: Romance of the Ages* HSP Publications, London, 1996. Accomplished photographer Javed Jafferji compiled this fascinating collection of archive photos from the late 19th and early 20th centuries – the text and captions were provided by Abdul Sheriff, Professor of History at the University of Dar es Salaam and Principal Curator of the Zanzibar Museums.

Fiction and autobiography

Bateman, G *Zanzibar Tales* Gallery Publications, Zanzibar, 2002. Another reprint from the industrious Gallery house; a collection of amusing (and sometimes confusing) Zanzibari folktales originally recorded and translated into English by George Bateman almost a century ago, and enhanced by lively illustrations by Walter Bobbett.

Haji, M M *Sowing The Wind* Gallery Publications, Zanzibar, 2002. This autobiographical novel explores life and politics on the islands of Zanzibar during the turbulent years which led to independence in 1963, and the revolution which followed.

Kaye, M M *Death in Zanzibar* Penguin, London, 1984 – first published as *The House of Shadows*, Longman 1959 and Kaye, M M, *Trade Wind* Longman, 1963, Penguin, 1982. Two historical romantic novels set in Zanzibar. *Death in Zanzibar* is also published with two other M M Kaye *Death in...* stories in a larger book called the *House of Shade*.

Field guides
Mammals and birds

Kingdon, J *The Kingdon Fieldguide to African Mammals* Academic Press, USA and UK, 1997. For animals on Zanzibar, a field guide to the more common species of east Africa is of limited use. However, Kingdon's book is by far the best, as it covers every species in Africa in detail, including those on Zanzibar, with excellent illustrations and background notes.

van Perlo, B *Illustrated Checklist of the Birds of Eastern Africa* HarperCollins, London, 1996 and Williams, J, and Arlott, N *A Field Guide to the Birds of East Africa* Collins, London. For birds, the field guide you choose is determined by your level of interest. Of the books listed above, the van Perlo *Illustrated Checklist* is complete, with illustrations of every bird occurring in Africa, including those on Zanzibar, while the classic Williams and Arlott also has fairly good coverage. The large and comprehensive *Birds of Kenya & Northern Tanzania* by Zimmerman is used by keen birders, and it includes most species which occur on Zanzibar, but it's quite heavy to carry around.

Marine wildlife

Richmond, M (ed), *A Guide to the Seashores of Eastern Africa and the Western Indian Ocean Islands* Sida/SAREC, 1997. This excellent book contains around 450 pages, including over 150 of colour illustrations. More than 1,600 species of marine plants and animals are illustrated, plus notes on geology, climate, ecology and human activities. This is an essential tool for scientists, and a useful handbook for all visitors to the region. Proceeds from the sales of this book are put towards marine education purposes in the region, administered by the SEA Trust. Although hard to find overseas (only specialist stores stock it), this book is readily available in Zanzibar from all good bookshops.

Forstle, A, and Vierkotter, R *Marine Green Book* Green Ocean, Zanzibar, 1997. This handy little pocket encyclopaedia covers everything you need to know about marine life (from algae to zooxanthellae) and marine activities (from anchor damage to the Zanzibar Sea Turtle Project) in and around the Zanzibar archipelago. It also covers snorkelling, diving, coral reefs, fish and marine habitats. It is available in Zanzibar bookshops at a very reasonable price, and all proceeds go to fund environmental education projects.

Manuals, guidebooks and phrasebooks

Bogaert, P *The Krazy Kanga Book* Gallery Publications, Zanzibar, 2002. An offbeat 'adult' study of the kanga or 'wrap', the ubiquitous and vital garment for the women of east Africa.

Briggs, P, and McIntyre, C *Tanzania: The Bradt Travel Guide* Bradt Travel Guides, 7th edn 2013. The most comprehensive guide to Tanzania, ideal both for those heading off the beaten track and travellers visiting the country's major attractions.

Dawood, R *How to Stay Healthy Abroad* Oxford University Press, Oxford, 2012

Benjamin, M *Swahili Phrasebook* Lonely Planet, London, 2008

Hatt, J *The Tropical Traveller* Pan, London, 1993

Koornhof, A *Dive Sites of Kenya & Tanzania, including Zanzibar, Pemba & Mafia* New Holland, London, 1997

Rattray, G *Access Africa: Safaris for People with Limited Mobility* Bradt Travel Guides, 2009. Covers everything relevant to planning a safari in Africa for those with limited mobility, including transport, accommodation, and access to restaurants and national parks.

Wilson-Howarth, J, and Ellis, Dr M *Your Child Abroad: A Travel Health Guide* Bradt Travel Guides, 2004, with updates on www.bradtguides.com

Wilson-Howarth, J and Levene, B *Bugs, Bites and Bowels* Cadogan, UK, 2006

BOOKSHOPS

The Travel Bookshop 13 Blenheim Cres, London W11 2EE, UK; ☎020 7229 5260; www.thetravelbookshop. co.uk. Stocks guidebooks, phrasebooks, history, fiction, maps, & anything else to do with travel publications. They can source old & out-of-print books, & operate a worldwide mail-order service.

Risborough Books 81 Manor Park Av, Princes Risborough, Bucks HP27 9AR, UK; ☎01844 343165. Specialises in 2nd-hand books on east Africa, & offers mail order only. Contact them by post (no fax or email) for a list.

WEBSITES If you've got access to the internet, you can get further information on Zanzibar from the following websites. Most have links to other useful relevant sites.

Africa Confidential (*www.africa-confidential.com*) gives the inside story on political events across Africa, including Tanzania and Zanzibar.

Africa Travel Association (*www.africa-ata.org*) has close links with the US-based *Africa Travel* magazine and is an interesting source of information on the whole continent.

African Travel and Tourism Association (*www.atta.co.uk*) represents many tour operators covering Africa, and is an excellent directory of useful contacts.

Internet Living Swahili Dictionary (*www.yale.edu/swahili*) is a very handy online Swahili–English dictionary, with links to other Swahili-related sites.

The Hunger Site (*www.thehungersite.com*) is not directly related to Zanzibar, but if you visit this site (no more than once per day) and click on a 'donate' button, the site's sponsors will give two *free* cups of food to a developing country.

Zanzibar Travel Network, also called **Zanzibar Net** (*www.zanzibar.net*) has sections on history, diving, touring, beaches, history, travel tips and so on. It also has a good selection of links to other sites which cover Zanzibar.

Zanzibar.org (*www.zanzibar.org*) is a gateway site with pages on several hotels in Zanzibar Town and around Zanzibar Island, plus coverage of various aspects of Zanzibar such as culture, history and wildlife.

Sites for general news and information

www.allafrica.com Huge pan-African news site with vast amounts of topical content.

www.theexpress.com Weekly newspaper based in Dar es Salaam.

www.tanserve.com Interesting and slightly offbeat Dar-based portal with a mix of news and information.

www-sul.stanford.edu/depts/ssrg/africa/tanzan.html Extensive listing of links for Tanzania and Zanzibar.

www.zanzibargovernment.org/ Official site of the government of Zanzibar.

http://home.globalfrontiers.com/Zanzibar/sights_to_see_in_zanzibar.htm Historical site on Zanzibar, with pictures and illustrations.

www.africa.upenn.edu/Country_Specific/Tanzania.html University of Pennsylvania African studies course – linking to useful Tanzania-specific sites.

www.zanzibar-travel-guide.com Online site where you'll find much of the text of this guide, plus many additional useful links.

Index

Page numbers in **bold** refer to main entries; those in *italics* refer to maps

INDEX OF ADVERTISERS